# A Companion to
# Continental Philosophy

# Blackwell Companions to Philosophy

This outstanding student reference series offers a comprehensive survey of philosophy as a whole. Written by today's leading philosophers, each volume provides lucid and engaging coverage of the key figures, terms, topics, and problems of the field. Taken together, the series provides the ideal basis for course use, representing and unparalleled work of reference for students and specialists alike.

## Published

**Forthcoming**

Copyright © Blackwell Publishers Ltd, 1998

First published 1998

2 4 6 8 10 9 7 5 3 1

Blackwell Publishers Inc.
350 Main Street
Malden, Massachusetts 02148
USA

Blackwell Publishers Ltd
108 Cowley Road
Oxford OX4 1JF
UK

*British Library Cataloguing in Publication Data*

A CIP catalogue record for this book is available from the British Library.

*Library of Congress Cataloging in Publication Data*

A companion to continental philosophy / edited by Simon Critchley and William R. Schroeder.
      p.   cm. – (Blackwell companions to philosophy)
      Includes bibliographical references and index.
      ISBN 0–631–19013–9 (hardback: alk. paper)
1. Philosophy, European.   2. Philosophy, European—20th century.   3. Philosophy, Modern—
19th century.   4. Philosophy, Modern—20th century.   I. Critchley, Simon, 1960.
      II. Schroeder, William Ralph.   III. Series.
                     B803.C66   1998
                     190—dc21                                    97–10146   CIP

Typeset in $10\frac{1}{2}$ on $12\frac{1}{2}$pt Photina
by Best-set Typesetter Ltd, Hong Kong
Printed and bound in Great Britain by MPG Books Ltd, Bodmin, Cornwall

This book is printed on acid-free paper

*Blackwell*
*Companions to*
*Philosophy*

# A Companion to Continental Philosophy

*Edited by*
SIMON CRITCHLEY AND
WILLIAM R. SCHROEDER

Advisory Editors    Jay Bernstein
Dominique Janicaud
Robert Bernasconi
Rodolphe Gasché
Bernhard Waldenfels

# Contents

vi

## PART III: THE PHENOMENOLOGICAL BREAKTHROUGH

## PART IV: PHENOMENOLOGY, HEGELIANISM AND ANTI-HEGELIANISM IN FRANCE

## PART V: RELIGION WITHOUT THE LIMITS OF REASON

## PART VI: THREE GENERATIONS OF CRITICAL THEORY

# PART IX: STRUCTURALISM AND AFTER

# Acknowledgments

I would like to express my gratitude to those without whom this *Companion* would not have been completed. First and foremost, I would like to thank my co-editor, Bill Schroeder, for joining the project at a relatively late stage and working swiftly, amicably, and extremely competently. It has been an intimate – albeit largely virtual – collaboration in the final stages of work. Secondly, I would like to thank my advisory editors for their help in the early stages of the project, particularly Robert Bernasconi and Jay Bernstein, who were crucial in shaping the volume, organizing the sections and suggesting and helping to select contributors. Others freely offered advice, notably Peter Dews. Thirdly, I would like to thank Noreen Harburt for her secretarial assistance during the final stages of the project. Fourthly, at Blackwell, I would like to thank Stephan Chambers for initially seducing me into taking on this task in his inimitable fashion, Steve Smith and Nathalie Manners for seeing the project through with great care and solving what seemed like insurmountable logistical problems at crucial moments, and Denise Rea, formerly of Blackwell, for a great deal of assistance early on. Fifthly, I would like to thank the Research Promotion Fund at the University of Essex for granting me a term's leave partially in order to work on the *Companion*. Finally, I would like to thank my contributors, many of whom made a special effort to find the time to contribute to this *Companion*.

**Simon Critchley**

# Contributors

Hans-Dieter Bahr, Department of Philosophy, University of Vienna, Austria

Ernst Behler, Department of German, University of Washington, Seattle, USA

Frederick C. Beiser, Department of Philosophy, University of Indiana, Bloomington, Indiana, USA

Geoffrey Bennington, Department of French, University of Sussex, Brighton, UK

Robert Bernasconi, Department of Philosophy, Memphis State University, Tennessee, USA

Rudolf Bernet, Department of Philosophy, Louvain Catholic University, Louvain, Belgium

Hauke Brunkhorst, Frankfurt am Main, Germany

John D. Caputo, Department of Philosophy, Villanova University, Pennsylvania, USA

Tina Chanter, Department of Philosophy, Memphis State University, Tennessee, USA

Fabio Ciaramelli, Department of Philosophy, University of Naples, Naples, Italy

Rebecca Comay, Department of Philosophy, University of Toronto, Ontario, Canada

Jean-François Courtine, Department of Philosophy, Ecole Normale Supérieure, Paris, France

Simon Critchley, Department of Philosophy, University of Essex, Colchester, UK

Steven Galt Crowell, Department of Philosophy, Rice University, Texas, USA

**Paul Davies**, Department of Philosophy, University of Sussex, Brighton, UK

**John Deigh**, Department of Philosophy, Northwestern University, Evanston, Illinois, USA

**Hent de Vries**, Department of Philosophy, University of Amsterdam, Amsterdam, The Netherlands

**Bernard Flynn**, Department of Philosophy, Empire State College, SUNY, New York, USA

**Thomas R. Flynn**, Department of Philosophy, Emory University, Georgia, USA

**Maurice Friedman**, Department of Philosophy, San Diego State University, California, USA

**Manfred S. Frings**, The Max Scheler Archives, Des Plaimes, Illinois, USA

**Edward Fullbrook**, freelance writer, Bristol, UK

**Kate Fullbrook**, School of Literary Studies, University of the West of England, Bristol, UK

**Mike Gane**, Department of Sociology, Loughborough University, Leicester, UK

**Moira Gatens**, Department of Philosophy, University of Sydney, Australia

**Pete A. Y. Gunter**, Department of Philosophy, North Texas State University, Denton, Texas, USA

**Marcel Hénaff**, Department of Literature, UCSD, California, USA

**Michel Henry**, Department of Philosophy, University of Montpellier III, Montpellier, France

**Stephen Houlgate**, Department of Philosophy, University of Warwick, Coventry, UK

**Richard Kearney**, Department of Philosophy, University College, Dublin, Ireland

**Douglas Kellner**, Department of Philosophy, University of Texas at Austin, Texas, USA

**Ernesto Laclau**, Department of Government, University of Essex, Colchester, UK

**Rudolf Makkreel**, Department of Philosophy, Emory University, Georgia, USA

**Gyorgy Markus**, Department of Philosophy, University of Sydney, Australia

**Brian Massumi**, Department of Comparative Literature, McGill University, Montreal, Canada

**Thomas McCarthy**, Department of Philosophy, Northwestern University, Evanston, Illinois, USA

**Paul Mendes-Flohr**, The F. Rosenzweig Research Centre, Hebrew University, Jerusalem, Israel

**Kelly Oliver**, Department of Philosophy, University of Texas at Austin, Texas, USA

**Paul Patton**, Department of General Philosophy, University of Sydney, Australia

**Max Pensky**, Department of Philosophy, SUNY, Binghampton, New York, USA

**Robert B. Pippin**, Department of Philosophy, University of Chicago, Illinois, USA

**Jacques Rancière**, Department of Philosophy, University of Paris VIII, Vincennes, Paris, France

**Robert Rethy**, Department of Philosophy, Xavier University, Cincinnati, Ohio, USA

**William J. Richardson**, Department of Philosophy, Boston College, Massachusetts, USA

**Jacob Rogozinski**, Department of Philosophy, University of Paris VIII, Vincennes, Paris, France

**Stanley Rosen**, Department of Philosophy, Boston University, Massachusetts, USA

**Kurt Salamun**, Department of Philosophy, University of Graz, Austria

**Robert Sasso**, Department of Philosophy, University of Nice, France

**Gunzelin Schmid Noerr**, Stadt- und Universitätsbibliothek, Frankfurt am Main, Germany

**Dennis J. Schmidt**, Department of Philosophy, Villanova University, Pennsylvania, USA

**William R. Schroeder**, Department of Philosophy, University of Illinois at Urbana-Champaign, Illinois, USA

**Charles E. Scott**, Department of Philosophy, Pennsylvania State University, Pennsylvania, USA

**Ludwig Siep**, Department of Philosophy, Universität Münster, Münster, German

**Lawrence S. Stepelevich**, Department of Philosophy, Villanova University, Pennsylvania, USA

**Philip Stratton-Lake**, Department of Philosophy, Keele University, Staffordshire, UK

**G. L. Ulmen**, Senior Editor, Telos Press Ltd, New York, USA

**Ben Vedder**, Department of Philosophy, University of Tilburg, The Netherlands

**Bernhard Waldenfels**, Department of Philosophy, Ruhr-Universität Bochum, Bochum, Germany

**Merold Westphal**, Department of Philosophy, Fordham University, Bronx, New York, USA

# Introduction: what is Continental philosophy?

## SIMON CRITCHLEY

### Rationale of volume and principle of selection

The purpose of this volume is to provide a high-quality, one-volume companion to the study of philosophy in the Continental tradition. At present, there is no volume which provides the analytically trained philosopher, the interested academic in the humanities and social sciences, the postgraduate and undergraduate student in philosophy and related areas, and the lay reader, with an introductory but authoritative account of what is distinctive and compelling about Continental philosophy and which gives an overview of its diverse historical movements, main figures, and distinctive themes.

In relation to other volumes in the Blackwell Companions to Philosophy series, the format of this volume is not that of a standard reference book, i.e. composed of alphabetically arranged short articles on a whole range of topics and organized under headwords. This volume contains 58 original essays of varying length, which deal with individual philosophers in the overwhelming majority of cases. To that extent this *Companion* has a closer family resemblance with Singer's *Companion to Ethics* and Goodin and Pettit's *Companion to Contemporary Political Philosophy*, than, say, with Dancy and Sosa's *Companion to Epistemology* or Kim and Sosa's *Companion to Metaphysics*.

A word of explanation is required on this principle of selection. By virtue of the nature of philosophy in the Continental tradition, and in particular the way in which it is taught, researched and simply *talked about* in the English-speaking world, it makes more sense to organize the Companion by proper names, philosopher by philosopher, in an approximately chronological sequence. As the reader will see from a glance at the Contents pages, this chronological sequence begins with Kant, who in many ways is both the final great figure common to both the analytic and Continental traditions and announces the parting of their ways. After an introductory survey essay on the context and problematic of post-Kantian philosophy, the Companion opens with a series of articles on the central figures in German idealism and romanticism (Fichte, F. Schlegel, Novalis, Schelling, Hegel). Part II deals with the various nineteenth and early twentieth-century critiques of the philosophical tradition, ranging from Schopenhauer, Feuerbach, and Kierkegaard, through the "masters of suspicion" (Marx, Nietzsche, Freud) to Bergson. After an essay on Neo-Kantianism, which was the dominant philosophical current on the Continent in the late decades of the nineteenth century and the early decades of the twentieth, Part III contains a series of essays on Germanophone phenomenology (Husserl, Scheler, Jaspers, Heidegger). Part IV looks at the singular development of phenomenology in France from the 1930s into the postwar period in the work of Levinas, Sartre, and Merleau-Ponty, a time characterized by both a strong Hegelianism in Kojève and Sartre and an anti-Hegelianism in Bataille, as well as the attempt to extend phenomenology into the areas of sexual difference (De Beauvoir) and literature (Blanchot). Parts V, VII and VIII deal respectively with three chronologically more disparate but none the less decisive themes in the Continental tradition: philosophy of religion (Rosenzweig, Buber, Marcel), hermeneutics (Schleiermacher, Dilthey, Gadamer, Ricoeur) and political philosophy (Lukács, Gramsci, Schmitt, Arendt, Lefort, Castoriadis). Part VI is a series of essays on philosophers more (Horkheimer, Adorno, Habermas) or less (Benjamin, Bloch, Marcuse) closely identified with the Critical Theory of the Frankfurt School and closes with a consideration of Third Generation Critical Theory. The *Companion* concludes with a long series of essays on Francophone thinkers more or less closely associated with structuralism and its aftermath (Lévi-Strauss, Lacan, Althusser), and habitually grouped together under the rather unhelpful and approximative labels of "poststructuralism" (Foucault, Derrida, Deleuze), "postmodernism" (Lyotard, Baudrillard) and "French feminism" (Irigaray, Kristeva, Le Doeuff), labels that often prevent rather than enable an appreciation of their work. Although the informed reader will quickly see that there are many philosophers worthy of interest who have been omitted because of lack of space, it is hoped that all the major traditions and figures in the Continental tradition are included and fairly represented.

Although organizing the *Companion* by proper names largely (and for good or ill) reflects the way the Continental tradition is taught and talked about in the English-speaking world, this principle of selection also avoids what I believe would be an insurmountable problem of overlap if a thematic principle were adopted. For example, an entry on "subjectivity" or "the subject" would inevitably repeat material from entries on Kant, Fichte, Hegel, Kierkegaard, Nietzsche, Freud, and Heidegger, to name just a few. Thus, the vast majority of contributors to the *Companion* were invited to write essays on specific thinkers, although this was only done as a way of organizing the thematic substance of their thought. An alternative thematic way of reading the *Companion* would be to begin by following through references and cross-references to particular philosophical concepts by using the specially prepared analytic index. So, there are two ways into the Companion, via proper names and via themes.

One more prefatory word is required on the historical period that has governed the selection. With admittedly broad brushstrokes, the ten sections of this *Companion* cover an approximately 200-year period in the history of philosophy. Of course, it would be possible to imagine a "Companion to Continental Philosophy" that might begin around 1900 with the publication of Husserl's *Logical Investigations* and Freud's *The Interpretation of Dreams*. Such an organization of the volume would have the virtue of reminding readers that the contemporary division (or gulf) between "analytic" and "Continental" traditions is essentially a division between traditions inspired by Frege's philosophy of logic and language and those traditions derived from an often critical confrontation with Husserlian phenomenology. Of course, what is peculiar about these seemingly divergent traditions is that they have a common ancestry in the work of Bolzano and Brentano, and in the critique of psychologism, scepticism, and relativism. Michael Dummett compares Frege and Husserl to the Rhine and the Danube, "which arise quite close to each other and for a time pursue roughly parallel paths, only to diverge in utterly different directions and flow into different seas."[1] Although it is clear, for Dummett at least, that Frege's Rhine is the right course for thought whereas Husserl's Danube debouches into the idealist Black Sea of the Continental tradition, this is an instructive and suggestive image, particularly at a time when the distinction between analytic and Continental philosophy appears increasingly unstable.[2] However, when planning the Companion, I decided at an early stage that the volume should begin with Kant, German idealism and romanticism, and the nineteenth-century critique of metaphysics for the following two reasons: (i) twentieth-century developments in Continental philosophy are largely unintelligible without reference to their nineteenth-century precursors, especially Hegel, Marx, and Nietzsche; and (ii) this period of the history of philosophy, in Britain at least, is woefully under-represented in syllabuses, where it is possible to receive a degree in philosophy without having read much, if anything, of Germanophone philosophy between Kant and Frege.

## The *de facto* distinction between analytic and Continental philosophy

What's in a name? Having got some preliminaries out of the way, I would like to address the vexed problem of nomenclature. What is Continental philosophy?[3]

The adjective "Continental," at least for the British reader, evokes associations with other uses of the adjective, such as a "Continental breakfast" or what used to be called a "Continental quilt." That is to say, it is a geographical term or toponym that refers to something that occurs in a particular place, namely the European Continent. The adjective opens up a distinction between the Continental and what is not Continental, a distinction that, from the British perspective, often risks hardening into an opposition between the British and the Continental, where the latter is defined as the foreign, the exotic, and the strange and the former as the homely, the native, and the familiar. As such, the notion of "Continental" alludes to seemingly intractable and frankly rather tiresome issues of political geography, namely as to whether Britain is adrift from the Continent or the Continent is adrift from Britain (recall the infamous newspaper headline, "Fog over the channel. Continent cut off").

Regardless of the philosophical validity of the distinction, which I shall have occasion to question below, there exists and has existed at least since the Second World War, a *de facto* distinction between analytic and Continental philosophy.[4] What must be emphasized here is that this distinction is essentially a *professional self-description*, that is, it is a way that departments of philosophy seek to organize their curricula and course offerings as well as signalling their broad intellectual allegiances. However, the problem with the distinction is that this professional self-description overlays and rehearses a more ancient cultural opposition, where perhaps justifiable questions of the identity of philosophical tradition become fatally enmeshed in the obfuscatory ideological prejudice of a political geography. In my view, the conflation of philosophical tradition with political geography leads to the ideological stereotyping and distortion that can be found in such labels as "British empiricism," "French rationalism," and "German metaphysics," labels which only seek to widen the gulf between philosophical traditions and block the possibility of dialogue.[5] Perhaps the gulf that seemingly separates the analytic and Continental traditions was most succinctly stated during the irritable and infamous discussion that followed Gilbert Ryle's paper at the Royaumont conference in France in 1960, where in response to Merleau-Ponty's plea "notre programme n'est-il pas le même?," Ryle answered, "J'espère que non."[6] It is this "I hope not," this steadfast "no" in the face of the perceived exoticism of the Continent, that is so revealing of an ideological prejudice that surely should have no home in philosophy.

Although there is no consensus on the precise origin of the concept of Continental philosophy as a professional self-description, it would seem that it does not arise as a description of undergraduate and postgraduate courses in philosophy before the 1970s. It is clear that this happened in the USA before Britain, where the first postgraduate courses in Continental philosophy were offered at the Universities of Essex and Warwick in the early 1980s, although undergraduate courses in Continental philosophy were available at Warwick from the mid-1970s. In the American context, and to a lesser extent in Britain, the term "Continental philosophy" replaced the earlier formulations, "Phenomenology" or "Phenomenology and Existential Philosophy." These terms are preserved in the names of the professional associations most closely associated with Continental philosophy in the English-speaking world, the Society for Phenomenology and Existential Philosophy founded in 1962 and the British Society for Phenomenology founded in 1967. It would seem, then, that in the postwar period, Continental philosophy was broadly synonymous with phenomenology (often in an existential garb), a fact that is also reflected by certain introductory American book titles from the 1960s: *An Invitation to Phenomenology* (1965), and *Phenomenology in America* (1967).[7] It is perhaps indicative that the latter title is both mimicked and transformed in 1983 with the appearance of *Continental Philosophy in America*.[8] The reason why "Phenomenology" is replaced with "Continental philosophy" is not absolutely clear, but it would seem that it was introduced to take account of the various so-called poststructuralist Francophone movements of thought that were increasingly distant from and often hostile towards phenomenology: to a lesser extent Lacan, Derrida, and Lyotard, and to a greater extent Deleuze and Foucault.

So, to summarize, Continental philosophy is a professional self-description that overlays a prior and more pernicious cultural opposition between the "British" or "Anglo-American" and the "Continental" and which has been pragmatically refined over the years.

This *de facto* divide between analytic and Continental philosophy can be observed in sundry philosophical epiphenomena such as job descriptions asking for

4

"Continentalists" and in publishers' catalogues where special pages are given over to "Continental Philosophy," usually towards the back of the catalogue. As John Searle complacently asserts, there is a near-complete professional hegemony of analytic philosophy in the English-speaking world, where types of non-analytic philosophy, like phenomenology, feel it necessary to define their position in relation to this hegemony.[9] However, despite this unquestionable hegemony, there are universities in the UK, Ireland, Canada, and Australia that specialize in Continental philosophy and many more in the USA, mostly amongst the Catholic universities, with some notable exceptions. In philosophy departments and faculties where the analytic tradition is dominant, there is often a course or paper on "Modern European Philosophy," "Post-Kantian Philosophy" or "Phenomenology and Existentialism," courses that were often initiated as concessions to student demand, which is rather significant in this area. Also, the influence of Continental philosophy in the English-speaking world, particularly in its more recent Francophone versions, is arguably much stronger outside philosophy departments than within them, where it has decisively influenced many theoretical innovations in the humanities and social sciences: in literary theory, art history and theory, social and political theory, cultural studies, historiography, religious studies, and anthropology, not to mention debates in fine art, architecture, feminism, and psychoanalysis. Revealingly and significantly, the acceptance of Continental thought in the English-speaking world has, for the most part, taken place outside of philosophy departments.

## Problems with the *de facto* analytic/Continental distinction

It would not take a genius to realize that there are grave problems with the *de facto* distinction between analytic and Continental philosophy. As a glance at the contents list to this *Companion* will reveal, Continental philosophy is a highly eclectic and disparate series of intellectual currents that could hardly be said to amount to a unified tradition. As such, Continental philosophy is an *invention*, or, more accurately, a *projection* of the Anglo-American academy onto a Continental Europe that would not recognize the legitimacy of such an appellation – a little like asking for a Continental breakfast in Paris.

However, if the concept of Continental philosophy is taken at face value as a toponym or geographical category, then other problems arise. As David Cooper points out, there are philosophers from the Continent, such as Frege and Carnap, who are not ajudged Continental, and philosophers from outside the Continent, like many of the contributors to this *Companion*, who are.[10] Also, geographically, matters can become nicely confused, as when Dummett rightly claims that the term "Anglo-American" (another toponym of no more obvious felicity than "Continental") has done more harm than good because it elides the Germanophone origins of analytical philosophy. Dummett rather mischieviously but accurately suggests in its place the term "Anglo-Austrian."[11]

A more far-reaching objection to the distinction between analytic and Continental philosophy is that raised by Bernard Williams, when he claims that the distinction rests upon a confusion of geographical and methodological terms, as if one were to classify cars into front-wheel drive and Japanese (one thinks here of recently founded "European Society for Analytic Philosophy" as a case in point).[12] Although analytic philosophy is often powerfully associated with certain places, habitually Oxford, it denotes a commitment to a certain method of philosophizing, to certain standards of argumentation, clarity and rigour, whereas Continental philosophy would seem to denote a commitment to a certain place regardless of methodology. Thus, for Williams, the distinction between analytic and Continental philosophy rests upon a confused comparison of methodological and geographical categories.

However, such confusion would not be rectified by recasting the terms of the opposition into either strictly geographical (i.e. Anglo-American/Continental) or methodological (i.e. analytic/phenomenological) categories. If the opposition were recast geographically, then this would make matters even muddier because it would fallaciously imply both that philosophy in the UK and USA was by definition non-Continental, and that the founding father of analytic philosophy (Frege) and its greatest representative (Wittgenstein) were exclusively Continental philosophers. If the opposition is recast methodologically, then this would hardly begin to account for the fact that, on one side of the divide, very few philosophers can be said to engage in traditional forms of philosophical analysis (not to mention all talk of "post-analytic" philosophy) and, on the other side of the divide, there is simply no category that would begin to cover the diversity of work produced by thinkers as methodologically and thematically opposed as Hegel and Kierkegaard, Freud and Buber, Heidegger and Adorno, or Lacan and Deleuze.

Williams is rightly sceptical about any such drawing of distinctions between philosophical schools and doctrines because it disguises and disarms a more profound and interesting possible debate about the identity of philosophy itself. Although, in criticism of Williams, it is clear that for him the identity of philosophy is best represented by analytic philosophy, with its rather manly virtue of "workmanlike truthfulness,"[13] which seems to be based upon a quite questionable analogy between philosophy and the procedures of the natural sciences,[14] he clearly has a point here and I shall come back to this theme in my conclusion. There is something ultimately parochial and intellectually cowardly about identifying oneself with either side of a perceived philosophical divide, because it prevents the possible intellectual challenges that would be the consequence of a dialogue outside of one's professional entrenchments.

## Stereotypical representations of the analytic/Continental distinction

However, although it should by now be evident that there are problems with the *de facto* distinction between analytic and Continental philosophy, it should not simply be pushed aside without exorcising a few of the lingering cultural stereotypes lodged within it. If this is not done, these stereotypes may well return to haunt and hinder future discussion. Stanley Rosen, with his tongue firmly in his cheek, deftly summarizes the stereotypical representation of the distinction: "precision, conceptual clarity and systematic rigour are the property of analytical philosophy, whilst the continentals indulge in speculative metaphysics or cultural hermeneutics, or, alternatively, depending on one's sympathies, in wool-gathering and bathos."[15] Such stereotypes are, I fear, only confirmed by debates in the press and by the remarks of some professional philosophers who really should know better. For an example of the latter, one need think no further than the Derrida affair in Cambridge in 1992, where certain prominent members of the university opposed Jacques Derrida's nomination for an honorary doctorate. On the day after the opposition had lost the vote, a "quality" British newspaper ran the headline "Cognitive nihilism hits English city."[16]

However, for a revealing example of the lingering prejudice with which Continental philosophy is still treated, one might take as a case study a pair of articles on analytic and Continental philosophy respectively by Anthony Quinton and published in the *Oxford Companion to Philosophy* as recently as 1995.[17] Quinton's piece on analytic philosophy is a fair summary of logical atomism and logical positivism, although it is too brief to be useful on postwar developments in the field. He concludes with reference to Hilary Putnam and Robert Nozick, "they think and write in the analytic spirit, respectful of science, both as a paradigm of reasonable belief and in conformity with its argumentative rigour, its clarity, and its determination to be objective."[18] It is a pity that such a determination to be objective was not manifested in Quinton's companion article on Continental philosophy. The article begins, reasonably enough, with Quinton rightly pointing out how recently the current meaning was attached to Continental philosophy, i.e. in Britain after the Second World War. Useful observations are also made on the unity of philosophical endeavour that characterized the Latin Middle Ages and the Renaissance, an admirably unproblematic dialogue between philosophers from Britain and the Continent that extended well into the Enlightenment, where Locke was a reader of Descartes, Gassendi, and Malebranche, Hume read Bayle and knew Rousseau, Mill studied Comte, etc. So far, so good. However, Quinton then goes on to claim that "there is really no perceptible convergence between the two philosophical worlds," and as if (unintentionally, of course) to prove his point he provides quite shocking summaries of existentialism, structuralism, and critical theory: the first is rejected, without adequate reference to phenomenology, for its reliance "on dramatic, even melodramatic, utterance rather than sustained rational argument;" the second is said to have "culminated with Foucault and to have transcended itself, shooting off into outer intellectual space, with Derrida;" the third is bewilderingly dispatched in the following terms: "The evident political intentions of the critical theorists ruled out any interest on the part of analytic philosophers, committed to neutrality."[19] If such comments can be said to exhibit a commitment to neutrality, not to mention the above-mentioned virtues of rigour, clarity, and a determination to be objective, then Quinton might very well be justified in his belief that there is no possible convergence between the two philosophical worlds. Needless to say, such remarks are not only incorrect, but, I believe, intellectually intolerant and simply serve to perpetuate pernicious cultural stereotypes and postpone the possibility of dialogue.

## Dislodging the stereotypes – or how, after all, might the analytic/Continental distinction be drawn?

It is clear that the distinction between Continental and analytic philosophy brings in its wake a whole range of vexed ideological issues in cultural politics and political geography. But, that said, can the distinction be recast in such a way that dislodges the stereotyping seen above?

Richard Rorty, one of the few English-speaking philosophers who has attempted to work across the distinction between analytic and Continental philosophy by rooting both in the tradition of Deweyan American pragmatism (and who has consequently been shot at by both sides), suggests that the distinction between traditions essentially consists in the fact that analytic philosophy deals with problems, whereas Continental philosophy deals with proper names.[20] This would seem to be initially confirmed by what I said above about the principle of selection for this *Companion* as a roughly chronological sequence of proper names beginning with Kant, rather than the problem-orientated series of concepts that one might find in the other Blackwell Companions to Philosophy. But, one must be cautious here because Rorty's criterion for distinguishing between traditions might justifiably be said to be a superficial generalization that confirms the ridiculous stereotype that the Continental tradition is somehow unconcerned by problems and their argumentation (how could it *not* be so concerned?).

However, Rorty's remark does reveal something interesting, insofar as books, papers, and discussions in contemporary Continental philosophy, both on the Continent and in the English-speaking world, have a tendency to focus around the texts of a particular canonical philosopher, or offer a comparative study of the texts of two or more philosophers. Thus, rather than writing a paper called "The concept of truth," one might write a paper on "Heidegger's conception of truth" or "The concept of truth in Husserl and Heidegger;" rather than writing a paper on "The communitarian critique of liberalism," one might write on "The relevance of Hegel's critique of Kant for contemporary political theory;" rather than write on "The limits of ethical theory," one might write on "the contemporary relevance of Nietzsche's genealogical critique of morality;" rather than write on "The problem of self-identity," one might write on "The concept of the subject from Kant to Derrida," and so on.

It is fair to say that this practice often mystifies and infuriates philosophers trained in the analytic tradition, who maintain that Continental philosophers are only doing commentary and not original thinking. Now, it is at least arguable that there is too great a propensity towards commentary to the detriment of originality in contemporary Continental philosophy in the English-speaking world. But what is lacking in such a criticism (and in Rorty's criterion) is the recognition of a distinct practice of philosophy with a quite different sense of the importance of translation, commentary, interpretation, tradition, and history for contemporary philosophical research. It is not that philosophy in the Continental tradition is dismissive of problems – far from it – it is rather that problems are often approached *textually and contextually*, and therefore demand a different mode of treatment, one that might *appear* more indirect.

Perhaps Stanley Cavell puts the point too strongly when he writes that philosophy is not a series of problems but a series of texts.[21] It is rather, I would contend, that the various intellectual traditions that have shaped contemporary Continental philosophy constitute *a determinate but ever-reconfiguring constellation of texts, a documentary archive of philosophical problems, with a distinct relation to their context and our own and marked by a strong consciousness of history*. Three examples of this: (i) the interest in Kant's *Critique of Judgement* in the 1980s and in particular in the Analytic of the Sublime was both the cause and the consequence of the problems posed by the modernity/postmodernity debate; (ii) some of the recent growth of interest in the texts of German Idealism, particularly the work of Schelling, arose out of perceived philosophical problems in the Anglo-American reception of French "poststructuralist" thought; (iii) the great contemporary interest in the work of Levinas seems to have been the direct consequence of the perceived ethical weakness and political myopia of Heidegger's thinking and the thinking which Heidegger inspired, notably Derridian deconstruction. Many other examples of the kind could be given, where the Continental tradition functions as a kind of vast textual archive for contextually specific philosophical problems.

In other words, for the Continental tradition, philosophical problems do not fall from the sky ready-made and cannot be treated as elements in some ahistorical fantasy of *philosophia perennis*. One's reading of a classic text from the philosophical tradition does not so much take the form of a collegial dinner conversation, as much as a meeting with a stranger from a distant land whose language one is only beginning to understand, and with difficulty. Philosophical problems are textually and contextually *embedded* and, simultaneously, *distanced*, which perhaps explains why seemingly peripheral problems of translation, language, reading, interpretation, and the hermeneutic access to history should take on such central importance in the Continental tradition. Of course, this often leaves one open to the bewildering charge that one is doing "literature" rather than "philosophy," as if a philosopher's propositions had some unmediated and transparent relation to experience, a notion which seems to be modelled upon what Wilfrid Sellars called "The myth of the given," or some outmoded positivistic philosophy of science.

Thus, although inadequate as a criterion, to identify the distinction between traditions in terms of a superficial difference between proper names and problems leads to deeper questions of tradition and history, and the centrality of the latter for the Continental tradition. Perhaps the easiest and most minimal way to characterize the distinction between analytic and Continental philosophy is in terms of what they each see as the shape of their tradition and which philosophers constitute that tradition. That is to say, what matters here is which tradition the philosopher feels part of, knowing who counts (and perhaps more importantly, knowing who doesn't count – sometimes without knowing why) as an ancestor or an authority, who's in and who's out. Thus, whereas an analytic philosopher might cite Frege,

9

Russell, and Moore as ancestral authorities, a Continental philosopher might cite Hegel, Husserl, and Heidegger.

But making the distinction in this way does not really get to the nub of the issue, because what is curious about analytic philosophy, from a Continental perspective, is that, until fairly recently, it has been singularly unselfconscious about its tradition. This is beginning to change and interesting work has been done on the origins of analytic philosophy, whether in relation to its Germanophone roots in Frege or in relation to Russell's critique of British Idealism.[22] Indeed, John Skorupski has interestingly argued that the analytic tradition's response to scepticism allows it to be situated within the wider cultural movement of modernism.[23]

To speak in doubtless unjustifiably general terms, I take it that the Continental tradition would refuse the validity of the distinction between philosophy and the history of philosophy operative in much of the analytic tradition, and would claim that philosophy as a conceptual practice is inseparable from a relation to its tradition. Furthermore – and crucially – this relation to tradition is not some conservative acquiescence in the face of the past, but rather takes the form of a *critical* confrontation with the history of philosophy, what Heidegger calls *Destruktion* or *Abbau*, words that Derrida renders into French as *déconstruction*.[24] It is a question here of a critical dismantling of the tradition in terms of what has been unthought within it and what remains to be thought. This is also why the focus on the post-Kantian tradition is so important for Continental philosophy, because, with the notable exception of Vico and the later and slightly different examples of Rousseau and Herder, it is here that the question of history becomes philosophically central in the work of Hegel. One might say that the gain of the Continental tradition is that it allows one to focus on the essential historicity of philosophy as a practice and the essential historicity of the philosopher who engages in this practice.

The consequence of the above, I take it, is that deep philosophical questions about the meaning and value of human life can no longer be legitimately referred to the traditional topics of *metaphysica specialis* – God, freedom, and immortality – topics regarded as cognitively meaningless (although morally defensible) by Kant's critique of dogmatic metaphysics. Rather, the recognition of the essential historicity of philosophy (and philosophers) implies: (i) the radical *finitude* of the human subject, i.e. that there is no God-like standpoint or point of reference outside of human experience from which the latter might be characterized and judged; and (ii) the thoroughly *contingent* or *created* character of human experience. Once this move has been made, that is, once the human being has been located as a finite subject embedded in an ultimately contingent network of history, culture, and society, then one can perhaps begin to understand a feature common to many philosophers in the Continental tradition, namely the *utopian* demand that things be otherwise. That is to say, the demand for a transformative practice of philosophy, art, poetry or thinking (what the young Hegel and Schelling referred to as a "mythology of reason") that would be capable of addressing, criticizing, and ultimately redeeming the present. Critique and utopia are two ends of the same piece of string. However, a couple of words of explanation are required here.

Kant bequeathes a problem to his idealist, romantic, and even Marxist inheritors

10

in the Continental tradition, a problem that he grapples with himself in the *Critique of Judgment* (parenthetically, it is arguable that much of the difference between analytic and Continental philosophy simply turns on *how* one reads Kant and *how much* Kant one reads, whether one is solely concerned by the epistemological issues of the First Critique or by the greater systematic ambitions of the Third Critique, where Kant attempts to throw a bridge between the faculties of the Understanding [epistemology] and Reason [ethics] through a critique of the faculty of Judgement, where the latter would be the mediator between the concepts of nature and freedom and would harmonize the elements of the critical project). The problem might be put in the following way: the Kantian critique of metaphysics, if justified, achieves the remarkable feat of both showing the *cognitive* meaninglessness of the traditional claims of speculative, dogmatic metaphysics, whilst establishing the regulative *moral* necessity for the primacy of practical reason, that is, the concept of freedom. Yet, the question that this raises is the following: how is freedom to be instantiated or to take effect in the world of nature, if the latter is governed by causality and mechanistically determined by the laws of nature? How is the causality of the natural world reconcilable with what Kant calls the causality of freedom?[25] How, to allude to Emerson alluding to the language of Kant's Third Critique, is genius to be transformed into practical power?[26] Doesn't Kant leave human beings in what Hegel might have called the *amphibious* position of being both freely subject to the moral law and determined by an objective world of nature that has been stripped of any value and which stands over against human beings as a world of alienation?

Such is the problem that Nietzsche will diagnose in the 1880s with the concept of *nihilism* – a concept that is absolutely decisive for a whole range of twentieth-century Continental thinkers: Heidegger, Benjamin, Adorno, Schmitt, Arendt, Lacan, Foucault, Derrida, and Kristeva – namely that the recognition of the subject's freedom goes hand in hand with the collapse of moral certainty in the world, that the highest values have devalued themselves.[27] Nihilism is the breakdown of the order of meaning, where all that was posited as a transcendent source of value in pre-Kantian metaphysics becomes null and void, where there are no cognitive skyhooks upon which to hang a meaning for life. All transcendent claims for a meaning to life have been reduced to mere values – in Kant the reduction of God and the immortality of the soul to the status of the postulates of pure practical reason – and those values have become, for Nietzsche, incredible, standing in need of "transvaluation" or "revaluation." Now, for Nietzsche, when we realize the shabby and all-too-human origin of our moral values, our *reactive* response – that is to say, our Christian response – is to declare that existence is meaningless. It is this declaration of meaninglessness that Nietzsche identifies as nihilism and which he detects in various nascent phenomena: in the Schopenhauerian pessimism or "passive nihilism" that Nietzsche often identifies as "European Buddhism," in the terroristic anarchism of "active nihilism," which, for Nietzsche, is the mere expression of decadence, and in a general cultural mood of weariness, exhaustion, and fatigue summarized in the memorable formula, "Modern society . . . no longer has the strength to *excrete*."[28]

For Nietzsche, nihilism as a psychological state is attained when it is realized that the categories (for Nietzsche, the Christian-Moral categories) by means of which human beings had tried to give meaning to the universe are meaningless. This does not at all mean that the universe is meaningless, but rather, in a possible allusion to Kant, that "the faith in the categories of reason is the cause of nihilism."[29] Thus, from a Nietzschean perspective, nihilism is the unforeseen consequence of the Kantian critique of metaphysics. That is to say, nihilism is the consequence of moral valuation. My values no longer have a place in the world – it is this self-alienation of the modern Stoic that Hegel calls "the moral view of the world,"[30] and which can lead to the resignation of nihilism, but which can also lead to the demand for a revaluation of values, the revolutionary philosophical demand that things be different.

To put this in other terms, the touchstone of philosophy in the Continental tradition might be said to be *practice*; that is to say, our historically and culturally embedded life in the world as finite selves. It is this touchstone of practice that leads philosophy towards a critique of present conditions, as conditions not amenable to freedom, and to the Utopian demand that things be otherwise, the demand for a transformative practice of philosophy, art, poetry or thinking. Perhaps this begins to explain a possibly puzzling feature of philosophy in the Continental tradition, namely the theme of *crisis* that, in different forms, runs like Ariadne's thread through German idealism, Marxism, phenomenology, psychoanalysis, and the Frankfurt School.[31] For the Continental tradition, philosophy is a means to *criticize* the present, to promote a reflective awareness of the present as being in crisis, whether this is expressed as a crisis of faith in a bourgeois-philistine world, a crisis of the European sciences, of the episteme of the human sciences, of nihilism, of the oblivion of Being, of bourgeois society, of the hegemony of instrumental rationality, of the technological domination of nature, or whatever. Philosophy as an acute reflection upon history, culture, and society can lead to the awakening of critical consciousness, what Husserl would call the reactivation of a sedimented tradition. To push this a little further, the responsibility of the philosopher – in Husserl's formula "the civil servant of humanity"[32] – is the *production* of crisis, disturbing the slow accumulation of the deadening sediment of tradition in the name of a reactivating historical critique, whose horizon would be an emancipated life-world. Philosophy in the Continental tradition has an emancipatory intent, and rightly so. For a philosopher, I take it, the real crisis would be a situation where crisis was not recognized – "Crisis, what crisis?" In such a world, philosophy would have no purpose, other than as a historical curiosity, an intellectual distraction, or a technical means of sharpening one's common sense.

The fact that philosophy in the Continental tradition can be said to respond to a sense of crisis in modernity and indeed tries to produce crisis insofar as it endeavours to awaken a critical consciousness of the present, perhaps also goes some way to explaining its most salient and dramatic difference from analytic philosophy, namely its *anti-scientism* (an attitude that is, of course, far from being anti-scientific). The critique of scientism here resides in the dual belief that (i) the procedures of the natural sciences cannot and, moreover, should not provide a model for philosophical method, and (ii) that the natural sciences do not provide our primary

12

or most significant access to the world. One finds this belief variously expressed in a whole range of Continental thinkers, in Nietzsche, Bergson, Heidegger, and the later Husserl, in the Francophone existential and hermeneutic phenomenologists (notably Levinas, Ricoeur, and Merleau-Ponty) and, in a different register, in the Frankfurt School (particularly Adorno's and Horkheimer's *Dialectic of Enlightenment*, but also in the early Habermas). Of course, it would be a misrepresentation to claim that this worry about scientism and the allied but not identical concern about the naturalization of philosophy was absent from analytic philosophy, where it arises in the Wittgensteinian tradition and has been strongly expressed in Putnam's recent work.[33]

From a Continental perspective, the adoption of scientism in philosophy fails to grasp the critical and cultural function of philosophy; that is, it fails to see the complicity between a scientific culture and what Nietzsche diagnosed as nihilism.[34] What this means is that philosophical scientism fails to see the role that science and technology play in the alienation of human beings from the world through the latter's objectification into a causally determined realm of nature or, more aggregiously, into a reified realm of commodities manipulated by an instrumental rationality. In a Heideggerian register, scientism rests on the false assumption that the scientific or theoretical way of viewing things – what Heidegger calls the present-at-hand – provides the primary and most significant access to ourselves and the world. Heidegger shows that the scientific view of the world is derivative or parasitic upon a prior practical view of the world as ready-to-hand, that is, the environing world that is closest, most familiar, and most meaningful to us, the world that is always already colored by our cognitive, ethical, and aesthetic values. That is to say, scientism or what Husserl calls objectivism, overlooks the phenomenon of the *life-world* which is the enabling condition for scientific practice. Although such an anti-scientism *can* lead to obscurantism – which in many ways is the inverted or perverted counter-concept to scientism – it *need* not do so. The critique of scientism, at least within phenomenology, does not seek to refute or negate the results of scientific research in the name of some mystical apprehension of the unity of the man and nature, or whatever; it rather simply insists that science does not provide the primary or most significant access to a sense of ourselves and the world. What is perhaps required here is what Heidegger referred to in *Being and Time* as "an existential conception of the science" that would show how the practices of the natural sciences arise out of life-world practices, and that the latter are not simply reducible to the former.[35]

## Professionalism and the identity of philosophy

To conclude, in many ways, this *Companion*, insofar as it forms part of the series of Blackwell Companions to Philosophy, very much reflects the professional place of what has come to be known as Continental philosophy in the English-speaking world. That is to say, it is an irritable and slightly swollen appendix within the corpus of Anglo-American philosophy. There are the major sub-divisions of philosophy, a dozen or so: logic, epistemology, metaphysics, philosophy of mind, philosophy of language, philosophy of law, ethics, philosophy of religion, political philosophy, aesthetics, and so on; and there is this odd addendum called "Continental philosophy" that doesn't readily or usefully fit into these divisions, for it seems to cut across them all. The fact that this appendix contains some of the best of what has been thought on the philosophically most fertile territory on the globe for the past two hundred years or so might perhaps be a greater cause of intellectual anxiety and embarrassment that it often appears to be.

However, things are improving, slowly. The various philosophical hegemonies, orthodoxies, and research programs on both sides of the philosophical divide that characterized philosophy in the decades that followed the Second World War have arguably come to a close, whether through the death or retreat of their major protagonists, through simply having run out of steam or into the sand, or by having suddenly and often inexplicably become tiresome and uninteresting. In a *fin-de-siècle* mood, it is unclear quite what the future holds, if anything at all. However, I would wager that there is the dim, but perceptible, prospect of a more bracing philosophical pluralism, where philosophy is recognized as a practice that (i) habitually takes place in relation to a specific tradition, and that the intellectual preferences that make up the canon of a tradition are recognized *as preferences* and not natural choices; (ii) that philosophy has more than one tradition and that assertions of philosophical exclusivism result, at best, in parochialism and, at worst, in intellectual imperialism; (iii) more normatively, but also more Socratically, that philosophy should form an essential part in the life of a culture, i.e. that philosophy be cultivated as that moment of critical reflection where citizens are invited to question the *doxai* that govern their *polis*: what is justice? More crudely stated, philosophy should have a civilizing, educative, emancipatory effect. It should be noted here that my talk of philosophical pluralism does not imply an abandonment of the search for truth in the name of a pragmatically driven desire for peaceful cohabitation. Rather, I take it that pluralism begins with a recognition of the specificity of one's philosophical approach and a tolerance of other approaches whilst engaging in the common pursuit of shared philosophical problems.[36]

The conditions for dialogue between philosophical traditions are not ideal – are they ever? – and the blame lies with both camps and their dual and reciprocal tendency towards insularity and intellectual sectarianism. Although it sometimes appears as if analytic and Continental philosophy are really two separate disciplines with nothing much in common, one might at the very least hope that in the future philosophers can do better than shout at each other across the gulf that separates them. Such dialogue is taking place here and there, and to the extent that it can continue, the future looks a good deal brighter than the recent past. The importance of such dialogue cannot be overestimated, because the very identity of philosophy as a practice is at stake. Both Continental and analytic philosophy are, to a great extent, sectarian self-descriptions of philosophy that are the lamentable consequence of the professionalization of the discipline, a professionalization that, in the view of this writer, has lead to the weakening of philosophy's critical function and its emancipatory intent, its progressive marginalization from the life of culture. It might be hoped that the overcoming of this marginalization is

14

something that all philosophers, whether "analytic" or "Continental," might agree upon.

## Notes

1 Michael Dummett, *Origins of Analytic Philosophy* (London: Duckworth, 1993), p. 26. In this regard, see Dermot Moran's "A case for philosophical pluralism: the problem of intentionality," in *Philosophy and Pluralism*, ed. David Archard (Cambridge: Cambridge University Press, 1996), pp. 19–32, where he tries to make a case for philosophical pluralism between the analytic and Continental traditions by taking up the theme of intentionality.

2 For a brief critique of Dummett's account of the emergence of analytic philosophy that, with some justification, argues for the centrality of Russell rather than Frege, see Ray Monk's "Bertrand Russell's brainchild. Analytical philosophy: its conception and birth," *Radical Philosophy*, no. 78 (July/August 1996), pp. 2–5. The same argument is presented at greater length by Monk in "What is analytic philosophy?," in *Bertrand Russell and the Origins of Analytical Philosophy*, ed. Ray Monk and Anthony Palmer (Bristol: Thoemmes, 1996), pp. 1–22.

3 For a book-length discussion of Continental philosophy, which appeared after this text was written, see David West, *An Introduction to Continental Philosophy* (Cambridge: Polity, 1996). Of particular merit in West's account is the way in which he refuses to identify Continental philosophy as a geographical category and seeks instead to reconstruct the rich historical context of post-Kantian Continental thought as a series of responses to the Enlightenment.

4 However, the notion of "Continental philosophy" can, at the very least, be traced back to the mid-nineteenth century. A decisive document in this regard is John Stuart Mill's 1840 essay on Coleridge, published in the *London and Westminster Review* as a companion to his 1838 essay on Bentham (in J. S. Mill and Jeremy Bentham, *Utilitarianism and Other Essays* [London and Harmondsworth: Penguin, 1987], pp. 177–226). In this essay, and in connection with the German influences on Coleridge, Mill speaks of "Continental philosophers" (p. 188) and "the Continental philosophy" (pp. 191 and 201). I owe this information to Jonathan Rée, who persuasively argues that the opposition between analytic and Continental philosophy is a good deal older and more native than is usually thought and might be rethought in terms of Mill's opposition between Bentham and Coleridge: that is, between the questions "Is it true?" and "What is the meaning of it?" (p. 177).

5 I allude here to a 1966 paper by Istvan Mézaros, where, in an exasperated and even desperate tone, he criticizes the philosophical exclusivism and implicit cultural parochialism of Ryle and Austin. He writes, "For how can one entertain even for a moment the idea of a dialogue if one's approach implies – however politely this may be put – that everyone else is conceptually confused." And again, "The elementary condition of a fruitful dialogue is, naturally, not the readiness to give up existing preferences, but the sober recognition that these preferences *are preferences*, however justified they may be." ("The possibility of a dialogue," in *British Analytical Philosophy*, ed. Bernard Williams and Alan Montefiore (London: Routledge & Kegan Paul, 1966), pp. 314, 333).

6 Cited in Leslie Beck's "avant-propos," preface to *La Philosophie analytique, Cahiers de Royaumont No. IV* (Paris: Editions de Minuit, 1962), p. 7.

7 *An Invitation to Phenomenology*, ed. James M. Edie (Chicago, IL: Quadrangle, 1965); *Phenomenology in America*, ed. James M. Edie (Chicago, IL: Quadrangle, 1967).

8 *Continental Philosophy in America*, ed. Hugh Silverman, John Sallis, and Thomas M. Seebohm (Pittsburgh, PA: Duquesne University Press, 1983).

9 John Searle, "Contemporary philosophy in the United States," in *The Blackwell Companion to Philosophy*, ed. Nicholas Bunnin and Eric Tsui-James (Oxford: Blackwell, 1996), pp. 1–2.

10 David E. Cooper, "Modern European philosophy," in *The Blackwell Companion to Philosophy*, p. 702. See also, Cooper, "The presidential address: analytical and Continental philosophy," *Proceedings of the Aristotelian Society*, 94 (1994), pp. 1–18.

11 Dummett, *Origins of Analytic Philosophy*, pp. 1–2.

12 This objection first appears in Williams's lead article in the inaugural issue of *The European Journal of Philosophy*, "Nietzsche's minimalist moral psychology," vol. 1, no. 1 (April 1993), p. 5; and is repeated and elaborated in Williams's survey article, "Contemporary philosophy: a second look," in *The Blackwell Companion to Philosophy*, p. 25.

13 Ibid., p. 27.

14 I allude here to Hilary Putnam's critique of Williams on this point in "Bernard Williams and the absolute conception of the world," *Renewing Philosophy* (Cambridge, MA: Harvard University Press, 1992), pp. 80–170.

15 Stanley Rosen, *The Question of Being: A Reversal of Heidegger* (New Haven, CT and London: Yale University Press, 1993), p. x.

16 *The Independent on Sunday*, May 17, 1992.

17 See *The Oxford Companion to Philosophy*, ed. Ted Honderich (Oxford: Oxford University Press, 1995), pp. 28–30, 161–3.

18 Ibid., p. 30.

19 Ibid., pp. 161, 163.

20 *Contingency, Irony, and Solidarity* (Cambridge: Cambridge University Press, 1989), p. 81.

21 "I have wished to understand philosophy not as a set of problems but as a set of texts," (*The Claim of Reason* (New York and Oxford: Oxford University Press, 1979), p. 3).

22 See Dummett, *Origins of Analytic Philosophy*; *The Analytic Tradition*, ed. David Bell and Neil Cooper (Oxford: Blackwell, 1990). In this regard, some very interesting work has been done on Russell and British idealism; see Peter Hylton, *Russell, Idealism and the Emergence of Analytic Philosophy* (Oxford: Oxford University Press, 1990), Nicholas Griffin, *Russell's Idealist Apprenticeship* (Oxford: Oxford University Press, 1991), and Ray Monk and Anthony Palmer (eds), *Bertrand Russell and the Origins of Analytical Philosophy* (Bristol: Thoemmes, 1996). Ray Monk's biographies of Wittgenstein and, more recently, of Russell, also merit consideration as part of an emerging history of the analytic tradition. See *Ludwig Wittgenstein: The Duty of Genius* (London: Jonathan Cape, 1990) and *Bertrand Russell: The Spirit of Solitude* (London: Jonathan Cape, 1996).

23 John Skorupski, "The intelligibility of scepticism," in *The Analytic Tradition*, pp. 1–29.

24 Jacques Derrida, "Lettre à un ami japonais," in *Psyche: Inventions de l'autre* (Paris: Galilée, 1987), p. 388.

25 *The Critique of Judgement*, tr. James Creed Meredith (Oxford: Oxford University Press, 1952), p. 37.

26 R. W. Emerson, "Experience," in *Selected Essays*, ed. L. Ziff (Harmondsworth: Penguin, 1982), p. 311.

27 Friedrich Nietzsche, *The Will to Power*, tr. W. Kaufmann and R. Hollingdale (New York: Vintage, 1966), p. 9.

28 Ibid., p. 32.

29 Ibid., p. 13.

16

30 "The moral view of the world" and "Dissemblance or duplicity" in *Phenomenology of Spirit*, tr. A. V. Miller (Oxford: Oxford University Press, 1977), pp. 365–83.

31 I would argue that one can also find such a mood of crisis in the culturally and politically more self-conscious areas of the analytic tradition, for example the Vienna Circle's fascinating 1929 Manifesto dedicated to Moritz Schlick and written collectively by Otto Neurath, Rudolf Carnap, and Hans Hahn, which argues for a scientific conception of the world and an overcoming of metaphysics as an element in a revolutionary social democratic transformation of society. See "Wissenschaftliche Weltauffassung: Der Wiener Kreis," in Otto Neurath, *Empiricism and Sociology* (Dordrecht: Reidel, 1973), pp. 299–318.

32 For this image, see Edmund Husserl, *The Crisis of European Sciences and Transcendental Phenomenology*, tr. D. Carr (Evanston, IL: Northwestern University Press, 1970), p. 17.

33 Putnam, *Renewing Philosophy*.

34 David E. Cooper, "Modern European philosophy," in *Blackwell Companion to Philosophy*, pp. 706–10.

35 Martin Heidegger, *Being and Time*, tr. J. Macquarrie and E. Robinson (Oxford: Blackwell, 1962), p. 408ff. It is at least arguable that such a position is approached by John McDowell, admittedly from the other end of the philosophical telescope, in his highly influential *Mind and World* (Cambridge, MA: Harvard University Press, 1994). McDowell borrows Aristotle's notion of second nature and Hegel's notion of *Bildung* in order to try and escape the traditional predicament of philosophy, namely the epistemological construal of how to relate thought to things and mind to world and, in particular, the naturalistic version of that construal. McDowell implicitly borrows at least four Heideggerian themes (via Gadamer – a revealing fact): (i) the unintelligibility of scepticism (p. 113), which recalls the argument of Paragraph 44 of *Being and Time*; (ii) the attempt to construe experience as "*openness* to the world" which recalls Heidegger's notions of *Offenheit* and *Lichtung*; (iii) the idea that human life in the world is structured environmentally (p. 115), which recalls Heidegger's idea that *Welt* is first and foremost an *Umwelt*; and (iv) the claim that language is the repository of tradition (p. 126), which recalls Heidegger's ideas about historicity.

36 I here borrow Dermot Moran's formulations in "A case for philosophical pluralism: the problem of intentionality," in *Philosophy and Pluralism*, p. 31.

PART I

# THE KANTIAN LEGACY

# 1

# The context and problematic of
# post-Kantian philosophy

## FREDERICK C. BEISER

### Kant and the crisis of the Enlightenment

Usually, the history of philosophy in the first two decades after the publication of the *Kritik der reinen Vernunft* (Critique of Pure Reason) in May 1781 is seen as little more than commentary upon and criticism of Kant's classic text. It is chiefly a story about how Kant's successors tried to defend and systematize, or criticize and dismember, his philosophy. The main theme of this story is the central outstanding problem of Kant's philosophy: the transcendental deduction, the problem of the possibility of empirical knowledge. The various approaches to this problem, their formation and demise, is essentially the history of the Kantian philosophy itself. Such, at any rate, is the picture that emerges from the solid studies of Karl Rosenkranz, Johannes Erdmann, Nicolai Hartmann, Josiah Royce, Richard Kroner, and Ernst Cassirer.

There is much to be said for this approach. After 1788 Kant's philosophy was usually – though certainly not always – the centre of attention in German intellectual life. But it is worthwhile to consider that, before 1788, the *Kritik* seemed to suffer the same fate as Hume's *Treatise*: "to fall stillborn from the press." It was only in 1786 that Kant's philosophy began to receive more attention due to the success of Reinhold's *Briefe ueber die kantische Philosophie* (Letters on the Kantian Philosophy), which popularized many of Kant's ideas. By 1788 Kant's philosophy had truly arrived. In that year several journals, dozens of books, and hundreds of articles appeared devoted to discussion of it. It was also the case that the problem of the Transcendental Deduction became *one* of the central concerns of Kant's successors. They were no less concerned with the foundations and implications of his moral, political, and aesthetic doctrines; but the problem of the Deduction loomed very large for some of the most eminent among them, such as Reinhold, Maimon, FICHTE (see Article 3), SCHELLING (Article 5), and HEGEL (Article 6). We shall attempt to do some justice to it in the next section.

So this classical approach does have a substantial, if not total, historical justification. What, then, is wrong with it? It suffers from myopia, a failure to see the broader context of German philosophy in the 1780s and 1790s. It is crucial to see that Kant's philosophy did not create this context, but was simply part of it. People criticized or defended Kant because his philosophy was seen as one interesting response to broader issues that dominated public attention. Indeed, Reinhold's

*Briefe* succeeded only because it portrayed Kant's philosophy as the only solution to the then raging "pantheism controversy." It is important to recognize that Kant's philosophy itself was largely formed in the maelstrom of controversy. Although the first *Kritik* was the product of "the silent decade," the 1770s, the second and third – *Kritik der praktischen Vernunft* (1788, Critique of Practical Reason) and *Kritik der Urteilskraft* (1790, Critique of Judgement) – were conceived only in the late 1780s in response to current criticisms and debates. Underneath the veneer of Kant's frozen architechtonic there raged a fiery polemic. The critical philosophy was not hatched from the eternal contemplation of reason, from rigorous adherence to the demands of system, as some Kantians would have us believe. Rather, it grew out of the demands of its age, the crises and controversies of late-eighteenth-century Germany.

The context of German philosophy toward the close of the eighteenth century was dominated by one longstanding cultural crisis: the decline of the *Aufklärung*, the German Enlightenment. This crisis threw into question its main article of faith: the sovereignty of reason. The *Aufklärung* was the German "age of reason," or, since reason was conceived as a critical power, "the age of criticism." The *Aufklärung* gave reason complete sovereignty because it claimed that reason could criticize *all* of our beliefs, accepting or rejecting them strictly according to whether there is sufficient evidence for them. This principle was confidently asserted by Kant himself in the preface to the first edition of the *Kritik der reinen Vernunft*:

> Our age is, to a preeminent degree, the age of criticism, and to criticism all of our beliefs must submit. Religion in its holiness, and the state in its majesty, cannot exempt themselves from its tribunal without arousing just suspicion against themselves.

Such was the bold programme – and dream – of the *Aufklärung*. Tragically, though, it carried the seeds of its own destruction. Simply to state its principle of the sovereignty of reason is to raise grave questions about it. For if reason must criticize everything on heaven and earth, must it not also criticize itself? And, if it does so, how does it prevent its self-criticism from becoming scepticism? A nightmare looms: that the self-criticism of reason ends in nihilism, doubt about the existence of everything. That fear was the sum and substance of the crisis of the *Aufklärung*.

That a crisis was impending was seen very clearly by Kant himself. His answer to it was nothing less than the *Kritik der reinen Vernunft*. The aim of the critical philosophy was to walk a middle path between dogmatism (belief upon authority) and scepticism (doubt about all belief). This middle path would consist in a tribunal to examine all of our beliefs according to "the eternal laws of reason." The tribunal would avoid dogmatism because it would rigorously examine all the claims of reason; and it would also escape scepticism since its eternal laws would be the necessary presuppositions of all discourse, even that of the sceptic. So, Kant hoped, the critical philosophy could finally bring reason's house into order, putting it upon a firm foundation for once and all.

But are there really any such eternal laws? Is there truly a middle path between scepticism and dogmatism? Or is it the case that if we examine the tribunal of critique itself, we end out in a new higher-order scepticism, a *metacritical* scepticism? These were the questions raised by Kant's early critics, and indeed the source of so much of the early controversy surrounding his philosophy. Upon them hung the very fate of the *Aufklärung* itself.

Although it had been simmering for decades, the crisis of the *Aufklärung* reached boiling point in 1786. The first bad omen was the death of Friedrich II, "the philosopher king," who had always supported the *Aufklärung* from the throne. The prospects that his successor, Friedrich Wilhelm II, would be as enlightened looked grim. But disaster truly struck when Jacobi published his *Briefe ueber die Lehre von Spinoza* (Letters on the Doctrine of Spinoza), which revealed Lessing's shocking confession of Spinozism. *Prima facie* there was little more to his book – a pastiche of textual exegesis, personal reminiscences, and correspondence – than juicy gossip. But Lessing was merely a vehicle or excuse for Jacobi to launch a full frontal assault on the *Aufklärung*. Jacobi saw Spinoza's philosophy as the paradigm of rationality because of its rigorous and uncompromising naturalism; but he also insisted that Spinozism ends in atheism and fatalism. He was therefore contending that rational enquiry, if it is only consistent, ends in the destruction of moral and religious belief. His argument for this conclusion was simple but worrisome: if we are complete naturalists, then we must universalize the principle of sufficient reason, such that for *any* event there must be some prior events that determine it into action of necessity; but then there cannot be spontaneous or first causes, which are required by the beliefs in God and freedom. In making this argument, Jacobi put his finger upon a common concern at the close of the eighteenth century: that the progress of science will undermine moral and religious belief. He dramatized the issue by confronting the *Aufklärer* with a dilemma: a rational atheism and fatalism or an irrational leap of faith (*salto mortale*). There was no comforting middle path, such as that postulated by Kant's critique, where it was possible to find a rational support for moral and religious belief.

It was this dilemma, so dramatically posed, that sparked off the storm of the pantheism controversy in the late 1780s. Among the participants in this debate were Goethe, Hamann, Herder, Mendelssohn, and Reinhold. The shock waves lasted into the 1790s and early 1800s when Fichte, Schelling, Hegel, and Kierkegaard took up the isues raised by it. It is no exaggeration to say that this controversy set one of the defining issues of the whole Continental tradition, the problem of the authority of reason. The so-called "postmodern predicament" really began, then, in 1786.

The crisis of the *Aufklärung* deepened in the summer of 1789 due to one momentous event: the storming of the Bastille. The subsequent bloody course of the Revolution – the September massacres, the execution of the king and queen, and the reign of terror – seemed to indict the *Illumination* and so, by implication, the *Aufklärung* itself. It was in the name of reason that the French radicals justified their *liberté, egalité et fraternité*, that they swept away the historical traditions and institutions of France, and that they conceived and executed the terror. But this raised

23

grave doubts in those who were appalled by the French apocolypse: does not reason, if applied rigorously and uncompromisingly, lead to anarchism? Here again it seemed necessary to question the value of reason, which had all the blood of the guillotine on its hands. Just as reason seemed to end in atheism in religion and fatalism in morality, so it appeared to result in anarchism in politics.

This question provoked a heated controversy in the early 1790s, the "theory–practice debate," which took place in many journals but chiefly in the *Berlinische Monatsschrift*, the most prominent mouthpiece of the *Aufklärung*. The occasion for the debate was the publication in 1793 of Friedrich Gentz's translation of Edmund Burke's *Reflections on the Revolution in France*. With its passionate attack upon "political metaphysicians," Burke's tract seemed to vindicate those conservatives who doubted the value of reason in politics. Burke's critique of rationalism in politics incited a reply by Kant himself in his famous 1793 essay *Ueber den Gemeinspruch: Das mag in der Theorie richtig sein, taugt aber nicht für die Praxis* (On the common saying: what might be true in theory is useless in practice). Kant was attacked by a host of talented conservative critics: A. W. Rehberg, Friedrich Gentz, Justus Möser, and Christian Garve, to name just a few. The fundamental question raised by this debate concerns the role of reason in politics. Does reason have the power to determine the first principles of the state? If so, does it also have the power to make people *act* on them? There were two opposing responses to these questions, reflecting the deeper differences between rationalism and empiricism in ethics. According to the rationalists, whose chief spokesman was Kant, pure reason does have the power to determine the first principles of morality; and since these principles are categorically and universally binding, they hold also in politics, providing the standards to which all institutions and practices should conform. In other words, practice should conform to theory, which consists in the standards of morality. According to the empiricists, however, whose main representative was Möser, the principles of morality are determinable only through experience, through knowing the consequences of our actions; and since experience shows that wholesale reform has bad consequences, disrupting the delicate social organism in all kinds of unpredictable ways, present institutions and practices should provide the standard to which all plans for reform should conform. In other words, theory should conform to practice.

This debate continued well into the 1790s and after. Fichte, Hegel, Feuerbach, and Marx would later all develop answers to it. The famous question of the relationship between theory and practice, which has been so important in the Continental tradition, ultimately goes back to this debate at the close of the eighteenth century.

Kant's philosophy became the centre of public attention in Germany because it seemed to provide a plausible solution to both the pantheism controversy and theory–practice debate. In his 1786 essay *Was heisst: Sich im Denken orientiren?* (What does it mean to orient oneself in thinking?) and in his 1788 *Kritik der praktischen Vernunft* Kant set forth his solution to the seething pantheism controversy. His doctrine of practical faith seemed to provide a middle path between the horns of Jacobi's dilemma. According to Kant, reason could not muster a *theoretical* justification for our moral and religious beliefs, because it could not provide demonstrations of the existence of God, providence, immortality, and freedom. Reason could supply a *practical* justification for our beliefs, however, because it could show them to be a necessary incentive to act according to the moral law, which is prescribed by pure reason alone. To many, such a solution appeared very attractive because it gave a rational foundation for belief, yet avoided the perilous enterprise of metaphysics with all its questionable proofs for the existence of God, providence, immortality, and freedom. In the realm of politics, Kant's philosophy also seemed to provide a powerful defense of the powers of reason. Some of his 1790 essays, especially the *Ueber den Gemeinspruch* and *Zum ewigen Frieden*, argue that the fundamental principles of the Revolution – *liberté, egalité et fraternité* – can be easily derived from the categorical imperative, the principle "Act only on that maxim that can be a universal law of nature." Reversing the charge of his conservative critics, Kant contended that it was empiricism, not rationalism, that invited the danger of rebellion and anarchy. Rationalism forbade rebellion since a maxim permitting disobedience, if universalized, would permit lawlessness, and so destroy itself. Empiricism, on the other hand, permitted, even encouraged, rebellion, because the people *ought* to rebel whenever it proves to be to their advantage.

But many of Kant's early critics – both friends and foes of the *Aufklärung* – were not so easily convinced. Their criticisms only deepened the crisis of the *Aufklärung*, making it seem even more irresolvable. One of the most common and troubling criticisms was that Kant's philosophy, if it were only consistent, ends in a total solipsism. This criticism was made most effectively by Jacobi in his 1799 *Brief an Fichte* (Letter to Fichte). According to Jacobi, Kant's first principle is that reason is a pure activity, an activity that knows only what it creates, or what it makes conform to its own laws. This means, however, that it knows only the products of its own activity and not a reality that exists apart from and prior to it. Hence, either we know ourselves or nothing, so that we are trapped inside the circle of our own consciousness. Of course, Kant does believe in the existence of the thing-in-itself, which is supposed to be the cause of our experience. But, Jacobi further argued, if Kant were only consistent, then he would have to admit that he knows nothing about its existence either. For if the categories are applicable only within experience – as Kant says *ad nauseum* – and if existence and causality are only categories, then how do we know that the thing-in-itself exists and is the cause of experience? With this attack upon Kant, Jacobi reformulated and reinforced his earlier attack upon the *Aufklärung*. Now, the paradigm of rationality was not Spinoza's naturalism but Kant's idealism. The dilemma was now a rational solipsism or an irrational leap of faith.

The charge of solipsism against Kant marks the beginning of a problem that will continue to haunt philosophy well into the nineteenth and twentieth centuries: nihilism. As early as the 1790s nihilism, "that most uncanny of guests" (as Nietzsche put it), was knocking at the door. It was Jacobi who first introduced the term during his polemic against Kant. To Jacobi, a paradigm nihilist is a Kantian who admits that he knows nothing more than his passing representations. The nihilist is therefore someone whose reason does not permit him to affirm the existence of anything – God, the external world, others' minds, even his own self – and

25

whose representations really represent nothing. In its original sense, then, the term "nihilism" denotes the alleged solipsistic consequences of all rational enquiry. The introduction of this theme dramatized the crisis of the *Aufklärung*: Kant's philosophy, once the very bastion of the *Aufklärung*, now seemed to represent nihilism itself, the extreme negation of all moral and religious belief.

The predicament of the *Aufklärung* became even more grave after the many attacks upon Kant's doctrine of practical faith, which were made by a whole host of critics throughout the 1780s and 1790s. This doctrine does not provide a middle path between dogmatism and scepticism, they charged, because it just begs the question against the sceptic. Its central premise is that we are all subject to the moral law, and so need the incentive of religion to uphold it. How, though, do we *know* that we are subject to the moral law? Kant says we know that we are obliged because we are free; but we know that we are free through our conscience. But our conscience believes – and cannot prove – that the moral law applies to us. A vicious circle! It is also questionable, these critics pointed out, that a Kantian has a right to believe in the *existence* of God, providence and immortality. According to the "Dialektik" of the first *Kritik*, such a belief would amount to hypostasis, the confusion of a regulative and constitutive principle, or the false assumption that there is some reality corresponding to a moral ideal. All that we can do, following Kant's strictures, is to act *as if* God, providence, and immortality exist. These ideas should be nothing more than regulative fictions to guide our conduct. They provide no escape, then, from Kant's solipsistic shell.

Kant's critics were no less relentless toward his political philosophy, which to them only typified the weaknesses of rationalism in politics. After a severe scrutiny of the critical philosophy, Möser, Gentz, Garve, and Rehberg contended that pure reason is powerless in the political sphere. They made three chief criticisms of Kant.

1  The categorical imperative is not an adequate criterion of moral or political value because it amounts to nothing more than the demand of universalizability; but all maxims, even evil ones, can be universalized.
2  Even if the categorical imperative could determine the general principles of the state, these are so general that they are compatible with all kinds of specific laws and institutions. Just knowing that all citizens are equal, for example, does not determine the respects in which they should be treated equally (economically as well as legally?); or just knowing that all mature citizens deserve the right to vote does not make clear under what conditions they should be given that right (age, wealth, sex?). To determine which specific laws and institutions are best, it is always necessary to consult experience.
3  Pure reason by itself does not have the power to motivate a person to do their duty. The main motives of political action are passion, imagination, and tradition.

These criticisms of Kant's rationalism were an important factor in the development of historicism, which flourished in the early nineteenth century in Germany with Friedrich Savigny's and Gustave Hugo's school of law. The fathers of this movement were Rehberg, Gentz, and Möser. The rise of historicism only completed the crisis of the *Aufklärung*, however, because it threw into question another central tenet behind its faith in reason: the doctrine of natural law. The historicist *credo* is that all characteristic human activities – language, literature, art, religion, and law – should be placed within their historical context and seen as the necessary result of their specific historical conditions. But once this approach is rigorously practiced, what becomes of the supposed universal and eternal laws of nature? They disappear, because all laws are really only the product of a specific time and place. The claim that a law is universal and eternal arises only by invalidly generalizing from the specific values of one's own culture, by forgetting the specific historical circumstances behind their genesis. Such an argument throws into question the very possibility of criticism as practiced by the *Aufklärung*. The attempt to criticize the values, beliefs, and traditions of the apparently superstitious and barbarous past now seems guilty of the fallacy of ethnocentrism, the questionable assumption that all cultures and epochs have the same beliefs, values, and traditions as our own.

The ultimate effect of the criticism of Kant's philosophy in the 1780s and 1790s was to make the *Aufklärung*'s faith in reason seem more questionable than ever. Kant seemed to many to be the best hope for sustaining that faith; yet his most basic doctrines now seemed problematic. His idealism led to solipsism; his practical faith was a *petitio principii*; and his categorical imperative was empty. According to many of his early critics, Kant was not thwarting but abetting reason's self-destructive march toward the abyss. Of course, it would be absurd to suggest that such pessimism is true, the final conclusion of the controversy. For when is anything decisive in philosophy? Yet the mere fact that the debates had ended in an *aporia*, a question mark, meant that the old faith and consensus of the *Aufklärung* had gone. Would it ever be possible to restore its faith in reason? That question will continue to preoccupy the Continental tradition well into the twentieth century.

## The fate of the Transcendental Deduction

The crisis of the *Aufklärung* in the 1780s and 1790s arose not only in the spheres of morality, religion, and politics. Its faith in reason was profoundly shaken in another area: the natural sciences. They were crucial to the *Aufklärung*'s confidence in reason because they seemed to demonstrate the power of reason to know and control nature. The more reason could know of nature's causes, the more it could control them to benefit the life of man, and the more superstition, ignorance, and prejudice would retreat. But in the 1780s and 1790s, the *Aufklärung*'s faith in science also came under unprecedented attack. What was now at stake was not the moral and religious consequences of the sciences, but their very possibility. Is it possible for reason to know nature, to have insight into the universal and necessary laws of its operation?

That there is a serious problem in the justification of natural science had long been recognized by the *Aufklärung*. The *Aufklärer* were well aware of the challenge of Hume's skepticism, which threatened to dissolve the relation of cause and effect into a mere fiction of habit and the imagination. There had been several German translations of Hume – both the *Enquiry* and *Treatise* – since the 1750s. Kant's famous remark about his "dogmatic slumber," which came from forgetting his

Hume, was more self-reproach than a comment upon his age. The problem of the justification of the principle of sufficient reason – the principle that there must be a reason or cause for every event, according to which it occurs of necessity – had been considered by Leibniz, Wolff, and Crusius, by Lambert, Tetens, and Mendelsohn.

As early as the 1760s, the examination of this topic had ended in an *aporia*. In the *Nouveaux Essais*, Leibniz had made it clear that the principle of sufficient reason cannot have an empirical justification. It ascribes a universal and necessary connection between events; but no amount of experience ever shows that something *must* be, or that it *always* will be, the case. In his *Entwurf der nothwendigen Vernunft-wahrheiten* (1745; Sketch of the necessary truths of reason) C. A. Crusius had also made it plain – at least to everyone but the most stubborn Wolffian – that there cannot be an a priori demonstration of the principle that derives it from the law of non-contradiction. For any presumed cause–effect relation, it is possible to affirm the cause and to deny the effect (or conversely). This then left the challenging question: if it is not possible to derive the principle from experience or from the law of non-contradiction, what possible justification can it have? All the options appeared exhausted; but the very possibility of natural science hung in the balance. Such was the impasse Kant confronted in the 1760s and 1770s. His final solution to it would be nothing less than the Transcendental Deduction of the first *Kritik*.

The problem of the justification of natural science became more acute in the 1780s and 1790s because it seemed that Kant's solution – the most sophisticated and thorough to date – was ultimately untenable. The attempt to repair his solution by some of his disciples, especially by Reinhold in his *Elementarphilosophie*, only served to make its deficiencies more apparent. It is indeed striking that the 1780s and 1790s witness a revival of Hume's scepticism. The list of thinkers who would invoke Hume as their witness was formidable: J. G. Hamann, Thomas Winzenmann, Ernst Platner, G. E. Schulze, A. W. Rehberg, and Solomon Maimon. In one form or another they all invoked the spirit of *le bon David* to cast a spell against the critical philosophy.

What, then, went wrong with Kant's solution? To answer this question we must first have some idea, no matter how rough, of the problem and argument of the most difficult section of the first *Kritik*, the Transcendental Deduction. Here, however, we only need to interpret it as it was first understood by Kant's contemporaries.

The problem of the Transcendental Deduction began with Kant's impasse in the 1760s. Sometime in the 1770s, Kant came to the conclusion that there are other principles essential to our knowledge of experience that, like the principle of sufficient reason, are not capable of formal or empirical justification. Among them were the principle of substance (that all change in time presupposes something permanent) and reciprocity (that all effects react upon their causes). Since these principles are also a priori (not derived from experience) and synthetic (not derived from the law of non-contradiction), Kant posed the general question: how are synthetic a priori judgements possible? He also formulated the problem in terms of his distinction between understanding and sensibility. According to Kant, the understanding is an active intellectual faculty, which is the source of our a priori concepts or categories; sensibility is a passive empirical faculty, which receives our sensations or intuitions. The problem of the Deduction was then posed in these terms: how do the categories of the understanding apply to experience, the intuitions of sensibility, if they are not derived from these intuitions?

Put in its simplest terms, the main argument of the Deduction is that the categories are valid of experience because they are necessary conditions of its possibility. If perceptions are to be more than my private passing sensations, if they are to give me experience of a world outside me, then they must conform to the categories, which confer objectivity upon them. They provide objectivity because they are universal and necessary, indispensable conditions for any intelligent being to have an experience. The categories must apply to experience, then, for the simple reason that they *create, make or impose* its order, structure, and form. We should not conceive of that order, structure, and form as something given, to which the categories conform. If we make this assumption, then we must resign ourselves to a complete scepticism, for we can never get outside our representations to see if they conform to things-in-themselves. The Deduction was therefore the proof of the central assumption behind Kant's Copernican Revolution: "that objects conform to concepts and not concepts to objects." It was the crowning achievement of his "new method of thought": that the understanding knows a priori only what it creates.

Such, at any rate, was the early understanding of the Transcendental Deduction among many of Kant's contemporaries. Its assumptions and arguments were soon subjected to severe scrutiny in the late 1780s and early 1790s. Among its early critics were H. A. Pistorius, J. A. Eberhard, Christian Garve, J. G. Feder, G. E. Schulze, Ernst Platner, and even Kant's loyal expositor, Johannes Schultz. The most important and influential criticisms, though, were those made by Solomon Maimon in his 1790 *Versuch ueber die Transcendentalphilosophie* (Essay concerning the transcendental philosophy). Kant regarded Maimon as his best critic; and Fichte believed that his criticisms had completely overturned the critical philosophy. Maimon's scepticism proved to be a powerful challenge to post-Kantian philosophy. Indeed, to study Fichte, Schelling or Hegel without Maimon is like studying Kant without Hume.

Maimon's critique of the Deduction is powerful because it is internal, beginning from Kant's own premises. Maimon accepts Kant's argument that the objectivity of knowledge cannot be measured by some standard *outside* experience. The question is, however, whether we can establish a standard *within* it. Maimon doubted that this could be the case. If we summarize his involved and intricate polemic, then we should stress the following points.

1  Kant's argument is a *petitio principii* because all that it shows is that the categories are a necessary condition of an objective experience; but the sceptic denies that there is any such experience in the first place. He happily admits that his experience is a phantasmagoria, consisting of nothing more than passing impressions without any universal and necessary order.

2  There is an insurmountable gap between the categories, as the principles of *any* possible experience, and the specific laws of science, which are true only of *our* experience. The categories are compatible with any particular order of experience, and do not by themselves determine *which particular* order prevails. The category

of causality, for example, is compatible with smoke being the cause of fire as much as fire being the cause of smoke.

3 Kant cannot provide a criterion to determine when, and indeed whether, his categories apply to experience. Since they are compatible with any specific order, the categories do not show when and how they apply; and since experience is never universal and necessary, it does not determine that a category applies.

4 Kant's dualism between understanding and sensibility is so drastic and deep that it prohibits the possibility of a priori concepts applying to a posteriori intuitions. If understanding is a purely intellectual faculty, formal, active and standing above space and time, and if sensibility is a purely empirical faculty, material, passive and within space and time, then how do they interact? Kant stressed that the interplay of understanding and sensibility is essential for knowledge – "concepts without intuitions are empty, intuitions without concepts are blind" – yet his faculties were too heterogeneous for any interaction to be possible. The old Cartesian mind–body problem thus returned within Kant's system.

Maimon's scepticism set the problematic for much post-Kantian philosophy, especially the systems of Fichte, Schelling, and Hegel. Its net result was that the problem of the Deduction is insurmountable in the face of Kant's dualisms (understanding/sensibility, form/matter, category/empirical law). The main challenge facing Kant's successors was therefore to find some more general principle to overcome these dualisms. It was necessary to find some higher faculty of mind, of which they were only appearances.

The first philosopher to see and confront these challenges was K. L. Reinhold, Kant's early publicist. Although he was once an enthusiastic disciple of Kant, Reinhold became increasingly worried about the foundation of the critical philosophy, even before the advent of Maimon's scepticism. The critical philosophy lacked a self-evident first principle, and it required more system and unity. Yet Kant himself had insisted that a science is a system organized around and derived from a single principle! What was needed, then, was nothing less than a new foundation for the critical philosophy, a single self-evident first principle immune to doubt and capable of unifying Kant's dualisms. If the categories could be only derived from this principle, then they would finally have their deduction. Reinhold duly turned to the task of rebuilding the critical philosophy, publishing his results in his 1789 *Versuch ueber einen neuen Theorie des menschlichen Vorstellungsvermögens* (Essay on a new theory of the human faculty of representation). The fruits of his labour were what he called the *Elementarphilosophie*, a philosophy of the first elements or presuppositions of any philosophy. The guiding idea behind the *Elementarphilosophie* is that the single unifying faculty of mind is representation (*Vorstellung*). All the concepts of the understanding, intuitions of sensibility, ideas of reason, and schema of the imagination are simply so many forms of representation. All of Kant's dualisms are then derived as necessary aspects of representation as such. The problem was then to find the single self-evident first principle true of representation in general. This was the central task of his next major work, his 1790 *Beyträge zur Berichtigung bisherigen Missverständnisse der Philosophen* (Contributions toward the correction of misunderstandings among philosophers). The first principle of representation, grandly dubbed "the proposition of consciousness" (*Satz des Bewusst-seins*), sounds banal and trite: "In consciousness, the representation is distin-guished from, and related to, the subject and object by the subject." Reinhold's main point was indeed simple: that all representation requires something repre-sented (the object), someone representing (the subject), the act of representing, and, finally, the possibility of self-awareness of each element. Essentially, his prop-osition was an interpretation of the necessary conditions of Kant's principle of the unity of apperception, that the "I think" must be able to accompany all my repre-sentations. For all its banality, Reinhold's proposition did have a deeper point. In his analysis of representation, Reinhold's constant aim was to examine only the neces-sary conditions of representation or consciousness, excluding all metaphysical and physiological speculations. The *Elementarphilosophie* was thus an early phenome-nology, a study simply of the structure of what is given to consciousness. Only by adopting such a rigorous phenomenological approach, Reinhold believed, would the critical philosophy remain within its self-imposed limits of possible experience and avoid stepping over the barely discernible boundary of the transcendental and into the forbidden realms of the transcendent.

Reinhold's *Elementarphilosophie* was doomed to a brief, but brilliant, career. Al-though it dominated the philosophical stage in Jena in the early 1790s – a period when Jena was the intellectual capital of Germany – it quickly came under merci-less criticism. In early 1792 a polemical work appeared that weakened the very foundations of the *Elementarphilosophie*, G. E. Schulze's *Aenesidemus*. The main thrust of Schulze's polemic is that the *Elementarphilosophie* cannot provide a sound foundation for the critical philosophy. If the critical philosopher subjects the *Ele-mentarphilosophie* to a thorough examination, Schulze contends, then he has no choice but to accept a complete scepticism – a scepticism not only with regard to knowledge of the world but a *meta-critical* scepticism with regard to the very possi-bility of epistemology itself. Although Schulze's attack upon Reinhold sometimes misses its target, resting upon a crude interpretation of the *Elementarphilosophie*, it also hits home in important respects. Schulze makes several telling points.

1   The proposition of consciousness is simply too vague and equivocal to be a first principle. This is especially apparent with its terms "relate" and "distinguish," since a subject can "relate" a representation to himself and his object in all kinds of ways: as a whole to its parts, as an effect to its cause, as matter to its form, as a sign to what it signifies. Reinhold equivocates between these senses, depending on what he wants to deduce.

2   Reinhold's entire program is unworkable because it attempts to infer the specific from the general. The concept of representation in general or as such determines nothing about any specific kind of representation. Hence Kant's gap between form and matter, universal and particular, reemerges as a gap between representation as such and the specific kinds of representation.

3   Reinhold equivocates about the status of his phenomenological program. If it consists in the examination of the facts of consciousness, as he sometimes says, then it cannot provide a self-evident first principle because it will be subject to falsification like any empirical judgement: but if it is a logical analysis of the *concept*

31

of representation, then we have no guarantee that it is anything more than the analysis of a word, whose reference is not guaranteed.

4   Although Reinhold insists upon remaining within the boundaries of possible experience, he violates his own strictures all the time. He maintains, for example, that the thing-in-itself is the cause of the matter of representation; and he writes that the faculty of representation is the source of experience but never given to it.

Reinhold's philosophy, and Schulze's examination of it, came under further scrutiny in a short review destined to have a great influence upon later post-Kantian thought, Fichte's 1792 review of *Aenesidemus*. Although he argued that many of Schulze's criticisms missed their target, Fichte admitted that enough had hit home to leave the *Elementarphilosophie* a ruin. Fichte then added two basic criticisms of Reinhold: (1) that the proposition of consciousness could not be the first principle because it expressed a mere fact, which must have arisen from a prior activity; and (2) that the subject is prior to representation because it is responsible for relating and distinguishing itself, the object, and the representation from one another. Fichte resisted Schulze's conclusion, though, that philosophy would have to resign itself to a complete meta-critical scepticism. All that Schulze had shown, he argued, is that the *Elementarphilsophie* is not the foundation for philosophy; but it is still possible to some find new foundation. Fichte's criticisms of Reinhold now suggested where that foundation would lie: in the active, self-determining subject. Fichte would soon explore this suggestion in his famous 1794 *Wissenschaftslehre*.

The collapse of the *Elementarphilosophie* under the weight of Schulze's and Fichte's criticisms, and the abiding challenge of Maimon's scepticism, made it necessary to rethink the whole foundation of the critical philosophy. Somehow, it was necessary to find a first principle, and a new method for unifying Kant's dualisms. Only then would the problem of the Transcendental Deduction finally be resolved. Such, at any rate, was the conclusion reached by Fichte, and many others, in the early 1790s.

The development of German idealism after Kant – the growth of the grand systems of Fichte, Schelling, and Hegel – arose from this problematic. In one form or another these systems attempted to resolve the outstanding problem of the Transcendental Deduction. It is important to recognize, however, that this problem had been completely transformed since its early formulation in the 1760s and 1780s. Now the problematic had shifted to the unification of Kant's dualisms, since this was seen as the *sine qua non* of ensuring that interchange between understanding and sensibility that is the precondition of all knowledge. This led to the search for what Fichte, Schelling, and Hegel called "the principle of subject–object identity."

The quest for this principle immediately posed another problem, however. If this principle is to unify Kant's dualisms, it also has to explain them, to do full justice to them. For it is just a blunt fact of experience that sensations are given and contingent, that what we see, hear or feel does appear independent of our conscious control; it is just a hard reality that we are finite beings, who cannot create all of our world. Fichte, Schelling, and Hegel all insist that a transcendental and critical idealism, as opposed to a transcendent and dogmatic one, must account for these basic facts of experience. Hence their problematic now seemed paradoxical: they had to unify *and* divide the subject and object. They had to unify them to explain the possibility of knowledge, which requires their intimate connection; and they had to divide them to explain the basic facts of experience. Somehow they had to find, then, some means of unifying both subject–object identity and subject–object non-identity. What they were looking for, to use Hegel's paradoxical language, was the "identity of identity and non-identity." This phrase summed up the basic desideratum of German idealism after Kant: to find an idealism that explains the possibility of knowledge *and* the basic facts of experience.

Such was the main problematic of German idealism as it arose from the criticism of Kant's philosophy in the late 1780s and early 1790s. Fichte, Schelling, and Hegel will all develop different solutions to it, different formulations for the identity of identity and non-identity. In Fichte, it will be the notion of the infinite striving of the ego; in Schelling it will be the concept of life; and in Hegel it will be the concept of spirit. Just how these systems resolve this problem is, of course, a much longer and even more complex story. Here our main task has been only to trace the growth and transformation of the problem itself.

Our story does suggest, however, one moral about Continental philosophy in general. The development of German idealism after Kant marks one of the major dividing points between the analytic and Continental traditions. The grand metaphysical systems of Fichte, Schelling, and Hegel have found little sympathy in the analytic tradition, which has been more influenced by positivism and empiricism. The distance between these traditions will not appear so great, however, if we return to the problems that German idealism attempted to resolve: the problem of the possibility of empirical knowledge of the Transcendental Deduction and the general crisis of reason of the *Aufklärung*. Perhaps once the systems of Fichte, Schelling, and Hegel are explained as serious attempts to resolve these classic problems, they will not appear to be sheer speculation and system-building for its own sake? Perhaps they will seem to have, no matter how untenable, some philosophical point. Perhaps, indeed, these are possibilities worth exploring.

## References and further reading

Beiser, Frederick C.: *The Fate of Reason: German Philosophy from Kant to Fichte* (Cambridge, MA: Harvard University Press, 1987).

——: *Enlightenment, Revolution and Romanticism: The Genesis of Modern German Political Thought, 1790–1800* (Cambridge, MA: Harvard University Press, 1992).

Cassirer, Ernst: *Das Erkenntnisproblem in der Philosophie und Wissenschaft der neueren Zeit. Band III: Die nachkantischen Systeme* (Darmstadt: Wissenschaftliche Buchgesellschaft, 1974).

Crusius, C. A.: *Die philosophische Hauptwerke*, ed. G. A. Tonelli (Hildesheim: Olms, 1964).

Erdmann, Johann: *Versuch einer wissenschaftlichen Darstellung der Geschichte der Philosophie*, vol. V: *Die Entwicklung der deutschen Spekulation seit Kant* (Stuttgart: Holzboog, 1977).

Fichte, J. C.: *Gesammtausgabe der bayerischen Akademie der Wissenschaften*, ed. R. Lauth and H. Jacob (Stuttgart: Fromann, 1970).

Garve, Christian: *Versuch über verschiedene Gegenstände der Moral* (Breslau: Korn, 1801).

———: *Abhandlung über die Verbindung der Moral under der Politik* (Breslau: Korn, 1788).

———: *"Kritik der reinen Vernunft," Allgemeine deutsche Bibliothek*, 37–52 (1783), pp. 838–62.

Gentz, Friedrich: *Schriften von Friedrich Gentz*, 6 vols, ed. Gustave Schlesier (Mannheim, 1838).

———: *Betrachtungen über die franzöische Revolution nach dem Englishcen des Herrn Burke, neu bearbeitet mit einer Einleitung, Anmerkungen, politis che Abhandlungen, und einem critischen Verzeichnis* (Berlin, 1793).

Hartmann, Nicolai: *Die Philosophie des deutschen Idealismus*, 3rd edn (Berlin: de Gruyter, 1974).

Hausius, K. G.: *Materialien zur Geschichte der critischen Philosophie* (Leipzig: Brietkopf, 1793).

Jacobi, Friedrich Heinrich: *Werke*, ed. F. H. Jacobi and F. Köppen (Leipzig: Weidmann, 1846).

Kant, Immanuel: *Schriften*, ed. Wilhelm Dilthey et al. (Berlin: de Gruyter, 1902ff).

Kronenberg, M.: *Geschichte des deutschen Idealismus* (Munich: Beck, 1909).

Kroner: *Von Kant bis Hegel* (Tübingen: Mohr, 1921).

Maimon, Solomon: *Gesammelte Werke*, ed. V. Verra (Hildesheim: Olms, 1965).

Möser, Justus: *Sämtliche Werke: Historisch-Kritiksche Ausgabe*, ed. Göttingen Academy of the Sciences (Berlin, 1944).

Platner, Ernst: *Philosophische Aphorismen* (Lepizig: Sigwart, 1784). (Third completely revised edn, 1794, in Fichte, *Gesammtausgabe*, II/4.)

Rehberg, A. W.: *Ueber das Verhältnis der Metaphysik zu der Religion* (Berlin: Mylius, 1787).

———: *Untersuchungen über die franzöischen Revolution* (Hannover, 1992).

———: *"Kritik der praktischen Vernunft," Allgemeine Literatur Zeitung*, 188/3 (August 6, 1788).

———: *"Ueber das Verhältnis der Theorie zur Praxis," Berlinische Monatsschrift*, 23 (1794), pp. 114–43.

Reinhold, K. L.: *Briefe über die kantische Philosophie* (Leipzig: Reclam, 1923).

———: *Versuch ueber einer neuen Theorie des menschlichen Vorstellungsvermögens* (Prague: Widtmann & Mauke, 1789).

———: *Beyträge zur Berichtigung bisheriger Missverständnisse der Philosophen* (Jena: Widtmann & Mauke, 1790–4).

———: *Ueber das Fundament des philosophischen Wissens* (Jena: Widtmann & Mauke, 1791).

Rosenkranz, Karl: *Geschichte der Kant'schen Philosophie* (Leipzig: Voss, 1840). (New edn by Steffan Dietzsch; Berlin: Akademie Verlag, 1987.)

Schulze, G. E.: *Aenesidemus oder über die Fundamente der von em Herrn Professor Reinhold in Jena gelieferten Elementarphilosophie*, ed. A. Liebert (Berlin: Reuther & Reichard, 1912).

Wizenmann, Thomas: *Die Resultate der Jacobischen und Mendelssohnischen Philosophie, von einem Freywilligen* (Leipzig: Göschen, 1786).

# 2

# Kant

### ROBERT B. PIPPIN

In the following, I want to suggest two different ways of understanding the relation between Kant's *Critique of Judgment* and the later German Idealist tradition. Commentators have long noted the *point d'appui* for any interpretation of this relation: Kant's remarks about an "intuitive intellect" (for him a divine, or creative intellect), and the interpretations of this doctrine offered by SCHELLING (see Article 5) and HEGEL (Article 6). The first interpretation I want to consider might be called the received or standard view about that relation. I shall summarize it in sections I and II below. Roughly, according to this view, what Kant proposed as a mere regulative doctrine, of no central importance in the third *Critique*, was inflated by Schelling and Hegel, in a philosophically unjustifiable way, into a positive metaphysical claim about reality itself as a self-positing divine mind.

The second view presents a different picture, and I shall begin defending it in the remaining sections. According to this second view, both the accounts of Kant and of Hegel in the standard view are wrong. Kant's views about the intuitive intellect are connected in a more positive and detailed way to the major claims about judgment made in the work as a whole (exactly as the Hegel of *Glauben und Wissen* claimed), and the position Hegel is beginning to defend, when basing his early formulations on these Kantian texts, is not a defense of the absolute reality of a divine mind.

The main interpretive issue raised by either possible direction is whether each could be said to represent "internal" developments of Kantian arguments in the third *Critique*, or whether they are motivated by non-Kantian, even non-"critical" commitments on the part of Schelling and especially Hegel. On the standard view, the answer is clearly that the appropriation is not an internal development, but stems from concerns external and hostile to Kant's critical philosophy. My claim will be that the suggested alternate or second formulation of Kant's influence does rely on an internal criticism and development of Kant's position. That claim will require a defense of the reading of Kant's text suggested by that appropriation.

My argument will not be that this suggested appropriation is wholly "Kantian;" Kant's position is too incomplete and there are too many *aporiai* to claim that, as I shall try to indicate; nor that the full implications of Hegel's attempted completion and resolution of the Kantian position are adequately worked out and defended in these early Jena texts. But I do want to defend the claim that the suggested reading of the third *Critique*'s influence on, especially, Hegel, is a more defensible reading of both the Kantian and Hegelian texts, and that it suggests both a more accurate and a more philosophically interesting reading of the early Idealist tradition.

# I

Many German philosophers of the last decade of the eighteenth and the first decade of the nineteenth century interpreted the *Critique of Judgment* in the light of what they perceived to be the great problem created by the Kantian revolution in philosophy. That problem, as they saw it, was: once "inside" the Kantian project, to find one's way "out" again.

To enter the project seemed to many simply unavoidable. It was to share in the spirit of Kant's revolutionary modernism, to destroy dogmatism, to assert the autonomy of human reason, its sufficiency in being a law unto itself. To be able to see all conscious, intentional relations to nature, or any normative relation to others as primarily a "self-determination" in relation to nature and others, would establish that free self-determination as the supreme condition of intelligibility and action.

Finding some way out, however, quickly seemed necessary to many. The main problem: Kant's transcendental skepticism, his denial that any knowledge of things in themselves was possible; that, instead, we knew only appearances. For some, taking their bearings from Kant's own remarks at the end of the first *Critique*,[1] this restriction still left unacceptably open the possibility of "Spinozism" and so did not sufficiently secure the ideal at the heart of the Idealist aspirations: the absolute reality of human freedom. For others, this restriction meant that Kant's account of the merely subjective conditions of experience could not finally be distinguished from an epistemologically inconsistent and still unsystematic psychologism; that philosophy had not really advanced much beyond Locke,[2] and that it must. For still others, Kant's skepticism meant that the essentially practical proof for the efficacy of pure practical reason, and the transcendental case for the subjective conditions necessary for nature to be a possible object of experience, could be integrated into no systematic whole. And without such a systematic account, Kantianism amounted to faith (*Glauben*), not knowledge (*Wissen*), finally just an expression of faith that the whole is as it must be, if we are to be able to act as we ought.

For the young Fichte, the young Schelling, and the young Hegel, the prominent charge that there was finally no way out of Kant's skepticism (most memorably formulated by the devious Jacobi)[3] was much more a challenge than a damning criticism, an invitation to formulate an internal criticism of Kant which accepted central aspects of his anti-empiricism and his attack on transcendental realism, but which avoided these putative skeptical problems.[4] They shared none of Jacobi's counter-Enlightenment, religious worries about transcendental philosophy, preferred to see themselves, in the Biblical terms first formulated by Reinhold, as avoiding the "letter," but embracing the "spirit" of Kant's philosophy, and all were spectacularly confident of success.

But everyone seemed to see a different sort of way out of the Kantian wilderness, and, eventually, a different philosophical promised land. Tickets were soon being sold to an *Elementarphilosophie*, a *Wissenschaftslehre*, an *Identitätsphilosophie*, a *Wis-*

*senschaft der Logik*, and so on. In my own view, the most interesting and philosophically suggestive of these journeys began with Fichte's radicalization of Kant's claims about the apperceptive or self-conscious nature of human experience and action. The direction of this transformation would eventually lead to a revision of Kant's founding distinction between spontaneity and receptivity (as one between conceptual and a wholly non-conceptual content) and so to an anti-skeptical argument for the "absolute" (or unconditioned, not exogenously limited) status of the mind's spontaneous self-positing. This direction, formulated by Fichte roughly between 1790 and 1797 or so, would form a key element, even, I think, the heart of Hegel's eventual absolute idealism.[5] (It is also, we shall see later, a key element in Hegel's understanding of the third *Critique*.)

But this Kantian–Fichtean heart is not the whole Idealist body.[6] And it is also true that the publication in 1790 of Kant's *Critique of Judgment* convinced many that *Kant himself* had found a way out of Kantianism, that Kant had conceived a way of defending a systematic or holistic position within which the possibility of moral agency and of living or organic beings, as well as of law-governed, dynamically moving matter, could all be understood consistently. Somehow, our ability to appreciate natural beauty (in a "subjective" but "universally valid" way) and the indispensability of our "estimations" of life, could help defend the possibility of the systematic philosophy devoutly pursued by the post-Kantians.

However, while there is widespread agreement that Kant's position in *Kritik der Urteilskruft* (*KU*) was at least as influential in the development of later Idealism as his theory of self-consciousness, transcendental deduction, or theory of autonomy, and substantial consensus about the terms and issues which formed the core of that influence, there does not, at least on the surface, appear to be much in the consensus account that is very philosophically interesting. The question, in other words, has pretty much become a wholly historical one, a question simply of the proper formulation of an episode in *Ideengeschichte*, an episode without much contemporary or perennial relevance. This is so because the standard picture looks like this.

Both Schelling and Hegel directly identify the passages and themes which are supposed to mark out Kant's way out of Kant. They both cite two sections from the *Dialectic of Teleological Judgment*, no. 76 and no. 77. These sections attempt to explore the implications of the unavoidability of the appeal to purposiveness in explanations of nature, or the unacceptability of the radical and infinitely detailed contingencies we would have to face in wholly mechanistic explanations. To have to conceive of nature as purposive is to conceive of parts as existing "for the sake of" wholes (or to think of the effects of causes as also the causes of those causes) (no. 63 and no. 64), or is simply to conceive of nature as intelligently designed. (Or, perhaps said in a more Schellingian way, as intelligently designing itself.)[7] When Kant comes to explain what thinking of nature this way amounts to, he says that,

> reason forever demands that we assume something or other (the original basis [*den Urgrund*]) as existing with unconditioned necessity, something in which there is no longer to be any distinction between possibility and actuality. (*KU*, p. 402)

37

This "necessity" appears to require that nature be conceived as the product of an "intuitive intellect" (p. 406); not, like ours, an understanding which must discursively judge, organize, and systematize "material" which pure thought itself cannot supply, but an absolutely "active" intellect, a "complete spontaneity of intuition" (p. 406), an *intellectus archetypus* (p. 408) or "intellectual intuition" (p. 409),[8] whereby "wholes" are not thought as dependent on, or as aggregations of prior "parts," but parts as dependent on, only intelligible in their existence and functioning, by reference to their relation to already thought "wholes."[9]

Now on one reading, this could all certainly sound like Kant might be claiming that human reason can determine what there really is or must be (the "*Urgrund*"); that it must be a living, self-organizing nature, and so in some sense a "spiritualized" nature. This approach would defend a conception of such an "original basis" or *Urgrund* which transcended the great Kantian dualism of *Geist* and *Natur* (such a nature must exhibit a purposively designing intelligence). And this direction would appear to have greatly revised the first *Critique*'s picture of reason's subjectively regulative function. We now appear, in other words, not to be making some claim about how "we must think" of nature such that our explanatory demands can be met, but how nature must be, such that our conceivings and demandings, not to mention our very "living," could be possible in the first place.[10]

This version of the direction is especially stressed by those (such as Burkhart Tuschling) who are particularly worried about the development of Kant's views about systematicity (after about 1787) and who see in Kant's own work increasingly strong claims that a non-human intuitive intellect is required to account for empirical concept formation, organic unity, and a system of scientific laws.[11] Tuschling even, rather startlingly, suggests that these claims in no. 76 and no. 77 represent the beginnings of a major turn in Kant's thought, leading him towards an acceptance of a Schellingian self-positing Divine Mind or "Absolute," and culminating in the *Opus postumum*'s otherwise bewildering affirmation that transcendental idealism is a "Spinozism," or that its "present" is represented as much by Schelling as its past is by Spinoza.[12]

What is clear is that the young Schelling, in the *Ich-Schrift*, was certainly very much excited by this version of a *Third Critique* revision of the *First*:

> The completed Science does not rely on dead faculties, which have no reality and exist only in an artificial abstraction; it rather much more relies on the *living unity of the I*, one which remains the same in all the external manifestations of its activity; in it all the different faculties and activities, which philosophy has always set out, become only one faculty, only one activity of the same identical I.[13]

Hence no transcendental skepticism; no unsystematic dualism, or lifeless mechanism or mere faculty psychology; but a holistic, speculative philosophy; a nature conceived of as actively intuiting itself (purposively organizing itself) with human thought as a manifestation of this activity, not a classifying, legislating machine, operating on "dead," passively received matter.

Hence, too, the great enthusiasm in commentaries on these passages. Here is Schelling again:

> There have perhaps never been so many deep thoughts pressed together on so few pages as occurred in the Critique of Teleological Judgment, section no. 76.[14]

In an 1801 letter of Fichte, Schelling formulated his own "idea of the Absolute" as the "identity of thinking and intuiting" about which he says that this is "the highest speculative idea, the idea of the absolute, the intuiting of which occurs in thinking, the thinking of which occurs in intuiting" and that he is, in articulating this idea, simply "relying" on section no. 76 of the *KU*.[15]

Hegel too, in *Glauben und Wissen*, identifies sections no. 76 and no. 77 as the place where Kant expresses most fully "the idea of Reason," the basis for a truly speculative, not merely reflective philosophy. He too notes with great enthusiasm that Kant was "led" (by the internal logic of his own position) to the idea of an "intuitive intellect" and led to it "as an absolutely necessary idea."[16] And he goes on to claim,

> So it is he himself who establishes the opposite experience, that of thinking a nondiscursive intellect. He himself shows that his cognitive faculty is aware not only of the appearance and of the separation of the possible and the actual in it, but also of Reason and the In-Itself. Kant has here before him both the idea of a reason in which possibility and actuality are absolutely identical and its appearance as cognitive faculty wherein they are separated. In the experience of his thinking he finds both thoughts. However in choosing between the two his nature despised the necessity of thinking the Rational, of thinking an intuitive spontaneity and decided without reservation for appearance.[17]

It is clear from these and from many other enthusiasts (especially Schiller) that many post-Kantians were not content to interpret the *Critique of Judgment* as a limited critical account of the "conditions for the possibility" of some possibly objective status for distinctive sorts of pleasure/pain responses to the world, or as a kind of expanded account of how we must, subjectively, think of nature if an appreciation of its beauty and an estimation of the living beings within it are to be possible. Aside from Schiller's insistence on its importance in supposedly revising Kant's moral theory, the direction suggested by these quotations points to the even more ambitious belief that Kant's analysis implied revisions and expansions in Kant's core transcendental project. As we have seen, that claim rests on putatively revisionary implications of the "necessity" for postulating an "intuitive intellect."

Hence the questions: *do* these remarks by Kant in no. 76 and no. 77 suggest such revisions and expansions in any central doctrines of the transcendental Aesthetic and Analytic of the *Critique of Pure Reason*; if they do, what are such revisions; and even if they do, do those revisions lead in any interesting philosophical direction, or instead towards a romantic metaphysics, even a hylozoism, or a panlogicism or wild apriorism, etc.?

39

## II

Officially of course, the answer most prominent in the text itself is "no." The idea of an intuitive intellect serves a very limited, still basically regulative, subjectively required function. It may indeed be that Kant, in his account of teleological judgments and reflective judgments in general, is going farther than the *First Critique*'s account of regulative ideas, treating the problem now not just as one of the organization of the results of empirical enquiry, but as involving a different sort of formation, subsumption, and application of concepts. Appeals to nature's purposes are not ways of systematizing the results of our empirical inquiries about efficient causation, and are not heuristic principles necessary to regulate such enquiries. There are phenomena, he now claims, that will never be adequately explicable mechanistically. The problem is not now just systematization, but the possibility of subsumption under concepts in the first place, and a new model for such subsumption.[18]

And he may be "upping the stakes" in introducing this topic, beyond what was claimed for similar issues in the "Appendix" to the "Dialectic of Pure Reason," suggesting now that without a legitimate warrant for such reflective judgments (its "a priori principle"), "our empirical cognition could not thoroughly cohere to form a whole of experience" (p. 23).[19]

But whatever argument Kant presents for the "necessity" of teleological explanation, and however he resolves the apparent dialectic of teleological and mechanical judgments, the invocation of the idea of an intuitive intellect appears of narrow, explanatory significance. In the first place, it can be introduced this way only because Kant is clearly wedded to a general intentional model of teleology, on the strict model of an agent doing A in order to achieve B. When he considers teleological functions in organisms, since hearts do not act in order to circulate blood, he must revert to that model by requiring that the heart be intentionally designed by an agent in order to circulate blood. And he claims that the analysis of such an intentional designer reveals it must be a non-discursive intellect.[20] In other words, Kant's position seems designed more to avoid the metaphysically idealist direction than to invite it.

Where then (where, at least in Kant) is Schelling getting the notion that by introducing this idea of an intuitive intellect Kant has also reformulated his notion of human subjectivity itself, proposed a new view of "the living I," or even an unconditioned condition of all intelligibility, an Absolute, the "producings" of which involve a collapsing of the key Kantian distinction between thinking and intuiting?

Where especially is Hegel basing his even more extravagant assertion that Kant's discussion in no. 76 and no.77 has something to do with *the human intellect*.

Kant also recognizes that we are necessarily driven to the Idea [of a non-discursive intellect]. *The Idea of this archetypal intuitive intellect is at bottom nothing else but the same idea of the transcendental imagination that we considered above.* For it is intuitive activity, and yet its inner unity is no other than the unity of the intellect itself, the category immersed in extension, and becoming intellect and category only as it separates itself out of extension. *Thus transcendental imagination is itself intuitive intellect.* [My emphasis][21]

It might be possible here to detect in this take on the issue of an intuitive intellect something vaguely Kantian, an echo of the first edition of the *First Critique* and its suggestion of "a common root" out of which, or by original reference to which, the dualism between understanding and sensibility can be understood, a common root suggested to be the "productive imagination."[22] But a vague echo is the most that could be said, and the standard view of this *point d'appui* for German Idealism would seem confirmed. Whether the move in question is to a divinely productive nature, or to some even more obscure claim about our divinely productive intellect, the moves seem motivated by non-Kantian commitments and non-critical expectations. This view is well stated by Düsing. In summing up the issue he writes,

> All the foundational principles and doctrines of Kantian aesthetics in the *Critique of Judgment* are accordingly transformed and exported into a different metaphysical system of meaning [*Bedeutungssystem*]. The critique made against Kant is therefore not immanent, but presupposes the soundness of Hegel's own conception, which Kant, as the opponent of doctrinal metaphysics, would have criticized.[23]

## III

So, it appears that one way of thinking about the possibility of a purposively ordered world (as intelligently designed by an intuitive intellect) is somehow being inflated into a thesis about the supersensible substrate of nature itself (i.e., Kant's warnings about the subjective, regulative character of this thought seem contemptuously swept aside), and even more importantly it is being treated as a thesis of direct relevance for the basic mind–world relation at stake in Kantian philosophy. Such an inflation would appear to rest on some independent commitment to the view that Kant's transcendental account must already rest on a prior theory of some absolute world-process posing or dividing itself from itself and then identifying with itself in some act of supreme self-realization, as in many standard views of Fichte, Schelling, and of course Hegel. Why else, apart from such a commitment, would no. 76 and no. 77 be read in this way? Düsing's view would appear confirmed.

What is noteworthy, however, about Hegel's treatment of these passages in *Glauben und Wissen* is that he does not frame his discussion of no. 76 and no. 77 in any way informed by the specific problem of mechanism and teleology or even the philosophy of nature in general.[24] As we have seen, the issue which seems to be suggesting to Hegel some "inflation" of the importance of the idea of an intuitive intellect is not the problem of organic wholes or functional explanation. In a way that can indeed be said to follow Kant's treatment without distortion, what interests Hegel throughout these passages is what is involved in *our* capacity to "estimate" (*schätzen*) nature as living (and, originally, to appreciate it as beautiful). His remarks make clear that it is *this* capacity for estimation and appreciation, and the relation between such a capacity and our capacity for determinative judgment and discursive systematization, which will require a revision in the intellect–sensibility relation originally proposed. This is why he says that it is the issue of *reflective judgment* (*not* "nature") which "exhibits the most interesting point in the Kantian system"[25] wherein the "reality of reason" (not its subjective regulation) is demonstrable, exhibiting as its "subjective side" the aesthetic judgment, and as its "objective side," organic nature.[26] *Our capacity to experience a beautiful and living nature* is what requires a revision in understanding the general relation between "the empirical manifold" and the "absolute abstract unity." And this is why he suggests that it is in our being driven or required to think of the possibility of an aesthetic appreciation of nature, and our being driven or required to think through the implications of a living nature, both in ways with some binding normative status, that the idea of reason as organizing or systematizing data breaks down, and, let us say, the idea of a reason (non-arbitrarily, non-subjectively) *determining its own data*, or an intuitive intellect, becomes unavoidable.[27] What is also interesting is that so much of what Hegel discusses in *GW* is inspired by Kant's discussion of *aesthetic* experience, aesthetic judgment and "aesthetic ideas," topics which, in Kant's presentation, stand far away logically and textually from no. 76 and no. 77. The Hegelian claim is:

> This [Hegel has been exploring various versions of the "authentic idea of Reason" in Kant] shows that the Kantian forms of intuition and the forms of thought cannot be kept apart at all as the particular, isolated faculties which they are usually represented as. One and the same synthetic unity . . . is the principle of intuition and of the intellect.  (GW, p. 70)

Clearly, Hegel is claiming that Kant is introducing something in his treatment of aesthetic judgments which alters in a fundamental way the empirical realism/regulative idea theory of the *First Critique*; that this claim requires an intellect which does not only conceptualize data in a passively received manifold or organize the results of empirical enquiry in a system, but which can itself be conceived as intuitive; and that this alternative way of conceiving the mind–world issue is most visible in Kant's doctrine of the productive imagination, Kant's "truly speculative idea" (*GW*, p. 71).

It is of course still true that Hegel is in some sense conflating what Kant is saying about the *idea* of nature's origins and a putatively *divine intellect* with a claim about the proper relation between the *human intellect* and sensibility. But this sort of claim about the divinity of the human is certainly not foreign to Hegel's idiosyncratic theology, and it is at least clear that the issues of life and beauty raise directly for Hegel questions about the Kantian concept–sensibility relation, and *not* about the possibility of a pre-subjective *Urgrund* expressing itself in human actions and thinking.[28] And he is also at least purporting to point to issues in Kant which *justify* this turn to the broad problem of our cognitive capacities.

## IV

On the face of it, this is still a sort of "frying pan into the fire" interpretation. It does not seem to help matters much to argue that Hegel is not leading us "out of Kant" towards a romantic monism, but is instead making use of the analysis of aesthetic judgments to establish that our intellect really is intuitive.

If we focus on what seems of most relevance to Hegel, the Kantian account of beauty, the questions suggested by this version of "the influence of no. 76 and no. 77" are straightforward. (1) Of what consequence for the core Kantian position on the intellect–sensibility relation is the general case for the "subjective universal validity" of aesthetic judgments? (This question is really dual; it involves the direct issue of the possibility of such inter-subjectively valid judgments, based as they are on sensible pleasures, and the separate issue of the implications of such a possibility for Kant's position on the general possibility of the intelligibility of the world for a human mind. It might, in other words, be possible that aesthetic objects are simply *uniquely* intelligible.) And (2), assuming Kant got something right about the radical and general implications of aesthetic intelligibility, did Hegel get something right in extending the implications in the way suggested? These are the questions involved, at any rate, in such typical Hegelian claims as:

> Since beauty is the Idea as experienced, or more correctly, as intuited, the form of opposition between intuition and concept falls away. Kant recognizes this vanishing of the antithesis negatively in the concept of a supersensuous realm in general. But he does not recognize that as beauty, it is positive, it is intuited, or, to use his own language, it is given in experience.   (*GW*, p. 87)

In this extraordinary phrase – "the form of opposition between intuition and concept falls away" – Hegel's overall interests begin to emerge. He is interested in the possibility of some intelligible appreciation of nature, *understanding* nature we might say, even, in general, grasping a meaning, all with some normative validity, without that normativity (= "all others, suitably situated, ought to understand in the same way") being a function of the application of a concept (or the imposition of an ideal) to a passively received manifold (or "on" a set of empirical concepts or regularities), and he is apparently interested in the implications of such a possibility for intelligibility as such.[29] If, in other words, a common intelligibility, a shareability of experience, is possibly in some way inconsistent with the general critical model of conceiving a passively received content, and if that intelligibility requires a different model for the engagement of our intellectual activity in such an intelligible experience, then, so goes this "direction," we are in effect proposing a different critical model of the relation of thought to reality in our experience, one of potentially wide relevance.[30] (Or: as we might expect in a Kantian idealism the content of aesthetic experience itself should not be clearly distinguishable from *our* actively "making sense" of what is occurring to us, or from the aesthetic judgment and its shareability. To be in a mental state, even to experience a feeling of pleasure, is to have taken up a position, to have evaluated or judged. But now, it is being suggested, the possibility of the latter no longer can appeal to concept application, regulation, or to an empirically given, common, non-conceptual content.)

Now, this reading, as we shall see below, highlights something clear from the surface of Hegel's remarks. He does not comment much on the problem of pleasure, or the affective dimension of Kant's case, suggesting that it is in appreciating, or in being reflectively aware of the harmony of our faculties that we experience pleasure, thus shifting a great deal of weight to the reflective evaluating supposedly going on *in* aesthetic experience.[31] Hegel does not note that this all implies that it is by means of this reflective appreciation that we are taking pleasure *in* the formal suitability of nature to our rational ends, or that pleasure can be intentional, and that we are therewith evaluating our experience in a way that can be shown to be universally subjectively valid.[32] Since there is conflicting evidence about Kant's meaning, with many passages suggesting that, for him, harmony simply produces pleasure, that pleasure is a qualitatively identical, non-intentional state, and that subjective universal validity involves an expectation about another's feeling, and not a claim about a warranted evaluation of nature, this is all extremely controversial if considered as an exercise in Kant scholarship.[33] My own view is that Hegel is very much on the right track in reading Kant, but I can only sketch the case for that here.

Such a sketch must at least indicate what reading of the deduction of aesthetic judgments Hegel must have had in mind to suggest this direction. And posed this way, with so many issues at play, it is hard to see how any sort of economical discussion is possible. We can, I think, begin to defend the extension Hegel is pursuing, but that will first require some giant steps over much contested terrain. Consider first the famous details of Kant's accounts.

According to Kant, the claim "this is beautiful" has a misleading surface structure. It appears to be a standard application of an empirical predicate to an object, but it is not. It really involves the claim that:

1  I am in a certain mental state, I feel something in the presence of an object, and, Kant wants to show, by being in such a state, under certain conditions, I am *ipso facto* warranted in claiming all others would be too, "if they had taste" (which I am justified in assuming they could have).
2  That state is a *pleasure* ("consciousness of a representation's causality, with respect to that state, so as to keep me in it").
3  It is *disinterested* (does not incite any desire directed at existence of the object occasioning such a state).
4  This pleasure is attendant to, or in Kant's somewhat clumsy phrase, "attaches to" a reflective awareness of a *harmony* of cognitive faculties (the imaginative reproduction of a manifold in harmony with what would have been required by the understanding for its unity).
5  Since there is such a harmony without the application of a concept, this harmony should be seen as a *"free play"* of such faculties, although Kant also claims, in some way that remains the subject of much controversy, that our appreciating a beautiful object must involve the activity of reflective judgment (the

attempt in general to find a universal for a given set of particulars, although in this case without any real prospect of, or progress towards, such a concept).

6   This is a reflecting occasioned by and in some sense directed upon the *formal properties* of the occasioning object(s), experienced in such judgmental striving to be purposively suited to our cognitive ends, without such a discovery requiring any specific discovery of "a" purpose ("*purposiveness without a purpose*"),

7   all occasioning the delight which accompanies the attaining of my cognitive ends, here unintentionally, not as a result of some conscious project.

8   In the most important aspect of this argument for our purposes, Kant goes on to claim that, in engaging in such a reflection, what I am doing is attempting to situate myself, or orient myself in experience "as anyone else would," to take account "of everyone else's way of representing" (*KU*, p. 293) and am, in feeling pleasure in this way, relying on a *sensus communis*. The universal communicability of such a state thus presupposes a common set of cognitive faculties and a shared ability, reflective judgment guided by, in some way, such a common sense. This assumption, he argues, is warranted because experience itself would not be possible without such a capacity.

I am therefore entitled not only to assume the universal communicability of my mental state, but to demand (*fordern*) that all others appreciate the beautiful, that they "ought" to find this beautiful ("as a duty, as it were"). The experience of beauty, in other words, involves a norm, binding on all with subjective universal validity. And again, for the purposes of our discussion, the important point is: without such normativity involving the *application* of a norm *to a content*, nor the *idea* of a possible norm which we "must think" applies.

These are the bare details. And, with this skeleton of the theory in mind, it is not hard to find passages, particularly in the published and unpublished Introductions, which show that Kant himself did believe that such an analysis was relevant to the larger issues which Hegel summarizes as the "authentic idea" or "reality" of reason. Those passages are all based on the claim that aesthetic judgments are a species of "reflective" judgments (given the particular, find, formulate, construct the universal) as opposed to determinative (where one has a concept and seeks to apply it) and on the general claims made on behalf of reflective judgments. The principle of such judgments is "purposiveness" and the claims made are very great. The Kantian language also calls to mind Hegel's remarks about our own reason spontaneously "giving itself its content," as if an intuitive intellect. For example,

> Judgment . . . provides nature's supersensible substrate (within as well as outside us) with determinability [*Bestimmbarkeit*] by the intellectual power . . . and so judgment makes possible the transition from the concept of nature to that of freedom. (*KU*, p. 37)

While Kant often claims that our intellectual powers "determine" nature, thus leading to the skeptically idealist claim that we should consider nature only as determined by us, this sort of claim about our originally providing (*verschafft*) nature *with* "determinability" in the first place is unique, as far as I know, to the third *Critique* and later works.[34]

And the direction of these remarks suggests that in appreciating the beautiful, we are providing ourselves with a sort of original "orientation" in experience that is not like reason's subjective self-regulation (again we don't "impose" a demand on nature but appreciate nature's suitability to our demands) and not like empirical apprehension (since we are talking about an original orientation required for there to be coherent empirical apprehension). It is the relation between a subjectively universally valid pleasure in the beautiful and this self-orientation which forms the core of Hegel's suggested direction. Perhaps the fullest Kantian statement of this direction occurs in the unpublished Introduction:

> Hence we must consider aesthetic judgment as a special power, necessarily none other than reflective judgment; and we must regard the feeling of pleasure (which is identical with the representation of subjective purposiveness) as attaching neither to the sensation in the empirical representation of the object, nor to the concept of that object, but as attaching to – and as connected with, in terms of an a priori principle – nothing but the reflection and its form (the essential activity of judgment) by which it strives to proceed from empirical intuitions to concepts as such. (*KU*, p. 249)

Now, in his 1786 essay "*Was heisst, sich im Denken orientieren?*," Kant, discussing spatial orientation, had noted that "To this purpose, I require above all the feeling of a difference in my own person."[35] These remarks on the reflective character of aesthetic judgment, and on the function of reflective judgment suggest that by the time of the third *Critique*, Kant had also realized that a more fundamental "orientation" in all the "activity of life" is needed, and cannot be the result of any inference or application of, or even obedience to, a rule.[36] It turns out that this fundamental orientation is also achieved by a "feeling", although Kant still insists on a "critique" of such a feeling and so on its universal normative force. Since, in no. 76 and no. 77, Kant appears to claim that the subsumability or general suitability of particulars to the application of our concepts is itself the result of the original, non-determinative, active engagements of our judgment-power (an original "self-orienting"), he seems to have at once conceded the general priority of such reflective activity in any account of the possibility of experience, and, as Hegel and Schelling suggested, to have undermined his own strict distinction between the divine and the human intellect. The broadest claim is at p. 404:

> were the power of judgment not to be able to recognize purposiveness with respect to particulars, were it not to have its own universal law [the law he identifies as purposiveness] under which to subsume particulars, *it could not make any determinate judgment about particulars.*[37]

But now we come to the most specific of the difficulties involved in trying to read Kant in this Hegelian direction, this link between the normative status of the experience of the beautiful, and this reflective activity, an activity which supposedly undermines or bypasses the standard Kantian picture of normativity (the application of a concept or principle). As alluded to earlier, the problem with such passages and claims has always been to understand the role of such reflection *in* aesthetic judgments, which, on the face of it, seem so much a matter simply of sensible pleasure, albeit occasioned in a unique way in the case of the beautiful.[38] There is no question that Kant himself goes very far in linking the experience of such pleasure with "reflective activity" and so, apparently, with the themes Hegel is interested in. But the question has always been whether he is entitled to such claims.

For example, in section no. 4,

A liking for the beautiful must depend on the reflection, regarding an object, that leads to some concept or other (but is indeterminate which concept this is). This dependence on reflection also distinguishes the liking for the beautiful from the agreeable, which rests entirely on sensation.   (p. 207)

In no. 8 Kant calls our aesthetic sensibility the "taste of reflection" to distinguish it from a mere taste of sense, and to further emphasize the role of our intellectual activity in the possibility of such pleasure (beyond, that is, some sort of passive "activation" of the understanding and the imagination) he notes that this capacity, taste, can be cultivated, indeed, in no. 32, that,

taste is precisely what stands most in need of examples regarding what has enjoyed the longest-lasting approval in the course of cultural progress in order that it will not become uncouth again . . . and taste needs this because its judgments cannot be determined by concepts and precepts.   (p. 283)

This "taste" is defined in no. 40 "as the ability to judge something that makes our feeling in a given presentation universally communicable without mediation by a concept" and that "taste is our ability to judge a priori the communicability of the feelings that (without mediation by a concept) are connected with a given presentation" (pp. 295–6).

Kant is undoubtedly very aware that by linking in this way aesthetic experience and the possibility of a distinct pleasure in the beautiful to some sort of reflective awareness of natural purposiveness, however non-standard and indeterminate such an awareness, he is in danger of intellectualizing the experience again (the "we get out of nature what we put there" model), or of making it very hard to see how, without a concept, the normative or common significance of such a vague appreciating can be preserved.[39] As noted, in addressing these concerns, he suggests that such a reflecting activity is not based on the a priori needs of reason, nor on a putative common "content," but is already and originally oriented from a "common sense," as if in appreciating the beautiful we already are appreciating its shareability. This "sense" is

a power to judge that in reflecting takes account (a priori), in our thought, of everyone else's way of representing, in order as it were, to compare our own judgment with human reason in general, and thus escape the illusion that arises from the case of mistaking subjective and private conditions for objective ones.   (p. 293)

Most famously, these considerations are concentrated in the passage Kant calls "the key to the critique of taste" (no. 9), where the question is "whether in a judgment of taste the feeling of pleasure precedes the judging of the object, or the judging precedes the pleasure," and the answer, causing great difficulty to many commentators, but consistent with the direction Hegel is pursuing, is the latter. That section is quite a tangle, and while a detailed consideration of its claims is central for the direction Hegel is suggesting, I want to conclude with a more general consideration of the issues Kant himself raises with these claims about the role of reflective activity in our appreciation of the beautiful.[40]

## V

The point at issue is the suggestion of a "reflecting" activity which is not the conceiving of a content, but an activity already engaged in the taking up of a manifold and so not checked by some externally received content, a thinking or "ability to judge a priori the communicability of the feelings that (without mediation by a concept) are connected with a given presentation," which thinking somehow reveals this "a priori communicability" of our feelings and so the normative status of the experience of the beautiful. According to Kant, "we have a merely aesthetic power of judgment, an ability to judge forms without using concepts and to feel in the mere judging of these forms a liking that we also make a rule for everyone, though our judgment is not based on an interest and also gives rise to none" (KU, p. 300).

Since this sort of reflective appreciating is not an application of a concept, nor a response necessitated or directed by some sensory impingement, nor a postulated ideal, Hegel claims it is like a *self*-orienting in relation to nature and others,[41] or a kind of "intellectual intuition," intellectual because actively established, and intuiting because not the projection of an ideal, but an experience, an orienting "in" an experience.[42]

I have already noted where, in the reading of Kant implied by Hegel's remarks, the controversial points of interpretation lie. They mostly have to do with the relation between reflective judgment and aesthetic experience itself, and each would require an extensive separate discussion. It is also true that the general significance of aesthetic experience for the "system" problem so important to later Idealists, or the way in which the possibility of universally valid aesthetic judgments implies a possible, comprehensive account of morally free agents, mechanically moving matter, living beings, and scientific systems is only suggested by this emphasis on the priority and centrality of such a reflective self-orienting, and its a priori principle, purposiveness, for any and all of these accounts.

In the KU of course, the specific "systematic" problem is the link between aesthetic and teleological judgments, and here again, Hegel only makes a suggestion: that the Kantian "sense" of purposiveness required in both appreciating and estimating is not the postulation of an Idea which we "require" in our experience of nature, nor the application of a concept to a manifold or set of empirical regularities. To be oriented in this way, to take up the natural world in its purposiveness suggests that we are both being responsive to what nature requires if we are to explain it, as well as "reflectively" active in such responding. To him this sounds like being "intellectually intuitive."

But, finally, besides these continuities with Kant suggested by this sketch of the direction opened up by nos 76 and 77, there is clearly a major discontinuity. As Kant himself implies when he discusses the kind of "sense" involved in the role of a common sense in appreciating the beautiful, and when he associates such a sense with everyday good sense, or prudence, or other examples of a capacity for judgment for which no rule can be given, this reflective activity is always indeterminate.[43] It yields no determinate concept or concepts of purposiveness in this aspect or that; just an orienting and pleasing "sense." He does say in the "Solution to the Antinomy of Taste" that "a judgment of taste must refer to some concept or other," but this concept is "intrinsically indeterminate and inadequate for cognition" and is only the "concept of a general basis of nature's subjective purposiveness for our power of judgment" and may be considered the concept of the "supersensible substrate of humanity" (KU, p. 340).

It is in commenting on such passages that Hegel objects to this "merely negative" conception of the supersensible and insists that Kant does not appreciate his own doctrine, that Kant

> does not recognize that as beauty, it [the supersensuous] is positive, it is intuited, or, to use his own language, it is given in experience. Nor does he see the supersensuous, the intelligible substratum of nature without and within us, the thing in itself . . . is at least superficially known when the principle of beauty is given an exposition as the identity of nature and freedom.   (KU, pp. 88–9)

Because, supposedly, Kant does not see a way of integrating what his exposition required into the standard Transcendental Idealist picture, he retreats, and claims,

> that the supersensuous, insofar as it is the principle of the aesthetic, is unknowable; and the beautiful turns into something strictly finite and subjective because it is only connected with the human cognitive faculty and a harmonious play of its various powers.   (p. 88)

Exactly as one might expect, Hegel is much more interested in that side of Kant's exposition of aesthetic experience which does allow for the possibility of some reflective grasp of determinacy, the expression of *aesthetic ideas* in fine art.[44] In Kant's presentation, although the "expression" of Juliet's love or Iago's jealousy allows for a great deal more determinate "play" in our "reflective powers," the possibility is still understood on an analogy with natural beauty and so an indeterminate play of such reflection is still all that is allowed. The aesthetic idea remains a representation of the imagination for which no conceptual exposition or definition can be given, just as an Idea of Reason is one for which no demonstration can

49

be given, "demonstration in the Kantian sense being a presentation of a concept in intuition" (p. 87). Hegel goes very far in summing up what he thinks can be derived from the implications of Kant's case, contra Kant's official line:

> As if the aesthetic idea did not have its exposition in the Idea of Reason, and the Idea of Reason did not have its demonstration in beauty.   (p. 87)

At this point, such a claim remains a promissory note, a promise to be able to show that certain sorts of rational "self-determinations" in relation to the contents of experience are, in their various determinate forms (which we might imagine as the categories of Hegel's *Logic*), not "empty forms" (but the famous "concrete universals"),[45] any more than aesthetic ideas or organic wholes are empty forms or subjective regulations. This promise already suggests the problems we appear headed towards: (1) an extreme coherentism, a network of categories and principles "unchecked" by intuitions or the pure forms of intuition because our intellect itself is already, supposedly, intuitive, and (2) how to explain the determinacy in such self-determination if we take the idea of such an "unboundedness of the conceptual" seriously.

These are serious problems, still very much with us in any of the many forms of philosophy which could be called post-Kantian by virtue of a common rejection of any comprehensive empiricism or "absolute" realism or naturalism. My point in this paper has been to show how Hegel must have been reading the *Critique of Judgment* in order to see such a promise implied in our capacity to appreciate the beautiful and to estimate life, and to suggest that his reading has a great deal to be said for it.

## Notes

1   A803/B831. For a good sense of the importance of these problems for the early idealists, especially the Spinozism issue, see Karl Ameriks, "Kant, Fichte, and short arguments to idealism," *Archiv für Geschichte der Philosophie*, 72 (1990), pp. 63–85.

2   It had, of course, advanced to some degree, since Kant proposed what later Idealists would characterize as an "immanent" account of the origin and inter-relation of concepts. He had insisted on the non-derived status of pure concepts (without a theory of innate knowledge) and so had at least proposed a theory of synthetic a priori knowledge. See the quotation from Locke in Hegel's *Glauben und Wissen*, *Gesammelte Werke* (hereafter *GW*), ed. Rheinisch-Westfälischen Akademie der Wissenschaften (Hamburg: Felix Meiner, 1968), vol. IV, p. 326; *Faith and Knowledge* (hereafter *FK*), tr. W. Cerf and H. S. Harris (Albany, NY: SUNY Press, 1977), pp. 68–9; and Jean Hyppolite's helpful discussion, "La critique hégélienne de la réflexion kantienne," *Kant-Studien*, 45 (1953–4), pp. 86ff.

3   Friederich Heinrich Jacobi, a major figure in the German counter-Enlightenment, formulated many of the most influential early criticisms of transcendental philosophy; for example, that its skepticism was inconsistent with its own claims to ground knowledge, that it was inadequate to the explanation of organic life, and that it dangerously undermined the centrality of religious faith in human life. Rolf-Peter Horstmann, in *Die Grenzen der Vernunft* (Frankfurt: Anton Hain, 1991), narrates the history of post-

Kantian philosophy in a way that reveals the importance of Jacobi. See also Frederick Beiser. *The Fate of Reason: German Philosophy from Kant to Fichte* (Cambridge, MA: Harvard University Press, 1987).

4   One strategy for achieving this goal; to rethink and radicalize the Kantian beginning, the supreme epistemic condition without which there could be no experience, by explication of which a variety of determinate conclusions about possible objects of experience could be derived. This is roughly the strategy adopted by Fichte and Reinhold. Another strategy would be to follow more closely what I am calling here "Kant's own way out of Kant" in the third *Critique*, or his reflections on the necessity of an intuitive intellect. This is the path pursued by Schelling and Hegel. See the summary in Rolf-Peter Horstmann, *Die Grenzen der Vernunft*, ch. IV: "Kant's 'Kritik der Urteilskraft' im Urteil seiner idealistischen Nachfolger," pp. 191–221.

5   Cf. my *Hegel's Idealism: The Satisfactions of Self-Consciousness* (Cambridge: Cambridge University Press, 1989). The idea that Hegel's position is best assessed in terms of his interpretations of, and his claims against, Kant is not, of course, a novel one. W. Bonsiepen, for example, has shown how dominating that issue already was for Hegel's contemporaries (see "Erste zeitgenössische Rezensionen der *Phänomenologie des Geistes*," *Hegel-Studien*, 14 (1979), and it is prominent in much of the best contemporary work on Hegel, such as that by Klaus Düsing. See his *Hegel und die Geschichte der Philosophie* (Darmstadt: Wissenschaftliche Buchgesellschaft, 1983), pp. 196–242, and "Aesthetische Einbildungskraft und intuitiver Verstand," *Hegel-Studien*, 21 (1986), pp. 87–128. Traditional and contemporary accounts such as Düsings' have not though, in my view, done full justice to the philosophical quality of Hegel's Kantianism, and that is especially true, I want to show, with respect to the question of his appropriation of third *Critique* themes.

6   In Hegel's case, for one thing, a final account of his trajectory would obviously also have to include his complex commitments to various elements of classical Greek philosophy and to Christian theology.

7   Kant himself says "nature organizes itself," but he is quick to stay clear of the hylozoism he would see in Schelling's formulations. See *Kritik der Urteilskraft* (hereafter *KU*) in *Kants gesammelte Schriften* (Berlin: Königlich Preussische Akademie der Wissenschaften, 1908–13) (hereafter *AK*), vol. 5, p. 288. I have mainly consulted the translation by Werner Pluhar, *The Critique of Judgment* (Indianapolis, IN: Hackett, 1987), though I have often made changes. (Page references to the unpublished Introduction are to vol. 20 of the *Akademie* edition.) See also p. 374. For a study of the relevance of the pantheism, life philosophy, and hylozoism controversies to the composition of *KU*, see John H. Zammito, *The Genesis of Kant's Critique of Judgment* (Chicago, IL: Chicago University Press, 1992).

8   Kant uses the *intellektuelle Anschauung* phrase rarely; this is the only occurrence in these famous passages, although, largely thanks to Schelling it would become the term of art for stating this problem and so come to play a large role in Fichte's 1797 *Introductions* and in Hegel's Jena writings. See Schelling's *Abhandlungen*, in *Sämtliche Werke* (hereafter *SW*), ed. F. W. J. Schelling (Stuttgart & Augsburg: J. G. Cotta'scher, 1856–61) vol. I, p. 402, and the discussion in Horstmann, *Die Grenzen der Vernunft*, pp. 210–19, and nn. 102–3. (Horstmann points out that while many of Schelling's criticisms of Kant's first *Critique* were common currency at the time, Schelling alone insisted that the third *Critique* notion of intellectual intuition could remedy those supposed deficits). Cf. also the heady pronouncements in the 1800 *System der transzendentalen Idealismus* (hereafter, *STI*) in *SW*, vol. III, p. 368: "Intellectual intuition is the organ of

all transcendental thinking." *System of Transcendental Idealism* (hereafter *ST*), tr. by Peter Heath (Charlottesville, VA: University of Virginia Press, 1978), p. 27.

9   In other words, a merely "strategic" purposive creator, with an intellect and will much like ours, only extremely powerful, could not explain the organic unity of nature and natural wholes. For the appeal to a creative intelligence to fill the great gap created by mechanistic explanations, "wholes" must really *be* prior to "parts" for such an *intellectus archetypus*, and that means it must create what it thinks immediately, rather than rely on some "material" to create for the sake of some causally motivating end. In the latter case we would not have appealed (even negatively and by contrast with our discursivity) to a purposively designing intelligence, but to a mind and will empirically motivated like ours and so would be back with the contingencies problem, which problem undergirds the claim that "it is just as indubitably certain that the mere mechanism of nature cannot provide our cognitive power with a basis on which we could explain the production of organized beings" (*KU*, p. 389; see also the famous remark on a "Newton for a blade of grass" at p. 400). Kant himself is clear about the only possible realization of this idea: "Es is schwer zu begreifen, wie ein anderer intuitiver Verstand stattfinden sollte als der göttliche" (*Reflexion*, no. 6048 in *Ak*, vol. XVIII). Cf. also the discussion in Henry Allison, "Kant's Antinomy of Teleological Judgment," *The Southern Journal of Philosophy*, XXX Suppl. (1991), pp. 25–42.

10  As we shall see, the exact difference between these formulations, of crucial importance for Schelling's insistence that the "system of idealism" include *both* a philosophy of nature and transcendental philosophy as co-equals, is extremely difficult to formulate. Cf. Schelling's attempt in the Preface to *STI*, vol. III, p. 330; *ST*, p. 1.

11  Tuschling takes his bearings from passages in the published introduction to *KU* which make claims such as: "particular empirical laws, must, as regards what the universal laws have left undetermined in them, be viewed in terms of such a unity as if they too had been given by an understanding (even though not ours) so as to assist our cognitive powers by making possible a system of experience in terms of particular natural laws" (p. 180). See B. Tuschling, "The system of transcendental idealism: questions raised and left open in the *Kritik der Urteilskraft*," *Southern Journal of Philosophy*, XXX, Suppl. (1991), p. 113.

12  See the quotations from the *Opus postumum* in Tuschling, op. cit., pp. 121–2, and see also his "Intuitiver Verstand, absolute Identität, Idee. Thesen zu Hegels früher Rezeption der "Kritik der Urteilskraft," in *Hegel und "Die Kritik der Urteilskraft,"* ed. Hans-Friederich Fulda and Rolf-Peter Horstmann (Stuttgart: Klett-Cotta, 1990), pp. 174–188. In the latter, Tuschling discusses a number of important differences between Hegel and Schelling on the "logic" of such a self-positing intellect, but as will be clear below, I disagree with the way he ropes Hegel and Schelling together. Moreover, when Tuschling asks whether this whole direction represents a "regress" into a pre-critical metaphysics or an "ontologization" of logic, he answers "no," for two reasons, neither of which seem to me persuasive. First, he claims that, internally, Kant himself had not solved the problem of the "determinability" of the empirical manifold, as if this alone in some way supports the Divine Substance solution. Kant's difficulties could be addressed in any number of ways, as we shall see, apart from a full-blown metaphysical philosophy of nature, and, anyway, there is no philosophical justification for any claimed connection between Kant's putative failure and a romantic metaphysics solution. The second reason Tuschling presents is that we should not understand Hegel's metaphysics as a kind of absolute apriorism, or as the derivation of analytic truths from concept analysis. The concept is supposed to be demonstrated as the "immanent struc-

ture of empirical existence," which "unites in itself the moments of identity with itself and relation to others" (p. 187). This might suggest that the *sort* of metaphysics to which Tuschling's analysis commits Hegel is unprecedented, but that, as far as I can see, does not address the "regress" question which would be raised by a Kantian (which is an epistemological problem).

13  *SW*, vol. I, p. 238.

14  Ibid., p. 242. See also p. 181.

15  Quoted in Horstmann, op. cit., pp. 214–15.

16  *GW*, p. 341; *FK*, p. 89.

17  *GW*, p. 341; *FK*, pp. 90–1.

18  For discussions of this difference, see Paul Guyer, "Reason and reflective judgment: Kant on the significance of systematicity," *Nous*, 24 (1990), 17–43; Hannah Ginsborg, "Reflective judgment and taste," *Nous*, 24 (1990), pp. 63–78; George Schrader, "The status of teleological judgments in the critical philosophy," *Kant-Studien*, 45 (1953–4), pp. 204–35; L. W. Beck, "Kant on the uniformity of nature," *Synthese*, 47 (1981), pp. 449–64; Christel Fricke, "Explaining the inexplicable: the hypothesis of the faculty of reflective judgment in Kant's third *Critique*," *Nous*, 24 (1990), pp. 45–62; Rudolf A. Makkreel, "Regulative and reflective uses of purposiveness in Kant," *The Southern Journal of Philosophy*, XXX Suppl. (1991), pp. 49–71; Max Liedtke, "Der Begriff der Reflexion bei Kant," *Archiv für die Geschichte der Phiosophie*, 48 (1966), pp. 207–16.

19  All of which was no doubt involved in the remarkable transformation of the planned, limited "Critique of Taste" in 1787, and the virtual invention of the topic of "reflective judgment." Cf. Rolf-Peter Horstmann, "Why must there be a Transcendental Deduction in Kant's *Critique of Judgment*?," in *Kant's Transcendental Deductions*, ed. E. Forster (Stanford, CA: Stanford University Press, 1989), pp. 157–76.

20  There is not, I think, any particularly good reason for Kant to think that all such teleological explanations must be understood in the intentional sense. Aristotle did not and Hegel's Aristotelianism provides him the basis for several effective criticisms of Kantian or subjectivist teleology in the *Science of Logic*. See Willem de Vries' article, "The dialectic of teleology," *Philosophical Topics*, 19 (1991), pp. 51–70; Klaus Düsing, "Naturteleologie und metaphysik bei Kant und Hegel," in *Hegel und "Die Kritik der Urteilskraft*," op. cit., pp. 141–157 and especially his *Die Teleologie in Kants Weltbegriff* (Bonn: Bouvier, 1968).

21  *GW*, p. 341; *FK*, p. 89.

22  For an exploration of the position on the imagination which emerges from the first and third *Critiques*, see Rudolf Makkreel, *Imagination and Interpretation in Kant: The Hermeneutical Import of the Critique of Judgment* (Chicago, IL: University of Chicago Press, 1990), part two. Makkreel's general position is that while Kant claims that the human understanding categorially sets the conditions for the possibility of an experience of nature, and that reason self-imposes laws for action, it is a reflective imagination which makes possible the apprehension of a wholeness and so an overall meaning in experience (this by way of what is called "reflective specification"). Makkreel links this orienting activity, especially in the apprehension of life, to the hermeneutical tradition. Hegel is close enough to Kant still to link such possible "meaning apprehension" with truth, and so is interested, with Kant, in the nature and basis of the claim that all others ought to appreciate the beautiful and estimate life (or "orient themselves meaningfully") as I do. Cf. also the discussion in J. M. Bernstein in *The Fate of Art: Aesthetic Alienation from Kant to Derrida and Adorno* (Cambridge: Polity Press, 1992) about the

various ways in which the reflective judgment doctrine strains the basic faculty divisions of the first *Critique*, pp. 44–55.

23 Düsing, "Naturteleologic und Metaphysik," p. 112. See also his comment: "Er [Hegel] nimmt hierbei die idealistischen Weiterführungen der Kantischen Konzeption der Vermittlung und des Übergangs von der theoretischen zur praktischen Vernunft, von der Natur zur Freiheit auf und schmilzt sie ein in sein spekulatives Identitätsprogramm" (p. 110). Another good summary of the position I am trying to oppose (at least with respect to Hegel) can be found in the Conclusion to Zammito, *Genesis of Kant's Critique of Judgment*.

24 Because I am interested here in the question of the early reception of *KU* in German Idealism, I shall concentrate on Hegel's *Glauben und Wissen* comments. In Hegel's posthumously published *Lectures on Fine Art*, he interprets *KU* in both a more friendly and more critical way and concentrates (appropriately) more on the aesthetic theory itself than on its implications for his own systematic philosophy, which is the topic I want to pursue here. His account there does though make clear the importance to him of the way in which "ideas" can be said to be "embodied" in, rather than applied to or derived from, art or the beautiful. See G. W. F. Hegel, *Werke in zwanzig Bände*, ed. Eva Moldenhauer and Karl Markus Michel, vol. 13 (Frankfurt: Suhrkamp, 1970), pp. 11–99; *Aesthetics: Lectures on Fine Art*, tr. T. M. Knox, vol. 1 (Oxford: Clarendon Press, 1975), pp. 1–90.

25 *GW*, p. 338; *FK*, p. 85.

26 "The objective side is the nonconscious intuition of the reality of Reason, that is to say, organic nature. In his reflection upon it in his 'Critique of Teleological Judgment,' Kant expresses the Idea of Reason more definitively than in the preceding concept of a harmonious play of cognitive powers. He expresses it now in the idea of an intuitive intellect, for which possibility and actuality are one" (*GW*, p. 340; *FK*, p. 88).

27 Kant himself, of course, is famously given to remarks about how "reason" in investigating nature is really "investigating itself." And in the first *Critique*, his concept–intuition divide does not prevent him from calling apperception itself an "indeterminate intuition." Cf. B422n.

28 These two questions are, of course, not incompatible and Hegel could be raising both issues, but the body of evidence, I am suggesting, shows that he only considers such an *Urgrund* in terms of our intellectual activity. The question is treated differently by Schelling and would require a separate treatment. On the one hand, in a work very much like Hegel's *Difference* essay, his 1797 *Treatise Explicatory of the Idealism in the Wissenschaftslehre*, Schelling also stresses the way in which Kant himself was supposedly led to the idea of *our* actively intuitive faculty, and that Kant really did not intend, for us, any "utter separation of the understanding and sensibility" (*SW* vol. I, p. 359; *Idealism and the Endgame of Theory: Three Essays by F. W. J. Schelling*, tr. Thomas Pfau (Albany, NY: SUNY Press, 1994), p. 73). However, on the other, he begins to stress that in order to account for such an activity, we must assume a "productive force" inherent in all things; and so that "it is a fundamental mistake to attempt a theoretical grounding of theoretical philosophy (SW, vol. I, pp. 387, 399; *Idealism*, pp. 93, 101). Hegel never gave up such a goal. In general, the issue of Schelling, and the relation between Schelling's and Hegel's position, is too complicated to discuss here. The "Hegelian direction" I am defending here is not, though, in any great opposition to the early Schelling, as is clear from Part Six of *STI*.

29 "Intelligibility," in this context, admittedly covers a great deal of territory. It is a more general term for what a Kantian would recognize as the question of the possibility of

experience or a possible representation of content at all, where experience is understood as the possibility of judgments, and understanding such a possible judgment is understanding what it would be for a judgment to be true. Cf. the best account of this dimension of the Kantian theory in Gerold Prauss, *Erscheinung bei Kant* (Berlin: de Gruyter, 1971).

30 The general suggestion toward which such revisions in the classic Kantian picture is leading is familiar: that what it is for any thinking to be about something, to be constrained in a way common to all, cannot be said simply to be the result of, or based on the direct impingement of the external world, or "its" just occasioning in some distinct way a pleasure. Since even receptivity or the passivity of aesthetic experience requires the activity of spontaneity, that constraint and so shareability is a matter of integratability into some whole. See the recent book by John McDowell, *Mind and Nature* (Cambridge, MA: Harvard University Press, 1994), especially his criticisms (in what seem to me a Hegelian spirit) of Davidsonean holism on the one hand, and "bald naturalism" on the other.

31 This emphasis is what allows him to shift attention somewhat from Kant's concern with the more formal issue of the exercise of our faculties in aesthetic experience, the "play" of the imagination and the "striving" of the understanding, to the concepts or ideas supposedly expressed in such "material." This shift is especially obvious in his treatment of Kant in the *Lectures on Fine Art*.

32 A way of explaining the intentionality of pleasure, one of much relevance for this "direction," is presented by Richard Aquila, "A new look at Kant's aesthetic judgments," in *Essays in Kant's Aesthetics*, ed. Ted Cohen and Paul Guyer (Chicago, IL: University of Chicago Press, 1982), pp. 87–114. See also the useful formulation by Jens Kulenkampff in *Kants Logik des äesthetischen Urteils* (Frankfurt: Klostermann, 1978), p. 88.

33 I defend the broader reading of Kant's strategy in my paper "The significance of taste: Kant, aesthetic, and reflective judgments" (forthcoming). The narrower and wider views also reflect what would become, in the post-Kantian European tradition, basic differences about the autonomy of art on the one hand, and its ever accelerating cognitive, moral, and political significance in later modernity on the other. All of which is the subject of Bernstein's valuable study, *The Fate of Art*, op. cit. See especially pp. 1–65.

34 See again Tuschling's claims about the *Opus postumum* in the articles cited above (see nn. 11 and 12). In the first *Critique* Kant does say that "reason thus prepares the field for the understanding" (issues A658/B685), although how that is supposed to happen (as opposed to reason systematizing the results of the understanding's work) is not explored.

35 *AK*, vol. VIII, p. 134.

36 Howard Caygill, in *Art of Judgment* (Oxford: Blackwell, 1989), connects Kant's account of this orientation with very broad themes in the role played by considerations of taste in earlier political and civil society traditions, and he concludes with characterizations of Kant's position which sound very much like the later Idealists (see ch. 5 especially and, for example, p. 299). Whether the historical Kant could accept this position (and the enormous implications which follow from it), and still remain the historical Kant, is, I think, another question, not settled by Caygill's speculation.

37 The sentence in which this claim occurs is extremely complicated. Pluhar has tried to help by re-arranging its order fairly radically. The quoted passage begins by saying that we would have no distinction between the mechanism and the technic of nature,

"wäre unser Verstand nicht von der Art, daß er vom Allgemeinem zum Besondern gehen muß, und die Urteilskraft also in Ansehung des Besondern keine Zweck-mäßigkeit erkennen, *mithin keine bestimmende Urteile fällen kann*, ohne ein allgemeines Gesetz zu haben worunter sie jenes subsumieren könne" (my emphasis).

38   The most influential contemporary accounts skeptical of such a connection are Kulen-kampff's book cited above (n. 32) and Paul Guyer, *Kant and the Claims of Taste* (Cambridge, MA: Harvard University Press, 1979), p. 33ff, *inter alia*.

39   He makes his concerns very clear in no. 9, at p. 218, insisting that it is most definitely not "intellectually, through consciousness of the intentional activity by which we bring these powers into play" that we "become conscious, in a judgment of taste, of a reciprocal subjective harmony between the cognitive powers." I discuss this passage in "The significance of taste" (see n. 33).

40   As noted above, the interpretive problem stems from those passages, as in Section VII of the published Introduction, or at p. 224 of the First, where Kant seems to claim that judgments of taste are based on a sensation, which is itself just "brought about" [*bewirkt*] by the harmony of faculties. What I am suggesting is that Kant is not claiming that this harmony simply causes a pleasure, nor that it is "through" or by means of pleasure that we attend to this harmony, but that it is *in* appreciating such a harmony as purposive that we feel pleasure. This implies that without "taste," a certain harmo-nious play could occur without pleasure in the beautiful, or could be appreciated only as the agreeable. I try to defend this reading independently in my "The significance of taste: Kant, aesthetic, and reflective judgments" (forthcoming).

41   When, in the "General Comment" after no. 22, Kant defines taste as "an ability to judge an object in reference to the free lawfulness of the imagination," he calls the activity of the imagination "productive and self-active [*selbstätig*]," and he says that it is "free and lawful of itself [*frei und doch von selbst gesetzmäßig*]" (pp. 240–1). See chapter 8 of Makkreel, *Imagination and Interpretation in Kant*, op. cit., for a discussion of the herme-neutical aspects of such an "orientational" view of reflective judgments. Cf. also Cay-gill's remarks in chapter 5 of *Art of Judgment*, op. cit. As noted earlier, Hegel would not agree with the reliance on an indeterminate "common sense" to explain such common orientation and claims to be able to provide determinate content to such common orientation, a topic that would lead to his theory of conceptual change and to his "logic." Cf. also Zammito's discussion of this "orientational" issue (*The Genesis of Kant's Critique of Judgment*, op. cit (pp. 237ff) especially on the relevance of Kant's "Was heißt: sich im Denken orientieren" essay.

42   To quote Hegel, "*Kant himself recognized in the beautiful an intuition other than the sensuous.* He characterized the substratum of nature as intelligible, recognized it to be rational and identical with all reason, and knew that cognition in which concept and intuition are separated was subjective, finite cognition, a phenomenal cognition" (my emphasis; *GW*, p. 343; *FK*, p. 91).

43   Cf. the claim at p. 340.

44   Cf. the discussion in no. 49, p. 314ff.

45   There is an interesting discussion of the relation between the Kantian notion of "aes-thetic object" and Hegel's "concrete universal" in G. Wohlfahrt, *Der spekulative Satz: Bemerkungen der Spekulation bei Hegel* (Berlin: de Gruyter, 1981).

# 3

# Fichte

LUDWIG SIEP

## I

Johann Gottlieb Fichte (1762–1814) was never Kant's student. But when he, as a private teacher without any university degree, anonymously published his first book, the *Kritik aller Offenbarung* (Critique of all revelation, 1791), even some of the most prominent German philosophers took it to be Kant's long-expected philosophy of religion. Three years later he became the successor of one of the most influential Kantian philosophers, Karl Leonhard Reinhold, at the famous University of Jena. There he taught and published his theory of the "Science of Knowledge," which the famous poet and critic Friedrich Wilhelm Schlegel hailed as among the "greatest influences of the age," together with the French Revolution and Goethe's *Wilhelm Meister*. It became the origin of post-Kantian philosophy, later called "German Idealism." Fichte himself supported the French Revolution and soon got into trouble with conservative student "orders" and with the church authorities (because of his Sunday lectures). In 1798, an article by a friend in his *Philosophisches Journal* was accused of atheism. Fichte defended it and withdrew from the university in Jena, after troubles with Goethe – the "minister of education" in Weimar – and Herder.

He went to Berlin and lectured privately. In 1807/8 his *Reden an die deutsche Nation* (Addresses to the German Nation) helped to arouse the German resistance against Napoleon, though by "German" he understood all the peoples using Germanic languages. Fichte was among the founders of the Friedrich-Wilhelm University of Berlin and was its first elected rector (1810). He resigned after new troubles with conservative students and colleagues. In 1814 he died in the typhus epidemic during the "war of liberation" against Napoleon.

## II

Like many philosophers of the modern age, Fichte claimed to have transformed philosophy into a scientific system. This system he called "Science of Knowledge" (*Wissenschaftslehre*). Throughout his lifetime, he continued to publish versions of it and to give public lectures, defending his conception against misunderstandings and criticism. Modern scholars distinguish between the early "Science of Knowledge" (1793–8) and different versions thereafter. Undoubtedly, the most influential version is the first, published in the *Foundations of the Entire Science of Knowledge (Grundlage der gesamten Wissenschaftslehre*, 1794) and the following writings of the

Jena period, among them his *Science of Rights* (*Grundlagen des Naturrechts nach Prinzipien der Wissenschaftslehre*, 1796/7) and his *System of Morals* (*System der Sittenlehre nach den Prinzipien der Wissenschaftslehre*, 1798).

The early "Science of Knowledge" revolves around the concept of the "Ich," i.e. the "I" or the "self." All knowledge must be based upon the spontaneity, the unity, and the self-certainty of the self, the "I." Self-consciousness can neither be caused nor explained by anything outside itself. It is a twofold act of spontaneity and reflection. In this sense, it "posits" itself. Most of his critics understood this self-positing as a sort of self-creation of the human being. As Fichte criticized Kant's concepts of receptivity and of the "thing in itself", he was accused of extreme subjectivism. As Bertrand Russell put it: Fichte "carried subjectivism to a point which seems almost to involve a kind of insanity" (Russell 1948, p. 744).

Fichte was not unfamiliar with this sort of criticism, as it had already been uttered by his contemporaries, such as Jacobi, Jean Paul and others. However, whoever reads his writings carefully will realize that he never confused the transcendental self-positing with individual self-creation – and that he did not reduce reality to a subjective creation (cf., for instance, his letter in reponse to Reinhold; *SW* vol. II, p. 509). His Self or "I" is supposed to be the general structure of consciousness for each individual – as, for instance, spatiality is for Kant a structure of each person's intuition – and individuality does not even belong to this "transcendental" structure. In the first instance Fichte is concerned with this structure, and only in later stages of his system does he "deduce" the concept of individuality (see below). Fichte's philosophy is primarily a transcendental theory of knowledge and science, not a "philosophy of mind." "Knowledge," however, refers to a concept which for Fichte is broader than the one we usually employ today: it refers to all representations which are "accompanied by a feeling of necessity" (cf. *HL*, p. 6; *SW*, vol. I, p. 423). This also includes, for example, the demands of conscience regarding our moral obligations. The "Science of Knowledge" is concerned with the explanation of this necessity – not, however, by means of a psychological but by a transcendental explanation.

According to Fichte, spontaneity, self-relatedness, and unity are the basic traits of knowledge. Kant had already discerned an intimate connection between the unity of knowledge and its self-relatedness. The doctrine of *transcendental apperception* contends that the unity of our representations is in the end derived from the "I think," which "must be able to accompany" all our representations. It is only because they are *"mine"* that they are conjoined – not because they belong to this cognizant individual, but because the act of representation is always capable of presenting itself in each of its representations. Fichte adopted this idea, but according to him the basic traits of the Kantian transcendental apperception are even more intimately bound to one another. Knowledge is based upon a unity which actively produces itself as a relationship to itself. This principle of all knowledge, which is the indivisible unity of those basic traits – spontaneity, unity, self-presence – is what Fichte calls the "I" or the "self."

To be transcendental does not mean that something is beyond the finite, terrestrial world (that it is "transcendent"), but that it is a precondition for the ability to think, speak, or know about the world or to act in pursuit of an end in the world. This is a basic tendency already in the medieval doctrine of "transcendentals." Without "beings," without a distinguishable "something," without "truth," and without something towards which one could strive (*bonum*, the good), there would be no thought, no acting, no human reality. Kant had located these transcendental conditions in the necessary structure of human reason – in its spatio-temporal forms of intuition, in its forms of connecting concepts and impressions mediated by temporal "schemes," and so on. These forms of conjunction are usually "at work" in thought, without themselves being an object of consciousness. We think causally without thinking about causality; we see things next to each other without giving a thought to the spatial character of our intuition. It is furthermore questionable whether we can ever conceive of these forms purely and as such apart from their application – for instance, of space without geometrical figures. To this extent, we can call these activities of reason "non-conscious." We have to resort to them in order to explain something which one cannot reasonably doubt, but which is not in itself immediately comprehensible. Even today this form of explanation is called "transcendental argumentation." However, "transcendental arguments" in analytical philosophy and transcendental thought in "critical theory" differ from those of Kant and Fichte in that the transcendental conditions discovered in the former theories are not a priori, i.e., valid and certain independently of any experiences gained in space and time. Regarding this demand for certainty, Fichte's standards are even higher than Kant's, as he couples the transcendental method with the demands of Rationalism since Descartes and Spinoza, i.e., that all knowledge must be founded in a single, supreme, self-grounded and indubitably evident principle.

The "I" in the first fundamental principle of the *Foundations of the Entire Science of Knowledge* is the foundation of all knowledge, and it exhibits itself – or at least can be demonstrated – to each person in his own knowledge as an activity which is necessarily "for itself" and whose "being-for-itself" is its own self-producing activity. It is indubitably certain for itself and for all knowing. Here Fichte is, of course, indebted to Descartes: one cannot conceive of the non-existence of one's thought without consciously thinking. He differs from Descartes in two respects. First, according to Fichte, the self is pure cognizant self-actuation and nothing else; it is not a "res," a thing; it has no Being which is not totally comprehended in its thinking itself. Second, Fichte does not view the certainty of the transcendental principle of the self as based on an act of "self-experience." Though it *can* be experienced by anyone under philosophical guidance, it is valid because, without it, there could not be anything like knowledge. To this extent, it is proven transcendentally, a proof which must be provided by the entire "Science of Knowledge." The first steps in this proof are supposed to demonstrate that, without such an activity of the self, neither knowledge's reference to reality nor the elementary laws of logic can be held valid.

Knowledge articulates itself in judgments. In very general terms, to judge means to distinguish concepts from one another and to place them in relationship to one another. One might assume – and Fichte discusses this possibility first – that the foundation for this "structure of judgment" is contained in the logical principles of identity (for all A: A = A) and contradiction (A ≠ Non-A). But for Fichte these principles are only conditionally valid: *if* there is something A that is knowable, *then* it holds that. . . . These principles tell us nothing about whether or not our judgment corresponds to reality, or whether distinguishing and relating are at all appropriate to anything. Judgment could perhaps hide reality from us, for instance if there were only complete change instead of self-sameness, or if the "real" being of the world were in fact without distinctions (Parmenides). Is there *anything* concerning which we can state with necessity that, "all by itself," it is the same in different respects and that it determines itself in its own self-actuation, by distinguishing itself from what it is not?

This is precisely the structure of the self in knowledge according to Fichte. It guarantees that knowledge primordially refers to something whose reality cannot be doubted: to its own activity. In the same act it necessarily distinguishes itself into knowing and being known, and knows both to be two aspects (or "senses") of one act. However, this solution seems to be a "trick." It seems that knowledge's reference to reality is supposed to be assumed precisely because it knows nothing other than itself; and thus, that it revolves around itself, absolved of all real content and objectivity. Would this not be an empty self-reflection rather than "knowledge"? The activity of the self must, however, not only distinguish between "I" and "Me," the activity as subject and object of its self-awareness. It must also distinguish itself from something which it itself is not, from a non-activity. There is no other way for it to apprehend or characterize itself. Only if the self distinguishes between "I" and "not-I" does it relate itself not merely to an indistinct pure activity, but to something determinable: a determinable *Self* and a determinable *Something*. Thus, the second principle states that the "I" opposes to itself a "Non-I," and the third that "in the self, I oppose a divisible not-self to the divisible self" (*HL*, p. 110; *SW*, vol. ɪ, p. 111). The determination of this "something" is, according to Fichte, either a "negation" or a "transmission" of aspects of the self (activity, unity, self-sufficiency, distinction, etc.) to the non-self or the object. All categories which are necessary for our knowledge result from this mutual demarcation between the self and the non-self. This demarcation also leads to the necessary conclusion that our knowledge is directed toward something independent of it and that our volition seeks to arrange something independent of it according to its own plans.

The result of the transcendental foundation of knowledge in the principle of the self is that our knowledge, which from the outset refers to reality (originally to its own reality), must distinguish something from itself on the basis of its own laws which it knows to be given *in* knowledge but is, at the same time, not completely dependent on it. Fichte called it a "check" (*Anstoß*). Even without the "thing in itself," Fichte does not dissolve reality into subjectivity. The basic determinations for that which is given must none the less be explainable through the distinction and the mutual limitation of "I" and "not-I."

Fichte's early work *The Foundations of the Entire Science of Knowledge* encounters at least two difficulties: first, if the "I" of the first principle contains no difference or opposition, how can it be self-conscious at all? Second, how can Fichte provide a reason for the transition from the "absolute I," which is *causa sui* and refers only to itself, to the second and third principle, the counterpositing of a Non-I and the mutual "limitation" of both? Hegel and Reinhold explicitly pointed out both of these difficulties, but it seems that the difficulties also soon became evident to Fichte himself. Reinhold suggested that Fichte's "I" could not be understood as "the I of consciousness" (cf. Fuchs 1978, p. 405). That the original I lacks reflection, and thus consciousness, can indeed be supported by passages in the *Foundations of the Entire Science of Knowledge* of 1794: "Pure activity is that which has no object at all, but rather reverts back to itself" (HL, p. 226; *SW*, vol. I, p. 256). In contrast, an ego which knows itself, which "posits itself as self-positing" or "as subject," is only "possible on the condition that it delimits itself by something opposed to it" (*HL*, p. 195; *SW*, vol. I, p. 218).

If, however, the pure activity of the first fundamental principle possessed no "for itself," then it could neither be certain, nor would its knowledge be "out of one piece," but rather a composition of activity and reflection. Fichte would not be able to insist, contrary to Spinoza, that there is a necessary being by means of itself ("*esse per se*") only *for* a "being for itself": "I exist only for myself; but for myself, I am necessary" (*HL*, p. 99; *SW*, vol. I, p. 98). We must suppose that – as Hegel later formulated it – a "distinction in that which is not distinguished" is meant in the first fundamental principle: as it were, an "internal" distinction within self-knowledge which is not a distinction by means of opposition or negation. This assumption does not, however, solve the second difficulty; that is, how one can proceed from this fundamental principle to the other two. Thus it contains only one of the transcendental conditions of knowledge, to which the others must be added; but then, Hegel objects, the transition from something which is purportedly absolutely independent and self-founded to something conditioned is grounded in a deficiency within the absolute. A deficient absolute is, however, a contradiction. This is why Fichte in his later philosophy (after 1801) understood the absolute fundament of knowledge as indeed completely void of distinction and thus – in terms of finite consciousness – as void of consciousness. At the same time, this ground is shown to be the only possible fundament for truth and reference in knowledge. Insofar as this knowledge is conscious by means of differences and oppositions, the absolutely simple "Being" ("*Sein*") in its appearance is "split" into differences.

## III

It seems difficult to understand how this abstract and alien speculation could have fascinated poets, politicians and theologians, lodges and salons, or how it aroused enthusiasm for the French Revolution and later on for rebellion against foreign domination under Napoleon. However, this may become clearer if one looks to the consequences of Fichte's principles and to the way they transformed Kant's moral and political philosophy.

Fichte himself has provided an excellent summary of this transformation in his early *Aenesidemus Review* (1792). It discussed a skeptical interpretation and critique of Kant written by a former student colleague, Gottlob Ernst Schulze. In this text Fichte proceeds from the "contradiction" in which the self is caught as far as it is, on the one hand, pure, completely independent self-positing; and, on the other, "empirical consciousness", which in its knowing is always bound to objects (or in Fichte's words: the intelligible). This contradiction would destroy the unity of the self if practical reason did not exist, which Fichte interprets as the self's "striving" to make "the intelligible dependent upon it." The goal of this striving is the unification of the "self which posits itself" and the "representational self." Fichte then proposes the brief sketch of a new foundation for the Kantian "moral theology" within a system that tries to grasp knowledge, action, and faith as a unity:

> The final goal of this striving is the unification of a self which, in its self-determination, at the same time determines all non-self (the idea of divinity); such striving, if its goal is conceived by an intelligent self to be external to itself, is faith (faith in an eternal duration). This idea cannot but be *believed*, i.e. the intelligence has as the object of its presentation not an empirical perception, but rather only the necessary striving of the *self*. . . . However, this faith is not merely a *probable opinion* but has the same degree of *certitude* as the indubitable proposition "I am," which infinitely surpasses all objective certainty that is made possible through the mediation of an intelligent ego.   (*SW*, vol. I, p. 22ff)

In these passages the Idea of an endless striving towards unification with God is given as the ultimate explanation for all human knowledge and action. The Kantian destruction of the proofs of God's existence and the reduction of religion to faith for the sake of morality are transformed in a way that faith is now founded in the immediate certainty of the proposition "I am." And finally, the striving towards unification with the divine is placed in a necessary connection with the striving for the self's absolute autonomy – a point of great importance for the contemporaries of the French Revolution and the literary movement of *Sturm und Drang*. A foretaste, so to speak, of this absolute self-sufficiency is possible for every person who performs the "intellectual intuition" of the self – that is, who abstracts from all object-directedness in his thought and action and thus gains an insight into the pure self-present activity spoken of above. According to Fichte, such insight does not transcend the bounds of reason and is not a mere product of the imagination. It is, in fact, at work – even if unconsciously – for example, whenever we feel the unconditional moral demand "you ought to. . . ." Such a demand that we, independent of desires, interests, and constraints, simply ought to do what is rational, what everyone else should do in such a situation – in short, such an awareness of the moral law, as Kant had called it – presupposes for Fichte the absolute autonomy of reason; though, of course, only as one moment of the categorical "you ought to. . . ." For this demand also includes the awareness of being determined by something external to pure reason. In empirical self-consciousness, the absolute self-sufficiency of reason emerges only in contrast to the continual dependence upon that which is non-rational: as something to be striven toward, not as something which is simply present.

However, the opposite is also true, as Fichte demonstrated more extensively in his *Science of Knowledge*: all knowledge of the constraints upon reason in acting as well as in knowing is only possible in contrast to the awareness of rational activity which is "in itself" unconditioned. Fichte demonstrated that everything which convinces us of the reality of objects – their resistance as a sign of their materiality, the way that our imagination is tied to the contours of objects, and so forth – must be explained as a boundary for our own "for itself" unbounded activity. The "feeling of necessity" in our knowledge and of the resistance of objects in our action are only explainable by means of a kind of unconscious comparison with the idea of an infinite active and cognizant being. The result of this comparison, the consciousness of limitation as something which does not correspond to the absolute in human knowledge and action, appears as something "offensive," as something which is contrary to the true determination of humanity. This determination instead demands a striving towards unification with that which is infinite, although this unification can neither be recognized nor explained theoretically since human consciousness is only conceivable in the opposition between the self and the non-self.

These are the essential elements of the image of humanity with which Fichte fascinated his contemporaries; this image captured both the internal tension and the indestructible dignity of human beings. Fichte was thus able to express the self-understanding of the generation of the French Revolution and the Romantic movement. In addition, in his attempt to demonstrate the practical striving of man after absolute self-sufficiency as the basis for the unity of all consciousness, Fichte radicalized Kant's theory concerning the primacy of practical reason in a way that had great impact on his philosophical "descendants" up until the present day (cf. Habermas 1968, p. 254).

The primacy of praxis means that, for Fichte, the human mind is in a broad sense "active" in all of its capacities. This is implicit already in the well-known concept of "positing," which is not clearly defined in the *Foundations of the Entire Science of Knowledge*. Concerning this concept, Fichte writes in a letter:

> This primordial positing, opposition and division is, note well, neither thought, nor feeling, desire, emotion, or the like; it is rather the complete activity of the human which is nameless, never occurs in consciousness, and is unfathomable; because, though it is determinable through every particular act (which only on account of this particularity can become a content of consciousness), it is never determinate. (*GA*, vol. III/2, p. 344)

Fichte occasionally employs the term "drive" ("*Trieb*") in a similarly broad sense, as in the essay "The spirit and the letter in philosophy" ("Über Geist und Buchstabe in der Philosophie", *SW*, vol. VIII, p. 278). This drive, according to Fichte, takes three forms: it is a drive for knowledge, a practical drive, and an aesthetic drive. As the drive for *knowledge*, "it is directed to knowledge as such, for its own sake. . . . In this realm representations have no other value and no other merit than to be completely adequate to their object." The *practical* drive, on the other hand, "is founded upon a representation in the soul which is generated by free self-activity, and the drive aims towards bringing forth a corresponding product in the sensible world. "The *aesthetic* drive, finally, is a medium between the two: it is directed towards a representation which is "its own end," which does not derive its "value from a correspondence with objects . . . but from the free and independent form of an image."

All three forms of this drive in man aim, then, towards self-sufficiency and self-activity. This includes not only moral freedom for everyone, but also independence of humanity from the threats of nature. The idea of an autonomous self, according to Fichte's work *The Vocation of Man*, thus explicitly entails domination over external nature in order to make humanity independent of catastrophes and shortages.

## IV

An outline of Fichte's early philosophy can be given without resorting to the concept of an *individual*. Personality and embodiment do not belong to the structure of the transcendental "I" in our knowledge and volition, but they are the conditions under which this structure can be experienced by an "empirical self." In this way, Fichte attempts a transcendental deduction of individuality and embodiment.

He first expounded this deduction in his *Science of Rights (Grundlagen des Naturrechts nach Prinzipien der Wissenschaftslehre*, 1796/7; sometimes translated as *Philosophy of Right*). He shows that a consciousness of oneself as determined (in "objective" representation) and at the same time free for self-determination (in volition) can only arise under the presupposition of a request ("*Aufforderung*"). In being requested to act, I experience the possibility of free self-determination as an "objective" and objectively bound representation (no mere phantasy) which nevertheless does not originate as an effect of some object. If I want to understand the request to act independently, then I must understand the author of this request as a rational being who limits his radius of action to the benefit of my possibilities for action – and thus recognizes me as a "potentially" rational being. Only such an author can induce me not to merely react, but to consciously accept my own possibilities for action. I can only accept them by conceiving of myself as one rational being among others – an *individual*. This comprehension of a request also implies for Fichte that I can only be known to someone else as a rational being if I recognize him in turn by limiting my radius of action. Together with the consciousness of individuality, the insight arises that rational beings in the sensible world can – as rational – only enter "into contact with one another" in a certain relationship of mutual self-limitation. This is a "*Rechtsverhältnis*," a relationship governed by the concept of right. Along with individuality and interpersonality, this relationship is another necessary condition for the possibility of experiencing self-consciousness.

But what does this have to do with embodiment? The fourth fundamental proposition of the *Science of Rights* states: "Rational beings cannot posit themselves as effective individuals without ascribing to themselves a material body and determining it in doing so" (K, p. 87; *SW*, vol. III, p. 56). This means that individual self-consciousness presupposes the consciousness of one's own "unmistakable" effects in the sensible world. The individual "sphere" of free actions which are intuited in the "productive imagination" is the body. Thus, for Fichte, individuality and corporality are both necessary conditions for the experience of pure self-activity or "being an I." The proposition "I am so and so" (e.g., Johann Gottlieb Fichte) combines the "mental mere selfness" and an "individual character". The expression "I" in such a proposition refers to a universal self – similar to Thomas Nagel's "objective self" (Nagel 1986) – but the phrase "so and so" must include the intersubjectively (publicly) identifiable characterization of a particular person. Personality and embodiment do not belong to the structure of the "I" in our knowledge and volition, but they are the conditions under which this structure can be experienced by an "empirical self."

The deduction of the mutual recognition of corporeal persons serves in Fichte's "Philosophy of Right" as the foundation for the right to bodily inviolability and to "possession" of one's own activity. In contrast to Locke and, later, Marx, Fichte did not, however, primarily derive from it a claim to possession over the "work of one's own hands;" instead, he concluded that the state must guarantee the opportunity for supporting oneself through one's own activity. The right to work and to secure one's living by it can be realized only by means of governmental control over professional choice in a planned economy. This consequence, which is indicated already in the second volume of the *Natural Law*, is then extensively developed in the *Closed Commercial State* (*Geschlossener Handelsstaat*), which appeared three years later in 1800. However, the result of this philosophical deduction is a paradox: in order to secure the lasting possibility of one's own activity, it is necessary to eliminate an important aspect of that which constitutes the proper character of self-activity in the sensible world, namely, the choice of a sphere for one's own activity, the choice of one's own profession. Although Fichte later came to see this as a major problem (cf. *SW*, vol. x, p. 535), he never found a satisfactory solution to it in any of his later works on the philosophy of the state.

## V

As for Fichte's impact on the history of philosophy, two main directions can be distinguished: first, Hegel adopts the idea of subjectivity as a unity of the self's dichotomy and synthesis of itself; secondly, Marx and the existential philosophers adopt the notion of man's self-generation.

For Hegel, the "principle" of subjectivity no longer means that every category and rule of thought and action must be derived from an activity which is present to itself; instead, all necessary developments and comprehensible connections in nature as well as in history, art, religion, and science are founded in a "self-like" structure – in an expulsion into opposition and a process of becoming transparent as a whole of mutually implicative oppositions. The precise determination of this structure is possible only in a systematic analysis of the basic concepts of being and knowledge – in a "Science of Logic" (in Hegel's sense).

In contrast to this concept of the self as a "logical" movement throughout all reality, philosophers after Hegel have taken the idea of self-positing as a key to the understanding of man as a being which is not fixed by nature, history, or culture; man is rather a being which makes or "projects" ("*entwirft*") himself, his cultural existence and self-understanding. The position of the transcendental self is replaced in Marx's early writings by man as a "species being," in Heidegger's and Sartre's thought by individual, "ownmost" existence. There is no doubt that the self-generation in all of these conceptions is not spontaneous, unconditioned, and completely independent, as is the case with Fichte's pure self. Instead, self-positing implies negation *and* acceptance of natural, historical, or social facticity. Still, the idea of attaining oneself only through a continually renewed attempt to overcome that which is alien within oneself ("être-pour-autrui," "*Man-selbst*") is an existentialist version of Fichte's theory, in which the self comes to be in extending the transcendentally posited boundaries of the non-self, of passivity. Nevertheless, these attempts to turn Fichte's theory of self-positing activity into a concrete activity of individuals or "species beings" obscured his transcendental epistemology.

## Writings

Fichte, J. G.: *Gesamtausgabe der Bayerischen Akademie der Wissenschaften*, ed. R. Lauth, H. Jacob, and H. Gliwitzky, 25 vols (Stuttgart/Bad Cannstatt: Fromann, 1962ff.) (quoted as *GA*, vol. I, etc.).

——: *Sämtliche Werke*, ed. I. H. Fichte, 11 vols (Berlin: de Gruyter, 1971) (quoted as *SW*, vol. I, etc.).

——: *Briefwechsel*, ed. H. Schulz (Hildesheim: Olms, 1967).

——: *Science of Knowledge*, with the First and Second Introduction, ed. P. Heath and J. Lachs (New York: Appleton-Century-Crofts, 1970) (quoted as *HL*).

——: *The Science of Rights*, tr. A. E. Kroeger (London: Routledge & Kegan Paul, 1970) (quoted as *K*).

——: *Foundations of Transcendental Philosophy* (*Wissenschaftslehre Nova Methodo*, 1796/97), ed. and tr. D. Breazeale (Ithaca, NY: Cornell University Press, 1992).

## References and further reading

Baumanns, P.: *Fichtes Wissenschaftslehre* (Bonn: Bouvier, 1974).

Breazeale, D.: "Fichte's *Aenesidemus* review and the transformation of German Idealism," *Review of Metaphysics*, 34 (1981), pp. 545–68.

Breazeale, D. and Rockmore, T. (eds): *New Perspectives on Fichte* (Atlantic Highlands, NJ: Humanities Press, 1996).

Cesa, C.: *Introduzione a Fichte* (Roma/Bari: Editori Laterza, 1994).

Claesges, U.: *Geschichte des Selbstbewußtseins* (The Hague: Martinus Nijhoff, 1974).

Fuchs, E. (ed.): *Fichte im Gespräch* (Stuttgart/Bad Canstatt: Fromann, 1978).

Girndt, H.: Forschungen zu Fichte seit Beginn und im Umkreis der kritischen Edition seiner Werke," *Zeitschrift für philosophische Forschung*, 38 (1984), pp. 100–10.

Guéroult, M.: *L'Évolution et la structure de la doctrine de la science chez Fichte* (Paris: Société d'édition Les Belles Lettres, 1930).

Habermas, J: *Erkenntnis und Interesse* (Frankfurt: Suhrkamp, 1968).

Hammacher, K. (ed.): *Der transzendentale Gedanke* (Hamburg: Meiner, 1981).

Henrich, D: "Fichte's original insight," In *Contemporary German Philosophy: I*, tr. D. R. Lathterman (University Park, PA: Pennsylvania State University Press, 1982), pp. 15–53.

Inciarte, F.: *Transzendentale Einbildungskraft* (Bonn: Bouvier, 1970).

Janke, W.: *Fichte* (Berlin: De Gruyter, 1970).

Kahlo, M., Wolf, E. A., and Zaczyk, R. (eds): *Fichtes Lehre vom Rechtsverhältnis* (Frankfurt: Klostermann, 1992).

Lauth, R.: *Die transzendentale Naturlehre nach Prinzipien der Wissenschaftslehre* (Hamburg: Meiner, 1984).

Léon, X.: *Fichte et son temps*, 3 vols (Paris: Armand Colin, 1954).

Nagel, T.: *The View from Nowhere* (New York/Oxford: Oxford University Press, 1986).

Neuhouser, F.: *Fichte's Theory of Subjectivity* (Cambridge: Cambridge University Press, 1990).

Philonenko, A.: *La liberté humain dans la philosophie de Fichte* (Paris: Vrin, 1966).

Pippin, R. B.: "Fichte's Contribution," *Philosophical Forum*, 19, nos 2–3 (1988), pp. 74–96.

Rohs, P.: *Johann Gottlieb Fichte* (Munich: C. H. Beck, 1991).

Russell, B.: *History of Western Thought* (London: George Allen & Unwin, 1948).

Schrader, W.: *Empirisches und absolutes Ich* (Stuttgart/Bad Canstatt: Fromann-Holzboog, 1972).

Siep, L.: *Hegels Fichtekritik und die Wissenschaftslehre von 1804* (Freiburg/Munich: Alber, 1970).

——: *Praktische Philosophie im Deutschen Idealismus* (Frankfurt: Suhrkamp, 1992).

Verweyen, H. J.: *Recht und Sittlichkeit in J. G. Fichte's Gesellschaftslehre* (Freiburg/Munich: Alber, 1979).

# 4

# Early German Romanticism: Friedrich Schlegel and Novalis

ERNST BEHLER

The word "romanticism" designates in German as in other European languages a broad movement in literature that originated at the beginning of the nineteenth century and has often been characterized as an opposition to the preceding age of rationalism and Enlightenment. Situated between the classicist schools of taste of the previous century and the realistic and naturalistic trends in literature of the later nineteenth century, Romanticism or romantic literature is the product of the creative power of the imagination; it appeals to the emotions, has a preference for the mysterious aspects of nature, and shows a strong predilection for the past, the Middle Ages, and mythological traditions. With its strong affinity to the novel, romantic literature departs from the classical forms and the classicist canon of literature, but when these classical forms were nevertheless used by the authors of this movement, something new was created – the romantic tale, the romantic drama, and romantic poetry. The great romantic authors in Germany were E. T. A. Hoffmann, Eichendorff, Brentano, Arnim, and Fouqué. There is both a narrower and a broader notion of Romanticism in Germany, the broader also relating to painting (Friedrich, Runge) and music (Schumann, Schubert, Mendelssohn, Bartholdy, Wagner). Romanticism had a great impact on the general view of the world and was influential in the rise of the historical consciousness, the revival of a religious spirit, and the emergence of a conservative political attitude. As far as philosophy and the sciences are concerned, Romanticism is associated with figures such as Schelling and Schopenhauer, the development of a philosophy of art, of nature, and of the subconscious. On the whole, Romanticism is one of those movements that shaped an entire age and manifested itself down to the most particular features of popular belief and scientific interest.

"Early Romanticism" is a category which applies only to the intellectual life of Germany, designating a period of about five years before the turn from the eighteenth to the nineteenth century. The term is obviously a creation by historians and was introduced to distinguish this phase from later forms of Romanticism. The main differences consist in the strongly theoretical and philosophical orientation among the members of this group and the future-oriented revolutionary character of their work. Their literary and critical ambition was not limited to German national literature, but had a broad historical and international direction toward world literature, including Oriental and Far Eastern literature. Above all, their work had a communal, collaborative character. This group formed a "school," or the "new school," as their contemporaries liked to call them. This school, located in the University town of Jena, entertained a close interrelationship with the philosophy of transcendental idealism, as it emerged in these years from Kant to Fichte and to Schelling. The term "Early Romanticism" has been used by critics since the rediscovery of this school at the end of the nineteenth and the beginning of the twentieth century. It became more established following the Second World War and is now the common designation for this special and early form of German Romanticism.

The formation of this school began in June 1796, when August Wilhelm Schlegel (1767–1845) and his wife Caroline decided to move to Jena, where Schlegel assumed a professorship of literature at the university. Their house in Jena became the gathering place for a group of young authors, all in their twenties, who were soon to be called by the collective name "the new school." Friedrich Schlegel (1772–1829) followed his brother in August 1796. He was a close friend of Novalis (1772–1801), the Baron Friedrich von Hardenberg, who had just finished his studies and assumed the position of an engineer in the saltmines at Weißenfels near Jena. When Friedrich Schlegel moved temporarily to Berlin in the summer of 1797, he established contact with a group of writers including Johann Heinrich Wackenroder, Ludwig Tieck, and Friedrich Schleiermacher. He also became acquainted with Dorothea (at that time, Brendel) Veit, the daughter of Moses Mendelssohn, who later became his wife. This move to Berlin led to the formation of the *Athenaeum*, the famous periodical of the Early Romantics, to which they all contributed. When Friedrich Schlegel returned to Jena in the autumn of 1799, he was followed by Dorothea and Tieck. Wackenroder had died in 1798, and Schleiermacher never came to Jena because of his obligations as a preacher in Berlin. This was the group of people designated by the term "Early Romanticism." Friedrich Schlegel describes their communal philosophizing and poetizing when he writes in Fragment 125 of the *Athenaeum*:

> Perhaps there will be a birth of a whole new era of the sciences and the arts if symphilosophy and sympoetry became so universal and heartfelt that it would no longer be anything extraordinary for several complementary minds to create communal works. (*KSFA*, vol. 2, 185; *LF*, p. 34)

August Wilhelm Schlegel was the oldest and most learned member of this group. His lectures at Jena University on aesthetics comprised the entire field of the philosophy of art, including sculpture, architecture, painting, music, and dance. His treatment of poetry and literature proceeded from a theory of language remarkable for its innovative features. His wife Caroline did not produce writings of her own, but she participated actively in the work of her husband. Several sections of his dialogue *Paintings* stem from her. Dorothea, Friedrich Schlegel's friend and later wife, wrote a novel in the romantic vein, *Florentine*, a pleasant and entertaining piece of romantic narrative. Wackenroder is the author of *Outpourings of an Art-Loving Friar*, comprising reminiscences and musings of a fictitious Italian monk about art, the painting of the Italian Renaissance, in particular Raphael, but also about paintings and engravings by Dürer. The text has the merit of having stimulated interest in the Italian Renaissance and so-called Old-German art among artists and theorists of the time. Tieck, a close friend of Wackenroder, the most gifted narrator of the early romantic school, was the author of novels and tales, and also lyric poetry of a new and astonishing character.

Friedrich Schlegel and Novalis are the two authors of this group most closely associated with philosophy. Both wrote novels, and Novalis was also a lyric poet of great talent, but their philosophical speculation always attracted attention because of a singular, innovative style of thought. Schleiermacher, too, is a philosopher in his own right, famous for his *On Religion: Speeches to its Cultured Despisers* of 1799. His theory of hermeneutics is renowned for representing the romantic phase of hermeneutics that was to be followed by Dilthey's foundation of the human sciences, Heidegger's "ontological turn" of hermeneutics, and Gadamer's "philosophical hermeneutics." Yet Schleiermacher never really participated in the school of Early Romanticism. His writings have the character of coming from outside rather than that of communal products. It is mainly for this reason that the following sections focus on Friedrich Schlegel and Novalis.

## Friedrich Schlegel's and Novalis' critique of Fichte

When Friedrich Schlegel moved to Jena in the summer of 1796, he renewed his friendship with Novalis, who lived near the city, and immediately established contact with the philosopher Fichte. This meeting of minds led to the first communal work of the two romantic critics in the field of philosophy. This work can be characterized as the first major response to Fichte – a response, however, which went far beyond the intentions of the philosopher and related his "Doctrine of Science" closely to the aims of the school of Early Romanticism. In his letters to Christian Gottfried Korner, a friend in Dresden, Schlegel is quite outspoken about his relationship to Fichte. On September 21, 1791, he reports that he is visiting Fichte frequently and finds him "occasionally better" in personal dialogue than in his writings or at the lecture podium. "At the latter I found him admirably trivial," he said (*KFSA*, vol. 23, p. 333). Schlegel also found him "weak and strange in every science that has an object." During their first conversation, Fichte earnestly told the young historian of Greek literature that he "would rather count peas than study history" (ibid.). Yet, Schlegel insisted that he defended, loved, and praised all of this not out of an "iron obstinacy, maintaining preconceived prejudices," but out of the conviction that nothing great ever happens "without such glaring onesidedness, without a certain limitation" (ibid.). On January 30, 1797, he told Körner that he was finished with "Fichte's system." He talked with him only about the external aspects and liked the person all the more since he had "separated himself truly and decidedly from the teacher of the doctrine of science" (*KFSA*, vol. 2, p. 343). To this experience one should add a letter of Fichte to Friedrich Schlegel of August 16, 1800. Fichte wrote in response to Schlegel's *Dialogue on Poetry* and took issue with the idea expressed at the beginning of the *Dialogue* that there are manifold individual views on poetry and that we should try to "grasp every other independent form of poetry" so that it may become a stimulus for our own imagination (p. 284). Fichte was not only upset by the asystematic character of this view, but also by its implied historicism. The friendship between Schlegel and Fichte had deepened during these years, but their completely diverging theoretical views could not be better expressed than by Fichte's letter:

> Having received the last two pieces of the *Athenaeum*, I now believe I understand completely your system of poetry that we discussed last winter in Jena. It is worthy of your mind, your love of hard work, and your historical research, although I myself consider it only provisional, only suitable for this time. Something in the material of poetry is, to be sure, individual; the main thing in it, however, its form, is thoroughly general; and in this regard, I would say contrary to you: just as there is only one reason, there is only one true poetry. Are we supposed to absorb the works of the great artists of previous times through study? It may be that in our desiccated age we can do no better. But where then did the source for the first artist who had no predecessors originate? Could it be possible that this original source has now dried up for all time? Oh, if only we had a pure aesthetics! (*FI*, vol. 4, pp. 282–3)

In the notebooks sent to him by Schlegel, Novalis read of how one could "almost always boldly contradict" what Fichte assumed as self-evident (*KFSA*, vol. 18, p. 31). Regarding his endless attempts at introducing his audience to the point of view of the doctrine of science, Schlegel wrote: "I have not yet found anybody who believed in Fichte, yet many who admire him, some who know him, and the one or the other who understands him. Fichte is somehow like the drunk man who does not tire of mounting his horse from one side and, transcendingly, keeps falling off on the other" (p. 32). In general, however, Schlegel believed that Fichte's doctrine of science was "too narrow": "Only Fichte's principles are deduced in it, that is, the logical ones, and not even these completely. And what about the practical, the moral or ethical ones? Society, learning, wit, art, and so on are also entitled to be deduced here". Fichte's theory of femininity appeared ridiculous to Schlegel, for whom true women were not "passive," but "antithetical, physically as well as morally" (p. 34). On the whole, Fichte's doctrine of science appeared to him "as rhetorical as Fichte himself: "With regard to individuality, it is a Fichtean presentation of the Fichtean spirit in Fichtean letters" (p. 33). In a more humorous vein, Schlegel considered the doctrine of science not to be the "*formative process of pure egohood*, but fancies and narrations of an oscillating, travelling, strolling mystic" (p. 35). Schlegel, in other words, raised the question of Fichte's own historicity, or the historicity of what was going on in his system, and felt that what was proclaimed here as absolute Ego or absolute thought was nothing more than Johann Gottlieb Fichte in Jena, including all his personal idiosyncrasies and prejudices.

In a more philosophical or theoretical formulation of his critique, Schlegel objected to Fichte's assumption of only one basic principle, one single axiom (*Grundsatz*), and insisted that, to be set in motion, the transcendental process has to proceed from two interactive principles, two reciprocal poles, or one axiom antithetical in itself (*Wechselgrundsatz*; *KFSA*, vol. 18, p. 36). In its philosophical orientation, his critique of Fichte already presupposes that absolute idealism of a full-blown interaction of subject and object, ideality and reality, ego and nature, which Schelling and Hegel made their own after the turn of the century. Yet, in a strictly philosophical sense, it was evident for him that idealism and realism, subject and object, Fichte and Spinoza, were not only complementary components, but also two poles that must "interactively make themselves possible, necessary, and real." And he added: "This may indeed be beyond Fichte; Schelling surmises as much" (p. 66). If we take later texts by Friedrich Schlegel into consideration, this aspect of his critique of Fichte can be characterized as an objection to making only the Ego the centre of "spirit, life, activity, movement, and change," and reducing the non-Ego or nature to a state of "constant calm, standstill, immobility, lack of all change, movement, and life, that is death" (*KFSA*, vol. 12, pp. 152, 190). Nature is thereby degraded to a "dead sensual world or a mere sediment of reflection," to a "mere restraint and limitation of the infinitely developing spirit," even to the "true non-being" (*KFSA*, vol. 8, p. 68). "Fichtean idealism proves its incompetence by not understanding and comprehending materialism", Schlegel said in a note of 1811 (*KFSA*, vol. 17, p. 269). Friedrich August Hülsen, an associate of the early Romantic circle, expressed this feeling most vividly when he studied the doctrine of science in the Schwarza Valley of the Thuringian forest, formerly one of Germany's most beautiful landscapes, and, on looking up from the book, said: "Nature approached me as if a distant friend had greeted me after a long absence."

Whereas Schlegel's position in relation to Fichte is one of distance, expressing a feeling of his own superiority, Novalis attempted to transpose himself into the interior of this philosophy and from there, sought to transcend it. His *Fichte-Studies* are recognized as one of the most peculiar products of Early Romanticism in the field of philosophy. Indeed, Novalis's *Fichte-Studies* conduct an intellectual struggle with a type of systematic thought that represents philosophy in exemplary fashion, and they come to show that, from the point of view of poetry as well as that of personal self-recognition, philosophy is immeasurably incomplete and thereby in need of support from all sorts of other quarters.

The central subject of interest in Novalis's study of Fichte is obviously that of philosophy, which for him was certainly not the only activity of the mind, nor even the most prominent of all intellectual experiences as it was for Fichte. For Novalis, philosophy should be seen in a larger context where faith, love, poetry, and religion have the same right to existence. These *Fichte-Studies* can therefore be characterized as attempts to analyze the "activities of the spirit" in a more comprehensive manner than Fichte had done and to create a theory of the ego with a much wider scope than the doctrine of knowledge had been able to establish. The real target, however, is philosophy as such. In his critique of philosophy, Novalis does not take on the whole of the history of philosophy, or an abstract, self-constructed notion of philosophy, but philosophy in its most recent expression, in its most advanced form. In his analyses, he concentrates on the theory of the ego and relates it to his own notion of personality; he sketches out a theory of the imagination in contrast to Fichte's thought process; he describes the poetic power in its distinctness from the philosophical faculty within us. In other instances, he attempts to distinguish the faculty of feeling from that of reflection, to compare "intellectual intuition" with "intellectual power of seeing," and he writes down everything that appears noteworthy to him and translates it into his own language and manner of thinking.

The most important theme emerging from these manifold observations is that of the relationship of philosophy to poetry, of the thinking to the poetizing power. Here Fichte maintained the absolute primacy of philosophy; for him, all questions boiled down to philosophical ones. Novalis, unlike Fichte, relativized the activity of philosophy or, rather, he gave other realms of experience autonomy, especially poetry. Many interpreters have seen the result of these studies as embodied in a fragment of a later date that seems to proclaim the absolute domination of poetry and reads: "Poetry is the absolutely real. This is the core of my philosophy. The more poetic, the more true" (*NO*, vol. 2, p. 647). This statement seems to reverse the relationship between philosophy and poetry as Fichte saw it, and to introduce the reign of poetry as the core of Early Romantic theory as expressed by Novalis. Yet, if one bears in mind the counter- or interactive quality of the notion of "real" in its relationship to "ideal," as well as other statements by Novalis, one can very well show that, like Schlegel, he understood the relationship between poetry and philosophy in terms of an interaction (*Wechselwirkung*) and conceived of the union or fusion of philosophy and poetry not in terms of subjugating one to the other, but as a full maintenance of the mutual tension between the two poles. One of these fragments states: "The poem of reason is philosophy – This is the highest élan that reason gives to itself. Unity of reason and imagination. Without philosophy, the human being remains discordant in his essential powers – There are two human beings – one reasonable being and one poet. Without philosophy, imperfect poet – without poetry, imperfect thinker, critic" (*NO*, vol. 3, p. 531). In another instance, Novalis describes the interaction of philosophy and poetry in the following way: "the philosopher becomes a poet. Poet is only the highest degree of the thinker, or the perceiver, etc. . . . The separation of poet and thinker is only fictitious – and to the disadvantage of both – it is a sign of a sickness – and of a sickly constitution" (p. 406). This thought continues to be formulated in the most varied contexts. Another of the fragments reads: "Poetry is the hero of philosophy. Philosophy elevates poetry to its principle. Philosophy teaches us the value of poetry. Philosophy is the *theory of poetry*. Philosophy teaches us what poetry is, that poetry is the one and the all" (*NO*, vol. 2, p. 591). If one isolated philosophy from this lively and essential interaction with poetry, as Fichte seems to propose, one would reduce philosophy to a "mere activity of the intelligence" (p. 269). The isolated, energy-specific activity of the intelligence, however, is its "proper mode of thought," the seeking of grounds, the desire of an absolute grounding (ibid.). Reduced to this tendency, philosophy becomes finite, petrified. Philosophy becomes free and an "infinite activity," an "infinitely free activity in us," once such a ground is no longer sought or the desire for it is satisfied only in a relative manner. This goal of a free philosophy could be called the "absolute postulate" of philosophy, whereas all "search for *one principle*" appears like an attempt to find the "squaring of the circle," the "perpetuum mobile," or "the philosopher's stone" (p. 270).

In general, one can say about Friedrich Schlegel's and Novalis's attitude toward Fichte's thought, that, after closer acquaintance with his doctrine of knowledge, they made a decisive distinction between the project in its philosophical scope and its reflective and animating thought process, between the dogmatic ballast of Fichte's theory of consciousness and the life of the intelligence, between what they called the "letter" and the "spirit" of the doctrine of science. They separated, in other words, Fichte as the promulgator of a new scientific edifice or system of philosophy from Fichte as the "inventor of an entirely new way of thinking – for which there is not yet a name in language" (*NO*, vol. 2, p. 524). They readily relinquished all the cognitive elements, categories of thought, and forms of self-consciousness that Fichte attempted to establish through his philosophical specula-tion, and focused almost exclusively on the "art of reflection," on the lively thought and counterthought which animated this philosophy. They also felt free to transfer this informed thinking to other realms of human experience, such as poetry, art, society, politics, but especially to literary communication. When Friedrich Schlegel attempted, shortly after the dissolution of the Early Romantic group, to give the readers of his Paris journal *Europa* (1803–5) some flavour of the spirit that had emanated from the new German literature and philosophy, he referred to Fichte as the most prominent figure but practically ignored all of the material part of his doctrine of science, its philosophical and systematic constructs. Instead, he focused solely on the reflective, agile character of Fichte's thought process and described his merit as having "entirely on his own and for the first time discovered and installed the proper method in philosophy by organizing free autonomous thought as an art" (*KFSA*, vol. 3, p. 6). He added that Fichte, "by upsetting consciousness in its inner-most creative depth," had provoked the "most significant changes and revolutions in all other areas of human thought and creation," and that there was "hardly an art or a science that had not yet been seized by the light of intellectual intuition and begun to experience the beneficial results of idealism" (ibid.).

## Novalis on the truly poetic

A major theme deriving from these *Fichte-Studies* is the nature of the truly poetic. When we focus on this theme in Novalis's writings, we soon realize that it is interrelated with many others, all of which are scattered among thousands of fragments. This makes it difficult to isolate one theme and pretend that it is distinct-ly individual, neatly separated from all the others. This basic difficulty of reading Novalis is, of course, a result of his fragmentary writing. In several instances he gives us to understand that his fragments were only of preliminary value and would be overcome by a "future literature," when we would read "nothing but the beau-tiful composition – literary works of art" (*NO*, vol. 3, pp. 276–7). But one wonders whether these images of transitoriness and a beautiful future were only ironic metaphors enabling its author to express himself all the more uninhibitedly in fragmentary writing.

One important result of this fragmentary style of writing for Novalis is that his thoughts never occur in isolation, but always in relationship to other, often opposite thoughts. His ideas on the nature of the poet are a good example of this manner of writing. He never talks about the poetic as such, but always in interaction with other things. Representation of objects is confronted with reflection on the part of the ego, free creation is brought in relationship with instinctual creation. In his *Fichte-Studies* we read:

> It is coarse and dull to communicate oneself simply because of content – content and material should not tyrannize us. We should communicate ourselves in a suitable manner – artfully – reflectively – our delivery should not be unworthy of ourselves – it should be appropriate to its public, to its aim. It should utilize the advantages of time and space.   (*NO*, vol. 3, p. 281)

This became more and more his model of the poetic activity. In another passage in his *Fichte Studies*, he analyzed the interaction of subject and object in poetic creation more precisely, although we have to consider that these reflections occur in the context of an exploration of Fichte's philosophy, and thereby show a natural inclination towards the side of the subject or the ego. This passage reads:

> If there is an independent representative power – which simply represents in order to represent – to represent in order to represent – then it is a *free* representation. This simply indicates that not the object as such but the ego as base of the activity should determine the activity. The work of art thereby assumes a free, autonomous, ideal character – an imposing spirit – for it is a *visible* product of an ego. The ego, however, posits itself distinctly in this manner because it posits itself as an infinite ego – and since it has to posit itself as an infinitely representing ego, it posits itself as free, as a distinctly representing ego. The object can only be the germ, the type, the point of investment – only the forming power develops creatively the beautiful totality at, in, and through the object.   (*NO*, vol. 2, pp. 282–3)

In his later fragments Novalis is inexhaustible in describing this particular power of the poet. One favourite example is the language used by the poet not in the sense of "general signs," but as "tones," or "terms of enchantment." He compares the poet's words to the clothing of saints that enclose "wondrous powers." We cannot really say that, for the poet, language is too poor but only that it is "always too general" (*NO*, vol. 2, p. 533). Another way of illustrating the particular nature of poetry is by comparing it with the other arts, especially painting and music. Like the painter who sees the visible things of this world with eyes different from those of the ordinary person, the poet sees the events of the inner and outer world in a manner different from others. No other art, however, can exemplify the nature of poetry more effectively than music. Novalis says:

> Nowhere is it more conspicuous than in music that it is only the spirit that poeticizes the objects, the modifications of the material, and that the beautiful, the subject of art, is not pregiven to us and does not lie readymade in the appearances either. All sounds produced by nature are hoarse – and spiritless – only a musical soul perceives the rustling of the forest, the whistling of the wind, the song of the nightingale, the babbling of the brook as melodious and significant. The musician takes the essence of

> his art from himself – not even the slightest suspicion of imitation can be incurred by him.   (*NO*, vol. 2, pp. 573–4)

This particular quality of perception also applies to the painter, the only difference being that he employs "an infinitely more difficult language of signs than the musician," that he paints with the eye. In the last analysis, however, "every human being is to a small degree already an artist." The main difference is that the artist is able to employ this particular susceptibility as he pleases and "without exterior solicitation," whereas the non-artist becomes susceptible only at the instigation of an external solicitation (p. 574).

In another instance, Novalis calls this artistic susceptibility by its proper name and says: "The imagination is that wondrous sense that can *substitute* for us all other senses – and is already to a large extent subject to our choice. While the outer senses are totally subservient to mechanical laws – the imagination is obviously not bound to the presence of and contact with outer stimulations" (p. 650). A little later, he compares the consciously artistic activity with the working of instinct, and observes: "Instinct is art *without intention* – art without knowing how and what one is doing. Instinct can be transformed into *art – by observing* the activity of art. What is done instinctively can eventually be learned to be done artistically. Art of producing the ridiculous and the romantic" (*NO*, vol. 3, p. 287). From this point of view poetry can be seen as the "intentional, active, productive employment of our organs," if we understand by "organs" our natural equipment as human beings, including the organs of perception and knowledge. Indeed, Novalis continues, "thinking perhaps would not be much different – and thinking and poeticizing are thereby one" (p. 563). The particular point in this fragment is, of course, that thinking is enlisted on the side of the natural, unconscious, instinctive activities of the mind, whereas poeticizing is ranked as an intentional, conscious action. Yet, the type of artistic intentionality advocated by the Schlegels is too radical for Novalis and lacks the natural component of an instinctive and unconscious creation. He comments on these relationships in a fragment on Shakespeare that reads:

> When the Schlegels talk about the intentionality and artificiality of Shakespeare's works, they overlook that art belongs to nature and is, as it were, nature contemplating, imitating, and forming itself. The art of a well-developed nature is of course miles apart from the artificiality of reason and a merely reasoning spirit. Shakespeare was no calculating mind, no scholar, he was a powerful and motley soul whose inventions and works, like products of nature, bear the impression of a thinking spirit and in which even the most penetrating observer will discover new agreements with the infinite structure of the universe, correspondences to ideas not yet discovered and relationships with the higher powers and senses of humanity. His works are metaphorical and polysemous, simple and inexhaustible like these [the works of nature], and nothing more senseless could be said about them than that they were works of art in that limited and mechanical meaning of the word.   (p. 569)

Taken together, the fragments quoted so far on the poetic faculty reveal a constant oscillation, a subtle shifting of balance in their alternate predilection for the artistic or the natural, the intentional or the instinctive tendency of poetry. Some of them, especially those from or close to the *Fichte Studies*, show a clear preponderance of the subjective side, whereas others, especially the fragment on Shakespeare, are more explicitly in favour of nature. Novalis appears to adopt this oscillating manner of viewing the interrelationship in order to avoid a "systematic" solution, a final result, as well as to keep reflection alive and open-ended for further discoveries.

Another characteristic way of describing the nature of poetry and the poetic is by analogy to the human mind (*Gemüt*). One fragment adopting this approach reads: "Poetry is true idealism – contemplation of the world as contemplation of a large mind – self-consciousness of the universe" (p. 640). That poetry is essentially a *"representation* of the *mind –* of the *inner world in its entirety"* is already indicated for Novalis by its medium, that is, its words, language, which are the revelation of this inner realm (p. 650). However, just as the "representation of nature" must be "spontaneous, peculiarly general, connecting, and creative," the "representation of the mind" should never aim at "how it [the mind] is, but how it could be, and ought to be" (ibid.). One fragment describes the mind's particular poetic manner of "weaving" (*verknüpfen*) more precisely:

> In our mind, everything is connected in the most peculiar, pleasant, and lively manner. The strangest things come together by virtue of one space, one time, an odd similarity, an error, some accident. In this manner, curious unities and peculiar connections originate – one thing reminds us of everything, becomes the sign of many things, and is itself signified by and referred to many things. Reason and imagination are united through time and space in the most extraordinary manner, and we can say that each thought, each phenomenon of our mind is the most individual part of an altogether individual totality.   (pp. 650–1)

Yet the investigation into the nature of poetry remains infinite and cannot be concluded with a firm result: "What actually constitutes the essence of poetry can definitely not be determined. It is infinitely composed and yet simple. Beautiful, romantic, harmonious are only partial expressions for the poetic" (p. 690). It is in this context that Novalis formulates his most avantgardist ideas about poetry. In one of these fragments, he characterizes poetry as the "art of exciting the mind" (*Gemütserregungskunst*), as an "inner *painting* and *music*" producing "inner moods and pictures or visual perceptions like a mechanical instrument in the mind – perhaps also *spiritual* dances, etc." (p. 639). In such a procedure, the poet uses "things and words like *piano keys,*" and his "entire poetry consists in an active association of ideas – of spontaneous, intentional, ideal production of contingencies" (*Zufallsproduktion*) (p. 451). Unity and connection appear to be suspended in such poetry. "A fairy tale," Novalis says, "is really like a dream image – without connection – an *ensemble* of wondrous things and occurrences – for instance a *musical fantasy* – the harmonious effects of an aeolian harp – *nature* itself." And he adds: "If a *story* is brought into a fairy-tale, this is already an interference from the outside" (p. 454). Then the fairy-tale assumes features of "reason," of "connection, meaning" (p. 455). In another instance, we read:

Narrations without connection, yet with associations, as in dreams. Poems – merely melodious and full of beautiful words – but also without any meaning and connection – at most, only some stanzas comprehensible – they must appear altogether like fragments of the most diverse things. True poetry can have at best an allegorical meaning on the whole and like music, exert an indirect effect: nature is therefore purely *poetic* like the chamber of a magician – of a physicist – a nursery – a storage room, a storage pantry. (p. 572)

## Friedrich Schlegel's theory of irony

The most salient step in Friedrich Schlegel's response to Fichte occurred when he began a fragment of the *Athenaeum* with the statement: "There is a kind of poetry whose essence lies in the relation between the ideal and real, and which therefore, by analogy to philosophical jargon, should be called transcendental poetry" (*KFSA*, vol. 2, p. 204; *LF*, p. 195). At this point, Schlegel had related the Fichtean form of transcendental philosophy to that artistic, reflective type of thinking which for him is an essential element of poetry. He saw the essence of this poetry as including "the producer along with the product", i.e., the poet together with his poem, thereby effecting an "artistic reflection and beautiful self-mirroring" for which he found the best examples "in Pindar, in the lyric fragments of the Greeks, in the classical elegy, and, among the moderns, in Goethe." Such a poetry should represent itself in all its representations and "always be simultaneously poetry and the poetry of poetry" (ibid.). In his long fragment on Romantic poetry as a universal progressive poetry, Schlegel described the "poetic reflection" of transcendental poetry in the image of an endless series of mirrors, saying that this poetry is able to "hover at the midpoint between the portrayed and the portrayer, free of all real and ideal self-interest, on the wings of poetic reflection, and can raise that reflection again and again to a higher power, can multiply it in an endless succession of mirrors" (*KFSA*, vol. 2, pp. 182–3; *LF*, p. 175). As is obvious from these statements, Schlegel understood the meaning of "transcendental" in its original sense. Kant had defined this term when, in the introduction to the second edition of his *Critique of Pure Reason*, he called "transcendental" that mode of cognition which is not so much interested in the mere cognition of objects, but in our manner of recognizing objects (*KA*, vol. 3, p. 43), and thereby joined the subject of knowledge and its object in an inseparable way. Fichte's usage of the term "transcendental" emphasized the reflective action on the part of the subject in this relationship. Friedrich Schlegel's new version of the term, however, abolished the distinction between philosophy and poetry by refer-ring the reflective part of this interaction also to poetry and by rephrasing the notion of reflection as a "poetic reflection" that includes "the producer along with the product" (*KFSA*, vol. 2, p. 204; *LF*, p. 195), "the portrayed and the portrayer" (*KFSA*, vol. 2, p. 182; *LF*, p. 175).

Nothing comes closer to this reflective type of literature than irony, and irony is virtually identical with that self-reflective style of poetry that became accentuated in Early Romanticism and constitutes a decisive mark of literary modernism. Irony is also the most famous part of the Early Romantic theory and became so closely associated with it that the two are often regarded as identical. Friedrich Schlegel's treatment of irony cannot be reduced to a ready-made theory, but consists of a great number of statements which certainly show coherence but also exhibit constant changes in emphasis and approach. The most productive way of dealing with this complex topic is the genetic way, the discussion in successive fashion of his three collections of fragments relevant to the notion of irony. These are the *Critical Fragments* (1797), the *Athenaeum Fragments* (1798), and the *Ideas* (1800).

When Friedrich Schlegel decided to extend the restricted use of irony, as encountered in the rhetorical tradition of Europe, to the works of Boccaccio, Cervantes, Sterne, and Goethe, and wrote in 1797 that "there are ancient and modern poems which breathe throughout, in their entirety and in every detail, the divine breath of irony" (*KFSA*, vol. 2, p. 152; *LF*, p. 148), he gave irony a completely new scope and effected a fundamental change in the concept in Western literary theory. The authors he mentioned certainly would have been astonished to hear him interpret their literary creations as displaying irony – to say nothing of Shakespeare and other older models of so-called ironic style. Schlegel himself described his novel treatment of literary works as a move away from the search for "beautiful instances and single images" which was so dominant in eighteenth-century criticism to the comprehension of the entirety of works of the imagination and the expression of this insight in words (*KFSA*, vol. 3, p. 296). Indeed, in this reference to the entirety of literary works, Schlegel's new understanding of irony bears a strong resemblance to his other innovations in literary criticism.

This change of meaning in the notion of irony can be dated in a precise manner and actually occurs in Fragment 42 of the *Critical Fragments*, beginning with the blunt statement: "Philosophy is the real homeland of irony, which one would like to define as logical beauty" (*KFSA*, vol. 2, p. 152; *LF*, p. 143). This statement implies that, contrary to the entire rhetorical tradition of Europe according to which irony is a distinct figure of speech, the real origin of irony is to be found in philosophy, more precisely in a particular philosophical type of argumentation practiced by Socrates and developed as a form of art by Plato. Schlegel calls this technique "logical Beauty," but the technical term for it is Socratic or Platonic "dialectics" – thought and counterthought as a progressive movement of thinking. In fact, Schlegel's statement continues directly with the argument that "wherever philosophy appears in oral or written dialogues – and is not simply confined to rigid systems – there irony should be asked for and provided." This is entirely in line with his general image of Plato. In his Paris lectures on European literature of 1804, he formulated this image of Plato more pointedly, saying: "Plato had no system, but only a philosophy. The philosophy of a human being is the history, the becoming, the progression of his mind, the gradual formation and development of his thoughts" (*KFSA*, vol. 11, p. 118). A little later in these lectures he says:

We have mentioned already that Plato only had a philosophy, but no system; just as philosophy in general is more a seeking, a striving for science than science itself, this is especially the case with that of Plato. He is never finished with his thought, and this constant further striving of his thought for completed knowledge and the highest cognition, this eternal becoming, forming, and developing of his ideas, he has tried to shape artistically in dialogues.   (p. 120)

Schlegel was, of course, aware of the rhetorical tradition in which irony was transmitted and had found its habitual place in Europe. But this rhetorical irony, bound to individual instances and to particular figures, appeared to him minor and insignificant compared with the philosophical homeland of irony where it could manifest itself "throughout." He said: "Of course, there is also a rhetorical species of irony which, sparingly used, has an excellent effect, especially in polemics; but compared with the sublime urbanity of the Socratic muse, it is like the pomp of the most splendid oration set against the noble style of an ancient tragedy." The most important sentence occurs in the middle of the fragment and states that it is not rhetoric but poetry that can equal philosophy in the use of irony "throughout," in the entirety of a work, and not simply in single and isolated instances. The sentence reads: "Only poetry can also reach the heights of philosophy in this way, and only poetry does not restrict itself to isolated ironical passages, as rhetoric does." After this equation of Socratic philosophy and modern poetry in the works of Boccaccio, Cervantes, Shakespeare, and Goethe is established, Schlegel concludes with the statement that actually constitutes the turning-point in the history of the concept of irony: "There are ancient and modern poems that are pervaded by the divine breath of irony throughout and informed by a truly transcendental buffoonery." What he understands by the "divine breath of irony" is described with reference to the internal mood of these works of literature. It is a "mood that surveys everything and rises infinitely above all limitations, even above its own art, virtue, or genius" (ibid.). The fragment, however, like all complex and condensed statements, also has an afterthought, which consists of the words "transcendental buffoonery." A buffoon is a clown, and after irony has been introduced in elevated fashion as Platonic discourse and Socratic incompletion, it appears appropriate to remind the reader of the human character of limitation and confinement, a feature which is also apparent in the outer appearance of Socrates and is expressed by Schlegel in the final words of the fragment, "the mimic style of an averagely gifted Italian buffo".

Fragment 108 of the *Critical Fragments* focuses more directly on Socratic irony, but it does not convey anything not already mentioned in Fragment 42 of the same collection, except for the paramount topic of communication. Schlegel now refers to the "impossibility and necessity of complete communication," which is mediated by irony. Instead of paraphrasing this fragment, it is perhaps best to reproduce some of its statements in their entirety:

In this sort of irony, everything should be playful and serious, guilelessly open and deeply hidden. It originates in the union of *savoir vivre* and scientific spirit, in the conjunction of a perfectly instinctive and a perfectly conscious philosophy. It contains and arouses a feeling of indissoluble antagonism between the absolute and the relative, between the impossibility and the necessity of complete communication. It is the freest of all licenses, for by its means one transcends oneself; and yet it is also the most lawful, for it is absolutely necessary.   (*KFSA*, vol. 2, p. 160; *LF*, p. 156)

There are some other passages in the *Critical Fragments* that illustrate this change in the meaning of irony from the classical, rhetorical concept to its modern connotation as being coextensive with speech, writing, and communication. These fragments add little to what has already been said. One of them, however, introduces a new note on the concept of irony, although the term itself does not occur in it. The reference is to a rhythm of "constant alternation of self-creation and self-annihilation" (*KFSA*, vol. 2, p. 151; *LF*, pp. 146–7) that becomes the dominant theme in the exposition of irony in the *Athenaeum* (e.g., *KFSA*, vol. 2, pp. 172, 217). In its dual movement of affirmation and negation, of enthusiasm and skepticism, this ironic alternation between self-creation and self-annihilation is simply another formulation for what had previously been presented as poetic reflection, as transcendental poetry, and it shows that Schlegel's notion of poetry and literature actually coincides with this dual movement in the creative mind. To underline this fact, one could add that practically all polarities which have occurred so far in the description of Schlegel's theory of literature can be related to this alternating rhythm of self-creation and self-annihilation, that is, the antitheses of classical and Romantic, poetry and philosophy, the Ego and the world. The speaker of Schlegel's *Speech on Mythology* refers to the "structure of the whole" in the works of Shakespeare and Cervantes and describes it as "this artfully ordered confusion, this charming symmetry of contradictions, this wonderfully perennial alternation of enthusiasm and irony which lives even in the smallest parts of the whole" (*KFSA*, vol. 2, pp. 318–19; *DP*, p. 86). A similar and recurrent formulation of the same phenomenon is the phrase "to the point of irony" or "to the point of continuously fluctuating between self-creation and self-annihilation" (*KFSA*, vol. 2, pp. 172, 217; *LF*, pp. 167, 205). In a certain respect, this is the point of highest perfection – a perfection, however, that is conscious of its own imperfection and inscribes this feature into its own text.

The collection of fragments with the title *Ideas*, which appeared in 1800 in the last volume of the *Athenaeum*, does not contain many entries on irony. There is one fragment, however, hardly more than one line long, that introduces a larger, almost cosmic view of irony. It reads: "Irony is the clear consciousness of eternal agility, of an infinitely abundant chaos" (*KFSA*, vol. 2, p. 263; *LF*, p. 251). If one stresses the feeling of one's own insignificance, transitoriness, and fragmentation implied in this fragment, one comes close to the notion of melancholic irony, which became a famous topic in Romantic theory after the turn of the century, although the fragment can, of course, also be read in a more confident vein. That Friedrich Schlegel's thought was inclined in that direction, or at least not closed off from it, becomes obvious in some of his later pronouncements on irony. In his Cologne lectures of 1804–6, he says in a philosophical context that irony brings to our attention the "inexhaustible plenitude and manifoldness of the highest subjects of knowledge" (*KFSA*, vol. 13, p. 207). In his Dresden lectures of 1829, delivered

81

shortly before his death, he claims: "True irony . . . is the irony of love. It arises from the feeling of finitude and one's own limitation and the apparent contradiction of these feelings with the concept of infinity inherent in all true love" (*KFSA*, vol. 10, p. 357).

## References and further reading

Fichte, Johann Gottlieb: *Gesamtausgabe der Bayerischen Akademic der Wissenschaften*, ed. Reinhard Lauth and Hans Jacob (Stuttgart: Gromann-Holzboog, 1964– ). [Cited as *FI.*]

Kant, Immanuel: *Werke*, 9 vols (Berlin: de Gruyter, 1968). [Cited as *KA.*]

Novalis: *Novalis Schriften: Die Werke Friedrichs von Hardenberg*, ed. Richard Samuel in collaboration with Hans-Joachim Mähl and Gerhard Schultz, 5 vols (Stuttgart: Kohlhammer, 1960–88). [Cited as *NO.*]

Schlegel, Friedrich: *Kritische Friedrich Schlegel Ausgabe*, ed. Ernst Behler in collaboration with Jean-Jacques Austett, Hans Eichner, et al., 35 vols (Paderborn: Schöningh, 1958– ). [Cited as *KFSA.*]

Schlegel, Friedrich: *Dialogue on Poetry and Literary Aphorisms*, tr. Ernst Behler and Roman Stone (University Park, PA: Pennsylvania State University Press, 1968). [Cited as *DP.*]

Schlegel, Friedrich: *Lucinde and the Fragments*, tr. Peter Firchow (Minneapolis, MN: University of Minnesota Press, 1971). [Cited as *LF.*]

# 5

# Schelling

JEAN-FRANÇOIS COURTINE

It might seem paradoxical to present Schelling's thought by emphasizing the practical dimension of his work when so many commentators are challenging the reality of this practical dimension. When one considers Schelling's position within modern European philosophy, or when one attempts to underline the importance and the contemporary nature of his thought, several themes repeatedly come to the fore: the existence of freedom (which asserts itself in the face of the system and of closure), positivity and factuality (which are irreducible to the self-movement of thought), and, lastly, creative temporality, the system of time, the organic nature of which is destined to make possible and thinkable the new beginnings that stem from an initial decision. I wish to propose that the problem of freedom – that is the freedom to do good *and* evil, as well as the metaphysics of evil which is introduced by this problem – constitutes the crux of Schelling's thought, capable of opening up a line of thought in classical German philosophy which deserves to be pursued again today, even if it is muddled by the theo-cosmological speculations of the later Schelling.

Throughout Schelling's work we find the enthusiastic affirmation of absolute freedom or of the absolute as freedom. But if the *pathos* of freedom undeniably represents one of the most constant fundamental traits of Schelling's thought – from the fiery proclamations of the young *Stiftler* (students of the *stift* in Tübingen: Hölderlin, Hegel, Schelling, etc.) to the final declarations of the *Philosophy of Revelation* (vol. XIII, p. 359) – this persistent theme cannot on its own constitute a moral philosophy.

There is more than just a simple change of metaphor in the following statements: in the first, Kant declares that "the concept of freedom . . . is the *keystone* of the entire edifice of practical reason" (*Kritik der praktischen Vernunft* [*Critique of Practical Reason*]); in the second, Schelling announces the project of his book *The Self as a Principle of Philosophy* to his former fellow student Hegel (letter of February 4, 1795) in these terms: "the highest principle of all philosophy is . . . the Self insofar as it is purely and simply Self, not yet conditioned by an object, but where it is formulated by *freedom*. The alpha and omega of all philosophy is freedom." With the abandonment of the sharp distinction between practical freedom and transcendental freedom goes the refusal of the Kantian articulation between moral law as the *ratio cognoscendi* of freedom and freedom as the *ratio essendi* of moral law. Clearly, this "step beyond the Kantian limit" enacted by Schelling's transformation of freedom into an absolute leads him to reduce the formula of obligation to its simplest expression. When the transcendental search for the conditions of possibility seeks to achieve a greater degree of radicality in the study of the unconditioned in human knowledge, the highest law for the absolute or infinite Self becomes "identity." In any case, such a law is a "natural law" for the absolute Self much more than it is a moral law. For the real and ultimate *imperative* that is necessary for the Self in its relation to itself, setting aside all interpersonal or intersubjective concerns, is *equality with itself, identity*:

> Insofar as the highest law, through which the *being* of the infinite Self is determined, is the law of its identity, the moral law must represent in the finite being this identity not as *what is*, but as what is demanded, so that in consequence the highest law for the finite being is the following: *Be absolutely identical to yourself.* (*Vom Ich*, no. vii, in *Sämtliche Werke* [hereafter *SW*], vol. I, pp. 177–9)

This return of the practical commandment to the constituent law of essence underlines the significance of Schelling's gesture – the very same one that supports the so-called Philosophy of Identity – reinstating the finite Self into the absolute Self. If "the essence of the Self is freedom" (ibid., no. viii), this means that the Self posits itself through its "self-will" and that it posits itself as "simple Self," prior to any determination in relation to what is *other* than itself. If Kant's caution emphasized both the factual nature of practical reason and the inconceivable nature of freedom to which we gain access only indirectly, Schelling's set of themes, in contrast, stresses intellectual intuition as intuition of freedom. Schelling indicates this clearly in his *Letters on Dogmatism and Criticism*:

> Within all of us there is the mysterious and marvellous faculty of being able to withdraw into the most intimate part of ourselves . . . in order to intuit the eternal within us in the shape of immutability. This intuition is the most intimate experience, the closest, that upon which all that we know and believe about the supersensible world depends. This is the intuition which first of all persuades us that something *is* in the real meaning of the term. . . . It is different from all sensory intuition in that it can only be produced by *freedom*. (Letter no. 8, *SW*, vol. I, p. 318)

By making an absolute of freedom, Schelling, together with Fichte, was logically led to define the Self as pure activity or as "act" (*Handeln*) without a prior transitive object. Thus, the Self is not only pure will which, through its self-determination and its own strength, posits itself and exists for itself; by way of unconstrained will, the Self is first of all "the will of the original act of wanting" (*SW*, vol. III, p. 541). In the philosophy of identity, liberty is always envisaged as absolute freedom or, better still, freedom of the absolute. Consequently, evil can only be understood negatively by way of imperfection. In truth, from the point of view (which is precisely no longer a "point of view") of identity, evil disappears entirely to become a pretence, and the finite nature of things itself becomes illusory:

> There is nothing positive in things, by virtue of which they are finite, only a simple privation, and this privation is only itself a manner of imagining or considering things according to relation. (*SW*, vol. VI, pp. 542–3)

Therefore, that which is free is the cause that acts in conformity with its essence or, rather, with the freedom of its essence; to act "freely" means always to act "in accordance with the law of identity." There is no room here for hesitation or for the sharp distinction of a real alternative ("or . . . or"), nor is there any possibility of envisaging something as a "beginning" – a break with all that has preceded it. If the only freedom is absolute or divine, and if the only real action is that which comes from the essence and the self-affirmation of one's identity, then no being can be considered free unless he identifies with God, or better still, unless it is God that is acting within him. Liberty only exists through the participation of the finite being in the divine or essential act: "Man is not free for himself, but for himself and considered according to his own life, man is the prey to necessity. . . . Only action which finds its origin in God is free" (ibid.).

In contrast, Schelling adds, in a remark which in a sense encapsulates the entire programme of *Of Humam Freedom* (1809), "closely associated with the concept of the individual freedom of man are the concepts of evil, sin, fault, punishment." In this treatise, the attention given to evil, to finitude, to the fall, and to sin represents a real break for Schelling with his early philosophy of absolute freedom. The attempt to understand liberty as human, to think though the possibility of the effectivity of evil, goes hand in hand henceforth with a historicization of freedom. The latter is henceforth taken to be freedom to do good *and* evil, and it is considered within its own temporality, in relation to a decision that is likely to open up a "higher" history. This, in turn, leads to "narratives" of the creation and the fall which always resist a reduction to conceptual analysis.

For the Schelling of *The Ages of the World*, returning to first principles within the framework of a "historical" and narrative philosophy means enquiring into the very will of God – defined as pure liberty beyond being – in order to make explicit the decision of creation: why does God decide to make space and time (that is, to withdraw in order to allow creation and the world of creatures); what is the role and the place of man in the process of creation? It is indispensable to reach this higher "point of view" of a unitary theo-cosmogonical process if one is to understand the general scheme of history in depth. In order to do that, it is necessary to return to the beginning, or better still to the pre-beginning – in a word, to the Fall. "Higher" history finds its real point of departure, its ultimate root, in the original event of the Fall (*Urthatsache, unvordliche That, SW*, vol. XIII, p. 385). History, in its initial appearance, must be envisaged as an entirely new world, a world of "mobility" (*neue Welt der Bewegung*), a new world which presupposes that man freely shook the very basis of creation (*Grundlage der Schöpfung*):

> Without this expulsion from the original Paradise, there would be no history. This is why the first steps of Man are the arch-event which alone makes possible the succession of other events, that is history. (Ibid.)

On this side of the theo-cosmological perspective developed mainly in the system of the ages of the world and in positive philosophy, Schelling's *Of Human Freedom* above all expounds his anthropology. However, through its central question, that of the conditions of the possibility of evil, the treatise of 1809 paradoxically signals a return to Kant. Within the bounds of practical philosophy, Schelling henceforth relates more closely to *Religion within the Limits of Reason* than to the *Critique of Practical Reason* or the *Foundations of a Metaphysics of Morals*. In the first two parts of *Religion* the "inherent nature of the principle of evil alongside good" was envisaged and the hypothesis of radical evil in human nature was formulated, before the "struggle of the principle of good with that of evil" was described. Thus it was *Religion within the Limits of Reason* that took the drama of Good and Evil as its main theme, and *Of Human Freedom* later continued this theme.

After having examined at the beginning of his book "the original predisposition to evil," then "the tendency toward evil in human nature," Kant establishes its effective reality according to a procedure that Schelling was later to follow. However, it is necessary to underline an important difference in their respective thematizing of the "tendency to evil." For Kant, moral evil is essentially the result of a perversion in the relation of the will to the law, whereas for Schelling evil is first of all revealed in fallen nature by way of a quasi-ontological principle:

> There is . . . a universal evil, which is not initial but which has been awake since the beginning of the revelation of God, through a deep-seated reaction, an evil which assuredly never reaches its implementation, but which constantly tends towards it. Only when this universal evil has been recognised is it possible also to understand good and evil in man. (*SW*, vol. VII, pp. 380–1)

As far as the question of "radical evil" is concerned, the comparison between Kant and Schelling is also enlightening: Kant tells us that radical evil is that which corrupts the foundation of all maxims. Wickedness is only the "corruption" or the "perversion" (*Verderbheit, Verkehrheit*) of the heart. By emphasizing the essentially spiritual dimension of evil, Schelling reserves, at least in *Of Human Freedom*, the possibility of an authentically diabolical aspect of the will that is disposed to want evil for evil's sake. But just as the real opposition does not result in any dualism in Kant, so with Schelling the distinction or the "ontological difference" between ground and existence – the cornerstone of *Of Human Freedom* – cannot muddle the still transcendental perspective which leads from the condition of possibility to that of the reality of experience and to the reality in experience:

> We have tried to deduce from first principles the concept and the possibility of evil, and to bring to light the general foundation of this doctrine, a foundation which resides in the distinction between the existant and the foundation of existence. But the possibility does not as yet imply effective reality: it is nonetheless this which constitutes the crux of the matter. Indeed, what needs to be explained is not just the way in which evil becomes effective in a given individual, rather it is the universal operativeness (*Wirksamkeit*) of evil, that is, how it was able to burst in upon creation as an incontestably universal principle, struggling against good everywhere. (*SW*, vol. VII, p. 373)

This shift in the question of effective reality in the direction of universal operativeness goes back, beyond Kant, to the general issue of theodicy and to the idea of a philosophy or theology of history. Schelling later called this "higher history" (*SW*, vol. XIV, p. 219), insisting on the "temporal" value of the opposition of principles, but above all giving it a theological or theogonic dimension which isn't found in Kant: "Since evil is undeniably effective, at least as a universal opposition to good, there can be no doubt whatsoever that it was necessary to the revelation (*Offenbarung*) of God" (*SW*, vol. VII, p. 373).

With this we have entered the theo-anthropomorphic circle that is characteristic of the treatise of 1809. If *Of Human Freedom* opens up first of all an "anthropological" perspective, Schelling immediately claims – as Heidegger justly pointed out in his commentary – the rights of anthropomorphism, by virtue of which the examination of the "situation" of man (in nature, in history, in the sphere of living creatures in general) always leads back to the process of creation and to the theogonic process. Man is "at the crossroads" because in him "the bond of principles is not necessary, but free" (*SW*, vol. VII, p. 374). However, this liberty or this indeterminate quality in the "bond" explains the possibility of evil: "Evil as such can only appear in the creature to the extent that there is only light and shadow within it, that is, the two principles can unite while remaining separable" (ibid.). The "creature," by which one must understand Man, is that which reveals evil *as such*, if it is true that the ground (*Grund*) – that fundamental, initial force that Schelling has shown to be present in everything that is, including in God – cannot be evil in itself. The "ground" is in effect present in God, even if it is that which is not God itself: it is the other-than-God in God, as soon as God is essentially understood as spirit or, better still, as love.

A further point must be made while we are thus emphasizing the Kantian background of *Of Human Freedom*: in this treatise, Schelling also undertook to criticize or rather correct what he considered to be the idealist concept of freedom, a concept that was only formal and to which Fichte had given a complete determination. Against subjective idealism, Schelling notes: "it in no way suffices to assert that 'activity, life and freedom alone constitute that which is really effective' . . . what is required is rather to show that, on the contrary, everything that is effective (nature, the world of things) is grounded in activity, life, freedom" (p. 351). However, not only is this first generalization insufficient, it also runs the risk of concealing that which is distinctive about human freedom:

> But on the other hand, when freedom becomes the positive concept of the in-self in general, research into human freedom is rejected once more into indeterminate generality since the intelligible which underpinned it is also now the essence of things in themselves. Thus, in order to bring out the specific difference, that is the determining element of human freedom, simple idealism is not enough. (p. 352)

In this conclusion Schelling certainly does not wish simply to refuse the superior concept of freedom that had been achieved by Kantian idealism: "For up until the discovery of idealism, the genuine concept of freedom has been missing from every modern system, whether it be that of Leibniz or of Spinoza" (p. 345). Rather, he tries to reinterpret it in the context of a "superior realism" for which nothing less is required than a "metaphysics of evil", the final developments of which are as visible in the *Philosophy of Mythology* as they are in the "Satanology" of the *Philosophy of Revelation.*

But if the purpose of the 1809 treatise *Of Human Freedom* is to make apparent the specific difference of human freedom – its very title is indicative of this – the key point is achieved precisely by the definition of freedom as "the power to do good *and* evil." "Idealism provides on the one hand the most general concept of freedom, and on the other its simply formal concept. However, the real and living concept of freedom is that of the power to do good *and* evil" (*SW,* vol. VII, p. 352).

To make the specificity of human freedom apparent in this way does not simply lead to a renouncement of the initial project to make of freedom "the One and the All of philosophy." However, it does involve the introduction of a more historical or narrative perspective that is capable of accounting for the possibility and the effective reality of evil. The great and remarkable paradox of the text of 1809 – which Schelling himself was fully aware of since it is here that the problem of pantheism and that of "human" freedom meet – is that in order to "save" Man's freedom (*SW,* vol. VII, p. 339), there is no solution other than "to look for refuge within the divine essence itself." Anthropology at this point becomes general ontology and theology, both of which stand against the cardinal distinction between "ground" and "existence." Now the problem shifts, since with such a distinction the issue henceforth becomes that of understanding in God that which is not God himself. This complex development within Schelling's research invalidates the following type of alternative: either an anthropological enquiry which strives to thematise finite human freedom, or a theological enquiry which focuses on life in God. Put another, more positive, way, this back and forth explains the "onto-theo-anthropo-cosmological" unity of the treatise and that also establishes the centrality of anthropomorphism. From this point, everything follows on logically: thanks to this distinction between ground and existence, God is cleared of fault, evil, and wickedness, and human freedom can assert itself in the face of the divine omnipotence – unconditioned power – without, however, being reduced to an "absolute passivity" (ibid.).

The two opposing arguments of the 1809 treatise then become apparent: the metaphysics of evil on the one hand and, on the other, what should no doubt be called the metaphysics of love. For the ultimate "definition" of God in the treatise is, indeed, love: God *is* love; and above all the supreme law is the law of love, the law that commands that the ground should not be prevented from acting. According to Schelling, this is the only possible way the idea of the "permission" of evil can be conceived.

For Schelling, the idea of revelation implies not only temporality and historicity, but also and above all the antagonism of forces. From *Of Human Freedom* on, and even more so in the *Stuttgart Lectures,* Schelling stresses that for there to be revelation, the ground must be allowed to give rise to the opposite of love or of universal will: property (*Eigenheit*), the specific-being, being.

What is played out on the theo-cosmogonic level before Man is repeated and dramatised in Him – He who is the summit of creation: "But the ground continues also to work ceaselessly in Man and moves (*erregt*) his specific-being (*Eigenheit*) and his particular will, for the very reason that in opposition to him the will of Love can arise." If the opposition of ground and existence has first of all a theological and especially a theo-cosmogonic significance – since it facilitates the formulation of the "fundamental law of opposition" which governs both divine life as well as its reve-lation in the world and in history – it also enables us in the end to account for the possibility of evil, as "discord" or "disjunction" (*Zwietracht*) of the two ultimate ontological principles (*SW*, vol. VII, p. 392). From this point on, the general possi-bility of evil consists in the fact that Man, instead of making "the base and the instrument" of his "ipseity," of his "specific-being" (the analogue of ground in him), seeks to raise this ipseity to the level of universal principle. It is also this "fundamen-tal law of opposition" that allows Schelling to put forward in turn a "dialectical" interpretation of identity and of the "copula," an interpretation which culminates in the proposition: "Good is evil." Good is, in effect, only a surmounting of the "ground":

> Only the surmounted ipseity . . . is good. . . . It can be said, with absolute rigour, that in a dialectical manner good and evil are the same. . . . He who does not have within him either the stuff or the energy of evil, is equally incapable of good.   (p. 400)

It is then necessary to integrate the argument for the universal necessity of evil and the argument that evil "always remains the particular choice of Man." As Schelling states, the "ground can never do evil as such" (p. 166). In effect, in nature evil is never *as such*, it is only as such if it is *spirit:* "Just as there is an enthusiasm for good, there is also a *Begeisterung*, an exaltation of the spirit for evil." It is the spiritual trait, capable of provoking this type of "exaltation," which characterises evil in its specifically human shape. Just as error, far from being a simple privation of truth, is something that is positive, betraying no lack of spirit but rather demon-strating a "perverted" spirit, so evil is not simply the privation of good, the absence of connection or harmony, but a genuinely "positive disharmony." Schelling notes that evil is from a certain point of view, "the purest type of spirit, for it wages the most savage war against all being, and seeks even to suppress the foundation of creation" (p. 468). *Evil is spirit*: this is the decisive formula if one needs to be able to conceive a "freedom for evil."

What holds theo-cosmogonic speculation, anthropology, and the metaphysics of evil together in *Of Human Freedom* is the analysis of the *situation* of human freedom in relation to ground, to nature in God, to everything that in God is not God: "Man is an undecided creature in the midst of original creation . . . and who can only decide himself through himself." Even if such an arch-decision might first of all be conceived outside time, according to the Kantian determination of the "intelligible character" (p. 385), the question of liberty finds itself intrinsically linked through it to the question of temporality, or more precisely of the beginning of time. In his late philosophy, Schelling asks – and thus reiterates the Kantian determination of tran-scendental freedom as the ability to begin from oneself – how is a real beginning possible? What is in actual fact "to begin," in the radical sense in which the begin-ning is always a non-foreseeable initiative, an inaugural break?

The elucidation of human freedom is the real main theme of a positive philosophy whose principal characteristic is the fact that it is a *historical* philosophy, that is attentive to the factor of time in God. A historical God (that is a God who literally makes Himself in time and enters history) must in effect allow himself to be affected by a state of becoming. The God who becomes and is revealed in history is precisely the Living God. We can only hope to understand the *Lebendigkeit*, the "live nature" of the God which according to the Scriptures is a living God, if we elucidate the possibility of this historical becoming of and in God Himself. In *Of Human Freedom*, Schelling asks "Does creation have a final aim, and if it does, why is this not achieved immediately, why is the conclusion not given from the beginning?" We can only attempt to answer this question satisfactorily by using the concept of life: God is life and not simply being; however, "all life has a destiny, and is subject to suffering and to a state of becoming. God has also freely submitted to this destiny from the moment He separated, in order to become personal, the world of light from the world of darkness. Being is only perceptible to itself in the state of becoming" (p. 403).

This theological or even scriptual determination of God as *living* God has decisive implications for any thinking about or philosophy of history. Faithful to the general argument of anthropomorphism, Schelling concludes in effect that "without the concept of a God that suffers as a human . . . the whole of history would remain incomprehensible" (ibid.). But if we must conceive of God as a being in a state of becoming – "God makes himself" (p. 432) – it is not simply because we cannot think God as an effective and personal being once we consider him as something "finished once and for all and which remains immutably," pure self-thought, never affected by anything whatsoever.

"If we desire a God that we can consider as a being that is fully alive and personal, then we must also consider God in a human way and admit that there is the strongest analogy between his life and human life; in God there is, next to the eternal being, a being in a state of becoming" (ibid.). Such is the principal theme of the *Stuttgart Lectures* which Schelling goes on to develop further in his *Ages of the World*. God is not "a dead and immobile being," but He is "the very highest life." And if there is no life without becoming and movement, without joy but also without suffering – in a word, without passion – then to assert that God is life is also to think Him as eternal becoming. But the idea of becoming also strictly implies the possibility of a distinction, of a dissociation, of a differentiation between beginning and end. It is not enough to remark that the state of becoming exists in time; it is also necessary to understand how, and which temporalisation will have each time made it possible. To become is first of all "to make time," to give oneself time, in the same way that one gives oneself space (*SW*, vol. XIV, p. 353).

In so far as Schelling's enquiry into the possibility of finite human freedom, and into its position within the absolute system, leads (through the general distinction of "ground" and "existence") to the linked meditation on life in God and on the "mobility" of creation which is relaunched by human decision, we can argue that the remarkable return to Kant in 1809, together with the emphasis on the anthropological and practical character of the enquiry, establishes a new conception of historicity and especially of temporality (the "system" or the organism of time). This is a clean break with the dominant metaphysical tradition in which time is first of all given as present, whereas history only allows a teleological interpretation.

In his commentary on the 1809 essay, *Of Human Freedom* – which in our view constitutes the real centre of Schelling's work – Heidegger in a striking phrase noted that the enquiry directed itself to that which in Man goes beyond Man toward freedom "beyond being and time." Because Schelling's reflection contemplates human freedom, it endeavours to elucidate freedom's central position and theological context. This is in order to understand the "possibility of liberty," which is founded in a temporality that is essentially determined as futurition.

It is undoubtedly for this reason that Schelling's thought – beyond the theosophical speculations of the later philosophy or the laborious metamorphoses of the doctrine of potencies – retains such fecund possibilities for current philosophy. As Heidegger noted, such possibilities emerge as soon as one proposes to thematise the *event* of the decision and its distinctive temporality, or again the irreducible positivity of that which is presented or *given* to think – the very thing that Schelling was fond of calling *das Unvordenkliche*, the immemorial or the unprethinkable, that no thought of thought would ever be able to join.

## Writings

Schelling, F. W. J.: *Sämtliche Werke*, ed. K. F. A. Schelling (1856–61; Munich: Beck, 1927).
——: *Die Weltalter, Urfassungen*, ed. M. Schröter (Munich: Beck, 1946).
——: *Grundlegung der positiven Philosophie, Münchner Vorlesung WS 1832/33 und SS 1833*, ed. H. Fuhrmans (Turin: Bottega d'Erasmo, 1972).
——: *Einleitung in die Philosophie*, ed. W. E. Ehrhardt (Stuttgart: Fromman-Holzboog, 1989).
——: *System der Weltalter*, ed. S. Peetz (Frankfurt: Klostermann, 1990).
——: *Urfassung der Philosophie der Offenbarung*, ed. W. E. Ehrhardt (Hamburg: Meiner, 1992).

Translations

Schelling, F. W. J.: *Of Human Freedon*, tr. with critical intro. J. Gutmann (Chicago, IL: Open Court, 1936).
——: *The Ages of the World*, tr. with intro. F. de W. Bolman (New York: Columbia University Press, 1967).
——: *System of Transcendental Idealism*, tr. P. Heath, intro. Michale Vater (Charlottesville, VA: University Press of Virginia, 1978).
——: *The Unconditional in Human Knowledge: Four Essays, 1794–1796*, tr. with commentary Fritz Marti (Lewisburg: Bucknell University Press, 1980).
——: *Bruno, or On the Natural and the Divine Principles of Things*, tr. with intro. Michale G. Vater (Albany, NY: State University of New York Press, 1984).
——: *Ideas for a Philosophy of Nature: An Introduction to the Study of this Science*, tr. E. E. Harris and Peter Heath (Cambridge: Cambridge University Press, 1988).
——: *On the History of Modern Philosophy*, tr. with intro. Andrew Bowie (Cambridge: Cambridge University Press, 1994).

## References and further reading

Bowie, A.: *Schelling and Modern European Philosophy: An Introduction* (London: Routledge 1993).

Courtine, J.-F.: *Extase de la raison: Essais sur Schelling* (Paris: Galilée, 1990).

Heidegger, M.: *Schellings Abhandlung über das Wesen der menschlichen Freiheit* (Tübingen: Niemeyer, 1971).

Kant, Immanuel: *Kritik der praktischen Vernunft* (*Critique of Practical Reason*), *Akademische Ausgabe*, vol. v, p. 4.

Kasper, W.: *Das Absolute in der Geschichte* (Mainz: Matthias Grünewald, 1965).

Marquet, J.-F.: *Liberté et existence; Etude sur la formation de la philosophie de Schelling* (Paris: Gallimard, 1973).

Schulz, W.: *Die Vollendung des Deutschen Idealismus in der Spätphilosophie Schellings* (Neske: Pfullingen, 1975; 2nd edn.).

Tilliette, X.: *L'Absolu et la philosophie: Essais sur Schelling* (Paris: Presses Universitaires de France, 1987).

——: *Schelling: Une philosophie en devenir* (Paris: Vrin, 1993; 2nd edn).

White, A.: *Schelling: Introduction to the System of Freedom* (New Haven, CT: Yale University Press, 1983).

# 6

# Hegel

## STEPHEN HOULGATE

G. W. F. Hegel (1770–1831) was the last and greatest of the German Idealists and exercised an unparalleled influence on nineteenth- and twentieth-century thought. His legacy includes the idea that human existence is essentially historical, that history is the development of the consciousness of freedom, and that true freedom involves living in an ethical community whose members accord one another reciprocal recognition and respect. Through his emphasis on human historicity and freedom, as well as his analysis of concepts such as "alienation" and "dialectic," Hegel's thought helped spawn such divergent philosophical movements as Marxism, existentialism, pragmatism, hermeneutics, and deconstruction. He also had a profound impact on modern social theory and modern (especially, Protestant) theology; and he has even been called the "father" of art history.

Although Hegel is clearly one of the most important modern thinkers, by no means all post-Hegelian philosophers have welcomed his contribution to their discipline. Many regard his work as obscure, sophistical and even dangerous: Bertrand Russell thought that most of what Hegel said was wrong, Karl Popper considered his political thought to be pernicious, and Schopenhauer dismissed him as a simple charlatan (in contrast to Fichte who was damned even more emphatically by Schopenhauer as an utter "windbag"). Nevertheless, there are also a great many modern philosophers who view Hegel's thought as a source of enduring insight and influence, and who think of themselves as continuing to work within a tradition which he inaugurated. Marx, Heidegger, Gadamer, Adorno, and Habermas all regard their work as inspired by Hegel and Derrida even goes so far as to say that his own thought of *"différance"* is located "at a point of almost absolute proximity to Hegel" (Derrida 1981 [1972], pp. 43–4) (see Article 50, DERRIDA).

One of the reasons why Hegel's thought has provoked such conflicting responses is that his texts are extremely difficult to read. This is not because Hegel cultivates difficulty or obscurity in order deliberately to bemuse his readers or to give his texts an air of pseudo-profundity. Hegel's belief is that philosophy should be "exoteric, comprehensible, and capable of being learned and appropriated by all" (Hegel 1977 [1807], p. 7). However, he also believes that the insights he wishes to communicate require the adoption of a mode of thinking and a style of writing (and speaking) which necessarily violate what "ordinary" understanding considers to be the minimal conditions of intelligibility. As a consequence, he frequently coins what – at least to English ears – seem to be impossible verbal nouns (such as "becoming-other-than-itself", *Sichanderswerden*), and his texts abound in what appear to

93

many to be blatant contradictions (such as the statement that "being . . . is in fact *nothing*, and neither more nor less than *nothing*" – Hegel 1989 [1812–16, 2nd edn 1832], p. 82). In feeling compelled to frustrate the expectations of "ordinary" understanding in this way, Hegel does not, of course, stand alone. Fichte before him, and Nietzsche, Heidegger and Derrida after him, have all felt obliged by what they have to say to adopt styles of writing which they know will mystify or offend those wedded to more conventional conceptions of clarity and common sense. Indeed, one might say that this conviction that philosophical truth cannot be expressed in clear and distinct propositions, such as those employed by a Descartes or a Hume, but requires a certain bending or dislocating of language, constitutes one of the central themes of European philosophy since Kant, and the one that has probably contributed more than any other to opening and sustaining the rift between "Continental" and "analytic" philosophy.

The fact that many continental thinkers share Hegel's belief that philosophical understanding requires an unconventional style may well explain why they on the whole have been much more open to Hegel's philosophical innovations than have philosophers trained in the analytic tradition. However, I believe that analytic critics of Hegel, such as Russell or Popper, might have been less dismissive of Hegel's achievements if they had been able to look past the obvious strangeness of Hegel's texts and appreciate *why* Hegel writes and thinks as he does. Had they done so, they would have seen in Hegel not a sophist or a charlatan, but a profoundly disciplined thinker who is forced to transform philosophical language by his conception of freely self-determining thought, and who is set on the path towards that conception by the work of Immanuel Kant (1724–1804).

In the *Critique of Pure Reason* (1781, 2nd edn 1787) Kant sets out to show how it is possible to have a priori knowledge, through concepts, of objects in the world. Such knowledge is possible, we are told, because a priori concepts of the understanding, or "categories," such as quantity, substance, and causality, are precisely what allow us to conceive of a realm of "objectivity" in the first place and so constitute the indispensable conditions of any experience of such a thing as an "object." That is to say, what we perceive can only be understood by us *as* an "object" at all in so far as it is thought of as a quantifiable substance in causal relations with other such substances. Since the categories lay down a priori what it means for something to be conceived as an object, such concepts must grant us a priori understanding and knowledge of objects (see Article 2, KANT).

For Kant, fundamental categories, such as substance and cause, are thus not derived from our experience of objects, but are what make such experience possible to begin with. To the extent that Hegel also believes that human experience presupposes concepts or forms of understanding through which we interpret everything we see and hear, he remains a loyal follower of Kant. Whether this specific thing causes this specific effect to occur, is, according to Hegel (as it is for Kant), a matter for empirical observation to decide; but the very idea that there is a *causal* relation to be encountered at all has its source in thought itself and is brought to bear on experience by our reason and understanding. Furthermore, not only are concepts such as cause and effect, or force and expression, a priori categories of thought for

Hegel, even the simple idea of an *individual* thing, or of something's *being there*, is brought to bear on what we perceive by thought. Things in the world are thus not just given to us as being there; rather, Hegel tells us, the mind takes what it perceives, distinguishes it from itself, and so itself "first gives it the determination of being" (Hegel 1971 [1830], §418). Hegel is a Kantian philosopher, therefore, for the simple reason that he believes that all empirical observation – to use contemporary jargon – is "theory-laden."

The fundamental concepts, through which what we perceive is understood to form an objective "world," constitute what Hegel calls our underlying "metaphysics": "for metaphysics means nothing other than the range of general determinations of thought, the diamond lattice, as it were, into which we bring all material and thereby first make it intelligible" (Hegel 1970 [1830], §246 Addition). Such a metaphysics is not decided upon by us and is not something we can simply change at will, but is something we are born into by virtue of the fact that we are beings that think and speak a language. Every educated consciousness thus has its metaphysics, and we give expression to our a priori metaphysical understanding of the world every time we utter a simple sentence: for "categories, like *being*, or *individuality*, are already mingled into every proposition, even when it has a completely sensible content: " 'This leaf *is* green' " (Hegel 1991 [1830], §3).

Hegel is not, however, an uncritical follower of Kant. His main point of disagreement with his predecessor is his contention that categories are not unambiguously universal forms of human understanding, but are conceived in subtly different ways in different cultures and in different historical epochs. Indeed, Hegel claims that some concepts (such as that of causality), which are employed by modern scientific consciousness, are not explicitly employed by certain civilizations and periods of history at all. He accepts that all the basic concepts enumerated by Kant are *implicit* in the very structure of human understanding; but, much like Plato, he thinks that such categories have to be "recollected" or brought to *explicit* consciousness over time, and he believes that the education of the human race is precisely this process of becoming explicitly conscious of the concepts inherent in human understanding. Fundamental developments and revolutions in science and history thus do not come from simply gathering more information about the outside world (though such gathering is important), but come from deepening our understanding of the nature of understanding itself and of its concepts. That is to say, human development involves teasing out new, more complex categories which are merely implicit in understanding and also coming to a more sophisticated conception of those categories which are already being explicitly employed. As the categories we employ become more nuanced and sophisticated in this way, so our view of the world itself changes and develops:

> The advance of culture generally, and of the sciences in particular, gradually brings into use higher relationships of thought, or at least raises them to greater universality and they have thus attracted increased attention. This applies even to empirical and natural sciences which in general employ the commonest categories, for example, whole and parts, a thing and its properties, and the like. In physics, for example, the

95

category of *force* has become predominant, but more recently the category of *polarity* . . . has played the leading part.   (Hegel 1989 [1812–16, 2nd edn 1832], p. 32)

Hegel's conception of human development is distinctive because he thinks that
we change and refine our understanding of the world by refining our understanding of the concepts that are inherent in our *own* understanding itself – that is to say,
by coming to a deeper understanding of *ourselves*. What we discover about
ourselves in this process, according to Hegel, is not only that we interpret what
we perceive in a variety of more or less sophisticated ways (as *being there*, as a realm
of *things* with *properties*, or as a realm of mechanical and chemical *objects*), but
also, and much more importantly, that we are intrinsically self-determining, *free*
beings.

Now, to discover that we are free is not to discover that we can, after all, simply
decide which categories we are going to employ: we do not have the untrammelled
"freedom" to make such a decision, because the categories through which we view
the world arise (with greater or lesser degrees of explicitness in different ages and
cultures) from the very structure of thought itself. However, precisely because the
concepts in terms of which human beings think are not imposed upon us by outside
forces but are inherent in, and so ultimately determined by, the nature of our own
understanding, we are in fact – though we do not always realize it – *self-*
determining beings; and determining oneself through one's *own* understanding
and reason – whether consciously or unconsciously – is precisely what freedom is
for Hegel. To discover that we are free is thus not simply to be alerted to the human
capacity for arbitrariness, but to become explicitly aware that the power determining what it is to understand (and therefore what is to be understood by "nature" or
"being") lies nowhere else than within *ourselves* and our *own* understanding.

It is important to note that human beings have to *discover* that they are intrinsically free and self-determining, and that they also have to learn what it means for
human freedom to be fully recognized in political, aesthetic, and religious life, as
well as in science and philosophy. Not all cultures acknowledge that human beings
are free and rationally self-determining (both the Hindu caste system and the medieval European system of feudalism, in Hegel's view, consign people to an externally
given social and spiritual order), and even those cultures or historical periods
which do acknowledge human freedom, do so in varying degrees. As Hegel famously puts it in the lectures on the philosophy of history, "the orientals knew only that
*one* is free, the Greek and Roman world that *some* are free, . . . while *we* know that
*all* human beings in themselves, that is, human beings as human beings, are free"
(Hegel 1956 [1837], p. 19).

With each shift in the awareness of the extent and nature of human freedom
comes a profound restructuring of human society. A civilization that accords freedom only to some of its members will allow a place for slavery and will obviously
not develop institutions and a legal code designed to guarantee the universal right
of citizens to rational self-determination. However, a society which is founded on
the principle of universal freedom will clearly allow no place for slavery and will
have to develop institutions and a legal code to protect the fundamental rights of all

its citizens. Indeed, Hegel thinks that not only the social and political structure of a civilization, but also the whole character of a civilization's art and religion, depends upon the degree of awareness of human freedom which permeates that culture: because, he argues, only a civilization which puts a premium on human freedom will represent freely self-determining dramatic characters (as opposed to allegorical ciphers) in their art, and will conceive of God (or the gods) as creating human beings to be free (rather than enslaved by divine necessity). To the extent that history is marked by the move from what Hegel regards as despotic, patriarchal civilizations (such as ancient China) to modern constitutional states based upon the principle of universal self-determination and right, world history, for Hegel, is simply "the progress of the consciousness of freedom" (Hegel 1956 [1837], p. 19).

It is evident that Hegel's philosophical conception of human existence unites a strong emphasis on the historicity of human life with an equally strong emphasis on human freedom. On the one hand (following Herder and anticipating Marx, Heidegger, and Gadamer), Hegel insists that "what *we* are, we are at the same time historically" (Hegel 1985 [1833–6], p. 9); on the other hand (following Rousseau and Kant and anticipating Sartre), he insists that freedom constitutes humanity's "ownmost nature" or "essence" (Hegel 1956 [1837], p. 18). One should recognize, however, that of the two concepts, "history" and "freedom," it is *freedom* which has priority in Hegel's account of human life. This is because, as we have seen, Hegel understands history itself to be nothing other than the process of social, political, aesthetic, and religious change which is generated as human beings come to understand more fully and explicitly *that* they are free and what it *means* to be free. As inhabitants of the modern, post-Reformation world, therefore, we must be acutely conscious of the fundamental historicity of human life, and of our own indebtedness to previous generations; but we must also understand that through our history we have become beings who subject all our inherited institutions and categories to critical scrutiny in the name of explicitly free, self-determining reason. This is why Hegel deems it necessary to write his *Science of Logic*.

Hegel considers the modern era to be the one in which humanity has come of age and has become fully "self-conscious." This means both that modern (i.e. Western) society is marked by a more fully developed sense of freedom than other ages and cultures, and also that we have a more fully developed understanding of the basic categories of understanding itself – that, as Hegel puts it, "logical objects and their expressions" (such as "cause," "force," and "polarity") are now "thoroughly familiar (*bekannt*) to educated people" (Hegel 1989 [1812–16, 2nd edn 1832], p. 33). We have become familiar with the basic categories of understanding by inheriting the results of the labours of previous generations who have helped to clarify precisely what it is to understand – results which, Hegel believes, have passed into the language of educated moderns and have become common property. However, the very fact that we now place such a strong emphasis on our rational freedom and self-determination means that we cannot remain content with becoming familiar through *inheritance* with the categories of understanding, but that we demand to see, as it were, with our own eyes, how (and to what extent) those familiar categories are indeed *freely* determined by thought itself.

97

The only way to satisfy that demand, Hegel maintains, is by undertaking a study of thought which initially makes no determinate assumptions about thought itself – which presupposes no familiar categories and no familiar laws of thought (such as the laws of identity and non-contradiction) – but which seeks to discover which categories and laws, if any, arise freely from the minimal character of thinking as thinking. The categories and laws which are seen to arise through the presuppositionless study of thought will thus be known to be ones that have not just been passed down to us through inheritance, but that have indeed been generated freely by thought itself. To the extent that such freely developed categories overlap with those with which we are familiar from ordinary and scientific discourse, such familiar categories will, of course, be thereby given their proper legitimation.

Hegel undertakes such a presuppositionless study of thought in his *Science of Logic* (1812–16, 2nd edn 1832). Most philosophers, including many who are sympathetic to Hegel's project, have rejected his claim to have produced a genuinely presuppositionless science. Schelling, for example, pointed out that Hegel in fact employs "common logical forms' (such as *S is P*) and "virtually *all* concepts which we use in everyday life" when setting out his "presuppositionless" account of thinking (Schelling 1994 [1856–61], p. 148). However, Schelling, like many others after him, misunderstands the nature of Hegel's claim. Hegel does not deny that the *Science of Logic* has to be written using a given historical language with its own "metaphysics," nor indeed that such a science presupposes a historical interest in freedom and in the critical study of thought. What he wishes to insist on is that no assumptions be made about the *subject-matter* to which we turn our attention – namely, thinking – beyond the fact that it is thinking. We must, indeed, employ ordinary language in our science of logic, as Schelling rightly pointed out, but we must employ such language to suspend, and abstract from, all that we ordinarily take thinking to be. This means that we must begin from the least we can think thinking to be: the idea that thinking is not necessarily the thinking of what is "possible," or "necessary," or "non-self-contradictory," but minimally the thought of *is* or *being*.

Thinking must at least be the thought of *is*, because, before we can arrive at a determinate understanding of any possibility, actuality, or necessity – that is, of anything at all – we must at least think of such an undetermined possibility, actuality, or necessity as *being* whatever it is. Precisely what is meant by this word "being," however, is not immediately clear. We cannot simply assume in advance that it means "existing," or "having a certain identity," or "subsisting over time;" and, without making such assumptions, we cannot tell, from the simple fact that we must always at least think "is," just how that "is" is to be understood. All we can say is that thinking is minimally the thinking of *being*, whose sense is as yet quite indeterminate.

The first category we come upon when we presuppose nothing whatsoever about thinking – except that it is *thinking* – is thus the simple category of being: being (as Hegel states it, using ordinary language) "without any further determination" (Hegel 1989 [1812–16, 2nd edn 1832], p. 82). Because of its sheer indeterminateness, however, the thought of pure being is in fact completely and utterly vacuous. Indeed, it is indistinguishable from the thought of *nothing whatsoever*. The first category we encounter thus immediately gives rise to a second category, because the thought of pure being slides immediately, through its own emptiness and lack of determinacy, into the thought of sheer and utter nothing. But, of course, nothingness itself *is* sheer emptiness and lack of determinacy, and so is itself nothing but indeterminate *be-ing*. Just as the thought of being slides immediately into the thought of nothing, therefore, the thought of nothing proves to be equally unsustainable and to slide immediately back into the thought of being. "Their truth", Hegel concludes, "is, therefore, this movement of the immediate vanishing of the one in the other: *becoming*, a movement in which both are distinguished, but by a difference which has equally immediately dissolved itself" (p. 83); and with the thought of such "vanishing' or "becoming," a third category has emerged through our presuppositionless study of thought. To think, as we have seen, is minimally to think "is;" but, if Hegel's analysis is correct, it turns out that to think is also minimally to think "becomes." With this insight, Hegel follows in the footsteps of Heraclitus and anticipates the thinking of Nietzsche.

Not every part of Hegel's philosophy is structured in the same way as this opening analysis of being–nothing–becoming, but one can nevertheless learn much from that analysis about how Hegel's philosophy proceeds. First of all, one can clearly see what it means to understand categories to be *dialectical*. In the first part of the *Encyclopaedia of the Philosophical Sciences* (1830) Hegel defines "the *dialectical* movement" as the "self-sublation of finite determinations" or, to put it in somewhat plainer language, "their passing into their opposites" (Hegel 1991 [1830], §81), and we are given a striking example of such a dialectical passage or "vanishing" right at the beginning of the *Science of Logic*. Dialectic remains a constitutive trait of all the concepts Hegel considers in his philosophy, and it is for this reason that his thought anticipates some of the features of Derridean deconstruction. For, like deconstruction, Hegel's dialectical analysis of the categories of thought calls into question the boundaries that have traditionally been drawn between concepts. If categories inevitably pass into their opposites, as Hegel's analysis suggests, then we can no longer hold apart such concepts as being-in-itself and being-in-relation-to-another, or form and content, or substance and accident, in quite the way they have been held apart in the past. Thus, whereas Kant can claim with confidence that "a thing in itself cannot be known through mere relations" (Kant 1929 [1781, 2nd edn 1787], B67), Hegel's analysis of categories leads him to the conclusion that "something *through its own nature* relates itself to the other" (Hegel 1989 [1812–16, 2nd edn 1832], p. 125), and that, consequently, it is precisely through the way it *relates* to other things that a thing is known *in itself*. Deconstruction is without doubt more "literary" and "playful" than Hegel's *Science of Logic*, but to the extent that Derrida wants to call all conceptual oppositions into question, he shares one of Hegel's main aims (see Article 50, DERRIDA).

The second feature of Hegelian thinking one can see clearly in the opening analysis of being is that dialectic is wholly *immanent* in the categories under consideration. It is not the philosopher who turns the thought of pure being into the thought of nothing, but the thought of pure being *itself* that slides into its opposite by virtue of its own indeterminacy. Hegel claims that all the categories generated through the presuppositionless study of thought are intrinsically and immanently dialectical in this way: "they investigate themselves, [and] they must determine their own limits and point out their own defects" (Hegel 1991 [1830], §41 Addition 1). The proper attitude for the philosopher to adopt is thus, according to Hegel, to surrender oneself to this immanent dialectical self-transformation and development of the concepts, and not to seek to direct it, control it, or pass judgment on it from one's own particular perspective. As a true thinker, therefore, "I give up my subjective particularity, sink myself in the matter, let thought follow its own course (*lasse das Denken für sich gewähren*); and I think badly whenever I add something of my own" (Hegel 1991 [1830], §24 Addition 2).

This conception of philosophy explains why Hegel's texts seem so strange to those who have been reared on classic examples of "balanced argument," such as J. S. Mill's *On Liberty*. For, unlike Mill, Hegel does not believe it to be the task of the philosopher to advance certain propositions and then consider arguments for and against those propositions: "it is not difficult to see that the way of asserting a proposition, adducing reasons for it, and in the same way refuting its opposite by reasons, is not the form in which truth can appear" (Hegel 1977 [1807], p. 28). For Hegel, "truth is its own self-movement," and all that falls to us as philosophers is to let the truth or the "content" – the categories under consideration – move spontaneously of its own nature (*ihn durch seine eigene Natur . . . sich bewegen zu lassen*) . . . and then to contemplate this movement" (p. 36). Consequently, the Hegelian philosopher is less of an active judge of what is true, and more of a passive follower of the truth – though, of course, such a philosopher is "active" in so far as he or she is the one who *lets* the truth unfold itself in thought. [It should be noted that Hegel's model of the philosopher is not without precedent and can be found in Spinoza's *Ethics*, and also in Descartes' Fifth Meditation where Descartes acknowledges that it is not "my thought" that makes it necessary that God exist, but "the necessity of the thing itself, namely the existence of God, which determines my thinking in this respect" (Descartes 1984 [1641], p. 46).]

The third feature of Hegelian thinking evident from the opening moves of the *Science of Logic* is also one that is likely to puzzle non-Hegelians. In Leibniz's *Monadology*, we begin with a definition of a monad (namely, that it is a "simple substance"), and we proceed through ninety paragraphs to learn more about the nature of such monads. At the end of Leibniz's analysis, we know much more than we did at the beginning, but in the process monads never cease being understood as monads; they do not turn out in the end to be anything other than they were first thought to be. They remain the fixed subjects of Leibniz's discourse, and his philosophical procedure is to provide us with a more sophisticated account of such fixed subjects. We can see from the beginning of the *Science of Logic* that Hegel's thinking does not work in the same way. For although we begin with the concept of being, the thought of being turns out in the process not just to be the thought of being after all but to be the thought of being as becoming. That is to say, the subject-matter of the *Science of Logic* actually *transforms itself* as the analysis proceeds. We thus do not simply learn more about a subject that is clearly identified to begin with; rather, it only becomes apparent *through* Hegel's analysis what the subject-matter of the *Science of Logic* actually is. It is because the subject-matter of Hegelian philosophy is not given at the outset, but unfolds itself and emerges in the course of philosophy itself, that it has to be presented by means of curious verbal nouns such as "self-positing" (*Sichselbstsetzen*) and "coming-to-self" (*Zu-sich-selbst-Kommen*). As Hegel himself acknowledges, the "abnormal inhibition of thought" which this method of philosophizing brings about "is in large measure the source of the complaints regarding the unintelligibility of philosophical writings from individuals who otherwise possess the educational requirements for understanding them" (Hegel 1977 [1807], p. 39).

If we learn the lessons of Hegel's *Science of Logic* and allow our own thinking to be transformed by what that text reveals about the categories of thought, then we will come into a "metaphysics" or "diamond lattice" which has not simply arisen through the implicitly free, *historical* development of human understanding, but rather through the explicitly free, *presuppositionless* self-determination of thought. Hegel thinks that such a transformed metaphysics is the only one that is appropriate for an age which emphasizes human freedom above all else. He also thinks that such a transformed metaphysics is the only one in which the true nature of being itself can be thought. Like Kant, Hegel believes that we understand the world through categories; but, unlike Kant, he thinks that those categories, when properly understood, disclose the nature of things in themselves and not just the character of things as they appear to us, that is, that "thinking in its immanent determinations and the true nature of things form one and the same content" (Hegel 1989 [1812–16, 2nd edn 1832], p. 45). In so far as Hegel's *Science of Logic* does indeed present the categories as they are properly to be understood, therefore, it does not just constitute a logic, or a study of the categories of thought, but at the same time presents an ontology, or a study of the nature of being itself.


Hegel's *Science of Logic* lies at the heart of his philosophical system, because it sets out in its purest form his conception of philosophical method. However, Hegel's system comprises three other parts in which that philosophical method is, as it were, "put to work" in the analysis of specific subjects. In his *Phenomenology of Spirit* (1807), which actually precedes the *Science of Logic* in the system, Hegel offers a dialectical analysis of consciousness and its objects (as opposed to the categories of *thought*). This text contains Hegel's famous discussions of the "master/slave" relation and of the "unhappy consciousness," and has greatly influenced subsequent continental philosophy through its reception by Heidegger, Alexandre Kojève, Jean Hyppolite, and Jean-Paul Sartre. Following the *Science of Logic* comes the *Philosophy of Nature* (1830), which presents Hegel's account of the fundamental features of nature, such as space, time, and matter, and which builds on the work of both Kant and Schelling. Then follows the largest part of Hegel's system, the *Philosophy of Spirit (or Mind)* (1830), which includes, amongst other things, his social and political philosophy, philosophy of history, aesthetics, and philosophy of religion. Probably the most important of these is Hegel's social and political philosophy

101

(contained in a text called the *Elements of the Philosophy of Right*, 1820) in which he develops his conception of legal, moral, social, economic, and political freedom.

Just as he understands the free self-determination of thought to involve letting thought follow its own course, so Hegel thinks that political and social freedom involves *letting* one's actions be guided by those institutional structures (such as the family, the corporations, and the state) which secure rights, welfare, and mutual respect between citizens. True freedom, for Hegel, thus does not consist in the frenzy of political activism, in personal "resoluteness" and "decisiveness," or in following the dictates of one's own conscience, but in "knowledge of the objective side of ethics," and in displaying that "self-forgetfulness and self-renunciation which seriously immerses itself in this objectivity and makes it the basis of its action" (Hegel 1991 [1820], §140). This stance clearly puts Hegel at odds with the existentialist emphasis on personal "authenticity" and choice and has led to the charge that he advocates a sinister form of political quietism. However, critics who level that charge invariably overlook the fact that Hegel only advocates the recognition and acceptance of those social, economic, and political structures which do *actually* secure freedom and welfare, and that he insists that a state which does not effectively secure the freedom and welfare of its citizens "stands on an insecure footing" (Hegel 1991 [1820], §265 Addition). In demonstration of this point Hegel offers a powerful analysis – which clearly influenced Marx – of the way an unregulated market economy geared to the pursuit of self-interest and the maximization of profit and growth necessarily leads to poverty and alienation. It is important to remember that – Nietzsche's caricature in his *Untimely Meditations* notwithstanding – Hegel always advocates letting oneself be determined by what is truly rational and free, not just by what is contingently given or arbitrarily asserted by those in power.

Hegel's emphasis on freedom and reason mark him as a child of the Enlightenment in the mould of a Rousseau or Kant. However, his dialectical method and his break with the conventions of "ordinary" language clearly set him next to Nietzsche, Heidegger and Derrida as a "Continental" – indeed, a "deconstructive" – philosopher. One of the most important lessons to be learned from studying Hegel's thought is that there is much more continuity and overlap between Enlightenment rationalism and allegedly "irrational" Continental philosophy than is usually recognized.

## Writings

Hegel, G. W. F.: *Phenomenology of Spirit* (1807), tr. A. V. Miller (Oxford: Oxford University Press, 1977).

——: *Science of Logic* (1812–16, 2nd edn 1832), tr. A. V. Miller (Atlantic Highlands, NJ: Humanities Press, 1989).

——: *Elements of the Philosophy of Right* (1820), tr. H. B. Nisbet, ed. A. W. Wood (Cambridge: Cambridge University Press, 1991).

——: *The Encyclopaedia of Logic* (1830), tr. T. F. Geraets, W. A. Suchting, and H. S. Haris; (Part One of the *Encyclopaedia of the Philosophical Sciences*) (Indianapolis, IN: Hackett, 1991).

——: *Philosophy of Nature* (1830), tr. M. J. Petry, 3 vols (Part Two of the *Encyclopaedia of the Philosophical Sciences*) (London: Allen & Unwin, 1970).

——: *Philosophy of Mind* (1830), tr. W. Wallace and A. V. Miller (Part Three of the *Encyclopaedia of the Philosophical Sciences*) (Oxford: Clarendon Press, 1971).

——: *Introduction to the Lectures on the History of Philosophy* (1833–6), tr. T. M. Knox and A. V. Miller (Oxford: Clarendon Press, 1985).

——: *Philosophy of History* (1837), tr. J. Sibree (New York: Dover, 1956).

## References and further reading

Avineri, S.: *Hegel's Theory of the Modern State* (Cambridge: Cambridge University Press, 1972).

Burbidge, J.: *On Hegel's Logic: Fragments of a Commentary* (Atlantic Highlands, NJ: Humanities Press, 1981).

Derrida, J.: *Positions* (1972), tr. A. Bass (Chicago, IL: University of Chicago Press, 1981).

——: *Glas* (1974), tr. J. P. Leavey and R. Rand (Lincoln and London: University of Nebraska Press, 1986).

Descartes, R.: *The Philosophical Writings of Descartes* tr. J. Cottingham, R. Stoothoff, and D. Murdoch, 2 vol; vol. 2: *Meditations on First Philosophy and Objections and Replies* (1641) (Cambridge: Cambridge University Press, 1984).

Findlay, J.: *Hegel: A Re-examination* (1958) (London: Oxford University Press, 1976).

Harris, H. S.: *Hegel's Development*, 2 vols; vol. 1: *Toward the Sunlight, 1770–1801* (Oxford: Clarendon Press, 1972), vol. 2: *Night Thoughts (Jena 1801–1806)* (Oxford: Clarendon Press, 1983).

Houlgate, S.: *Hegel, Nietzsche and the Criticism of Metaphysics* (Cambridge: Cambridge University Press, 1986).

——: *Freedom, Truth and History: An Introduction to Hegel's Philosophy* (London: Routledge, 1991).

Hyppolite, J.: *Genesis and Structure of Hegel's Phenomenology of Spirit* (1946), tr. S. Cherniak and J. Heckman (Evanston, IL: Northwestern University Press, 1974).

Jaeschke, W.: *Reason in Religion: The Foundations of Hegel's Philosophy of Religion* (1986), tr. J. M. Stewart and P. C. Hodgson (Berkeley, CA: University of California Press, 1990).

Kant, I.: *Critique of Pure Reason* (1781, 2nd edn. 1787), tr. N. Kemp Smith (London: Macmillan, 1929).

Kojève, A.: *Introduction to the Reading of Hegel* (1947), tr. J. H. Nichols, ed. A. Bloom (New York: Basic Books, 1969).

Lauer, Q.: *A Reading of Hegel's "Phenomenology of Spirit"* (New York: Fordham University Press, 1976).

O'Brien, G.: *Hegel on Reason and History* (Chicago, IL: University of Chicago Press, 1975).

Pippin, R.: *Hegel's Idealism: The Satisfactions of Self-Consciousness* (Cambridge: Cambridge University Press, 1989).

Schelling, F. W. J.: *On the History of Modern Philosophy* (1856–61), tr. A. Bowie (Cambridge: Cambridge University Press, 1994).

Waszek, N.: *The Scottish Enlightenment and Hegel's Account of "Civil Society"* (Boston, MA: Kluwer, 1988).

White, A.: *Absolute Knowledge: Hegel and the Problem of Metaphysics* (Athens, OH: Ohio University Press, 1983).

# PART II
# OVERTURNING THE TRADITION

# 7

# Feuerbach and the young Hegelians

## LAWRENCE S. STEPELEVICH

### Hegelians vs Hegelians

Alexandre Kojève well understood the view that Hegel had of Hegelianism:

> In defining the Wise Man, the Man of absolute Knowledge, as *perfectly* self-conscious – i. e., *omniscient*, at least potentially – Hegel nevertheless had the unheard-of audacity to assert that he *realized* Wisdom in his own person.

This would also be the view that Hegelians had of HEGEL (see Article 6), for to be a Hegelian is to take Hegel at his word – which is that with him philosophy had finally reached its long-sought goal. The centuries-long quest for ultimate knowledge, the love of wisdom, had ended successfully with Hegel's philosophy. Philosophy now was, as Hegel defined it, no longer the mere love of wisdom, but the "actual possession of wisdom."

And so, when Hegel died in 1831, it was natural for his most dedicated followers to believe that philosophy itself had died. The graveside eulogy of Friedrich Förster compared Hegel to an intellectual Alexander the Great, whose followers henceforth needed only "to confirm, to proclaim, and to strengthen" their recently inherited "Kingdom of Thought." After him, as one of his disciples later said, philosophers had only the choice to be either Hegel's "gravediggers or monument-builders."

That Hegel would have agreed with this assessment seems certain. It is only necessary to read his introduction and conclusion to his lectures on the history of philosophy to know that he believed his own philosophy to have cumulated the whole course of philosophic history. Each of the first two ages of the philosophic spirit, the ancient, from Thales to Proclus, and the medieval, from the Christian Middle Ages to the Reformation, ended with a reconciliation – the first with the reconciliation of the finite and infinite, the second reconciling the human and divine. The third age extended from Descartes to Hegel. It was the final age. What had hitherto only been sought, in love or in faith, was now reached in an all-comprehending reason. The same eschatological impress can also be found in the conclusions of the *Phenomenology of Spirit*, the *Logic*, and the *Encylopedia*.

However, facing this "end of philosophy," there still remained the matter of ongoing history. In what way was Hegel's perfected theory related to ongoing practice? Was the course of history merely to be philosophically understood, passively contemplated from the high ground of Hegelianism. or was it to be directed in its course to accord with those principles? And so it was, that within a few years after his death, in a suggestively dialectical manner, two antithetical Hegelian schools emerged. The so-called "Old Hegelians" who found satisfaction in the retrospective analysis and conservation of their philosophic inheritance, and the "Young Hegelians" who, unhappy with the evident disconformity of speculative rationality and actual practice, sought the radical reform of that practice.

Using Hegel's own dictum that "What is rational is actual and what is actual is rational" as a principle of division, the Old Hegelians found existential reality to be rational, whereas the Young found it otherwise. For the former, who were later labelled "Right Wing" Hegelians, a philosophic "quietism" prevailed, a Panglossian "accommodation" to the actual world wherein present evils were taken as merely superficial epiphenomena under which rationality could be discerned. This was one way of reading Hegel that Hegel himself seemed to have recommended. Certainly, his famous metaphor of philosophy as "The Owl of Minerva," which flew only at the twilight of a historical epoch, implied that philosophers were not suited as reformers or revolutionaries. However, not all of Hegel's first disciples had the patience to merely contemplate the course of history. As the young Marx expressed it, "Hitherto Philosophers have *interpreted* the world in various ways; the point however is to *change* it." For these disciples, the present state of the world resembled that of the French Monarchy – which had been "real" but not "rational." If that world of aristocratic scorn and religious folly had fallen to the forces of reason, so could their world – and as it would be Hegelian reason, so much the better. For the Young Hegelians, a philosophic "activism" prevailed in which Hegel's theory served as merely the basis of a program for the rationalization of present political and cultural forms. The Young Hegelians differed only as to the nature and implementation of this "rationalization." But despite their disagreements in these respects, there was a general agreement among the Young Hegelians that atheism, expressed as a radical humanism, was the *condition sine qua non* for any "world-transforming" activity. And finally, among all Hegelians, Young or Old, Left or Right, it was agreed that "with Hegel philosophy comes to an end."

It can be argued that these two schools of "hostile brothers" still exist as vital elements within contemporary philosophy, the Young Hegelians finding their recent representatives in such as Habermas (who knows and admires the "Critical Philosophy" of Bruno Bauer) and others within the "Frankfurt School," and the Old Hegelians finding themselves represented among such academics as Werner Marx, Charles Taylor, Otto Pöggler, and many others. Indeed, the recent public debate over Francis Fukayama's Old Hegelian thesis defending the end of political history bears witness to the continuing relevance of the debate within Hegelianism.

The first "Old Hegelians" were mainly those who had established academic careers, such as Karl Friedrich Göschel, Georg A. Gabler, and Johann Henry Erdmann, and most of those who edited the first and second editions of Hegel's collected works. They were primarily concerned with conserving Hegel's philosophy as it had been received from him. As they added little more than erudite commentaries upon the work they inherited, their names are now forgotten, and they exercised little effect upon the subsequent course of philosophic history.

The delicate accommodation of the Old Hegelians to the actual state of religious belief and political correctness was severely tested when, in 1835, D. F. Strauss's theologically shocking *Life of Jesus* was published. In it, the historic Jesus was separated from the Christ of faith, a Christ generated entirely from the myths of Messianic expectations. Unhappily for the conservative Hegelians, Strauss claimed his work had been inspired by his reading of Hegel. It created an immediate uproar among the orthodox clergy who felt that their earlier suspicions of the dangers of Hegelianism were now vindicated. The painful efforts of the academic Hegelians to deny Strauss's contentions that Hegel had provided the principles by which Christ's history was but a mythic accretion proved less than convincing. *The Life of Jesus* was but the first of a series of revolutionary works by radical Hegelians which finally made it impossible for Hegelianism to be supported, as it had been, by enlightened governmental ministries. In 1841, just one decade after the death of Hegel, Prussia's new King, Friedrich Wilhelm IV, decided to restore orthodox philosophic order by calling the aged Friedrich Schelling to Berlin. It was hoped that his authority and his conservative philosophic temper would put an end to both Young Hegelian radicalism and Old Hegelian hypocrisy. But the King's effort failed, perhaps not so much because of Schelling's disappointing lectures but because philosophy in the grand tradition of absolute systems seemed increasingly irrelevant in the face of scientific and technical advances. By 1866, the Hegelian historian Johann Erdmann half-humorously referred to himself as the "Last of the Mohicans." At that time it clearly seemed that Hegelianism, in all of its forms, Old and Young, had passed away forever.

## Turning Hegel on his head

Ludwig Feuerbach has the distinction of being the first of the Young Hegelians. Among those who followed him, in time if not in thought, were such as David Friedrich Strauss, Bruno and Edgar Bauer, August von Cieszkowski, Moses Hess, Karl MARX (see Article 8), Friedrich Engels, Max Stirner, Arnold Ruge, and Karl Schmidt.

But Young Hegelianism, just as the "Old," at least as a recognized philosophic movement, did not endure beyond the first two decades after Hegel's death. Ludwig Feuerbach, if nothing else, is a reflection of the whole course of Young Hegelianism, from its optimistic and outspoken beginnings to its pessimistic and silent ending.

It was Hegel who determined that his philosophy was the culmination of all past thought, but the first signal of what it might mean for the future came from Feuerbach. In November of 1828, Feuerbach enclosed a letter along with a copy of his recent doctoral dissertation. Both were testaments of his devotion and indebtedness to Hegel, with Feuerbach praising Hegel's thought as being nothing less than the "Incarnation of the pure Logos." Nevertheless, in his letter, the twenty-four-year-old rather bluntly (considering Hegel's reputation) presented his own views as to what *should* be the role played by Hegelianism. First, it should not

be directed to academic ends [the direction of Old Hegelians], but to mankind – for the least, the new philosophy can make the claim that it is compelled to break through the

109

limits of a school, and to reveal itself as world-historical, and not simply to be the seed in every spirit of a higher literary activity, but rather to become the expressed universal spirit of reality itself, to found as it were, a new world-epoch, to establish a kingdom. . . . There is now a new basis of things, a new history, a second creation, where . . . reason will become the universal appearance of the thing.

The central principle of Young Hegelianism is here expressed: that Hegelian theory should be used to establish a new world-order, a "second creation." Although there will be little agreement upon the exact nature of that "new basis of things," the unquestioned eschatological belief that a new order was immanent defined the emotional appeal of Young Hegelianism. Although no letter from Hegel replying to Feuerbach's predictions has been found, it is difficult to imagine that Hegel would have agreed to Feuerbach's future visions. For Hegel, it was not for philosophy to say what "should" or "ought" to be. However, there is another side to the matter, a side even suggested by Hegel himself: if the dialectic, inexorably pressing onward as "the portentous power of the negative," was universal in its advance, then even Hegelianism itself was fated for destruction. But in accord with this very dialectic a new beginning would emerge, a new "thesis," a new philosophy. This overall destructive yet optimistic messianic vision is the inspiration of Feuerbach's prediction of "a new basis of things, a new history, a second creation. . . ." Feuerbach and Hegel and almost all of the first Hegelians had studied to become biblical theologians. That their theological studies might have affected their philosophical thought is not impossible, and analogies can, and have, been drawn between Hegel's triads and the Trinity, between the Absolute Spirit and the Holy Spirit, and between the messianic expectations of the coming "Kingdom of God" and the eschatology of Young Hegelianism. Certainly, there is hardly a better example of this "secular theology" than that found in *The Communist Manifesto*.

The title of Feuerbach's doctoral dissertation, *De Ratione, une, universali, infinita*, was intended to suggest the 1584 work of Giordano Bruno, *Della causa, Prinzipio et uno*. Feuerbach's admiration of Bruno found expression in the dissertation itself, which read Hegelianism as a pantheism. It was a monistic reading that Feuerbach never abandoned. At the time, Feuerbach's understanding of Hegelianism as a pantheism was not an uncommon one, being held by the earliest critics of Hegel, and a view which formed the permanent basis of the Catholic rejection of Hegel.

However, Feuerbach's revision of Hegelianism as a pantheism was only the first step. A further series of revisions would continue on until his views seem to have departed entirely from Hegelianism and to have evolved into a programmatic atheistic humanism based upon the rejection of all philosophy. But throughout his career, Feuerbach's relationship to Hegel remained essential to his own development, and is the model upon which all Young Hegelian "rejections" of Hegel can be understood.

The basic criticism of Hegel's philosophy, which defines the whole of Feuerbach's thought, is the rejection of what he perceived to be Hegel's abstract idealism. For Feuerbach, Hegel had begun his *Phenomenology of Spirit* with the sensuous

110

world of the "here" and the "now," – but only so as to dialectically reduce it to a final emptiness and abstraction termed "Absolute Knowledge." This idealism, which was perfected in Hegel's philosophy, had theoretically eviscerated the content of the actual world, and had become totally blind to the present reality of physical and sensuous objectivity. Feuerbach's "new basis of things" was intended to restore man and his world to their actual significance. What had hitherto been taken from the world and man and given to Heaven and God through the activity of the alienating thought of idealistic religion (whose last and greatest representative was Hegel), was now to be returned to the world and man. Nevertheless, to his credit, it was only through Hegel that the last and final stage of alienated thought had been reached. He alone had perfected, and so put a radical end to, all further speculative thought. It was only left for such as Feuerbach to recall mankind back to its truth, which was not the abstract truth of philosophy, but the concrete truth of the senses. In one of his final programmatic works, *The Principles of the Philosophy of the Future*, Feuerbach set out the relationship of his "new philosophy" to Hegel's philosophy:

> The new philosophy has, according to its historical origin, the same task and position toward modern philosophy that the latter had toward theology. The new philosophy is the realization of the Hegelian philosophy or, generally, of the philosophy that prevailed until now, a realization, however, this is at the same time the negation, and indeed the negation without contradiction, of this philosophy.

In 1830, Feuerbach imprudently decided, against his father's advice, to anonymously publish *Thoughts on Death and Immortality*. In it, Feuerbach rejected the Christian belief in personal immortality because such belief had emptied our real lives of meaning. He also attacked what he considered to be the superficial and hypocritical lives of clergy and theologians of his time. Intended or not, the work succeeded in fulfilling his father's prediction: it assured the end of any hope for an academic career that young Feuerbach might have entertained. Its anonymous author was soon discovered, and he was discharged from his position of lecturer at the University of Erlangen. He was then only 26 years old. In his career-destroying move, he anticipated that act of early academic suicide common to most Young Hegelians. In 1835, at the age of 27, Strauss's imprudent publication of his *Life of Jesus Critically Examined* ended his chances for either a clerical or an academic life. At the age of 34, in 1841, Bruno Bauer's publication of his unorthodox *Critique of the Synoptic Gospels* put an early end to his promising academic career. Unhappily for Karl Marx, he was then known to be a close friend of Bauer. Bauer's ejection from the University of Bonn also insured that Marx, at 23 years of age, could forget about future academic appointments. It was the same with Johann Caspar Schmidt, as even his pseudonym Max Stirner could not protect him from the career-destroying notoriety of his anarchic text *The Ego and His Own*. The same story repeats itself with Arnold Ruge, whose ever-more radical forays into journal editing led him, just as with Bruno Bauer's brother Edgar, into a prison cell.

In regard to its speculative content, Feuerbach's *Thoughts* retains the same stress upon pantheism found in his dissertation. For him, Christianity's egoistic tendencies were doctrinally supported by the belief in the immortality of the individual soul. This meant not only an emphasis upon a socially destructive egoism of self-salvation, but an equally destructive impact upon the very meaning of the world in which humanity found itself. Feuerbach casts his more formal arguments in Hegelian terminology, as with this tortured closing argument intending to prove that death gives value to life:

> Death is no positive negation, but a negation that negates itself, a negation that is itself empty and nothing. Death is itself the death of death. As it ends life, it ends itself. . . . Only the negation that takes away something is real. . . . Thus death, as a total negation, is a self-negating negation, a negation that, because it takes all, takes nothing. . . . Death has no value, no significance, no reality, no determination, and yet certainly its lack of value and significance, its unreality and lack of character, are the clearest testimony and verification of the value, significance, and substantiality in the character of life.

But if Feuerbach employs Hegel's dialectic, his style and intent are radically different than anything which might be expected from Hegel. The language throughout is passionate and personal, being directed to a "thou," to "thou, dear reader." In an even more romantic vein, the work includes a lengthy poem, whose "overall effect," in the words of an otherwise admiring commentator, "is more that of a college student filling up spare time than the celebration of death depicted in the great romantic poetry that Feuerbach may have had in mind (such as Novalis's *Hymns to the Night*)." The heated tones of this early work of Young Hegelianism anticipates those that will follow. With the exception of Strauss's *Life of Jesus*, the literature of Young Hegelianism is more often than not caught up in a passionate informality that borders on bombast. Even Franz Mehring, the sympathetic biographer of Marx and Engels, had to admit that their anti-Feuerbachian and anti-Stirnerian work *The German Ideology* was "an oddly schoolboyish polemic." Bruno Bauer's anonymous *Trumpet of the Last Judgement Against Hegel the Atheist and Antichrist*, described as "a perfect example of Young Hegelian writing," is not only marked by an excited excess of bold and italic types, of exclamation points and dashes, but even employed arrows and pointed fingers to illustrate its more important passages. In reading these works, Karl Löwith's observation concerning the works of Feuerbach and the Young Hegelians seems appropriate:

> In spite of its numerous "consequently's" his system hovers in a mystic darkness which is not made more transparent by his emphasis on "sensibility" and "perceptibility." This characteristic is true not only of Feuerbach, but of all the Young Hegelians. Their writings are manifestos, programs, and theses, but never anything whole, important in itself. . . . Whoever studies their writings will discover that, in spite of their inflammatory tone, they leave an impression of insipidity.

The conclusion of Feuerbach's "Thoughts" further advanced the position he had taken in his dissertation. His earlier emphasis on pantheism gave way to intimations of a radical humanism, a humanism which stressed that sensuous and physical life was the solution to the ancient Christian sundering of the soul from the body, of heaven from earth. Christian idealism was to be cast aside for a new secular realism. From this point in his thought, Feuerbach would only have to take a short step to see that the alienations introduced by Christians were in fact supported by the idealistic philosophy of Hegel. In the concluding paragraphs of the work, the argumentative links are all present:

> Then how should one call those who take transitoriness to be a predicate of this life, who believe that they say something, that they pass a judgment on this life, when they say that it is temporal, it is transitory? . . . How should one designate those who take as their object that which is nothing . . . ? They call themselves the pious ones, rationalists, even philosophers. Leave the dead among the dead!
>
> God is life, love, consciousness, Spirit, nature, time, space, everything, in both its unity and its distinction. As a loving being, you exist in the love of God . . .

In 1833, the first of three volumes on modern philosophy was published, with subsequent volumes appearing in 1836 and 1838. Because of their somewhat pedestrian quality, these studies have attracted little scholarly attention. However, for at least one commentator, Marx Wartofsky, the first volume, *A History of Philosophy from Bacon to Spinoza*, "is a crucial work in understanding Feuerbach's development. In it, Feuerbach comes to discover his own views in the course of his critique of major philosophical figures." In sum, this work is reminiscent of Hegel's own phenomenological approach to philosophic history. The result of Feuerbach's journey of self-discovery in his examination of philosophic history reached its final conclusion in his 1839 work *A Critique of Hegelian Philosophy*. This work marked Feuerbach's conscious and definitive turn from idealistic philosophy toward the statement of his own thought.

In 1841, Feuerbach published, if not his most important, then certainly his most influential and popular work, the *Essence of Christianity*. Its general thesis is simple enough: that the traditional idea of God is nothing more than the abstract and therefore alienated essence of the idea of man set over and against man as an object of worship. In Feuerbach's words:

> Man – and this is the mystery of religion – projects his being into objectivity, and then again makes himself an object to this projected image of himself thus converted into a subject; he thinks of himself as an object to himself, but as the object of an object, of another being than himself.

Not unexpectedly, the *Essence* was greeted with enthusiasm by most of the Young Hegelians. By June of 1842, a youthful Marx, who had been Feuerbach's disciple since 1839, was heatedly proclaiming the pun that "there is no other road for you to *truth* and *freedom* except that leading *through* the stream of fire [the Feuerbach]. Feuerbach is the *purgatory* of the present time."

Feuerbach's work was again suggestively Hegelian insofar as it proposed a phenomenology of the religious consciousness. What was unHegelian was his intention to actively promote the advance of that consciousness. His exhortations were intended to press the natural religious consciousness onward to a breaking point where it would finally understand *itself* to be the ultimate object of its own pious longings. Feuerbach, just as all of the Young Hegelians, had no interest in standing alongside the slow course of the "World Spirit" as a "phenomenological observer" – that cynical passivity was only for Old Hegelians to enjoy. If they chose only to philosophize when "the dusk begins to fall," it was for the Young Hegelians to prepare for a new dawn. Within two years after *The Essence of Christianity*, Feuerbach set forth two major programmatic essays: *Provisional Theses for the Reform of Philosophy* (1842) and the *Principles of the Philosophy of the Future* (1843). These works define Feuerbach at the height of his creativity and influence.

Feuerbach's goal was to press the consciousness of his readers to the point where they would fully understand that "Man is the true God and Savior of Man". His intention, as he stated it, was to change "the friends of God into friends of man, believers into thinkers, worshippers into workers, candidates for the other world into students of this world, Christians, who on their own confession are half-animal and half-angel, into men – whole men." But this humanistic truth was not to be found in abstract ideas, in philosophical speculation, but in immediate physical feeling, in a direct sensuous love of Man as Man–God.

The pantheism found in his first reading of Hegel was now transformed into a radical humanism which dialectically reversed the Christ, the "God–Man" into the "Man–God." What was earlier known only through the lens of alienating thought, the theory of Christianity, was now to be directly apprehended in sensuous feeling. Unlike all previous philosophy, this philosophy

> places philosophy in *the negation of philosophy*. . . . This philosophy has for its principle, not the Substance of Spinoza, not the *ego* of Kant and Fichte, not the Absolute Identity of Schelling, not the Absolute Mind of Hegel, in short, no abstract, merely conceptual being, but a *real* being, the true *Ens realissimum* – man; its principle, therefore, is in the highest degree positive and real. It generates thought from the *opposite* of thought, from Matter, from existence, from the senses; it has relation to its object first through the senses.

The new religious truth for the new age would be "the realization and humanization of God – the transformation and dissolution of theology into anthropology."

## Beyond Feuerbach

However much Feuerbach's new philosophy of radical humanism and sensuousness might appeal to the Young Hegelians, it was infected with a fatal flaw – an ambiguity which in short order ended his influence upon them. The ambiguity is this: if the true object of religious feeling, the basis of all notions of divinity, is termed not God but "man," then is this term "man" to be understood as referring to the concrete human individual or to the whole class of men, to that abstraction termed "mankind"? In short, is the term "man" to be taken distributively or collectively? The ambiguity is evident in such statements as the 59th "Principle of the Philosophy of the Future": "Solitude is finiteness and limitation; community is freedom and infinity. Man for himself is man (in the ordinary sense); man with man – the unity of I and thou – is God." Certainly man as "the unity of the I and thou," is not the individual that is sensuously perceived – unless, perhaps, as Engels archly notes, Feuerbach's God is the sex act. But if the individual, as a concrete and visible being, is subordinate to the community, then Feuerbach has deified relationship, a community, and not the actual individual human. The ambiguity regarding what he meant by the term "man" rendered Feuerbach defenseless against the very charge which he had so confidently directed against Hegel: Feuerbach's new philosophy was, under questioning, nothing but the old philosophy in disguise, a covert theism playing such "etymological tricks" as substituting the term "Man" for "God," which underneath its radical surface still retained the old abstract attitudes. That this was the case with Feuerbach was first made clear by Max Stirner.

In 1845, in *The Ego and his Own*, Stirner accused Feuerbach of being nothing more than a dangerous "pious atheist" whose whole task had been to deceptively, if unconsciously, re-present "God" as "Man." The situation of having a new god, this time earthbound, did not bode well for individual freedom. The "God–Man" of Feuerbach, unlike the relatively impotent "Man–God," long banished to Heaven, would find his will directly and painfully expressed in the secular power of the state. It would have been better had Feuerbach left things as they were, with the original "God" set at a safe distance from individual affairs. In two brief paragraphs, Stirner states his position as well as his understanding of Feuerbach:

> Let us be brief, and set Feuerbach's theological view and our contradiction over against each other: "The essence of man is man's supreme being; now by religion, to be sure, the *supreme being* is called *God* and regarded as an objective essence, but in truth it is only man's own essence; and therefore the turning point of the world's history is that henceforth no longer *God*, but man, is to appear to man as God."
>
> To this we reply; The supreme being is indeed the essence of man, but, just because it is his *essence* and not he himself, it remains quite immaterial whether we see it outside him and view it as "God," or find it in him and call it "Essence of Man" or "Man." I am neither God nor Man, neither the supreme essence nor my essence, and therefore it is all one in the main whether I think of the essence as in me or outside of me . . .

Before 1845 it seemed clear to all that Feuerbach's charge was correct, and that Hegel's philosophy was indeed a covert theology. After 1845, it seemed clear to all that Stirner's charge was correct, and that Feuerbach's philosophy was but a covert religion. Feuerbach's dissertation can be said to have initiated what Engels described as "the decomposition process of the Hegelian school" which characterized Young Hegelianism. Ironically, Feuerbach was the first to be expelled from this school. His attempt to rebut Stirner took the form of a brief unsigned article of a dozen pages. It was not an effective effort, little more than reiterations, in a higher voice, of his previous arguments, or arguments mainly intended as a *reductio ad absurdum* – intending to show that Stirner "also belongs to the 'pious atheists!'" Feuerbach's rebuttal was unconvincing, and Stirner's reading of Feuerbach soon became the accepted reading.

After reading Stirner, Marx reconsidered his relationship to Feuerbach, and his *Theses on Feuerbach* mark his departure from the interest in "alienated man" and Feuerbachian "love" which had characterized his earlier work. He now turned toward "critical-revolutionary praxis" – an attitude which Marx saw had "no meaning" for Feuerbach.

In 1845, other than his brief reply to Stirner, Feuerbach wrote nothing. He thereafter turned from what Sidney Hook termed his "historically significant thought" to a "degenerate sensationalism," or the "most 'vulgar' of 'vulgar materialisms.'" As many scholars agree, it seems certain that Stirner's criticism put a virtual end to Feuerbach's further influence. Indeed, even a half-century later, Engels was still repeating Stirner's charge: "He [Feuerbach] by no means wishes to abolish religion: he wants to perfect it."

A survey of the dates in Feuerbach's bibliography and the events of his career would support the thesis that Stirner's criticism definitively ended Feuerbach's desire to further promote his philosophy. In his recent study of Feuerbach, Eugene Kamenka concludes:

> The general view was, and to a large extent remains, that Feuerbach had said everything of importance that he had to say by 1845, and that his subsequent work is either a mere repetition or a falling-away into positions (such as "vulgar materialism") which he had effectively criticized earlier.

It seems that Stirner had won a victory of sorts. It was not to last, however, as even Stirner within a few years was charged by his even more radical colleagues as being covertly religious, in this case a charge of "Ego-worship." Pure atheism required total disbelief – even in one's own ego.

It is of the essential nature of Young Hegelianism that each new proposal for changing thought or the world should, in its time, be displaced by the criticism of a new, more radical proposal. The ideology of Modernity had entered into the world, and the old order was not only passing away, but the past itself no longer had anything to give to the present. Feuerbach unconsciously predicted the end of his own "Philosophy of the Future" when, in 1842, he wrote:

> The period of breakdown of a historical world view is necessarily filled with conflicting demands: some think it necessary to preserve the old and banish the new, others think it necessary to realize the new. Which party recognizes the true need? The one which sees the need of the future – the anticipated future – the one which shares in forward progress [the Young Hegelians?]. The need for preservation is something artificial, something itself evoked – reaction [the Old Hegelians?]. . . . Only he who has the courage to be absolutely negative has the strength to create something new.

If Hegelianism is to be taken only as a program for the future, then all that has passed and is now present must be rejected. As Engels well understood, "In accordance with all the rules of the Hegelian method of thought, the proposition of the rationality of everything which is real resolves itself into the other proposition: All that exists deserves to perish."

It was not long before Stirner's radical egoism was supplanted by even more radical programs. The last significant Young Hegelian was Karl Schmidt. In his 1846 work *The Realm of the Understanding and the Individual*, Schmidt traced the logical exhaustion of Hegelianism after Hegel, and, going beyond Stirner, concluded the process by drawing forth the modest truth that "I am only myself." With this, the school which began so loudly and hopefully ended in silence and cynicism.

## Writings

Feuerbach, L.: *The Essence of Christianity*, tr. G. Eliot (New York: Harper Torchbooks, 1957).
——: *Principles of the Philosophy of the Future*, tr. M. H. Vogel (Indianapolis: Bobbs-Merrill, 1966).
——: *Lectures on the Essence of Religion*, tr. R. Mannheim (New York: Harper & Row, 1967).
——: *The Fiery Brook: Selected Writings of Ludwig Feuerbach*, tr. Z. Hanfi (New York: Anchor Books, 1972).

## References and further reading

Brazill, W. J.: *The Young Hegelians* (New Haven, CT: Yale University Press, 1970).
Löwith, K.: *From Hegel to Nietzsche: The Revolution in Nineteenth-Century Thought* (New York: Holt, Rinehart & Winston, 1964).
Mah, H.: *The End of Philosophy: The Origin of Ideology* (Berkeley, CA: University of California, 1987).
McLellan, D.: *The Young Hegelians and Karl Marx* (London: Macmillan, 1969).
Rosen, Z.: *Bruno Bauer and Karl Marx* (The Hague: Martinus Nijhoff, 1977).
Stepelevich, L. S.: *The Young Hegelians: An Anthology* (Cambridge: Cambridge University Press, 1983).
Towes, J. E.: *Hegelianism: The Path Toward Dialectical Humanism, 1805–1841* (Cambridge: Cambridge University Press, 1980).
Wartofsky, M.: *Feuerbach* (Cambridge: Cambridge University Press, 1977).

# 8

# Marx

## MICHEL HENRY

Marx's work is dual, and includes both a philosophical and an economic aspect. The philosophical work was developed with great speed between 1842 and 1846 in a series of extraordinary texts, notably the *Critique of the Hegelian State*, the third manuscript of 1844, and *The German Ideology* (1845–6). It is a philosophy unlike anything that had gone before it and is without equal. It was destined to shake the foundations of Western thought. Such is its originality, in fact, that it remains misunderstood even today.

Unfortunately, these crucial texts were neither known nor published before the period 1929–34. So-called Marxism was developed without a knowledge of them. Instead, Frederick Engels' text *Ludwig Feuerbach and the End of Classical German Philosophy*, which was written after Marx's death, was taken as its foundation. In the absence of the above-mentioned texts, this claimed to present a summary. However, it is intellectually feeble and contains serious historical errors, such as a reversal in the order of Feuerbach's and Stirner's influences on the evolution of the "young Marx's" thought, and the introduction of concepts like "dialectical materialism," which one will not find in Marx's work. Thus, the text that was in effect destined to serve as a support for Marxist ideology has no connection with Marx's key insights. This explains the conflict between Marxism and Marx's actual thought. For example, in Marxism it is society or social class which determines the individual, leading to a general devaluing of the individual, who is reduced to a mere effect of "socio-economic conditions"; these, in turn, are treated as objective relations, "reality" becoming economic reality, etc. All of these are propositions that Marx either criticized or ridiculed. Therefore, this first methodological postulate needs to be advanced: *the intelligence of Marx's thought presupposes that Marxism be put to one side*. This needs to be set against the Marxist approach to Marx, such as that of the Althusserian school, which on the contrary advocates eliminating anything from Marx which does not conform to the Leninist, Stalinist, or Maoist catechism. This means, in particular, the philosophical work, which is said to be the production of a "young German bourgeois."

Marx's economic work explicitly sets out to be a "critique of political economy." In Marx's time, political economy was undergoing an extraordinary revival in England. The critique of political economy is therefore equivalent to a critique of the English school, a thoroughgoing consideration of its important theoretical contribution, and the rejection of some of its theses. If it is understood in this way, the critique of political economy that Marx undertakes is much less radical than it is often said to be. Even though Marx corrected Smith and Riccardo on certain important points – on the theory of wages, the separation of labor and its value, the organic composition of capital, etc. – it must not be forgotten that he strove above all to safeguard their fundamental assertion concerning the creation of value exclusively through labor. Moreover, this took place at a time when this notion seemed to be contradicted by events and to be in decline.

Nevertheless, Marx's critique of political economy is radical. Not only does it challenge some of Smith's and Riccardo's propositions, which belong to a certain type of political economy, it also calls into question political economy itself, of whatever type. Thus, the study that Marx began cannot be classified under political economy or put itself forward as a science, without falling foul of its own critique and canceling itself out. It cannot do so because it questions political economy's very right to exist, that is as knowledge defined by the thematization and emergence of an independent economic object, by the elucidation of specific economic phenomena and their laws, circumscribed and studied as such. For Marx, there are no economic laws, no specific economic phenomena, and there is no independent economic science. Marx's critique is radical not because it is first of all a critique of political economy but because it is a critique of economic reality itself.

What does a critique of economic reality itself signify? Despite the illusion of economists – Marx calls this fetishism or sometimes economic materialism – it signifies that there is simply no such thing as economic reality in the sense that reality is usually understood, that is as something that exists by itself and that has, in a sense, always done so. Reality, precisely, is not in itself economic. But where can such an assertion be formulated? Obviously not in political economy, which only has knowledge of economic phenomena and is defined by their thematization. Only a primary philosophy, in the sense of a radical and absolute knowledge of what reality intrinsically is about and which claims to be able to express it, could unhesitatingly define reality as foreign to the economy and its realm. A critique of political economy in Marx's terms – in other words, a critique of economic reality – begins outside the economy and from that standpoint formulates a critique of it, explaining and understanding it.

It is just this absolute reality, which is prior to the economy and from which both economic reality and the science of that reality derive, that Marx's philosophical thought defines at the end of the extraordinary itinerary of 1842 to 1846. As this thought shakes the foundations of Western philosophy, it can only be decoded to begin with through its antitheses. Thus we note in the *Theses on Feuerbach* – a text which represents the point of greatest tension in the process of Marx's thought coming into its own – that this reflexion still uses two presuppositions that it jointly rejects. It uses Hegelian idealism and dialectics in order to reject Feuerbach's sensible intuition, materialism; and makes use of Feuerbach's materialism in order to reject Hegel's dialectics. Materialism and dialectics are together exactly what Marx challenges, although through lack of other means to do so, he pitches them one against the other. Then, in this final confrontation between two dying concepts, the key insights blaze forth: praxis, subjectivity.

Praxis is the word that Marx uses in order to develop the notion of real action.

Praxis denotes action as something that excludes both intuition and the dialectical process. The dialectical process is not a real action, but a pseudo-action. Thus, when, for example, in order to attain its reality the Idea appears in the form of Truth in objective particularity and determination, in nature, thought is in fact alienated and conceives of itself as other; but this alienation is not different from the actual action of thought. What thought has before it is nothing less than itself. In relation to thought, this otherness and this outsideness are only a pseudo-otherness and a pseudo-outsideness. In no way do they constitute a reality that is in fact different from thought.

That is why such alienation, which is in fact but a pseudo-alienation, is so easy to overcome. What is necessary to its elimination? It is enough to know that the object that thought places in its objectivization as other than itself, as nature, is in reality none other than itself. As soon as thought is made aware of that, as soon as knowledge knows that what it has before it only appears to be other, it knows that its object is in reality only itself; it knows that in front of its object, with its object, it is in reality with itself, that it remains with itself in the other.

What does it signify to have overcome this alienation, to have negated the being-other of nature, of the object? It signifies the negation of the *meaning which this had of being other* and its replacement by a new meaning, according to which this being-other is in reality the same as thought.

Thus the action in question here is only an action that concerns ideal meanings, propositions; it is an action that is itself ideal and abstract and which does nothing to change reality because it is not an action in reality, an action of the body, a real action. It is an action of thought, of what Marx calls "consciousness;" it is the operation of a *Sinngebung* (bestowal of sense), which does not involve changing the real being but rather consists of interpreting it in another way. In Marx's view, this action of thought characterizes German ideology. First, with Hegel: in Hegel, the real world, the alienated world of politics, of the State, of religion is not eliminated. On the contrary, it is maintained as soon as it is accorded the meaning, of being not the other of the mind, but rather its objectivization and realization. Thus, the critique of Feuerbach's religion also centers on a displacement of meanings that eventually leads to no longer considering God as God but as the objectivization of the human essence, of the *Gattungswesen*. Thus also the critique of Stirner's State, which consists in no longer considering the State as something that one must serve, but as that which one uses according to interest or inclination. The neo-Hegelians declared that they were only contending with words; we see here how, as Marx pointed out, they themselves were only able to oppose them with yet more words.

Intuition – Feuerbach's materialism – does not constitute real action any more than the dialectical process does. First, the possibility of such real action, the possibility of gaining access to the power that it brings into play – in other words, access to the body – does not reside in sensible intuition. On the contrary, sensible intuition supposes as a precondition a positioning in the body, in sight, touch, hearing and movement. Secondly, the unfolding of action itself, the reality of its performance, is in no respect intuition. Intuition perceives the object, discovers it, contemplates it. In as much as we live within this vision, we are not acting.

What is action then if it excludes from itself all intuition? The first sentence of the first thesis on Feuerbach expresses it. Materialism is reproached precisely for merely grasping reality "in the form of object or intuition, but not as activity . . . not as practice, in a subjective manner." The metaphysical determining of actual reality in terms of praxis advances the entirely new concept of a subjectivity that is neither intuition nor thought, composition of sense nor intentionality – which is neither consciousness nor its dialectical movement; neither is it representation nor its ecstatic foundation; it carries within it neither Difference nor Otherness. Reality as subjectivity of praxis, exclusive of any Difference, as pure immanence and affection of self, Marx henceforth terms life.

Life designates a subjectivity which is founded in the body. It is not a consciousness open to an external world but a force that is immersed in itself and which feels itself at once and without distance. In this way, life is in possession of itself and of each of the powers that make up its organic subjectivity: it is in a position to exercise them. Action, real action, is possible as living subjective praxis, the actual putting into practice of the motor potential with which this subjectivity coincides. Moreover, life, which is pressed up against itself, and from which all self-directed negativeness is absent, finds it impossible to separate from itself, to escape from itself and from any oppressiveness and heaviness its being might have. Radically passive when it comes to itself, it is given up to each of its impressions: cold, hunger, suffering, need in all its forms. Under the effect of its own burden, the suffering engendered by this need is transformed into an effort to satisfy it. Thus, in life's pathetic ordeal, the movement towards auto-satisfaction is born. The endless iteration of desire, of labor, and of satisfaction distinguishes this as the hidden principle driving and causing the development of every conceivable historical community.

Life is also in essence individual. Although Marx did not concern himself with providing the theory of the life development of the individual, he none the less interpreted life as a multiplicity of "living individuals" who form the only reality that exists. If Marx rejects the traditional concept of an individual defined by thought, consciousness, or reason, it is in order to put in its place that of the real, concrete individual who is subject to need and capable of action. This is the individual that is elaborated in the admirable polemic against Stirner and which will form the "presupposition . . . of all human history" as well as of society. And, in actual fact, of the economy.

Reality – praxis, living praxis, which Marx in the *Grundrisse* calls "organic subjectivity" and in the economic texts the "subjective force of labor," "living labor," "subjective labor," "real labor," "individual labor" – is not in itself economic at all; nor is its correlative, the nature that has been modified by it. Walking, running, breathing do not carry within them an economic value. Eroticism cannot be analyzed, but if it could one would not find prostitution within it. A lump of sugar can be analyzed: the price will not be found in it. Reality has established itself, living individuals live, but no economic reality has appeared on the horizon of their world. Maybe they will continue to live and economic reality will exist no longer. The question is therefore the following: When and how in human history did economic reality establish itself?

121

When groups of human beings produced a little more than was necessary to their subsistence, they exchanged it. These use values became commodities: the economic universe was born. How was the production of an economic universe possible? This is a transcendental question, and because the possibility of an economic universe resides in reality itself, the exposition of this possibility is only discernible by the philosophical elucidation of the adequate concept of reality.

This explains the fundamental criticism that Marx directs at the English school: that is, that they were confused when talking about labor. How did the economic universe appear, how was exchange possible? The English economy states: $x$ of commodity $a$ is exchanged against $y$ of commodity $b$ so long as the same amount of labor was necessary for each to be produced. Labor, measured by the objective amount of time required and by its nature, is the unit, the measure, the universal which, subsuming products that are qualitatively different, facilitates the overcoming of their heterogeneity. In other words, it establishes an equivalence between them and makes possible their exchange.

However, in a philosophy of praxis, *labor* in this sense does not exist; it is neither objective nor universal. It is not itself a measurement, and cannot be measured; it is not the being that several different things have in common. Rather, it is unique to each single thing; it is integral to each and to the radical singularity of each. Labor is the accomplishment of a subjectivity that is delivered up to the ineffable of its night. This explains why the temporalness of this accomplishment has nothing to do with the objective time of the universe, nor indeed with the ecstatic time of which objective time is the ontological representation. It is an immanent temporalness which relates only to the rhythm of its effort and suffering. We are aware of Marx's crucial distinction, from *The Holy Family* onwards, between "empty time," which wages take account of, and the "time of accomplished labor," which is the real time of real labor. As for the nature of this real labor, it is not objective at all, but uses itself up in the auto-affection of phenomenological systems and in the lines of force along which organic subjectivity expends its effort. All of this means that, when we witness the variety of commodities available on the market and wish to refer back to the labor underlying them in order to determine their value and to be able to exchange them, we do not in fact find a unit that can overcome and reduce this diversity. Rather, we have before us a still more radical diversity, the irreducible diversity of real instances of labor. In other words, of isolated bodily subjectivities.

In a manuscript of 1857 Marx was confronted with the transcendental question of exchange and formulated the following dazzling summary of it: "In itself labour time only exists in the subjective form of activity . . . subjectively, this comes down to saying that [the worker's] labour time cannot be exchanged against any other's. In order to be universally exchanged, first of all it must have an intermediary and take on a different form." Take on a different form, become another: this is indeed alienation. Here, only the philosophy of praxis can guide us and prevent any confusion. The worker's labor is not alienated in the sense of a process that would affect it in its very being and which would be a component of its being. For the reality of praxis is unaware of the being-outside-itself and, shut up in its radical subjective immanence, invincibly rejects it. This is unlike the Hegel of the Jena manuscripts, for whom labor includes within itself the objective moments which confer being – instrument, method, work object – and which make it a universal. Hegel was a prisoner both of his own philosophical presuppositions and of the economic fetishism that he inherited from Adam Smith; he mistook the objective and social elements of labor for labor itself, so that the reality of production and labor becomes economic reality and contributes towards defining it, just as in turn economic reality defines reality. Marx, on the other hand, thanks to the key insight of praxis, perceived in the blaze of the metaphysical vision that economic labor is not real labor, but is in fact opposed to it. With economic labor – objective, universal, recognized, and which has overcome the singularity of individuals – all economic reality, founded on economic labor and identical to it, falls outside reality and is projected a long way from it, into unreality and phantasmagoria, like life's irrational and ghostly double.

How is this uncanny double of life possible? Since a worker's labor cannot be exchanged, it is made to take on a different form, said Marx; its ideal substitute is constructed, as the result of an abstraction that abandons all its real characteristics and reduces it to a certain type of labor – the way of doing that Hegel discusses. Moreover, this real praxis is made to fit universal time, which slips over it without changing it, without a bearing on the intensity of effort expended. What it does do is to add external boundaries to it so that it can be compared to any praxis that is enclosed within the same boundaries: thus, eight hours of labor. What does it mean to subject praxis to a norm, to boundaries which in no way change its real being? It means: to imagine praxis. Economic labor – Marx calls it "social," "abstract" – is that representation of real labor which overlooks its reality and puts in its place a pure meaning: "so many hours of such and such a labor (simple or complex, qualified or not)." The exchange value is this pure meaning added to the object produced. It designates it as "produced by so much labor of such and such a type." Economic reality as a whole is the *theoria* of praxis and it is because the *theoria* in principle overlooks the real being of praxis that economic reality is an abstraction in a radical sense, in the sense of the loss of all reality.

All Marx's economic analyses have a single aim, which is to establish that only *real* labor (and in this way the English thesis is not only modified but reversed) produces economic value, in other words the exchange value of which the pure form is money. It is a question of making the being of value appear within its transcendental genesis, as a quantifying and qualifying representation of real praxis, as its pure meaning and, inherent in the latter, its total impotence to found itself.

Take, for example, the famous critique of surplus value. When in the movement of commodities a value appears that is higher than that which immediately precedes it, the transcendental view solves this economic aporia in the following way. No surplus value is possible in a movement which presupposes the equality of exchanged values. In fact, the capitalist has not exchanged one exchange value, the wage, against another exchange value. Rather, he has exchanged it against a use value (which is why this exchange of capital and of labor is not an exchange, for this always takes place between exchange values) or, more accurately, against the fundamental use value. This is the usage of the worker's force of labor, the operation of his organic subjectivity. It is because the latter has the property of producing more use value than it needs during production, that this fundamental property of life, this extra-economic fact, Marx says, has the following economic meaning: the force of labor produces more value (of exchange) than that which is necessary for its subsistence; the capitalist derives surplus value from the usage of that force.

However, it is far from being the case that only the paradoxical shape of surplus value refers the economic universe back to its secret foundation. Just as much as enhanced value, the simple maintenance of value implies the continual action of living labor. Here the illusion that is characteristic of the movement of commodities must be exposed: the semblance that value is preserved in it, because exchange presupposes the equality of the values exchanged. It is important to oppose the tautological reappearance of the same ideal quantity with the real preservation of value. For every exchange value is based on a use value; it deteriorates and disappears with it: tea goes moldy, a tool rusts, ports silt up, civilizations die. Just like its production, the preservation of value is achieved outside the economic sphere, where a concrete praxis grappling with the usage values that are thrown into the process of production, maintains the form of these usage values, and as a result, maintains their value. Each value at every moment, each of its modifications just as much as its permanence, each economic phenomenon, in consequence, refers back ceaselessly to its source. This origin does not cease either, as a result of the indefinite reiteration of praxis in its eternal present, the "living present," says Marx, "living labor."

The heterogeneity of the economic universe and of its foundation is overwhelming when political economy comes up against the crucial problem of the value of labor. Thus, the unfathomable statement that "labor has no value" ensues. As the source of all values, labor (real labor, living labor, life) stands this side of those values, this side of the whole economic universe. Only thought that returns to a place located before the economy and before science can allow us to understand one and the other. It is not only the critique of political economy, but of all science that finds here one of its most brilliant formulations.

Marx is one of the greatest Western thinkers. However, his thought completely eludes the history of Western philosophy, because it eludes the phenomenological presupposition upon which this philosophy has been based since the Greeks. It is a stranger to the conceptualizations of philosophy, but not to reality, the essence of which it grasps in the concept of "living praxis." What can this thought do for us today? Nothing less than allow us to understand the world in which we live – and in which we die: on the one hand, the recent failure of the communist regimes, and on the other, the impending collapse of capitalism.

Those communist regimes were based on Marxism: on the devaluing of the individual and on the correlative primacy of a society whose reality is objective economic reality. An objective science of that reality was consequently thought possible; it was considered necessary to found society upon such a science, upon the objective knowledge of economic and social laws. Hence, the decisive role attributed to the concept of "organization." Hence the Plan, the state-controlled economy.

It is important at this point to recall Marx's polemic with Proudhon, in *The Poverty of Philosophy*, in which he scornfully took issue with the concept of a society considered as an autonomous reality, as a primitive totality with its own nature and laws, distinct from individuals, located beyond them and no longer taking its reality from them: where henceforth, the individuals would take their reality from society. Marx fiercely rejected this absurd reversal of the order of things, this definition of the individual's reality which was built up from the reality of an allegedly transcendent society that determined the individual from the outside. It was as if the individual had desires and needs because society had them, as if "the life of that person [society] obeyed laws that conflicted with the laws that determine the actions of man as an individual."

We only have to look at the decaying communist societies to recognize a striking illustration of Marx's criticism. In as much as reality resides in life and in radically immanent subjectivity, everything that is placed outside of this and is transcendent to it – regardless of whether it be an object or an ideal – is an automatic unreality, an "abstraction." It is because Society, the State, its various bodies, its institutions, its ideology have been molded to the principle of social organization that this organization has found itself powerless, left to ruin. Everywhere concepts, plans, products of thought, in short, abstractions can be found that are foreign to life and as such deprived of force and effective strength. What we are witness to in the collapsed communist regimes is not the failure of a conceptual analysis of economic phenomena, with as a result the various plans that have been founded upon it. Rather, it is an obvious "practical" element, that refers back to the principle governing any society: the inhabitants of those countries are no longer doing anything and do not want to do anything. It is because the individuals no longer do anything that nothing is achieved, that in reality nothing corresponds to the various forecasts and programmes, that all the "plans" go up in smoke.

What we see happening in the crisis-ridden capitalist countries is not so very different. There is of course an important distinction between capitalism and the planned, state-controlled Marxist economy. While the second implies a continual under-estimating of the individual and his capacities, capitalism (we are speaking here of real capitalism and not of the ideologies that attempt to legitimate it after the event) has not misjudged the principle that produces economic value: in other words, capital itself. It is through systematically exploiting the force of the individual's living labor that capitalism achieves its goal: its indefinite expansion. In spite of its economic discourse, capitalism agrees *in practice* with Marx's key insight that the individual produces the totality of economic wealth through the operation of his strength alone. It is precisely because capitalism has seized hold of that strength, forcing it to exert itself to its limits, that it has managed to transform the earth's surface in a few centuries.

It cannot be forgotten that capitalism is an advanced form of the market economy and is embedded within it: from the beginning capitalism has involved the whole range of constituent substitutions of the market. Equally, it is made up of

125

abstract ideals – "labor," money, capital, costs, multiple rates – which all refer back, however, to reality, to the subjective force of living labor which is put into effect by "productive forces." In fact, Marx's analysis of productive forces brings out not their simple development but their internal modification, the growing importance within them of objective elements, of technical and instrumental devices, the correlative decline in importance of the subjective element, of living labor. Economically, the progressive decline of living labor means that the production of exchange value, of money, and of capital is increasingly problematic. Thus appears, prophetically announced by Marx, the contradiction of capitalism and technology, resulting in the progressive decline of capitalism under the growing pressure of technology. Over a long period, this brings about its eventual dissolution. The invasion of the real process of production of use values by technology means the gradual exclusion of living individuals, their "unemployment," or the suppression in each individual of the essential connection between need, labor, and enjoyment, and thereby the disturbance of one of life's great laws.

The transcendental genesis of the economy is located this side of any conceivable economy, whether it be capitalist or Marxist. The examination of both with an external critical gaze is made possible by it. Beyond the obvious contrasts, and however strong these might be, the transcendental observation recognizes a curious common destiny between the system which founders and that which attempts to replace it. This destiny is the result of the theoretical and practical elimination of the individual.

The theoretical debasing of the individual in Marxism, its replacement by ideological abstractions that are incapable of producing anything, these are the causes of the collapse of communism. Corresponding to this debasing of the individual in Marxist theory is its sidelining in capitalism, a capitalism which has its driving force progressively weakened by Galilean technology. We see all around us today the effects on the individual of this theoretical debasing on the one hand and of the progressive practical elimination on the other. Marx is not only one of the great thinkers of all time, he is also one of the few that has really been a prophet, a "seer," because of that "eagle's gaze" which he mentioned on November 10, 1837 in a letter to his father.

## Writings

Marx, K.: *Historisch-Kritische Gesamtausgabe* (MEGA) (Frankfurt, 1927–72), vols I–VIII.
——: *Werke*, vols 1–39 (Berlin, 1956–67).
——: *Gesamtausgabe* (Berlin: 1972).

## References and further reading

Althusser, L.: *Pour Marx* (Paris, 1965).
Calvez, J. Y.: *La pensée de Karl Marx* (Paris, 1956).
Cottier, G.: *L'Athéisme du jeune Marx: Ses origines hégéliennes* (Paris, 1959).
Croce, B.: *Materialismo storico ed economia marxista* (Bari, 1899).

Engels, F.: *Herrn Eugen Bühring's Umwaltung der Wissenschaft. Philosophie. Politische Oekonomie. Sozialismus* (Leipzig: Dietz).

——: *Ludwig Feuerbach und der Ausgang der klassischen deutschen Philosophie* (Stuttgart, 1888).

Fromm, E.: *Marx's Concept of Man* (New York, 1961).

Gentile, G.: *La filosofia di Marx, Studii critice* (Pia: E. Sperri, 1899).

Henry, M.: *Marx*, vol. I: *Une philosophie de la réalité*; vol. II: *Une philosophie de l'économie* (Paris, 1976/1991; English translation, Bloomington, 1983).

Horkheimer, M.: *Kritische Theorie, gestern und heute* (Frankfurt, 1970).

Hyppolite, J.: *Etudes sur Marx et Hegel* (Paris, 1955).

Kautsky, K.: *Ethik und materialistische Geschichte auffassung* (Stutgart: Dietz, 1906).

Labriola, A.: *Del materialismo storico: Delucidazione preliminiare* (Rome, 1897).

Löwith, K.: *Von Hegel zu Marx* (Zurich, 1941).

Lukács, G.: *Geschichte und Klassenbewusstsein. Studien über marxistische Dialektik* (Berlin, 1923).

Marcuse, H.: *Reason and Revolution in Hegel and the Rise of Social Theory* (New York/London, 1941).

McLellan, D.: *The Young Hegelians and Karl Marx* (London, 1969).

Ollman, B.: *Alienation – Marx's Critic of Man in a Capitalist Society* (Cambridge, 1971).

Popitz, H.: *Der entfremdete Mensch, Zatkritik und Geschichtsphilosophie der jungen Marx* (Basle, 1953).

Richter, H.: *Zum Problem der Einheit von Theorie und Praxis bei Karl Marx. Eine biographisch-systematische Studie über den frühen Marx* (Frankfurt/New York, 1978).

Rubel, M.: *Marx critique du marxisme* (Paris, 1974).

# 9

# Kierkegaard

MEROLD WESTPHAL

History provides us with at least four ways of describing the writings of Søren Kierkegaard (1813–55). In the 1840s, along with the writings of FEUERBACH (see Article 7) and MARX (see Article 8), they belonged to the rebellion of the sons against the Hegelian father to whom they all were so deeply indebted. In the first half of the twentieth century, especially between the two World Wars, they played such a formative role in the emergence of existentialism in philosophy and theology that Kierkegaard came to be seen as the father of existentialism. Now, at the turning of the century and the millennium, his critique of modern society is increasingly becoming a dialogue partner for a variety of discourses that can be called critical social theory; and his critique of reason is increasingly becoming a dialogue partner for the postmodern assault on logocentrism (the belief that our concepts can be totally lucid in themselves and totally adequate to the realities they intend). In his massive corpus there is plenty of support for all of these overlapping readings: Kierkegaard the anti-Hegelian, Kierkegaard the existentialist, Kierkegaard the critical social theorist, and Kierkegaard the postmodernist. As we turn to the texts, we do well to pay special attention to two requests he makes of his readers, both related to his understanding of authorship.

First, there is the matter of pseudonymity. Because Kierkegaard published many of his most widely read works under a variety of pseudonyms, there is a plethora of voices in the writings. In the two volumes of *Either/Or*, for example, there are five distinct voices, none of them Kierkegaard's own. His goal is clearly not the usual one of hiding his identity. For it is precisely when he publicly acknowledges that the pseudonymous works come from his pen that he pleads most vigorously that we not attribute to him even "a single word" from the authors he has created (Kierkegaard 1992, pp. 625–7).

The different kind of anonymity Kierkegaard seeks is best seen by treating his pseudonyms as *personae* rather than as disguises (Mackey 1971, p. 247). They are like the characters in a novel, who tell their own story and spin their own theories. This means that reading Kierkegaard is in many respects like reading fiction. Imagine the incoherence that would result if we attributed to Dostoyevsky the thoughts and beliefs of all three brothers K, along with those of their father, of Smerdyakov, and, for good measure, of the holy man Zossima!

Of the several reasons Kierkegaard has for writing this way, the most basic is expressed by the Hongs, when they say that "no thinker and writer ever tried as Kierkegaard did to leave the reader alone with the work" (Preface to Malantschuk

1971, p. viii). Victor Emerita, the pseudonymous editor of *Either/Or*, says the same with reference to two other pseudonyms, "The point of view ought to speak for itself. . . . Thus, when the book is read, A and B are forgotten; only the points of view confront each other" (Kierkegaard 1987, vol. I, p. 14). Anticipating Husserl's passion to return "to the things themselves" (see Article 15, HUSSERL), Kierkegaard wants his readers to engage the (many) points of view presented in his writings directly, without being influenced for or against them by what we (think we) know about his personality.

Kierkegaard's request that he not be confused with his fictitious creations has been more honored in the breach than in the observance, sometimes with dreadful results. When reading the secondary literature it is usually best to let "Kierkegaard" stand for a body of texts rather than for the melancholy Dane who produced them, unless the context is explicitly biographical. Twentieth-century literary theory has prepared us in a wide variety of ways to separate author and text in this way.

Given this plurality of voices and Kierkegaard's zeal in preserving it, it may seem surprising that he also insists that his writings form a coherent whole with a unified meaning. He is quick to deny that this derives from his intention. At the time of writing he did not see the religious telos that governs the texts from start to finish, and he attributes the resultant unity of his corpus to divine providence. In so doing he makes it clear that with the hermeneutics, structuralism, and poststructuralism of the twentieth century he rejects the notion that the intention of the author (*mens auctoris*) is the meaning of the text. Rather than claim authorial privilege over his own writings ("I know what's in there because I put it there"), he takes the stance of a co-reader with his readers, whom he treats as co-authors. His second request of us is that we look for the religious unity he claims, as co-reader, to find in his writings.

At the heart of the authorship are the presentations of the three stages or spheres of existence, the aesthetic, the ethical, and the religious. "Stages" is not a happy name for them because neither developmentally (psychologically) nor dialectically (logically) is there any inevitability to the progression of the stages. The transition from one to another is a leap, which means that human reason can neither explain it in terms of causal necessity, nor justify it in terms of conceptual necessity. For this reason, the leap, which is neither blind nor restricted to the religious sphere, exhibits human freedom (as the intersection of risk and responsibility) in an especially powerful way. Conceptual undecidability requires personal decision. It is not that reasons cannot be given to support the move to the ethical or to the religious. It is just that they are hermeneutically circular (see Article 18, HEIDEGGER) and presuppose the sphere to which they point.

The spheres of existence are language games (= forms of life) or modes of being-in-the-world (see HEIDEGGER) that are more or less integrated patterns of belief and practice. What identifies each one vis-à-vis the others is the criterion by which it answers the question, what is the good life?

We quickly realize that the aesthetic sphere has no special link to the arts. Like the Kantian usage, the Kierkegaardian points back to the ancient Greek distinction between sense and intellect and suggests a kind of immediacy prior to judgment.

But we realize just as quickly: (1) that it is not sensible immediacy that is at stake; (2) that the notion of immediacy is not itself immediately helpful, since the aesthetic life is usually presented in highly reflective forms; and (3) that the aesthetic is only prior to certain forms of judgment.

Sometimes the aesthetic criterion for a successful life is identified as pleasure. This nicely captures *Either/Or*'s discussion of erotic immediacy in Mozart's operas and of reflective eroticism in "The Seducer's Diary." But it doesn't fit so well with the suggestion that interesting/boring is a primary aesthetic category, nor with the suggestions in *Concluding Unscientific Postscript* that fortunate/unfortunate is an aesthetic criterion and that philosophical speculation belongs to the aesthetic sphere.

What all the phenomena presented as aesthetic have in common is a criterion that is pre-ethical. Notions of right and wrong, good and evil, virtue and vice play no role in the aesthetic evaluation of life. It is better described as amoral than as immoral, for it is not so much the refusal to obey ethical norms as the refusal to take them seriously. The aesthetic life can be described as hedonism only if pleasure serves as the generic term for all pre-ethical goods, including everything usually called good fortune; and it can be described as an immediacy, however reflective it may be, only as being prior to ethical categories and judgments.

As in the Platonic dialogues, the "leap" to the ethical comes when moral norms are given priority over pleasure (in this extended sense) as the criteria of the good life. It may seem that this move is at least developmentally necessary. Is not socialization unavoidable? Yes, but this may mean no more than that as children we learn to be "good" as the most effective or least painful way of getting the goodies our family and larger society have to offer. If the good life means getting the goodies, even if we have to be good to do so, we are still at the aesthetic stage.

This is why the boundary between the aesthetic and the ethical is marked by despair and self-choice. Here despair means giving up so radically on the aesthetic project that the moral life is no longer seen as a means to its ends but replaces it as the purpose of life. Self-choice is the deliberate decision to reorient oneself in this way. Hence the slogan, "Choose despair." The infant whose existence revolves around a full tummy and a dry bottom is aesthetic by birth. We become ethical only by choice.

As a continuous act of self-choice the ethical is a form of self-relation. But this does not signify autonomy, for my relation to myself is mediated by my relation to another. The formula is this: to enter the ethical is to choose oneself, to receive oneself, and then to become the self one has chosen to receive (Kierkegaard 1987, vol. II, p. 177). The dialectic of choosing and receiving oneself signifies that I am not in the domain of self-legislation, much less of self-creation (Kierkegaard 1987, vol. II, p. 270). Rather, "I choose the absolute that chooses me" (Kierkegaard 1987, vol. II, p. 213). Whether this absolute is to be understood as society or as a God who transcends the social order concerns the boundary between the ethical and the religious.

This means that in the ethical and religious spheres Kierkegaard presents us with a relational theory of the self. He presents a dialectical individualism diametrically opposed to the compositional or atomistic individualism of Cartesian episte-mology and Lockean social theory, according to which discrete and self-sufficient entities are the building blocks out of which the complexity of the world is con-structed (see Westphal 1987, ch. 3). Thus the radical loneliness of the Kierkegaar-dian self is not the isolation of an ego locked into a consciousness with no content but its own ideas, or the independence of a bearer of rights marching out to defend those rights; it is rather the inwardness of a self, whose relation to itself is in any case mediated by its relationships with others, that is called upon to accept as its own the responsibility for choosing how all those relationships will be structured. Far from presupposing an atomic, pre-existing individual self, such a call requires that one break free from one's absorption in what "they" say and what "everyone" is doing (see Article 18, HEIDEGGER). True community can only be among those who have in this way accepted their freedom (see Westphal 1987, ch. 4).

We can now define the boundary between the ethical and the religious in terms of two questions, neither of which arises for the aesthetic self. Is "the absolute that chooses me" society or God? Is the voice with which I choose this absolute the voice of my social milieu or my own voice? For Kierkegaard it is the latter alternative in each case that distinguishes the religious from the ethical. The crucial text is *Fear and Trembling*, where the story of Abraham's (near) sacrifice of Isaac (Genesis 22) is the basis for an understanding of the religious as the teleological suspension of the ethical.

A teleological suspension is something like an Hegelian *Aufhebung* (see Article 6, HEGEL). To be suspended or *aufgehoben* is not to be obliterated but to be relativized by being contextualized in a larger whole whose governing principle comes from elsewhere. Thus, in an Aristotelian human being, the vegetative and animal souls are teleologically suspended in a context whose essential principle is the rational soul. They have their place, but they are no longer self-sufficient or self-governing.

Abraham shows that he is willing to kill his son Isaac. How shall this act be characterized? Ethics calls it murder; religion calls it sacrifice. Only if religion is the teleological suspension of the ethical, that is, only if the former can trump the latter in this kind of situation, can Abraham be a hero, the father of the faithful that both the Jewish and Christian Bibles take him to be.

But what kind of situation is this, and what is the ethical that the religious would trump? Johannes de Silentio, the pseudonym (who importantly does not take sides in the dispute between the ethical and the religious but only insists on their differ-ence), calls the ethical the universal. This has misled many to assume that it is a Kantian conception of ethics that is placed over against religious self-understanding. But the evidence is overwhelming that it is rather the Hegelian conception, according to which the ethical universal is the concrete universal, the laws and customs of a people. For Hegel the abstract universal of KANTIAN (see Article 2) ethics (*Moralität*) is always teleologically suspended in the concrete uni-versal of such social institutions as family, civil society, and the state (*Sittlichkeit*). Kantian ethics is the fallacy of misplaced concreteness.

The evidence that Kierkegaard's texts concern the ethical in a Hegelian rather than a Kantian sense is threefold. First, the formal account of ethical self-choice in

*Either/Or* as receiving myself from the absolute that calls me, does not easily lend itself to the Kantian notion of autonomous self-legislation. Secondly, that formal account is embedded in an institutional context; it belongs to an extended description and defense of traditional marriage, the first moment of Hegelian *Sittlichkeit*.

Thirdly, and most important, beyond the fact that Abraham's ethical duties (to Isaac and Sarah) are those of family life, *Fear and Trembling* is doubly specific about its Hegelian understanding of the ethical. One the one hand, Silentio identifies the ethical with "social morality," (Danish *Sædelighed* = German *Sittlichkeit*). What distinguishes Abraham from Agamemnon, who actually sacrificed his daughter but remained securely within the ethical, is that the Greek subordinated his family ties to his duty to his people (nation, state), a higher moment of *Sittlichkeit*, while the Jew had no such national interest to justify his act.

On the other hand, Silentio mentions Hegel by name in each of the three "problems" which contain the primary reflection on the Abraham story. Each begins with this dilemma: if the ethical universal is the highest, then Hegel is right; but Abraham is lost, for we will have to understand the killing of Isaac as murder and not sacrifice. There is no room for Abraham's faith in Hegel's rational society (see Westphal 1987, ch. 5).

It becomes clear that we must substitute "society" for "universal" and "God" for "absolute" in the following accounts of the religious. In each case it is the paradox of faith

> that it is the single individual who, after being subordinate as the single individual to the universal, now by means of the universal becomes the single individual who as the single individual is superior, that the single individual as the single individual stands in an absolute relation to the absolute.   (Kierkegaard 1983, p. 56)

> that the single individual . . . determines his relation to the universal by his relation to the absolute, not his relation to the absolute by his relation to the universal.   (Kierkegaard 1983, p. 70)

In other words, to call the religious the teleological suspension of the ethical is to say that from within the religious we have an absolute duty toward God and only a relative duty toward our nation, our people (Hegel's *Volk*). The knight of faith will only pledge allegiance to the flag with fingers crossed, and will never be able to say, "My country, right or wrong."

It is here, and not in the articles published during the 1850s, that Kierkegaard's "attack upon Christendom" begins. It is a dual attack: first on a society that by virtue of its religious identity takes its laws, customs, and institutions to be the highest norm for human life; secondly on a Hegelian philosophy that provides theoretical justification for such an attitude. The critique of Hegel that runs throughout the corpus is ideology critique just because these writings treat Hegel as the legitimizer of a certain arrogant modernity.

This last sentence could just as easily have been about the texts MARX (see Article 8) was writing simultaneously. Of course Marx has an anti-religious motivation and a communist aspiration that Kierkegaard does not share. But these obvious differences should not obscure the latter's identity as a critical social theorist. What Kierkegaard calls Christendom is pretty much the same set of phenomena that Marx calls the bourgeoisie. Both see deep pathologies in this dominant aspect of European modernity, and both seek to expose and undermine its Hegelian self-legitimation. But whereas the other target of Marx's ideology critique is political economy, Kierkegaard's other target is the preaching of the Danish clergy.

This reflects the fact that the two offer different diagnoses of modernity. For Marx, its deepest ill is capitalism, while for Kierkegaard its deepest ill is its tendency to absolutize itself, to confuse itself with God. It is the "how" of modernity's institutions, the metanarrative that makes them the meaning and goal of the historical process, more than their "what" that is most highly problematic; this means that even what may be substantively good about those practices becomes corrupted.

Like NIETZSCHE (see Article 11), Kierkegaard seeks to expose a will to power in the Western world that is more subtle than the will to economic growth and political domination. If Marx's historical materialism uncovers a materialistic will to power, what we might call Kierkegaard's historical spiritualism, his hermeneutical key to interpreting "the present age," reveals a moral will to power, the desire to be the ultimate standard of the Good and the Right. While the former might lead to war, the latter is even more dangerous, for it can lead to holy war. Hence the importance of the teleological suspension of the ethical. Is there a divine reality higher than our social order to which it is answerable, or are we, somehow, collectively, God?

Some find it difficult to think of anything as critical social theory that is not directly descended from the Marxian critique of capitalism. In the spirit of one of his pseudonyms, Kierkegaard might well reply, "You want to maintain a monopoly on the title Critical Social Theory for your own project? Fine. It's all yours. If you like I'll call my project Uncritical Social Theory to make sure no one confuses it with yours. A rose by any other name. . . . Now let's get down to the serious debate over which diagnosis is deeper, which provides a more radical hermeneutics of modernity."

If such a debate were to occur, Kierkegaard would insist that in spite of the dialogical and utopian elements that distinguish the HABERMASIAN (see Article 34) conception of rationality from Hegel's, by virtue of its linguistification of the sacred it remains essentially Hegelian. The form of rationality implicit in modernity is the highest criterion of truth and justice. After all of the qualifications are spelled out, the voice of the people remains the voice of God (see Matuštík et al. (forthcoming), chs 1, 11, 12, 14; and Westphal 1987, ch. 7).

At this point the epistemological question can no longer be ignored. A number of Kierkegaardian voices consider with utmost seriousness the possibility of a voice beyond and different from the voice of the people and their practices. But how could one know anything about such a voice? Johannes de Silentio assures us Abraham knew that the voice commanding the sacrifice of Isaac was God's voice; but far from telling us how this is possible, he emphasizes its impossibility, humanly speaking, by stressing the "paradox" of a faith which acts "by virtue of the absurd." The writings of Johannes Climacus, *Philosophical Fragments* and *Concluding Unscientific*

*Postscript*, are best read as further explorations of the religious sphere in terms of this posing of the question of faith and reason. At this point Kierkegaard the critical theorist becomes Kierkegaard the critic of logocentrism.

*Fragments* contrasts two accounts of how we might know transcendent, divine Truth. From Athens comes the Socratic notion of knowledge as recollection, while from Jerusalem comes a very different account, recognizably Lutheran, but more broadly speaking, Augustinian. Throughout the Kierkegaardian corpus, Socrates is presented as a prophetic challenge to Athenian *Sittlichkeit*. The God he serves, like Abraham's, is not the voice of the Athenian people, however democratic, but the occasion for a teleological suspension of the ethical.

But for Socrates, the religious is the rational rather than the paradoxical or the absurd, because the Truth is within us and needs but to be recollected. Like the slave boy in relation to mathematical truth, we have the inherent capacity to recognize the Truth that contains the highest criterion for human life. The Socratic version of critical social theory is post-Hegelian, having made the "leap" from the ethical to the religious; and it is metaphysical, because it posits both (1) an eternal reality beyond social practice and democratic discourse, and (2) the capacity, in principle at least, of the human intellect to have an adequate apprehension of this reality.

The Augustinian alternative is post-Hegelian and quasi-metaphysical. It affirms a God beyond the social order, but denies the univocity of the human logos and the divine Logos. On the one hand, the human logos is finite, caught up in a herme-neutical circle that leaves its grounds ever ungrounded. For example, we can prove the existence of God from his works only if we have first interpreted the world as the handiwork of God, which is not how the world appears "directly and immediately" (Kierkegaard 1985, p. 42). The immediacy to which every foundationalism appeals is unavailable. On the other hand, the more basic reason we lack the ability to recognize and articulate the Truth is sin. Questionable desire and dubious interests shape what we see and are able to see. For the Augustinian hermeneutics of suspicion (see Article 39, RICOEUR), here set over against Socrates, Creation generates a deep continuity between the human mind and divine Truth, but the Fall represents a disruption we can cause but cannot cure. If we are ever to know the Truth it will have to be by virtue of a grace that restores the condition for recognizing it, whether God's self-revelation takes place in nature or in history. Faith, both in God as creator and in Jesus as God incarnate, is not so much a lower stage on the Platonic divided line as a miracle of regeneration or recreation.

Climacus does not choose sides between Socrates and Augustine; but he seeks to undermine a quick dismissal of the latter from the Socratic side. Philosophers have often charged various religious worldviews with being unreasonable, even irratio-nal. The appropriate Augustinian response, Climacus thinks, would be something like this: "You wish to monopolize the notion of 'Reason' for the philosophical project of epistemic self-sufficiency? Fine. We will call ourselves the Paradox, to be sure no one confuses the two views. But when you say that the Paradox is in conflict with 'Reason' there is something of an acoustical illusion. For this is but an echo of what the Paradox has been saying about its relation to that philosophical project since at least the time of the apostle Paul." For Climacus, once the difference between the two standpoints is clear, the debate between them can begin. But calling one's own view "Reason" is not an argument, and the Paradox can rightly respond, "It is just as you say, but the amazing thing is that you think that it is an objection" (Kierkegaard 1985, p. 52).

The distinction between Religiousness A (the recollection of the eternal) and Religiousness B (the paradoxical entry of the eternal into time in Jesus) in *Postscript* is an extended commentary on the structure, the resources, and the mutual opposition of these two positions. But it is what they have in common that sets the stage for the anti-Hegelian and existentialist features for which the text is famous. As religious, both presuppose the teleological suspension of the ethical; but they also presuppose the formal features that set the ethical off from the aesthetic. In *Postscript* these are called subjectivity, inwardness, and existence, terms that refer to the self's relation to itself as being responsible for itself to another (be it society or God). "Existence" thus becomes a technical term. Not only does it apply uniquely to humans, but it applies as a task and not a fact. We can fail to exist, can fail to accept the kind of responsibility the term implies. The name for this failure is the aesthetic life.

Much of *Postscript* is Climacus's argument that Hegelian speculation is a mode of the aesthetic life. Whereas Silentio suggests that Hegel has not gotten beyond the ethical, Climacus argues that he has not even gotten to it. In both cases the claim of Hegelian philosophy to have the content of Christianity but in a more adequate conceptual form becomes problematic. The difference of form turns out to be a difference of existence spheres and not simply the difference between representational and conceptual thought (*Vorstellung* and *Begriff*). Even if there is some sense in which the content remains the same, doesn't such a change of form change the totality beyond recognition? Like Socratic philosophy, Christianity is an "existence communication," a mode of reflection in the service of self-choice and self-reception. But the goal of Hegelian philosophy, the objective possession of Absolute Knowledge, is pre-ethical and leads away from existence.

Climacus has a "postmodern" critique of Hegel as well as an existentialist critique. The Hegelian System is an ontotheology, a theory of the total intelligibility of the totality of being on the basis of the highest being, Spirit. Synchronically, the truth is the whole as expressed in a logic which is simultaneously a metaphysics. Diachronically, the truth is the whole expressed in a philosophy of world history which presents modernity as the telos of the entire process. In both dimensions the System is logocentric as defined above.

The critique of foundationalist immediacy in *Fragments* is irrelevant to this project, whose holistic strategy finds truth not at the outset but at the completion of reflection, whether logical or historical. But Climacus challenges the assumption that human thought can escape the finitude of its temporality by bringing reflection to completion (as distinct from just stopping for a while) in either dimension. Reality may be a system for God, who sees the whole *sub specie aeternitatis*, but it cannot be for us. Like Heidegger and Derrida, Climacus stresses the ineluctably temporal character of human thought; he then draws the conclusion, not just that the

Hegelian project is a pipe dream but that it involves the comical confusion of the human with the divine logos.

This is the point at which the postmodern critique and the existentialist critique intersect. It is precisely at the logocentric blurring of the distinction between ourselves and God that the System engenders a radical forgetfulness of existence. The deification of the human logos is the lapse into existential oblivion. For like the rocks and trees, God does not exist. Even if God, as *ens realissimum*, is more fully actual than the rocks and trees, only humans exist; and we flee that task both in any naturalism that tends to confuse us with rocks and trees and in any idealism that tends to confuse us with God.

In the existentialist critique of Hegelian speculation, Socrates is an ally. But in the postmodern critique of its exaggerated claims for human thought there is an implicit critique of Socratic recollection and its many cousins. Recollection is supposed to be pure reason, the direct contact between a soul and a truth both of which are unconditioned by the limits of the cave. But if Climacus is on target in pointing to both radical finitude and sin as the site of every human enterprise, what we recollect will be human, all too human. It will bear the marks of our language and culture, and it will be distorted by our individual and collective will to power. Nor will its historical specificity be surpassed by the historical finality Hegel requires. What philosophy often refers to as Reason is very likely to be ideological false consciousness. Loudly proclaiming its universality and its purity, it manages not to notice its perspectival particularity and its contamination by interests and desires. The "irrationalism" for which Kierkegaard is famous is his refusal to take the bona fides of philosophical Reason at face value. In this regard he is deeply akin not only to philosophical postmodernism but also to both hermeneutics and ideology critique as traditions in continental philosophy, to say nothing of pragmatism, the later Wittgenstein, and post-positivist philosophy of science.

In his later writings, especially *Practice in Christianity*, Kierkegaard describes what we might call Religiousness C (see Connell et al. 1992, ch. 7). The writings regularly point out the ease with which religion, like Hegelian speculation, lapses into the aesthetic. The focus in Religiousness B on the paradoxicality of a savior who is both human and divine poses a challenge to the ultimacy of human reason. But it also risks reducing the religious life to a metaphysical theory and seducing the believer into forgetting existence. In Religiousness C, orthodoxy is teleologically suspended in orthopraxy. Christ is no longer primarily the Paradox to be believed, but the Pattern or Paradigm to be followed and imitated. He is a threat to Christendom and to every established order by virtue of his compassion for the poor and the powerless, those pushed to the margins of every society.

> Sausage peddlers will consider that in being compassionate it is descending too far down to go to paupers in the poor-house and express equality with them; the compassion of sausage peddlers is trapped in . . . consideration for other sausage peddlers and then for Saloon keepers. Thus their compassion is not totally reckless. (Kierkegaard 1991, p. 59)

The religious telos that Kierkegaard claims for his authorship culminates in a challenge to the church to link faith essentially with a compassion for suffering that goes beyond class loyalty. Faith is the intersection of epistemic risk and reckless social equality.

## Writings

Kierkegaard, S.: *Either/Or* (1843), tr. H. V. and E. H. Hong (Princeton, NJ: Princeton University Press, 1987).

——: *Fear and Trembling/Repetition* (1843), tr. H. V. and E. H. Hong (Princeton, NJ: Princeton University Press, 1983).

——: *Philosophical Fragments* (1844), tr. H. V. and E. H. Hong (Princeton, NJ: Princeton University Press, 1985).

——: *Concluding Unscientific Postscript* (1846), tr. H. V. and E. H. Hong (Princeton, NJ: Princeton University Press, 1992).

——: *Works of Love* (1847), tr. H. and E. Hong (New York: Harper & Row, 1962).

——: *The Sickness Unto Death* (1849), tr. H. V. and E. H. Hong (Princeton, NJ: Princeton University Press, 1980).

——: *Practice in Christianity* (1850), tr. H. V. and E. H. Hong (Princeton, NJ: Princeton University Press, 1991).

## References and further reading

Collins, J.: *The Mind of Kierkegaard* (Chicago, 1953; Princeton, NJ: Princeton University Press, 1983). (Good overall introduction.)

Connell, G. B. and Evans, C. S. (eds): *Foundations of Kierkegaard's Vision of Community: Religion, Ethics, and Politics in Kierkegaard* (New Jersey and London: Humanities Press, 1992).

Dunning, S. N.: *Kierkegaard's Dialectic of Inwardness: A Structural Analysis of the Theory of Stages* (Princeton, NJ: Princeton University Press, 1985). (Shows formal links to Hegel.)

Elrod, J. W.: *Kierkegaard and Christendom* (Princeton, NJ: Princeton University Press, 1981).

Evans, C. S.: *Kierkegaard's "Fragments" and "Postscript": The Religious Philosophy of Johannes Climacus* (Atlantic Highlands, NJ: Humanities Press, 1983).

——: *Passionate Reason: Making Sense of Kierkegaard's "Philosophical Fragments"* (Bloomington: Indiana University Press, 1992). (Focus on the arguments of Climacus.)

Kirmmse, B. H.: *Kierkegaard in Golden Age Denmark* (Bloomington, IN: Indiana University Press, 1990). (Best placing of Kierkegaard in his historical setting.)

Mackey, L.: *Kierkegaard: A Kind of Poet* (Philadelphia, PA: University of Pennsylvania Press, 1971).

Malantschuk, G.: *Kierkegaard's Thought*, (1968), tr. H. V. and E. H. Hong (Princeton, NJ: Princeton University Press, 1971).

Matuštík, M. and Westphal, M. (eds): *Kierkegaard in Dialogue* (forthcoming from Indiana University Press). (Essays relating Kierkegaard to major twentieth-century thinkers.)

Perkins, R. L. (ed.): *International Kierkegaard Commentary: The Sickness unto Death* (Macon: Mercer University Press, 1987). (The subtitle of each volume in this series identifies the volume in the Princeton translations to which its essays are devoted.)

Roberts, R.: *Faith, Reason, and History: Rethinking Kierkegaard's Philosophical Fragments* (Macon: Mercer University Press, 1986).

Taylor, M. C.: *Kierkegaard's Pseudonymous Authorship: A Study of Time and the Self* (Princeton, NJ: Princeton University Press, 1975).

Westphal, M.: *Kierkegaard's Critique of Reason and Society* (Macon, 1987; University Park, PA: Pennsylvania University Press, 1991). (Challenges traditional readings of Kierkegaard as individualist and irrationalist.)

——: *Becoming a Self: A Reading of Kierkegaard's "Concluding Unscientific Postscript"* (West Lafayette, IN: Purdue University Press, 1996).

# 10

# Schopenhauer

ROBERT RETHY

## I

Arthur Schopenhauer (born 1788 in Danzig, died 1860 in Frankfurt am Main), was the son of Heinrich Floris Schopenhauer, a wealthy merchant, and Johanna Trosiener, who was later to become a well-known member of Goethe's circle in Weimar and, subsequently, a popular novelist whose collected works, published in 1831, filled twenty-four volumes. The death of his father (a probable suicide) in 1805 led to the future philosopher's ultimate abandonment of the plan that he should enter business. After further study, he attended the University of Göttingen in 1809 where he studied with G. E. Schulze, whose *Aenisidisumus* (1796), with its critique of Kant's conception of the thing-in-itself, had played a crucial role in the early development of Fichte's *Wissenschaftslehre*. It was through Schulze that he became acquainted, not only with Kant, but with Plato and Schelling (see Hübscher 1989, pp. 159ff). The connection between Plato and Kant, a crucial thesis of his philosophy as a whole, is the subject of some of his earliest and most penetrating notebook entries (Schopenhauer 1988, vol. I, nos 17, 228, 442). Schopenhauer left Göttingen for Berlin to attend Fichte's lectures. Despite apparently serious attempts, testified by his voluminous notebooks (preserved in Schopenhauer 1988, vol. II), Schopenhauer found himself deeply out of sympathy with the Fichtean philosophy of reflection, and his distaste for German idealism, which only increased with the years, dates from this encounter. On the heels of Napoleon's invasion of Berlin, Schopenhauer retired to a small town outside of Weimar, where (June–November 1813) he wrote his dissertation *On the Fourfold Root of the Principle of Sufficient Reason*, whose simplification and transformation of the Kantian doctrine of the concepts of the understanding into a third "form of intuition" next to space and time forms the basis of his distinctive epistemology and its difference from Kant's. (This difference is most clearly expressed in §21; see also the "Critique of Kantian Philosophy", the Appendix to *The World as Will and Representation*, vol. I, pp. 437–451). The "ideality of sensation" is the theme of *On Vision and Colors*, written in 1815 under the influence of his encounter with Goethe's *Farbenlehre* (a sympathy not reciprocated by Goethe for the younger man's contribution). At this time, Schopenhauer moved to Dresden, where for four years he worked out *The World as Will and Representation* in intellectual isolation. In addition to the dual influence of Plato and Kant, Schopenhauer had also been introduced to doctrines of Eastern religion by F. Meyer in Weimar (1813), and is often said to be the first

Western philosopher seriously to incorporate Eastern thought into his system (see Schopenhauer 1988, vol. I, no. 564). The "work" is announced in a note that is even earlier, from 1813, which begins:

> Beneath my hands and rather within my mind a work is growing, a philosophy, which is going to be ethics and metaphysics *in one* [*in Einem*], though they have previously been so falsely separated, like soul and body. (Schopenhauer 1988, vol. I, no. 92)

After the completion of his major work at the age of thirty, Schopenhauer hoped to teach at the University of Berlin, where Hegel had only recently (1818) been installed. Although unimpeded in his appointment by Hegel, Schopenhauer chose to lecture at the same time as the more senior philosopher and attracted at first few, and then no students. Schopenhauer's deep antipathy for Hegel dates from this event, thus post-dating the publication of *The World as Will and Representation*. All references to him in that work or the earlier dissertation were added to the later editions. Schopenhauer published nothing further until *On the Will in Nature*, seventeen years after the publication of *The World as Will and Representation*. In the 1830s he had tried to interest publishers in various translations both to and from English. His prosecution for an assault on a seamstress neighbor who would not leave his parlor as he prepared for an assignation with his mistress, as well as his final move to Frankfurt a. M. (1833), where he was to remain almost uninterruptedly for the last twenty-seven years of his life, also date from this period. In 1837 he encouraged the separate publication of the first edition of Kant's *Critique of Pure Reason*, establishing himself as the first publicly to recognize the importance of the divergence between the first and second editions, a commonplace of Kantian scholarship today (see Schopenhauer's own account, Schopenhauer 1969, vol. I, Appendix, p. 435). The two writings devoted to ethics, *On the Freedom of the Will* (1839) and *On the Foundation of Morality* (1840), were both submitted as responses to public competitions. The former was awarded first prize, the latter, athough the only entry, was pointedly refused any award. Schopenhauer had them published together, in 1841, as *The Two Fundamental Problems of Ethics*, and characterized them (in the Preface) as a "supplement to the Fourth Book of my main work as my writing 'On the Will in Nature' is a very essential and important supplement to its Second Book." In 1844 the second edition of *The World as Will and Representation* appeared at Schopenhauer's insistence. The first edition had gone out of print and had also aroused little interest among reviewers and the academy. The second edition comprised additions (there were no substantive corrections) to what was now Volume I, and a second volume whose chapters were keyed to sections of the first. Schopenhauer's fortunes with the public slowly began to change at this point, Schelling's famous lectures in 1842 perhaps marking the beginning of the decline of Hegelianism in the German academy (Hübscher 1989, p. 352). However, it was the disillusionment that followed upon the failure of the left-Hegelian-inspired Revolutions of 1848 – in which he had been a willing, if minor, participant on the side of the government's forces – along with the publication (1851) of the popular essays contained in *Parerga and Paralipomena* whose title indicates their frankly secondary philosophical importance, that led to the phenomenal growth of Schopenhauer's fame in the last decade of his life. Characteristically, it was a discussion of this work in the English *Westminster Review*, Oxenford's "Iconoclasm in German Philosophy," which was then translated into German, that paved the way for his recognition. Schopenhauer himself announces this ultimate vindication ("their Caspar Hauser has escaped") in his Preface to the second edition (1854) of *On the Will in Nature*. In 1859 he published a third edition of his major work, and died one year thereafter.

## II

Schopenhauer emphasized the *unitary* nature of his philosophy in his earliest Preface to *The World as Will and Representation*, as in the early note already quoted. "What is supposed to be communicated by [this book] is a single thought" which, "viewed from different sides, shows itself as what people have called metaphysics, what they have called ethics, and what they have called aesthetics" (Schopenhauer 1969, vol. I, p. xii). However, to call it a "single" thought is not to imply that it is "singular." Its formal unity of purpose is matched by a thoroughgoing material duplicity. The Kantian insight, said to be both his greatest discovery and the core of Schopenhauer's philosophy, is the discovery precisely of the *duality* of "appearance" and "thing-in-itself" (Schopenhauer 1969, vol. I, App. p. 417), a duality mirrored in the fundamental dualism of Schopenhauer's "system," that of world as representation and world as will. Of these two "aspects" of "the world," neither is itself a unit. Owing to its "essential division within itself" (Schopenhauer 1969, vol. I, p. 146), the will, the "single" thing-in-itself, is not itself a unit. And knowledge, forming the other structural axis of the system, is divided between knowledge "in accordance with the principle of sufficient reason" in its first two books (knowledge of appearance and the will) and knowledge "independent" of this principle in its last two books (the intuitive knowledge that constitutes art in Book III and the insight that leads to morality and saintliness in Book IV). This duplicity is connected with the "duplicity of our essence" (Schopenhauer 1969, vol. I, p. 278), which "does not rest in an absolute unity" and thus makes unitary self-consciousness, the Holy Grail or Philosopher's Stone of German Idealism, impossible in one sense, the miracle κατ'ἐξοχήν (par excellence) in another. (See Schopenhauer 1969, vol. II, ch. 19, pp. 201–3, where he also refers to a similar passage in the *Fourfold Root*.) These various dualities of consciousness seem to go back to one that pervades the early notebook entries, and whose presence, despite the terminological changes, is felt throughout Schopenhauer's writings: the opposition of the "better consciousness" and "empirical consciousness." The former is a timeless, transcendent state of awareness in direct and fierce opposition to empirical awareness and its objects. It is the obvious source of the impersonal, contemplative vision common to the artist of Book III and the philosopher-saint of Book IV. In 1813, prior to the publication of any of his books, Schopenhauer wrote:

> The source of all true happiness, of all comfort that is secure and not built upon shifting sand but rather on an unshakeable foundation (the better consciousness) is, for our empirical consciousness, total destruction, death, and annihilation. No wonder, then, that we can gain no comfort from it as long as we remain on the standpoint of the empirical consciousness. . . . Hence, in order to be true to that better consciousness, we must renounce this empirical consciousness and separate ourselves from it. Self-mortification [*Selbstertötung*].   (Schopenhauer 1988, vol. I, no. 128; Zint 1954)

Schopenhauer, then, begins his philosophy from this characteristically modern experience of self-division, an experience designated by Hegel, in his *Differenz-Schrift* (in 1800), as that which gives rise to the "need for philosophy" and which is particularly characteristic of everyone after Kant. Schopenhauer, however, certainly did not place himself in such systematic proximity to any of these near-contemporaries, whom he mercilessly pilloried throughout his works. He rather urges his readers to view him as a follower of Kant alone among the moderns, correcting and completing the latter's grand work. He marks himself as a "critical" philosopher in his epistemological beginning: "The world is my representation" is the assertion with which *The World as Will and Representation* begins. This statement signifies, according to the first section of the book, that everything that belongs to the world is conditioned by the subject of knowledge, without whom there could be no object. Schopenhauer identifies three "forms of intuition," space, time, and causality, that constitute the world of representation as a world of inter-related, individual objects. By including causality as one of the sensuous forms of intuition, Schopenhauer makes a fundamental revision in Kant's epistemology, which separated a priori sensuous forms of intuition (space and time) from categories of the understanding (causality being one of the twelve). Through their transcendental deduction, the categories guarantee the objectivity of knowledge for Kant. For Schopenhauer, on the other hand, causation as a form of intuition that proceeds from the body is present equally in humans and animals (Schopenhauer 1969, vol. I, p. 21). These forms constitute a screen, a "Veil of Maja" (this Hindu term is used as early as Schopenhauer 1969, vol. I, p. 8) that is placed between "the world inside my head and the world outside my head" (Schopenhauer 1969, vol. II, p. 3). The world of representation thus lacks true objectivity ("the world is *my* representation"): "if it [causality] is a priori given, as Kant has more correctly taught us, then it is of *subjective* origin, and then it is clear that we always remain in the *subjective*" (Schopenhauer 1969, vol. II, p. 11). Due to this focus on non-discursive, receptive intuition, Schopenhauer views Kant on a continuum with the English empiricists (Schopenhauer 1969, vol. II, pp. 11f). The elevation of intuition is also coordinate with the subsidiary role that both understanding and reason play for Schopenhauer, in both experience and philosophy. Schopenhauer summarizes this in chapter 7 of Volume II of *The World as Will and Representation* (Schopenhauer 1969, vol. II, p. 72), "Of the Relationship of Intuitive to Abstract knowledge":

> To intuit, to let the things themselves speak to us, apprehend new relationships among them, only afterward to deposit and store this all in concepts in order to possess it securely: this yields new knowledge. . . . The inmost core of every genuine and

actual knowledge is an intuition, every new truth is also the product of one. All originary thinking happens in images. [*Alles Urdenken geschieht in Bildern.*]

This last sentence, added in the third edition (and repeated, significantly, in the chapter on [artistic] genius), shows clearly the way in which this view of the relation of thought, intuition and knowledge leads to the apotheosis of art as "objective knowledge" in Book III (see Schopenhauer 1969, vol. I, pp. 184ff). Its denial of the spontaneity of reason and understanding will clearly entail the impotence of reason as a force against the passions or as a source of goals for action.

## III

According to the famous chapter 17 of the second volume of *The World as Will and Representation*, "On the Metaphysical Need of Man": "Only to thoughtless beasts do the world and existence seem to be self-understood. For human beings, on the other hand, they are a problem" (Schopenhauer 1969, vol. II, p. 171), and this problem leads beyond investigations that follow the principle of sufficient reason, beyond the knowledge we share with animals, to metaphysics, which attempts to solve the "riddle of existence" by discovering "the correct, universal understanding [*Verständnis*] of experience itself, the true interpretation of its sense and content. This is the metaphysical" (Schopenhauer 1969, vol. II, p. 183). The image of experience as a riddle or cipher whose meaning needs interpreting, and whose solution is the thing-in-itself, indicates Schopenhauer's attempt to construct an "immanent metaphysics" that does not violate the Kantian strictures against "transcendent speculation" (see Schopenhauer 1969, vol. I, Appendix, pp. 426–8). It also indicates the "anthropological" turn characteristic of Schopenhauer. He may lay claim to be the originator of the "metaphysics of meaning" since, according to him, the concern for the metaphysical is neither for the being of beings nor for the indubitable foundation of knowledge, but for the meaning of an otherwise phantom-like existence (Schopenhauer 1969, vol. I, pp. 98f, 119; see Simmel 1988, p. 5). Schopenhauer claims that he has discovered the answer to this riddle by avoiding two traditional errors, the rationalist's error of identifying being and thinking and the dogmatist's error of identifying an (external) appearance with the thing-in-itself. Contra rationalism, Schopenhauer offers an "inverse proportionality of knowability and genuine reality":

> The more necessity that knowledge bears along with it . . . the clearer and more sufficient it is, the less pure objective content it has or the less genuine reality is given to it. And on the other hand, the more that must be grasped in it as purely contingent, the more that impresses itself upon us as merely empirically given, the more genuinely objective and true reality there is in such knowledge.   (Schopenhauer 1969, vol. I, p. 122)

In asserting the "primacy of will over self-consciousness" and denying the hegemony of consciousness, Schopenhauer believes he is reversing millennia of philosophical presumption that set knowledge, a mere tool of the will, over the will. He does not mention such characterizations, of which Hume's is only the clearest, that "reason is, and ought only to be the slave of the passions, and can never pretend to any other office than to serve and obey them." As for the metaphysical elevation of the will, it is certainly anticipated, if not independently articulated, in Schelling's *Abhandlung Über das Wesen der menschlichen Freiheit* (1809), with its assertion that "Willing is primordial being [*Wollen ist Urseyn*], and all predicates of the latter belong solely to it: groundlessness, eternity, independence of time, self-affirmation. The whole of philosophy strives for nothing but the discovery of this supreme expression." Schopenhauer was well acquainted with this essay before writing *The World as Will and Representation*. He mentions this passage, only as something quoted by critics interested in the "question of priority," in the *Parerga* (1851), *Fragments on the History of Philosophy*, where he characterizes it as a mere "foreshadowing of my doctrine, without consequence, connection and execution" (Schopenhauer 1974b, vol. I, p. 132).

In contrast to the dogmatist, Schopenhauer claims to have taken a "pathway from the inside," in which we are able to become "immediately acquainted" with our will as that groundless "thing-in-itself" (Schopenhauer 1969, vol. II, p. 196; vol. I, pp. 100, 111), the animating essence, first of my body, which is its immediate objecthood (*Objektität*), and then the essence of all representations (Schopenhauer explains the distinction between objecthood [*Objektität*] – as inherent in the objects themselves – and objectivity [*Objektivität*] – as a matter of judgment – in Schopenhauer 1988, vol. I, no. 286 [1814]). The immediacy of my acquaintance with my will allows me to identify it as thing-in-itself without fear of the deception inherent in other such (dogmatic) assertions.

Just as the will as thing-in-itself is not subject to the principle of sufficient reason and is thus groundless and unfathomable, so is it independent of the forms of space and time, which are now, in the discussion of the will (Book II), characterized by Schopenhauer as the *principium individuationis* (principle of individuation). The two negative characteristics: groundlessness and independence of the principium individuationis, permit Schopenhauer to assert two crucial elements of the will as thing-in-itself: its unity and purposelessness. Not subject to the *principium individuationis* the will is one, something like the metaphysical One of Parmenides, Plato, and the neo-Platonists (see Schopenhauer 1969, vol. I, pp. 129f). Secondly, Schopenhauer interprets the groundlessness of the will as entailing its inaccessibility to any purpose: no answer can be given to the question "why we will," so that "absence of any goal, of any limits belongs to the essence of the will in itself." It is only at this point that the stage is set for Schopenhauer's "pessimism," a term today inextricably associated with his philosophy and which becomes central in his works only with the *Parerga* of 1851 and the third edition (1859) of *The World as Will and Representation* (see Hübscher 1989, pp. 257ff). The will as that which initiates and impels action in living beings, as that which resists penetration in inorganic nature and which maintains itself in motion and life in all beings, is goal- and purposeless. From the infinite and goalless motion of the heavens to the plant and animal and human world, the will is a "blind pressure [*Drang*], a dark, dull driving force

[*Treiben*] . . . striving deprived of knowledge [*erkenntnisloses Streben*]" (Schopenhauer 1969, vol. I, p. 149), and as such cannot reach satisfaction: having no goal, it has no end, and without either, it has no purpose. But that such restless activity is an evil is only clear once the unitary essence of the will is recalled. The striving of the manifold of living things to maintain and augment themselves in life, the "will to life," is then seen not merely as purposeless, but as self-defeating, since it is the one will that is at odds with itself and attempts to take its satisfaction by doing violence to itself. In a passage added to the third edition, Schopenhauer writes that "the will must consume itself because nothing exists other than it and it is a hungry will." It is only a short step from the dual assertion of the will as an endless striving and the will as a self-divided and self-consuming entity, to the final assertion, echoed by Freud in *Beyond the Pleasure Principle*, that "death" is the "genuine result and to that degree the purpose of life" (Schopenhauer 1974b, vol. I, p. 223: "Transcendent Speculation on the Apparent Purposiveness in the Destiny of the Individual"; see also vol. II, p. 637. See Freud 1955b and the remark in Freud 1964).

## IV

In turning from knowledge and will in their empirical manifestations to a "second consideration" of each, independent of the principle of sufficient reason, or in turning from the "empirical consciousness" to the "better consciousness," Schopenhauer must also turn away from Kant, for whom knowledge that was independent of these a priori conditions of the possibility of experience was impossible. It is thus not surprising that at the beginning of Book III of *The World as Will and Representation* Schopenhauer speaks of the fundamental identity of Kant and Plato (Schopenhauer 1969, vol. I, p. 170). In one of his early "marginalia to Kant," Schopenhauer had observed that "it is perhaps the best expression of Kant's inadequacy if one says that he was unacquainted with contemplation," and he notes the complementarity of the "negative insight" of Kant and the positive, intuitive knowledge of Plato (Schopenhauer 1988, vol. I, no. 17). Having given content to the necessarily formal Kantian conception of the thing-in-itself, Schopenhauer proceeds to fill in the chasm that separates it and its appearances with the "(Platonic) idea," the "immediate and hence adequate objecthood of the thing-in-itself" that is independent of the conditions of space, time, and causality and is determined as an object merely by the presence of a subject of knowledge opposed to it (Schopenhauer 1969, vol. I, p. 175). The Schopenhauerian system thus takes on a decidedly neo-Platonic structure, with its ineffable One "thing-in-itself," its many (Platonic) ideas, and its indefinite individual appearances. (Cf. Plato, *Philebus*, 15bff, a passage quoted at the beginning of Schopenhauer's dissertation as giving Plato's "rule for the method of all philosophizing." See also Schopenhauer 1969, vol. I, pp. 63f, 82.) Correlative to the object released from its empirical conditions is the subject of such knowledge, the "better consciousness" of Schopenhauer's notebooks (cf. Schopenhauer 1988, vol. I, no. 86), a "pure subject" no longer determined by the will and its search for causes that will be useful for the satisfaction of its needs. Once one discards concepts of reason and gives "the whole power of one's spirit over to intuition," one's "whole consciousness is filled by the calm contemplation of the natural object present." Having "totally lost oneself in this object," i.e. having forgotten one's will, the subject remains "only as pure subject, as clear mirror of the object," the "pure, will-less, painless, timeless *subject of knowledge*" (Schopenhauer 1969, vol. I, p. 179), the "eternal world-eye" (Schopenhauer 1969, vol. II, p.371). The object of contemplation that was "veiled" by the "forms" of intuition in science is liberated in such "artistic intuition." It is thus the artistic genius, that human being capable of such contemplation, rather than the scientist, who merely pursues the relations constituted by the subjective forms of intuition in the pragmatic service of the will, who is the one able to apprehend and present the world in its true objectivity. Art

> repeats the eternal ideas apprehended in pure contemplation, what is essential and enduring in all the appearances of the world. . . . Its sole origin is knowledge of the ideas; its sole goal the communication of this knowledge. (Schopenhauer 1969, vol. I, pp. 184ff)

Such contemplation involves a two-fold paradox, both epistemological and metaphysical. In the first place, it is a knowledge that is devoid of all forms of intuition (and *a fortiori*, concepts, for Schopenhauer). Given Schopenhauer's sympathy for the English empiricists, one might hazard that it is the Schopenhauerian equivalent of "knowledge by acquaintance." Metaphysically, the pure subject is "will-less," and yet the will is the "thing-in-itself." The genius, then, is at odds with the very ground of being. This has several significant consequences. First, because the self-consuming will is the ground of suffering, the genial moment, in the artist as well as the audience, is a moment of unmixed and supreme pleasure, which is fundamentally negative for Schopenhauer, a release from pain. (This analysis of pleasure is also, significantly, a Platonic one, and the images he uses, e.g. the sieve of the Danaids, is Platonic as well.) Released from the will, we experience the "state of the gods. For that moment we are released from the harsh pressure of the will, we celebrate the sabbath of the penal servitude of willing" (Schopenhauer 1969, vol. I, p. 196). Secondly, since the aesthetic intuition involves a turn away from the shared reality of appearance and its spatio-temporal, causal relations as well as from the insistent reality of the will, genius is akin to madness (Schopenhauer 1969, vol. I, pp. 196ff; vol. II, pp. 386ff). Finally, the aesthetic pleasure is of necessity temporary, since alienation from the ground of being, or "knowledge turning against will," cannot be sustained (Schopenhauer 1969, vol. I, p. 321) without a turn against life itself, that is, without the artist becoming a saint. And it is just for that reason that art, particularly in its highest (discursive) form, tragedy, functions as a "quietive of the will" that leads to resignation and the renunciation "not merely of life, but of the whole will to life," introducing us to the problematic that forms the climax of Schopenhauer's philosophy: the affirmation or negation of the will to life itself.

146

# V

In a note written at the age of twenty (1808–9), Schopenhauer asks: "If we take the few moments of religion, art and pure love from life, what remains but a series of trivial thoughts?" (Schopenhauer 1988, vol. I, nos 12 [8]). Art as the contemplation of Ideas, the pure love that is pity and the human good, and the godless religion of renunciation are the subjects of the last two books of *The World as Will and Representation*, relieved as they both are of the "trivial" concerns of the "empirical consciousness" in favor of those of the "better consciousness." The intermittency of the contemplative state and the insubstantiality of Schopenhauer's "Platonic Ideas" lead us from art to the Fourth Book's twin themes of love and renunciation. At this climax, the various threads of Schopenhauer's philosophy are brought together, animated by fundamentally ethical concerns. Here, Schopenhauer answers both the particular ethical question of what constitutes goodness in human action and behavior, and the larger, most properly religious question of "the worth or worthlessness of . . . existence" (Schopenhauer 1969, vol. I, p. 271). Goodness is the love that is pity [*Mitleid*] (Schopenhauer 1969, vol. I, p. 375), the negation of the will's egoism determined by an understanding of and involvement in the suffering of all creatures. This leads to the ultimate question of the value of the "will to life". Since "essentially *all life is suffering*" [*Leiden*] (Schopenhauer 1969, vol. I, p. 310), and since the only way to diminish this suffering is to renounce one's own particular will to life by renouncing one's attachment to one's own self (love as pity), then life itself, and its metaphyscial principle, the will to life, must also be valueless, and "ought not to be." Such a renunciation of the will to life does not entail suicide of the individual, which is in fact the affirmation of life and the will, since here it is the individual will that exercises itself on a disappointing existence. It rather involves an ascetic withdrawal from active participation in and appreciation of the pleasures of life, as exemplified by the sexual desire, or physiologically the genitals, according to Schopenhauer "the focus of the will" (Schopenhauer 1969, vol. I, p. 330; vol. II, p. 394). Such asceticism ultimately leads to a withdrawal from life itself. The final stage of human goodness is thus "saintliness": or "holiness" [*Heiligkeit*] and "the inner essence of saintliness, self-denial, mortification of willfulness [*Eigenwille*], *askesis* . . . [is] negation of the will to life" (Schopenhauer 1969, vol. I, §58, S. 520).

> The greatest, most important and significant appearance which the world can display is not he who has conquered the world, but he who has overcome the world, thus in fact nothing other than the quiet and unnoticed way of life of such a man in whom that knowledge [of the unity of the will] has dawned.   (Schopenhauer 1969, vol. I, p. 386)

Finally, and despite Schopenhauer's express atheism and his characterization of traditional philosophy as a mere cover for theological speculation (in, for example, the Preface to "On the Will in Nature"), philosophy must nevertheless give way to religion if its ultimately self-contradictory and negative teaching is to have any content. As the epistemic emptiness of sensuous reason must be supplemented by the Platonic ideas of art, so the inevitable formalism of reason must be supplemented by the visions of the mystics of Christianity and the Eastern religions, whose intuitions function as evidence for the truth of Schopenhauer's teaching (Schopenhauer 1969, vol. II, p. 610). This mystical apprehension at the peak of godless reflection is one of the most striking points of contact between Schopenhauer, Nietzsche, and Wittgenstein (see Clegg 1978, p. 45).

But if the interconnection of the various strands of Schopenhauer's analysis is clear, the mechanism of the negation of the will to life is less so. The subtitle of the Fourth Book, the "Second Consideration of the World as Will," is instructive in this regard: "Upon Attaining Self-Knowledge, Affirmation and Negation of the Will to Life." Since, as we have noted, the will, through violence (suicide) cannot negate itself, the negation of the will to life must come about through something else: namely, knowledge. The will comes to know its own nullity, either through an insight into the subjective source of individuation, or through the experience of suffering. Yet, owing to the essential weakness of the intellect and its subordination to the will, it is only the very few whose intellect can see through the will (Schopenhauer 1969, vol. I, p. 392). For the majority, then, it is the second case, the experience of suffering, that may lead to insight into the will's nullity. For them,

the final mystery of life has been revealed in the excess of pain, that woe and evil, suffering and hatred, the tormented and the tormenter, however different they appear in the knowledge that follows the principle of sufficient reason, are in themselves *one*, appearances of the one will to life that objectifies its conflict with itself by means of the *principium individuationis*.   (Schopenhauer 1969, vol. I, p. 394)

It is only when the will, through such knowledge of itself, however attained, sees its own self-contradiction and turns away from itself, that the true self-negation of the will and the destruction of the will to life itself, as manifested in that individual, can be said to occur. This "self-negation of the will" involves Schopenhauer in affirming two events that deeply contradict his general teaching: the "identity of the subject of knowing and the subject of willing," and the advent of freedom of the will, the choice of self-renunciation, in the strictly deterministic realm of appearances (see Rethy 1986–7, pp. 366ff). Knowledge in its empirical state cannot escape from the duality of subject–object, and this is the grounds of the criticism of Fichte's philosophy (see Weimer 1982, pp. 37ff); the will, considered "according to the principle of sufficient reason," or in its phenomenality, is totally determined (see "On the Freedom of the Will," pp. 27ff). At its peak, however, Schopenhauer's philosophy must accept precisely these two "miracles," cornerstones of the post-Kantians he rejected so harshly: the binding miracle (the miracle κατ'ἐξοχήν of the unity of the self grasped in self-consciousness, and the dissolving miracle of the advent of freedom in the realm of necessity (Schopenhauer 1969, vol. I, pp. 288, 395), the two transcendent characteristics of the notebooks' "better consciousness" (see Schopenhauer 1988, vol. I, nos 274, 278 [1814].) Beyond the determined and determinate realm of objects and its complement of subjects, the newly unified, transparent and self-determining self floats free, into a nothingness that is merely its invisibility to the dull eyes of embodied, impulsive men.

> We freely admit it. What remains after complete destruction [*Aufhebung*] of the will is, for all those who are still full of the will, certainly nothing. But on the contrary for those in whom the will has turned and negated itself, this our so very real world with all its suns and galaxies, is – nothing.   (Schopenhauer 1969, vol. I, pp. 411f)

## VI

There is no philosopher for whom the disparity between influence and academic reputation is as great as it is for Schopenhauer. It is possible that the almost proverbial contradictoriness of Schopenhauer's philosophy (see Hübscher 1989, pp. 379ff) has something to do with its easy dismissal, as well as the harshness of his polemic against "academic philosophy" (see "On University Philosophy" in *Parerga and Paralipomena*, vol. I). Today, too, his undeniable misogyny (memorialized in another infamous essay of the *Parerga*, vol. I, "On Women") and the anti-Semitism for which his name became a by-word in the nineteenth century (see Nietzsche's comments in *Gay Science*, aphorism number 99) are certainly unappealing elements as well. It is nevertheless striking that many of the founders of modernity in its contemporary guise, from Wagner in music and Mann and Proust in literature to Nietzsche and Wittgenstein in philosophy to Freud in psychiatry, owe their deepest intellectual debts to Schopenhauer or, in Freud's case, found themselves uncannily anticipated by him. The connection with Wagner is indisputable (see Magee 1983, pp. 326–78). In fact, the themes of the last two books of *The World as Will and Representation*: art, love, and renunciation, read almost as subtitles to Wagner's last three operas. Wagner's attraction to Schopenhauer, and especially his epoch-making theory of music, which elevates it above all the other arts, as imaging, not the (formal) ideas but the (formless) thing-in-itself, the will (Schopenhauer 1969, vol. I, p. 257), is not hard to understand, and Schopenhauer's theory of music had an important influence, not merely on other composers, but on Nietzsche (in *The Birth of Tragedy*: see Rethy 1988, pp. 14–36), Mann (for Mann's indebtedness to Schopenhauer, see his essay "Schopenhauer" [1938], reprinted in Mann 1947, pp. 372–410), and Proust (in his accounts of the Vinteuil Sonatas and Septuor: see Beckett 1958, pp. 70–2; and on Beckett–Proust, see O'Hara 1988, pp. 273–92). It is not surprising that so many and such significant artists should have found themselves influenced by Schopenhauer (and we have just scratched the surface here: see Magee 1983, p. 379) since, as Thomas Mann says, "the philosophy of Arthur Schopenhauer has always been regarded as pre-eminently creative, as an artist-philosophy *par excellence*" (Mann 1947, p. 373). The artist is not necessarily bothered by the glaring inconsistency in Schopenhauer's theory of music (which delights *as* image of the terrible will), is honored by the Schopenhauerian elevation of the artist over the scientist and of intuition over reason, and is stimulated by the vigor and passion of Schopenhauer's presentation.

More striking is the fact that three of the great intellectual revolutionaries who helped shape twentieth-century thought were more deeply influenced, or in Freud's case, anticipated, by the (Restorationist) Schopenhauer than by any other philosopher. Although at one time the relation of Wittgenstein and Schopenhauer had forcibly to be brought to the attention of his rather incredulous disciples, for whom the history of philosophy, and certainly German metaphysics, held nothing positive, today, the fact of Schopenhauer's influence on Wittgenstein, particularly the latter portions of the *Notebooks* and the *Tractatus Logico-Philosophicus*, is beyond dispute, although its extent and significance are still a matter of controversy (see Janaway 1989, pp. 317–42).

Things are rather different with Nietzsche. The influence of Schopenhauer upon Nietzsche is too wide-ranging and all-encompassing to be treated with any adequacy in this space. An ardent disciple in his early works, despite specific differences in, for example, *The Birth of Tragedy*, he wrote a homage to Schopenhauer as "the philosopher," *Schopenhauer as Educator* (1875), and if his later works are sharply critical of Schopenhauer as exemplification of the nihilism of Western philosophy, his own philosophical coinages, e.g. "the will to power," the "eternal return of the same" as the "supreme affirmation," bear the unmistakable stamp of a constant regard for Schopenhauerian terms, as does the whole problematic of *Toward the Genealogy of Morals*, culminating as it does in the question of the meaning of ascetic ideals, the Schopenhauerian ideal of "saintliness." It is fair to say that it is impossible correctly to understand Nietzsche without an understanding of Schopenhauer, the only philosopher whose complete writings he read, and to whom he is indebted for his whole conception of the history of philosophy. The fact that relatively little attention has been paid in recent years to Schopenhauer's continuing influence on Nietzsche is probably due to Heidegger's comments in his Nietzsche book – originally published in 1961 but based on lectures delivered in 1936 – which turn attention away from Schopenhauer to Schelling and Hegel as the true sources of the conception of the will to which Nietzsche (misled, according to Heidegger, by Schopenhauer's perfidy) is "truly" indebted. This has led many to reject Nietzsche's true – if in their minds humble – philosophical predecessor in favor of grander, if false, relations. (There is some evidence that this situation is changing; see Blondel 1991.)

Perhaps the strangest case is that of Freud. Although Freud claims not to have read Schopenhauer's main work, nor to have realized its congruence with his own until after it was pointed out to him by Otto Rank in 1911, the parallels between the two are uncanny, and were noted by Freud himself (see Freud 1957, 1955a). The Schopenhauerian anticipation of the unconscious and the Freudian "id" in the will, of the ubiquity (and unconsciousness) of the sexual motive in human action (see Schopenhauer 1969, vol. II, pp. 513–16), as well as the conception of the weak yet not powerless ego or "intellect," along with the similarity in their (negative) conceptions of pleasure and hence their agreement about the connection of happiness and death (Freud's death instinct, Schopenhauer's "negation of the will to life"), as well as Schopenhauer's own anticipation of the Freudian theory of repression (Schopenhauer 1969, vol. II, pp. 400f) point to their striking agreement. And yet, no monograph has been written on this generally known, but highly underestimated relation. (See Thomas Mann (1936) in Mann 1947, pp. 415–19; also Brandell 1979.)

Completeness would demand that mention, at least, be made not only of other philosophers, such as Bergson, but also of historians and social philosophers like Jacob Burckhardt and Max Horkheimer. Horkheimer's conversion from left-wing activist to conservative Schopenhauerian pessimist (see Horkheimer 1980) might be said to have heralded the decline of European Marxism, a function performed by Schopenhauer a second time, more than one hundred years after the abortive Revolutions of 1848. Horkheimer's position is even more relevant thirty-five years later. Our current social and political, as well as intellectual condition can only be clearly comprehended if the often unmentioned, but ever-present role of Schopenhauer is understood. It may be that an account of the character, contradictions, and the impasses of our age can best be undertaken through an examination of the attactions, contradictions, and impasses of his thought.

## Writings

Schopenhauer, A.: *On the Freedom of the Will*, tr. Konstantin Kolenda (Indianapolis–New York: Bobbs Merrill, 1960).

——: *The World as Will and Representation*, tr. E. F. J. Payne, 2 volumes (New York: Dover, 1969). (All translations in the text are the author's, but references are to the pagination of this generally fine translator's editions.)

——: *On the Fourfold Root of the Principle of Sufficient Reason*, tr. E. F. J. Payne (La Salle, IL: Open Court Press, 1974a).

——: *Parerga and Paralipomenta*, tr. E. F. J. Payne, 2 volumes (Oxford: Clarendon Press, 1974b).

——: *Manuscript Remains in Four Volumes*, tr. E. F. J. Payne (London–New York–Hamburg: Berg Publishers, 1988); vol. I: *Early Manuscripts, 1804–1818* (references to vol. I are by note number); vol. II: *Critical Debates, 1809–1818*.

## References and further reading

Beckett, Samuel: *Proust* (New York: Grove Press, 1958).

Blondel, Eric: *Nietzsche: Philosophy as a Philological Genealogy*, tr. Seán Hand (London: Athlone Press, 1991; Stanford, CA: Stanford University Press, 1991). (The discussions of Nietzsche's relation to Schopenhauer are particluarly valuable.)

Brandell, Gunnar: *Freud: A Man of His Century*, tr. Iain White (Sussex: Harvester Press/ Atlantic Highlands, NJ: Humanities Press, 1979).

Clegg, J. S.: "Logical Mysticism and the Cultural Setting of Wittgenstein's *Tractatus*," *Schopenhauer Jahrbuch*, 59 (1978), pp. 29–47.

Freud, Sigmund: *The Complete Psychological Works of Sigmund Freud* (London: Hogarth Press); vol. xvii: *A Difficulty in the Path of Psycho-Analysis* (1917; 1955a); vol. xviii: *Beyond the Pleasure Principle* (1920; 1955b); vol. xiv: *History of the Psychoanalytical Movement* (1914; 1957); vol. xxii: *New Introductory Lectures on Psycho-Analysis* (1933; 1964).

Heidegger, Martin: *Nietzsche*, 2 vols, tr. David Farrell Krell (San Francisco, CA: Harper & Row, 1991).

Horkheimer, Max: "Schopenhauer Today," in Michael Fox, *Schopenhauer: His Philosophical*

*Achievement* (Sussex: Harvester Press/New Jersey: Barnes & Noble Books, 1980), pp. 20–33. (The only translated essay (originally published in 1960) of four contributions to the *Schopenhauer Jahrbuch* made by the erstwhile member of the Frankfurt School between 1955 and 1971.)

Hübscher, Arthur: *The Philosophy of Schopenhauer in its Intellectual Context: Thinker Against the Tide*, tr. Joachim Baer and David E. Cartwright (Lewston, NY: Edwin Mellon Press, 1989). (A valuable testament of the great editor and biographer, whose appearance in English should be welcomed.)

Hume, David: *A Treatise of Human Nature* [1739], ed. L. A. Selby-Bigge (Oxford: Clarendon Press, 1967).

Janaway, Christopher: *Self and World in Schopenhauer's Philosophy* (Oxford: Clarendon Press, 1989). (Perhaps the best-informed full-length work on Schopenhauer written in English.)

——: "Nietzsche, the Self, and Schopenhauer," in *Nietzsche and Modern German Thought*, ed. Keith Ansell-Pearson (London and New York: Routledge, 1991), pp. 119–42.

Magee, Brian: *The Philosophy of Schopenhauer* (Oxford: Clarendon Press, 1983).

Mann, Thomas: "Freud and the Future" (1936); "Schopenhuaer" (1938), in *Essays of Three Decades* (New York: Alfred A. Knopf, 1947).

Nietzsche, Friedrich: *Kritische Gesamtausgabe Werke*, ed. G. Colli and M. Montinari (Berlin: de Gruyter, 1967).

O'Hara, J. D.: "Beckett's Schopenhauerian Reading of Proust," in Eric von der Luft (ed.), *Schopenhauer: New Essays in Honor of His 200th Birthday* (Lewston, NY: Edwin Mellon Press, 1988).

Rethy, Robert: "The Metaphysics of Nullity," *Philosophy Research Archives*, vol. XII (1986–7), pp. 367–86.

——: "The Tragic Affirmation of the *Birth of Tragedy*," in *Nietzsche Studien*, 17 (1988), pp. 1–44.

Safranski, Rüdiger: *Schopenhauer and the Wild Years of Philosophy*, tr. Ewald Osers (Cambridge, MA: Harvard University Press, 1990). (A stimulating intellectual biography whose presence in English is a surprise and a delight.)

Schelling, F. W. J.: *Abhandlung Über das Wesen der menschlichen Freiheit* (1809), in *Friedrich Wilhelm Joseph von Schellings sämmtliche Werke* (Stuttgart and Augsburg: J. G. Cotta'sher Verlag, Abt. I/7), pp. 331–416.

Simmel, George: *Schopenhauer and Nietzsche*, tr. Helmut Loiskandl, Deena Weinstein, and Michael Weinstein (Amherst: University of Massachusetts Press, 1988).

Weimer, Wolfgang: *Schopenhauer* (Darmstadt: Wissenschaftliche Buchgesellschaft, 1982).

Zint, Hans: "Schopenhauers Philosophie des doppelten Bewußtseins," in *Schopenhauer als Erlebnis* (Munich–Basle: Ernst Reinhardt Verlag, 1954).

# 11

# Nietzsche

## CHARLES E. SCOTT

### Nietzsche's legacy

We can appreciate the strength of Friedrich Nietzsche's thought in the transformation of many of the ideas and values that have formed our Western heritage. This
strength is figured in part by the questions that Nietzsche generated concerning
traditional concepts of reason, nature, God, time, religion, memory, and morality.
Hans-Georg GADAMER (see Article 38), a leading continental philosopher speaking
when he was ninety years old, remarked that an entire generation of thinkers and
artists in early twentieth-century Europe found in Nietzsche's writings their entry
into the ideas and images that incited their creative work. These writers range from
Karl JASPERS (Article 17) and Jean-Paul SARTRE (Article 21) to Thomas Mann, Nikos
Kazantzakis, and Maurice BLANCHOT (Article 25). Martin HEIDEGGER (Article 18),
Michel FOUCAULT (Article 49), Gilles DELEUZE (Article 51), Jacques DERRIDA (Article 50),
and Luce IRIGARAY (Article 54) are among those continental philosophers who have
been considerably influenced by Nietzsche and who have considerably influenced
contemporary readings of Nietzsche. In England and the United States his work
gained gradual acceptance particularly after the Second World War and after people came to understand that the use of his writings by the Third Reich in Germany
constituted a shameless perversion of his thought. German National Socialism's
interpretation of Nietzsche's philosophy constituted a most flagrant of many misreadings of him. But his influence has been amplified by other misreadings in
addition to many careful interpretations of his thought. His thought has been seen
as a species of process metaphysics and compared to that of Bergson, Whitehead,
and neo-Darwinians. He has been read as an ethicist and as a strange theologian
who replaced God as He is traditionally conceived with the will to power. His
philosophy is frequently presented as nihilistic, as a body of beliefs and observations
that leaves us with nothing to affirm and nothing to support hope and confidence
for living.

We shall see, however, that Nietzsche is not a metaphysician, ethicist, theologian, or nihilist in any usual senses of those words. The force of his thought, rather,
is found in the manner in which it turns through and beyond the values, ideas, and
nihilism that formed his religious, moral, and philosophical tradition (and hence
formed his own actions and beliefs). In that turning he opened up a way of thinking
and valuing that grows out of the transformation process itself. His way of thinking
is formed and empowered by the transvaluing processes that develop through his

153

critical encounter with the ideas and values that are central in our traditional western culture. As we follow that turning in his thought we discover that we lose the possibility of claiming that his work constitutes a definitive origin for proper contemporary continental thought and find instead that we can follow him best in learning how to turn through his thinking to ideas and values that are outside of his perview. His work requires for its understanding the loss of the authority and value that would accrue to it were he considered to be the founder of a philosophical movement.

In order to elaborate his thinking I shall consider a number of his leading ideas and show how those ideas require their own transvaluation. The best way to learn from him is to engage his thought thoroughly enough to be able to follow its process of self-overcoming. This dynamic of self-overcoming brings one face to face with both Nietzsche's philosophy and his philosophical legacy. His philosophy is not constituted primarily by a group of ideas which are to be taken literally and defended, amended, contrasted, and, in their "best" formulation, advocated. Rather his philosophy is a process of self-overcoming in which the western experience of identity is transformed and in which the priority of "difference" and "differing" replaces the priority of clarification, identification, and reconciliation for thought. The priority that is frequently given to home and homeland also withers in his thought, and with that withering the importance of the hero, national ethos, and permanent presence begin to fall away.

## The performative dimension of Nietzsche's thought: self-overcoming and the will to power

In order to consider the manner in which Nietzsche puts in question the idea of essence, I shall begin with an interpretation that claims that his thought is essentialist.

One might interpret Nietzsche as saying that the essence of life is will to power. He often writes that will to power is a continuing force throughout all transformations. *Will to power* can be read in his work as synonymous with *life*. To complement his claims about will to power, he seeks to construct an order of values on the basis of their comparative forces, their valencies. Will is the force of creation, liberation, and self-affirmation. Knowledge and truth are kinds of willing, he says, and the value of knowledges as well as of truths is found in their force of will and their energy for creation, not in their correspondence to reality or their accuracy of judgment. Will is the basis for moralities, and it is beyond good and evil. His thought is thus organized around conceptions of will and will power which are not primarily human realities. Will to power constitutes the force of nature of which human volition and energy are parts. Physics, for example, according to Nietzsche is properly a science of the will to power. He thus seems to be making claims about the nature of things, claims that sound quasi-theological in contrast to other claims that say, for instance, that the human will is founded in and reflects the act of a loving God or that life is a movement toward final reconciliation of its own destructive conflicts or that life is essentially reasonable.

154

I shall suggest that Nietzsche's genealogical way of approaching traditions emphasizes the construction and psychology of morality, religion, and philosophy. They are kinds of practice and knowledge that are historical, imaginative, and contingent in their historical development. Moreover these descriptive claims also apply to Nietzsche's own work – indeed, they apply to themselves. This elaboration of his genealogical approach and the claims associated with it will add an important dimension to these observations. For now it is enough to show that the essentialist side of Nietzsche's thought must be seen as subordinate to his thought of self-overcoming and that his idea of will to power requires its own self-overcoming.

Self-overcoming is a process whereby one constellation of values is transformed into another one by means of powers and conflicts within the first constellation. Nietzsche finds, for example, in the values that emphasize the intelligibility of all beings or altruism and self-sacrifice, a strong even virulent will to power that is hidden within our rhetoric and knowledge and in the values' cultural lives (Nietzsche, *Thus Spoke Zarathustra*, Part II, Section 12, pp. 113ff). While rational neutrality or a primary concern for the other's welfare might appear to define these values, in fact they seek control, domination, and self-aggrandizing strength. Not only does a colonizing culture of both domination and self-delusion eventuate from such values, but also the will to power of these values makes possible Nietzsche's own conception of will to power. The self-overcoming, in Nietzsche's thought, of our dominant experiences of rationality and morality arises from the unacknowledged drive to power within our rationalities and moralities. The force of these movements is toward the formation of ideas and values that give emphasis to dominance, control, and self-enhancement in the guise of disinterestedness or altruism. Their force actually moves them away from the disinterestedness or altruism that they appear to support.

Further, Nietzsche makes the descriptive claim that self-overcoming characterizes the movement of will to power. In his perception of the combination of sacrifice and power in our rationalities and altruisms he is able to say that "life sacrifices itself – for power" (Nietzsche, *Thus Spoke Zarathustra*, Part II, Section 12, pp. 113ff). In the course of Nietzsche's developing this claim the Hebrew–Christian value of self-sacrifice in obedience to God turns into new formulations, and sacrifice occurs for the enhancement of life. That life, as will to power, lives for its own sake. Nietzsche thus claims that the meaning of self-sacrifice is self-enhancement (or selfishness). And in this overturning of moral and religious altruism he finds expressed and enhanced the non-moral, physical life that is sacrificed in the ascetic, spiritual intentions of the West's dominant moral traditions. Life – will to power – comes to the fore and is intensified in the self-overcoming (or, one could say, the self-sacrifice) or self-sacrificial values.

The idea and image of will to power do not require a foundational reality that transcends their own movement. In one of the most telling aspects of Nietzsche's thought, and one in which its performative dimension is clearest, the thought of will to power requires its own self-overcoming. "Whatever I create and however much I love it – soon I must oppose it and my love . . . verily my will to power walks also on the heels of your will to truth" (ibid., p. 112) The *must* in this quota-

155

tion arises from the movement of self-overcoming that characterizes the will to power and with which the author seeks rational accord. The claim that Nietzsche's idea of will to power makes regarding itself is that it cannot remain in its formulation and remain fully alive. It must move through itself and beyond itself if it is "consistent" with itself – Nietzsche called this aspect of his thought dionysian (Nietzsche, *The Birth of Tragedy*, p. 176: "Attempt at Self-Criticism"). In other words, will to power cannot be conceived as the essence of life except in the ironic sense that its own overturning will show its power of life, its contingency, and its "truth."

One finds the performative movement of self-overcoming throughout Niezsche's thought of the 1880s. Throughout *Beyond Good and Evil*, for example, he allows in the same paragraph contradictory ideas to combine and yet remain unresolved and unreconciled. He thereby incites movements of opposition – small crises – in his paragraphs that show both the metaphysical elements in his thinking and a direction for overcoming those elements. As he thinks in such tensions, his thought becomes a continuous process which unsettles those structures of thought that make possible reasonably certain ideas and values and which also make possible one's thinking further in the uncertainty and critique that eventuates in the destructuring process. The forces for these crises arise from the opposition and contradiction that are hidden in the values, ideas, and beliefs that have traditionally presented themselves as clear and without destructive ambiguity.

## Genealogy and the ascetic ideal

Nietzsche's performative work plays an important role in his genealogical studies. For example, in his account of the western lineage of the ascetic ideal he identifies himself as an ascetic priest and sacrifices his own values to the process of self-overcoming that has been both promulgated and truncated by the ascetic ideal (Nietzsche, *On the Genealogy of Morals*, "Third Essay," pp. 97ff). His account of the ascetic ideal brings together much of his characteristic thought and also gives emphasis to part of his influence in the twentieth century by way of his critique of ascetic practice and thought. He finds this practice and thought throughout both our secular and religious traditions in the forms of abstractness, disembodied images of the human spirit, altruism, and above all, the search for transendent meaning that gives a stable basis for contingent life. His account also influences Continental thought because it offers a way of thinking that does not require transcendental grounds. We will consider the ascetic ideal in this section and turn to the processes of losing transcendental grounding in the following section.

For Nietzsche *ascetic* refers to disciplines and values of self-denial. The abstinence and disciplines on which Nietzsche focuses, in addition to the obedient, anti-sensual "angelic ones" of chastity, poverty, and humility, are those that either claim or assume noncontingent meaning for life, especially for suffering human life. His broad claim is that our knowledge and values have been developed largely in the desire to dominate life and death through giving them meaning that allegedly originates outside of the limits of mortality and the historical lineages of these values. The values that maintain transcendent meaning for life are accompanied by depreciation of our enjoying, suffering, dying bodies – their subsumption under values that presume that contingent life in its suffering, death, sensuousness, and lack of meaning is inferior to something that transcends it and is deathless. Our lives are to be sacrificed in order that we might find access to higher (i.e., death-less) life. Such sacrifice can occur through adopting values that emphasize the importance of the "soul," eternity, or altruistic love (as distinct from love based on one's own intensity and fullness of life), or meanings for life that are based on something other than mortal lives. (The preparation for this claim in Nietzsche's thought can be found in his early book *The Birth of Tragedy*, as well as in *Thus Spoke Zarathustra*. His fully developed ideas on the subject are in the Third Essay of *On the Genealogy of Morals*). In this will to dominate mortality, Nietzsche finds that the requirement that life have such meaning amounts to a destructive form of self-denial and life-denial. Our lives happen in their passage. We find our sameness in our sensuous, utterly physical desire to be, a desire that happens only under the conditions of momentary passage, loss, and affirmation. To affirm our lives in their own movements of coming to be and passing away requires "sacrificing" those meanings that are designed to hide from us our lives that are without transcendence of pleasure, suffering, and death. The way to such affirmation is the self-sacrifice (or self-overcoming) of the ascetic ideal.

The ascetic ideal on Nietzsche's account has had enormous force in the formation of our culture. Separation of mind and body, the ideal of clarity without ambiguity, the expectation of timeless, universal grounding for our "highest" values and beliefs, knowledge gained by methods of exact inference from specific occurrences, truth and goodness as values founded on foundations that transcend sensuality, interest, lineage, and death: such articulations of the ascetic ideal have constituted the warp and weft of our lives. Its force is felt in the perhaps unavoidable sense that our ability to love people and things and to affirm life depends on presence and meaning that transcend physical existence. For Nietzsche such sensibility constitutes a virulent and unconscious nihilism – a deeply ingrained denial of life in life's happening and an inability to affirm life in its (and our) own occurrence. Hence, the self-overcoming of the ascetic ideal is a passage through nihilism  – a radical transvaluation of western asceticism – toward an undetermined way of being that presumably will be created in the process of overcoming the nihilism of the ascetic ideal.

Nietzsche uses "Resentment" to name an unconscious feeling in people whose lives are controlled by life-denying values. It is the feeling that accompanies the nihilism of western thought and practice. By that word Nietzsche describes a predisposition torwards fear of the strength required to affirm life in its deathly ambiguity and constant danger. He includes in the word's meaning a predisposition to recognize various kinds of spiritual weaknesses as forms of strength. In such predispositions an individual lives in contradiction to his or her energy for life, which is an energy that is predisposed to affirm the power of life, its creativity, and its own continuous self-transformation. Resentment is the affective aspect of such an embodied contradiction.

157

Nietzsche calls "Free spirits" those people who now struggle to overcome their own resentment and to live in affirmation of their own self-overcoming. Some of Nietzsche's best and most influential work lies in his accounts of the free spirit (Nietzsche, *Beyond Good and Evil*, pp. 33ff).

"Genealogy" names the process whereby Nietzsche achieves a transvaluation of the ascetic ideal and brings to realization his own free spiritedness. His genealogy is a study of the lineages of moral practices, disciplined knowledges, and religious beliefs that have formed our recognition of sound methodology, truth, and proper behavior. By showing, for example, in the first chapter of *On the Genealogy of Morals* the connection between the activity of naming and the power of self-affirmation, Nietzsche shows also the intrinsic connection between the power of recognition and the power of life-affirmation or of life-denial. He shows in this book that our disciplines that provide certainty and common recognition of things and people are themselves the products of a subtle fear of life in its dangerous mortality and suffering. The self-overcoming of the ascetic ideal thus means the self-overcoming of our disciplines of knowledge and thought as well as the self-overcoming of our moral and religious practices. Since Nietzsche's genealogy in *On the Genealogy of Morals* shows itself to be within the ascetic lineage that it describes, we may expect a self-overcoming movement in his genealogical studies as those studies undercut the force and authority of the ascetic ideal. The undercutting takes place as the systematic principles of intellectual and moral endeavor are shown to include insights, interests, and emotions opposite to those that the endeavors promote. He shows, for example, that our western altruism is formed in fear of creative strength, terror before the meaninglessness of life, a resentment born of weakness in the face of strength, a reversal of life-promoting values (i.e., a deep nihilism), and protection of spiritual and physical weakness. As he uncovers this lineage of western disciplined effort, the authority of his own genealogical descriptions falls into question on its own terms. Its primary function of observation – the abstract cleanliness of such distance – its suggestion of life's continuing, unbroken, and thus seemingly timeless presence as force of will, its own attachment to the values that it so passionately opposes – such characteristics of genealogical research should raise questions as they develop a knowledge and presentation of the life-resisting character of the ascetic ideal. They also incite within genealogical knowledge interest in transforming the values that structure and animate this knowledge. Such transformation is initiated by the conflicts that constitute genealogical knowledge and that are exposed by it. In this sense, Nietzsche's genealogy of the ascetic ideal participates in the self-overcoming movement that it identifies in the value of self-denial in the name of something higher than the self's life. It performs the movement that it also identifies, and by this movement effects within its own text a process of self-transformation.

## The overman and eternal return

Nietzsche's thought of eternal return might be understood as a literal claim about the movement of time (see Nietzsche, *Thus Spoke Zarathustra*, Pt III, Section 3, pp.

158

155ff, and Section 13, pp. 215ff). He says that time moves in a circular manner, that events and all their detail are repeated eternally in their cycles. Destiny is found in infinite repetition. Nothing essentially changes. Hence, all metaphysical hope is illusory as well as eternally recurrent. On a literal reading, Nietzsche's statements are descriptive claims that are either accurate or inaccurate.

If, however, one gives emphasis to Nietzsche's own statements about truth, namely that truth and truths are values that humans develop and that express greater or lesser degrees of will to power and life-affirmation, one sees that no statement properly can be read only literally. Words and grammars are creations just as meanings and values are, and their occurrences are as marked by the loss of what is said as they are characterized by an imaginative creation of what is said. Truth is an imaginative and often powerful estimate of what "reality" is or ought to be.

Such Nietzschean claims mean that his own account is as much an estimate as all other knowledge and truth. His estimate is that his transvaluation of truth allows for a transformation of human being away from the ascetic ideal and toward a way of being that is free of the ascetic ideal's nihilism: a life that is beyond humanity as we know it and that, perhaps, is formed in a much greater appreciation for life than is now possible for humans. The overman is the name that Nietzsche gives such a way of being.

Eternal return is an image that interrupts and counters the ascetic ideal's bestowal of transcendent meaning on temporal events. To affirm eternal return in an understanding of truth as imaginative construct means in this case to give importance – a high estimate – to an image of time that has no ultimate purpose or meaning. Nietzsche says that to make such an affirmation throughout one's values, beliefs, and knowledge not only requires enormous effort but also takes an incalculable emotional toll. To live with no sense of ultimate meaning and with the sense that life's meanings arise as cultural images from no meaning at all and still to want to live in affirmation of life opposes western understanding of affirmation. Life-giving hope, love, and justice have required an ultimate justification in most segments of our tradition. To love unsparingly without further justification? To create for creation's sake? To feel genuine happiness while *accepting* the image of eternal return? Nietzsche thought that such questionable possibilities were beyond western humanity's capacity – perhaps beyond all humans' capacity.

And yet to learn at least the beginning steps of such affirmation suggested to Nietzsche a possibility for a kind of creature that is different from humans as we know them. This would be a being whose formation begins to develop in the trauma of losing the ways of life that the ascetic ideal has produced, i.e., it can begin with free spirits. It can also develop in such an interruption of the ascetic ideal as we find in his thought of eternal return. In such interruptions forces that are freed from the control of the ascetic ideal can begin to change the form and substance of our way of being. On this basis Nietzsche can speculate – he can create an image – that the overman's affirmations will not be dominated by self-denial and that the overman will love differently from the ways we are able to love. He guesses that the overman will not develop a knowledge that is dominated by judgment and hence by calculation, that a sense of play will replace the spirit of seriousness that is the overwhelming mood in a culture dominated by the ascetic ideal. Perhaps holding and keeping will be less important than is presently the case in our culture and psychology. Perhaps the overman will live with no sense of divinity, holiness, or transcendence of time. He or she would probably live without need of ritual, without the thoughts of will to power and eternal return, and without an effective memory of an era when events, if they were to be affirmed, needed a meaning other than that provided by their own passing, historical occurrences. The overman would be unaffected by the value and experience of God.

## The death of God

This phrase is the one for which Nietzsche is best known in popular culture. Nietzsche understood himself not to have caused God's death but rather to perceive that God had died in western cultural life, the only site where western divinity could have lived. God's life is measured by the degree to which the sense and image of God give creative energy and direction in human lives. Emphasis must fall on *creative*, because according to Nietzsche God does not live in repetitions, rituals of "remembrance", and reverence for texts that record what God has done. God's life is found in the creation of values and ways of life – for us, above all in the creation of western morality, religion, and philosophy – but not in the continuance of those creations. After the creation, there may well be inventiveness in adapting and refining the various values, practices, and thoughts. But when the power to inspire genuine creation moves elsewhere, God is dead. God's greatest feat was in the transvaluation of ancient Greek and Roman culture, inverting many of its values, and engendering a culture that saved people from a sense of cosmic meaninglessness. God served the ascetic priest well.

Now, however, our greatest threat is found in our satisfactions and loss of creative passion. Nietzsche calls us in our distance from God's creation the "last men." We are condemned by our values to perpetuate God's death, to live as though God were alive, and thus to transfer from one generation to the next ways of life that require no radical creation but only the perpetuation of modified versions of values that at one time had the power to transform the world.

Nietzsche's work is an effort to overcome such nihilism through the fragile energy for self-overcoming that remains in it. This overcoming requires individuals now to live in full self-awareness in the power of God's death and to redirect creative energy away from God and the ascetic ideal and toward other images that arise through the effort and process of self-overcoming. Nietzsche's hope rested with the creative artist. He thought that in the work of great artists the death of God could issue in another kind of life that would not be God's creation.

## Writings

Nietzsche, F.: *Thus Spoke Zarathustra*, tr. W. Kaufmann (New York: Penguin, 1966).
——: *The Birth of Tragedy*, tr. W. Kaufmann (New York: Vintage Books, 1967).

———: *"On the Genealogy of Morals" and "Ecce Home"*, tr. W. Kaufmann and R. S. Hollingdale (New York: Vintage Books, 1967).

———: *Beyond Good and Evil*, tr. W. Kaufmann (New York: Vintage Books, 1989).

## References and further readings

Allison, David B. (ed.): *The New Nietzsche, Contemporary Styles of Interpretation* (London: MIT Press, 1985).

Andreas-Salome, Lou: *Nietzsche* (New York: Gordon & Breach, 1970).

Deleuze, Gilles: *Nietzsche and Philosophy*, tr. Hugh Tomlinson (New York: Columbia University Press, 1983).

Derrida, Jacques: *Spurs: Nietzsche's Styles*, tr. Barbara Harlow (London/Chicago: University of Chicago Press, 1979).

Foucault, Michel: *Language, Counter-Memory, Practice*, tr. Donald F. Bouchard (Ithaca, NY: Cornell University Press, 1977).

Heidegger, Martin: *Nietzsche*, 4 vols; vol. 1: *The Will to Power as Art*, tr. D. F. Krell (New York: Harper & Row, 1979); vol. 2: *The External Recurrence of the Same*, tr. D. F. Krell (London: Harper & Row, 1984); vol. 3: *The Will to Power as Knowledge and as Metaphysics*, tr. Joan Stambaugh, D. F. Krell and F. A. Capuzzi (London: Harper & Row, 1987); vol. 4: *Nihilism*, tr. F. A. Capuzzi and D. F. Krell (London: Harper & Row, 1982).

Hollingdale, R. J.: *Nietzsche: The Man and his Philosophy* (London: Ark Paperbacks, 1985).

Irigaray, Luce: *Marine Lover of Friedrich Nietzsche*, tr. G. C. Gill (New York: Columbia University Press, 1991).

Jaspers, Karl: *Nietzsche: An Introduction to the Understanding of his Philosophical Activity* (Tucson, AZ: University of Arizona Press, 1965).

Kofman, Sarah: *Nietzsche and Metaphor*, tr. Duncan Large (Stanford, CA: Stanford University Press, 1993).

Krell, David Farrell: *Postponements, Women, Sensuality, and Death in Nietzsche* (Bloomington, IN: Indiana University Press, 1986).

Magnus, Bernd: *Nietzsche's Existential Imperative* (Bloomington, IN: University of Indiana Press, 1978).

Sallis, John: *Crossings, Nietzsche and the Space of Tragedy* (Chicago, IL: University of Chicago Press, 1991).

Scott, Charles E.: *The Language of Difference* (Atlantic Highland, NJ: Humanities Press International, 1987).

———: *The Question of Ethics, Nietzsche, Foucault, Heidegger* (Bloomington, IN: Indiana University Press, 1990).

# 12

# Freud

JOHN DEIGH

Sigmund Freud (1856–1939) created a theory of psychology that has had a more profound influence on twentieth-century thinking about human life and human culture than any other produced in this century. Freud presented his theory as the product of scientific work. He did not offer it as part of a philosophical system and did not advance philosophical arguments to defend it. Rather he based it on evidence he gathered from the observations he made as a physician specializing in nervous disorders, and he enlarged and modified it on the basis of further observations and reflections. Consequently, it is necessary first to explain how the theory developed and what its central ideas are before discussing its philosophical import.

## The development of Freud's theory

Freud grew up in Vienna, where his family had moved when he was four. He was born in Freiburg, Moravia, which is now part of the Czech Republic, and lived there for three years, followed by a year in Leipzig, before going to Vienna. At seventeen he entered the University of Vienna as a medical student. He was drawn to medicine, not from a desire to become a physician, but rather from an interest in science. The coursework of his first two years reflected this interest. It consisted of a steady diet of lectures in physics, chemistry, biology, physiology, botany, anatomy, and so forth, though he did manage during this period to take a few courses in philosophy from Brentano. Midway through his third year he began to do research in zoology but by the end of the fourth he had switched to physiology. His imagination and commitment to science had been captured by Ernst Brücke, the director of the physiology laboratory, and he remained Brücke's student and a member of his Institute for the next five years. During this time he focused in his research on the nervous system and, *en passant*, received his MD. While there can be no doubt as to the success of his research, he had no realistic hope of advancing to any of the higher positions within the Institute. In 1882 he left and began preparing for a career as a practicing physician.

His expertise in neurophysiology equipped him for specializing in nervous diseases. He became a resident at Vienna's General Hospital, where he concentrated on brain anatomy and neurology while also acquiring the broad knowledge and skill necessary for his new career. At the end of his residency, in the summer of 1885, he won a six-month travel grant for the purpose of studying with Jean

Martin Charcot at his clinic in Paris. Charcot, one of Europe's leading neurologists, was at that time lecturing on hysteria and demonstrating its treatment through hypnosis. The impact of these lectures and demonstrations on Freud's thinking cannot be overstated. On the one hand, Charcot presented a symptomatology of hysteria that, in Freud's view, established it as a true neurosis, for previously it had been widely considered to be merely a grab-bag diagnostic category, equally applicable to faking as to genuine nervous disorders. On the other, seeing Charcot use hypnotic suggestion to induce as well as remove the physical symptoms of hysteria – anesthesia, convulsions, paralysis, etc. – convinced Freud of the importance of psychological factors in the etiology of the neurosis, at least in certain of its forms. Thus, the idea of psycho-neurosis took hold in his mind and became the inspiration for the subsequent theoretical and clinical work that constitutes his extraordinary intellectual legacy.

The heart of that legacy is the theory and practice of psychoanalysis. It took Freud a long time, roughly a dozen years after he returned to Vienna and started a private practice, to arrive at its fundamental principles and techniques. To relate how he did so would require recounting the many twists and turns his thinking took as he wrestled with ideas for which there was very little sympathy in Vienna's medical community. Suffice it to say, he developed the theory of psychoanalysis from successive attempts to fit the hypothesis of psycho-neurosis to both the clinical observations he made from the cases he treated and the understanding of neurophysiology he retained from his studies and research at the university and the hospital. And he developed the therapeutic techniques of psychoanalysis through discovery of ways to elicit from his patients material that provided insight into the ideas and impulses at the root of their illnesses and also ways to relieve his patients of their suffering by making them aware of those ideas and impulses and helping them to work through them. *Studies in Hysteria*, a book that he wrote with his friend and older colleague Josef Breuer, and published in 1895, contains his early theoretical ideas and the case histories from which they were drawn. It was his first book on psychopathology. The full flowering of his psychoanalytic researches in this formative period appeared four years later in his next book, his masterwork, *The Interpretation of Dreams*.

The last chapter of this work lays out the basic structural features of psychoanalytic theory. Although Freud significantly revised these in later works, the essential ideas remained constant throughout his subsequent writings. Thus, to begin with, Freud divided the mind into conscious and unconscious parts. On this scheme, the workings of the latter explain many of the thoughts and feelings that occur in the former and the behavior that manifests them. The principal explanations center on conflict between the mind's conscious and unconscious parts. The unconscious part contains thoughts and wishes that would be painful and distressing if one were conscious of them. Indeed, their having become unconscious is itself due to the necessity of ridding oneself of the pain and distress they cause. The memory of a traumatic experience, for example, or the wish to see a loved one dead can be so upsetting that, to regain peace of mind, one must not only banish it from consciousness but also block it from returning. One must exclude the painful

163

memory or wish from the field of conscious experience and then repress it. In this way one gains an immunity from its pain and distress, though renewed exertions of repressive force are necessary to keep up the immunity. They are necessary, according to Freud, because unconscious thoughts and wishes are themselves invested with psychic energy in consequence of which they would force themselves into consciousness if left unimpeded. The conflict between the mind's conscious and unconscious parts is therefore to be understood as a clash of these psychic forces. On the one side is the force with which unconscious thoughts and wishes are invested, and on the other is the force that is exercised in repressing those thoughts and wishes by the conscious part of the mind, more exactly, the agency that Freud assigned to it and that he called the ego. And this clash continues as long as the repression is successful.

The principal explanations of psychoanalytic theory consist then in citing the dynamics of this conflict and following out its effects. Because of the force with which unconscious thoughts and wishes are invested, the ego's mastery of them is never total. They do not, in other words, completely succumb to the repressive force the ego applies but rather continue to exert pressure within the mind. Being blocked from becoming conscious, they exercise influence in other ways. The pressure they continue to exert finds alternative outlets, and both their force and their content, albeit in distorted and disguised forms, are communicated through these outlets. As a result, they affect their subject's conscious thought and behavior while remaining unknown to him. The effects of their influence include emotions with inappropriate objects, abnormally strong desires and urges, dreams and delusions, and other disturbances of thought and behavior. The symptoms of the psychoneuroses Freud treated are prime examples. Dreams too, which Freud took to be disturbances of thought that occurred when the ego's defenses were temporarily weakened during sleep, are examples of first importance in the development of his theory. In either case the phenomenon is traced back through associations and ideational transformations to its origins in the subject's unconscious thoughts and wishes, and accordingly what seems pointless or incoherent in a person's life is shown to be meaningful in the context of that life. The triumph of these explanations is that they make such familiar but disturbing phenomena of human life as compulsions, obsessive thoughts, excessive fears, and dreams, which were once regarded as the products of alien spiritual forces or the expressions of mysterious somatic disorders, intelligible as effects of the human struggle to escape pain and achieve happiness.

Freud, having anchored his theory with the explanations of these disturbing phenomena, proceeded to extend its reach. In *The Psychopathology of Everyday Life* and *Jokes and their Relation to the Unconscious*, two books he published soon after the appearance of *The Interpretation of Dreams*, he offered distinctively psychoanalytic explanations of other familiar but more innocuous types of human behavior. These included accidents, mistakes, slips of the tongue, acts of forgetfulness, jokes, and comical behavior. Surveying a broad range of examples, he illustrated the workings of the unconscious in the production of these actions. Later he considered religious rituals and presented a psychoanalytic account of these on which they were understood as analogous, in both their genesis and their forms of expression, to the thoughts and behavior characteristic of obsessional neurosis. And then, in 1913, he published *Totem and Taboo*, his groundbreaking work on the origins of religion and morality in human society. Using anthropological studies of aboriginal cultures, Freud proposed an account of the primitive religious practices and moral norms of these cultures according to which they represented resolutions of conflict between parents and children that each person, as a child, had internalized and repressed. Freud then suggested that this account could be extended to the religious practices and ethics of his own, Judeo-Christian society, that they too represented resolutions of such conflicts. *The Psychopathology of Everyday Life*, with its deeper explanations of human actions that to common sense seemed like chance events or the results of mere lapses in thought, had attracted favorable interest from a general, educated public. *Totem and Taboo*, by contrast, with its unflattering account of the origins of religion and morality, added to Freud's notoriety as a purveyor of shocking and dangerous ideas.

Freud had originally gained such notoriety from the hypotheses about human sexuality that he ultimately adopted in developing his theory of the psycho-neuroses. He had come to the conclusion from his clinical work with hysterics that sexual trauma was at least partly responsible for his patients' condition, and as he delved more deeply into the material these patients provided, he became increasingly persuaded that this trauma occurred in early childhood. He initially formed the hypothesis that the patients, as small children, had been the victims of sexual abuse and that the memory of this experience, now repressed, was at the root of their illness. As alarming as this hypothesis was, he replaced it with an even more alarming one, that the trauma, in many cases, resulted from fantasies the patient had as a small child. After all, Freud noted, whether the illness was due to repressed childhood memories or repressed childhood fantasies would not affect the character of its manifestations in the adult patient. It would, however, say something about the character of the child's sexuality, and this implication is what made the new hypothesis even more alarming. For the fantasies that, on the new hypothesis, Freud attributed to small children, unlike the memories that on the old one he attributed to them, expressed sexual desires. In other words, where the old hypothesis merely implied that small children were sometimes the objects of another's sexual interests, the new one implied that such children themselves had sexual interests and experienced sexual impulses. To the members of a society whose moral view of human nature required belief in the sexual innocence of the prepubescent child, Freud's new hypothesis was nothing short of scandalous.

Freud expounded and defended this new hypothesis and its auxiliaries in *Three Essays on the Theory of Sexuality*, which appeared in 1905. Next to the basic structural features of psychoanalytic theory outlined above, these hypotheses are its most significant elements. The structural features identify the theory as a representative of psychological hedonism, and as such it descends from theories of human motivation that originated in the thought of the ancient Greeks. By using his hypotheses about human sexuality to fill in the structure that these features defined, Freud was then able to advance this tradition in a remarkably fertile way. For one thing, filling in the structure with these hypotheses enabled him to organize the theory around common, age-specific patterns of experience in infancy and early childhood. Thus the content of the unconscious thoughts and wishes to which distinctively psychoanalytic explanations appealed could be systematically determined in relation to the infant's or child's experiences of sexual gratification and frustration at different stages of its development and, moreover, in relation to the different aims and objects of the infant's or child's sexual interest at those stages. For another, it enabled Freud to locate the psychic energy with which those thoughts and wishes were invested in a single source, namely the sexual instinct or libido, and consequently to unify psychoanalytic explanations under the general idea of tracing the transmission and discharge of this energy under conditions of repression.

Nowhere did these developments in his theory prove more fruitful than in the elaboration of his famous idea of the Oedipus complex. The hypothesis of infantile sexuality created for Freud a problem that did not arise on the traditional view of children as asexual until puberty. Both the dramatic physical and psychological changes that occur at puberty and the absence in adults of any memory of their having experienced prepubescent sexual impulses gave powerful support to this traditional view. Since Freud too regarded puberty as a time of sexual awakening and recognized the absence of such memories in adults, he faced the problem of how to square these phenomena with his hypothesis. He did so by assuming a period of sexual latency in childhood at the onset of which all memory of the prior impulses and experiences of infantile sexuality was repressed. This period ended with puberty, though the repression with which it began continued. The assumption fitted his hypothesis to the problematic phenomena, and the question then was what could bring this period of sexual latency about. What, that is, could bring about repression of such strength and scope as to block from coming into consciousness memories, thoughts, and wishes that have accumulated over several years and that carry the vital force of the libido? Clearly, to explain such repression required very frightful fantasies and wishes, and the Oedipus complex, with its fantasies and wishes concerning incest and parricide, met this requirement.

Accordingly, Freud placed the Oedipus complex in the final stage of infantile sexuality. At this stage the child, on the simplest exposition of the Oedipus complex, sought sexual union with the parent of the opposite sex, and came to regard the parent of the same sex as a hated rival whom it wished to see dispatched. The emotional conflict within the child that these incestuous and parricidal wishes and their related fantasies reflected could not be sustained indefinitely, and its resolution, Freud proposed, came about through their sharp and lasting repression. This resolution of the complex not only brought the period of infantile sexuality to an end and initiated that of sexual latency but also created the store of unconscious thoughts and wishes that were chiefly responsible for any psycho-neuroses the child might later develop. The Oedipus complex, as Freud liked to say, was "the nucleus of the neuroses."

Two other principal outcomes that Freud attributed to the Oedipus complex signal a growing interest in general psychology. The first is the adult choice of a spouse and other lovers; and the psychoanalytic explanations Freud offered of such choices, while direct extensions of his theory of psycho-sexual development, also depended on the role parents have as their children's first ideals. The second is the acquisition of a sense of guilt; and the psychoanalytic explanation Freud offered of this phenomenon depended on the child's relations to its parents as authorities who set and enforced the bounds of right and wrong in its young life. In developing these explanations, Freud increasingly focused on the processes by which individual ideals and moral precepts became internalized, and as he deepened his account of these processes, he found it necessary to revise the basic structural features of his theory. Specifically, he concluded that the representative of parental ideals and parental authority in the mind was neither entirely conscious nor entirely unconscious and thus was not happily located in either of the mind's two parts. And concurrent with this conclusion, he realized that the ego itself was not entirely conscious and, indeed, that a satisfactory account of repression required that it be partly unconscious. The upshot of these points was a new model of the mind's structure on which it was divided into three parts, ego, id, and superego. The advent of this new model, which received its fullest statement in Freud's 1923 monograph *The Ego and the Id*, completed the shift in his interests from the study of the psycho-neuroses and other disturbances of thought and behavior to the general study of human personality.

In working out this new model, Freud, for the reasons mentioned above, abandoned the idea of defining the mind's parts according to the conscious or unconscious quality of the thoughts and feelings they contained. Instead, he defined them by their functions. The ego's functions corresponded to those it had on the old model, and the id's corresponded to those of the unconscious. Thus the ego was the agent of such conscious activities as deliberation and decision-making about how best to adapt to the environment, and also the unconscious action of repression, and the id functioned as the storehouse of repressed thoughts and wishes as well as the source of instinctual energy. The superego, then, which had no counterpart on the old model, was assigned the functions of conscience and maintaining the individual ideals to which the ego aspired. Repression remained a central dynamic in the explanations of psychoanalytic theory, but the three-part division of the mind yielded a more complex account of this dynamic on which the ego, in effecting repression, acted under the direction and the pressure of the superego. This difference reflects the general thrust of the changes Freud made to the basic structural features of his theory: conflict between the mind's conscious and unconscious parts gave way, as the basis of psychoanalytic explanation, to more complex interactions among ego, id, and superego.

At the same time as Freud was making these changes he was also revising his theory of the instincts. Initially, he had assumed two, those of sex and self-preservation, and conceived of repression as a site of opposition between them. That is, on his original conception of repression, the sexual instinct supplied the psychic energy with which unconscious thoughts and wishes were invested, and the self-preservative instinct explained the activities of the ego in its efforts to block those thoughts and wishes from becoming conscious. Later, Freud saw that, on his way of understanding the instincts, the self-preservative instinct might derive from

167

the sexual one. For crucial to his understanding of the instincts, the sexual instinct in particular, is the idea that they do not have fixed objects. Indeed, their lability is necessary to Freud's account of how, under repression, the psychic energy with which unconscious thoughts and wishes are invested is communicated and reinvested in new thoughts and wishes such as those that lie behind the symptoms of the psycho-neuroses. The derivation, then, of the self-preservative instinct from the sexual instinct followed directly once Freud realized that the ego itself could become invested with libidinal energy. Freud advanced this hypothesis of ego libido in his seminal paper of 1914, "On Narcissism: An Introduction," and for the next several years he proceeded in his theoretical work on the assumption that libido was the sole instinct in human life. This assumption, however, clashed with his conception of repression as a site of opposing instincts, a conception he regarded as fundamental to his theory. He eventually resolved this difficulty with his postulation of a death instinct and his subsequent treatment of it as the source of the aggressiveness with which the superego impressed its demands on the ego. The postulation, by restoring dualism to Freud's theory of the instincts, thus allowed him to give an account of repression that conformed to his fundamental conception of it.

Freud first postulated the death instinct in his 1920 monograph *Beyond the Pleasure Principle*, and then, in the final chapter of *The Ego and the Id*, he examined its role in the superego's relations to the ego and the sense of guilt that characterized those relations. This chapter combines the revisions Freud made to the basic structure of his theory with the revisions he made to his theory of the instincts, and its theoretical brilliance amply demonstrates the great fecundity of these changes. With the exception of a revision to his account of the death instinct noted below, these were the last major changes he made to his theory.

## The philosophical import of Freud's theory

Freud's theory belongs to the tradition of naturalism in Western thought. The tradition stretches back to antiquity. Its founders are several pre-Socratic philosophers, most notably the atomists, who advanced programs for understanding all phenomena as the products of natural forces. This tradition, after disappearing into the darkness of the medieval period, resurged with the rise of modern science. Accordingly, the naturalist ideal has become that of bringing all that is observable in nature within the scope of the natural sciences. Freud, who developed psychoanalysis as a natural science, repeatedly identified it as a contribution to the realization of this ideal. His theory, to be sure, was not the first in the modern period to explain the workings of the human mind as entirely the products of natural forces. Both Hobbes and Hume, for instance, expounded comprehensive naturalistic theories of human psychology. But it surpassed these predecessors in its explanations of the phenomena that opposing traditions regularly advanced as proving the untenability of naturalism in psychology. Above all, it surpassed them in confronting the objections of Christian spiritualism, the dominant tradition in Western philosophy. Indeed, the apparent success of psychoanalysis in dispatching the doctrines of this tradition, doctrines about the essential mysteriousness to science of the elevated aspects of human thought and conduct, secured its claims to having advanced the naturalist ideal farther than any previous scientific theory of the mind.

The advantages that Freud's theory has over its predecessors within the tradition of naturalism derive from its structural features. First, its conception of the mind as divided into parts – tension between which produces various thoughts, feelings, and behavior – introduces dynamic relations within the mind that have no counterparts in earlier naturalistic theories. The introduction of these relations enabled Freud to give cogent explanations of inner conflicts – the struggle against sin, say, or the combat of reason and passion – that spiritualists since Plato had adduced as evidence against a wholly naturalistic understanding of human psychology. Secondly, the theory's assumption of unconscious thoughts and wishes whose psychic force affects conscious thought and feeling gives depth to its explanations that is alien to theories like Hobbes's and Hume's. And the possibility of these deeper explanations enabled Freud to treat the civilized motives that people offered as explanations of their own behavior and that the opponents of naturalism regarded as revealing a dimension of human existence unaffected by natural forces as surface movements whose underlying causes sprang from the more primitive drives of animal life and thus qualified fully as forces of nature.

Of these two advantageous features, the second is generally regarded as Freud's most original contribution. Yet arguably the first is the bolder innovation. The bare assumption of unconscious thoughts and wishes had precedents in other psychological work, precedents that Freud readily acknowledged, and its germ is already evident in such devices as Hume's notion of a calm passion. By contrast, the idea of incorporating the conception of a divided mind into a naturalistic theory of psychology was wholly new. Before Freud such a conception was the intellectual property of spiritualism, and Freud, one might say, raided this tradition's domain of one of its most valuable possessions when he incorporated it into his theory. Before Freud, disputes between naturalism and spiritualism regularly turned on the question of the mind's structure, specifically whether it was unified or divided, for the tendency of naturalist thinkers like Hume was to identify the mind with a single, uniform field and to organize the great variety of mental phenomena in human life around a few simple principles that operated co-ordinately in this field. With Freud's innovation, the terms of this dispute changed completely.

Of course, a conception of the mind as divided is not essential to Christian spiritualism. Paul, after all, may have had no such conception in mind when he warned of the contrariety between spirit and flesh (Galatians 5:17), and Descartes, who made spiritualism a cornerstone of his philosophy, can plausibly be read as adhering to Pauline doctrine in maintaining the unity of the mind and its absolute division from the body. Still, Descartes's position was not that far removed from a conception of the mind as divided, his assertions to the contrary notwithstanding. For to preserve the dualism in human nature that *is* essential to Christian spiritualism, Descartes had to give a novel account of human weakness (Descartes 1989 [1649], pp. 44–6). On this account, such weakness involves direct conflict between mind and body in which the mind's power to move the body yields to the automatic forces at work in the body's animal movements, whereas on the standard account,

169

it involves conflict internal to the mind in which the force of reason yields to that of desire or emotion. And the obvious correspondence between these two accounts makes it clear that Descartes was in fact applying the model of a divided mind even while denying its truth. The irony is that his account of human weakness, once the model he was applying becomes apparent, can be seen to contain its own version of unconscious thoughts and wishes.

A more orthodox defense of Christian spiritualism in modern philosophy is found in Kant's work, his ethics in particular. Kant divided the mind into two faculties, reason and desire. Typically, the two operate harmoniously, as they do, for instance, when reason shows one how best to satisfy some desire. Hence, they typically cooperate in the formation of plans and schemes for pursuing happiness. Sometimes, however, they oppose each other, and to exemplify their opposition Kant turned to occasions when one desires something that is forbidden by a moral principle to which one adheres. Analysis of such conflicts, Kant argued, shows that the constraint on desire one experiences must be due to the force of reason as it operates in one's recognition of the principle's validity. Hence, Kant concluded, the principles of morality are dictates of reason, and moral motivation is an expression of the practical force of reason in the lives of human beings. That this force sometimes opposed the force of desire and that neither was resolvable into the other meant that the two forces were absolutely distinct. And from this conclusion Kant's division of the mind followed immediately.

Kant then built upon this division a metaphysics of clearly spiritualist inspiration. Human beings, he maintained, belong to two worlds. On the one hand, they belong, in virtue of possessing the faculty of desire, to the natural world. The faculty comprises the natural appetites and passions that humans share with other animals, and its operations are determined by the forces of nature. On the other, human beings belong, in virtue of possessing reason, to the intelligible world. Because the operations of reason when it opposes desire are disconnected from natural appetites and passions, they occur spontaneously, undetermined by the forces of nature. Thus the faculty of reason implies a capacity for freedom that distinguishes human beings from other animals. In exercising this freedom, human beings act from principles whose validity their own reason endorses rather than on impulses whose stimulation occurs regardless of reason's approval. Their choices, in other words, are determined by the legislative processes of their reason rather than by the external stimulation of their appetites and passions. As inhabitants of the natural world, humans live as integral parts of a system of nature. As inhabitants of the intelligible world, they live as independent members of a community of rational souls, a kingdom of ends. These metaphysical doctrines, which echo similar doctrines in the works of Plato and Augustine, secure Kant's place in the spiritualist tradition of Western philosophy.

As long as naturalist theories conceived of the mind as undivided, their responses to Kant's challenge were limited to various attempts to resolve moral motivation into natural desire. They then faced the following difficulty. Natural desires, the desire for warmth, the desire for food, the desire for companionship, and so forth, while they might differ in intensity or felt urgency, did not differ in rank or felt authority. Moral motivation, by contrast, when it clashed with some natural desire, was experienced as a constraint on the latter and, hence, as superior to it. How, then, could one resolve moral motivation into natural desire without loss of its felt superiority? The question stymied naturalists who conceived of the mind as undivided, but it posed no similar difficulty for Freud. Freud's mature theory especially, with its three-part division of the mind and its revised account of the instincts, could answer Kant's challenge directly, and it did so quite powerfully.

The key to Freud's answer is the identification of the experience of moral constraint with a sense of guilt. Freud, on his mature theory, explained a sense of guilt as tension between the ego and the superego, tension that is modeled on tension between subject and governing authority. Accordingly, the features of moral constraint that Kant invoked in his argument for the irresolvability of moral motivation to natural desire are found in a sense of guilt. The felt superiority of moral motivation to natural desire is captured by the superego's authority over the ego, and the opposition between moral motivation and natural desire is captured by the harshness with which the superego deals with the ego. Both features are then explained through Freud's explanation of how the superego is formed, which is to say, his explanation of how the child resolves the Oedipus complex. The first feature results directly from the internalization of parental authority at the heart of this process. The second results from what happens to the aggression the child directs toward the hated parent of the Oedipus complex. As aggression directed toward a figure who is loved as well as hated, it is emotionally difficult to sustain. To resolve the difficulty the child invests this aggressive energy in the parental authority it internalizes, the superego, and the harshness of the superego in its dealings with the ego is then explained as an expression of the aggression that now powers the superego. This account of the superego's harshness has an obvious affinity to Nietzsche's conjecture, advanced in the second essay of *On the Genealogy of Morals*, about the origins of bad conscience in man, so much so that one could justly characterize it as a substantial elaboration of that conjecture. Indeed, Freud's overall account of how the superego is formed and how it draws its power from the aggressive instincts – more exactly, the death instinct – constitutes a naturalistic answer to Kant that was already budding in Nietzsche's wry remark in that essay about the smell of cruelty in the categorical imperative (Nietzsche 1967 [1887], p. 65).

It was not until Freud wrote *Civilization and its Discontents* (1930), however, that he fully articulated these Nietzschean themes. They emerged in his thought once he came to regard the death instinct as the source of human aggression in general, though it took him ten years after he introduced the instinct into his theory to reach this view. The question that he then faced, in light of his attributing human aggression to the death instinct, was how human beings could live together peaceably given this natural drive toward hostility. How did civilization sustain itself? The answer, Freud held, lay in the way civilization, conceived of as a natural process by which social relations among human beings are fostered and regulated, turned the aggressive instincts in human beings to its own advantage. It did this principally through the formation of the superego, which, as the internal agent of morality, as conscience, drew its power from those very instincts. The real work of the superego, Freud held, was therefore to block and deflect the aggressive instincts so that they did not realize their socially destructive potential. As counterpoint to Kant's notion of conscience, this idea could not have been more apposite. Where Kant saw conscience as a form of intelligence that transported its possessor beyond the determinations of nature, Freud saw it as a device that nature implanted in human beings for her own purposes. And where Kant celebrated the transcendental freedom that the possession of a conscience brings, Freud regretted the unhappiness that its possession made inevitable, the unhappiness that nature made the lot of humankind as the price of being civilized.

The pessimism that runs through the argument of *Civilization and its Discontents* reflects the greater role the death instinct had acquired in Freud's theory. It marked as well the declining condition of his health and of the political situation in Europe. In 1938 the Nazis invaded Austria, and Freud was forced to leave Vienna. He went briefly to Paris and then to London, where he died the following year.

## Writings

Freud, S.: *The Standard Edition of the Complete Psychological Works of Sigmund Freud*, ed. James Strachey (London: Hogarth Press, 1953–71).

——: *The Origins of Psycho-Analysis: Letters to Wilhelm Fleiss, Drafts and Notes, 1887–1902*, eds Marie Bonaparte, Anna Freud, and Ernst Kris (New York: Basic Books, 1954).

## References and further readings

Deigh, J.: *The Sources of Moral Agency: Essays in Moral Psychology and Freudian Theory* (Cambridge: Cambridge University Press, 1996).

Descartes, R.: *The Passions of the Soul* (1649), tr. S. Voss (Indianapolis, IN: Hackett, 1989).

Hume, D.: *A Treatise of Human Nature* (1739–40), ed. L. A. Selby-Bigge (Oxford: Oxford University Press, 1888).

Jones, E.: *The Life and Work of Sigmund Freud* (New York: Basic Books, 1957).

Kant, I.: *The Critique of Practical Reason* (1788), tr. L. W. Beck (Indianapolis, IN: Bobbs-Merrill, 1956).

Neu, J. (ed.): *The Cambridge Companion to Freud* (Cambridge: Cambridge University Press, 1991).

Nietzsche, F.: *On the Genealogy of Morals* (1887), tr. W. Kaufmann and R. J. Hollingdale (New York: Random House, 1967).

Wollheim, R.: *Sigmund Freud* (Cambridge: Cambridge University Press, 1971).

# 13

# Bergson

PETE A. Y. GUNTER

Henri Bergson was born in Paris on October 18, 1859, the son of a Polish father (Varsovie Michael Bergson) and an English mother (Katherine Levinson Bergson). Both Michael and Katherine Bergson were Jewish, and they shared a Hasidic background. Though Henri Bergson did not consider himself Jewish in any orthodox sense, he conceded that the awareness of belonging to an unfairly treated minority was to have a lasting influence on his life. While his father was a pianist – a popularizer of Chopin – and composer, his mother was deeply interested in the arts, especially the contemporary literary world.

Until the age of nineteen, Bergson held British citizenship through his mother. At that time his family moved to England and Bergson chose to remain in France and assume French citizenship. The young scholar's career had already shown great promise, culminating in prizes in English, Latin, Greek, philosophy, and mathematics at the Lycée Condorcet. His mathematics professor, Desboves, published a proof by Bergson in his book on Blaise Pascal and contemporary geometry, and in the same year a national prize-winning paper by Bergson was published in the *Annales de mathématiques*. The young man turned to philosophy, however, instead of going into the sciences. "You might have been a mathematician," Desboves grumbled, "but you will only be a philosopher."

In the last decades of the nineteenth century, French philosophy was divided between a rationalistic spiritualism and positivism. At the École Normale Supérieur, where Bergson enrolled, these tendencies were represented by Kantianism, taught by Emile Boutroux, and by mechanistic evolutionism, represented by the writings of Herbert Spencer. Spencer's scientific erudition, his effort to "bring philosophy back to the ground of fact" attracted the young *normalien*, who was regarded by his classmates as a positivist or a materialist.

In 1883, Bergson published a translation of Lucretius' celebration of atomistic materialism, *On the Nature of Things*, and began work on his dissertation. The next year he took a teaching position at a *lycée* in the provincial town of Clermont-Ferrand, where he studied the infinitesimal calculus with the mathematician Constantine, investigated hypnosis with a circle of colleagues, and puzzled over a fundamental conundrum he had discovered. Though a follower of Herbert Spencer, Bergson found Spencer's thinking imprecise. A more careful conceptual analysis was needed, one which, he hoped, would bring Spencer's ideas in line with recent physics.

According to Spencer, everything that takes place, from the diffusion of a drop of ink in a glass of water to the emergence and evolution of life, can be explained through the "concentration" and "diffusion" of mass particles. Such processes were said by the English philosopher to take place in "time." But the more Bergson studied Spencer's time concept – especially the more carefully he compared it with experienced time – the less it appeared to be a concept of time at all.

For Spencer – who on this point follows a very long tradition – time is a geometrical dimension, analogous to space. This dimension is held to be made up of instants, and the movement from one moment to the next (succession) is reduced to the following of one instant upon another. Not only is time, on this widely prevalent view, presumed to be made up of unchanging parts; it is reduced to the endless repetition of the same. Bergson was intrigued. When he examined his experience of time something quite different appeared to be happening. In listening to language or music – or simply following the succession of our psychological states – we do not find crisp, clearcut units or sharp breaks. Rather, we find a constant progression, whose overwhelming impression is that of continuity. Suppose, by contrast, we consider experienced time (which Bergson was to term "duration") in terms not of instants but of units (minutes, seconds . . .) having breadth. Unlike the instants of which time is said to be composed, the lived present contains breadth; but this breadth, unlike that of quantitative units, contains no sharp boundaries and is dynamic throughout. When we strip aside conventional spatial associations and probe into our personal duration we find a surprising reality:

> A qualitative multiplicity with no likeness to number; an organic evolution which is yet not an increasing quantity; a pure heterogeneity in which there are no distinct qualities. (Bergson 1910b, p. 226)

The moments of inner duration, unlike space, are not external to one another.

The distinction between quantitative ("clock") time and duration is the key to Bergson's first work, *Essai sur les données immédiates de la conscience* (1889), translated into English as *Time and Free Will*. An adequate grasp of our inner duration, he argues in this work, can free us from a host of needless assumptions. If our inner lives cannot be adequately conceived as strictly repetitive or as made up of factors that repeat themselves, then some aspects of our careers must be such as to escape prediction:

> To say the same inner causes will reproduce the same effects is to assume that the same causes can appear a second time on the stage of consciousness. Now if duration is what we say, deep-seated psychic states are radically heterogeneous to each other, and it is impossible that any two of them should be quite alike, since they are two different moments in a life-story. (Bergson 1910b, p. 220)

Our ordinary behavior, Bergson grants, may be habitual: even to the point of automatism. But this cannot always be the case. In crises in which our future and our very concept of ourselves are threatened, we may overcome our habitual lethargy and our conventional roles, and express ourselves freely. We are reluctant to

174

be free, he points out, in a way that had undoubted impact on later French existentialism. We are ordinarily freer than we want to be.

The problem of human freedom involves not only the existential character of volition; it is made difficult also by our inveterate tendency to conceive of freedom in spatial terms. To take only one example: It is natural to represent freedom as a decision to follow one path, already laid out for us, rather than another equally pre-existent ("Two roads diverged in a yellow wood . . ."). When the question of "free will" is posed in this way, whether by the determinist or the libertarian, the stage is already set for the victory of the determinist. For then it will be necessary either to postulate forces ("causal factors") driving the chooser down one path or the other, or to suppose some sort of spontaneity which opts, arbitrarily, for one route or the other. But we should not be misled, Bergson insists, by simple visual clarity. Underlying our hesitations between apparent pre-existing alternatives there are not two tendencies or directions, but a

> . . . self which lives and develops by means of its very hesitations, until the free action drops from it like an over-ripe fruit.   (Bergson 1910b, p. 176)

"Choice" is less a matter of seizing pre-ordained possibles than it is a matter of self-creation.

Though such reflections, and others like them, have been thought to provide an ingenious and challenging defense of human liberty, the context in which they are developed presents a serious and inescapable problem. Within us, Bergson asserts, there is "succession without externality"; but outside us, in the world, there is "externality without succession" (Bergson 1910b, p. 108). This means that the nature of the self, with its freedom, is radically different from that of the world in space. The self is said to endure; the world is said to lack duration. If this very Cartesian contention is true, how can freedom possibly be expressed in human behavior? Human behavior, to consider only one of its aspects, certainly does involve succession.

The task of *Matter and Memory* (1911c) is to sweep away Bergson's earlier, very problematic, dualism. This is done by recasting not only the traditional notions of mind and matter, but also many presuppositions about their possible interrelations. The idea behind this new approach is straightforward. We have thought about mind and matter in overwhelmingly spatial terms. It is time, however, to think about them as being, or possessing, different concrete durations.

Whether one considers Newton's simply-located mass particles (internally unchanging), his rigid absolute space, his abstract absolute time, or his linear trajectories and reversible deterministic linear equations, one finds an accent on the static, the stable, the atomic. From Bergson's vantage-point Newtonian physics is based on concepts which are thoroughly – one might say almost exhaustively – spatial. His response is to invert all of these features, replacing particles with wavelike phenomena, absolute space with changing spatial relationships, absolute time with pulsational phenomena, reversibility with irreversibility, physical determinism with an element of indeterminism. Physical nature would thus be comprised of

175

"rhythms" of duration; matter would be seen as "*modifications, perturbations, changes of tension* or of *energy* and nothing else" (Bergson 1911c, p. 266).

Bergson's suggestions are interesting from the vantage-point of twentieth-century physics. From the vantage-point of the mind–body problem, they become interesting precisely because they make mind and matter, mind and world, similar in principle. Both become processes, and their interrelations thus become, at least in principle, intelligible. This possible intelligibility is increased by a subtle but far-reaching transformation of his concept of "inner duration."

Though in *Time and Free Will* Bergson insists on the breadth of the experienced present, he treats each present moment as merging continuously with the next. In *Matter and Memory* , however, he relaxes this extreme emphasis on continuity and depicts duration – both "inner" and "outer" – as occurring in successive rhythms. Though he never treats these as sharply cut off from one another, it is clear that they possess an element of real discontinuity. The rhythms of matter, he points out, are much briefer than those of human consciousness. The rhythms of consciousness, though far longer than those of matter, are extremely varied. When conscious to a high degree, our duration broadens, when dulled or unfocused our present will contract, approaching – through what some contemporary psychologists call "temporal disintegration" – the extreme brevity of material events. Mind, Bergson speculates, is neither so foreign to the order of nature as we have suspected; nor is it so alien to the "extensity" of the world-as-experienced.

In still another respect *Matter and Memory* enlarges the concept of duration. *Time and Free Will* had explored inner time consciousness with an almost exclusive focus on the present. Bergson now placed a strong emphasis on the past, distinguishing two sorts of memory by which the past becomes available to us: habit memory, consisting of learned conceptual and behavioral patterns, and involuntary memory, which retains our entire past. Both are necessary. But while the former is clearly stored in our brain and nervous system, the latter, he argues, is not.

If we knew all brain mechanisms and their activities in minute detail, we would find there, Bergson argues, only habit-patterns: stored behavioral potentialities which enable us to ride a bike, walk, or repeat our multiplication tables. Established in the past through efforts of attention, these "memories," far from recalling the past, exist in the present. Far from being conscious, they tend to be automatic. We value them *because* they are unconscious. (As a rule, one does not have to cogitate when one rides a bike or searches out the multiplicand of six times eight.)

The contrast with involuntary memory is striking. Involuntary memory – so named because it involves no special effort of attention – automatically accumulates our past, which therefore remains with us. We are not usually aware of this; but occasionally concrete memory images will slip into our awareness, reminding us of events, names, faces we believe have slipped away. Like Freud, and like Marcel Proust – who attended Bergson's lectures on memory – Bergson insists that our present is to a great extent made up of our past.

If unexpected concrete recollections are the exception, it is because the ordinary role of concrete memory is to provide us a sense of familiarity with the world around us. Much that we do – opening a door, walking into a room – is habitual. But when a question arises – What is that object on the desk? – we call not only upon a clearer visual focus but upon a host of memories of similar past situations, for recognition. Sense perception, Bergson insists, is selective, picking out features of our world that interest us; so also is our memory, which goes forward to meet perceptual images with which it can cohere, and through which we can orient ourselves.

We could not effectively "focus" our memories, Bergson believes, without the aid of the brain. That is, the brain and its neural mechanisms, on his view, both hold back a flood of memories which otherwise would overwhelm us, but allow through those which can assist us to recognize objects, and to respond to them effectively. Word-recognition, object-recognition, person-recognition require a superabundance of concrete memory; but, equally, concrete (involuntary) memory requires the choke-filter mechanisms of the brain for its actualization.

This picture of the interrelation of concrete memory and brain structure can be related effectively to what is known about brain damage. The most intensively studied amnesias (maladies of memory) are the aphasias, the maladies of word memory. It is natural to assume that when word memory is lost, memories – presumably lodged in the affected area of the brain – are lost also. Bergson argues, however, that what has been lost is not the memories themselves but the capacity to realize them. Damage to the filtering mechanism might (as for example in cases of *dementia praecox*) let through multitudes of useless recollections, clouding the mind. Damage to motor mechanisms (e.g. those connected with speech acts) might make word recall impossible. People with brain damage, Bergson points out, act not as if their memories have simply disappeared, but as if they are present, dimly recognized, but cannot be retrieved.

The interaction of mind and body (i.e. of memory and brain) involved in speech acts and other coping behaviors is also involved in Bergson's theory of perception. In asserting that involuntary memory is not in the brain and that in recognizing objects around us we focus our memories in terms of them, he is also suggesting that perception is not so thoroughly "trapped" in the brain, nor is consciousness so isolated as we have traditionally – whether as materialists or idealists – assumed. It is not possible to deal in depth with this issue in the present essay. It is important to point out, however, Bergson's contention in *Matter and Memory* that in "pure perception" we are outside ourselves, in the world. Bergson thus holds – in a manner reminiscent of Sartre and doubtless influencing him – that perception is in-the-world: that is, ec-static.

But just as perception is no stranger to the world, neither, for Bergson, is freedom. The memories we carry with us – memories of everything we have felt and thought – *are* our character, the sum of everything we have thought and willed. Our personal past is neither a stamp collection of memory images nor a set of causal factors more or less mechanically impelling us. It is a culmination of wider possibilities which funds our freedom. Retaining the past more and more effectively, we "organize it with the present in a newer and richer decision" (Bergson 1911c, p. 249).

The investigations of *Time and Free Will* and *Matter and Memory* remain within a psychological – in fact, phenomenological – horizon. This part of Bergson's philosophy was to influence projects as diverse as the phenomenology of the "lived body," the stream of consciousness novel, and (as noted above) the existentialist concept of freedom. In *Creative Evolution* (1907) his thought moves inexorably towards a metaphysics – though not quite a metaphysical system – on a grand scale.

Most strikingly, *Creative Evolution* is a critique of Darwinism. That is how it was seen by its contemporaries: as an attack on a fundamental pillar of modern science. It was, however, much more than this. *Creative Evolution* proposes a broadened epistemology in an evolutionary setting. And it treats evolution not as the hit-or-miss result of mutation mediated by natural selection but as a process exhibiting "purposiveness": not a search for pre-determined goals, but a creativity vectored towards greater levels of consciousness and freedom.

Darwinism, Bergson insists, rests uneasily on the horns of a dilemma. Either it must assume that evolution moves in giant leaps, suddenly (that is, in evolutionary time) producing whole new organs and organisms – but such a concept (an extreme form of which was to be labeled the "hopeful monster hypothesis" by later biologists) seems less like a scientific explanation than an exercise in magic; or (the other alternative) Darwinism must propose that evolution occurs slowly, through the accumulation of slight mutations. The problem here is that of explaining how minimal mutations can be accumulated, in the right order, at the right time, and so as to "reinforce" each other. Either (a second dilemma) the mutations required will hinder organ function and the organism will be eliminated; or, if the organ is improved only minimally, the organism possessing it will have no significantly improved chance of surviving and leaving descendants.

Explaining the emergence of life is difficult enough on these terms. But the difficulty is compounded by the problem of convergent evolution: that is, the appearance of like organs on unlike organisms, or simply of like organisms, at widely separated points on the evolutionary tree. The example Bergson used is that of the human eye and the eye of the pecten, a mollusk. That man and mollusk are quite different creatures no one will deny. Yet both have eyes containing corneas, lenses, and retinas: inverted retinas in both cases. Can this striking convergence really be explained *via* chance *via* natural selection?

Bergson's critique of Darwinism (that is, of Darwinism plus Mendelian genetics) was sufficiently effective to play a part in its reformulation as "Darwinism, the Modern Synthesis" in the 1930s and 1940s. His critique of prevailing theories of knowledge, though equally radical, received less attention. In reasoning about reason, Bergson protests, we have traditionally viewed human intelligence as a pure faculty, suspended in a noetic void, whose task is simply to know for the sake of knowing. But to make this assumption is to reason as if our own particular brain and nervous system had nothing to do with our place in the evolutionary scheme or with the kind of organism we are.

Bergson's theory of knowledge depends not only on his insistence that human ways of thinking have their roots in man's biological makeup, but on his distinction between instinct, as developed by the arthropods (especially the social insects), and intelligence, developed most fully by the vertebrates and culminating in man. Intelligence proceeds by the increasingly effective manipulation of material objects; in man manipulation finally becomes manufacture: a process involving analysis into parts and reconstruction from these parts. The end result of this tendency is an atomistic, analytical approach to experience, which Bergson finds most highly developed in modern science. There it is termed "intellect."

Contrasted with intelligence is instinct, which Bergson believes is not only an unlearned behavior but a mode of knowing. In each species capable of using it, instinctive knowledge is narrowed, primitive, and pragmatic in focus. The specoid wasp that stings a caterpillar precisely on its nervous centers so as to cause paralysis but not death "knows" (recognizes) something essential about its victim. But its awareness is limited to certain aspects of one species, and is little more than a sort of behavioral trip-hammer, releasing a behavior pattern. Instinct, Bergson states, knows its object from "within"; but this within is profoundly limited.

By arguing that instinct can be found throughout a significant sector of the animal kingdom, Bergson makes a place for intuition as a mode of thought having biological roots. Man, he argues, is the intelligent animal *par excellence*; but he brings with him vague, unfocused instinctual capacities which could be generalized and made reflective. This would be intuition. Intuition may have roots in instinct; but unlike fixed instincts of insects, solitary or social, it escapes biological provincialism and pragmatism by becoming reflective, capable of application to a wide variety of phenomena. If developed, he believes, it would open the door to all sorts of knowledge we do not now possess.

The sudden fame brought by *Creative Evolution* was a mixed blessing. Bergson's lectures, already popular, swelled to unmanageable proportions. Isaiah Berlin recounts:

> they came an hour before and attended the lecture of say, some Professor of Assyrian archeology; he and others were very surprised to find the lecture hall so full of odd-looking people, very unlike academics. No sooner was the lecture over than the audience rose to its feet and made room for smart ladies who crowded in to hear Professor Bergson. There has been nothing like this in England since the lectures of Thomas Carlyle.

One wag, after a series of progressively larger auditoriums proved inadequate, suggested that the Paris Opéra might suffice.

Bergson's status and prestige brought him unexpectedly into world history. In 1917 the French government (with the concurrence of Great Britain) sent the philosopher on a secret mission to the United States, authorized to promise President Wilson that if he would bring the United States into the First World War on the side of the Allies, after the war Britain and France would back the creation of a League of Nations, dedicated to maintaining world peace. Philippe Soulez's careful scholarship has demonstrated that Bergson's mission played a decisive role in Wilson's decision to enter the war.

After the war Bergson's work as president of the League of Nations International Commission on Intellectual Cooperation (forerunner of UNESCO) was cut short by a disastrous decline in his health, due to crippling arthritis. Though he continued to correspond, and to work, when possible, on his next major study, he was forced into virtual seclusion. In part this forced exile from the intellectual life of Europe explains the declining fortunes of his philosophy, which by the end of the 1920s passed out of fashion – a fact which the award of a Nobel Prize for Literature, in 1928, did little to reverse. In part it also explains why his final statement, *The Two Sources of Morality and Religion* (1932), is separated from *Creative Evolution* by 25 years.

In an interview with a *New York Times* reporter in 1925 Bergson argued that, beset with rapid technological and social change and with the specter of warfare on an unprecedented scale, the world needed a new ethics. Though it was in this direction that his thought was taking him, he confessed, finding and articulating such an ethics was extremely difficult. Bergson might have been surprised if he could have foreseen the extent to which his pursuit of a new ethics would lead him to the re-exploration of a very old one. This re-exploration would lead to a new way of envisioning the phenomena of religion as a struggle between two impulses, one leading to the "open," the other to the "closed."

*The Two Sources of Morality and Religion* begins with an analysis of the emergence of religions which sustain, and express, essentially closed societies. The earliest religions – if we can call them that – consist of little more than belief in the continued existence of ancestors after death, a belief sustained by occasional visions (perhaps shadowy images) of these ancestors. If this was illusory, it was also inescapable. Small hunting–gathering bands are literally made up of individuals. How can the authority of the band endure if it can summon up no authority greater than that of its present impermanent membership? From such beginnings to the highly developed religions of Greece or Rome – or India – there is a long history, exhibiting the emergence of gods possessing ever more vivid and unique personalities, gods which participate in increasingly elaborate mythologies.

If we probe beneath the surface of this historical process, Bergson suggests, we will find closely similar causes at work. Possibly some animals commit suicide. It does not seem possible that other animals can foresee clearly that they must die or know they may fail to reach objectives. Such awareness interrupts the forward momentum of life; it is a "downer" and must be dealt with. Religions respond to this destabilizing influence by neutralizing it. That is, closed religions are "defensive reactions" which offer images suggesting hope, and continued existence, along with punishments for social disobedience. Especially in this latter guise, natural religion functions not only to sustain effort but as a sort of social "glue," creating cohesion in societies which might otherwise tend to unravel. Such religions function through a collusion of individual psychology and social pressure. Their gods guard the city gates.

Charles Hartshorne has argued that Bergson must be viewed as a sociobiologist: that is, as one of those who have thought about human history in biological terms. This claim goes even deeper than Hartshorne suggests, however. Bergson thinks of humankind not only in biological terms but in genetic terms as well. He concludes, arguing against archeologists like his friend Lucien Lévy-Bruhl, who believed man had changed genetically through the inheritance of acquired characteristics, that humankind has changed genetically very little since its first appearance. The long, many-sided development of the "static religions" of closed societies, he believes, simply brings out what was already present in man as a natural creature. Biologically, though we inhabit mass societies founded on sophisticated technologies, we remain hunter–gatherers: creatures of small groups dependent on group authority, insisting on hierarchy and group closure for our security and identity.

Bergson's treatment of natural man, therefore, is hardly flattering. In a state of nature *Homo sapiens* is no noble savage. Human societies are, if nothing more intervenes, controlled by alpha males or their surrogates, armored against outsiders, and ever ready for defense – or attack. The corollary of closure is war.

The natural response to such a philosophical anthropology is to ask whether, after all, there is not more to man than his genetic limitations, more to religion than a series of strategic ruses supported by social pressure. Besides static religion, Bergson believes, there is a movement towards dynamic religion and its natural corollary, the open society. In the words of Lezlek Kolakowski:

> This march towards an open society in which we are able to see humanity in everyone, and where all are equal in moral obligations and claims, was initiated in various civilizations: Greek sages, Jewish prophets, Buddhist and Christian saints have paved the way towards a universally human morality. Unlike nature, these great spirits do not command or exert pressure. They appeal to all, they find followers, and thus they prove that in our soul there is a potential force, however embryonic, that goes beyond the tribal mentality towards human fraternity. The closed soul can evolve into an open one – not by broadening its field of bonds with other people, but by acquiring another, truly human nature.   (Kolakowski 1985, p. 76)

It takes a creative emotion to open oneself to the human race and to abandon a life in which we can love some people only by hating or excluding others, Kolakowski observes. It is this emotion – rich in ideas – that Bergson believes the great mystics discovered and developed.

Bergson neither disregards nor otherwise denigrates the great mystics and sages, whether of Greece, the Orient, or elsewhere. He finds, however, that their very real achievements were incomplete. Complete mysticism, he holds, responds to its encounter with deity not only through rapture and enlightenment but through action. Receiving love, its natural impulse is not only to teach but to bestow love. A complete mysticism lends itself to social concern – and action. It is in these terms that we must understand his contention that the open society has found its fullest development among the Christian saints and mystics.

Bergson's life was to end both heroically and on a note of bitter irony. Possibly he might have converted to Roman Catholicism in the 1930s. Foreseeing the wave of antisemitism about to break so disastrously over Europe, however, he refrained, confessing that under such conditions he "preferred to remain among those who are to be the persecuted." With the collapse of France in 1941 Jews were required to register with the authorities. The French Chamber of Deputies tried to shield Bergson from this rule, conferring on him the title "Honorary Aryan." Bergson refused the title, resigned all honors and positions, and registered on the street with other Jews. He died two days later, January 7, 1941, of pulmonary congestion.

## Writings

Bergson, Henri: *Mind-Energy* (New York and London: Macmillan, 1910a).
——: *Time and Free Will* (New York and London: Macmillan, 1910b).
——: *Creative Evolution* (New York: Holt; London: Macmillan, 1911a).
——: *Laughter* (New York and London: Macmillan, 1911b).
——: *Matter and Memory* (New York and London: Macmillan, 1911c).
——: *The Two Sources of Morality and Religion* (New York: Holt; London: Macmillan, 1935).
——: *The Creative Mind* (New York: Philosophical Library, 1946).

## Further reading

Antliff, Mark: *Inventing Bergson* (Princeton, NJ: Princeton University Press, 1993).
Capek, Milic: *Bergson and Modern Physics* (New York: Humanities Press; Dordrecht, Holland: Reidel, 1971).
Kolakowski, Lezlek: *Bergson* (Oxford: Oxford University Press, 1985).

PART III

# THE PHENOMENOLOGICAL
# BREAKTHROUGH

# 14

# Neo-Kantianism

## STEVEN GALT CROWELL

Neo-Kantianism, a movement with roots deep in the nineteenth century, dominated German academic philosophy between 1890 and 1920. Though it carried
the impulse of German Idealism into the culture of the twentieth century and set
the agenda for philosophies which displaced it, the movement is little studied now.
One encounters it primarily in liberation narratives constructed by those whose
own thinking took shape in the clash between neo-Kantianism and the "rebellious"
interwar generation spearheaded by JASPERS (see Article 17) and HEIDEGGER (see Article 18). Thus, before Heidegger – so Hannah Arendt (Arendt 1978, p. 294) –
"philosophy was not so much communicated as drowned in a sea of boredom." And
with Heidegger – so Hans-Georg Gadamer (Gadamer 1977, p. 214) – "the compla-
cent system-building of neo-Kantian methodologism" gave way; its "calm and
confident aloofness . . . suddenly seemed to be mere child's play" (Gadamer 1977,
p. 230). Here neo-Kantianism is the *terminus ad quem* of a "liberation from the
unbreakable circle of reflection" toward recovery of the "evocative power of conceptual thinking and philosophical language" (Gadamer 1977, p. 202). It thus
enters the lore of Continental philosophy as the father who had to be slain in order
that philosophy might live.

No doubt testimony from those who were there reflects well enough their experience of the matter, even if it leads some (like Gadamer) to stigmatize neo-Kantian
motifs in Heidegger's thought as inauthentic. Meanwhile, however, projects such
as fundamental ontology or philosophical hermeneutics, which heralded the
liberation, have developed internal aporias which suggest that reassessment of
their triumphal claim to have transcended the dead-end questions obsessing their
neo-Kantian fathers may be in order. It is a commonplace of contemporary Continental philosophy, for example, that epistemology (the neo-Kantian project of ultimate grounding) is dead. Already in 1962 a writer could characterize the time as
one in which "epistemology is seen as the ultimate stage of philosophy's degeneration" (Brelage 1965, p. 74), so pervasive was the ontological (Heideggerian) revolution. Heidegger's claim, however, was not that knowledge needed no grounding,
but that it needed *ontological* grounding. Subsequently, E. Tugendhat questioned
the adequacy of this position, and K.-O. Apel began to interrogate the "hermeneutic
turn" in light of the neo-Kantian philosopheme "validity" (*Geltung*). Heidegger had
been deeply concerned with such questions. His anti-foundationalist heirs – the
deconstructionists, the pragmatists, the hermeneuticists – find in this concern only
residual "philosophy," an incomplete liberation. Rorty (1980, pp. 134f, 393) right-

ly ties the rhetoric of the "end of philosophy" to the collapse of the neo-Kantian programme which sought, by becoming theory *of* science, to establish an autonomous place for philosophy among the positive (empirical and mathematical) sciences. Depending on one's sympathy for what is announced in that rhetoric, one might well feel that the neo-Kantian paradigm has not been altogether superseded. A balanced assessment of neo-Kantianism might reveal questions with which the onto-hermeneutic turn is burdened by its very nature but which, as transcending all its powers, it is also not able to answer.

The present essay will neither carry out such an assessment nor pretend to encompass the movement as a whole. In reconsidering the neo-Kantian heritage one should be aware that Continental philosophy defines itself through a largely distortive and reductive reading of the neo-Kantians, but here the aim is simply to indicate something of what is at stake in such readings by situating a few theses characteristic of "classical" neo-Kantianism within the horizon of a particularly contested point, namely, the dispute between the neo-Kantians and their phenomenological critics over the *autonomy* of philosophy. Both movements lay claim to the mantle of "scientific philosophy," but neo-Kantianism differs from phenomenology in maintaining a *continuity* between positive science and philosophy. As theory of science, neo-Kantian epistemology wants to provide grounds for a principled ("scientific") *Weltanschauung*; phenomenology (here, Husserl and the early Heidegger), on the contrary, locates the autonomy of philosophy precisely in its *discontinuity* with positive science and with the aims of worldview formation.

## The neo-Kantian movement

In 1912 the Rickert-student Heidegger opened his review of current trends in the philosophy of logic by referring to a longstanding controversy over the meaning of Kant's first *Critique*: the once-dominant "psychological interpretation of Kant," with its "naturalization of consciousness," has now been displaced by the "transcendental-logical conception advocated since the 1870s by Hermann Cohen and his school as well as by Windelband and Rickert," according to which "Kant in his critique did not inquire into the psychological origin of knowledge but into the logical value of its validity" (Heidegger 1978a [1912], p. 19). Here one sees that by the turn of the century "Kant" had come to govern a semantic field by no means restricted to an historical figure. The neo-Kantian movement did yield an efflorescence of Kant-philology, but the issue dividing psychological and transcendental (aprioristic) readings of Kant was ultimately systematic, not philological: Where does philosophy stand in the economy of the sciences? That Kant, with some justification, had been enlisted on both sides reflects the pluralism of the neo-Kantian movement, its diverse agendas and competing claims jostling throughout a nearly eighty-year period. Some orientation is therefore indispensable if the implications of the debate between "classical" neo-Kantianism and phenomenology are to be seen.

The beginnings of neo-Kantianism have been identified with O. Liebmann's *Kant und die Epigonen* (1865), in which the phrase, "Thus we must go back to Kant," repeatedly occurs. As Köhnke (1991) has shown, however, Liebmann's work is a rather *late* instance of what had been, since 1850 and in step with fluctuating fortunes of philosophy in the academy (and the academy in German politics), a whole series of "programmata" in which Kantian motifs played enormously varied roles. Thus the earliest neo-Kantian authors (J. B. Meyer, H. Helmholtz, E. Zeller, R. Haym, F. A. Lange, K. Fischer) diversely exploited idealist, realist, critical, sceptical, naturalistic, and metaphysical possibilities contained in Kant's philosophy. Further, as Lehmann (1987) has shown, the notion that neo-Kantianism arose out of the "collapse of German Idealism" needs to be tempered by the recognition that the Kant to whom these authors "returned" owed much to a "late idealism" (I. H. Fichte, C. H. Weiße, H. Lotze) of the 1830s and 1840s that had not yet succumbed to the divorce between "scientific" (i.e. academic) philosophy and *Weltanschauung*. Its impulse would be felt again in the late 1870s when the neo-Kantian "critique of German idealism changed into a new idealism" and "again laid claim to its own systems, to the absolute validity of its foundations, metaphysics, an unassailable apriorism, and theories of ethics and values" (Köhnke 1991, pp. 280–81).

This new idealism is the classical neo-Kantianism identified with the Marburg School (H. Cohen, P. Natorp, E. Cassirer, N. Hartmann), noted for its focus on the logic of the exact sciences, and the Southwest German (or Baden) School (W. Windelband, H. Rickert, E. Lask, B. Bauch), known for its interest in the historical, cultural sciences and its theory of transcendent value (*Wert*). The views of these schools concerning the relation between philosophy, science, and *Weltanschauung* evolve, in turn, over three distinct periods.

In the first period (1871–8), characterized by an "extremely broad palette of possibilities for the contemporary realization of Kant's theories of apperception and apriority" (Köhnke 1991, p. 239), there is a certain continuity between apriori and empirical inquiry. The autonomy of philosophy *vis-à-vis* positive science has not yet become the decisive issue. Cohen, for instance, whose "transcendental" reading of the ideality of space and time in Kant permitted the realistic thesis that scientific knowledge reaches the *thing* and not merely "representations," could contribute to the positivist *Vierteljahresschrift für wissenschaftliche Philosophie*; and Windelband, whom Heidegger described as rejecting all inquiry into the "origin" of the apriori as irrelevant to the "logical value" of its "validity," could propose a Darwinian evolutionary explanation of categories in terms of ethno-psychology (Köhnke 1991, pp. 237f). A version of this realistic or quasi-positivistic strain of neo-Kantianism, developed by A. Riehl at this time, survived into the later idealistic period, though Riehl never established a school. In line with Lange's influential *Geschichte der Materialismus* (1866), "scientific philosophy" is limited in this period to theoretical reason; interest in Kant's ethical philosophy, and the motives toward idealism and *Weltanschauung* stemming from it, emerged only in the second period, from 1878 to the end of the First World War.

During this second period the two schools developed their salient doctrinal differences. Equating Kant's concept of experience with the *account* of the object in scientific judgments, Cohen's *Kants Theorie der Erfahrung* (1871) elaborated the characteristic Marburg view of the *Critique of Pure Reason* as a "theory of science." Philosophy has only indirect access to being, mediated by cognitions achieved in first-order scientific theorizing (= "the fact of science"). Unable to deduce truth speculatively from its own principle (Hegel), philosophy is to reflect upon the principles governing independent sciences. By extending to all reality Kant's thesis concerning the constructed character of mathematics, Cohen's *Das Prinzip der Infinitesimalmethode* (1883) established the Marburg understanding of transcendental logic as a theory of knowledge which (in Natorp's words) brings "ultimate unity" to the system of sciences by uncovering the principles (categories) according to which they construct being. In E. Cassirer's *Philosophie der symbolischen Formen* (1923–9) this approach undergoes an anthropological extension, from the logical construction of the object of knowledge to the symbological construction of all cultural unities.

In its identification of thought with logical form, Marburg idealism's understanding of Kant's Copernican priority of thought over being recalls both Plato (cf. Natorp's controversial *Platons Ideenlehre* [1903]) and Hegel. The value-philosophical idealism of the Baden School, on the contrary, drew upon the subjectivist, Fichteanized Kant of Windelband's teacher, Kuno Fischer, and advanced a more Aristotelian logic emphasizing the bi-polarity of form and material. Its conception of the relation between philosophy and science thus reflects Fichte's *Wissenschaftslehre* and the "primacy of practical reason" of Kant's second *Critique*. Both sources are evident, for example, in Rickert's theory of judgment (Rickert 1915, pp. 135ff). With roots going back to Windelband's idea of logic as the "ethics of thought" and ultimately to H. Lotze's theory of "validity" (*Geltung*) as a "value," Rickert's view holds that cognitive judgment involves two moments: first, a moment *immanent* to the subject, in which alogical, irrational material (the "content of consciousness") is combined via categories (logical form); and second, a moment of *affirming* or *denying* what is so synthesized, in light of the subject-*transcendent* "value" of cognitive validity, or truth. The "object of knowledge" is thus not a function of thinking alone (Marburg formalism), but of interest, position-taking, and decision; being is what "ought" to be affirmed; *Sollen* has priority over *Sein*.

Southwest German idealism's appeal to the primacy of the practical opened it to *Weltanschauung* motives transcending Kant's epistemology, including elements derived from the *Critique of Judgment*. Thus Rickert (1934, pp. 13–14) argued that though for Kant "scientific philosophy must base itself on the theory of knowledge," it would be "the gravest misunderstanding" to think that "Kant intended to substitute a theory of science in place of metaphysics." From the outset the Baden School projected a general philosophy of culture (of cognitive, ethical, and aesthetic validity) grounded in the concept of transcendent *Wert* as philosophy's specific theme, and in its more inclusive epistemology it came to grapple with the question of *historical* knowledge. Developing Windelband's distinction between "nomothetic" and "ideographic" sciences, Rickert's *Die Grenzen der naturwissenschaftlichen Begriffsbildung* (1896, 1902) maintained that the "generalizing" and "homogenizing" concept-formation found in natural science (and the Marburg constructivism based on it) encounters an unsurpassable limit in the "heterogeneous continuum," the ultimately "irrational" material, of reality. To approach it, historical concept-formation must proceed in an opposed – "individualizing" –

direction, its interest being not in general laws but in *understanding* unique "value-individualities."

The third phase of classical neo-Kantianism begins with the outbreak of war in 1914 and continues through the NS (National Socialist) intervention in the German university system in the 1930s. Reflecting the collapse of cultural optimism, this period is characterized by an assault upon academic idealism in the name of *Lebensphilosophie* (a catchall term invoking the theses of philosophical "outsiders" like Nietzsche, Bergson, and Dilthey). In the neo-Kantian schools this appears as a conflict between the epistemological framework of transcendental logic and ontological issues asserting priority over such a framework – e.g., the infinite manifold of particular reality that escapes derivation from the concept, and the concrete or "factic" subject, whose life overflows the transcendental consciousness postulated in logical idealism.

In the Baden School, E. Lask's *Logik der Philosophie* (1911) and *Die Lehre vom Urteil* (1912) anticipate themes of the third period. Abandoning Rickert's immanentist interpretation of the form/material schema (and so also the primacy of practical reason [Lask 1923a (1908)]), Lask adopts the "standpoint of transcendence" to give an ontological interpretation of the object as a unity of categorial form and alogical material. Objects are *themselves* "truths, unities of meaning, not cognitions, judgments, propositions" (Lask 1923b [1911], p. 41). In contrast to Cohen, for whom the object is constructed in the scientific judgment, Lask (1923b [1911], p. 185) argues that "the most basic problems of logic reveal themselves only if pre-theoretical cognition is included in the investigation." In Marburg, N. Hartmann offered the *Grundzüge einer Metaphysik der Erkenntnis* (1921), a quasi-phenomenological "realistic" theory of the subject–object relation intended to *account* ontologically for what is merely *presupposed* in Natorp's logical idealism, namely, the subject's ability to "transcend" its own sphere. In Kant-philology, H. Heimsoeth (1924) began to uncover the "metaphysical motives" of Kant's critical philosophy, an interpretation pursued in Heidegger's 1927/28 lecture course on Kant and in *Kant und das Problem der Metaphysik* (Heidegger 1929).

The neo-Kantianism that began as a "theory of science" continuous with the positive sciences and hostile to "anti-scientific" philosophy (metaphysics = *Weltanschauung*), and that grew into an idealistic worldview based on an *incomplete* autonomization of philosophy (transcendental reflection on the constructions of natural or historical science), is thus challenged, in the third period, by a resurgent metaphysics laying claim to sources more "primordial" than what has been elaborated theoretically. But with what right? Are such claims anything more than uncritical speculation, rhetoric, edification, or mysticism? Rickert (1922, pp. 36, 50–51), for example, rejected phenomenology's appeal to intuition because it lacked any *principle* for the systematic ordering of *Erlebnisse*, which alone could render an approach to them "scientific." The concern of philosophy "is not life, but *thought about* life" (Rickert 1922, p. 59). Can philosophy go back behind the critical, epistemological starting point – in this sense abandon neo-Kantianism – without losing its identity as a principled claim to truth, an autonomous "science"? The debate between Natorp's critical idealism and phenomenology, at whose heart lies

189

the issue of what constitutes "scientific" philosophy, exemplifies what is involved in trying to answer this question positively.

## Natorp's Critical Idealism

In 1911 – the same year Husserl published his 'Philosophie als strenge Wissenschaft" in Rickert's *Logos* journal – Natorp opened his *Philosophie, Ihr Problem und ihre Probleme* by observing that the younger generation, schooled in scepticism *vis-à-vis* all "merely traditional wisdom," yearns after a "truth armored with the impenetrable steel of genuine science," one able "to satisfy not only the calculating intellect but also to answer the secret, innermost doubts and questions of the soul" (Natorp 1911, p. 1). *Critical* idealism is to address this yearning by exploiting the "close unity between science and philosophy," whose differences are but "opposite directions of one and the same path" (Natorp 1911, p. 3). Progressing systematically from logical through ethical, aesthetic, and religious principles, Natorp abjures any move into "the suspicious land of metaphysics"; nevertheless, the goal is a "reconciliation between experience and idea" that will fulfill "the demands of a *Weltanschauung*" (Natorp 1911, pp. 173, 184). In continuity with the positive sciences, philosophy can satisfy both intellect and soul.

To "reduce the manifold to law" is the "inner law of knowledge itself"; hence philosophy and science, as modes of knowing, have this in common (Natorp 1911, p. 13). In philosophy, however, the manifold consists of sciences themselves, and its laws are logical, not natural. Philosophy seeks the "unity and ground" of science, but it does not propose an explanatory theory of the fact of knowledge (*questio facti*) as might be found, say, in psychology or anthropology. Its distinctive task is the *critique* of knowledge (*questio juris*), a reflection on the principles which, as necessary conditions of any knowledge of objects at all, make science possible, provide the "justification" of its claim to truth.

The first condition of scientific validity is the priority of *methodological thinking* over being (where "thinking" does not refer to individual subjectivity but to thought, logical form, as such); and because the factic subject is not at issue, the resulting idealism is "critical," not "subjective" (Natorp 1911, pp. 38f). If "by thinking one understands the infinite process in which being is posited as object and first of all receives its concrete determination," then "being becomes a function of thinking"; to ask for a "being in itself" apart from the process of scientific knowing is to ask for something "internally contradictory" (Natorp 1911, pp. 14–15). Being "resolves itself into becoming" as the correlate of the *process* of "objectification," the "construction" of being as object through conceptual determination (Natorp 1911, p. 16). The "fact of science" is the fact of objectification at its most developed stage, and philosophy's task is to grasp the categories of objectification governing scientific development. The logic of science is thus transcendental, i.e., it concerns conditions under which *objects* can be known; "logical" principles are simultaneously principles of *being* (Natorp 1911, p. 44). It is in the (diachronic) coherence of this system of categories, not in any single principle, that the answer to the *questio juris* is demonstrated (Natorp 1911, pp. 23ff).

Natorp's projection of a transcendental logic contrasts, in important respects, with Kant's. First, by jettisoning the so-called "subjective deduction" of the first edition of the *Critique of Pure Reason* in favor of the second edition version, psychological and anthropological elements of the doctrine of synthesis are purged from logic such that the concept of the thing-in-itself loses its "sceptical" implications. The thing (or object) in itself is simply the limit of the infinite process of objectification. Subjectivist elements are further eliminated by incorporating the Transcendental Aesthetic into logic. On Natorp's reading, Kant makes the space–time order depend not merely on "pure intuition" but on "the entire system of synthetic functions of thought" (Natorp 1911, p. 63). Because intuition is not an *independent* cognitive faculty, there is no independently given realm of "phenomena" which would have its own laws. The wholly indeterminate, intuitively "given" is, in Natorp's phrase, only *aufgegeben*, i.e., presented as a *task* (Natorp 1910, p. 7). There is, then, no ultimate hiatus between the "form" (universal) and the "material" (particular) of knowledge: "particularity" signifies nothing but "completed determination . . . in which nothing remains to be determined" (Natorp 1911, p. 65). This panlogism, the effacement of all dualistic elements in Kant's theory of knowledge, invites the thesis that neo-*Kantianism* is often equally a neo-*Hegelianism*. It also indicates the primary point of disagreement between Natorp and phenomenology.

This is most clearly seen in Natorp's distinctive re-working of Kant's concept of apperception into the doctrine of transcendental psychology. Natorp accepts the "Kantian" view that "it is from the inner life that all things must spring" but argues that inner life is "in itself formless" and hence cannot be grasped in immediate reflection (Natorp 1911, p. 50). Nor can it be approached (as the "leading psychology currently does") as a field to be objectified, reduced to law, since this destroys its character precisely *as* the (flowing) subjective (Natorp 1911, pp. 153–4). Mental life can only be *re-constructed*, via a process of "subjectification." Only by a "regress from an objectification accomplished from its sources in the subject and its mental life [*Erlebnis*] can these latter be brought to cognition" (Natorp 1911, p. 50). Like Kant's unity of apperception but unlike Husserl's transcendental consciousness, the "ego of *Bewusstheit*" is "neither a fact nor something existing nor a phenomenon"; it is, rather, "the *ground* of all fact, the ground of all existence, all givenness, all appearance" (Natorp 1912, p. 32).

The formal structure of *Bewusstheit* (ego – formless content [task] – object) can be traced in two directions, one of which has teleological, the other foundational, priority (Natorp 1912, pp. 200–2). Object-determination has teleological priority: I objectify my experience by attributing the red I see to the apple. But as knowledge progresses I come to see that what is objective at one stage is in fact only subjective, that the redness of the apple is a function of my subjective life. Though it has foundational (transcendental) priority, this subjective life cannot be described; it is accessible only by working back from a given stage of objectification (abstraction) to *re-construct* a previous, richer, more "subjective" stage. The subjective is not a distinct *region* of being; there is only being itself, which can be grasped in two cognitive directions.

191

Critical idealism thus fulfills the yearning for philosophical wisdom, for *Weltanschauung*, by demonstrating a systematic, progressive constructivism as the "methodology" of science, grounded in a re-constructive transcendental psychology as the source of "the living mutual relations of the logical, ethical and aesthetic" (Natorp 1911, p. 153). In both form and aim, this neo-Kantian version of scientific philosophy contrasts sharply with that developed in the phenomenological movement.

## Critical idealism and phenomenology

In *Ideen I* (1913) HUSSERL (see Article 15) claims, with only slight irony, that "we are the genuine positivists" (Husserl 1983, p. 39). Under Brentano's tutelage Husserl's initial attitude toward Kantian apriorism had been altogether negative and, in harmony with neo-Kantianism's own early positivist period, he instead proposed a psychological account of the apriori (e.g., in *Philosophie der Arithmetik* [1891]). By the 1890s, this kind of continuity between philosophy and positive science had been abandoned in Marburg for transcendental idealism. Husserl nevertheless established close ties with Natorp, who was instrumental in steering him away from psychologism and would later inspire Husserl's move from "static" to "genetic" phenomenology. By 1913 Husserl had developed his own phenomenological "transcendental idealism," but it remained distinct in principle from Marburg neo-Kantianism. While the latter defined the scientific character of philosophy in terms of a transcendental *logic*, a systematic presentation of the apriori principles ("method") of empirical science, the former retained the anti-systematic, "empirical" cast of its founder's early period, grounding its theory of the apriori on a philosophical appeal to *intuition*.

In his treatment of Natorp's psychology in the first edition of the *Logical Investigations* (1900, 1901), for example, Husserl rejects Natorp's doctrine of the pure ego of apperception. In the second edition (1913), however, he claims that he has "since managed to find it," i.e., has "learnt not to be led astray from a pure grasp of the given through corrupt forms of ego-metaphysic" (Husserl 1970, p. 549). If the more idealistic Husserl no longer associates the Kantian ego with the "corrupt ego-metaphysic" of speculative idealism, his note also advances the very *un*-Natorpian claim to have *found* the pure ego in a "pure grasp of the given," i.e., in *evidence*. Another note states that the pure ego is "apprehended in *carrying out* a self-evident *cogito*" (Husserl 1970, p. 544). Natorp had denied the phenomenality of the ego; it can neither be objectified, nor present itself at all, without ceasing to be genuinely "subject." For Husserl, however, this argument is merely verbal: the ego is there as a fact, an object, in a manner appropriate to *it*. To claim otherwise is tantamount to consigning the ego to the realm of myth (Husserl 1970, pp. 549–51).

This episode indicates how Husserl remains a "positivist" by insisting on a *philosophy of evidence*; whether as correlate of empirical intuition or phenomenological reflection, givenness is no mere "task" but an ultimate *Rechtsquelle*. To define the scientific character of philosophy in terms of a distinction between empirical and apriori dimensions of positive science already presupposes an uncritical (unclarified) concept of science. Only the phenomenological *reduction* can establish a truly presuppositionless scientific philosophy by bracketing questions of *being* and disclosing the field of phenomenological *experience*. Phenomenology reflects on the intentional (neither logical nor causal) interconnections wherein the intelligibility (meaning, *Sinn* ) of things is constituted. It is therefore able to clarify the meaning-structure of scientific validity claims, but can it also provide a theory that *justifies* the claim of positive science to a progressive grasp of being? While phenomenology censures neo-Kantianism for presupposing too much, the latter objects that phenomenology does not really ground the *validity* of knowledge at all.

Because Husserl does not identify the task of scientific philosophy with the *questio juris*, transcendental phenomenology, unlike critical idealism, introduces a radical *discontinuity* between philosophy and positive science. It is the world-horizon as such – the life of meaning and not the fact of science – that phenomenology, as a reflection on "evidence," claims for itself. If, as Husserl writes to Natorp in 1909, the Marburg School operates with "fixed formulas" that serve as first principles governing all investigation, "we in Göttingen work from an entirely different attitude and, though we are genuine idealists, it is an idealism from below" – not the "false empiricistic and psychologistic" ground but "a genuinely idealistic one from which one may ascend, step by step, to the heights" (Schuhmann 1994, p. 110). Natorp however, like Rickert, doubts that Husserl's idealism "from below," based on intuitive givenness, is in a position to claim scientific – i.e., *ultimately grounded* – status for its own assertions. Phenomenological empiricism cannot, according to Natorp, provide the necessity and universality demanded of any philosophical cognition worthy of the name. The question of whether philosophical cognition is grounded in concepts (logic) or intuitions (evidence) remains a crucial point of contention between phenomenological and neo-Kantian modes of thought.

If the foundations of neo-Kantian and phenomenological conceptions of scientific philosophy are different, so are the motivations and aims. In the tradition of German idealism, Natorp seeks a scientific philosophy that will satisfy the soul as well as the intellect, while Husserl's idealism retains, somewhat reluctantly, its positivist character. Ethical, social, and existential situations demand a *Weltanschauung* – "we cannot wait . . . we have to take a position" (Husserl 1965 [1911], p. 141) – but it is illusory to think that this goal, "set in the finite," can be attained by scientific philosophy. To seek a scientific philosophy that will "satisfy both intellect and feeling" (Husserl 1965, p. 142), to hope "to have [a] system . . . soon enough to be able to live by it" (Husserl 1965, p. 143), is to conflate two distinct goals. The first, the aim of *Weltanschauung* philosophy, is *wisdom* (Husserl 1965, p. 144); the second, the only legitimate motivation of scientific philosophy, is "*responsibility* . . . in regard to humanity" (Husserl 1965, p. 141). Hence Natorp's position must be rejected: "To the extent that this is intended as a reconciliation calculated to erase the line of demarcation between *Weltanschauung* philosophy and scientific philosophy, we must throw up our defense against it" (Husserl 1965, p. 142).

Husserl's refusal to subordinate scientific responsibility to individual wisdom had its origin in a positivist, empiricist apprenticeship which Heidegger, trained in Southwest German neo-Kantianism at Freiburg, did not share. It might be expected, then, that as he began to develop his own postwar theory of "concrete subjectivity," Heidegger would retain the sympathy for neo-Kantian *Weltanschauung* tendencies he expressed, for example in his *Habilitation*-thesis reference to "the deeper, worldview essence of philosophy" (Heidegger 1978b [1916], p. 410). Instead, the lecture courses of 1919–23 introduce the "hermeneutics of facticity" as an extension of the phenomenological principle of evidence, and they cultivate Husserl's radical 1911 distinction between scientific philosophy and *Weltanschauung*. At least rhetorically, Heidegger resists the spirit of the age. He proposes to reform the University by recovering the roots of genuine "science" and in this context offers detailed criticisms of both Marburg critical idealism and Baden *Wertphilosophie*.

Both schools "exhibit a non-scientific tendency toward *Weltanschauung*" and an "overhasty striving toward systematic closure" (Heidegger 1993a [1919/20], p. 9). Lacking the "phenomenological criterion" of "understanding evidence and evident understanding," neo-Kantianism "lacks a genuine scientific problematic" (Heidegger 1987 [1919], pp. 125, 126). It is a "standpoint philosophy' that confuses reflection on science with scientific philosophy (Heidegger 1993b [1920], p. 142). It mistakenly restricts "the transcendental problem to the constitution-form 'science'" and sees "all domains of life through this filter" (Heidegger 1993a [1919/20], p. 23). Natorp's method is merely the uncritical "radicalization of the theoretical"; defining itself by the *questio juris*, it does not permit anything "outside the theoretical attitude" to be seen as a philosophical problem (Heidegger 1993b [1920], p. 143).

Husserl's non-formal concept of transcendental consciousness represented an initial break with the "theoretical" in this sense, but it shared with the neo-Kantian formal-logical subject the status of being "apriori," related to the world as an intentional ground, not as a natural, empirical item. Can this discontinuity – which defines the character of phenomenology as an *autonomous* science – be maintained when phenomenology becomes the *Urwissenschaft* of *factic* (i.e., historical, finite, situated) "life"? Early Heidegger thought so and recognized the "methodological" demand to show how "life as *Erleben* becomes *rationally* accessible for philosophy" (Heidegger 1993b, p. 88).

In this regard, Natorp's method of subjectification represents the "antipode" (Heidegger 1993b, p. 96) to Heidegger's own phenomenological approach. The argument that phenomenological description objectifies, and hence destroys, the subjective character of the life-flux "is correct from the constitutive [*sc.* Natorp's constructive] perspective," but phenomenological description – initially defined only negatively, against natural-scientific causal and genetic methods – is not equivalent to constructive objectification (Heidegger 1993b, p. 194). No doubt Natorp is right that "the ego cannot become an object of thought" (= logical construction), but "the question is whether it must become an object of thought, whether what it 'is' is determined in thought" (Heidegger 1993b, p. 143). This is not, however, to "resign" the ego, with the Baden School, to the conceptual limbo of being an "irrational remainder," for such "resignation" arises from the same constructive, theoretical standpoint (Heidegger 1993b, p. 143). Phenomenology does not ask that one "abandon thinking" in favor of "enthusing and intuiting" in some irrational immediacy; it invites one to explore "a more original form" of "theory" or thinking, one not driven by the "standpoint" of "neo-Kantian logical methodology" (Heidegger 1993b, p. 144).

It is beyond the scope of this chapter to lay out how the early Heidegger approaches this "more original" thinking in terms of "formal-indicating concepts" which arise "in life and on life itself," adumbrating an "evidence situation" where *philosophical* interpretation of factic life becomes possible as a responsible *Wiederholung* of the meaning (*Sinn/Sein*) presupposed in any encounter with entities. The salient point is just that this approach remains, for Heidegger, "categorial research" into an existential apriori and, like Husserl, he holds the demand for *Weltanschauung* to be a corruption of the genuine motive of philosophy (Heidegger 1993b, p. 170). Heidegger's appeal to an *ontological* ground for philosophical science thus also encounters the neo-Kantian *questio juris*: Upon what is grounded the validity of those categories factic life employs in understanding itself *philosophically?* Heidegger (1977 [1927/28], pp. 314ff) argues that a phenomenological account of the *origin* of categories renders the question of their *validity* otiose. But if that origin is finite, factical, and situational, can it suffice to *ground* those judgments that, in science and philosophy, lay claim precisely to trans-situational truth? At their famous 1929 Davos "dispute," Cassirer posed this question to Heidegger: If truth is ontologically relative to finite Dasein, must we not give up the idea of necessary truth? How can a finite being be the ontological ground of apriori validity (Heidegger 1991 [1929], p. 278)? Heidegger replied that his thesis of ontological relativity merely maintained that "truth only has meaning [*Sinn*] when Dasein exists" (Heidegger 1991, p. 281). Still, he did not go on to say where the distinction – between the "scientific" validity claimed by his own categorial analysis of "life" and those interpretations which belong merely to *Weltanschauung* – is itself grounded in the ontological theory of truth.

In the 1920s Heidegger did not wish to substitute *Weltanschauung* wisdom for scientific philosophy, but to *expand* the reach of reason beyond the limits of a logic of science. That he later abandoned the claim to philosophy (scientific or otherwise), though without ceding his claim to a certain rigor, does not demonstrate that the neo-Kantian problematic is either degenerate or irrelevant. It signals, instead, the truculence of issues that must reappear whenever Continental philosophy seeks to maintain contact with *philosophy*.

## References

Arendt, Hannah: "Martin Heidegger at eighty," in *Heidegger and Modern Philosophy*, ed. Michael Murray (New Haven, CT: Yale University Press, 1978).

Brelage, Manfred: *Transzendentalphilosophie und konkrete Subjektivität: Eine Studie zur Geschichte der Erkenntnistheorie in 20. Jahrhunderts*, in *Studien zur Transzendentalphilosophie* (Berlin: de Gruyter, 1965). (The best critical study to date.)

Gadamer, Hans-Georg: *Philosophical Hermeneutics*, ed. and tr. David E. Linge (Berkeley, CA: University of California Press, 1977).

Heidegger, Martin (1912): "Neuere Forschungen über Logik," in *Frühe Schriften*, in *Gesamt-*

*ausgabe*, vol. 1, ed. Friedrich-Wilhelm von Herrmann (Frankfurt: Vittorio Klostermann, 1978a).

——(1916): "Die Kategorien- und Bedeutungslehre des Duns Scotus," Conclusion, in *Frühe Schriften*, in *Gesamtausgabe*, vol. 1, ed. Friedrich-Wilhelm von Herrmann (Frankfurt: Vittorio Klostermann, 1978b).

——(1919): "Phänomenologie und transzendentale Wertphilosophie," in *Zur Bestimmung der Philosophie*, in *Gesamtausgabe*, vol. 56/57, ed. Bernd Heimbüchel (Frankfurt: Vittorio Klostermann, 1987).

——(1919/1920): *Grundprobleme der Phänomenologie*, in *Gesamtausgabe*, vol. 58, ed. Hans-Helmuth Gander (Frankfurt: Vittorio Klostermann, 1993a).

——(1920): *Phänomenologie der Anschauung und des Ausdrucks*, in *Gesamtausgabe*, vol. 59, ed. Claudius Strube (Frankfurt: Vittorio Klostermann, 1993b).

——(1927/28): *Phänomenologische Interpretation von Kants Kritik der reinen Vernunft*, in *Gesamtausgabe*, vol. 25, ed. Ingtraud Görland (Frankfurt: Vittorio Klostermann, 1977).

——(1929): "Davoser Disputation zwischen Ernst Cassirer und Martin Heidegger," in *Kant und das Problem der Metaphysik*, in *Gesamtausgabe*, vol. 3, ed. Friedrich-Wilhelm von Herrmann (Frankfurt: Vittorio Klostermann, 1991).

Heimsoeth, Heinz: "Die Metaphysischen Motive in der Ausbildung des Kritischen Idealismus," *Kant-Studien*, vol. xxix (1924).

Husserl, Edmund (1900–1; 2nd edn 1913): *Logical Investigations*, tr. J. N. Findlay, 2 vols (London: Routledge & Kegan Paul, 1970).

——(1911): "Philosophy as rigorous science," tr. Quentin Lauer, in *Phenomenology and the Crisis of Philosophy* (New York: Harper Torchbooks, 1965).

——(1913): *Ideas Pertaining to a Pure Phenomenology and to a Phenomenological Philosophy, First Book*, tr. F. Kersten, (The Hague; Martinus Nijhoff, 1983).

Köhnke, Klaus Christian; *The Rise of Neo-Kantianism: German Academic Philosophy between Idealism and Positivism*, tr. R. J. Hollingdale (Cambridge: Cambridge University Press, 1991).

Lask, Emil (1908): "Gibt es ein 'Primat der praktischen Vernunft' in der Logik?", in *Gesammelte Schriften*, vol. I, ed. Eugen Herrigel (Tübingen: J. C. B. Mohr, 1923a).

——(1911): *Die Logik der Philosophie und die Kategorienlehre*, in *Gesammelte Schriften*, vol. II, ed. Eugen Herrigel (Tübingen: J. C. B. Mohr, 1923b).

——(1912): *Die Lehre vom Urteil*, in *Gesammelte Schriften*, vol. II, ed. Eugen Herrigel (Tübingen: J. C. B. Mohr, 1923c).

Lehmann, Gerhard: "Kant im Spätidealismus und die Anfänge der neukantischen Bewegung," in *Materialien zur Neukantianismus-Diskussion*, ed. Hans-Ludwig Ollig (Darmstadt: Wissenschaftliche Buchgesellschaft, 1987). (This volume contains several excellent articles on various aspects of neo-Kantianism.)

Natorp, Paul: *Logik in Leitsätzen zu akademischen Vorlesungen* (Marburg: N. G. Elwert'sche Verlagsbuchhandlung, 1910).

——: *Philosophie, Ihr Problem und ihre Probleme: Einführung in den Kritischen Idealismus* (Göttingen: Vanderhoek & Ruprecht, 1911).

——: *Allgemeine Psychologie nach kritischer Methode, Erstes Buch: Objekt und Methode der Psychologie* (Tübingen: J. C. B. Mohr, 1912).

Rickert, Heinrich: *Der Gegenstand der Erkenntnis: Einführung in die Transzendentalphilosophie*, 3rd edn (Tübingen: J. C. B. Mohr, 1915).

——: *Die Philosophie des Lebens: Darstellung und Kritik der Philosophischen Modeströmungen unserer Zeit* (Tübingen: J. C. B. Mohr, 1922).

——: *Die Heidelberger Tradition und Kants Kritizismus* (Berlin: Junker und Dünnhaupt, 1934).

Rorty, Richard: *Philosophy and the Mirror of Nature* (Princeton, NJ: Princeton, University Press, 1980).

Schuhmann, Karl (ed.): *Edmund Husserl: Briefwechsel*, vol. V: *Die Neukantianer* (Dordrecht: Kluwer Academic Publishers, 1994).

## Further reading

Beck, Lewis White: "Neo-Kantianism," in *The Encyclopedia of Philosophy*, ed. Paul Edwards (New York: Macmillan, 1972).

Gadamer, Hans-Georg: *Philosophical Apprenticeships*, tr. Robert R. Sullivan (Cambridge: MIT Press, 1985).

Kern, Iso: *Husserl und Kant: Eine Untersuchung über Husserls Verhältnis zu Kant und zum Neukantianismus* (The Hague: Martinus Nijhoff, 1964).

Ollig, Hans-Ludwig: *Der Neukantianismus* (Stuttgart: J. B. Metzlersche Verlagsbuchhandlung, 1979). (Contains concise sketches of the major figures and useful bibliographies of the primary texts.)

Schnädelbach, Herbert: *Philosophy in Germany, 1831–1933*, tr. Eric Matthews (Cambridge: Cambridge University Press, 1984).

Wagner, Hans: *Philosophie und Reflexion* (Munich: Ernst Reinhardt, 1959).

Willey, Thomas E.: *Back to Kant: The Revival of Kantianism in German Social and Historical Thought, 1860–1914* (Detroit: Wayne State University Press, 1978).

# 15

# Husserl*

## RUDOLF BERNET

Edmund Husserl (1859–1938) is the founder of the phenomenological movement which has profoundly influenced twentieth-century Continental philosophy. The historical setting in which his thought took shape was marked by the emergence of a new psychology (Herbart, von Helmholtz, James, Brentano, Stumpf, Lipps), by research into the foundation of mathematics (Gauss, Rieman, Cantor, Kronecker, Weierstrass), by a revival of logic and theory of knowledge (Bolzano, Mill, Boole, Lotze, Mach, Frege, Sigwart, Meinong, Erdmann, Schröder), as well as by the appearance of a new theory of language (Peirce, Marty). This context is thus very like that which gave birth to the Vienna Circle. Though Husserl's study of classical thinkers began with the British empiricists (Locke, Berkeley, and in particular Hume), he later turned almost exclusively to the writings of Kant, Descartes, and Leibniz. As for his contemporaries outside the phenomenological movement, Husserl's closest – though always critical – engagement was with the neo-Kantians (Rickert and, above all, Natorp).

In view of this historical setting and the fact that Husserl's intellectual formation was mathematical (Weierstrass) before it was philosophical (Brentano), it is hardly surprising that his earliest writings concerned arithmetic and logic and dealt with them from a perspective that was psychological (even psychologistic) before it became phenomenological. However, though his thought later developed from a descriptive, to a static transcendental, and finally to a genetic transcendental phenomenology, Husserl remained faithful throughout to his initial interest in the epistemological elucidation of ideal objects on the basis of intentional consciousness. The "phenomena" analyzed by his "phenomenology" always remain givens or lived experiences of consciousness – even though the status of this consciousness will change more than once. In the same way, what is manifested in the phenomena of intentional consciousness will always remain an object, whether it be a logical object, an object of sense perception, a temporal object or a cultural one. Thus it can be said that Husserl's phenomenology is the science of the intentional correlation of acts of consciousness with their objects and that it studies the ways in which different kinds of objects involve different kinds of correlation with different kinds of acts.

What is the point of such a phenomenological study of this intentional correlation? Indeed, what is the goal of Husserl's phenomenology? One might answer that

*Translated by Lilian Alweiss and Steven Kupfer.

its concern is always to account for the "validity," that is to say, the "being-true" of objects on the basis of the way in which they are "given" or "constituted" in the lived experiences of consciousness. Some lived experiences are more suitable than others when it comes to guaranteeing the "being-true" of their intentional objects: these are the acts that not only "intend" their objects but also intuitively apprehend them. Husserl's phenomenological science is thus above all concerned with the study of intuitive acts (be they sensuous or intellectual) and with the way in which non-intuitive acts achieve an intuitive givenness of their objects by means of a "synthesis of intuitive fulfillment." This synthesis of intuitive fulfillment thus has the role of a verifying synthesis, that is to say, a synthesis which confirms or corroborates what, at first, was no more than an empty pretension to validity. Obviously this will usually involve a process having several stages; it thus becomes possible to refer to "degrees" of truth varying in proportion to the greater or lesser intuitive "fulfillment" of the intentional directedness of an object. "Adequate" ful-fillment, that is, the case in which an intended object is intuitively given exactly and in every respect just as it was intended, is the exception, not the rule. According to Husserl this can come about only in the case of an "internal perception," that is, in a "reflection" by consciousness upon itself.

If the object of phenomenology is defined in this way as the intentional correla-tion between acts of consciousness and their objects, and if its aim is defined as the search for an intuitive correlation which is to account for the truth of acts of consciousness, it then remains to be shown how phenomenology becomes the science of genuine knowledge. The first difficulty is that of understanding how there can be a science of consciousness if consciousness is a collection of multifarious psychic lived experiences which ceaselessly appear and disappear. As Husserl puts it: how can there be a science of a "Heraclitean flux" of acts of consciousness? Husserl answers that this is possible only if these acts are described in respect of their invariant or "essential" structure. Phenomenology will henceforth differenti-ate itself from empirical psychology by becoming an "eidetic" science (a science that deals with the essence) of acts of consciousness, or "pure psychology." We shall see that this first break with the "psychologistic" empiricism of his time was not an easy one. Husserl saw this as a real "breakthrough" which enabled him to deal with the correlation between lived experiences of consciousness and the ideal objects of logic without falling prey to the contradiction of making the subject-matter of logic, the "truths of reason," dependent upon the "factual truths" which are the subject-matter of empirical psychology. However, this new eidetic phenom-enology could not avoid new difficulties since it risked losing sight of the temporal character of lived experiences, especially those which are essentially temporal in character, such as acts of memory. We shall return to this matter.

A second decisive "breakthrough" in the development of phenomenological sci-ence came with the introduction of the "phenomenological reduction." Just as in the case of the "eidetic" reduction of lived experiences, so this new reduction was primarily motivated by methodological considerations. Indeed, if phenomenologi-cal science is to account for the possibility of a genuine knowledge of reality, and if, to do so, it turns to the study of the way in which consciousness relates itself intuitively to objects of reality, then the analysis of consciousness must be free from all presuppositions as to its own reality. In other words, if the aim is to show how reality acquires its validity, that is, its being-true, from consciousness, then this consciousness can no longer be understood as a reality of the same kind without falling prey to a vicious circle. Therefore it is necessary to "purify" consciousness of all empirical apperception, so that it ceases to be something belonging to the real world. This is why Husserl often presents the phenomenological reduction as a move which produces an exclusion, a "bracketing" of the world. But greater precision is necessary: if the validity of the world is "suspended" and if consciousness is purified of all worldly apperception, then this is precisely in order to account for the reality of the world and for genuine knowledge of the world in a critical, that is, non-dogmatic fashion.

This "justification" of genuine knowledge of reality on the basis of a purified intuitive consciousness is the object of "transcendental" phenomenology. It is a "phenomenology" since its concern is exclusively with "pure phenomena", that is, with the manner in which reality appears or is intuitively given in a purified consciousness. This pure phenomenology is "transcendental" insofar as it describes the correlation between the phenomena of consciousness and corresponding intentional objects in order to show how a synthetic collection of phenomena progressively "constitutes" or constructs the meaning and validity of real objects. Indeed, Husserl himself believed he needed to give an "idealist" interpretation to this process of constitution, a move which gave rise to objections among his students, from Heidegger, for example. None the less, the transcendental idealism of constitutive phenomenology is a direct consequence of the "transcendental phenomenological reduction" since it amounts to claiming that the being-true of objects is reducible to the way in which they appear and constitute themselves in pure consciousness. This pure and constitutive consciousness is thus the "origin" of the being (in the sense of the "being-true") of objects.

It could be said that Husserl's phenomenology was dominated from beginning to end by this question of the origin of objects in consciousness. The various stages in the development of Husserl's thought are thus so many different ways of rethinking this question of the origin of objects, in particular of ideal objects. The meaning of the notion of "origin" changes progressively in line with developments in the treatment of the origin of ideal objects – first, within a phenomenology still tainted by psychologism, then within a static phenomenology (static even as regards temporality), finally within a genetic phenomenology which opens out onto a philosophy of history. The status of the "ideal object" evolves in the same way: from an initial misunderstanding (its reduction to a consciousness understood in terms of empirical psychology), toward a logicist or Platonic conception (the claim that it is independent of any lived experience of consciousness), arriving finally at a transcendental-constitutive analysis which takes all constituted objects (those of logic but also cultural objects and those of sense perception) to be ideal objects. In the course of this evolution, the concept of "phenomenology" itself undergoes several changes: conceived to begin with as a kind of empirical psychology, phenomenology becomes next a pure or eidetic psychology, then a static transcendental phenomenology (which analyzes the correlation between constituting consciousness and constituted objects), and it finally turns into a transcendental genetic phenomenology (which investigates the formation of acts of transcendental consciousness on the basis of a "passive synthesis," and describes their "habitualization" and the historical transmission of ideal objects of science and culture from one generation to the next).

More detailed consideration of the historical development of Husserl's thought reveals that its *first* stage was characterized by a considerable hesitation between psychologism and logicism in the phenomenological analysis of the ideal objects of arithmetic and logic. Husserl's psychologism, so much criticized by Frege, consisted in his accounting for the concept of number on the basis of its psychological genesis in acts of selective perception and collection. This position, defended in his *Philosophy of Arithmetic* (1891), was quickly abandoned in the first volume of *Logical Investigations* (*Prolegomena to Pure Logic*, 1900) and replaced by a position diametrically opposed, a Platonic logicism which affirmed the independent existence of logical idealities. The antagonism between these two positions exemplifies Husserl's difficulty in reconciling his program of providing an analysis of the subjective origin of the objects of arithmetic and logic with his recognition of their objective and ideal character. Only in the second volume of *Logical Investigations* (1901) did he succeed in overcoming this difficulty with the introduction of eidetic phenomenology (which transformed the lived experiences of consciousness into *sui generis* idealities) and with the conception of "categorial intuition" (as a *sui generis* intuitive act relating to an ideal object).

The *second* stage in the development of Husserl's thought was dominated by its introduction of the transcendental phenomenological reduction and by its static phenomenological analysis of sense perception. These investigations were given expression in his key work *Ideas Pertaining to a Pure Phenomenology* (1913). From a methodological viewpoint this work is characterized by its idealist presentation of the transcendental phenomenological reduction and by a constitutive analysis which appeals throughout to the correlation between the intentional lived experience (or "noesis") and its object (or "noema") just as it is intended by lived experience. Henceforth, the "pure phenomena" studied by phenomenology will include, not only acts of consciousness but their intentional objects insofar as (and just as) they give themselves in those acts. The real world itself thus progressively becomes a phenomenon, which gives itself and constitutes itself in the course of the experience of a community of transcendental subjects. If the clarification of the possibility of a genuine knowledge of the world is the primary concern of transcendental phenomenology, it is easy to see why such a phenomenology attaches so much importance to the analysis of sense perception. Taken in its transcendental signification, that is to say, as constituting, sense perception is more than a discovery of a thing in the world, it is the intuitive justification of its meaning and its reality. Since the perceived thing is the noematic correlate of noetic lived experience of perception and since this correlate is phenomenologically given, there is no more room for doubt about its reality. The thing perceived may prove to be different, my actual perception may prove to have been mere illusion, nonetheless, inasmuch as I perceive it and inasmuch as it is intuitively given to me, it cannot not exist for me.

The transcendental analysis of perception not only makes a decisive contribution to a phenomenological resolution of the old "enigma" concerning the existence of the world and genuine knowledge of it, but also enables Husserl both to develop his original conception of the finitude of the transcendental subject and to provide a phenomenological analysis of other forms of intentional lived experiences (imagination, memory, empathy) and of their temporal structure. Surely, Husserlian phenomenology's most fruitful and lasting contribution to contemporary philosophy is provided by these meticulous analyses of the different forms of intentional consciousness, of their common temporal substrate, and of the different modes of being of the transcendental subject (ego, monad, person, intersubjective and generative community) which they imply. These analyses provide an opportunity for the reader to gain some idea of the extraordinary investigative scope of a phenomenology of transcendental consciousness.

In contrast to the "internal" perception of a lived experience of consciousness or to the "pure reflection" which is put to work by the phenomenological science of transcendental consciousness, the "external" perception of a spatial thing is characterized by an intuitive directedness which is essentially "inadequate." While intending the thing as a whole each perception must content itself with a partial givenness of the thing or, to use Husserl's term, with a simple "adumbration" (*Abschattung*) of it. It is true that in the course of the perceptual process new adumbrations offer themselves to the subject, one after the other, but it also remains true that none of them (nor their sum total) brings about a complete and definitive givenness of all aspects of the thing. The process of perception of a spatial thing is thus marked by an insurmountable finitude, and this finitude is manifested in the form of an indefinite, that is, infinite progress of the perceptual process. The real thing thus functions as an "idea in the Kantian sense," that is, as an anticipation or goal in accordance with which the perceptual process is regulated without ever attaining or realizing it intuitively. The essential finitude of the subject of perception of a spatial thing ensures that perception becomes "an infinite task." Husserl acknowledges that the same holds good for the perception of the temporal flux of consciousness and thus for transcendental phenomenology itself, which, while being a science, finds itself harnessed to an infinite task. Nothing can do away with this finitude of the transcendental subject of knowledge: neither the transition to an intersubjective historical community involving many generations, nor the hypothesis of the existence of an absolute transcendental subject whose nature is divine. However, it must be added that Husserl is at pains to transform this experience of an essential lack on the part of the transcendental subject into the idea of an indefinite progress of knowledge, a "universal teleology of reason."

Even if intuition in its twofold meaning of sense perception and categorial intuition (or "intuition of essences") is indeed the fundamental mode of transcendental knowledge, Husserl nonetheless takes the greatest pains with the analysis of derivative forms of intuitive consciousness, such as memory, imagination, and empathy (*Einfühlung*). These are what Husserl calls acts of "presentification" (*Vergegenwärti-*

*gung*), that is, intentional acts whose object, though intuitively given, is not immediately present (Husserl says, for instance, that empathy is an "appresentation" of the lived experience of another). Doubtless, memory is the simplest and most illuminating example of such an act of presentification. The intentional object of memory is a past object or, more exactly, the object of a past experience. This object is intuitively given to me in the present act of memory, not, however, as being present but as being past. In remembering, consciousness thus solves the riddle of making the past present without integrating it into the present, that is, it preserves the past's quality of pastness. For Husserl, memory is different from perception in that it is the lived experience of the "reproduction" of a previous perception. He claims that intuitive imagination is to be understood in terms of the same model: it is a "quasi-perception," that is, the perception of something absent "as if" it were present. Thus, instead of being, like memory, the reproduction of a previous perception, imagination is the productive reproduction of a fictitious perception. However, imagining is like remembering in that the person who is imagining knows that the intentional object, which is intuitively given to her, is not an object belonging to her present real environment.

In the case of empathy, present consciousness takes a further step in the phenomenological conquest of what is absent. While the intentional object of memory and imagination, though absent, remains essentially linked to my consciousness, this is not the case with the consciousness of the other as represented in my act of empathy. Nevertheless, the other's consciousness is not inaccessible since it is given to me through the "expressive" stratum of her body. Even though I can never intuitively perceive the other's lived experience, I can nonetheless perceive its trace through her bodily behavior. The expressive body of the other thus gives me access to her lived experience while making me realize, as Husserl emphasizes, that, as a direct perception, this lived experience remains inaccessible to me (not, however, to the other). Empathy is thus a presentification of what is absent *qua* invisible.

At least two things should be borne in mind concerning this phenomenology of the invisible, with its highly innovative analyses of a present consciousness which intends something that cannot be made present: first, that it is a mistake to characterize Husserl's phenomenology of transcendental consciousness as a "metaphysics of presence" (as Derrida does, following Heidegger); secondly, that Husserl's phenomenology in its most radical expression is a phenomenology of the temporality of consciousness. Indeed, it is from its temporal essence that consciousness derives its capacity to transcend itself towards what is absent (be it toward past or future, an imagined world or the inaccessible lived experience of another subject). Far from resembling a self-enclosed bubble, consciousness, from the start, is open to otherness, since, thanks to its temporal essence, it is always already an alteration in itself. From the first instant, consciousness passes beyond the present and distances itself from its point of departure. Husserl adds that this past of consciousness is nonetheless not lost since consciousness, while passing, can at the same time "retain" its past and return to it in memory. Holding on ("retention") to its past experiences with one arm, and stretching out the other ("protention") towards future experiences still to come, consciousness never coincides with its present lived experience.

203

Strictly speaking, there is no such thing as present consciousness. In other words, present consciousness is always the heir of a past consciousness and its presence consists of passing, and so, of surpassing itself, as it opens itself up to new experiences. It is clearer now how this meditation on the temporal essence of consciousness is the source of a new foundation for phenomenology, which leads to the abandonment of the static analysis of an atemporal correlation of noesis with noema in favor of a genetic phenomenology of transcendental consciousness.

With genetic transcendental phenomenology we arrive at the *third* stage in the development of Husserl's thought. Of his published works available in English translation, *Cartesian Meditations* ([1931]; 1960, §37–9) is the most suitable reference text. Genetic phenomenology deals with the "genesis" of acts of transcendental consciousness and of their intentional objects. It thus invokes forms of experience which precede and render possible those intentional correlations which were investigated by static phenomenology. Since every intentional act has a genesis it bears within itself the inheritance of other acts which have preceded it, and thus it never appears in isolation and complete. In particular, Husserl insists on the fact that this genesis of acts is a matter of passivity or "passive synthesis." This passive synthesis which forms the connections between the lived experiences of consciousness is prior to any voluntary activity or "position taking" on the part of the subject and is carried out especially in the form of "associations": a lived experience associates itself of its own accord (through resemblance or temporal contiguity) with another lived experience and "awakens" the subject to an active and explicit intending of that which these passive associations have done no more than suggest to the subject. It must, however, be emphasized that, within the framework of genetic phenomenology, these laws of association are not psychological but transcendental and that they are laws of "intentional motivation", which govern transcendental life by providing it with its dynamic unity.

Genetic phenomenology's study of passive synthesis not only leads to a new foundation for static phenomenology but also opens up a whole series of new phenomena. First, there are phenomena which concern the awakening of subjective activity (sleeping and waking, birth, a conversion leading to a new style of life). Then there are phenomena concerning the preservation of what has been acquired by means of subjective activity (formation of habitualities of transcendental life, of subjective competences, and of individual styles of life). It is thus apparent how the study of passive syntheses leads to a reshaping of the concept of transcendental subjectivity (and intersubjectivity): since every act is embedded in an associative chain with other acts (past, future, actual, and possible ones) and since the subject is inseparably linked to this infinite ensemble of acts, transcendental subjectivity, far from being a simple pole of identity (as with Kant), is filled with experiential content and is individualized. In Husserl's own words, the transcendental subject becomes a "monad" or "person." Since, further, this transcendental monad is always already associated with the life of other monads in the course of its subjective experience, subjectivity, as understood by genetic phenomenology, is always already "intersubjectivity," that is, a community of transcendental life.

However, genetic phenomenology is not concerned only with the genesis of subjective activities, with the birth and development of a transcendental personal life, with the formation of ever larger transcendental communities; it is also concerned with the genesis of objects. Exactly like subjective lived experiences, intentional objects are never isolated but are linked and refer to one another. This had already been established by static phenomenology, which had shown how every intentional object is part of an "intentional horizon," which implies other objects. This is why static phenomenology had referred to the world as the "horizon of all horizons." What is new about genetic phenomenology is that this horizonal givenness of the world (along with every object in this world) is questioned as to its genesis. Similarly, it turns out not only that the givenness of an object refers to the givenness of other objects (past, future, implicitly "co-intended," apparent, or hidden) but that it always already presupposes the "pre-givenness" (*Vorgegebenheit*) of the world. This pre-givenness of the world is to be understood as a transcendental "pre-constitution" (and not as a dogmatic assumption of the existence of the world), and is the result of prior constitutive activities by an intersubjective community. It is now easier to see how genetic phenomenology, having put in evidence the forms of a transcendental community comprising several generations, came to be transformed into a phenomenology of history.

Before moving to the final stage in the development of Husserl's thought, further reference should be made to that other vast area of genetic phenomenological research which deals with the genesis of judgments and of the objects of logic on the basis of "pre-predicative" experiences. Husserl's great work *Formal and Transcendental Logic* (1929) is exemplary of such a "genealogy of logic" and brings out clearly the way in which logical thinking is indebted to sense experience and the "life world" (*Lebenswelt*).

The key work of Husserl's final phase, when he was led to become increasingly interested in the phenomenology of history, is without doubt *The Crisis of European Sciences* (1936–7). In the context of a crisis simultaneously affecting the internal foundation of the objective sciences and their contribution to the "needs of life," Husserl became convinced of the need for phenomenological research into the history of scientific thought and the reasons for its decline. This "questioning back" (*Rückfrage*) into history led inevitably to a "reactivation" of the "originary evidence" on the basis of which scientific thought had developed. The aim is thus still to provide a phenomenological foundation for the validity of the ideal objects of science on the basis of an original transcendental intuition. Now, however, this transcendental origin is to be understood as a historical fact, or, more precisely, as a "transcendental historical fact." This means at least three things: (1) that this intuitive transcendental origin is accessible only by means of an intentional questioning which is historical in kind; (2) that this intuitive origin is embedded in the historical context of a particular "life world"; (3) that phenomenology is led to question itself about the meaning and possibility of a historical "transmission" of an original evidence. It is a shared feature of these new tasks that they make transcendental phenomenology particularly attentive to an original entanglement of transcendental intuition and empirical event. That is to say, by bringing out the importance of a "transcendental facticity," this new phenomenology of history is

205

led to thoroughly rethink its own eidetic character. Nonetheless, according to Husserl, the phenomenology of history does not abandon the study of history's essential structures, but must take account of the fact that these essential structures are themselves historical in kind.

This new conception of a transcendental historicity brings out very well the tension between empiricism and transcendental idealism which runs through all of Husserl's work. On the one hand, with his usual meticulousness, Husserl analyzes the "sedimentation" and "embodiment" of transcendental intuitions in written language and emphasizes forms of "self-objectification" (*Selbstobjektivation*) and the "enworlding" (*Verweltlichung*) of the transcendental subject. On the other hand, he never abandons the idea that the history of facts belongs to a "universal teleology of reason" whose guardian is transcendental phenomenology. On the one hand, then, there is phenomenology's focus on facticity, embodiment, the life-world, and the loss of meaning; and on the other, phenomenology proclaims itself as a science of essences, of the transcendental constitution of every kind of being, an absolute science which serves as the foundation of all human endeavor (be it theoretical, axiological, or practical).

It is therefore not at all surprising that this tension is reflected by the phenomenologists who succeeded Husserl and were inspired by him. There is no doubt that most of them have been more sympathetic to the empirical phenomenology of facticity and embodiment than to Husserl's transcendental and idealist phenomenology. This is particularly true of such outstanding figures in the phenomenological movement as HEIDEGGER (see Article 18), SARTRE (Article 21), MERLEAU-PONTY (Article 23), and LEVINAS (Article 20). Other phenomenologists such as Fink, RICOEUR (Article 39), Gurwitsch, and DERRIDA (Article 50) have shown more concern to resist this existentialist version of Husserlian phenomenology. Only more recently has there been interest in the convergences between Husserl and the "analytic" thought of Frege, Wittgenstein, and Searle.

## Writings

Husserl, E.: *Cartesian Meditations: An Introduction to Phenomenology*, tr. Dorion Cairns (The Hague: Nijhoff, 1960).

——: *Formal and Transcendental Logic*, tr. Dorion Cairns (The Hague: Nijhoff, 1969).

——: *Logical Investigations*, tr. J. N. Findlay (London: Routledge & Kegan Paul, 1970).

——: *The Crisis of European Sciences and Transcendental Phenomenology. An Introduction to Phenomenological Philosophy*, tr. D. Carr (Evanston, IL: Northwestern University Press, 1970).

——: *Ideas Pertaining to a Pure Phenomenology and a Phenomenological Philosophy. First Book: General Introduction to a Pure Phenomenology*, tr. Fred Kersten (The Hague: Nijhoff, 1982).

## Further reading

Bell, D.: *Husserl* (London/New York: Routledge, 1988).

Bernet, R., Kern, I., and Marbach, E.: *An Introduction to Husserlian Phenomenology* (Evanston, IL: Northwestern University Press, 1993).

Boer, Th. de: *The Development of Husserl's Thought* (The Hague: Nijhoff, 1978).

Cobb-Stevens, R.: *Husserl and Analytic Philosophy* (Dordrecht: Kluwer, 1990).

Kolakowski, L.: *Husserl and the Search for Certitude* (Chicago, IL: University of Chicago Press, 1987).

Mohanty, J. N.: *The Concept of Intentionality* (St Louis, MI: Warren Green, 1972).

——: *Husserl and Frege* (Bloomington, IN: Indiana University Press, 1982).

—— and McKenna, W. (eds): *Husserl's Phenomenology: A Textbook* (Lanham: Center for Advanced Research in Phenomenology, and University Press of America, 1989).

Smith, B. and Smith, D. W. (eds): *The Cambridge Companion to Husserl* (Cambridge: Cambridge University Press, 1995).

Sokolowski, R.: *The Formation of Husserl's Concept of Constitution* (The Hague: Nijhoff, 1964).

——: *Husserlian Meditations: How Words Present Things* (Evanston, IL: Northwestern University Press, 1974).

Welton, D.: *The Origins of Meaning: A Critical Study of the Thresholds of Husserlian Phenomenology* (The Hague: Nijhoff, 1983).

Willard, D.: *Logic and the Objectivity of Knowledge* (Athens, OH: Ohio University Press, 1984).

# 16

# Scheler

## MANFRED S. FRINGS

The philosopher Max Scheler was born August 22, 1874, in Munich. His mother was of Jewish extraction, his father Lutheran. He became a member of the Roman Catholic Church early in his youth, probably because of its concept of love. He studied medicine and philosophy in Munich and Berlin, and received his doctorate at Jena University in 1899 where he began teaching from 1900 to 1906. He then joined the fledgling phenomenological movement but, in his own phenomenological researches, he remained independent of it. Due to a divorce in 1910, the predominantly Catholic University of Munich discontinued his contract. He remarried in 1912, but remained without a university affiliation until 1919 when he was hired by the University of Cologne as professor of philosophy and director of the Institute of Sociology. During this period he produced an unusual amount of work, which quickly drew attention throughout Germany. In 1924 he married Maria Scheu, who, after his demise on May 19, 1928, was the devoted curator of thousands of posthumous manuscripts. Scheler's work was suppressed by the German Nazi regime.

During his first period of productivity, roughly until 1922, most of Scheler's writings center on problems of ethics. Among separate lengthy treatises on repentance, shame, ressentiment, the tragic, problems of population, etc., he published his *Zur Phänomenologie und Theorie der Sympathiegefühle und von Liebe und Hass* (*On the Nature of Sympathy and of Love and Hatred*), (1913; enlarged 1921), and *Der Formalismus in der Ethik und die materiale Wertethik. Neuer Versuch der Grundlegung eines Ethischen Personalismus* (*Formalism in Ethics and a Non-Formal Ethic of Value: A New Attempt Toward the Foundation of an Ethical Personalism*) (1913/16). He reinstated (1) the phenomenological significance of values in moral experience, and (2) the being of the person as a foundation of the discipline of ethics.

His thought, which remained independent of the phenomenological movement that revolved around Edmund Husserl, had the following characteristic features: (1) Phenomenology must not primarily be methodological but should be based on core intuitions upon which a method can only be applied. In any phenomenological reduction, sensory data, too, must be set aside. (2) The act-being of the person is the condition for both consciousness and an ego. (3) The experience of time is generated in the self-movement of the center of activity of universal and individual life, without which there can be no time-consciousness and perception. (4) All objectivating experiences are preceded by an experience of values.

# I

In the first part of his *Der Formalismus in der Ethik*, Scheler shows that values are noematic correlates of acts of feeling, which, in turn, are antecedent to all other acts not in terms of sequence but in terms of their order of foundation. Therefore, the nature of value-feelings must be part of an elucidation of moral experience. In its second part, he shows that each person has a different and irreplaceable self-value, which, too, must be accounted for (1) in variable moral situations and (2) in exploring specific forms of human associations such as a life-community or a society.

All his moral writings are characterized by the absence of an imperative or a moral law telling one what ought to be done morally. Instead, moral comportment exclusively consists in "preferring" and realizing values that are higher than those given. "Preferring" is not the same as choosing. It is an emotive act that comes close to one's "leaning toward" something prior to deliberation and willing. And since such emotive preferring is vulnerable to value-deceptions, Scheler closely examined such deceptions, most notably in his study, *"Die Idole der Selbsterkenntnis"* (*"The Idols of Self-Knowledge"*) (1911) and *Das Ressentiment im Aufbau der Moralen* (*Ressentiment in the Structure of Morals*) (1914). And his phenomenological researches became even more subtle when it was shown that value experiences were riveted in love, and that love and respective feelings had a logic of their own. In this he explicitly acknowledged Blaise Pascal's *"le coeur a ses raisons."* *Der Formalismus in der Ethik* is therefore rooted also in the phenomenological demonstration of the person as *"ens amans."* Or, there is an *"ordre du coeur,"* an order in every person's heart that is the seat of his or her rankings among values. To explain this point, Scheler makes use of the analogy colors have with values: Just as colors require a surface for their appearance, so also values require substrates for them to exist, while both colors and values remain independent of what they appear on. Yellow, for instance, can be a cloth or a bird, holy can be the value of God, of gods, or of a fetish. Nevertheless, without substrates neither colors nor values exist.

One can add to these analogies that just as all colors and colorations rest on few spectral colors, so also all values and valuations rest on spectral value-ranks. The distinction made among five value-ranks bears heavily on moral experience because what one "ought" to do, or what "ought" to be done, must, in light of the pre-givenness of value experience, presuppose the *value* of what one ought to do or what ought to be done.

In ascending order, the five value-ranks are: (1) The lowest value-rank, which pertains to feelings of the value of bodily comfort or discomfort; they are pleasure values. (2) The next higher rank, pertaining to value-feelings of what is useful or not useful; they are pragmatic values. The values of these two ranks are manageable, quantifiable, and calculable and can be willed. The more humans are occupied with these divisible values, the more humans are divided. (3) The next rank is that of life-values, encompassing values of the noble and the ignoble; this rank also contains values of heroism and can pertain to personal qualities. The two highest value-ranks are given only to feelings of the person. They are (4) mental values of

209

justice, beauty, and of the cognition of truth; and (5) the highest value-rank, which is holiness.

While the lower value-ranks are related to the lived-body and to life, the two higher ranks are of personal being only. This distinction can be corroborated by the fact that, for instance, pain can only be felt in the lived body, while pangs of conscience are strictly personal feelings. The ranks among values also possess exterior distinctive criteria: The higher the rank, the less can its values be willed or otherwise technically produced, managed, and divided because such values have little or no dependence on material substrates.

It is within this timetic framework that Scheler now determines the nature of good and evil: Good and evil are not correlates of feelings but appear with the preferring act that realizes a positive value, or with a non-preferring act realizing a negative value. Therefore, good and evil "ride on the back" of value realizations. In this, they appear exclusively with the temporality of the person. In essence, they are not objects of the will; deliberately pursuing a particular good can be morally good only when there is no pharisaical, egocentric, or other self-deception involved. But the temporality of *being*-good can be genuine only when it occurs in the very inception of preferring, spontaneously coupled with emotive "readiness" to realize a good without condition.

The second part of Scheler's *Der Formalismus in der Ethik* focuses on the being of the person. The form of any mind, spirit or consciousness – human, divine, or fictional – is being in-person. Hence, Scheler rejects all German idealism and phenomenology, holding there to be "pure" consciousness, mind, or spirit. Personal being exists solely in the *executions of acts*. Personal being – itself indifferent to gender, race, or culture – therefore, executes its existence. Yet, each act is tinged with a person's individuality. On the one hand, all persons act out the same types of acts such as thinking, willing, remembering, loving, hating, expecting, etc.; but, on the other, each act is acted out in a unique way peculiar to the individual person. This individual distinction existing between the act-executions of persons is called the "qualitative direction" of a person's acts. In Scheler's early phenomenological studies, consciousness exists only in *personalizing* executions of acts; no two persons execute the same act in the same way. Therefore, the a priori order of value-ranks experienced in the "*ordre du coeur*" is individually *refracted* in each person's moral tenor. This, however, implies that all persons are morally *unequal* no matter how equal they may be under the law.

Specifically, a person's moral readiness spontaneously to prefer higher values is implicit in what Scheler refers to as the forgotten moral category of the "call of the hour," summoning the person to prefer and realize positive values in the moral situation. This call is strictly individual and is intertwined with the individual refraction of the order of values. Even in such cases as a child spontaneously leaving his toys behind to pick a daisy for his mother, there is, no matter how unnoticed by the child, a call of preferring the mother's value over toys. It is the mother's value which exercises a moral tug on the child. Indeed, as a rule, it is the parents' function as models for the child which will engender lasting proper patterns of love and hate in the child's later life. If there is no such moral "tug" of model persons, negative values will more easily grow into a person's "consciousness of models." Scheler developed a classification of basic exemplary and model persons that corresponds to the five ranks among values. The most effective vehicle for individual and collective moral growth is the exemplarity of good persons; neither obedience to a moral law nor education can match their moral force.

One central tenet is also, however, that lower positive values ought to be realized also, but only toward the goal of an equal distribution of earthly goods for all and equal rights among persons. If, however, the manageable lower values are predominantly pursued for the production of pleasure values and their enjoyment, says Scheler, such fixation betrays a deep internal unhappiness in a society. On the other hand, the higher values of the person ought to be realized in a way that brings into relief the moral *difference* among persons so that their self-values are not subjected to egalitarianism. "Aristocracy 'in heaven' does not preclude democracy 'on earth.'" Scheler also extended his personalist ethics to social forms in which the person may find himself, such as in a "mass," a "life-community," "society," or in a "collective personality." It is in the last of these as represented by a nation, culture, or a religion that persons are both co-responsible and self-responsible in gradually forming "solidarity" with an Absolute, or God. This point led Scheler subsequently to write his phenomenology of religion, entitled, *Vom Ewigen im Menschen* (*On the Eternal in Man*, 1921), the last work of his first period.

## II

His second period of productivity reveals novel aspects that go far beyond his Value-Ethics and which culminated in a projected *Metaphysics* and *Philosophical Anthropology*. Both remained unfinished but their fragments were posthumously published in the *Gesammelte Werke* (the German Collected Edition). There are two introductions, Scheler tells us, to these projected works. They are *Probleme einer Soziologie des Wissens* (*Problems of a Sociology of Knowledge*) (1924–6), and *Erkenntnis und Arbeit* (*Cognition and Work*) (1926).

In *Probleme einer Soziologie des Wissens* Scheler showed that sociological and historical "ideal factors" such as art, philosophy, religion, and science that have their roots in *spirit* (*Geist*), are dependent for their historical realizations on "real factors," such as race, geo-politics, population, power politics, and economy, and have their roots in drive-life. The roles that drives have for bringing ideal factors into existence undergo variations over three extended eras of history. These begin with an early genealogical era, when the procreative drive was predominant and made people feel strongly about the preservation of their communal blood and tribal identification. Then follows the era of power aspirations and global struggles, resulting from a predominance of the power drive, and finally, the era of economic factors, resulting from a predominant role of the nutritive drive. This sequence of the predominant roles of the three major drives is not identical with a linear historical development, but the inceptions and durations of each era can also overlap over vast stretches of historical time. Thus, there are still vestiges of the first genealogical era among primitive and presocietal communities living today. The sequential structure itself – the three shifts of the predominant roles of the drives of procreation, of power, and of nutrition – remains, however, everywhere the same. Throughout these subliminal shifts in drive life, ideal and real factors possess dynamic interdependence. The process of this interdependence is characteristically accompanied by steady growth of knowledge and spiritual potential.

In *Erkenntnis und Arbeit* – one of the most complicated works Scheler wrote – the theme of three basic *types* of knowledge is resumed. In the sequence of their historical significance, these types are: "Knowledge of Salvation," "Knowledge of Essence," and "Knowledge of Controlling Nature." All human cognition, i.e., the mental processes *leading* to knowledge, derives its nature and goals from these kinds of knowledge. This pertains especially to Pragmatism, of which *Erkenntnis und Arbeit* is a fresh but critical re-evaluation and on which Scheler had lectured as early as his Munich years. On the one hand, Pragmatism is a viable philosophy because it is rooted in one type of knowledge, the "Knowledge of Control," but on the other, it utterly fails to do justice to the potentials of the other two types of knowledge. Scheler's subtle investigations into human drives and perception foreshadow one of two principles of human existence: the unity not only of the major drives but also of more than twenty of them as to what constitutes their vital motion – a vital, meta-biological energy in individual organisms and life in general. This vital energy and power is called *Drang*, "impulsion." Without impulsion spirit remains "impotent" to account for the reality of something. Despite the maze of thought offered in his *Erkenntnis und Arbeit*, there are two continuous threads running through the text:

1　The metaphysical genesis of impulsion and spirit. It is seen in "blind" impulsion as the principle that realizes spiritual contents while spirit itself seeks its realization. This is followed by the unfolding from impulsion to differentiations of drives and their vague internal objects. These stream forward into the field of perception, which, for this reason, is "drive-conditioned," and finally, the genesis reaches goals of cognition and knowledge. The entire complicated argument is sprinkled with pungent critiques of scientific theories of sensation, especially that of Ernst Mach. While Scheler displays an almost incredible familiarity with the foundations of the natural sciences, whenever he touches upon them, he does not lose sight of society's one-sided fixation on knowledge of control.

2　The genesis given becomes more convincing when seen in the light of Scheler's philosophy of *gestalts*. *Gestalts* originate from *phantasy* that is inherent in impulsion. They are "phantasmic images" (*Bilder*) in drives, which transfer into perception and the highest forms of thinking such as pure mathematics.

Quite a number of unsolved problems kept unspooling from these threads. These led to *Metaphysics* and *Philosophical Anthropology*. His sketches for their solution provide a comprehensible compass that shows the directions his thought was taking in the final fragments: into a "*Wesensschau*" (essence-intuition) of the *coming unity between man, world, and Deity in absolute time.*

After having been repeatedly urged to do so, Scheler published a small book that contained a brief summary of this direction of his thought. It was entitled, *Die*

*Stellung des Menschen im Kosmos* (*The Place of Man in Nature*) (1928). The summary hardly reflects the meta-anthropological dimension Scheler set out to explore.

There is ample speculation as to what, precisely, precipitated Scheler's change of direction in his second period when his rejection of traditional religious conceptions, such as a perfect creator-God, emerged. The claim was that spirit cannot bring anything into existence *without* impulsion and sociological real factors moored in impulsion must apply to the spirit of a Deity also. The Deity, therefore, must possess the two poles of spirit and impulsion to realize its own existence. Spirit and impulsion in the Deity, in humans, and in nature as a whole are the ultimate sources of reality in that they are in tension and resist one another. Reality is possible only when something has the capacity to resist something else. This capacity Scheler locates in the essence of individual and "All-Life," which is another name for impulsion. The theory of reality *qua* resistance had been latently in the making for many years, and Scheler acknowledges in this regard the works of Wilhelm Dilthey, Maine de Biran, Thomas Reid, and Arthur Schopenhauer among others.

While spirit, which historically occurs only in groups, is tethered to the phantasy in impulsion with which it seeks to realize itself, and while "blind" impulsion, in turn, seeks spiritualization, man, world, and God are one process of becoming. In this process the human being has its "place" (*Stellung*) in absolute time. Without this place God remains "absconditus," unknowable. The new direction of thought leading into this process is, therefore, determined by "absolute" time. Scheler's posthumous manuscripts dealing with Martin Heidegger's ontological explication of time break off at the point when he wanted to illuminate Heidegger in terms of absolute time. What is absolute time? One can only approximate its nature because human beings as bearers of history are part of it themselves.

There are three criteria of absolute time: (1) Its phases are *inseparably conjoined* with contents. For example, while this entry is being read, meanings are rolling along filling their time-phases. In contrast to measurable clock time, whose chosen units of hours, etc., are vacant but can be filled at random with contents, absolute time is the flux of the contents themselves. (2) Absolute time originates in alterations of states of life, not in time-consciousness. That is, while each phase of growth, for example, emerges, it simultaneously fades away while a new phase is again becoming, and so on. Absolute time is, therefore, both becoming and unbecoming (*Werden und Entwerden*). (3) In the becoming–unbecoming structure, there must, at first sight, be passages of time *between* any two phases, no matter how close these are taken to be. Concurrent becoming and unbecoming of phases, however, does not allow for gaps between them; rather, becoming and unbecoming is an uninterrupted continuum that grows into ever new phases via smooth transitions. The absolute time of transition is also at hand in all changes taking place, from potency to action, from inanimate to animate nature in plant life, during the realization of spiritual contents and the process of aging.

Its origin lies in the "four-dimensional" manifold of pure variations (*Wechsel*) in impulsion, in which time and space are not yet separated. They begin to disjoin in the drives in which there occurs (1) reversible movement (spatiality) and (2) irreversible alteration (temporality). Before objective time and space are conceived as separate, vestiges of impulsion's four-dimensionality still linger on, for instance, when in the visual field of perception two parallels "meet" at the horizon.

Are there signs of the becoming unity of man, world, and the Deity in absolute time? Scheler sees a sign of this in the first planetary awareness humanity had of itself as a whole. This happened during the eruption of World War I early in the twentieth century. This century beckons an incipient phase of the new era of a slow but unstoppable, global adjustment process among cultures, nations, social classes, genders, races, ethnic groups, intellect and body-consciousness, capitalism and socialism, East and West, and much more. Scheler lectured on this in 1926 and entitled his 1928 publication, *Der Mensch im Weltalter des Ausgleichs* (*Man in the World Age of Adjustment*). The background of this world age is the interpenetration between impulsion and spirit having reached a "mid-point" (*die Mitte der Zeit*). Like thousands of rivers flowing from the past into one common stream they will form in the future, the process of inter-cultural confluence is suffused, however, with "blood and tears" and humanity's "fate." At least in the relative short run, humans will have a capitalist mind-set because of the predominating drive to amass controls and power over "things" in nature through technology and economics. This mind-set is both negative and positive. It is negative in that it results in excessive production of things of the lower level of values and is in conflict with values of life, such as the environment and agriculture. It is positive in that bringing nature under maximum control *deflects* the drive of seeking power over humans as in war. The mind-set of capitalism necessarily leads to a global insight that war does not pay. Global peace is not impossible. History is bound to become "less historical."

A keen observer of what was happening in his time, Scheler engaged its controversial problems. He addressed the awesome dilemma of overpopulation, the confusion of values in society, the waning of faith; the causes of hatred of Germans. By 1927 he had warned in public of rising fascism and communism; he pleaded for a European university to enhance international understanding and the idea of a "United States of Europe"; he warned of a possible World War II, and valued highly the supra-partisan statesman who would be able to lead and guide the ship of state over the high tides of the era of confluence.

## Writings

The *Gesammelte Werke* (*Collected Works*) of Max Scheler, edited by Maria Scheler and Manfred S. Frings, have been published in Berne by Francke Verlag, 1954–86; and Bonn by Bouvier Verlag, 1986– .

## References and further reading

Barber, M. D.: *Guardian of Dialogue: Max Scheler's Phenomenology, Sociology, and Philosophy of Love* (Lewisburg: Bucknell University Press, 1993).
Bershshady, H. J.: *Max Scheler on Feeling, Knowing, and Valuing* (Chicago, IL: University of Chicago Press, 1992). (Contains an up-to-date list of English translatiochs of works by Scheler.)

Frings, M. S.: *Max Scheler: A Concise Introduction into the World of a Great Thinker* (Pittsburgh, 1965; 2nd edn, Milwaukee, WI: Marquette University Press, 1944).

——: *Person und Dasein: Zur Frage der Ontologie des Wertseins* (Person and Dasein: the question of an ontology of the being of values), *Phaenomenologica*, vol. 32 (The Hague: Martinus Nijhoff, 1969).

——: "Toward the constitution of the unity of the human person," in *Linguistic Analysis and Phenomenology*, ed. W. Mays and S. Brown (London: Macmillan, 1972).

——: "The background of Max Scheler's 1927 reading of *Being and Time*: a critique of a critique through ethics," *Philosophy Today*, Summer 1992.

——: "Capitalism and ethics: the world age of adjustment and the call of the Hour," *Phänomenologische Forschungen*, 28/29, eds W. Orth and G. Pfafferott (Freiburg: Alber Verlag, 1994).

Gabel, M.: *Intentionalität des Geistes: Der phänomenologische Denkansatz bei Max Scheler* (Intentionality of spirit: Max Scheler's inception of phenomenological thought) (Erfurth: Benno Verlag, 1991).

Good, P. (ed.): *Max Scheler im Gegenwartsgeschehen der Philosophie* (Max Scheler and present-day philosophy) (Berne: Francke Verlag, 1975).

Kelly, E.: "*Ordo Amoris*: the moral vision of Max Scheler," *Listening*, XXI (1986).

Leonardy, H.: *Liebe und Person: Max Scheler's Versuch eines "phänomenologischen" Personalismus* (The Hague: Martinus Nijhoff, 1976).

Luther, A. R.: *Persons in Love: A Study of Max Scheler's Wesen und Formen der Sympathie* (The Hague: Martinus Nijhoff, 1972).

Ranly, E. W.: *Scheler's Phenomenology of Community* (The Hague: Martinus Nijhoff, 1966).

Schütz, A.: "Scheler's theory of intersubjectivity and the general thesis of the alter-ego," in *The Problem of Social Reality*, vol. 1 of *Collected Papers*, ed. Maurice Natanson (The Hague: Martinus Nijhoff, 1962).

——: "Max Scheler's Philosophy," in *Studies in Phenomenological Philosophy*, vol. 3 of *Collected Papers*, ed. Ilse Schutz (The Hague: Martinus Nijhoff, 1975).

Shimonisse, E.: *Die Phänomenologie und das Problem der Grundlegung der Ethik* (The Hague: Martinus Nijhoff, 1971).

Spader, P. H.: "The primacy of the heart: Scheler's challenge to phenomenology," *Philosophy Today*, XXIII (1983).

——: "A change of heart: Scheler's *Ordo Amoris*, repentance and rebirth," in *Listening*, XXI (1986).

Stikkers, K.: "Phenomenology as psychic technique of non-resistance," in *Phenomenology in Practice and Theory*, ed. W. S. Hemrick (Dordrecht: Kluwer, 1985).

Vacek, Edward, S. J.: "Personal development and the *Ordo Amoris*," *Listening*, XXI (1986).

——: "Scheler's evolving methodologies," in *Morality within Life and Social World*, in *Analecta Husserliana*, ed. Anna Teresa Tymieniecka (Dordrecht: Kluwer, 1987).

Wojtyla, K. (Pope John Paul II): *Primat des Geistes: Philosophische Schriften* (The primacy of spirit: philosophical writings), Introduction by Manfred S. Frings, ed. Juliusz Stroynowski (Stuttgart: Seewald Verlag, 1980).

# 17

# Jaspers

## KURT SALAMUN

Karl Jaspers (1883–1969) is generally known as one of the two great German existentialists together with Martin HEIDEGGER (see Article 18), but Jaspers's existentialist approach is very different from that of Heidegger. While Heidegger intends to construct a fundamental ontology of Being by means of phenomenological method and to highlight some fundamental existentials of human being (*Dasein*), Jaspers rejects every kind of ontology. His existentialist approach is therapeutic: By his philosophizing he intends to appeal to every human being to realize his or her genuine existential possibilities, "possible Existenz" or "true selfhood." The formative influences on his basic thinking include Plato, Plotinus, HEGEL (Article 6), SCHELLING (Article 5), NIETZSCHE (Article 11), KIERKEGAARD (Article 9), DILTHEY (Article 37) and HUSSERL (Article 15). In contrast to Heidegger, Jaspers also developed a political philosophy in the liberal tradition that draws particularly upon the thought of Kant and Max Weber.

Jaspers started his academic career as a psychiatrist and psychologist before becoming a professional philosopher at the University of Heidelberg in 1920. His former professions provided him with many subtle insights into psychological phenomena, and influenced the development of the basic ideas of his existential philosophy. During his research activities as a psychiatrist he published his first major book, *General Psychopathology* (1963 [1913]), a methodological study that focuses on the relevance of hermeneutic understanding for specific fields of psychiatric research. Jaspers's second major book, *Psychologie der Weltanschauungen* (1919), is a study in hermeneutic psychology which argues that a necessary condition of the process of realizing true humanity is to struggle permanently against the dogmatizing tendencies of our world-views. Non-rational forces and life-impulses constitute dynamic elements which help us resist the absolutization of world-views. In this idea Jaspers was obviously influenced by Nietzsche and Dilthey. He already anticipates in this work two key concepts of his later existentialism: boundary situations (other translations of the German word "*Grenzsituation*" are "ultimate situation," "limiting situation," or "borderline situation") and existential communication.

*Existential self-realization and transcending philosophizing*: Jaspers's existentialism was developed in detail in his three-volume *Philosophy* (1969–71 [1932]), whose fundamental ground is a specific hypothesis of philosophical anthropology. Combining some ideas of Kant and Kierkegaard, Jaspers understands a human being as both an empirical and a non-empirical phenomenon. While the empirical dimension of man can be researched by the sciences (e.g., biology, psychology, sociology), the non-empirical dimension cannot be described and explained in scientific terms. Jaspers calls this non-empirical dimension of humanity "Existenz," that is, the non-objective actuality of self-being, true self-hood, existential freedom, undetermined moral decision, or the genuine and authentic self. No doctrines of philosophical anthropology, ontology, or ethics can give an adequate understanding of this dimension of subjectivity and humanity. Such an understanding is possible only by realizing Existenz in one's own life and (or) by elucidating it through transcending thinking.

In connection with Jaspers's project of a transcending philosophizing there arises a severe methodological problem: he proposes to relativize all the descriptive meanings and informative contents of propositions concerning Existenz. This position is similar to Ludwig Wittgenstein's ladder-argument in the *Tractatus*: If all sentences in the *Tractatus* have only the function of climbing the steps of a ladder and their cognitive and descriptive content is absolutely irrelevant – in other words, if they have only the therapeutic function of learning to see the world in the right perspective – then a discussion of the descriptive content of those sentences is of no purpose. They are not meant as propositions, but rather have only a therapeutic function, a sign-post function. Whether or not they can fulfill their function cannot be examined or proven because their sign-post dimension is non-objective and cannot be verbally communicated. This mystical consequence of Jaspers's transcending philosophizing can be avoided only by not accepting his demands for relativizing the content of his philosophy in a strict sense. The best way to interpret him here is to see his position as an appeal to an anti-dogmatic way of philosophizing and to an openness which does not reduce all Being to that which can be objectively articulated.

An urgent question in Jaspers's existentialism is: How can one realize Existenz? Jaspers's answer is that Existenz cannot be planned or managed because it is finally a gift from a non-objectifiable Being, which he calls Transcendence. One becomes aware of Transcendence through acts of existential freedom and self-realization. Such acts have no lasting temporal dimension, but are of only momentary duration. Thus, Jaspers prefers to speak of "possible Existenz" in order to convey the open-ended process of human becoming and realization of freedom and Existenz. Realization of Existenz in specific moments of life is possible only under two conditions. First, through the experience of the boundary situations of death, suffering, struggle, and guilt. Second, through existential communication between two persons such as friends, lovers, a married couple, parent and child, teacher and student, etc. Both conditions are necessary but insufficient for one's realization of Existenz.

*Boundary situations and existential communication*: Boundary situations are evident in the inevitable fact that we are always in situations and cannot escape the historicity of our existence. We cannot live without struggling and suffering. We cannot

217

avoid guilt. We must die. It is in these boundary situations that we either open our being to Transcendence or close ourself off to the truth of our Existenz. Boundary situations cannot be overcome merely by objective and rational solutions. They require a radical change in attitude and in one's common way of thinking. The adequate way to react within boundary situations, as Jaspers notes, "is not by planning and calculating to overcome them, but by the very different activity of *becoming the Existenz we potentially are*" (Jaspers 1970 [1932], vol. 2, p. 179). Jaspers tries to make clear that all intellectualizations of boundary situations prevent us from realizing our Existenz (Jaspers 1971a [1919], pp. 229–80; and 1970 [1932] vol. 2. pp. 177–222).

Jaspers distinguishes four types of communication operative in the four modes of being by which we exist. In the dimension of naive vitality and spontaneous instinctive life (*bloßes Dasein*) the human being lives in primitive communities with other human beings. One uses other people only to reach vital ends, for example, to satisfy basic needs of sex, power-wanting, etc. The second dimension, consciousness in general (*Bewußtsein überhaupt*), is linked to a type of communication based on logical and rational categories. Scientific discussions by experts with the aim of solving technical problems are examples of such universal communication. In the third dimension, spirit (*Geist*), the human being experiences communication as an "idea of a whole," of a certain state, family, society, university, religion, etc. While these three types of communication are objective forms of human interaction, the highest and most valuable form is authentic communication between oneself and another. This is a type of communication which cannot be adequately described in an objectifying language (Jaspers 1970 [1932], vol. 2, pp. 3–27).

*The Encompassing, Transcendence, and philosophical faith*: Self-realization as Existenz, which implies personal authenticity and existential communication and freedom, is experienced as a gift from a transcendent source. This experience directs the person to a dimension of Being, what Jaspers calls Transcendence, absolute Being, Being as such, God, the Encompassing. The concept of the Encompassing functions in Jaspers's philosophy to distinguish the various modes of the appearance of Being, on one hand, and to point indirectly to an infinite unity of Being, on the other hand. Therefore, Jaspers prefers to speak of "periechontology" rather than ontology to capture the non-objectifiable reality of infinite being. The concept of the Encompassing includes the idea of living within the various modes (open horizons) of Being without absolutizing one mode over another. Reason exercises a balance within and among these various modes. Jaspers's metaphysics rejects every type of system or philosophical speculation that collapses the dialectic between immanent and transcendent being by fixating on one dimension or the other. Such approaches are illegitimate objectivizations and anthropomorphizations of a sort of Being which is in a radical sense unknowable and cannot be objectified in rational categories. Therefore traditional symbols of God, the Transcendent, and the Absolute must be understood only as ciphers of transcendence and not as direct embodiments of Transcendence. For Jaspers everything in the world can become a cipher, although he mentions explicitly nature, history, creations of the arts, metaphysical systems, myths and religions, and, most important, man.

The ciphers of transcendence represent an important aspect of Jaspers's conception of philosophical faith. This sort of faith has no objectively guaranteed proof of the existence of transcendence and is not bound to rituals, churches, priests, and theologians, who pretend to be the interpreters of God's revelation. Philosophical faith is a kind of optimistic credo and confidence in the possibility of freedom and humanity and in the existence of a meta-empirical dimension of Being. Jaspers rejects such standpoints as theism, atheism, or pantheism when they are not understood as ciphers of transcendence. As he explicates (Jaspers 1967 [1962], pp. 15–60) in detail, he does not accept any conception of a revealed God as we find it, for example, in Christian faith. An historical revelation of God necessarily implies a claim to the position of an objectively guaranteed absolute certainty and an absolutely true knowledge of God. These claims breed intolerance, fanaticism, various restrictions of individual freedom, and an incapacity for a genuine mutual communication with persons of other religious beliefs. For Jaspers, God is hidden for ever and cannot speak to us in an objectifying language through mediators.

*Reason and politics*: With the publication of *Reason and Existenz* (1956 [1935]) the concept of reason rather then Existenz became prominent in Jaspers's philosophy, and he even viewed his comprehensive treatment of truth, *Von der Wahrheit* (1947), as an extensive study of the widest possible dimensions of reason. Jaspers's political philosophy developed as a reaction to his experience of the Nazi regime in Germany after the Second World War (Jaspers was married to a woman of Jewish origin, and at the end of the war was in great danger of being deported to an extermination camp with his wife). While Jaspers's earlier existentialism is a philosophy of Being, his later political philosophy is concerned with a coming world order, "world philosophy", world peace, German re-unification, and the future of German politics in the mid-sixties. Jaspers applies his concept of boundary situations to the political sphere and holds the thesis that mankind as a whole stands in a boundary situation requiring a radical change in politics and political consciousness. Politics needs to be governed more and more by reason. Because of the twin threats of nuclear annihilation and political totalitarianism, the new reasonable politics must have as its priority the promotion of conditions leading toward a world peace and world federation. Jaspers's central intention is not to trace out a plan for the institutional structure of this world federation, but rather to point to the needed "Umkehr" (transformation or conversion) in science, politics, and religion necessary for world peace and a new global communication. Jaspers's book *The Atom Bomb and the Future of Man* (1961 [1958]) remains one of the only systematic philosophical reflections on the nuclear problem and its moral implications by a contemporary thinker.

*The liberal ethos of humanity*: Jaspers's existential philosophy as well as his reflections on reason and politics portray a liberal ethos of humanity. This ethos is apparent in a number of moral attitudes which are not postulated as explicit moral norms or general ethical rules. He only seeks to stimulate them by his philosophizing. Five moral attitudes (or values) may be identified: First, courage without self-deception, composure, patience, self-possession, and dignity. These attitudes are not only the basis for adequate reactions to the boundary situations of death and suffering, but are also important in so far as they enable the individual to act within the social, political, and economic realms without ideological bias or dogmatic fanaticism. Second, a permanent readiness to assume personal responsibility for consequences of our actions in the world. Responsibility is the only adequate existential reaction to the ultimate situation of guilt. In various political contexts this responsibility corresponds to what Weber (1972, p. 2) called the "ethics of responsibility", i.e., the willingness to accept the consequences of one's own political actions and to stand up for them. Third, a sincere intention to accept communication-partners in their own personal freedom and potential for self-realization, and not to force one's own dogmatic standards of behavior upon them. Jaspers speaks of "existential solidarity" (1970 [1932], vol. 2, p. 63) between oneself and another. In the political sphere this means respecting other persons, groups, and peoples in their cultural and ethnic diversity, and creating a climate in which they have the same opportunity to develop their cultural and ethnic identity as does one's own group. Fourth, the non-egoistic intention to help the communication-partner to realize Existenz without using the other as a mere instrument for one's own purposes of self-realization. Jaspers speaks of a mutual "loving struggle" (1970 [1932], vol. 2, pp. 59–61) between those who share "existential solidarity". Assistance to economically less developed countries, without ignoring the dignity of their people and without using them as instruments for imperialistic purposes, exemplifies this moral attitude in the social and political realm. Fifth, an intellectual integrity and open-mindedness which enable a person to struggle against prejudices and political tendencies that suppress personal freedom such as freedom of speech, assembly, opinion, inquiry, travel, etc. For Jaspers, as for other liberal philosophers of our time, like Karl R. Popper (1974 [1945]), freedom of information and of critique are dominant features of authentically democratic political systems.

The influence of Jaspers on twentieth-century philosophical thinking is difficult to estimate. His works have been translated into over 25 foreign languages, and the German paperback editions have sold more than one million copies. Perhaps from this perspective, Jaspers may be one of the best read Continental philosophers of our age. We do well to recall that Jaspers rejected the idea of a philosophical school to which disciples could be recruited. For him true philosophizing is always original. Nevertheless, his works have provided fruitful impulses to prominent thinkers of the twentieth century such as the historian Golo Mann, the political scientists Dolf Sternberger and Eric Voegelin, and the female philosophers Jeanne Hersch and Hannah ARENDT (see Article 43). Prominent Continental theologians, such as Karl Barth and Paul Tillich, have engaged Jaspers's philosophy of religion, and Rudolf Bultmann was also involved in a public discussion with Jaspers concerning the problem of demythologization of religion (Jaspers/Bultmann 1958 [1954]). Finally, Jaspers has had a significant influence on hermeneutical and phenomenological thinkers like GADAMER (Article 38), RICOEUR (Article 39), and HABERMAS (Article 34), and, in the philosophy of education, on the work of Bollnow (1958). The present activities of the Jaspers Society of Japan, the Jaspers Society of North America, the Jaspers Foundation in Switzerland, and the Jaspers Society of Austria indicate the continuing reception and influence of Jaspers's ideas by contemporary philosophers worldwide.

## Writings

Jaspers, K.: *Allgemeine Psychopathologie* (Berlin, 1913); tr. J. Hoenig and M. W. Hamilton, *General Psychopathology* (Chicago, IL: University of Chicago Press, 1963).

——: *Psychologie der Weltanschauungen* [*Psychology of World-Views*] (Berlin, 1919); 6th edn, (Berlin, 1971a).

——: *Philosophie*, vols 1–3 (Berlin, 1932); tr. E. B. Ashton, *Philosophy*, vols 1–3 (Chicago, IL: University of Chicago Press, 1969–71b).

——: *Die Atombombe und die Zukunft des Menschen. Politisches Bewußtsein in unserer Zeit* (Munich, 1958); tr. E. B. Ashton, *The Future of Mankind* (also as: *The Atombomb and the Future of Man*) (Chicago, IL: University of Chicago Press, 1961).

——: *Der philosophische Glaube angesichts der Offenbarung* (Munich, 1962); tr. E. B. Ashton, *Philosophical Faith and Revelation* (Chicago, IL: University of Chicago Press, 1967).

—— and Bultmann, R.: *Die Frage der Entmythologisierung* (Munich, 1954); tr. N. Guterman, *Myth and Christianity* (New York: Noonday Press, 1958).

## References and further reading

Bollnow, O. F.: *Existenzphilosophie und Pädagogik* [*Existentialism and Education*] (Stuttgart: Kohlhammer, 1958).

Ehrlich, L.: *Philosophy as Faith* (Amherst: University of Massachusetts Press, 1975).

—— and Wisser, R. (eds): *Karl Jaspers Today: Philosophy at the Threshold of the Future* (Lanham: University Press of America, 1988).

Hersch, J.: *Karl Jaspers: Eine Einführung in sein Werk* [*Karl Jaspers: An Introduction*] (Munich: R. Piper, 1986).

Jaspers, Karl: *Basic Philosophical Writings: Selections*, ed., tr., with introductions by L. H. Ehrlich, E. Ehrlich, and George B. Pepper (Athens, OH: Ohio University Press, 1986).

Long, E. E.: *Jaspers and Bultmann: A Dialogue between Philosophy and Theology in the Existentialist Tradition* (Durham, NC: Duke University Press, 1968).

Olson, A. M.: *Transcendence and Hermeneutics: An Interpretation of Karl Jaspers* (The Hague: Nijhoff, 1979).

Penzo, G.: *Il comprendere in Karl Jaspers e il problema dell' ermeneutica* (Rome: Armando editore, 1985).

Popper, K. R.: *The Open Society and Its Enemies* [1945], 2 vols (London: Routledge & Kegan, 1974).

Salamun, K.: *Karl Jaspers* (Munich: C. H. Beck, 1985).

Samay, S.: *Reason Revisited: The Philosophy of Karl Jaspers* (Notre Dame, IN: University of Notre Dame Press, 1971).

Saner, H.: *Karl Jaspers in Selbstzeugnissen und Bilddokumenten* (Reinbeck: Rowohlt, 1970).

—— (ed.): *Karl Jaspers in der Diskussion* (Munich: R. Piper, 1970).

Schilpp, P. A. (ed.): *The Philosophy of Karl Jaspers* (Lasalle, IL: Open Court, 1957).

Schrag, O. O.: *Existence, Existenz, and Transcendence* (Pittsburg, PA: Duquesne University Press, 1971).

Tilliette, X.: *Karl Jaspers: Théorie de la vérité, Métaphysique des chiffres, Foi philosophique* (Paris: Aubier, 1959).

Walraff, Ch. F.: *Karl Jaspers: An Introduction to His Philosophy* (Princeton, NJ: Princeton University Press, 1970).

Walters, G. J.: *Karl Jaspers and the Role of "Conversion" in the Nuclear Age* (Lanham: University Press of America, 1988).

Weber, M.: *Politik als Beruf* (Munich, 1920); tr. M. Weber, *Politics as a Vocation* (Philadelphia, 1972).

Wisser, R. and Ehrlich, L. N. (eds): *Karl Jaspers, Philosopher among Philosophers* (Würzburg: Königshausen & Neumann, 1993).

Young-Bruehl, E.: *Freedom and Karl Jaspers's Philosophy* (New Haven, CT: Yale University Press, 1981).

# 18

# Heidegger

## JOHN D. CAPUTO

Martin Heidegger was born in 1889 in the rural farmlands of southern Germany. Raised in a conservative Catholic family, his earliest aspirations were to the Catholic priesthood. His earliest philosophical interests were in medieval scholastic logic, which first brought him in contact with HUSSERL's *Logical Investigations* (see Article 15). Seeing in phenomenology the antidote to the "unphilosophy" of psychologism, his habilitation dissertation (1916) interpreted the speculative grammar of Thomas of Erfurt, a fourteenth-century Scotistic logician, in the light of Husserl's theory of a pure a priori grammar.

In 1919, Heidegger broke with the Catholic confession and in that same year, in his lectures at Freiburg during the "War Emergency Semester," made a breakthrough to his fundamental project. Speaking of a "hermeneutics of facticity," Heidegger sought to trace the genesis of logical categories back to the "facticity" of "life," in contrast to the pure logical foundation of meaning and the categories he had previously defended under the influence of Husserl and scholastic logic. Philosophy, the young Heidegger contended, is subverted from within by a systematic blindness to the genesis of its own terms. This failure is connected by Heidegger with the academic setting of philosophy, with the "hermeneutic situation" of philosophical activity. Philosophical questions can be raised only by raising the question of the university, the status of which concerned him throughout his life. Academic philoso*phy* has no heart for the radicality of philoso*phizing*, for radical, revolutionary *questioning*. Philoso*phy* is a normalizing, institutional discourse that is never ultimately disturbed by the debates, however lively, that transpire within this discourse. But philoso*phizing* is a living act (*Vollzug*), a personal form of life, in which the philosopher seeks for himself to make things questionable and to do so radically.

Philosophy is institutionally and constitutionally blind to its own *pre*philosophical sources. Philosophical disputes occur in a space that has already been constituted by distilling the substance of "factical life" into a set of categorial "ghosts." The "hermeneutics of facticity" has a formidable, even paradoxical task, to make philosophy take into account the sphere of life before it is touched by philosophical conceptuality, a region of *non*philosophy or *pre*philosophy. How to philosophize about the prephilosophical without turning it into just more philosophy, without distorting and mummifying it, was the substance of the revolution the young philosopher had in mind.

The burden of leading this revolution fell to what Heidegger called "formal indication." Unlike the traditional concept or category that purports to seize or comprehend its object, the formal indication is but a projective sketch that traces out in advance certain salient formal features of an entity or region of entities. Instead of a conceptual mastery of its material that reduces the individual to an instance of the general, the formal indication is related to the factical region as the imperfect to the perfect, as an anticipatory sketch to the idiomatic fullness of concrete life. Fully to "understand" the factical would require a certain act or engagement, giving oneself to the factical matter at hand, which would no longer be the business of philosophy.

Heidegger identified two such *prephilosophical* sources as particularly important: the early Christian experience of time and the ethical experience of life in the Greek *polis*. To be sure, access to these "revolutionary" experiences could be gained only by means of the most traditional texts, the *New Testament* and the *Nicomachean Ethics*. Accordingly, such texts could not be approached by conventional academic reconstructions but required a new, more radical method Heidegger called *"Destruktion."* A "destruction" does not destroy but breaks through to the originary factical experiences from which the text arises, the term being suggested to him by Luther's notion of a *destructio* through the crust of scholasticism to the life of the New Testament. Lecturing on the "phenomenology of religion," Heidegger analyzed the temporality of the *parousia* in Paul's letters to the *Thessalonians*. The "second coming of Christ" is not a "when" to be calculated but a "how" to be lived, a matter not of reckoning a definite time in the future, but of being ready, existentially transformed, and radically open to an indefinite possibility that must be preserved in its indefiniteness. Recast in terms of a relationship to one's own death, this analysis became a centerpiece of *Being and Time*.

Although initially describing himself as a Christian theologian, Heidegger broke off his lectures on the Scriptures (and Augustine) in 1921 and turned to the texts of Aristotle's *Ethics*, noting that philosophy needed to be "methodologically atheistic." Reading Aristotle with the help of Kierkegaard, an important "impetus" for the young philosopher, Heidegger sees human existence as a matter of *kinesis*, of movement or being-moved, in the sense not of local motion but of "existential motion." Factical Life is unrest and care (*Sorge*), stirred (*bewegt*) always by needs and lack (*privatio*). As such, factical life seeks to make itself secure (*sine cura*) and so to cover itself up as the care-filled being it is. Thus the movement of factical life is simultaneously a "falling" out of itself, a proneness or inclination into the world, which tends to make things easy for itself and to shield itself from the "difficulty of life." As Aristotle says (*Ethics*, 1106b 28), it is easy to miss the mark of *arete* and hard to hit it, for there are many ways for factical life to fail to become itself (*Selbstsein* is what *arete* means in these lectures) but only one way to be itself. Heidegger devoted intensive analyses to the meaning of *techne, phronesis,* and *sophia* in Book Six, seeking to identify the sort of "understanding" that is capable of settling into the idiosyncrasies of the factical situation and making its way about without the help of formal rules.

In 1924, now teaching at Marburg and in dialogue with the theologian Rudolph Bultmann, retreating to his *Hütte* in the *Schwarzwald* during the holidays, Heidegger began making the first drafts of *Being and Time*, many of whose most important features first emerged in the 1919–23 lectures at Freiburg. The publication of *Being and Time* in 1927 in Husserl's *Jahrbuch* was hastened by Heidegger's need to publish something in order to have his appointment to a professorship at Marburg confirmed. Beginning with the remarkable "Introduction," the whole investigation has a more distinctly ontological, transcendental, and oddly academic tone. The "radical questioning" of the early Freiburg lectures is now formalized into the "question of the meaning of Being," making questionable every inherited understanding – of mere things, of the artifacts of everyday life, of human beings themselves. Philosophical inquiry is subverted in advance if it fails to ask into the meaning of the Being of the sort of entities with which it deals, and that is itself possible only if one inquires into what it means to be at all (*überhaupt*), what Being in general or as such itself means.

Such questioning starts with that entity whose very Being consists in raising such a question, and the first work of the inquiry will be to track down the implicit clues by which this entity is guided when it understands being. The idea is not to wipe the slate clean of inherited presuppositions, as in Husserl's pure "presuppositionless" phenomenology, but rather to penetrate all the more deeply into the presuppositions which shape any factical understanding. "Hermeneutic phenomenology" makes explicit the implicit clues that organize understanding, identifying the horizon of Being that allows entities to appear as they are, and then explicates the implicit clue around which that horizon is organized and by which it is nourished, which is the "meaning" of the Being of those entities. The contention of *Being and Time* is that those clues are always temporal, and hence that "meaning" is always a function of time, somewhat analogously to the way that the temporal schemata organize the categories in Kant's *Critique of Pure Reason*.

This temporal project enjoins a twofold task upon the treatise, one "systematic" and the other "historical," but carried out in such a way as to make this traditional distinction questionable. In the "First Half," an "existential analytic" will show that the Being of the entity that raises the question of Being is temporality itself, the very happening of time, and in virtue of this every understanding of Being is shaped by some sense of time. This analysis leads up to the key section of the entire book, "Time and Being," never published by Heidegger and the subject of endless controversy, in which the temporality of Being itself would be laid bare. In the "Second Half," Heidegger would demonstrate the temporal structure of every historical understanding of Being, a structure that needs to be forced out since the temporal clues operating in these historical texts are hidden. That is the famous "destruction of the history of ontology," which follows a reverse chronological order, from Kant, credited with awakening us to the temporal meaning of Being and with guiding this historical regression, to Descartes, to Aristotle. While the Kant analysis appeared separately in 1929 (*Kant and the Problem of Metaphysics*), we have only traces and drafts of the other sections of the Second Half.

Inasmuch as the book we now know as *Being and Time* is for the most part a "torso," consisting of the "existential analytic" of the projected First Half (in 1953 the heading "First Half" was struck), Heidegger was understandably regarded for

225

the next two decades as an "existentialist," particularly in view of the heavy (and usually unacknowledged) borrowings of the existential analytic from Kierkegaard. This reputation was more incomplete than false, failing as it did to take into account Heidegger's ultimately ontological aims. Even in its truncated form, *Being and Time* was by any standards a sensational success, catapulting Heidegger into the center of Continental philosophy, his fame rapidly eclipsing even that of his mentor Edmund Husserl, whose chair at Freiburg Heidegger filled, chiefly through Husserl's recommendation, when Husserl retired in 1928.

The existential analytic deals with the entity that we ourselves are, a being Heidegger calls "Dasein," in order to emphasize his ontological aims and to preempt an anthropological interpretation of the treatise. The Being of Dasein is "to be" (*zu sein*) the "there" (*da*) of the world, that is, to be the place where the world is disclosed or manifested as a world, on a certain analogy with Husserl's notion of the "constitution" of the world. Dasein is the event or happening of the world's manifestness, so that as soon as there is a being like Dasein, there is (*es gibt*) a world. The "essence" of Dasein is said to lie in its "existence," a Kierkegaardian term to which Heidegger gives a characteristically ontological twist. "Existence" means neither something factually occurring, nor some finished entity, but a being with the power, the potency (*dynamis, Seinkönnen*) to fashion its Being, to "be" itself in the active sense of taking over and "actualizing" its own, "authentic" (*eigentlich*) possibility to be – or to fail to do so. As a being that "falls," Dasein tends not to be itself, and to cover up its own being as existence. Hence the method of the existential analytic is to counter this tendency to fallenness by moving from Dasein's fall into the world of average everydayness back to the hidden and founding structures of Dasein's most primordial authenticity, thus echoing the Aristotelian method of gaining the ontologically prior by way of what is more manifest to us.

Dasein's average everydayness is systematically passed over in the tradition where the worldliness of the everyday world, the simple, hence highly elusive, character of "being-in-the-world," has never been a worthy object of philosophical inquiry. The tradition privileges the mode of "knowing" (*erkennen*) or looking on (*anschauen*) at the world as a kind of inert visible object or "static presence." The most extreme form of this tendency is found in the modern problem of knowledge (*Erkenntnistheorie*), where the very existence of the world is the issue. But in *Being and Time*, the "world" is a systematically linked concatenation of "instruments" leading out and leading back to Dasein, to which Dasein belongs more primordially than it can say, with which Dasein is always already pragmatically involved, so that the epistemological problem of the existence of this world makes no sense. "Pure knowing" is an abstract construction achieved only by suspending or interrupting this prior and ultimately incessant operation of being-in-the-world. The world is, moreover, a world shared with others, so that far from being a solipsistic ego requiring an epistemological proof of the existence of others, Dasein finds itself always already among others. Indeed, "others" are not those who are other than the I but those among whom the I is *also*, by whom Dasein is in fact dominated like an anonymous "they" (*das "man"*) and from whom it must learn to differentiate itself into an authentic self.

Upon analysis, being-in-the-world proves itself to be a phenomenon of "care," which has a tripartite structure of: (a) *projection* upon or towards its possibilities to be, local and everyday possibilities, but ultimate ones also; (b) *thrownness* into and among these possibilities, so that while Dasein is free, it is not free from the ground up but finds itself in a situation not of its making; and (c) *fallenness* among fascinating worldly possibilities and idle curiosities, to the neglect of its own deepest possibility to be itself. The unity of this tripartite structure is phenomenally manifested in the famous analysis of "anxiety" (*Angst*), the disturbing sense of uncanniness by which Dasein is overtaken (thrownness) when it finds that there is nothing other than Dasein's own freedom to sustain its projects (projection), an uncanniness from which Dasein is constantly taking flight (falling).

But if the determination of Dasein as "care" has uncovered the "Being" of Dasein, it has done so chiefly in terms of Dasein's everyday possibilities, leaving the deeper structure of Dasein, the "meaning" of its Being, in darkness. For that possibility, towards which Dasein is ultimately running, is its own possible impossibility, its own death or being-there-no-more. In a manner strongly reminiscent of Augustinian and Lutheran spirituality, Heidegger describes Dasein as fetched back out of its fall into the dissipation of worldly possibilities by freeing itself for its own mortality, taking over its projectedness into death instead of taking flight from it. Projection upon "my death" breaks the quiet tyranny the "they" exerts over Dasein, stripping Dasein down to its own resolve to be itself, exposing the vanity of worldly curiosities and the depth of Dasein's own quiet resolve.

This resolute running forth upon Dasein's own mortality proves to have the structure of temporality. Dasein does not "have" temporality as a defining feature, but Dasein is temporality, the very process of temporalizing, of tim-ing (*Zeitigung*). The temporality of Dasein is the unity of three temporal "ecstasies," upon which the tripartite structure of care is founded, so that temporality is the "meaning" of care and so of the Being of Dasein. For Dasein is radically *futural*, standing open (*ekstasis*) towards an indefinite possible which, unlike what is merely "not yet," is always approaching, always coming-towards Dasein and drawing it out of itself. In being drawn out of itself into what is coming, Dasein comes back to itself, to the possibility that it all along has been, so that far from being something over or "no more," the past is what Dasein *has been* all along and comes toward it. Thirdly, Dasein opens out towards that which it has been all along in the "moment" (another Kierkegaardian term) in which it catches sight of and seizes upon that very possibility to be itself which tends to withdraw under the cover of everydayness. The tripartite ecstatic structure of temporality provides the basis for an analogous theory of historicality, in which an entire "generation" can "repeat" or seize upon the historical possibility (or "destiny") which is sent to it as a collective unity from its own deepest historical having been.

*Being and Time* struck like thunder and, almost overnight, Heidegger became an international philosophical celebrity. But soon after this celebrity had set in, there followed Heidegger's darkest days, raising questions about his personal character and casting a shadow over his work that has persisted ever since. Undergoing a personal crisis detectible in the 1929–30 lectures, which bore the subtitle "World –

Finitude – Loneliness," Heidegger's disaffection with the bourgeois culture of the Weimar Republic, already detectable in his critique of the "they," by then in a state of near economic collapse, reached an extreme state. The upshot of this crisis was an enthusiastic embrace of National Socialism, although most people who knew Heidegger personally had not seen in him before this time a particularly political personality. Once again, for a second time, Heidegger launched a project of radical revolutionary renewal, this time involving the political overthrow of "this moribund culture." Heidegger seems always to have been, both personally and philosophically, a man of radical and revolutionary extremes, of utter upheaval and total transformation, resisting piecemeal reform. His life and writings represent a history of such upheavals. Indeed, the Nazis themselves, although delighted to enjoy the support of such a prestigious professor, were wary of Heidegger, wondering whether all this radical questioning would not eventually lead Heidegger into questioning the National Socialist revolution itself and calling for a still newer "new order."

The most notorious moments of this period in Heidegger's life were his political activities as Rector-*Führer* at Freiburg and his energetic leadership of the Nazification of the university in cooperation with radical student elements. Philosophically, this period took the form of an heroic voluntarism, forged in a dialogue not with Aristotle and Kierkegaard but with the extremism of Ernst Jünger and Nietzsche, and of an ultra-nationalism that exceeded the formal-ontological character of the existential analytic. Heidegger enlisted *Being and Time* into national service, calling for a "resolve" for the *Führer* in this "moment" of historical "choice." Much to the perplexity of the Nazis, Heidegger even put the "question of Being" to work as the "spiritualizing" element of the revolution – he opposed Nazi biologism – arguing that Germans alone possessed the spiritual mettle to raise this question. Called by a distant command originating in the Greeks, to which the Germans bear an inner spiritual relationship, it was the historical "destiny" of this "people" to save the West through radical questioning. The rectorship lasted only ten months. Heidegger's critics say Heidegger was an inept administrator who was worth more to the Party as a famous professor who left the running of the revolution to them. Heidegger and his supporters contend he resigned the rectorship because he saw that he could no longer "protect" the University from these "impossible people," which, as he would argue after the war, was the only reason he "accepted" the post. While this controversy flares up from time to time, the recent work of Hugo Ott and Victor Farias has been the most damaging, raising questions both about Heidegger personally and about the ethical and political import of his writings.

In 1936 Heidegger seems to have undergone still another upheaval, a third and more or less final transformation, which is now recorded for us in the publication in 1989 of his *Beiträge* (*Contributions to Philosophy: On the Event of Appropriation*), notes and drafts worked up in 1936–8. Out of power politically, disillusioned by what he considered the benighted elements who had taken over the Party, the movement, and even the *Führer* himself, Heidegger's thought took a deeply poetic tone, sometimes described as "inner migration." In a startling reversal of his earlier voluntarism, Heidegger renounced human "willing," not in the narrow sense of a particular mental faculty but in the sweeping sense of the whole range of human subjectivity. He undertook a critique of Nietzsche's "metaphysics of willing," on the one hand, and a series of provocative reading's of the poetry of Hölderlin and the fragments of the "early Greek" (pre-Socratic) philosophers, whose "poetic thinking" he now aligned with poetry itself, on the other hand.

Heidegger criticized the "representational" (*vorstellend*), subject–object paradigm of Enlightenment rationality for reducing the unencompassable power and upsurge of *physis* to an "object" over which the human subject held juridical authority. Unless a reason is rendered to the representational subject, entities have no right to be – thus speaks Leibniz's *principium rationis*. To this calculative or representational thinking – which lays bare the inner tendency, the "will to power" of "metaphysics" itself, which is itself what "philosophy" really is, which is itself more or less what the "West" amounts to – Heidegger opposes a gentler "meditative" possibility, sometimes just called "thinking," and sometimes identified as "*Gelassenheit*," "letting be," a venerable term from Meister Eckhart, whom Heidegger had studied in his Catholic youth. *Gelassenheit* is thinking "without why," emptying itself of the willful demands that cut Being to fit the human subject. Meditative thinking "lets" "things" rise up out of concealment, "whiling" for a while, only to sink away again into the shadows, in a process called "coming to presence" (*Anwesen*) or *a-letheia*, emerging-into-unconcealment. He mediates the "rose" of Angelus Silesius, which lives "without reason" or "without why," which "blossoms because it blossoms," in a range of freedom, of "the free," beyond the sphere of influence of Leibniz's mighty principle. Released from the power of ontico-causal thinking, which links beings with beings, thinking lets Being be, releasing "gods and mortals, heavens and earth" into their free play in a space–time of the "Fourfold." These texts, among his most powerful, beautiful, and spellbinding, have often been compared to certain Buddhist traditions.

This other, "second" (third?), "later" Heidegger burst upon the postwar scene in 1947 with the publication of the famous *A Letter on Humanism*. Heidegger's thunder had struck again, revealing a Heidegger unknown to all but the few who heard his lectures during the war years. One might thus identify three fundamental upheavals in Heidegger's life and work: (1) the discovery of the "hermeneutics of facticity" in 1919, the final upshot of which is *Being and Time*; (2) the heroic voluntarism of the early 1930s which pushed *Being and Time* into the politics of the Third Reich; (3) the metapolitical meditation upon dwelling poetically on the earth found in the postwar publications, which remained in place from 1936 until his death in 1976.

In *A Letter on Humanism*, which is a radical reinterpretation of *Being and Time* from the post-1936 perspective, Heidegger scolds his perplexed readers for the "existentialist misinterpretation" of the book, trying to create the impression, not that his thought had been importantly altered in the meantime, but that the numerous interpreters of the most obvious tendencies of the 1927 text itself were mistaken. "Resoluteness," for example, is said to mean not resolute choice but "unclosedness" (*Ent-schlossenheit*) to the advance of Being, "understanding" to mean "standing under" Being's truth, "thrownness" is explained as being thrown into

229

the place of Being's self-disclosure, while "Dasein" is said to mean that thinking provides the "place" (*des "da"*) of "Being" (*Sein*). In truth, if in *Being and Time* Heidegger had displaced the Cartesian, epistemological subject with being-in-the-world, he had by 1947 radicalized the critique of subjectivity by eliminating even the resolute, *Angst*-filled, existential subject, significantly altering the position of *Being and Time* in the process.

A *Letter on Humanism* was addressed to a French audience. For while the existentialist reading of the text prevailed everywhere, this was especially true in France, owing to the influence of Sartre, for whom "existentialism is a humanism." Although Heidegger's errant political fortunes had cost him his job and his peace of mind in postwar Germany, it had not cost him a hearing in France, which has to this very day been his central base of philosophical support. From this French center, Heidegger's critique of humanism, of human subject-ism, has set the stage for all subsequent Continental European philosophizing – hermeneutics, structuralism, and poststructuralism – and if we today are asking "who comes after the subject?" that is because we are all still standing in Heidegger's shadow.

Heidegger's "overcoming" of "subject-ism" or "humanism" or "metaphysics" involved showing that the dominion that the subject enjoyed in modernity from Descartes on was not the doing of the subject, not of Descartes or Leibniz, Kant or Husserl. The great power of the mighty principle of reason is not the power of Leibniz's thought, but the power of Being as it comes to language in Leibniz's words. Something stirred quietly and unobtrusively in Plato and Aristotle, lying more or less dormant over the centuries, that awakened in Leibniz, and it was the gift of Leibniz to hear it and to give it words. The rule of the subject is a happening, an event of "withdrawal" on the part of Being that makes itself felt in the texts of the great metaphysicians. The age of the "subject" is an historical movement in which Being is given, not as *physis* and *aletheia*, as in the age of the early Greeks, but as the "objectivity of objects," as an object laid out before the view of a juridical subject. The power awakening in Leibniz's principle was already alive in the discursive reason (*logos*) of Aristotle, which displaced the poetic thinking of the early Greeks; it grew more potent still in the metaphysical theology of the Middle Ages, and today it rages all around us in the unleashed fury of the will to power, of the technological domination of the earth. The essential thing to see is that the "history of metaphysics" is not a human history of human opinions about Being but the "history of Being," Being's own history as Being sends itself to and withdraws from human thought. Sending *and* withdrawing, all in one, since the sending of Being "is" its withdrawal, rather the way in theology the manifestation of God *in* creation is also God's concealment *by* creation. The crucial disanalogy here is that, unlike God, Being is no higher supreme entity standing autonomously above or behind the process of giving and withdrawing. Being is nothing more than this process of sending and withdrawing, this "epochal" (*epoche* means cutting off or withdrawing) happening of sending–withdrawing.

In its most careful formulation, in the celebrated 1962 lecture "Time and Being," the septuagenarian philosopher speaks of the *Ereignis*, the event of "letting be" or "giving" Being and time, which gives Being over to what is proper (*eigen*) to it –

hence the translation of *Ereignis* as the "event of appropriation" – even while it itself remains concealed, in "expropriation." Of entities we may say that they "are," and of Being only that "there is Being" (*es gibt Sein*), that "it" (*Ereignis*) "gives" Being, lets the Being of Beings happen epochally. But of *Ereignis* – since "it" is not really some higher-order thing or cause, but a "sheer" subjectless happening – we may say only "*das Ereignis ereignet,*" the event comes to pass, or appropriates.

In this formulation, "Being" is displaced as a master word for Heidegger and is said to belong to metaphysics, while the task of thought is to think something beyond Being, which "gives" Being, even as, in *Being and Time*, fundamental ontology sought the "meaning" of Being, that in terms of which Being becomes understandable. In this way, the "history of metaphysics" is exposed in its structural limits, or is delimited, its "end" marked off, which is what is meant by the "end of metaphysics," a misleading expression which by no means signifies a chronological termination. On the contrary, the present end-state, the technological domination of the earth, which for Heidegger is the last stage of "metaphysics" as willing and subject-ism, may go on indefinitely, while the possibility of an "other" beginning is dark and uncertain. The "other beginning" means a re-establishment of poetic dwelling, of a poetic–thoughtful relationship to the world, in which everything from Anaximander to "cybernetics" will be granted a fresh start, in some loose sense analogous to the first start with which the Western tradition was first set off in early Greek thinking. Thought thinks forward to the other beginning by thinking back upon (*an-denken*) the traces of the first beginning left behind in words of elemental power like *physis* and *aletheia* and in certain poets whose words echo the forgotten beginning. This "other beginning" is the focus of the third and final version of "revolutionary transformation" in Heidegger's thought, but this revolution is a turn to be taken in and by Being, and nothing subject to human control.

The "aftermath" of Heidegger's thought is immense, both inside and outside philosophy. In the broadest sense, every important Continental movement today stands under Heidegger's shadow and has to define itself in terms of his "destruction" of metaphysics. The two most important continuations of his thought are to be found in the philosophical hermeneutics of Hans-Georg GADAMER (Article 38) and in Jacques DERRIDA's notion of "deconstruction" (see Article 50). Gadamer's is the more conservative version, seeing in "destruction" a way of "retrieving" the "truth" of the tradition over and against the attempt to master tradition by way of historical-critical "method." For Gadamer, we belong to the happening of language and tradition more profoundly than we can say, and our task is to let ourselves be instructed by the otherness of our past, which is also our identity, to let tradition happen again in our dialogue with it.

In deconstruction, the more radical wing of post-Heideggerian thinking, which is sharply critical of Heidegger's valorization of the "primordial" and "proper," *Destruktion* is a way not of unearthing the deep truth of the tradition, but rather of loosening the grip of the most prestigious and powerful elements of tradition. A deconstruction frees up the repressed senses, the silenced voices, the excluded and marginalized elements that succumb to the violence of the tradition. In an interesting way, deconstruction sees itself as answering a call for justice for the singularity

231

of the "other," and hence as aligned with Emmanuel LEVINAS (see Article 20), Heidegger's most famous and relentless critic. Levinas argues that the thought of Being erases ethical alterity, a critique given a powerful impetus by the recent revelations about Heidegger's National Socialist years. Wherever the various commentators stand on this issue, Levinas has made it impossible to discuss Heidegger today without wrestling with the question of ethics.

Heidegger died in 1976 and was buried between his parents in the churchyard in Messkirch, the small town in which he was born. A Mass of Christian burial was held in St Martin's Church where the world renowned philosopher's father once served as sexton. The celebrant, Bernard Welte, a theologian and fellow townsman, read verses from Hölderlin and the Scriptures and described Heidegger as a "seeker" whose thought has shaken our century. In the end, Heidegger had indeed succeeded in starting a revolution.

## Writings

Books

Heidegger, M.: *Basic Writings*, 2nd edn, ed. David Krell (New York: Harper & Row, 1992). (Contains "A Letter on Humanism" and other essays central to the "later" Heidegger.)
——: *Being and Time*, tr. John MacQuarrie and Edward Robinson (New York: Harper & Row, 1962).
——: *The Principle of Reason*, tr. Reginald Lilly (Bloomington, IN: Indiana University Press, 1991).
——: *On Time and Being*, tr. Joan Stambaugh (New York: Harper & Row, 1972). (See especially the lead essay "On Time and Being.")
——: *The Question Concerning Technology and Other Essays*, tr. W. Lovitt (New York: Harper & Row, 1977).

Foreign titles, not translated

Heidegger, M.: *Gesamtausgabe* (Frankfurt: Klostermann, 1975ff). (Projected to reach some 70 volumes, this edition of the collected works includes all previously published works, including the author's marginalia, and unpublished lectures and essays, but, supposedly at Heidegger's request, it provides no critical apparatus.)

## References and further reading

Arendt, Hannah: "Martin Heidegger at eighty," in *Heidegger and Modern Philosophy*, ed. Michael Murray (New Haven, CT: Yale University Press, 1978), pp. 293–4. (Insightful reflections of one of Heidegger's first and most famous students.)
Biemel, Walter: *Martin Heidegger: An Illustrated Study*, tr. J. L. Mehta (New York: Harcourt, Brace, Janovich, 1976). (An affectionate intellectual biography with photographs.)
Derrida, Jacques: *Of Spirit: Heidegger and the Question*, tr. Geoffrey Bennington and Rachel Bowlby (Chicago: University of Chicago Press, 1989). (An interesting treatment by the most famous post-Heideggerian of all.)
Dreyfus, Hubert: *Being in the World: A Commentary on Heidegger's "Being and Time," Division I* (Cambridge: MIT Press, 1991).

Gadamer, Hans-Georg: *Heidegger's Ways*, tr. John Stanley (Albany: SUNY Press, 1994). (The reflections of one of Heidegger's first and most famous students.)

Guignon, Charles (ed.): *The Cambridge Companion to Heidegger* (New York: Cambridge University Press, 1993). (A good collection of recent studies with an excellent bibliography.)

Haar, Michel: *Heidegger and the Essence of Man* (Albany: SUNY Press, 1993).

Kisiel, Theodore: *The Genesis of Heidegger's "Being and Time"*, (Berkeley, CA: University of California Press, 1993). (A comprehensive study of the pre-*Being and Time* period, unmatched by any other work available in any language, including accounts of texts unpublished even in the German *Gesamtausgabe*. Contains a good bibliography and a revised list of Heidegger's courses and seminars.)

Ott, Hugo: *Martin Heidegger: A Political Life*, tr. Allan Blunden (New York: Basic Books, 1993). (Contains the essentials of the account of Heidegger's involvement with the Nazis.)

Poeggeler, Otto: *Heidegger's Path of Thinking*, tr. Daniel Magurshuk and Sigmund Barber (Atlantic Highlands, NJ: Humanities Press, 1987). Still widely regarded as the best single-volume introduction to Heidegger's thought as a whole; the first edition (1963) was written in some collaboration with Heidegger, who made unpublished manuscripts available; the second edition has an important postscript on the Nazism controversy.)

Marx, Werner: *Heidegger and the Tradition*, tr. Theodore Kisiel (Evanston, IL: Northwestern University Press, 1971). (Another of the classic introductions to Heidegger's works.)

Richardson, William: *Heidegger: Through Phenomenology to Thought* (The Hague: Martinus Nijhoff, 1963). (Contains Heidegger's well-known letter to the author as a "Preface." The work that largely introduced Heidegger to the English-speaking audience.)

Sallis, John (ed.): *Reading Heidegger: Commemorations* (Bloomington, IN: Indiana University Press, 1993). (A distinguished, international collection of contributors commemorating Heidegger's Centenary.)

Schürmann, Reiner: *Heidegger on Being and Acting*, tr. Christine Marie Gros and Reiner Schürmann (Bloomington, IN: Indiana University Press, 1987). (Skillful Foucauldian reading of Heidegger.)

PART IV

# PHENOMENOLOGY, HEGELIANISM AND ANTI-HEGELIANISM IN FRANCE

# 19

# Kojève

## STANLEY ROSEN

**I**

Alexandre Kojève, née Kojevnikov, was born in pre-revolutionary Russia; his uncle was the painter Kandinsky, and Kojève planned originally to study art history. He was traveling in Italy when the Russian Revolution occurred, an event that caused him to change his plans and to devote himself to philosophy. He spent some years in Germany before emigrating to France, and was able to pursue the life of an independent scholar until the worldwide economic depression led to the loss of his family income. Upon the invitation of Alexandre Koyré, Kojève began a series of lectures on Hegel in 1933 at the École des Hautes Études. These lectures lasted until 1939; ostensibly devoted to Hegel's philosophy of religion, they in fact provided an exhaustive commentary on the *Phenomenology of Spirit*.

Kojève's seminar soon became the most important philosophical event in Paris; his lectures were attended by Maurice Merleau-Ponty, Raymond Aron, Jacques Lacan, Georges Bataille, Father Gaston Fessard, Pierre Klossowski, André Breton, and Raymond Queneau, among others (but not by Sartre, as is sometimes claimed). Queneau, author of *Zazie dans le métro*, later became an editor at Gallimard, and arranged for the publication of the Hegel lectures, which first appeared in 1947. The bulk of this publication is derived from notes taken at the lectures, which were subsequently reviewed by Kojève. It is noteworthy that Kojève did not write out a complete set of lectures; his other posthumously published works, with one exception also issued by Gallimard, are taken from typed manuscripts which Kojève produced at odd moments during World War II and in such time as could be spared by his postwar duties as an official in the Gaullist government. One of the students in Kojève's seminar, Robert Marjolin, subsequently became minister of foreign economic affairs under de Gaulle and brought his teacher into the ministry, where he remained until his death in 1968. As Kojève put it, he was a weekend philosopher. During the week, I would describe him as a French Mycroft Holmes. His official duties included a wide range of responsibilities, not only in the ministry but as chief adviser to André Philip, head of the French delegation to GATT, and as an economic spokesman for France at the United Nations.

Kojève was not only a philosopher of extraordinary gifts but a self-taught economist of world stature. I remember very well visiting him at his office on the Quai d'Orsay each Monday afternoon during the year 1960–61. Our conversations on Plato and Hegel were periodically interrupted by telephone calls; after one of these,

237

Kojève smilingly told me: "That was New Zealand; they want to know how much to charge for butter." André Philip and Raymond Aron both confirmed independently Kojève's assertion to me that he was second only to de Gaulle in the decision-making process of the French government. I can also testify that he was perhaps the most respected, and in many ways feared, philosopher in France during his mature years. Kojève did not suffer fools gladly, although he was not polemical. He carried himself with the dignity of a self-professed "god," by which he meant a sage (a word used in the English-speaking philosophical world as a term of opprobrium, to the disgrace of our tradition). Kojève's comprehensive intelligence and range of knowledge, which extended from Oriental languages to modern mathematics and physics, in addition to philosophy, economics, and literature, were enough to intimidate all but the most powerful spirits in Paris. Nor did Kojève have a high estimation of professional philosophers; he told me that he associated only with priests (his closest friend among them was Gaston Fessard, SJ) and he advised me to do the same. In this connection, I should note his remark: "Everyone will tell you to study the pre-Socratics, but I, Kojève, tell you to study the post-Socratics!" He was referring in particular to the early Church fathers, among whom he especially valued Clement of Alexandria, and whom he saw as a kind of anticipation of the Hegelian system.

Kojève continues to be known primarily for his discussion of Hegel, published in France under the title *Introduction à la lecture de Hegel*. He was engaged for many years in composing a history of philosophy that would serve as a comprehensive supplement to the interpretation of the *Phenomenology*. From this long work, which was brought to varying degrees of completeness, he sanctioned the publication of the *Essai d'une histoire raisonnée de la philosophie paienne*, which appeared posthumously in three volumes (1968, 1972, 1973). Especially valuable in this work is the Introduction, which contains a good general statement of Kojève's philosophical position. In a footnote, Kojève also acknowledges his debt to Heidegger's *Sein und Zeit*, the only such acknowledgment of a contemporary by him of which I am aware.

In 1973, Gallimard published a long essay on Kant, found in Kojève's papers, originally written as part of his history of philosophy, and entitled simply *Kant*. This is a work of unusual power and originality, and discusses in detail the relation between Kant and Hegel. In 1981, there appeared, also under the imprint of Gallimard, an essay entitled *Esquisse d'une phénoménologie du droit*. This essay was written in 1943 but never revised, although, according to the editor, Kojève regarded it as finished. I know of two other posthumous works, both published in 1990: *L'Idée du déterminisme dans la physique classique et la physique moderne* (Librairie Générale Française); and *Le Concept, le temps et le discours* (Gallimard). In addition to these books, Kojève published a number of important reviews and articles which are extremely helpful, and in one or two cases perhaps indispensable, for an understanding of his thought. I mention in particular the long review of Leo Strauss's study of Xenophon's dialogue *Hiero*, entitled *On Tyranny*. The review and Strauss's reply to it appeared together with Strauss's original study under the title *De la Tyrannie* (Gallimard, 1954). I also recommend the important review article "Hegel, Marx et le Christianisme" in *Critique*, 3–4 (1946).

## II

It is essential to begin a discussion of Kojève's thought by commenting directly on his ambiguous persona as a public figure in Parisian intellectual life. I have already observed that Kojève was very widely respected and feared; the respect increased with the intelligence and spiritual power of those who judged him. The orthodox academic historian of philosophy is inclined to dismiss Kojève as a typical Parisian café philosopher, whose interpretation of Hegel is forced and inaccurate. This judgment fails to take into account two crucial points. Kojève was a philosopher, not a historian; he knew perfectly well that his interpretation of Hegel was arbitrary and argued that the decisive historical question is which interpretation of Hegel will be accepted in the future, thereby determining human destiny in accord with the genuine Hegelian principle that the truth is what is manifested in the actuality of world history. The second point is that philosophy is a spiritual activity, not a pastime for devotees of libraries. One must have experienced the vitality of Kojève's spiritual presence and the power of his discourse in order to understand adequately his philosophical nature.

Unfortunately these are not qualities that can be communicated by a written description. In addition, one has to admit that there was a streak of hyperbolical playfulness in Kojève's nature, characteristic of those who are entirely superior to their associates but too self-confident to enforce that superiority by unmitigated demonstrations of its existence. I can also testify that he was marked by a Slavic openness and freedom from intellectual pomposity that one did not always associate with the Parisian mandarins or the German academic stars. It is a striking fact that although Kojève made the Hegelian dialectic of master and slave the center from which all of his philosophical teaching radiated, he himself never engaged in the effort to reduce his friends to the status of slaves. His practice belied his theory, and gave the palm to those for whom philosophy is friendship rather than the struggle for recognition.

Kojève took the master–slave dialectic, or the struggle for recognition, as central not only to Hegel's *Phenomenology*, but to the Hegelian system altogether, and therefore to wisdom itself. This is a consequence of his view of the *Phenomenology* as a fundamentally anthropological text; otherwise stated, Kojève held that thought, not Being, is dialectical. In a way that owes much to Hobbes, Kojève identified man as the thinking animal, not in the Aristotelian sense but as rooted in the peculiar nature of human desire. According to Kojève, man is "absolute negating negativity" (p. 27): "Man, real presence of nothing [*néant*] in being (time), is action, that is to say, struggle and work: – and nothing else. The man who *knows* himself to be nothing (no survival, therefore atheism) is a nothing annihilating [*néantissant*] within *being*. He may achieve satisfaction (*Befriedigung*) in the present; the satisfaction of the bourgeois (citizen) in the state" (p. 91).[1]

This passage, when properly supplemented, contains the core of Kojève's thought. The human being is pure negation in the sense that the individual transcends the givenness of insentient being as well as of the brutes. Kojève as it were radicalizes Nietzsche's assertion that man is the not yet completed animal; desire as articulated by speech drives man to transform the given into the satisfaction of his desires. But human desire is not primarily physical; in Kojève's terminology, what we desire is not, like that of the brute, the satisfaction of an immediate appetite but rather desire itself. We desire to be desired by others who are capable of transcending the given in the effort to achieve satisfaction. This defining desire is for recognition, and leads human beings into the struggle for mastery.

The struggle is to the death; otherwise it is not serious. But it cannot terminate in death, since then recognition of the victor is suppressed. The triumph of the stronger establishes the spiritual relation of mastery and bondage that underlies all social and political structures and customs. The instability of these structures is a direct consequence of the negativity of human being, which cannot be satisfied until all of reality is transformed into recognition of its own mastery. This is obviously impossible for more than one individual; but it is also impossible for an individual tyrant, because recognition granted by slaves is inadequate to establish the tyrant's worthiness. This can be accomplished only through the recognition of other masters. To this must be added the fundamental difficulty that the masters inevitably become decadent by transferring their annihilating negativity – in plain English, the need to work – to the slaves, who accordingly overthrow the masters and take their place, thereby preparing the next stage of overcoming. As Kojève puts it, "history is the history of the worker–slave" (p. 26).

This process is obviously related to Nietzsche's analysis of human life as an expression of the will to power. But whereas human existence is for Nietzsche cyclical or Greek, and determined by the work of masters rather than slaves, Kojève accepts an atheistic version of the Christian interpretation of human existence as temporal and historical, and of history as the dialectically cumulative self-emancipation of the meek, not of course by prayer but by the sweat of their brows. The dialectic of master and slave leads to the progressive satisfaction of human desire, or the transformation of nature in the image of human desire. At this point, Kojève, like all philosophers of history, has recourse to prophecy; in a quasi-Marxist manner, he infers from the struggle for recognition the eventual establishment of the universal homogeneous state, in which there will, so to speak, be no slaves but only masters, or rather one master (a global Napoleon or his extension in the Napoleonic code) whose comprehensive satisfaction through universal recognition serves to equilibrate the desires of his subject-citizens into mutual recognition.

The individual citizens are like monads in the substance of the universal homogeneous state; otherwise put, all citizens are supermen, if not in their own persons, then by participation in the state; but, as rendered entirely equal through their mutual recognition, and entirely satisfied by the expression of Hegelian theoretical wisdom in the legal code and social structure, they will be friends rather than the friendly enemies that they are in the Nietzschean doctrine to which Zarathustra gives voice. This of course raises the question of the nature of Hegelian wisdom, and in particular, of how it can be satisfied by human action. It is easy to see that Kojève's atheistic and anthropological interpretation of Hegel, as well as his denial that nature, or non-human being, is dialectical, leads to the replacement of the Absolute Spirit by the annihilating or transformative negativity of human work,

240

itself understood in the sense just explained as the struggle for recognition. What is for Hegel the dialectical excitation of the Absolute Spirit as omnipresent within temporality, or in other words eternity as structurally isomorphic to history, is for Kojève the pulsation of temporality and nothing but temporality.

It is accurate to refer to Kojève as an anthropological thinker (pp. 307ff) because human desire is at the center of his teaching. In this light, it is not wisdom or the love of wisdom that is primary for Kojève but rather pride or the love of honor. On the other hand, it is insufficient to refer to Kojève as an anthropological thinker because he contends that pride, the peculiarly human form of animal desire, leads by its inner dynamic to the pursuit, and more important, to the achievement, of wisdom. In slightly different terms, the condition of human freedom is the identity of the concept with time, an identification first made by Hegel (pp. 364ff). The structure of time is therefore accessible to human self-consciousness, which is the temporalized and so historical version of Hegel's reciprocally transformative excitation of the concept and Absolute Spirit. Kojève, in other words, humanizes the negative activity of the Absolute; this is the basis for the famous, and more recently notorious, doctrine of the end of history. The circularity of the Hegelian concept is demoted from eternity to historicity, thereby bringing Kojève closer to Nietzsche than to Hegel, thanks to the mediation of Feuerbach and Heidegger.

Despite Kojève's repudiation of eternity in all its forms, it is evident that he cannot be entirely assimilated to the Teutonic grimness of the Heideggerian doctrine of *Sein und Zeit*. Kojève retains the Socratic irony and, among the moderns, the Nietzschean sense of life as play, together with the Hobbesian or political transformation of Marxist romanticism that is expressed in his prophecy of the universal homogeneous state. In addition, what one could call the Heideggerian melodrama of Protestant resolution and post-Protestant authenticity is represented in the equally tedious form of the boredom of the universal homogeneous state, in which all desires have in principle been satisfied, and everyone experiences full self-contentment. In a famous footnote to the second edition of his Hegel commentary, Kojève grants that the achievement of satisfaction, which is for him equivalent to the possession of conceptual wisdom (i.e. knowledge of the structure of temporality), leaves man scarcely distinguishable from the completeness of the brutes. Nothing is left for the Kojèvian epigone but love-making and the Japanese tea-ceremony (pp. 436ff). This is a distinctly non-Heideggerian touch, despite recent sensational revelations of the great ontologist's extra-curricular activities, and to some of us at least provides a hint of the superiority of Paris to the Schwarzwald.

The views just summarized are the source of the French postmodernist doctrines of the end of history and of post-anthropological man, which, together with the famous dialectic of master and slave, have played such a crucial role in Continental thought after 1968. In order to understand the transition from Kojève to the next generation as simply as possible, one has only to revise the Hegelian formula of the identity of identity and difference into the difference of identity and difference. When identity is conceived primarily as different from difference it becomes the Deleuzian "différentiel" of *Différence et répétition*. Despite his fondness for circles, Kojève prepares the way for this shift by the identification of the concept with time.

The result is obvious in Deleuze's misinterpretation of Nietzsche's eternal return as the repetition of difference. The fundamental connection between Kojève and his epigones, however, is that his own doctrine of the end of history is a playful expression of the world-weariness of worldly wisdom; when properly understood, it implies the inner bankruptcy of philosophy and the futility of the satisfaction of desire. Kojève's postmodern students conceal this blend of cynicism and resignation in a thick rhetoric of quasi-Nietzschean doctrines of continuous self-overcoming. For Kojève, there is no "new beginning" in Heidegger's sense, no new way of thinking but only fragmentary and incoherent repetitions of old ways of thinking. Because the inner emptiness of human existence as continuous striving is concealed by the rhetoric of freedom and creativity, post-Kojevian postmodernism has a greater appeal to the young, whereas Kojève's analysis is directed to the mature person who retains the playfulness of youth.

Before we reject Kojève's doctrine of the end of human striving in the death-throes of its success, let us pause for a moment and ask ourselves what are the consequences of the modern blend of atheism, materialism, and positivism on the one hand, and neuraesthenic aestheticism married to egalitarian liberation on the other. The reduction of human existence to the status of an unintelligible illusion, whether as an epiphenomenon of extension, figure, and motion or of the inarticulateness of pure difference, reduces scientific enlightenment on the one hand and the free play of difference on the other to the level of a simulacrum: an image of an image for which there is no original.

Kojève, with all his playfulness and despite his frequent surrender to the spirit of dramatic oversimplification, preserves eternity and purposiveness in the circularity of the conceptual structure of temporality. But in addition to asserting the unsatisfactory nature of satisfaction, Kojève almost explicitly grants the inner tragedy of the philosophical life when he denies that man is by nature a philosopher (p. 398) and acknowledges that history is normally created by those who are not philosophers (p. 404). Even more fundamentally, "language is born of discontent. Man speaks of the nature that kills him and makes him suffer" (p. 117). Philosophy, or the pursuit of wisdom, is thus an unnatural suffering, whereas wisdom itself terminates in boredom, which can be escaped only by an aestheticized version of eroticism.

On balance, then, with all of Kojève's conceptual elegance and despite the genuinely illuminating details of his idiosyncratic interpretation of the history of philosophy, despite, in other words, his detailed exhibition of his own philosophical genius, Kojève teaches us that life is a tragedy; and on this point he is a late-modern thinker who runs the risk of deteriorating into an intellectual and an aesthete. In my opinion, Kojève's greatest service is his manifestation of the dilemma of modernity at the level of philosophical reflection. Kojève repudiated religious faith, metaphysical fantasy, and political ideology. He was a realist *par excellence*, a man with no illusions except one: that life is an illusion. And he disguised this illusion, if not from himself, certainly from his disciples, in the mask of extraordinary conceptual clarity and precision. There is no whisper in Kojève of the fatuous self-congratulation that defaces so much of even the most brilliant writings of his students. His effortless expression of superiority was enacted at the level of political power, not ideological chanting. Unfortunately, by making all too clear the tragic core of power, he left a void that was filled by rhetoric; by showing the unsatisfactory nature of the satisfaction of the desire for desire, he left open the space that has subsequently been filled by the vulgar emancipation of mere desire.

This tragic situation becomes clear from a reflection on one of Kojève's most interesting essays, his long review of Leo Strauss's study of Xenophon's *Hiero*, entitled *On Tyranny*. I want to mention here only the most salient point of the debate between Kojève and Strauss. Strauss presents the classical, i.e. Socratic, position that philosophers seek the truth independently of historical fashions and that they are prevented from the madness of solipsism by associating with their friends. To this, Kojève rightly replies that even madmen have friends, namely, other madmen; the only secure verification of the truth of one's doctrines is that they are made true by historical success, that is, by political enactment, not by the agreement of private intellectuals.

In my opinion, Strauss has no effective reply to Kojève's criticism on this point, because, in the Aristotelian version of the Socratic position defended by Strauss, we choose our friends on the basis of a common love, and in the Socratic version as presented by Plato, love is a form of madness. In more sober terms, the noetic vision of pure Ideas or species-forms can only be verified by discourse; we have to say what we have seen, both to ourselves and to others. But speech is a political act on the classical analysis: political, not "intersubjective" in the post-Hegelian terminology. I can only give a brief indication here of why this is so. In the Platonic dialogues, there is no plurality of philosophical positions but only philosophy: all philosopher-kings in the *Republic* are Platonists. This is why the Eleatic Stranger says in the *Sophist* (242c 4–9) that all those who have spoken hitherto on the nature of being have expressed themselves carelessly, and talked to us as if we were children. The truth, as spoken to adults by adults, is one, not many. Incidentally, the same point is made by Hegel when he says that there are no philosophical opinions but only one true philosophy.[2]

Hegel, however, and Kojève after him, infers from this fact that speech demands practical implementation, not, as seems to be the case in Plato, in order to "solve" the political problem or to bring justice to the non-philosophers, but in order to preserve philosophy by transforming it into wisdom, and hence by transforming the non-philosophers into philosophers. When friends speak frankly to one another, they are transformed into citizens or potential citizens, in particular through those who overhear these conversations: their students and disciples. If on the other hand the philosophers practice extreme esotericism, or communicate to one another only by hints and the various devices of Aesopic speech, the dangers of madness or solipsism are not averted, because hints can be misunderstood, just as is the case with hinted responses to hints.

One can therefore say that Strauss avoids the tragedy of human existence by refusing, despite his ostensible interest in politics, to enter into history, and so a fortiori, into politics, except by the promulgation of salutary hints to the disciples who are entrusted with the political defense of the exoteric perimeter of philosophy.

243

But despite the constant reference to the fact that Socrates laughs (or smiles) twice in the *Phaedo* and never weeps, this is tantamount to an admission of tragedy. Kojève's victory, unfortunately, is pyrrhic, for reasons that we have now seen. The debate between Strauss and Kojève, fascinating in its details and worthy of endless reflection, is nevertheless at bottom a kind of comedy in which two protagonists of *Heiterkeit*, one of Socratic and the other of what I shall call Goethean irony, reveal on the one hand the pointless and on the other the impossible nature of wisdom.

This is the deeper meaning of Kojève's remark in his Hegel commentary that there is no comic satisfaction: that Greek tragedy shows the master to be an imposter and that comedy is the summit of Greek art (pp. 252–4). Kojève presents us with the strange spectacle of a *farceur* who impersonated the wise man on so high a level that he succeeded in becoming a philosopher, if not the sage or god that he claimed (ironically) to be. One must therefore wonder whether his friend Leo Strauss does not score the penultimate, if not the ultimate, point in their long conversation. Whereas philosophy is necessarily political, this seems to be true in a paradoxical sense. The city inhabited by the philosophers is a city restricted to friends of the Platonic Ideas; it cannot be populated by friends of the "ideas" of the *ego cogitans* or the historical subject because these are infinite and mutually contradictory. The abolition of eternity through the identification of Being as temporality thus leads to the annihilation of philosophy. It leads, not to the satisfaction of desire, but to its emancipation.

It would therefore seem that the annihilating negativity identified by Kojève as the essential nature of human being achieves nothing by its historical and conceptual labors of transformation: *ex nihilo nihil fit*. Otherwise put, the heaven of the sage turns out to be as boring as the heaven of the saint. A philosophy that is grounded in anthropology, and that seeks, above all, human salvation, is like an imaginary bridge between two crumbling towers of sand. Before we dissolve entirely into the abyss, should we not reconsider the eternity which Kojève, in the name of freedom, strove to deny us? Is it possible that the Hegel-philologists, whom Kojève scorned and to whom he was indeed superior in the depth of his intelligence and the sharpness of his wit, were in the last analysis closer to the Absolute than he?

This last question can be answered in the affirmative if and only if we reject the temptation to secularize Hegel, to transform him into a thinker of intersubjectivity, and so into a resident of post-Hegelian decadence. Despite his brilliance, Kojève contributed to the spread of decadence. What is perhaps most difficult to understand is that he did so by virtue of the extraordinary philosophical feat of thinking through to its end the life of philosophy. Just as Hegel's version of the Absolute was too lofty for his successors, so too with Kojève's demonstration of boredom.

## Notes

1 Numbers in parentheses identify the pages of the citations from the *Introduction à la lecture de Hegel* (Paris: Gallimard, 1947).
2 As, for example, in *Einleitung in die Geschichte der Philosophie* (Hamburg: Felix Meiner Verlag, 1959), p. 27.

# 20

# Levinas*

## HENT DE VRIES

In sharp contrast with Heidegger's insistence that the metaphysics of presence, in particular the objectivation of beings in terms of their being "ready at hand" culminating in the techno-scientific world-view, be destructed and overcome in light of a more fundamental thinking of "presencing" or "coming into presence" (*Anwesen*), the philosophy of the infinitely Other introduced (or should we say: rearticulated) by Emmanuel Levinas marks a radical rupture with all ontology. Indeed, it breaks away from every thought of Being, from the notion of the event or eventhood (*Ereignis*) of Being, but also from the notion of the gift implied in Heidegger's formula that Being "is" what "there is," that Being "is" what essentially "gives," or, finally, that Being "is" (what is) fundamentally given (*Es gibt das Sein*). From the publication of his earliest phenomenological studies in the 1930s and late 1940s onwards, but especially since the appearance, in 1961, of his first major book *Totalité et Infini: Essai sur l'extériorité* (*Totality and Infinity: An Essay on Exteriority*), Levinas has left no doubt that the central concern of his philosophical thinking was to leave the parameters – indeed, the very "climate" – of Heideggerian thought behind. This flight, as it were, not merely from ontology but also from Heidegger's later thinking-of (*Andenken*) of Being consists, in its first phase, in the reorientation rather than destruction or deconstruction of traditional Western philosophy – a tradition which, according to Levinas, has been by and large a philosophy of the Same (*le Même*) – in the direction of the Other (*l'Autre*) or, more precisely, other human beings (*autrui*). At first glance, therefore, Levinas's first major work is characterized by the attempt to establish ethics as the genuine first philosophy. The ethical relation here is at once the *primum intelligibele* that puts an end to the essential arbitrariness and the anarchy of the world of opinions and truths, of appearances and idealized constructs. For all its apparent abstraction, it signals itself in the concrete event of obligation, more specifically in the introduction of a responsibility that precedes and exceeds contracts and rules, reciprocity and recognition, norms and conventions. In *Totality and Infinity* this relation of the self to the other is described in terms of the asymmetrical structure of discourse, of dialogue, and, most importantly, of the face-to-face with the other's *visage*. For, so the argument goes, it is solely in the face-to-face that the Desire (*désire*) for the other arouses, provokes, or evokes. It is in this singular relation without relation alone that the self is accused and made responsible.

---

*Translated by Dana Hollander.

In the later writings, notably in the second major book, entitled *Autrement qu'être ou au-delà de l'essence* (*Otherwise than Being or Beyond Essence*) and published in 1974, Levinas shifts the emphasis that was put in the first work on ethical discourse, desire, the face-to-face, in short on transcendence, in favor of a relentless exploration of the passivity – on this side and beyond all interiorty and intentionality – that singles out the responsible self, and does so to the very point of its substituting itself for the other in becoming its hostage: more responsible than all others and responsible for all others, indeed for *everything* that concerns *every* other. The earlier assumption that non-violent and non-rhetorical discourse could somehow found, inspire, or judge all cognition and action is in the later work qualified in a sense that runs counter to any – Greek or transcendental – architectonics that continues to place the ethical Saying (*le Dire*) in the position of the *archè*, the principle or point of origination, of the *Said* (*le Dit*). On the contrary, Levinas now explores an *anarchy* of an ethics – or, rather, ethicity of ethics – that unsettles the very structure of first philosophy, in its onto-theological no less than in its modern transcendental guise. It is especially this disorienting feature of the Other who is no longer simply thought of as exterior, intelligible, or even ethical, but who leaves a trace – a transcendence to the point of absence – in the intrigue of the *In-finite* in the finite, which makes it possible and urgent to read Levinas's work in a radically antimoralist way.

In the same vein, it must be noted that while the obsession of responsibility is, in a sense, the "latent birth" of religion, it reveals itself "prior to emotions or voices, prior to 'religious experience' which speaks of revelation in terms of the disclosure of being."[1] To argue, with the Pascal of the *Pensées* and the *Mémorial*, that the God of the Bible, that is to say of Abraham, Jacob, and Isaac, is not properly "thinkable" and is thus to be radically distinguished from the conceptual God of the philosophers and the scholars, leaves ontology intact. In the same essay from which I am quoting here, namely "Dieu et la Philosophie" ("God and Philosophy"), Levinas says as much: "in staying or wanting to be outside of reason, faith and opinion speak the language of being. Nothing is less opposed to ontology than opinion and faith."[2] Without relapsing into fideism or irrationalism, one should ask therefore "whether the meaning that is equivalent to the *esse* of being, that is, the meaning which is meaning in philosophy, is not already a restriction of meaning."[3] In this contribution I will show that this position can already be found in what – with an oblique reference to one of Levinas's most implicit influences, namely the work of Franz Rosenzweig – can be called the Levinasian *Urzelle*. It is in this "germ cell" that we find the basic features of the thought that epitomizes Levinas's later philosophy as it distances itself ever more radically from the categories (and existentials) of ontology and theology. The alternative to these traditional and modern coordinates is neither the blind submission to the other of reason, of the *metaphysica generalis* and *specialis* that center around the most general and the highest concept of Being, nor is it the return to an archaic or mythical past. On the contrary, the religion of adults that transpires through Levinas's writing is from the start and in the final analysis in keeping with a disenchanted modern – indeed, modernist – experience whose contours will be described in the following.

# I

Levinas's early independent writings contain, *in nuce*, a number of the most interesting themes and figures of thought of his oeuvre as a whole. As has been pointed out, religious inspiration plays a surprisingly minor role, if any, in these texts.[4] This is especially so for the *Urzelle* of Levinas's oeuvre, the essay *De l'évasion*, which appeared in 1935 in the *Recherches philosophiques*, an avant-garde journal edited by Alexandre Koyré, Gaston Bachelard, and Jean Wahl among others. In this essay Levinas, referring to contemporary literature, evoked the specifically modern experience of a "mal du siècle,"[5] a "malaise" of existing, a sickness unto being that marks this century.

Retrospectively, this unabashed critique of the period – which relies heavily on phenomenological analyses of the subject's being-thrown-back-upon-itself – may be read as an idiosyncratic reception and implicit critique of Heidegger's analyses of "thrownness" and "anxiety." Jacques Rolland makes clear that the "fundamental mood" (*Grundstimmung*) of "anxiety" in Heidegger's "What Is Metaphysics?" is comparable to the "indeterminacy" (*Unbestimmtheit*) in Levinas's characterizations of malaise and disgust. These states are determined neither by something particular in the world nor by the subject's psycho-physical state.[6] Yet one also finds in *De l'évasion* an echo of the threat to Jewish existence during the 1930s.[7] In this and other modes of experience Levinas discerns the *horror* of living in a world without hope, a world stigmatized by what Benjamin and Adorno called the "ever same of the new" (*Immergleiche des Neuen*) and which thus revives antiquity's obsession with fate.[8]

Levinas combines his interpretation of oppressed modern existence with a preliminary description of a demand that is central to his early and late work: the demand for an *escape* (*évasion, excendance*) *from Being as such*, "leaving Being by a new way at the risk of reversing certain notions that to the common sense and the wisdom of nations seem the most evident" (p. 99). This early motif, then, is reason enough to reject the view that the question concerning the "otherwise than Being" and the "turn" that Levinas's work seems to take in the period after 1963 are without precedent in the development of his thought, as Stephan Strasser believes.[9]

The desire (for which the text of *De l'évasion* still employs the word *besoin*, but for which later on Levinas, in keeping with a Platonic, anti-Hegelian affect, will use the concept of *désir*) for breaking out of Being is, Levinas asserts, most apparent in modern literature. Such an appeal to literature is not unusual in Levinas's work. Here, he celebrates the relentless imagination and brilliant language of Louis Ferdinand Céline's *Voyage au bout de la nuit*. By evoking a "sad and desperate cynicism" (p. 86) that seems to permeate modern experience, this work had stripped and liberated the world of all ornament. The directionlessness of the mode of weariness that derives from the experience expressed by this novel could, Levinas suggests, be called an escape "without an itinerary and without an end"[10] whose indeterminate feeling was already probed long before Céline, above all by Baudelaire: "Like for Baudelaire's true travellers, it is a matter of parting for the sake of parting."[11]

Although Levinas hardly succeeds, in this *Urzelle*, in finding a clear point of departure, a point from which the *possibility* and the *modality* of a way out of Being can be described "concretely" or "positively," he does indeed draw a "negative" line of demarcation between traditional and contemporary philosophy. In *De l'évasion* as well as in the later writings, he argues that though philosophers since Aristotle and up to Bergson and Heidegger had repeatedly noted and emphasized the finitude of Being, they had never put Being itself into question. Occidental philosophy, Levinas says, voiced ontological critique only in the interest of a "better Being" ("être meilleur"), i.e., with a view to community with the infinite Being, the I's correspondence with the world, and an inner harmony of the subject that realizes itself by resisting oppression. However, this pathos of freedom and this desire to be at peace with oneself presuppose the *self-sufficiency* of Being. Levinas counters this self-sufficiency with a radical question: "Does Being suffice for itself?" (p. 94).

Being is, perhaps, not the final *ground* or the *highest level* of our philosophical reflections (p. 74). Indeed, Levinas continues, a civilization that puts up with the ineluctable tragedy and desperation of Being, as well as with the crimes that Being justifies, deserves to be called *barbaric* (p. 98). One might unhesitatingly endorse one of idealism's deepest aspirations – the search for ways of transcending the world of things on which Being was first modeled. But the course that idealism wound up taking toward this goal led to a vanishing point at which all its discoveries – the dimensions of the ideal, the notions of consciousness and becoming (p. 96) – quickly fell prey to a renewed *ontologization*. In *De l'évasion*, Levinas already tries to disrupt this ontological imperialism, this tendency toward a concept of *Being* (one which in its very dynamic is rather static) which is itself no more than a "mark of a certain civilization" (p. 74, cf. p. 98):

> The insufficiency of the human condition has never been understood otherwise than as a limitation of Being. . . . The transcendence of these limits, the communion with the infinite Being remained its sole preoccupation. . . . And yet the modern sensibility grapples with problems that indicate, perhaps for the first time, the abandonment of this concern for transcendence.  (p. 69)

According to Levinas, neither the classical-modern response to the age-old question of Being, nor the Romantic revolt against this response, ever broke with a *harmonizing* ideal of being-human, an ideal which reached its highest expression in the ideology of the late bourgeoisie. Levinas's first independent reflection on the problem of subjectivity (apart from his earlier influential commentaries on Husserl and Heidegger) is thus already prompted by a critique of that self-sufficiency of the bourgeois "I" whose constant striving to enrich and complete itself corresponds to the industriousness that formed the contours of Western capitalist societies. Here already, we are dealing with what Derrida, in his first essay on Levinas, "Violence and Metaphysics," would come to describe as an other than merely Marxist critique of ideology. In a different context and in a later essay, Levinas will even cite as the deeper motive behind the 1968 students' and workers' revolt the moral consciousness of the continuous stifling of the modern atmosphere by way of such "progress."

For a closer look at that event reveals that there too it was the conditions of possibility of an achievement- and consumption-driven society that were subjected to critique. Levinas interprets this society with the help of an "ontology of the false present," to use an expression of Adorno's, and unmasks the blind collective striving for individual self-preservation, "which no religious breath any longer succeeds in rendering egalitarian."[12] To put it more strongly: "Behind the capital of *having* weighed a capital of *being*."[13] And it is this overinvestment in Being that inspires, motivates, and necessitates the evasion and ethical disinterestedness that, according to the later work, is the condition of possibility of the critique of ideology and ontology as such.

Yet at the same time Levinas stresses, in *De l'évasion* and in the other early essays, that the modern epoch no longer allows anyone to simply retreat from the impenetrable inner workings of the universal (ontological, symbolical, and political) order. In the bustle of the modern age, everyone is mobilizable and it is no longer possible to withdraw from the *game* or to restore to things their innocent character. But this also means that modernity is defined by a relentless *earnestness* and by a premature adulthood:

> Temporal existence takes on the ineffable flavor of the absolute. The elementary truth *that there is Being* [*qu'il y a de l'être*] – Being that has value and weight – reveals itself with a depth that is a measure of its brutality and seriousness.   (p. 70)

The *two extremes* of modern experience – the experiential mode of naked being on the one hand and the desire for escape that this being provokes on the other – both share a structure *sui generis*. The analogous words with which Levinas first describes the burden of naked being and then evokes a flight that can barely hope to effectuate a real break serve to rigidify these two dimensions into something like *mirror images* of each other. If the transitions in Levinas's presentation are not entirely convincing, it is because of this kind of *absolutization* of extremes, making them something *more* than purely critical or rhetorical motifs. The idea of a *pure* Being of things or of a frightening *neutral* dimension that would remain if one were to subtract the world of things, but also the idea of a possible break with this Being and thus the retreat to an Otherwise-than-Being – all these risk becoming *abstract*. In particular, these complementary figures signal the very limits of their phenomenological description, in a gesture that will be reiterated in the later analyses of the polarity between the *il y a* (*there is*) and *illeity* as two different but co-originary modalities and possibilities, if one can still say so, of one and the same transcendence,[14] as well as of the up and down movements, *en-deça* (hither side) and *au-delà* (beyond), or, indeed, the movements of *transdescendence* and *transascendence*, to cite the notions that *Totality and Infinity* will borrow from the metaphysical treatises of Jean Wahl.

Yet, whatever the difficulties that lurk behind these complex notions, one cannot deny the great *heuristic* power of Levinas's findings. The words he chooses in this early essay have the potential to explode the tradition of onto-theology – a potential that needs, if one may say so, only to be ignited.

249

The problem of Levinas's thought, then, cannot be reduced to the question concerning the existence of God, His way of being, and His essential properties. This much is already clear from the *Urzelle* (cf. p. 97):[15]

It is not toward eternity that escape accomplishes itself. Eternity is only the accentualization or the radicalization of the fatality of being bound to itself. And there is a profound truth to the myth of the eternity that weighed on the immortal gods. (p. 95)

According to Levinas, the classical-metaphysical and modern *antithesis of the finite and the infinite*, of permanence and becoming, of nothing and eternity can only apply to *that which is*, i.e., to the world of things and its nature (p. 69). This antithesis operates within a conceptuality or a *metaphorics* which allows for a certain extension, for certain properties of objects of thought and experience to be determined in a process of mutual comparison, a process ultimately reflected in the ideal of perfection. But the *Being of things*, the bare fact of the existence of beings refers only to itself and in doing so takes on the character of an absolute (p. 76). This Being betrays an even "deeper flaw" (p. 69). With this, a decisive break with any philosophy of *finitude* is announced: "Existence of itself harbors something tragic, something which is not there only because of its finitude and which death cannot resolve."[16]

The malaise of Being is expressed in the *desire* for a way out. Levinas even calls this desire "the fundamental category of existence" (p. 88). The suffering which gives rise to it is an all-encompassing awareness that it is impossible to let the treadmill stand still. The oppressive feeling associated with the analogous phenomena of shame and disgust, for instance, attacks us from within; it is a "revolting presence of ourselves to ourselves" (p. 89). Shame consists of the impossibility of breaking away from oneself, no matter how much one would like to do so (p. 87). Disgust, of which Levinas gives a subtle analysis long before Sartre's *La Nausée*, corresponds to the impossibility of affirming the being that one is (p. 90). The modern experience of Being's permanent affirmation and self-reference, of its being fundamentally monadic in the Leibnizean sense, that is to say, "closed toward all the rest without a window on any other thing" (p. 92), which Levinas illustrates in a concentrated manner here, does not yield a new array of the properties of our existence. What is central is not the fact that, in our projects, we always already leave unrealized a number of possibilities, or, to put it more clearly, that we have a need for "innumerable lives" (p. 73). The desire for escape doesn't attempt, by a creative activity, to skirt the obstacles that it encounters on its way, but rather withdraws from the weight of Being only by breaking through the prison within itself (cf. p. 73). No romantic or nihilistic revolt, no nostalgic longing for death, and certainly no desire for a fulfilled Being, in sum: no new founding of the I (cf. pp. 71, 73) and no escape from the originary guilt of which Heidegger speaks in *Sein und Zeit* can adequately express the desire that Levinas means here. For these ultimately regressive figures of human striving are in search of a secure abode, they are a mere means of evading a forbidding "*definition*" (p. 71) of existence. And Levinas will not hesitate to point out that this holds true for Heidegger's (and, for that matter,

Sartre's) philosophy of freedom as well. The proper escape is not a search for the proper.

The true flight is a movement that is not directed at *any goal*. It prefigures or echoes an exodus (or the journey undertaken by Abraham, as opposed to that of Ulysses, about whose destination and return to Ithaca there is never any doubt). The malaise and the desire for a way out concern "an attempt to leave without knowing where one is going" (p. 78). What is sought is not so much a *satisfaction* but rather a *deliverance* (p. 78):

> The desire for escape finds itself . . . to be absolutely identical at all the resting points
> where its adventure leads it, as if the route completed had in no way diminished its
> non-fulfillment.   (pp. 71–2)

It is in this *unsublatable inadequacy* of every satisfaction of this desire that the *sublimity* of this gesture resides (p. 79). In other words, the quenching of the desire never removes the restlessness of the malaise. With this, we have, in a sense, the *photographic negative* of what Levinas will describe as metaphysical-ethical *désir* in his later work.

A description of the supposed satisfaction of desire in *pleasure* shows that pleasure's (closed) dialectic is in the final analysis condemned to failure (pp. 82–4). Even though its dynamic breaks away from the fixed forms to which the beings conform, and even though its effect points to a third way between thinking and acting, the path of gratification remains a "deceptive escape" (p. 83). Levinas's later ambivalence toward the *erotic*, his tendency to focus on *agape* and, indeed, on love in general as a model of absolute transcendence, is already in evidence here.

Psychology, by contrast, which misunderstands desire as a need in the sense of "privation" (pp. 73, 76), as a weakness or a defect of our human condition, rests, according to Levinas, on an untenable metaphysical assumption. For it identifies the ground of desire with an emptiness, a vacuum, a lack of Being, while interpreting the actual in terms of fullness, of a wholeness of Being. In doing so, it absolutizes a metaphorics that makes sense only in the world of things that exist as a part of nature (pp. 77–8). And this is precisely what desire seeks to free itself from (p. 83): "Desire expresses the presence of our being and not its deficiency" (p. 81). Desire concerns, in other words, "the purity of the fact of being which already announces itself as escape" (p. 76).

## II

The early text *De l'évasion* thus allows us to read *in nuce* a problematic leitmotif that will become ever more manifest in the development of Levinas's thought. This leitmotif is the *aporia* that the flight from Being is on the one hand conceived as the *internally produced mirror image* of Being, while on the other hand, as Levinas stresses, flight is not only *called for* but ultimately also *impossible*. This impossibility, however, is not simply a failure. More precisely, it is the structure of the failure of a certain metaphysics that is reread and made productive here. The impossibility for beings to escape from Being or from their being-there corresponds in the later writings to an impossibility for thought, experience, or language to grasp, let alone determine, the other in its ambiguity as the face of the neighbor and the stranger, as the idea or the trace or the enigma of the Infinite, as the intrigue of the Other in the finite totality of the Same.

Yet, while the formalism of the original structure of the escape is thus concretized as an ethical movement towards the Other, this Other "is," paradoxically, that which – or the One who – continues to escape. Let me conclude by briefly analyzing these two moments which in the later work come to be presented as two aspects of one and the same movement.

In *De l'évasion*, we said, Levinas attempts in the first place to understand the flight or evasion as the "internal structure" (p. 75) of Being's own self-positing. On this view, Being – which is brought back to the phenomena which testify to its ineluctability – produces its own opposite by a contradictory movement, in the "experience itself of pure being" (p. 90). In a combined moment of malaise, pleasure, shame, and disgust, it gives rise to an experience of *revolt* (p. 71):

> This "there-is-nothing-more-to-do" is the mark of a limit-situation in which the futility of any action is precisely the indication of the supreme instant in which there is nothing left to do but leave. The experience of pure being is at the same time the experience of its internal antagonism and of the escape that imposes itself.   (p. 90)

It would seem, then, that it is powerlessness and, in the same sense, the finitude of Being itself, that kindles the desire for a flight. In other words: that Being is a burden for itself (cf. p. 88) and consequently the "source of all desire" (p. 93). But it is no less obvious that, when one follows the progression of this type of reflection, a real way out of or beyond Being cannot be found. The question as to what kind of utopia of happiness and dignity (p. 74) such an escape might promise must remain unanswered. The escape remains an internal possibility of Being and thus, in a sense, remains in its very essence tainted by Being and existence.

It is only by turning to the *concretion* of the ethical dimension and by articulating the modality of transcendence with the help of the metaphor, or rather, the figure of the trace in his later philosophy, that Levinas is able to break out of this impasse. Or so it seems at first glance. For the trace of the Other allows one to think the modality of transcendence otherwise than by an abstract negation that presupposes an identity that precedes the very act of this negation.[17] The trace is not an essential possibility inherent in the structure of Being and existence as such. If anything, the trace "is not"; it signals the very impossibility for Being and existence to come into their own.

## III

Unlike this later thought of the trace, then, Levinas's earliest attempts to put the frightening and oppressive "experience" of Being into words remain ensnared in irresolvable problems. The same is true for the middle period of Levinas's oeuvre, which centered on the opposite pole of a moral *primum intelligibele* and thereby on an ethical transcendental philosophy.[18]

In the main work representative of this middle period, *Totality and Infinity*, Levinas rethinks exteriority in terms of an infinite Being. In a sense, he thereby retreats behind the position put forward by *De l'évasion*. The fact that the later philosophy of the trace of the ethical takes up again the radical critique of ontology contained in this early essay – and so to speak turns it against itself – serves once again to emphasize the essay's importance. Studying this text, then, as Rolland notes, is hardly an exercise in "archeology" or "paleography,"[19] for the most radical features of the later writing are indeed anticipated and prefigured in this "texte de jeunesse." In Levinas's own words: one can discern in *De l'évasion* a vigilant awareness of the modern experience of the "no exit" (*sans-issue*) that goes hand in hand with the "obstinate awaiting of impossible new thoughts."[20] While the later work explicitly takes its distance from the figure of the escape or flight that played such a central part in *De l'évasion*, it will also reaffirm that one "impossible new thought" that has interested us here: that of a movement beyond Being's essence that does not know where it is going:

> The task is to conceive of the possibility of a break out of essence. To go where? Toward what region? To stay on what ontological plane? But the extraction from essence contests the unconditional privilege of the question "where?"; it signifies a null-site [*non-lieu*]. Essence claims to recover and cover over every ex-ception – negativity, nihilation, and already since Plato, non-being, which "in a certain sense is."[21]

That the exception "is" an ethical one in this passage from *Otherwise than Being or Beyond Essence*, whereas in *De l'évasion* the primacy of the Other is not yet that of the other (*autrui*), of the Infinite, or of the "Divine Comedy," matters little. For the evocation and articulation of these later motifs are linked up with the experiences described above. Paradoxically, these experiences in their turn serve to concretize the modality of ethical transcendence.

## Notes

1  E. Levinas, "Dieu et la philosophie," in *De Dieu qui vient à l'idée* (Paris: Vrin, 1982), p. 118; "God and Philosophy," *Collected Philosophical Papers*, tr. Alphonso Lingis (Dordrecht: Martinus Nijhoff, 1987), p. 168.

2  Ibid., pp. 96/155.

3  Ibid., pp. 95/154.

4  Fabio Ciaramelli is right to note that Levinas, even before pointing to (Jewish) religion – and ethics – as the *via regia* to the critique of ontology, sought routes of escape from Being. The text that concerns us here is the best illustration of this. Thus, for instance, *De l'existence à l'existant* (1947) already contains the "messianic motif." "De l'évasion à l'exode. Subjectivité et existence chez le jeune Levinas," *Revue Philosophique de Louvain*, 80 (1982), pp. 553–78, 554.

5  *De l'évasion* (Monpellier: Fata Morgana, 1982), p. 70. All page numbers in the text refer to this edition.

6  See Jacques Rolland, "Sortir de l'être par une nouvelle voie," published as an introduction to the re-edition of *De l'évasion*, p. 23. In his annotations to the text, Rolland notes that Levinas is here already interested in a "putting in question . . . not of Being in its being-there . . . , but of being-there in its Being" ("mise en question, . . . non pas de l'être dans l'être-là . . . , mais de l'être-là dans son être" – ibid., p. 111, n. 6).

7  See ibid., pp. 103, 104.

8  *Ethique et infini: Dialogues avec Philippe Nemo* (Paris: Fayard, 1982), p. 18.

9  Cf. Stephan Strasser, *Jenseits von Sein und Zeit. Eine Einführung in Emmanuel Levinas' Philosophie* (The Hague: Martinus Nijhoff, 1978), pp. 220, 223. Incidentally, Strasser also identifies a turn (*Kehre*) in Levinas's later work toward positions whose radicality is comparable to the earlier work (ibid., p. 225).

10  *De l'existence à l'existant* (Paris: Vrin, 1978), p. 32; *Existence and Existents*, tr. A. Lingis (Dordrecht: Kluwer, 1988), p. 25.

11  Ibid.

12  "Sans identité," *Humanisme de l'autre homme* (Montpellier: Fata Morgana, 1972), p. 110, n. 9; "No Identity," *Collected Philosophical Papers*, tr. A. Lingis (The Hague: Martinus Nijhoff, 1987), p. 150, n. 9.

13  Ibid.

14  Cf. my "Adieu, à dieu, a-Dieu," ed. Adriaan T. Peperzak, in *Ethics as First Philosophy: The Significance of Emmanuel Levinas for Philosophy, Literature and Philosophy* (New York and London: Routledge, 1995), pp. 211–20.

15  In this sense Levinas might even be called, according to Rolland, a thinker of the "death of God." Rolland, "Sortir de l'être," p. 117.

16  *De l'existence à l'existant*, p. 21; *Existence and Existents*, p. 20 (translation modified); *De l'évasion*, pp. 93, 94.

17  Cf. *Autrement qu'être, ou au-delà de l'essence* (The Hague: Martinus Nijhoff, 1978), p. 142, n. 16; *Otherwise than Being, or Beyond Essence*, tr. A. Lingis (Dordrecht: Kluwer, 1991), p. 195, n. 16: "Every idea of evasion, as every idea of malediction weighing on a destiny, already presupposes the ego constituted on the basis of the self and already free."

18  Cf. Theodore de Boer, "An ethical transcendental philosophy," in Richard A. Cohen (ed.), *Face to Face with Levinas* (Albany: SUNY Press, 1986), pp. 83–115.

19  Rolland, "Sortir de l'être," p. 12.

20  The quote is from Levinas's 1981 letter to Rolland published as a preface to the re-edition of *De l'évasion*, p. 8.

21  Cf. *Autrement qu'être*, pp. 9/8.

## Writings

Levinas, E.: *Totality and Infinity: An Essay on Exteriority*, tr. Alphonso Lingis (The Hague: Nijhoff, 1979).

——: *Otherwise Than Being or Beyond Essence*, tr. Alphonso Lingis (The Hague: Nijhoff, 1981).

——: *Basic Philosophical Writings*, ed. Robert Bernasconi, Simon Critchley, and Adriaan Peperzak (Indianapolis, IN: University of Indiana Press, 1996).

## Further reading

Bernasconi, Robert and Critchley, Simon (eds): *Re-reading Levinas* (Bloomington, IN: Indiana University Press, 1991).

Derrida, Jacques: "Violence and metaphysics: an essay on the thought of Emmanuel Levinas," in *Writing and Difference* (Chicago, IL: University of Chicago Press, 1978), pp. 79–153.

Llewelyn, John: *Emmanuel Levinas: The Genealogy of Ethics* (London: Routledge, 1995).

Peperzak, Adriaan: *To the Other: An Introduction to the Philosophy of Emmanuel Levinas* (West Lafayette, IN: Purdue University Press, 1993).

# 21

# Sartre

## THOMAS R. FLYNN

The political notoriety and literary fame of Jean-Paul Sartre (1905–80) (he was awarded but refused the Nobel Prize for Literature in 1962) have tended to eclipse his philosophical accomplishments, at least in the eyes of the public at large. This is unfortunate, since Sartre's philosophical writings are original and insightful, especially in those areas where the philosophy of being (ontology), philosophical psychology, and ethics overlap – the very space in which the literary imagination operates. In fact, there is probably no philosopher of the twentieth century who so personified the creative tension between philosophy and literature as did Jean-Paul Sartre. His enthusiasm for phenomenology as a method for philosophizing about concrete experience was doubtless born of that tension. After discussing Sartre's work as a phenomenologist, I shall analyze his thought in the areas of ontology, psychology, and ethics, as well as related fields of philosophical inquiry, concluding with several observations about the contemporary relevance of his philosophy.

## Sartre as phenomenologist

Sartre's erstwhile friend Raymond Aron is said to have introduced him to phenomenology upon the latter's return from a term at the Institut français in Berlin. Sartre pursued this new methodology by succeeding Aron at the Institut in 1933. There he read HUSSERL (see Article 15), HEIDEGGER (Article 18), SCHELER (Article 16), and others, and composed a seminal essay, "The Transcendence of the Ego" (1937), that was among his first philosophical publications. This piece, like several of his subsequent works, displayed a deep admiration for Husserlian phenomenology, especially the concept of "intentionality." As Sartre saw it, this defining characteristic of the mental, namely, intentionality as the "presence to an other than itself" (even when that other was the subject of reflective consciousness) rendered unnecessary the many arguments adduced to meet the difficulties of an inside–outside understanding of consciousness. In other words, intentionality, the feature that all consciousness is consciousness *of* an other than itself, opens the entire world of experience to philosophical investigation. Whether it be the recalcitrant facts of history, the elusive fictions of literature, or the nuances of our emotional life, all this is grist for the phenomenologist's mill. It seemed as if philosophy was opened once more to the kinds of questions that had given it birth in ancient Greece but which had been strangled by dogma and system across the intervening centuries. Above all, philosophy should make a difference in the philosopher's life. It was not a mere curiosity or an interesting adornment to a beautiful soul. Though he had not yet coined the term "committed literature," this early essay already displays traces of Sartre's existentialist tendencies. Nowhere was this more evident than in his interpretation of Husserl's "phenomenological reduction" or *époché*.

The *époché* or "bracketing of being" is the basic philosophical act that, as it were, retains the world's melody but changes its key. Husserl could agree with Wittgenstein that philosophy leaves the world just as it found it, except that he would leave us the "reduced world" as phenomena, impervious to Humean skepticism and subject to philosophical description of the most rigorous sort. What is changed is not the world but our "natural attitude" toward it, namely, our common sense belief that the world is there, in itself, without reference to any mind/consciousness whatsoever. This naive, realistic view has been subject to devastating critiques since Berkeley, Hume, and Kant. Husserl's reduction discounted this belief and avoided its liabilities by focusing on the world "as given" in its various modes of "givenness." It was the task of descriptive phenomenology to bring this givenness to our attention as accurately and indubitably as possible. Though the original form of givenness was sense perception, and to this extent Husserl was an empiricist, other modes of givenness were accepted as legitimate objects of philosophical analysis so long as their respective modes of givenness were acknowledged. This obviously held great promise for such traditionally problematic areas of investigation as aesthetic and moral experience, social and political relations, number theory, and existence itself. One suspended the question of their being "in themselves" and limited oneself to painstaking descriptions of the phenomena as such.

Sartre accepted the descriptive phenomenology that Husserl proposed, but joined Heidegger, MERLEAU-PONTY (see Article 23) and others in rejecting the "transcendental ego" as the subjective remainder of the phenomenological reduction. The concept of a transcendental ego, the so-called "subject that cannot be an object," was part of Husserl's Kantian heritage. In its stead, Sartre spoke of consciousness as a "pure spontaneous upsurge" that required no overarching ego to hold it or the world together. He espoused a non-egological conception of consciousness: "transcendental consciousness is an impersonal spontaneity" (Sartre 1962 [1937], p. 98).

So the title of Sartre's "Transcendence of the Ego" employs both an objective and a subjective genitive. The transcendental ego has been transcended, that is, rendered superfluous, and the "empirical" ego – the object of reflective consciousness and of introspective psychology – is shown to be a transcendent object, that is, a "thing" in the world as much as any other object of intentionality. Sartre elaborates these claims in his existentialist masterwork *Being and Nothingness* (1943).

But what reveals the existentialist flavor of Sartre's early essay is his understanding of the transcendental–phenomenological reduction as an act of human *freedom*. He reads the natural attitude as one of flight from the freedom of the philosophical act (the reduction) toward refuge in the empirical ego: "perhaps the essential role of the ego is to mask from consciousness its very spontaneity" (1962 [1937], p. 100). The existentialist themes of responsibility, anguish, and flight from freedom are already at work in this apparently epistemic and psychological piece. Sartre offers a

257

preview of coming attractions when he concludes this essay with the opinion that his newly articulated position should suffice to construct "an ethics and a politics which are absolutely positive" (1962 [1937], P. 106).

## Phenomenological ontology

While Sartre's ethical theory and political commitment were gestating during the war years, he published his existentialist landmark, *Being and Nothingness*. Subtitled "An Essay on Phenomenological Ontology," it used the descriptive method to lay the foundations for a new philosophy that would respect the irreducible difference between consciousness and the world, the mental and the nonmental, without falling into a two-substance ontology of minds and things that has plagued philosophy since Descartes.

Sartre's descriptions yield three fundamental types of being, namely, being-in-itself (*l'être-pour-soi*) or roughly consciousness, being-for-itself (*l'être-en-soi*) or the nonconscious, and being-for-others (*l'être-pour-autrui*) or the realm of the interpersonal and the public. Each is irreducible to the others and all, he insists, are of equal ontological importance, though he devotes more attention to the for-itself than to the other two. Indeed, twenty-five years later, he would criticize his thought of this period as being a "rationalist philosophy of consciousness" (Sartre 1974, p. 41).

The key to Sartre's phenomenological ontology is, of course, the phenomenon itself. In accord with his robust realism, he argues that "the being of the phenomenon cannot be reduced to the phenomenon of being," in other words, that there is always something more to any phenomenon than meets the eye and that "more" is the being of the phenomenon, its being-in-itself. Yet, he continues, there are some experiences, boredom, for example, and nausea (as portrayed in his novel by that title), that yield "some kind of immediate access" to being. These are the phenomena of being *par excellence*, but they are scarcely the concepts of rationalist philosophy. In fact, Sartre insists that "knowledge can not by itself give an account of being" (1948a [1943], pp. xlviii–xlix). What the phenomena of being reveal is the "transphenomenality of being," the something more (or better, "other") than meets the eye. None the less, Sartre does not wish to leave us with a dualism of appearance and reality à la Kant. The being of the phenomenon, "although coextensive with the phenomenon, can not be subject to the phenomenal condition – which is to exist only in so far as it reveals itself – and that consequently it surpasses the knowledge which we have of it and provides the basis for such knowledge" (1948a [1943], p. 1).

The counter-phenomenon to the in-itself is the for-itself or consciousness. If phenomenological description reveals the in-itself to be inert, identical, and factical, the for-itself emerges as spontaneous and non-self-identical – the locus of possibility, negativity, and lack. The title, *Being and Nothingness*, captures this fundamental duality of inertia (being) and spontaneity (consciousness), since the for-itself is essentially the negation of the in-itself. If the latter is "thingness," the former is fundamentally "no-thingness," the internal negation of the in-itself. Thus Sartre can insist that whatever human reality (the human being) is, it is in the manner of not-being it. Because consciousness is never identical with itself, it projects "otherness" wherever its attention is directed. Some of Sartre's most arresting passages are devoted to analyzing the various forms of the negative that populate our lives owing to this "nihilating" function of being-for-itself. This inertia/spontaneity duality in one form or another will continue to mark Sartre's thought for the rest of his life.

Sartre follows Heidegger in speaking of three temporal "ekstases," namely, the past as facticity (Heidegger's "thrownness"), the future as transcendence or projection (Heidegger's "existenz"), and the present as presence-to (Heidegger's "immersion" in the everyday). But unlike Heidegger, he follows Husserl in ascribing these dimensions to the work of consciousness itself. The for-itself is not "in time" in the manner of a physical substance; rather, it "temporalizes itself" according to these temporal ekstases. Consciousness is thoroughly temporal, but its temporality is ekstatic or existential, qualitative rather than quantitative. This is the "lived time" of personal experience, not the "clock time" of objective measurement. The "inner distance" that characterizes human reality, the otherness that it projects on its very self – these are functions of the temporalizing character of being-for-itself. Such are the insights gained by Sartre's phenomenological description of human consciousness.

In order to respect the clarity of consciousness that Descartes left us but without subscribing to his two-substance ontology, Sartre speaks of the for-itself as a "nonsubstantial absolute." The certitude that phenomenological description yields follows from the intuitive power of consciousness. But this consciousness is divided into the reflective and the prereflective. Prereflective consciousness is the original awareness that one has before adverting to that fact. As intentional, it is in-the-world, involved in one's ongoing projects and focused on the specific objects those projects reveal. Prereflective consciousness is "prepersonal" in the sense that the ego or self in this phase is only implicitly on the scene. Once consciousness reflects on itself, the ego moves to center stage and becomes the object of a reflective act. Sartre claims that explicit or thetic consciousness of an object is implicit or nonthetic consciousness (of) self. (He parenthesizes the "of" to indicate that the self is not an object for nonthetic awareness.) So there is no need for a second, reflective act in order to be conscious; one is always "aware (nonthetically) that one is aware." This short-circuits any need to reflect on one's reflecting . . . to infinity (or to stop at a transcendental ego, the subject that cannot be an object). Simple awareness is quite enough. It follows that every reflective act (which Sartre calls "knowledge" properly speaking) is always prereflectively self-aware. This means both that we are aware of more than we know (Sartre will later say that we "comprehend" more than we know) and that our mental acts and states are always (except, perhaps, for moments of apodictic evidence) "troubled" by this lack of complete coincidence of consciousness with its object or its very self. One can either live this unstable condition authentically or flee it in bad faith.

Sartre adopts the poet's "I am more than myself" to capture this insight into the profound lack of self-identity that characterizes consciousness and human reality in general. It is the root of our ontological freedom ("man is free because he is not a self but a presence-to-self" [1948a (1943), p. 440]), the occasion of existential anguish (for we are always forming our selves by creative choices), and the source of bad faith (since we try to avoid anguish by telling ourselves that we coincide with our selves or with what others take us to be).

"Human reality" is Sartre's term for the human way of being in the world. We are in the world "projectively," that is, via a basic project that directs all other choices as means to a single unifying end. Consequently, we exist in-situation. "Situation" denotes the facticity or "givens" of our lives along with the transcendence or "surpassing" of these givens in our fundamental project. For example, my geographic location, racial features, and religious upbringing are part of my *facticity*, so too is the way I have dealt with these givens up to the present. The way I am in the process of dealing with them now, however, is my *transcendence*. Sartre believes that we evidence a basic but futile tendency to coincide with ourselves consciously, that is, to be at once fully factical and totally transcendent. But this urge to collapse our ekstatic temporality into a timeless moment is a contradiction in terms. Sartre calls it our "futile desire to be God." It warrants his famous observation that "man is a useless passion."

Bad faith is the act or state of denying either term of the facticity/transcendence duality that defines our human condition. It is a form of self-deception made possible by the dividedness of consciousness and the dual nature of situation. It is a "lie" about one's situation repeated by reflective consciousness, though prereflective consciousness "knows" better. There can arise an entire *Weltanschauung* of bad faith. In fact, Sartre's description of Second Empire French society in *The Family Idiot* is an extended portrayal of collective bad faith.

Most people tend to deflate their transcendence into facticity by some form of determinism or by simply explaining, "That's just the way I am!" This is an obvious flight from freedom and the responsibility that Sartre believes is coterminous with it. Less widespread is the tendency to volatilize facticity into transcendence, as if wishing could make it so. This is the bad faith of the student who claims he or she wants to be a doctor but does not bother to open a chemistry text. By denying the reality of their past choices, these people pretend they can float above the facticity of their situation.

Being-for-others is the dimension of being that arises from the contingent fact of the presence of other subjects. Because we exist in our bodies and do not merely "have" them, we are liable to the meanings that others care to ascribe to our activities. These are public and beyond our control. The sheer presence of others is an empirical fact that can be experienced but not deduced a priori.

One of the most famous passages in *Being and Nothingness* contains Sartre's phenomenological description of shame consciousness and its experiential "proof" of the existence of other minds. An individual gazing through a keyhole on a couple is like a transcendence transcending the pair whose freedom it qualifies by the interpretation it ascribes to the actions it is witnessing. Suddenly, she hears footsteps from behind. Immediately she experiences shame in her body objectified under the other's gaze. Sartre's analysis of the experience reveals that in one and the same act, the voyeur experiences the *other as subject* and herself as objectified. Far from some weak analogy, Sartre urges, this is an immediate awareness of another subjectivity. It is as indubitable as the blush one senses mounting on one's face.

A whole realm of relationships becomes possible with the advent of the other, which Sartre likens to our "original fall." That most of these are relations of inequality, that "the essence of the relations between consciousnesses" is not the *Mitsein* (Heidegger's "being-with"), it is conflict" (1948a [1943], p. 429), can be taken as the pessimistic prospect for a social philosophy based on *Being and Nothingness*. It found its emblem in the infamous line from his play *No Exit*: "Hell is other people."

## Social and political philosophy

The ontological root of Sartre's pessimism was the looking/looked-at model of interpersonal relations, generated by his reliance on the gaze. He replaced that paradigm by a *praxis* model in the *Critique of Dialectical Reason*, vol. 1 (1960). Now he could speak of group praxis and common individuals in a way that would have been impossible in his earlier work. No doubt, the fundamental form of praxis is human labor – the inspiration is Marxian. And there is considerable emphasis on class struggle and structural exploitation in the *Critique*. But Sartre, who saw his project at that time as an attempt to "reconquer man within Marxism" (1963 [1960], p. 83), was careful to preserve the vintage existentialist values of individual freedom and responsibility by insisting on the primacy of free organic praxis in the midst of the most alienating forms of impersonal social causation. The *Critique* constructs a social ontology that proclaims the primacy of individual praxis and responsibility in the ontological, the epistemic, and the moral realms (see Flynn 1984, pp. 105–12). It thereby provides a theoretical underpinning for the political polemics in which Sartre engaged during the early years of the Cold War, the Algerian revolution, and the Vietnamese conflict. It is the nature of social reality, he argues, to enhance, not undermine, individual responsibility. Though he gradually came to acknowledge the socioeconomic limitations placed on organic praxis, he continued to insist that "a man can always make something out of what is made of him" (Sartre 1974, p. 35). We may take this as the maxim of Sartrean humanism.

The cardinal categories of the *Critique* are praxis and the practico-inert. Praxis denotes historical human activity in its cultural and economic context. The practico-inert refers to that context, including the sedimentation of past praxes. These are the heirs of being for-itself and in-itself respectively. The latter terms are virtually absent from the *Critique*, though they reappear in *The Family Idiot* (1970–72). It is the fact of scarcity of material goods that modifies the *practico-inert* into an instrument of violence and changes cooperation into conflict. A certain degree of alienation or otherness is inevitable wherever the practico-inert mediates human activity. This mediation becomes destructive in a society like our own, ruled by material scarcity. Sheer material scarcity converts each person into a competitor and a threat, as Sartre makes clear with his famous example of potential riders too numerous for the places on a bus. Relations mediated by such practico-inert (collective) objects as the bus, the postal system, and the evening television news, Sartre calls "serial" and the persons so related "serial individuals." His project is to study how seriality can be overcome and people disalienated. He believes this can be initiated by group praxis, where each is "the same" as the other in a common project and where "free alterity" reigns among the members. But such spontaneous moments as the storming of the Bastille are short-lived, and the group must reintroduce the practico-inert in the form of pledges and organization in order to survive its victory over its enemies. Only a "socialism of abundance" (Sartre 1993 [1988], vol. 5, p. 171) seems to be enough to make this collective freedom long-term. And even then Sartre is ambivalent as to the disappearance of alienation in all its forms (see Sartre 1976 [1960], p. 307, n.).

## Existential psychoanalysis/biography

Returning to *Being and Nothingness*, in its concluding chapters Sartre introduces his concept of existential psychoanalysis, admitting that it has not yet found its Freud. Its basic premise is that human reality is a practical totalization (not an inert totality) that organizes the other elements of its life into a meaningful whole by means of its fundamental project. We all share the futile desire to be God, that is to coincide consciously with ourselves, but each does so in his or her own way. It is the work of an existentialist hermeneutic of the agent's works and actions, including his or her speech acts, to determine that idiosyncratic way. Psychoanalysis interprets the meaning–direction (*sens*) of a life and whether one is pursuing it in good or bad faith. Sartre implies here, and especially in his posthumously published *Notebooks for an Ethics* (written in 1947–8), that in a society of scarcity, authenticity is the exception and bad faith the rule. His imaginative reconstructions of the lives of Baudelaire, Genet, Mallarmé, and Flaubert as well as his own autobiography, *The Words* (1962), are exercises both in existential psychoanalysis and in social critique. The latter dimension of these undertakings became increasingly evident as Sartre's command of and commitment to dialectical thinking increased in the 1950s and 1960s.

## Methodology

We have observed Sartre's early use of the phenomenological method. He never set aside this instrument that seemed so suited to him. But as his ontological focus shifted from consciousness to praxis, dialectical thinking, familiar to him at least since his reading of Hegel in the 1930s, appeared more convenient and congenial. In 1958 he published *Search for a Method*, which in revised form would constitute the Preface to Volume One of the *Critique*. There he developed an amalgam of phenomenology, existentialist psychoanalysis and historical materialism that he called the "progressive–regressive method." It comprises three stages.

Significantly, the first stage consists in a rigorous phenomenological description of the object to be investigated. But Sartre now sees that this is not enough. Description must be completed by explanation. So the second stage moves from the fact, Flaubert's "feminization of experience," for example, to the conditions of its possibility in the events and relationships of his infancy and early childhood. This "regressive" movement resembles a mixture of Freudian psychoanalysis and historical materialism in its search for the family relationships that "mediate" socioeconomic structures at a certain stage of history. What were the possibilities open to a would-be author from a provincial bourgeois family during the age of Louis Philippe? And what were the younger Flaubert's specific choices given the history and dynamics of his particular family? These are the questions to be answered by the regressive method. But they are still rather structural and "abstract" by Sartre's reckoning. So a third, more existential, stage is called for: the progressive determination of how Gustave himself, in our example, "chose" to interiorize these conditions and re-exteriorize them dialectically in his novels. Sartre sets before himself (at the start of his multi-volume study of Flaubert and his times) nothing less than the task of uncovering the "necessary" connection between the author and the work, specifically, between Flaubert and *Madame Bovary*. Although Sartre will undertake similar progressive–regressive movements in the *Critique* – where the sought-for connection is between Stalin and Soviet Communism of the 1930s – and elsewhere, his massive study of Flaubert, *The Family Idiot*, is his most detailed and ambitious use of this method. As a synthesis of the categories and theses of *Being and Nothingness* and of the *Critique of Dialectical Reason*, it could well be considered Sartre's crowning achievement.

## Sartrean ethics

Sartre is above all a moralist. So-called "existentialist ethics" in its various forms is deeply indebted to his writings. We have noted the moral twist he gave to the Husserlian *époché* and watched him introduce into his phenomenological ontology what (despite his protests) are the moral concepts of authenticity and bad faith. At the end of *Being and Nothingness* he promised an ethics of authenticity and deliverance from bad faith. Though he composed hundreds of pages in fulfillment of that promise, his *Notebooks for an Ethics* were not published until after his death. By then he had fashioned a second, "dialectical" ethic, more in conformity with the categories of the *Critique*, and at the time of his death he was hard at work on yet a third, "an ethic of the we," in collaboration with Benny Lévy. Since the first ethic is best known and has been substantially completed by the appearance of the *Notebooks*, we shall concentrate on it and consider the other two in more summary fashion.

Whatever their limitations as partial, sketchy, and being deliberately withheld from publication by their author until after his death, the *Notebooks* make a major contribution to Sartre's existentialist ethics. Their emphasis on good faith, authentic love, the gift-appeal relationship among freedoms, and the like require that we seriously revise our coffee table notion of Sartre as nihilist and prophet of insuperable bad faith. Take the following as an example:

> Here is an original structure of authentic love . . . : to unveil the Other's being-within-the-world, to assume this unveiling and to set this Being within the absolute [the for-itself]; to *rejoice* in it without appropriating it; to shelter it in my

freedom and to surpass it only in the direction of the Other's ends. (Sartre 1992 [1983], p. 508)

This affirming and supportive ideal is a far cry from the mutual stare-down proposed in *Being and Nothingness* as the model for interpersonal relations. The latter justified at most the rather formal concept of authenticity described in *Anti-Semite and Jew* (1946), namely, "having a true and lucid consciousness of the situation, in assuming the responsibility and risks that it involves" (1948b [1946], p. 90). It led many to view Sartrean authenticity as more a style than a content and generated such counter-examples as the "authentic Nazi" and the like. To be sure, a careful analysis of Sartrean "situation" would reveal the impossibility of authentically denying another's freedom, but Sartre never mounted a clear defense against such objections.

Two considerations intervened to give the ethic elaborated in the *Notebooks* a more positive content. The first was a contextualizing of the question in its historical, socioeconomic setting. The earlier work took no account of the conditioning of personal relations by the class struggle (which Sartre was beginning to allow for). As he later observed, the relations described in *Being and Nothingness* and in *No Exit* were proper to individuals in an alienated society.

The second consideration was the "nonaccessory reflection" or *époché* introduced in "The Transcendence of the Ego." Sartre now calls this a "conversion" and a "catharsis." It entails "a new, '*authentic*,' way of being oneself and for oneself, which transcends the dialectic of sincerity and bad faith" (1992 [1983], p. 474). What we have described as nonthetic consciousness (of) self, Sartre now points out, "is always the possible occasion for a secondary and nonaccessory reflection" (1992 [1983], p. 366). This conversion entails the willingness to "get rid of the I and the Me" (1992 [1983], p. 417), to live the tension of the presence-to-self. Although it is utopian to expect that humankind will simultaneously experience such a conversion, Sartre hopes that such a turning might be fostered by a "socialism of abundance."

In the 1960s Sartre prepared a series of lectures that contained what he called his second or "dialectical" ethic. It was more realist and "materialistic" than the ethic of authenticity, which he now criticized as idealistic and subjectivist. It was avowedly Marxian in inspiration, being grounded in the reality of human need, and need, as Marx observed, is its own justification. It took as its ideal "integral humanity" or the human being in its full biological and cultural development. Pursued with the progressive–regressive method, Sartre's second ethic is more socially committed and historically sensitive than his vintage existentialist position. Still, despite a certain naturalism in his account of the genesis of moral imperatives out of true human needs, he retains the existentialist thesis that it is human reality that brings values/norms into the world. This ambiguity of the "given" and the "taken" in any situation is a constant feature of Sartre's mature thought. His "Marxism," even at its apogee, always remained adjectival to his existentialism.

If the second ethic is elusive, being confined to three unpublished manuscripts, only one of which is conserved in the Bibliothèque Nationale in Paris, Sartre's third, the "ethic of the we," is even less available. On the basis of several interviews granted near the end of his life, we may conclude that this ethic favors the social dimension of human activity, contains a holistic critique of his ethic of authenticity, and still fails to reconcile the unavoidable concepts of fraternity and violence. But owing to the paucity of material as well as the hermeneutical morass created by Sartre's having co-authored the work with Benny Lévy, one should probably regard this phenomenon as mainly of biographical significance.

## Sartre today

With the eclipse of Marxist philosophy and the rise of postmodern and post-structuralist thought, the question of Sartre's contemporary relevance seems particularly apt. Is he the last nineteenth-century philosopher, as Foucault once quipped? Or is he a postmodern thinker despite himself, as others have claimed? And what of the existentialist movement that he inspired and led? Has it been absorbed by the very tradition it endeavored to question?

To the extent that the issues of Sartrean existentialism, such as the freedom and responsibility of the organic individual, the relationship between freedom, need, and structural (practico-inert) conditioning, the dialectic between biography and history, the contingency of our existence, and the "inner distance" that undermines any attempt to constitute ourselves as mental substances or finished selves – insofar as these and similar matters are permanent acquisitions of our philosophical culture in the West, to that extent Sartrean existentialism is alive and well in contemporary debates and not just conserved in the galleries of the history of philosophy.

Moreover, Sartre's urge to uncover the roots of individual freedom–responsibility amidst the most unyielding structural necessities and impersonal historical conditioning not only tempers the deterministic impulse of the social and natural sciences but reaffirms the humanistic ideal that lay at the core of Western philosophy ever since Socrates directed its attention from nature to the human. In fact, there is an ironically Sartrean ring to Foucault's recommendation near the end of his life that we "create" our moral selves.

It was Sartre's concept of praxis as totalizing and his interest in the historical dialectic as much as his fascination with Flaubert, Mallarmé, and other nineteenth-century authors that occasioned Foucault's remarks. No doubt, as a thinker of historical totalizations and organic wholes, Sartre is out of step with the multiplicities and particularizing movements of postmodern thought. But his concept of the practico-inert is structuralist in character. In fact, at the very start of the *Critique* he asks, "Do we have today the means to constitute a structural, historical anthropology?" (1963 [1960], p. xxxiv). What distinguishes him from pure structuralists like Althusser, Barthes, and Lévi-Strauss is his characteristic insistence on the ontological, epistemic, and moral primacy of totalizing organic praxis. Structure was not enough. The subsequent history of the structuralist movement has proven him right, just as the recent "post-structuralist" search for an ethic of responsibility seems to have vindicated his convictions in this regard.

Though it would be excessive to claim that Sartre was a postmodernist before his time, he defends several theses compatible with recent postmodern discourse. Most notable is his anti-substantialist concept of presence-to-self. This introduces a certain fluidity into subjectivist language and enables Sartre to speak of the self as an achievement rather than an origin. Postmodern critics of the Cartesian subject have failed to exploit the possibilities of this Sartrean concept. Other postmodern aspects of Sartre's writing include his dialogue between philosophy and literature (roughly, concept and image), his concern to draw upon aesthetical notions in service of his ethics, and his interest in varieties of rationality as exhibited in the *Critique*. Sartre's profoundly "moral" approach to the concrete problems of historical individuals continues to speak to those who look to philosophy for hope and guidance, and not just for diversion.

*See articles on* KIERKEGAARD, NIETZSCHE, FREUD, BERGSON, HUSSERL, HEIDEGGER, SCHELER, KOJÈVE, MERLEAU-PONTY, and DE BEAUVOIR.

## Writings

For a complete annotated bibliography of Sartre's works see Michel Contat and Michel Rybalka (eds), *The Writings of Jean-Paul Sartre* (Evanston, IL: Northwestern University Press, 1973), updated in *Magazine littéraire*, 103–4 (1975), pp. 9–49, and by Michel Sicard in *Obliques*, 18–19 (May 1979), pp. 331–47. Michel Rybalka and Michel Contat have compiled an additional bibliography of primary and secondary sources published since Sartre's death in *Sartre: Bibliography, 1980–1992* (Bowling Green, OH: Philosophy Documentation Center; Paris: CNRS Editions, 1993).

### Books

Sartre, J.-P.: *La Transcendence de l'égo*, first published in *Recherches Philosophiques*, 6 (1936–7), reprint ed. Sylvie le Bon (Paris, 1965); tr. Forrest Williams and Robert Kirkpatrick, *The Transcendence of the Ego* (New York: Noonday Press, 1962).

——: *L'Être et le néant* (Paris, 1943); tr. Hazel E. Barnes, *Being and Nothingness* (New York: Philosophical Library, 1948a).

——: *Réflexions sur la Question Juive* (Paris, 1946); tr. Eric de Mauny, *Portrait of the Anti-Semite* (London, 1948b); tr. George J. Becker, *Anti-Semite and Jew* (New York: Schocken, 1948c).

——: *Between Existentialism and Marxism* (essays and interviews, 1959–70), tr. John Mathews (London: New Left Books, 1974).

——: *Critique de la Raison Dialectique, précédé de questions de méthode*, vol. I: *Théorie des ensembles pratiques.* (Paris: 1960), reprinted in new annotated edition (1985); prefatory essay tr. Hazel E. Barnes, *Problem of Method* (London: Methuen, 1964), and *Search for a Method* (New York: Alfred A. Knopf, 1963); vol. 1, tr. Alan Sheridan-Smith, *Critique of Dialectical Reason*, vol. I, *Theory of Practical Ensembles* (London: New Left Books, 1976).

——: *L'Idiot de la famille*, 3 vols (Paris, 1971–2), vol. 3, revised edn (1988); tr. Carol Cosman, *The Family Idiot*, 5 vols (Chicago, IL: University of Chicago Press, 1981–93).

——: *Cahiers pour une morale*, composed 1947–8 (Paris, 1983); tr. David Pellauer, *Notebook for an Ethics* (Chicago, IL: University of Chicago Press, 1992).

——: *Critique de la Raison Dialectique*, vol. II (inachevé), *L'Intelligibilité de l'histoire*, ed. Arlette Elkiaim-Sartre (Paris, 1985); tr. Quintin Hoare, *Critique of Dialectical Reason*, vol. II (unfinished), *The Intelligibility of History* (London: Verso, 1991).

## References and further reading

Anderson, T. C.: *Sartre's Two Ethics: From Authenticity to Integral Humanity* (Chicago, IL: Open Court, 1993).

Aronson, R.: *Sartre's Second Critique* (Chicago, IL: University of Chicago Press, 1987).

——and A. van den Hoven (eds): *Sartre Alive* (Detroit, IL: Wayne State University Press, 1991).

Barnes, H. E.: *Sartre and Flaubert* (Chicago, IL: University of Chicago Press, 1981).

Beauvoir, S. de: *La Cérémonie des adieux, suivi de Entretiens avec Jean-Paul Sartre* (Paris, 1981); tr. Patrick O'Brian, *Adieux: A Farewell to Sartre* (New York: Pantheon Books, 1984).

Bell, L.: *Sartre's Ethics of Authenticity* (Tuscaloosa, AL: University of Alabama Press, 1989).

Busch, T.: *The Power of Consciousness and the Force of Circumstances in Sartre's Philosophy* (Bloomington, IN: Indiana University Press, 1990).

Cannon, Betty: *Sartre and Psychoanalysis: An Existentialist Challenge to Clinical Metatheory* (Lawrence, KA: University Press of Kansas, 1991).

Catalano, J.: *A Commentary on Sartre's "Being and Nothingness"* (New York: Harper & Row, 1974).

——: *A Commentary on Sartre's Critique of Dialectical Reason*, vol. I (Chicago, IL: University of Chicago Press, 1986).

——: *Good Faith and Other Essays* (Lanham, MD: Rowman & Littlefield, 1996).

Cumming, R.: *Phenomenology and Deconstruction*, 3 vols; vol. 2: *Method and Imagination* (Chicago, IL: University of Chicago Press, 1992).

Detmer, D.: *Freedom as Value: A Critique of the Ethical Theory of Jean-Paul Sartre* (La Salle, IL: Open Court, 1988).

Desan, W.: *The Marxism of Jean-Paul Sartre* (New York: Doubleday, 1965).

Fell, J.: *Emotion in the Thought of Sartre* (New York: Columbia University Press, 1965).

Flynn, T. R.: *Sartre and Marxist Existentialism: The Test Case of Collective Responsibility* (Chicago, IL: University of Chicago Press, 1984).

——: *Sartre, Foucault and Historical Reason*, vol. 1: *Toward an Existentialist Theory of History* (Chicago, IL: University of Chicago Press, 1997).

Goldthorpe, R.: *Sartre: Literature and Theory* (Cambridge: Cambridge University Press, 1984).

Hollier, D.: *Politique de la prose: Jean-Paul Sartre et l'an quarante* (Paris: Gallimard, 1982); tr. Jeffrey Mehlman, *The Politics of Prose: Essay on Sartre* (Minneapolis, MN: University of Minnesota Press, 1986).

Howells, C.: *Sartre: The Necessity of Freedom* (Cambridge: Cambridge University Press, 1988).

——(ed.): *The Cambridge Companion to Sartre* (Cambridge: Cambridge University Press, 1992).

Jameson, F.: *Sartre: The Origin of a Style* (New Haven, CT: Yale University Press, 1961).

Lévy, B.: *Le Nom de L'homme: dialogue avec Sartre* (Lagrasse: Verdier, 1984).

McBride, W.: *Sartre's Political Theory* (Bloomington, IN: Indiana University Press, 1991).

Santoni, R.: *Good faith, Bad faith, and Authenticity in Sartre's Early Philosophy* (Philadelphia, PA: Temple University Press, 1995).

Schilpp, P.: *The Philosophy of Jean-Paul Sartre*, The Library of Living Philosophers (LaSalle, IL.: Open Court, 1981).

Silverman, H. and F. Elliston (eds): *Jean-Paul Sartre: Contemporary Approaches to his Philosophy* (Pittsburgh: Duquesne University Press, 1980).

Verstraeten, P. (ed.): *Sur les écrits posthumes de Sartre*. Annales de l'Institut de Philosophie et des Sciences morales (Brussels: Éditions de l'Université de Bruxelles, 1987); English version of one essay, R. V. Stone and E. A. Bowman, "Dialectical ethics: a first look at Sartre's unpublished 1964 Rome lecture notes," *Social Text*, 13/14 (Winter/Spring 1986), pp. 195–215.

# 22

# de Beauvoir

KATE AND EDWARD FULLBROOK

## Introduction

Long recognized as the twentieth century's foremost feminist thinker, Simone de Beauvoir's place in philosophy which takes as its ground the universal human subject is now a major area of debate. What is at issue currently is how much of the philosophical system previously credited to Beauvoir's lifelong partner JEAN-PAUL SARTRE (see Article 21) was really her invention. Some of the controversy's basic facts have been long known, but the cultural bias against regarding women as possible sources of major mainstream philosophical ideas has greatly impeded realization of the import of those facts.

This essay on Simone de Beauvoir divides into four parts: a biographical sketch, a summary of the aforementioned controversy, an exposition of those philosophical theories for which overwhelming evidence exists that Beauvoir was the primary originator, and, finally, an account of how Beauvoir applied those theories in *The Second Sex* to an explanation of the cultural and social position of women.

## Life

Simone Lucie Ernestine Marie Bertrand de Beauvoir – philosopher, novelist, essayist, biographer, autobiographer, playwright, journalist, editor, and pre-eminent feminist theorist – was born in Paris on January 9, 1908. She was the elder of two rebellious daughters of the lawyer Georges Bertrand de Beauvoir, and his wife, Françoise (née Brasseur). The split between her father's religious skepticism and her mother's conventional piety was cited by Beauvoir as one of the main impetuses behind her rejection of her parents' values in adolescence and her early determination to forge for herself a life in opposition to the eroded *haut bourgeois* standards of her family. Although Beauvoir was to prove herself a student of remarkable brilliance, she regarded her initial education as inferior. In her early years, Beauvoir was sent to a Catholic girls' school, the Institut Adeline-Désir, which provided little more than a good deal of religious instruction coupled with an introduction to the limited educational accomplishments deemed suitable for a girl of her social class. Subsequently, and despite her parents' reservations, Beauvoir began training for a career as a philosophy teacher in 1925. She attended the Institut Sainte-Marie at Neuilly and the Institut Catholique in Paris, and later studied philosophy at the Sorbonne and École Normale Supérieure. Among her fellow students were Simone

Weil, Maurice MERLEAU-PONTY (see Article 23 – who was to be a valued close associate for many years), future Catholic philosopher Maurice de Gandillac, and the structuralist anthropologist Claude LÉVI-STRAUSS (see Article 46).

As a student, Beauvoir read Plato, SCHOPENHAUER (Article 10), BERGSON (Article 13), and Hamlin with care, worked closely on Kant and Hume, developed a youthful enthusiasm for NIETZSCHE (Article 11), and was deeply influenced by the Cartesian rationalism associated with the teaching of Alain. In 1928 she began her studies for the *agrégation* in philosophy while simultaneously preparing for her teaching diploma. On the advice of her supervisor at the Sorbonne, the Kantian scholar and feminist supporter Professor Léon Brunschvig, one of the most important figures in French philosophy at the time, Beauvoir prepared a dissertation on Leibniz as part of the requirements for the diploma. In 1929 Beauvoir was invited by her first lover, René Maheu, to join him and his friends Paul Nizan and Jean-Paul Sartre (all students at the elite and exclusively male ENS), in preparing for the *agrégation*. The relationship between Beauvoir and Sartre, one of the paradigmatic intellectual associations of the century, lasted until Sartre's death in 1980. Although Sartre had failed the *agrégation* in the previous year, this time he came first and Beauvoir second (though evidence suggests that the panel may have been swayed by sexist principles in the rankings). Whatever the case, Beauvoir was the youngest of all philosophy *agrégées*, and the ninth woman to pass the examination.

Beauvoir's career as a secondary teacher, which took her to Marseilles and Rouen until her final transfer to Paris in 1936, ended in 1943, after which she supported herself with her writing until her death in 1986. With Sartre, and their associates Albert Camus and Merleau-Ponty, Beauvoir was at the centre of the postwar existentialist movement in France. Internationally known, she was the most famous woman intellectual of her generation and an influential voice for non-aligned leftist principles during the period of decolonization and the Cold War. Her work as a founding-editor for the journal *Les Temps modernes* provided her with a platform for continuing commentary on contemporary social and political as well as philosophical issues.

Beauvoir's novels, essays, sociological and cultural studies, biographical and autobiographical works are all deeply inflected with the philosophical principles which she worked out, some before and some after a careful reading of Husserl in 1934. Her first published novel, *She Came to Stay* (1943), is structured around debates regarding freedom, the self, and the Other – the configuration of philosophical issues which was to remain peculiarly hers. The success of Beauvoir's fiction (especially that of *The Mandarins*, which won the *Prix Goncourt* for 1954) was matched by that of her four volumes of autobiography (*Memoirs of a Dutiful Daughter* (1958), *The Prime of Life* (1960), *Force of Circumstance* (1963), and *All Said and Done* (1972)), which provide an invaluable cultural history of France grounded in the key Beauvoirian interests of freedom and intersubjectivity in all its forms. Further books on the deaths of her mother (*A Very Easy Death* (1964)) and of Sartre (*Adieux* (1981)) extend Beauvoir's life-long commentary on the intersection of the self and the Other in highly personal terms. Beauvoir's most influential work is her foundational feminist exploration of the situation of women, *The Second Sex* (1949), which is one of the most significant publications of the century. This account of the cultural situation of women grew directly out of Beauvoir's work on ethics in the 1940s (see *The Ethics of Ambiguity* (1947)), as well as out of her continuing development of her interest in intersubjectivity; her intense awareness of the impact of history on individual lives, fostered by World War II; and her appraisal of her own situation as a woman.

Beauvoir's later years saw an increase in active political commitments. With Sartre, she campaigned against the war in Algeria in the late 1950s and early 1960s; worked for rapprochement between communist and non-communist countries; supported the students in the demonstrations of May 1968. She also actively supported feminist campaigns, particularly the effort to legalize contraception and abortion in France in the 1970s and 1980s. Her later fiction, *Les Belles Images* (1966) and *The Woman Destroyed* (1968), attends closely to the condition of women's consciousnesses in late twentieth-century culture.

## The controversy

It was the English translator of Sartre's *Being and Nothingness*, Hazel Barnes, who first unwittingly undermined Sartre's claim to the philosophical system contained in that work. Barnes's *The Literature of Possibility* (1959), a comparative study of the works of Beauvoir, Sartre, and Albert Camus, treated Beauvoir's novel *She Came to Stay* as a philosophical text. By doing so, Barnes was merely applying to the woman writer a practice that was already a standard method of analysis for Sartre's fiction. Mary Warnock has explained the logic behind this method.

> This insistence on the particularity and concreteness of descriptions, from which ontological and metaphysical and general statements may be drawn, is what most clearly characterizes existentialist writing – and what, incidentally, makes it perfectly plausible for Sartre to use novels and plays as well as straight philosophical expositions to convey philosophical doctrines.   (Warnock 1965, pp. 72–3)

Beauvoir's *She Came to Stay* was published in 1943, the same year as Sartre's *Being and Nothingness*. Barnes's reading of Beauvoir's novel demonstrated that it contained a full statement of the theories of bad faith and of intersubjectivity (Being-for-Others) found in Sartre's treatise. The latter point is, with hindsight, particularly significant. Over a third of Sartre's text (pp. 219–430) is taken up by his statement of the theory of intersubjectivity, which, writes Warnock, "is by far the richest and the most extraordinary part of the whole book" (Warnock 1965, p. 63).

Barnes commented as follows on the resemblances between Beauvoir's and Sartre's philosophical expositions:

> For our study of bad faith in human relations we are fortunate in having both Sartre's formal analysis in *Being and Nothingness* and de Beauvoir's *She Came to Stay* (L'Invitée), a novel which follows so closely the pattern outlined by Sartre that it serves almost as a textbook illustration.   (Barnes 1959, p. 113)

271

And

> This emotional labyrinth [the theory of intersubjectivity found in *Being and Nothing-ness*] is all faithfully illustrated for us in Simone de Beauvoir's novel, *She Came to Stay*. Although this book and *Being and Nothingness* were published in the same year (1943), the similarity between them is too striking to be coincidence. As with all of de Beauvoir's early fiction, the reader of *She Came to Stay* feels that the inspiration of the book was simply de Beauvoir's decision to show how Sartre's abstract principles could be made to work out in "real life."   (Barnes 1959, pp. 121–2)

In fact, however, Barnes had no evidence that "Sartre's abstract principles" really were his invention rather than Beauvoir's. Nor did she really know that it was *She Came to Stay* "which follows so closely the pattern outlined by Sartre" in *Being and Nothingness*, and not the other way around. Instead, Barnes, like Sartre commentators before and since, shared in the cultural assumption that it is men, not women, who are the source of important philosophical ideas.

But in 1960 Beauvoir provided information to the contrary. In the second volume of her memoirs, *The Prime of Life*, she tells how in 1931, still only 23 and living at the opposite end of France from Sartre, she took up the problem of the existence of the Other (Beauvoir 1965, pp. 101–5). She also explains how she persisted with her "investigations" through to the writing of *She Came to Stay*, which, in October 1938, she carefully planned around the "discoveries" that had resulted from her seven years of research (Beauvoir 1965, pp. 337–45, 360). Beauvoir says she finished revising *She Came to Stay* in early summer 1941, "but the novel had belonged to past history as far as I was concerned ever since January of that year" (Beauvoir 1965, pp. 369, 540).

These dates are highly significant. In *The Prime of Life* Beauvoir relates how it was only following her discussions with Sartre during his army leave in February 1940 that he began making notes for *Being and Nothingness* (Beauvoir 1965, pp. 428–9, 433–4). In May of that year he was taken prisoner by the Germans and held until March 1941. But upon resumption of his life in Paris he still, says Beauvoir, had not begun to write his "philosophical opus" (Beauvoir 1965, pp. 484, 497). The earliest date she gives for Sartre working on his "philosophical treatise" is autumn 1941 (Beauvoir 1965, p. 501).

Writing again about *She Came to Stay*, Barnes notes:

> in this novel de Beauvoir has so carefully and so skillfully developed the human complexities that it is only after finishing the book that one notes with amusement its step by step correspondence with Sartre's description of the subject–object conflict.   (Barnes 1959, p. 385)

But if Beauvoir's account of the genesis of the two works is true – and Sartre never disputed it – our "amusement" with their "step by step correspondence" should be directed towards Sartre's work, not Beauvoir's.

For a long time, however, Beauvoir's potentially seditious account of the origins of these major philosophical works and Sartre's acquiescence to it were ignored.

This was encouraged by Beauvoir, who refused for herself the appellation "philosopher." However, in interview in 1979, Beauvoir explained that she used the terms "philosophy" and "philosopher" in a highly idiosyncratic way, with the latter term only applicable in her view to authors of formal treatises that set out "grand" philosophical systems. She also stated categorically that Sartre had no influence on her writing of *She Came to Stay*, or any of her other novels, and that, in particular, her treatment and solution therein of the problem of the Other's consciousness was exclusively hers. "It was I who thought about that!" said Beauvoir. "It was absolutely not Sartre!" (Simons and Benjamin 1979, pp. 338–9).

In 1986, Margaret A. Simons, now writing to an audience that included readers who did not *a priori* rule out women as possible sources of important philosophical ideas, staked out claims on behalf of Beauvoir for philosophical contributions previously credited to Sartre. Most notably, Simons pointed out that the postwar extension of the theory of the Other into the social realm, where it proved a powerful and soon much-used tool for analysis of oppression, had been deployed in *The Second Sex* before appearing in any work by Sartre.

But it was the publication of the letters and diaries of Beauvoir and Sartre following their deaths in the 1980s that brought the controversy about their relative philosophical contributions to a boil (Beauvoir 1990, 1991; Sartre 1984, 1992, 1993) These documents show beyond all doubt that Beauvoir did indeed write *She Came to Stay* before Sartre wrote *Being and Nothingness*. They also chart Sartre's introduction to and absorption of many of Beauvoir's philosophical ideas for his own use. In a letter to Beauvoir in January 1940 he wrote of his frustration and inability to come up with philosophical ideas of his own (Sartre 1993, p. 19). Beauvoir's diaries show that on his leave the following month, Sartre spent eight sessions reading her manuscript of *She Came to Stay*. (Merleau-Ponty also read her manuscript in December 1940 [Beauvoir 1991, pp. 356, 364].) Sartre's diary entries for the days following his return to his army camp include an outpouring of philosophical ideas from *She Came to Stay*, which became major components of *Being and Nothingness* (Fullbrook and Fullbrook 1993, 1994). To date, Sartre scholars have failed to offer any evidence that the disputed ideas and theories originated with the man rather than the woman.

## Theories of self and intersubjectivity

In the early 1930s, Beauvoir and Sartre became interested in cataloguing common forms of self-deception and "playing a part" (Beauvoir 1965, p. 128). Their early works abound with illustrations of these two categories of human behavior, which together have been widely discussed under Sartre's term "bad faith" (*mauvaise foi*). What is significant, however, is not the pair's depictions of these specific patterns of conduct, nor Sartre's catchy name for them, but rather the theory that their works offered as to how such human behavior is possible. That theory is based on the then novel hypothesis that the conscious human personality is non-self-identical, or what Beauvoir called the "split between two halves of the self" (Beauvoir 1965, p. 223).

Beauvoir describes the theory's genesis as taking place in two phases: her personal conquest of bad faith during her year alone in Marseille (1931–2) and, a year later, the reading of Dos Passos's novel *The 42nd Parallel* (Beauvoir 1965, pp. 223–5, 136–7). The American novelist, says Beauvoir, "had worked out a bifocal perspective for the presentation of his main characters, which meant that they could be, at one and the same time, drawn as detailed individuals *and* as purely social phenomena," that is, both as to freedom and as to situation (Beauvoir 1965, p. 137). Beauvoir transformed Dos Passos's narrative technique into a theory regarding the nature of human reality, namely, that it rests on a twofold division between freedom (transcendence) and situation (facticity). In a series of short stories (especially "Chantal" and "Marguerite") written between 1935 and 1937 (Beauvoir 1983 [1979]), she explored the implications of this divided self from the point of view of consciousness, clarified the notions of situation and freedom, and documented experiences of non-self-identity. Because the Beauvoirean self is posited only as an *object* of consciousness, rather than its subject as in the Cartesian legacy, these works, together with Sartre's article "The Transcendence of The Ego" (1936–7), were an important break with philosophical tradition. Beauvoir's stories describe individuals divided not between mind and body, but between facticity (aspects which resemble inert objects, for example, the past, social circumstance, and body-as-object) and elements of freedom, such as projects, values, and the body-as-subject. In Beauvoir's fiction, bad faith arises when individuals fail to coordinate these two dimensions of their reality, that is, when they pretend that they are facticity without freedom or freedom without facticity. This split in human being makes self-identity an illusive goal: our freedom keeps our sense of self, including even how we see our past, from ever being complete and final. One is always separated from one's "self" by one's freedom to do, imagine, or believe differently. As with all objects of consciousness (for example, in "Chantal" Beauvoir uses the image of a person in a gallery of mirrors), the number of possible points of view one may adopt toward one's "self" is unlimited.

Beauvoir's theory of Others or intersubjectivity carried still further her dismantling of the Cartesian subject. Her multi-layered theory, developed over nearly two decades, grew initially out of her efforts to solve the problem of other minds. We can observe "other people from without, through the shape of words, gestures and faces," but we cannot observe that they have thoughts and sensations like ourselves (Beauvoir 1984 [1943], p. 135). Philosophy's traditional argument for the existence of other minds was the argument from analogy founded on individual experience, but as this was a generalization based on a single instance, it never inspired confidence, nor, more significantly, an ontological foundation from which to erect a theory of intersubjectivity. HEGEL (see Article 6), at the beginning of the nineteenth century, had briefly introduced the Other into philosophy, but without resolving the ontological problem which this concept entailed. A century later, HEIDEGGER (see Article 18), although concerned with the idea of a collective Other, did not provide a *direct relation between concrete individual consciousnesses*. Beauvoir overcame this centuries-old impasse by employing a methodological device used to famous advantage by Descartes. His *cogito*, "I think, therefore I am," offers no proof that I exist, but identifies a fundamental experience which leads me to believe that I exist. Similarly, Beauvoir ignored the problem of proving the existence of other minds, in favor of asking; What universal experience leads us all to believe other people to be conscious beings like ourselves?

For Beauvoir, the basis of our belief in the subjectivity of the Other, i.e., the self who is not myself, is not an argument from analogy, but the phenomenological event of experiencing myself as the object of another's look. To be conscious of being looked at or judged by another person can actually *cause* a metamorphosis in my consciousness: I am made aware that I have another self, an objective one which exists only for the Other. My self-for-the-Other is revealed to me as an awareness that the Other has an image of me, as an object in a world whose center of reference is no longer my consciousness. This experience of being an object entails the Other-as-subject: only another consciousness could cause this decentering of my sense of self.

Beauvoir's novel *She Came to Stay* is structured in part around six categories of Being-for-Others (masochism, love, sadism, hate, desire, and indifference) and provides numerous illustrations and extensive analysis of each. For Beauvoir, the philosophical significance of these common experiences is that they all presume a direct *internal* relation *between* consciousnesses. For example, the flush of embarrassment one undergoes when caught in an unseemly act is not founded on an analogy which probabilistically induces the existence of other consciousnesses, rather it manifests itself instantaneously as the consequence of a *causal relation internal to my consciousness and the Other's*. My embarrassment arises from a sudden transformation in the mode of my consciousness, from one where I experienced myself wholly as subject, that is, as the point of view around which the world is organized, to a mode where I am an object in a world organized by the Other.

This asymmetrical *subject/object relation* provides the ontological basis of Beauvoir's theory of intersubjectivity. It is the innate reversibility of the property of asymmetry – I may cause you to experience yourself as my object, but you may subsequently do the same to me – which, with the greatest possible economy, furnishes the theory with its integral dynamism.

Emergence of my self-for-the-Other adds a second dimension to the previously noted division of self. In an interpersonal encounter there is my self as the subject, with its own division between freedom and facticity, and there is my experience of my self as the Other's object. And there are also the selves I remember or dream of being for other people. Because, under Beauvoir's theory, no self is ever more than an object of consciousness, none of these possible selves is ontologically privileged. This places us in an existential realm far removed from the self-identity of the Cartesian subject.

Further complications follow. In *She Came to Stay* Beauvoir explores how the two dimensions of the division of self, freedom/facticity and subject/object *vis-à-vis* the Other, can interact in diverse ways. Assumption of the role of object in relations with the Other is one way of denying (and being denied) one's freedom. Analysis of this mode of bad faith proved particularly important for Beauvoir's later work in feminist theory. Against relations founded on bad faith, she argued for the possibility of reciprocity between subjects, such that they recognize and encourage each other as sources of meaning.

Part of the modern Continental tradition is that philosophy should consort with social science, as it did with natural science in the formative age of Leibniz and Descartes. No twentieth-century thinker's work displays more conspicuously the benefits of this cross-fertilization than Beauvoir's. On the basis of the subject/object relation she built a theory of social interaction which, besides underwriting her *Ethics of Ambiguity* (1946–7) and her analysis of woman's oppression, has the widest possible implications for the social sciences.

Beauvoir's extension of the subject/object relation from pairs of individuals to groups began in *She Came to Stay*, which takes the trio as one of its central structures. The group dimension begins to appear when a third person C, is brought into the framework of the relation. A and B may form a subject-group which causes C to experience herself as its object. Or, conversely, C may cause A and B to experience themselves as members of an object-group. When four or more people are involved, groups may comprise both terms of the intersubjective relation, and, crucially, with the reversible asymmetry property preserved. In this way a whole morphology of groups with a built-in dynamic may be created on the basis of the one binary relation.

Beauvoir's socially extended theory of intersubjectivity (the theory of the Social Other), whose development was much influenced by her association in the 1940s with the African-American novelist Richard Wright, as well as by her reading of the Swedish social scientists Alva and Gunnar Myrdal, has immense import for what has long been the central and preponderant methodological issue in the social sciences: the divide between holist and individualist methodologies. Both traditional approaches are based on opposing doctrines of uni-directional causality: the former explains the behavior of individuals as a function of some "whole" to which they belong, such as, language, economy, society, or history; whereas the latter treats individuals as autonomous agents whose independent acts determine language, society, etc. These methodological extremes arise out of their shared absence of a method for analyzing direct interaction between subjectivities, an absence that is a direct correlative of philosophy's failure, prior to Beauvoir, to identify an internal relation between subjectivities. Beauvoir's subject/object relation with its reversible asymmetry introduces to social science both a method of intersubjective analysis and an indeterminate bi-directional causality. It is the latter characteristic that makes Beauvoir's methodology inherently subversive of social hierarchies, as it points to the means by which any culturally oppressed group may bring about their own liberation, namely by reclaiming their subjectivity *vis-à-vis* their oppressors.

Space does not permit discussion of Beauvoir's ethics, except to note that her *Ethics of Ambiguity* was first published in *Les Temps modernes* in the November, December, January, and February issues of 1946–7, and originally drafted in the late winter and early spring of 1946 when Sartre was absent in America. Sartre, on the other hand, did not begin writing his *Notebooks for an Ethics* (1983), which repeats and elaborates some Beauvoirean ideas and themes, until 1947.

In concluding this section, it is salutary to note that more than her studies of Husserl and Hegel and her readings of her fellow existentialists, Beauvoir's theories of self and intersubjectivity show the influence of her original grounding as a Leibniz scholar. The seventeenth-century philosopher conceived of the universe as composed of "monads," the ultimate units of being. Each monad is a realized set of perceptions defined by its particular point of view. Perception is continuous, and therefore a monad is not self-identical over time. Monads interconnect with each other by a relation analogous to mirroring and which today we regard as causal. This relation between two monads is asymmetric, one monad entering the relation in a relatively active mode, the other in a relatively passive one. The state of a monad arises not from its nature alone, but rather from its interrelation with other monads. When in these Leibnizian propositions "human being" is substituted for "monad," the broad ontological outline of the distinctive Beauvoirean universe emerges.

## The Second Sex

As in *She Came to Stay* the analytic union of the two ontological polarities, freedom/situation (or transcendence/facticity) and subject/object, provides the philosophical foundation for Beauvoir's great pioneering study of the condition of women, *The Second Sex* (1949). Published first in *Les Temps modernes* in 1948 and 1949, and appearing in book form in two volumes (vol. 1: *Facts and Myths*; vol. 2: *Women's Lives Today*), Beauvoir worked on the project from October 1946 until June 1949. Written immediately after *The Ethics of Ambiguity*, and concurrently with *America Day by Day* (1948), *The Second Sex* draws not only on the philosophical principles which Beauvoir had formulated in preparation for writing *She Came to Stay*, but on her careful working out of the moral and social implications of these principles and her intense awareness of race, gender, and class in her experience of America. Overshadowed in recent years in France by the dominance of neo-Heideggerian thought, Beauvoir's classic work has been of continuing use and interest to feminists working in the Anglo-American tradition. A hugely popular best-seller since its publication, translated into 18 languages, *The Second Sex* has never been out of print. For Beauvoir, it was "the book that has brought me the greatest satisfaction of all those I have written" (Bair 1990, p. 655). At the time of its appearance, *The Second Sex* – and Beauvoir – were reviled; after more than a generation it is clear that the book is one of that select handful which have directly changed lives and affected the course of history.

In recent years, *The Second Sex* has been attacked for its "masculine" thought, its dated existentialist jargon, its focus on the experience of privileged women of Beauvoir's era, nation, and class, and, most of all, for being subserviently constructed according to a Sartrean template. This critique, which has become ritualized in some feminist circles influenced by the psychoanalytically oriented work of Luce IRIGARAY (see Article 54) and Hélène Cixous, is contested by Michèle LE DOEUFF (see Article 56) in her study of women and philosophy, *Hipparchia's Choice* (1989). Le Doeuff outlines the crucial differences between Beauvoir's and Sartre's philosophical positions at the time of the composition of *The Second Sex*. Once again, Le Doeuff stresses the difficulties attendant on judging Beauvoir's work as a philosopher when she ("a tremendously well-hidden philosopher") is invariable read as the disciple of Sartre, "the century's most visible philosopher" (Le Doeuff 1991, p. 139).

In her analysis, Le Doeuff stresses Beauvoir's "perspectival" philosophical method, that is, one in which the "task is to explore a section of social and intersubjective reality, not to build a system' (Le Doeuff 1991, p. 89), a choice of method which radically challenges the traditional philosophical assumption of the philosopher's removal from personal engagement with the matter under scrutiny. The radical break with this tradition which *The Second Sex* enacts, by assuming the position of the *situated* philosopher, is of extraordinary interest. Further, Beauvoir's insistent attention to the material condition of women, to the facticity of the place they occupy, to the search for the means for change, when allied to the ethical principles of reciprocity, which grows directly from her philosophy of intersubjectivity, gives *The Second Sex* a startlingly original philosophical cast which is only just being recognized.

There are two major points which organize the mass of information on women's biology, psychology, history, myths, and culture which comprises *The Second Sex*. The first is succinctly stated in the much-quoted opening line of the second volume of the text: "One is not born, but rather becomes, a woman" (Beauvoir 1972, p. 296) ('On ne naît pas femme, on le devient"), which rejects absolutely the idea of woman as an essential natural category and treats gender as a matter of cultural, and thus changeable, production. Secondly, by casting her treatment of women in terms of the issues regarding the self and the other which so heavily informs her previous writing in *She Came to Stay* and *The Ethics of Ambiguity*, Beauvoir points the way out of the impasse which defines woman as the eternal Other to men, and suggests the ways in which intersubjectivity both for men and for women is a matter of shifting consciousness and reversible polarities. As in *She Came to Stay*, Beauvoir's solution to the problem of the Other revises Hegel's master/slave dichotomy and places women (in this case) in a new phenomenological position, one which allows for their reversal of the condition of oppression by assuming their subjectivity. However, *The Second Sex* also takes due account of the facticity of women's position as well as correcting theoretical accounts of their ontological status. Indeed, the two are inextricably intertwined. Beauvoir's stress on the need for women's financial independence, control of their fertility, equal education, etc. partakes of a notion of subjectivity which sees freedom as always situated, with the experience of the body and of consciousness as indivisible contributions to the definition of the self.

Beauvoir's early work was rejected by Sartre's publishers explicitly on the grounds that its intellectual content – what women thought, felt and wanted – was too subversive. This blanket of censorship under which Beauvoir and many others of her gender were forced to begin their intellectual careers should not be erased from historical memory, nor left out of the reckoning of who contributed what to humankind's stock of philosophical ideas.

## Writings

Beauvoir, Simone de: *She Came to Stay* (1943), tr. Yvonne Moyse and Roger Senhouse (London: Flamingo, 1984).

——: *The Ethics of Ambiguity* (1947), tr. Bernard Frechtman (New York: Citadel Press, 1970).

——: *The Second Sex* (1949), tr. H. M. Parshley (Harmondsworth, Middx: Penguin, 1972).

——: *Memoirs of a Dutiful Daughter* (1958), tr. James Kirkup (Harmondsworth, Middx: Penguin, 1963).

——: *The Prime of Life* (1960), tr. Peter Green (Harmondsworth, Middx: Penguin, 1965).

——: *Letters à Sartre*, ed. Sylvie Le Bon de Beauvoir, 2 vols (Paris: Gallimard, 1990).

——(1979): *When Things of the Spirit Come First: Five Early Tales*; tr. Patrick O'Brian (London: Flamingo, 1983).

——: *Letters to Sartre*, tr. Quintin Hoare (London: Radius, 1991).

## References and further reading

Bair, Deirdre: *Simone de Beauvoir: A Biography* (London: Jonathan Cape, 1990).

Barnes, Hazel: *The Literature of Possibility: A Study in Humanistic Existentialism* (London: Tavistock, 1959).

Bergoffen, Debra: *Gendered Phenomenologies, Erotic Generosities: The Philosophy of Simone de Beauvoir* (New York: SUNY Press, 1996).

Fallaize, Elizabeth: *The Novels of Simone de Beauvoir* (London: Routledge, 1988).

Francis, Claude and Gontier, Fernande (1985): *Simone de Beauvoir*, tr. Lisa Nesselson (London: Mandarin, 1989).

Fullbrook, Kate and Fullbrook, Edward: *Simone de Beauvoir and Jean-Paul Sartre: The Remaking of a Twentieth-Century Legend* (Hemel Hempstead: Harvester Wheatsheaf, 1993; New York: Basic Books, 1994).

Fullbrook, Edward and Fullbrook, Kate: *Beauvoir: A Critical Introduction* (Cambridge: Polity Press, forthcoming 1997).

Lundgren-Gothlin, Eva: *Sex and Existence: Simone de Beauvoir's "The Second Sex"* (London: Athlone, 1996).

Le Doeuff, Michèle (1989): *Hipparchia's Choice: An Essay Concerning Women, Philosophy, etc.*, tr. Trista Selous (Oxford: Blackwell, 1991).

Moi, Toril: *Simone de Beauvoir: The Marking of an Intellectual Woman* (Oxford: Blackwell, 1994).

Sartre, Jean-Paul (1943): *Being and Nothingness: An Essay on Phenomenological Ontology*, tr. Hazel Barnes (New York: Philosophical Library, 1956).

——(1983): *War Diaries: Notebooks from a Phoney War, November 1939–March 1940*, tr. Quintin Hoare (London: Verso, 1984).

——(1983): *Witness to my Life: The Letters of Jean-Paul Sartre to Simone de Beauvoir, 1926–1939*, ed. Simone de Beauvoir, tr. Lee Fahnestock and Norman MacAfee (New York: Charles Scribner's Sons, 1992).

——(1983): *Notebooks for an Ethics*, tr. David Pellauer (Chicago, IL: University of Chicago Press, 1992).

——(1983): *Quiet Moments in a War: The Letters of Jean-Paul Sartre to Simone de Beauvoir, 1940–1963*, ed. Simone de Beauvoir, tr. Lee Fahnestock and Norman MacAfee (New York: Charles Scribner's Sons, 1993).

Simons, Margaret A.: "Beauvoir and Sartre: The philosophical relationship," *Yale French Studies*, 72 (1986), pp. 165–79.

——(ed.): *New Feminist Essays on Simone de Beauvoir* (Philadelphia, PA: Pennsylvania University Press, 1995).

——and Benjamin, Jessica: "Simone de Beauvoir: an interview," tr. Véronique Zaytzeff, *Feminist Studies*, 5:2 (Summer 1979), pp. 330–45.

Warnock, Mary: *The Philosophy of Sartre* (London: Hutchinson, 1965).

# 23

# Merleau-Ponty

## BERNHARD WALDENFELS

To speak of Merleau-Ponty means to speak of phenomenology in France. If French phenomenology found its own idiom in the 1930s, one which dominated French thinking until the 1960s and even left its mark on the structuralist break with phenomenology, that is very largely due to the patient philosophical work of Merleau-Ponty. A philosophy which, as Merleau-Ponty himself points out, dwells in a world to which there are several modes of access, not all of them open to the philosopher, will find its place "where the transition from one's own self into the world and to the other occurs; at the place where the roads cross."

Merleau-Ponty, who was born in 1908 in Rochefort-sur-Mer, was a contemporary of Jean-Paul SARTRE (see Article 21) Simone de BEAUVOIR (Article 22), and J. Hyppolite, and studied with them at the École Normale Supérieure. Despite his brilliant philosophical début, at first all the political establishment would grant him was a chair in child psychology and pedagogics at the Sorbonne. He was then appointed to the Collège de France in 1952, and until his sudden death in 1961 he remained with that illustrious institution, where BERGSON (Article 13) and Lavelle taught before him, Hyppolite and FOUCAULT (Article 49) after him, and LÉVI-STRAUSS (Article 46) as his contemporary. Like Sartre, Merleau-Ponty grew up in an academic climate marked by critical rationalism in the style of L. Brunschvig. The methodical keyword was "reflection," that is to say the mind's incessant return to itself through the cultural works it produces. Bergson's thinking, which was orientated by the inventive faculty of life, was respected by the younger generation but did not represent an adequate alternative. In this transitional climate, the writings of Husserl and Heidegger had a liberating effect. The idea of "things themselves" seemed to promise greater riches than were contained in the categories of thinking, the constructions of the sciences and the traditional shapes of bourgeois culture and education. The special characteristic of French phenomenology, which emerged about three decades after German phenomenology, was that from the outset it established a link with the historical and social thinking of re-awakening Hegelianism and Marxism, and moreover that its temperature was dramatically raised by the existential climate of the prewar and postwar periods. The lectures on Hegel delivered by KOJÈVE (Article 19), which attracted much attention among later phenomenologists, represented a mixture in which phenomenological themes threatened to decline into mere accessories.

These features of the period certainly did not pass Merleau-Ponty by, leaving no trace, but he maintained a certain aloofness from them, an aloofness that is connected with his basic phenomenological orientation. He was not only the first to visit the Husserl Archive in Leuven as early as 1939, when it had just been founded, becoming acquainted with central writings such as Husserl's *Ideen II* and *Krisis* long before their publication; he also kept returning to the writings of Husserl and Heidegger until the end of his life. He increasingly took phenomenology to its limits, but did not exchange it for anything else. If we were to assign a guiding theme to Merleau-Ponty's widely branching oeuvre, it would have to be the "guide of the body" already recommended by Nietzsche, a guiding thread not only leading us through the labyrinth of life but implicating itself in that labyrinth. A characteristic of phenomenology as a whole is that objective themes and the mode of access to them cannot be separated. The mode of being of the *body*, which cannot be assigned unequivocally to nature or mind, nature or freedom, forces us to think in terms of *both/and also*; it requires a sense of ambiguities, transitions, and nuances which resists the blunt *either/or*. Keeping the decision open gives rise to a particular kind of resistance which favors the diversity of phenomenology. This casts light on Merleau-Ponty's preference for the tentative brushwork of Cézanne, the winding paths of Proust's *A la recherche du temps perdu*, and the splintering element in Valéry's writings as essayist. It also casts light on the way Merleau-Ponty merges *existentialism* into a "phénoménologie existentielle" without abandoning himself to the up and down swings of elation and despair, all or nothing; the way he demands a rethinking of *Marxism* to break the hold of inflexible historical laws; and finally, the way he turns his attention to *structuralism* without sacrificing the un-thought to a structural system as a result. In all these various arguments, Merleau-Ponty's phenomenology shows a power of transmutation which keeps it in constant movement.

Merleau-Ponty found the tone of his thinking very early. In a paper written in 1934 he is already speaking of a *third dimension*, a dimension this side of subject and object, activity and passivity, in which philosophical reflection and positive knowledge can meet (cf. *Titres et Travaux*, quoted from Geraets 1971, p. 37). The supremacy of philosophy over the sciences, or conversely the supremacy of the sciences over philosophy, is transformed in such an area of intersection into a *reciprocal relationship* open to mutual anticipations and stimuli. From this there proceeds an *implicit phenomenology* already at work in the sciences as well as in art, politics, and everyday life before it takes explicit shape. Feuerbach's demand for non-philosophy to be taken into the text of philosophy is thus validated.

This methodological perspective is tried out in the two doctoral theses *La Structure du comportement* (1942) and *Phénoménologie de la perception* (1945). In the first of these major works, Merleau-Ponty enlists the research of neurologists, behavioral scientists, and Gestalt theorists such as F. J. J. Buytendijk, W. Köhler, V. von Weizsäcker, and above all the studies in brain pathology of A. Gelb and K. Goldstein, to develop a theory of behavior which is as far from a mechanical theory of reflexes or learning as it is from a pure theory of consciousness. The third dimension which is being sought takes form in the basic concepts of *shape* and *structure*, which are neither things nor ideas but ways of organizing reality itself, matched by a corresponding self-organization on the part of the organism. Parallelism of inner and outer processes, inner and outer observation, is no less radically rejected than, for instance, in the work of G. Ryle. These studies toward a non-behaviorist theory of behavior, which have their parallels in the German anthropologist H. Plessner, are continued later in Charles Taylor's work *The Explanation of Behaviour* (1964) and my own investigations in *Der Spielraum des Verhaltens* (1980).

Merleau-Ponty's second early work, *Phénoménologie de la perception*, remains his *magnum opus*, despite certain provisional aspects of it. Like Heidegger's *Sein und Zeit* and Sartre's *L'être et le néant*, it is laid out on a broad scale and opens up many perspectives; like them again, it is one of the basic texts of phenomenology. Here the author moves more markedly away from the outer view of the scientist to the "inner view" of the phenomenologist; the latter does not shrink from passing through the sciences, but gives priority to referring back to experience as lived. The *perception* of the title does not denote one phenomenon among others but – as in Husserl before him – an exemplary and fundamental phenomenon: exemplary, because certain characteristics of perception, such as its open indeterminacy and its spontaneity, are also found elsewhere; fundamental because it establishes an original contact with reality, initiates into truth, thus forming a background against which all active endeavors and operations are seen. Perception is to be taken in the sense of Husserl's "*Urdoxa.*" Once again we are moving in the field of a third dimension, since perception cannot be reduced to either a vital substructure or a rational superstructure. Structures, shapes, sense, and sensory areas are born of a spontaneous process of organization with no previous model. It can thus be said of the shape occurring for the first time: "It is not a condition of the possibility of the world, but a phenomenon of the world itself, not the fulfilment but the creation of a norm" (Merleau-Ponty 1962 [1945], p. 74). In this, "original perception" differs from an empirical, secondary form of perception which recognizes only what is familiar. Original perception concentrates on a sense *in statu nascendi*, which, in its incompletion and inexhaustibility, is the focal point of phenomenology. Neither empirical recourse to completed facts nor rationalist recourse to completed categories is adequate to do justice to the "genealogy of being" (Merleau-Ponty 1962, p. 67).

Corresponding to the open nature of perception is the *bodily existence* that anchors us to the world and, in the various aspects of space, movement, sensual receptivity, linguistic and non-linguistic expression, and sexuality opens up a way of access to ourselves, to the world, and to others. This results in a constant revision of familiar concepts. The bodily self appears as a "pre-self" or "natural self" preceding itself in birth, bringing with it a "primitive past, a past that was never present" (Merleau-Ponty 1962, p. 280), submerged in an anonymity that will never become fully individual and personalized. In expression, and particularly in language, nature changes to culture and vice versa. As corporeal beings, humans are engaged in a constant *dialogue with the world*, beginning with the communication of the senses, where the sentient and that which is sensed get in contact, even before a subject confronts an object. The dialogue with things is finally intensified in the *dialogue with others*. The anonymity of the body represents itself as "intercorporality" (*intercorporéité*), in relation to an "interworld" (*intermonde*) in which our own experiences are interwoven with those of others, our own expressions with those of others, even before the self confronts the other as a strange subject. Sociality permeates us like an atmosphere in which we live. These interchanging relationships do not rule out an original *strangeness*, but that strangeness is part of one's own self, its reverse side.

The phenomenal field in which the body, the world, and others unite into a structure of relationships and events involving relationships finally shows itself *as such* in the form of a transcendental field where "being-to-the-world" appears as "being-for-itself." This "phenomenology of phenomenology," in which Merleau-Ponty takes up ideas from Husserl's *Cartesianische Meditationen* and from E. Fink, ends not in a self-consciousness transparent to oneself, but in a *cogito* which is founded on *silence* and is divided from itself by the *density of time*, and it concludes in a *field of freedom*. The freedom of the person acting depends on situations to which it responds, and fits into structures in which it is incorporated. There is no trace here, then, of Sartre's freedom as pure negation. The power of negativity is counter-balanced by a play of differences, delays, anticipations, and resumptions. We are not a "hole in being," as Sartre's interpretation of Hegel puts it, but a "hollow" (*creux*), a "fold" (*pli*) (Merleau-Ponty 1962, p. 249). There is an autochthonous sense of the natural and historical world, but not a completed sense detached from all non-sense. "We cannot say *everything has a sense* or *everything is non-sense*, but simply, *there is sense*" (Merleau-Ponty 1962, p. 342). "There is order," as Foucault later said. An embodied freedom, set in a certain situation, responding to what is offered in situations and fields of action, is incompatible with an idea of all or nothing.

This "philosophy of ambiguity," as A. de Waelhens has called it, is not raised above all doubt, as Merleau-Ponty himself admits. Like *Sein und Zeit*, *Phenomenology of Perception* can be read as a concretization of transcendental philosophy in which the authority of the transcendental consciousness is delegated to the body, and thus to a "pre-self" running after its own achievements. Questions regarding the event of sense foundation would thus be shifted to a pre-history without ever really being asked. We find similar tendencies in a system of hermeneutics relying on pre-given traditions. Merleau-Ponty himself, in his candidacy paper for the Collège de France, distinguishes between good and bad ambiguity (cf. Waldenfels 1983, pp. 174ff). A bad form of ambiguity would consist of a "blend of finality and universality, of the internal and the external." The *both/and also* would slacken to a compromise, shown by Foucault in chapter IX of *Les mots et les choses* to be a continual self-duplication of man. Merleau-Ponty later seeks a good form of ambiguity in the tension between sense as pre-given and sense creation, which he describes as a paradox or marvel of expression.

These questions continue in Merleau-Ponty's political thinking. In 1945 Merleau-Ponty and Sartre took over as editors of the recently founded *Temps Modernes*. Politically close to the French Communist Party, Merleau-Ponty was frequently active in current affairs as a journalist, as we can see in his collection of essays entitled *Sens et non-sens* (1948), and more particularly in the controversial essay on Communism which appeared in 1947 under the title *Humanisme et ter-*

*reur*. Trying to think in terms of politics as such, beyond the mere politics of the day, he looks for a theory of political action which, like the theory of perception, will open up a third way between the extreme of a moralism with humanistic trimmings, referring to pure principles, and a pragmatic realism talking its way out of objective constraints. To quote Arthur Koestler, it is a matter of avoiding the alternatives of the yogi or the commissar. Merleau-Ponty seeks the requisite middle way in the proletariat as a concrete "lived universality" (Merleau-Ponty 1969 [1947], pp. 124f), as "true co-existence to which language and a voice must be given" (p. 120). Of course he does not defend Communism as it actually was, as he has often been accused of doing; instead, he assesses it by its unfulfilled claims. In this sense he admits to a "*marxisme sans illusions tout expérimental*" (Merleau-Ponty 1964a [1948], p. 219). Later, Sartre rightly saw his position as that of a Marxist "*faute de mieux*," and it is true that at this time Merleau-Ponty's political insights lagged behind his insights as a phenomenologist.

A change comes with the publication of the essay *Les Aventures de la dialectique* in 1955, which led to the final break with Sartre. Later, Sartre described the course of this quarrel in his obituary of Merleau-Ponty (see *Situation IV*, Sartre 1961) with great lucidity and fairness. Merleau-Ponty now gives up his waiting game. He subjects the Marxist historical philosophy he pursues from the early Lukács to Stalin, and finally to Sartre's voluntaristic "ultra-Bolshevism," to a rigorous criticism which disposes of the illusions of a revolutionary world solution and world salvation. He also now finds in history a "third order" between subject and object, between humanity and things, and finds it in the shape of a *symbolical interworld* which transforms every action into indirect action. Certain kinds of progress are possible but not *the* progress which would lead once and for all from mere prehistory to a history of mankind. With the opening of dialectic, history recovers its plurality, ambiguity, and contingency. This political thinking, referring expressly to Max Weber and Raymond Aron, clearly left its marks on LEFORT (see Article 44) and CASTORIADIS (see Article 45), long before the "nouveaux philosophes" struck up their not particularly new song, and long before the wind of the Zeitgeist changed in France as well as elsewhere.

While this political rethinking was going on in public, a gradual but equally effective reorientation was in progress in the background of Merleau-Ponty's activities in teaching and research, something we can follow in the transcripts of his Sorbonne lectures (published in book form in 1988), in many essays in the volume of articles entitled *Signes* (1960), and in his inaugural speech at the Collège de France (*Éloge de la philosophie*, 1953) when he was on particularly brilliant form. Merleau-Ponty not only continues his earlier project by making wide use of the researches of the 1920s and 1930s in the human sciences and showing them to be convergent with his phenomenological questions, he also makes some entirely new points. He attacks the "monopoly" of established and traditional reason by recognizing, in particular in discussion of J. Piaget's ideas on development, the rights of the child as against the adult, the psychopath and the sick against the healthy, the so-called primitive against the civilized. Rationalization turns out, as previously in Husserl, and in K. Goldstein and G. Canguilhem, to be a process of normalization which by no means follows a straight line and which is constantly producing anomalies. Like history, child development obeys a "stumbling logic" which is groping to find its way. The form of differential phenomenology thus created is reinforced by reference back to those sciences too abruptly set up by Foucault (in *Les mots et les choses*) in opposition to the human sciences as "counter-sciences," i.e. *psychoanalysis, ethnology,* and *linguistics.* Freudian psychoanalysis, a companion to Merleau-Ponty's work from the first, now has new emphasis placed on it. The "polymorphism" of infantile sexuality, the body language of symptoms, and the family background of the Oedipus complex come to the fore, with express reference to Lacan's early works. The cultural variants of relationship structures inevitably lead to the field of ethnology and the vicinity of Lévi-Strauss, for whose acceptance by the Collège de France Merleau-Ponty successfully campaigned.

And finally, Merleau-Ponty was the first of the French philosophers to take up the structural linguistics of F. de Saussure and R. Jakobson. The name of Saussure first occurs in his 1948 collection of essays, *Sens et non-sens.* Merleau-Ponty here builds a bridge from the organization of experience in Gestalt theory, which starts up with the difference between figure and background, pre-Gestalt and post-Gestalt, to the organization of language which arises from the differentiation of a sign system. Here we can see how closely phenomenology and structuralism interlocked before the structuralist vogue opened up gulfs between the two ways of thinking. Merleau-Ponty increasingly transforms his existential phenomenology into a *structural phenomenology,* which, however, resists any hypostasing of structures and any tendency to make structural models absolute. As Merleau-Ponty emphasizes in his essay "De Mauss à Lévi-Strauss," all structural models go back to "practiced" structures, and it is indeed true that they "have" the subject, rather than that the subject "has" them (Merleau-Ponty 1964b [1960], p. 147). Not for nothing did Lévi-Strauss dedicate his work *La Pensée sauvage* to Merleau-Ponty (it appeared shortly after the latter's death), thus showing his deep respect for a way of thinking which – as he himself writes in his obituary of Merleau-Ponty – seeks its place at the "border where experience as lived exceeds knowledge."

The influences of structural thinking are also evident in Merleau-Ponty's ideas about language, which come increasingly to the fore in his later writings, particularly in the essays on such subjects in *Signes* and the posthumously published fragment *La Prose du monde.* The structural consideration of language leads beyond the early concept of a symbolic behavior and a bodily linguistic gesture. Our speech moves within certain structures in such a way that its sense always unfolds in a differential, allusive, and indirect manner. What we mean is removed from all direct access and every straightforward intuition; it appears only as a "*certain emptiness* which is to be filled with words" (Merleau-Ponty 1964b, p. 112). Merleau-Ponty's consideration of language derives its particular emphasis from this idea. The accent is on *functioning, living language,* on the *parole parlante,* which goes beyond the mere *parole parlée* of a conventional system of rules or signs. Phenomenological reduction here takes on a linguistic shape itself, in that it breaks not only with the prejudice of a completed world but also with that of a completed language. This leads to a dispute with *ordinary language philosophy,* which is evident in the critical questions Merleau-Ponty put to Ryle at the Congress on Analytical Philosophy in Royaumont (cf. the publication *Philosophie analytique* in the *Cahiers de Royaumont*, 1962), a dispute which was not settled in Merleau-Ponty's lifetime. Later, RICOEUR (Article 39) tried to bring phenomenology and linguistic analysis together, but his efforts remained unilateral.

When Merleau-Ponty stresses the limits of an existing language he does not refer to pre-linguistic facts or meanings beyond language, but rather insists that language itself refers back to what has already been said and forward to what is un-said. If language is everything, then it is only as a language coming into existence, which says more than any existing language. The tendency of language to exceed itself can be seen in *creative language*, which Merleau-Ponty sees operating chiefly in poetry and literature but also in the practical language of politics and the child's first stammering attempts to talk. Creation and innovation are seen, in the wake of Russian formalism but also echoing Valéry's poetics, as a coherent deformation (*déformation cohérente*) or a deviation (*déviation, écart*), so that every first word takes on features of a second word, and there can be no last word. In this connection, Merleau-Ponty speaks of a paradox or marvel of expression: "To talk and to write means to *translate* an experience, which, however, becomes text only through the word that it awakens" (Merleau-Ponty 1970 [1968], p. 41). This is as far from pure reproduction, rendering only the sense that already resides in things, as it is from pure production, which creates sense out of nothing, freely designs or constructs it, and thus forces it upon things. In contrast, creative speaking means that something is put *into language* while at the same time something else is condemned to *silence*.

Husserl says, in the *Cartesianische Meditationen* (*Husserliana I*, p. 77): "In the beginning there is the pure and as it were still mute experience, which is to be brought to the pure expression of its own sense," or in French: "C'est l'expérience muette encore qu'il s'agit d'amener à l'expression pure de son propre sens." This remark, frequently quoted and commented on by Merleau-Ponty, contains a paradox. If the experience were entirely mute, then one could only say something *about* it; it could not find its *own* sense. If the experience itself were already endowed with speech, and if it expressed itself as it were *of* itself, there would be nothing to say which had not basically already been said. Speech would become entangled in its own constructions, or sink into a murmur of being. Merleau-Ponty does not resolve the paradox as Husserl tried to do in similar cases; rather, he moves it to the interior of a *language as practiced*, which – never without violence – breaks the silence without abolishing it (Merleau-Ponty 1968 [1964], p. 230). In this transition from experience to language, a transition which must always be mastered anew and which in a way defines phenomenology itself, Merleau-Ponty once again finds a "good ambiguity" in which the weakness and strength of our language unite. Not only our relationship to things but our relationship to others and to history are nourished by the event of this expression, of which the speaker is never master because it has already begun in "pre-language." The result is a new kind of concept of truth, a truth to be made. This *vérité à faire* responds to the call of things, other people, and the world, proceeding from "restlessness in the world of what has already been said," to quote the foreword of *Signes*.

287

Language is not bound to words. The painter, too, speaks in his silent manner. The "riddle of visibility" is embodied in painting; the act of painting, which makes the invisible visible, itself enters visibility as a picture in which something becomes visible. Sensuousness is heightened to become the "reflectivity of the sensuous," so that the painter paints not only what he sees but also "what sees itself in him." In his essay *L'Oeil et l'esprit*, an essay on painting which was written in Le Tholonet in the shadow of Cézanne, and which appeared in the year of Merleau-Ponty's death, painting is raised to the status of a kind of pictorial ontology (cf. Waldenfels, in Métraux and Waldenfels 1986). Like poetry and literature, painting does not lead to another world of aesthetic appearance, but refers to the same world in which we all live, except that it is freed from the natural weight that makes our glance sink into the things. It would be not inappropriate to speak here of a kind of pictorial époché transferring us to a zero point of visibility equivalent to R. Barthes's "zero point of literature." Not by chance were the proponents of *minimal art* stimulated by Merleau-Ponty's phenomenology of perception, regarded as a linguistic art of making visible.

All these approaches to an indirect form of language operating on the borders of the visible and expressible, paradoxically expressing mute experience, culminate in the late ontology which Lefort published in 1964 under the title of *Le Visible et l'invisible*. Half of this fragmentary work consists of working notes made in the last three years of the author's life, which give a particularly vivid impression of the style of this thinking. Merleau-Ponty here tries to subject the results of the *phenomenology of perception* to an ontological interpretation, doing away with the old residue of a philosophy of consciousness. Husserl's genetic phenomenology and Heidegger's thought of Being are raised again, further reinforced by Saussure's theory of diacritical signs, Freud's and Lacan's deciphering of the unconscious, and Lévi-Strauss's structural concept of history and society. The interrogative thinking tested here does not aim to fill gaps in our knowledge but to make things themselves speak. This thinking does not move towards Being but proceeds from the questionability of Being, like a glance testing things out, stimulated and fascinated by the sight of them. Interrogative thinking resists all attempts to bring questioning to an end, whether in an ordinary belief, in a scientific survey, in the transparency of a reflecting subject, in a dialectic of being and non-being, in a pure intuition of essence, or in merging with the life stream.

In the course of the attempt to find an intermediate sphere which no longer functions as a preceding area of consciousness or an antechamber to the ego, the earlier phenomenology of perception and one's own body (*corps propre*) becomes an ontology of seeing (*vision*) and flesh (*chair*). Seeing is no longer a subjective act but an event which occurs between the seer, the visible, and the co-seer, enveloped in a sphere of visibility called "flesh." This flesh of the world, one's own body and the body of others, of time or language, must be thought of not in terms of substance, but functionally, as *texture, articulation, framework, joints*, as an *element* in which we live and move, as a field in which something appears as something and someone as someone, and in which meanings arise as certain deviations. Subject, object, ego, and individual are placed in inverted commas; they are no longer prime agencies. This diacritical ontology preserves itself from slipping into a structuralistic formalism by holding firmly to a simultaneous *ontogony*. The formations which arise are not only bound to each other by deformations and transformations; they point back to a background of indifference and polyvalence from which they emerge without ever leaving it behind. Thus the body refers to itself in an original form of narcissism without the circle of selfhood closing. In bodily backward reference I grasp more in myself than myself, and thus I touch what is other than me, and other people. An *intertwining* (*entrelacs*) forms between things, others and myself, a *chiasmus* or a *chiasma*, as Merleau-Ponty calls it with reference to Valéry. What is one's own and what is not constantly more or less overlap but never entirely coincide with each other. This non-coincidence keeps the play of differences open. It goes back to "an inaugural 'there is'" (Merleau-Ponty 1968 [1964], p. 292), which opens up a certain field of structures, without that event's finding a place in the field itself.

Open structuring processes lead to an endless play of presence and absence. Some *invisible* element underlies the visible, something that is not just invisible in fact, as something in the world, or absolutely invisible as something beyond the world, but which instead belongs to *this* world as being invisible. This "original form of elsewhere" causes the consciousness itself to show a blind spot, an "unconscious of the consciousness" (Merleau-Ponty 1968 [1964], p. 308). Here the search for a lost origin comes to an end. The original lies before us, in the present itself; it no longer manifests a uniform stamp, "the original shatters" (Merleau-Ponty 1968 [1964], p. 165). What eludes in this way our seeing and saying shows only as excess. Phenomenology becomes *indirect* ontology. Being can be grasped only in deviation from beings and their order, as a "wild being" which cannot be exhausted by any culture. At this point Merleau-Ponty clearly moves away from Heidegger's thinking of being, to which he knows himself linked in many respects. The fact that in thinking and speaking we proceed from "being" does not mean that after all Being itself speaks. Even that which exceeds and shatters the realm of the visible and sayable shows itself in its withdrawal as an "original presentation of what cannot be originally presented," again referring to Husserl. With its reference back to what shows itself, this indirect ontology remains a *phenomenological* ontology, even where it touches the "non-apparent."

Merleau-Ponty's endeavors end in an open process of re-thinking which hints at much that makes itself felt more strongly, but often also more unilaterally, in thinkers like Levinas, Foucault, and Derrida: for instance, the abandonment of a philosophy of consciousness, the subject, the ego, the presence, the origin . . . and on the other hand the emergence of new themes such as the dispersion of reason, the violent element in all order, shifts of time, disruptions of the ego, and the inevitable claim of the other and the strange. We may apply to this phenomenology, which makes its way to the borders of non-phenomenology, what Merleau-Ponty says in his essay on Husserl: "The philosopher carries his shadow with him and it means more than merely the actual absence of future light."

## Writings

Merleau-Ponty, M.: *La Structure du comportement* (Paris, 1942); 2nd edn (Paris: Presses Universitaires de France, 1949); tr. *The Structure of Behavior* (Boston, MA: Beacon Press, 1963).

——: *Phénoménologie de la perception* (Paris: Gallimard, 1945); tr. *Phenomenology of Perception* (London: Routledge & Kegan Paul, 1962).

——: *Humanisme et terreur* (Paris: Gallimard, 1947); tr. *Humanism and Terror* (Boston, MA: Beacon Press, 1969).

——: *Sens et non-sens* (Paris: Ngel, 1948); tr. *Sense and Non-Sense* (Evanston, IL: Northwestern University Press, 1964a).

——: *Les Aventures de la dialectique* (Paris: Gallimard, 1955); tr. *Adventures of the Dialectic* (Evanston, IL: Northwestern University Press, 1973).

——: *Signes* (Paris: Gallimard, 1960); tr. *Signs* (Evanston, IL: Northwestern University Press, 1964b).

——: *Le Visible et l'invisible* (Paris: Gallimard, 1964); tr. *The Visible and the Invisible* (Evanston, II: Northwestern University Press, 1968).

——: *Résumés de cours: Collège de France, 1952–1960* (Paris: Gallimard, 1968); tr. *Themes from the Lectures at the Collège de France, 1952–1960* (Evanston, IL: Northwestern University Press, 1970).

——: *La Prose du monde* (Paris: Gallimard, 1969); tr. *The Prose of the World* (Evanston, IL: Northwestern University Press, 1973).

——: *Merleau-Ponty à la Sorbonne: Resumés de cours, 1949–1952* (Dijon: ed. Cynara, 1988).

——: *Texts and Dialogues: Maurice Merleau-Ponty*, ed. and with an introd, by H. J. Silverman and J. Barry Jr (Atlantic Highlands, NJ: Humanities Press International, 1992).

——: *Le nature: Notes cours du Collège de France* (Paris: Seuil, 1995).

## References and further reading

*Actualités de Merleau-Ponty*, Les Cahiers de Philosophie, no. 7, Lille 1989.

Barbaras, R.: *De l'être du phénomène: Sur l'ontologie de Merleau-Ponty* (Grenoble: Millon, 1991).

Burke, P. and van der Veken, J. (eds): *Merleau-Ponty in Contemporary Perspectives* (Dordrecht: Kluwer, 1993).

Derossi, G.: *Maurice Merleau-Ponty* (Turin, 1965).

Dillon, M. C. (ed.): *Merleau-Ponty vivant* (Albany, NY: SUNY, 1991).

Edie, J. M.: *Merleau-Ponty's Philosophy of Language, Structuralism and Dialectics* (Washington, DC: University Press of America, 1987).

Geraets, Th. F.: *Vers une nouvelle philosophie transcendantale. La genèse de la philosophie de Maurice Merleau-Ponty jusqu'à la "Phénoménologie de la perception"* (The Hague: Nijhoff, 1971).

Heidsieck, F. (ed.): *Merleau-Ponty. Le Philosophe et son langage* (Paris: Vrin, 1993).

Kruks, S.: *A Study of the Political Philosophy of Merleau-Ponty* (Paris: Vrin, 1993).

Lannigan, R. L.: *Phenomenology of Communication: Merleau-Ponty's Thematics in Communicology and Semiology* (Pittsburgh, PA: Duquesne University Press, 1988).

Lefort, C.: *Sur une colonne absente* (Paris: Gallimard, 1978).

Madison, G. B.: *The Phenomenology of Merleau-Ponty: Search for the Limits of Consciousness* (Ohio: Ohio University Press, 1982).

*Maurice Merleau-Ponty, Esprit*, 66 (June 1982).

Métraux, A. and Waldenfels, B. (eds): *Leibhaftige Vernunft: Spuren von Merleau-Pontys Denken* (Munich: Fink, 1986).

Richir, M. and Tassin, E. (eds): *Merleau-Ponty: Phénoménologie et expérience* (Grenoble: Millon 1992).

Sartre, J. P.: "Merleau-Ponty vivant," *Situations IV* (Paris: Gallimard, 1961).

Waelhens, A. de: *Une philosophie de l'ambiguïté: L' Existentialisme de M. Merleau-Ponty* (Louvain: Publications Universitaires de Louvain, 1951).

Waldenfels, B.: *Phänomenologie in Frankreich* (Frankfurt: Suhrkamp, 1983).

——: *Deutsch-Französische Gedankengange* (Frankfurt: Suhrkamp, 1995).

291

# 24

# Bataille

ROBERT SASSO

## A transgression of philosophy

Writer, thinker, essayist, Georges Bataille (1897–1962) was not a "professional" philosopher. But he "always, above all else, turned towards philosophy," as he himself stressed (Chapsal 1961, p. 34); and "philosophers" can hardly remain indifferent to the radical calling into question of their discipline that his *heterological* body of work occasions, in its devotion to the other and to the subversion of the Logos. It is no longer possible to trivialize, or even to reject Bataille's contribution, as Sartre once did under the label of "new mysticism" (Sartre 1943). In 1970, while presenting the *Oeuvres Complètes* (*Complete Works*) [henceforth *OC*], Michel Foucault stated: "We owe to Bataille a large part of that which is our present moment; but without doubt we also owe to him that which remains to be done, to be thought and to be said, and this will be the case for a long time to come" (*OC*, vol. I, p. 5). If such a prophecy is by its nature difficult to verify, Bataille's contribution to philosophical "modernity" is nonetheless largely recognized, in as much as it deals with the destruction of the Hegelian "closure" of Discourse (Derrida 1967) and, more generally, with the emancipation of thought from the limits of Reason (Habermas 1984).

A few biographical details will allow us to retrace the circumstances in which he who wished to "embrace the totality of the possible," and whose only *ambition* was "to *be*, and to be *sovereignly*" (*OC*, vol. VII, p. 462), found himself confronted with philosophy and was able to envisage its "*transgression.*"

At the age of seventeen, Bataille successfully completed a baccalaureate in philosophy by correspondence course. At first he planned to become a priest or a monk (without having received a religious education at home, he converted to Catholicism in 1914). But after one year at the seminary, he opted to study at the École Nationale des Chartes (National Charter School) (Paris 1918–21), which opened up the career of librarian to him. In various capacities, he carried out the functions of librarian all his life: first in Paris (Bibliothèque Nationale (National Library), 1922–42) then, after quite a long period of sick leave, in the libraries of Carpentras (1949–51) and of Orleans (1951–61). Alongside this career as a minor public official – which did allow him, it is true, to move in the world of books – Bataille developed an intense activity as a writer and intellectual, often in an "excessive" vein. Between the wars, in particular, he either participated in or was the instigator of several avant-garde "revolutionary" movements: his relations with André Breton and the Surrealists (1929–30) were often difficult: he was a member of the Democratic Communist Circle (1931–4), an "anti-Stalinist" group led by Boris Souvarine; he created Counter-Attack, an antifascist political grouping of "Revolutionary Intellectuals" (1935–6); he founded, with Pierre Klossowski, a staunchly "Nietzschean" "secret society" as well as the journal *Acéphale* (after the name of a symbolic beheaded man, the head being taken as the center of the principles of subservience); he created, along with Roger Caillois and Michel Leiris, a College of Sociology (1936–9) to study the "sacred" and seek out the violence inherent in irrational social phenomena. After the war, Bataille founded the journal *Critique* with the apparently more moderate ambition of making it a modern *Journal Des Savants*.

Over the years, Bataille continued to teach himself philosophy and gradually acquired determining, albeit limited, philosophical knowledge. For different yet complementary reasons, three names stand out: BERGSON (Article 13), NIETZSCHE (Article 11), and HEGEL (Article 6).

Bataille often described how he became acquainted with the ideas of Bergson. While on a short visit to London in 1920, during which he was to meet Bergson at a dinner party, he borrowed the philosopher's shortest book, *Laughter*, from the British Museum. Reading it was a revelation. Not so much because the philosophy of Bergson appealed to Bataille, but because he became convinced that laughter constituted "The key question, the enigma which, once solved, would of itself solve everything (Bataille 1954 [1943], p. 86), opening up "the core of the world," beyond the "sensible," "logical," "rational" world. It was shortly afterwards that he enthusiastically discovered Nietzsche (first through personal reading, then, from 1923 to 1925, in the continuation of discussions with the Russian philosopher Leon Chestov – who initiated him into Plato, Pascal, and Kierkegaard). Bataille, filled with wonder, believed that he had found the perfect and definitive expression of a philosophy which, in asserting that that which has "not caused laughter at least once" (Bataille 1961 [1944], p. 40) – including the "tragic" – is *false*, made laughter the measure of truth. Bataille felt such a "community" of thought with Nietzsche, perhaps his only "earthly companion" (1945a, p. 33), that for a short while he considered giving up his own thinking and writing (*OC*, vol. VIII, p. 562). Things could have ended there, with Bataille engaged only in a perpetual commemoration of Nietszche (as in the volume of Nietzschean maxims which he published under the title *Mémorandum*, Bataille 1945b), cleansing the latter in particular of the "Nazi stain." That is, if he had not from 1929 developed an interest in Hegel. This interest was long-lasting and grew in intensity, leading him to attend Koyré's seminar on Hegel's religious philosophy (1932–3) at the École des Hautes Études (School of Advanced Studies), followed by six years (1933–9) at Alexander Kojève's seminar on *The Phenomenology of Mind*. There too, he was filled with wonder and fascination: Hegel was perhaps that which is "self-evident," even if it is "difficult to bear" (Bataille 1961 [1944], p. 146); no other doctrine can compare to his, "it is the summit of positive intelligence" (Bataille 1954 [1943], p. 140): it would have been necessary "without Hegel, first of all to be Hegel" (Bataille 1961 [1944], p. 149).

After having been passionately "Nietzschean," had Bataille become uncondi-
tionally "Hegelian"? In a surprising about-turn, had he gone from an aphoristic
philosophy of singularity and the instant to a systematic philosophy which made
everything a "moment" subordinate to the developing totality? In fact, the situation is much more "dialectical." Given that Bataille set out to attain the limits of the
thinkable, it is clear that Hegelianism represented a rigor and *effort* of thought that
precluded either "sentimental facileness" (*OC*, vol. XII, p. 542) or a "literary evasion" (*OC*, vol. VIII, p. 583). What is more, through a movement of thought that
relates to the universal, Hegel's philosophy answers to an immanent and indisputable "principle of totality" (*OC*, vol. VII, p. 531) within us. However, if Hegelianism
effectively realizes the "sum of the possible" – which, by definition, philosophy
should aspire to be (Bataille 1957a, p. 280) – thought only gains access "to the
summit of being" (p. 306) when it ends "in excess" (*OC*, vol. III, p. 12). What "is,"
in effect, at the "summit" and at the precise moment when thought completes its
"construction" is the "impossible," the inconceivable, the ineffable. To reach this
point, philosophy must free itself, *in the end*, of the "servile" tasks involved in the
constitution of "knowledge" through the discursive sequence, and, giving thought
over to the *experience* of what is beyond the sayable, become the "transgression of
philosophy" (Bataille 1957a, p. 305) and abolish itself in silence.

## An abundant body of work

However, it is clear that Bataille did not choose silence. Together with numerous
unpublished manuscripts, the twelve volumes of his *Oeuvres Complètes* contain
more than 6,500 pages of text. Besides philosophy, they concern art, literature,
psychology, politics, economics, sociology, history, ethnology, religion – all of a
very varied nature: there are articles (over two hundred, including numerous
accounts of books read); texts of lectures; stories (often suited to the forbidden
books department in the library), like *Histoire de l'oeil* (1928), *Madama Edwarda*
(1941) – published under pseudonyms; *L'Abbé C* (1950), and *Le Bleu du ciel* (1957);
collections of private thoughts in various stages of development and connected-
ness, in the form of meditations, diary entries, aphorisms, poems, like *L'Expérience
intérieure* (1943), *Le Coupable* (1944), *Sur Nietzsche* (1945); essays on specific
themes, such as *La Part maudite*, *Essai d'économie générale* (1949), *Lascaux ou la
naissance de l'art* (1955), *Manet* (1955), *L'érotisme* (1957), *Théorie de la religion*
(posthumous, 1973).

From the outside, such an abundance of different texts does not suggest a unity
of inspiration. Upon reading, however, one is quickly struck by the fact that the
same problems and the same arguments return almost obsessively, despite the
contextual differences. These can be summarized as follows: in a variety of ways
and at the risk of death, man aspires to the *instant* in which life is delivered from
need, necessity, or usefulness; but located beyond the "realm of objects" and removed from the temporal developments of "work" and of "knowledge," this *sovereign existence*" implies the dissolution of "*discursive reality*."

In wishing to testify to the extra-discursive dimension of human life, Bataille not only sought to envisage the "entirely other" of the Logos, within the framework of a general *heterology* (see *OC*, vol. II), but sought also to abolish "discourse" in favor of "silence" in his own texts. As a result, his work is subjected to the permanent contradiction of a language devoted to that which normally eludes language and leaves one *speechless*. In one sense, the "literary" part of his work would be enough to *communicate* the silence. One could say of Bataille's shocking "erotic" stories what he himself said about Sade's *Cent vingt Journées*: "unless you remain deaf to them," you will inevitably finish them "sick" (1957b, p. 143). They are fantastical stories relating to obsessive elements of his autobiography: the sight of a blind and paralyzed father, or of the mother's moments of "madness"; experiences of debauchery and sexual passion; violent deaths. But Bataille came up against apparently insurmountable theoretical and practical difficulties in trying, not to communicate *emotion* through words, but to *describe* and give a *theoretical* overview of extra-discursive experience. In effect, how can one "speak" of silence without betraying it, and how can one argue objectively in favor of the primacy of "subjectivity"? It appears that Bataille attempted to overcome these difficulties by using three main procedures, each of which constitutes a *transgression* of "discourse." The simplest and most immediate procedure is the break in the continuous sequence of the argument (which is signalled either by the explicit abandonment of a development that is under way, or by *suspension* marks that appear within or interrupt the sentence, or by aphoristic expression). The second procedure is the interference (very un-Aristotelian) of different types of expression within a single work (analyses and poems, stories and theoretical considerations, studies and personal confessions). Finally, and most frequently, is the procedure which one could term homeopathic. This involves emphasizing the argument's discursive nature right up to breaking point, with the idea that the largest "assembly" of language attains a limit at which the essential eludes its cohesion and invalidates it. Hence, the generally classical structure of Bataille's sentence, alongside an occasionally "sententious" turn of phrase which contributes to a "florid tone" and a certain heaviness – which are deliberate (*OC*, vol. III, p. 382). Hence also the proliferation of projects to regroup different writings into large collections; each time these were reconstituted and reorganized, but never completed. In fact, the *Oeuvres complètes* as a whole constitute the sole, discontinuous "text" for the expression of Bataille's thought; an immense text where below a surface "disorderliness" (one thinks of Pascal's *Pensées*) all the notions and statements are profoundly organized.

However, we are here concerned with Bataille's principal *theses* and the way in which they are articulated *theoretically* (those who wish to possess the "carnal keys" of his work – *Madama Edwarda* is one such, according to Bataille, for a chapter of *L'expérience intérieure* – are invited to read the relevant "literary" texts). So we will limit ourselves to the most explicitly analytical and reflective texts, noting three closely complementary themes: the subjective experience of that which is beyond the Logos (for Bataille this is a primary experience); the objective history of "self-consciousness" (for Bataille any individual consciousness is an expression of the totality of human experience given in history); the sovereign existence on the scale of the Universal "game" (according to Bataille, clear consciousness discovers its real relation to the excessive material energy of the Universe at the end of history and can at that moment imagine harmonizing with the violence of Being).

## Atheological experience and non-knowing

"Experience" is of course the principal theme of *L'Expérience intérieure*. This is a highly composite work and the author himself recognized its "obscurity." None the less, it is possible to identify its central argument; in doing so we will occasionally have recourse to complementary texts with which it forms, or should form, a *"Summa Atheologiae"*: *Méthode de méditation, Post-scriptum 1953, Le coupable, Sur Nietzsche, Conférences sur le non-savoir.*

Bataille defines the interior experience as a *mystical* experience which implies *no mysticism*. This experience answers fundamentally to that incontestable human particularity which calls everything into question, leading thought, without reservation, to the limits of the "possible," outside any specific "project." In effect, it is not possible to subordinate this movement of thought to the search for some sort of "goal," whether it be intellectual, moral, or aesthetic, without immediately betraying it. Nor is it possible to articulate it in relation to an entity that serves as a point of reference and is considered indubitable (such as the "self" or "God"). Consequently, beyond any passing similarities, the experience challenges any form of thought which presupposes the result of its processes. Thus philosophy, whether it be Descartes' or Hegel's or even the phenomenology of Heidegger, subordinates in advance the exercise of thought to the problem of knowledge; Christian spiritual exercises organize themselves beforehand around a particular religious confession and aim at a "satisfaction"; Hindu mental techniques have a utilitarian dimension (a "hygiene"); mythological, theatrical, or poetic approaches cannot do without "images." By way of a "method," the "meditation" that is the interior experience is not so much a question of rules and specific procedures (even though it might attempt to reproduce the conditions in which it has already taken place). Rather, it is an *arbitrary* and "sovereign operation" (Bataille 1954 [1947], p. 237), which looks to no "authority" other than itself, and through which "thought puts a stop to the movement that subordinates it and, laughing – or abandoning itself to some supreme effusion – identifies with the breaking of the ties that subordinated it (Bataille 1954 [1947], p. 232). Once we specify that, besides laughter, the sovereign "effusions" to which Bataille alludes are, for example, those of ecstacy (to which many mystics testify), of eroticism, of poetry or, more prosaically, of drunkenness, we come to understand that the experience amounts to a delivering up of thought, in such "shattering" moments, to a complete "eruption." In each case, without giving in to "madness," but without trying to avoid the "fear" to which the "totality of thought" leads, it is a matter of braving the *worst*, in the "halo of death" (Bataille 1954 [1943], p. 93), and of leading *reason* itself to "undo its work" before the inconceivable.

If, as a hypothesis, Hegelian "absolute knowledge" – a general composition of all that is possible, within which the sovereign moments in question are dialectically "cancelled out" (as negativities of which the negation gives a positive result) – was admitted, it would also be necessary to admit the hypothesis of an "absolute non-knowledge": we would know definitively that there would be nothing left to know. At its ultimate limit, knowledge would open out onto its "heart of darkness," confronting thought with a negativity that is irremediably removed from all *comprehension*. In fact, in the interior experience, the accomplished accumulation of all that is possible and the complete totalization of sense are brutally reversed into the "impossible," into the absence of ultimate sense. And if it is inevitable that, at some point, the non-sense itself makes a kind of sense, the latter, in as much as the experience continues, becomes non-sense again immediately afterwards. All knowledge, as soon as it is "seized," leaves one thus in a state of total "deprivation" as regards the non-known and loses itself in it. This explains why non-knowing transmits the anguish and the ecstasy of a "free fall" (Bataille 1954 [1943], p. 71). But in accordance with the very nature of laughter, "leap of the possible into the impossible – and of the impossible into the possible" (Bataille 1961 [1944], p. 139), this authentically *catastrophic* movement corresponds just as much to a *sliding* into the "illuminated heart of laughter" (Bataille 1954 [1943], p. 47).

Moreover, such are the effects of non-knowing: in discovering that *nothing* is revealed at the high point of human questioning, other than that man is a "plea without response" (Bataille compares it to the *lamma sabachtani* of Jesus of the cross), the only possible result is anguish and laughter, indefinitely formed, alone in corresponding to the scale of the harrowing vision of the unintelligible. In this agonizing silence, the experience becomes *divine*, but in a strictly *atheological* sense, outside all *mysticism*.

In this experience, Bataille undoubtedly sought to *see* beyond all that can be seen, in a similar way to "blind eyes" or to an eye opening at the top of our skull and pointing towards the "sun" (fantasy of the *pineal eye*, at the end of the 1920s, cf. *OC*, vol. II) – *see* and even *be* "God." Yet, with Bataille this "term" is in the end only the nominal correlative of a potential limit of the possible and the thinkable. Sometimes quoting Dionysus Areopagitica, Meister Eckhart or Angela of Foligno, Bataille asserts that "God" is literally "nothing" and that He *is unaware* of Himself (Bataille 1954 [1943], p. 131). If "God" was not in essence an "atheist" (Bataille 1954 [1943], p. 131), if he managed no longer to "hate" himself, thereby achieving a full presence, and a self-presence that is "satisfied" with the accomplished possible, a high point of sense and a high point of being, he "would immediately cease to be God." In fact, a God who coincided with the possible and the reasonable would condemn "the unlimited right to foolishness and to infinite, discordant laughter" (Bataille 1954 [1947], p. 207). But in excluding from himself these insane forms as incompatible with the perfection of his being, he would immediately be finished, overwhelmed by the "impossible." All in all, being *inconceivable*, the unknown to whom the experience brings back the known cannot be "enslaved" to any idea of plenitude, satisfaction or *perfection* (Bataille 1954 [1943], p. 14).

In fact, nothing is "revealed" at the limits, other than that *nothing* answers to the requirement of an infinite addition of sense – nothing, or the most insane *obscenity* of "what is" (like the prostitute in *Madama Edwarda* who offers the "rags" of her sex to view). Nothing or *no-one*, only a "terrible absence."

## A history of self-consciousness

Making use of history or ethnology and clearly inspired by the ideas of Bergson, Hegel, or Marx regarding anthropogenesis, works such as *La Part maudite*, *L'Érotisme*, *Théorie de la religion*, or *Lascaux* link the interior experience with the universal search for a sovereign existence, within the framework of a *history* of *self-consciousness*. In effect, Bataille stresses that man as a being has, through his technical activity (*Homo faber*), gradually freed himself from animality and gone on to acquire, with the intelligence of the nature of things and of their relations (*Homo sapiens*), *self-consciousness*. But this consciousness conceals a contradiction: the consciousness of being a non-object, a "subject," and the consciousness that this is not immediately and naturally the case, but is achieved through the intermediary of *work*, the institutor of an "order of things." On the one hand, therefore, *human* existence finds itself subordinated to the production and maintenance of this order – which is why, in every society, acts that are likely to threaten it (such as relations to death and to sexuality) are subject to "taboos." But on the other hand, men aspire to a full, full, sovereign existence, which would be removed from this order, independent of objects and unconcerned about any activity or "useful" knowledge. This is testified to in general and in every form by the *transgression* of taboos or by the many useless activities which are tantamount to unproductive *expenditures*, such as feasts and celebrations, luxury, spectacles, lavish constructions, wars, sacrifices, arts, eroticism. In other words, in any form of human existence and social life there is an *accursed share*, devoted in a paradoxical manner to what is "bad": not in order to possess something or to increase control, but for *nothing*. Thus man, nostalgic for a "lost intimacy" with the world (by definition (Bataille 1973) every *religion* is searching for this), constantly aspires to the removal of all that which separates him from it. It is clear, however, that a complete reduction of man's "transcendence" to the world would suppress "man" and reduce him to pure "animal" immanence.

Bataille assimilates the development of this contradiction to a "history of self-consciousness," underpinning the history of a humanity that is driven towards self-knowledge and emancipation. We are at this point obviously very close to Hegel, and in the *Théorie de la religion*, in particular, Bataille openly sought to write a kind of counterpart to the *Phenomenology of Mind*, setting out the different steps and forms of the dialectical opposition between subject and object in a new manner, until the opposition itself ceases through the absolute *effectivity* of the subject. But this had a very different meaning from that in Hegel.

Choosing examples from extreme types of civilization, Bataille makes a distinction in history between four principal forms of relation to the "divine." Archaic societies are in essence societies that "consume," subordinating their production to unproductive acts of destruction. The importance attributed to sacrifices and lavish celebrations, during which lives and material wealth are conspicuously destroyed (Aztec human sacrifices, the prodigal gift of the *potlatch* – studied by Marcel Mauss – among the Indians of North America) highlights the fact that the "sacred" is located beyond the "profane" world of specific beings and distinct objects, in a *continuum* to which one gains access but fleetingly, on suppressing the integrity and individuality of discontinuous entities. A "principle of loss" seems to be accepted as the condition of access to the "divine." But religions founded on the principle of consuming are limited in that any institutionalized and consecrated violence tends towards a community's self-destruction – unless, that is, it is carried out through "trickery" on substitutes (slaves), thereby removing its sacred element.

In contrast, societies based on "military conquest," which devote their resources to the growth of a universal empire, direct this destructive violence outwards (from this angle, Bataille analyzes in particular the historical expansion of Islam, but he also has Rome in mind). In its founding principles, military expansion extends to the whole world, but it is only able to maintain its "empire" through a "universal" and "rational" management of the "order of things." Informed by "morality" and "law," the useless destruction of goods becomes an "evil" that is deprived of any religious virtue. A pronounced metaphysical dualism is established: divinity becomes a pure reality (intelligible good), which totally transcends the material world. As a result, *mediation* is necessary to gain access to the divine, either through an appeal to a vengeful god who punishes crime, or through the sacrifice of that which, in the divinity, stems from the world of things (the body). This relation to the divine is none the less ambiguous since it is established via the "productive operations" mode that belongs to the profane world. The "solution" to this has apparently been found by a third form of society, the "disarmed society," which only uses violence to destroy its own productions, *without destroying itself*. Tibetan Lamaism is a perfect example of this, in which all resources are devoted to the *contemplative* life of the monks. Such a society clearly testifies to the fact that *activity* in and of itself has no value, and that the essential (the "divine") is absent from it. However, it may only exist in complete "isolation" (1967a [1949], p. 157), in a geographically and historically exceptional situation that allows one to conceive of a "limit" in general to what is a *currently unlimited* human activity.

In world history, it is with the development of capitalism and the Protestant negation of the divine value of "endeavors" (Bataille takes up the ideas of Max Weber), that the possibility of a total split between human activities and the divine appeared: if "salvation" is always in the other world, this world becomes the site for an activity that only draws meaning from itself and whose only aim is its own development. With this, we have reached a unique situation in the history of humanity. For the first time, in the capitalist or post-capitalist industrial society, there is no longer any "religious" limitation to the production and accumulation of wealth. In an entirely profane world, from which the sacred has been lost – or in which "sacrifice" has been deprived of its meaning, which comes down to the same thing – the "will to pure power" can continue uninterrupted. However, this becomes the opposite of what is claimed for it: as "indefinite production," it is not unconditional liberty but the manifestation of the *servile* spirit which implicitly accepts being linked to "things" and dominated by them (Bataille notes in particular (see 1967a [1949]) the paradox of "communist man" who is committed to continual labor with "future" liberation in mind). This is the stage at which the "age-old quest for lost intimacy" (Bataille 1973, p. 121) might be abandoned. Man,

299

no longer giving himself up to anything other than industrial development and having no "sovereignty" other than a collaboration in the "common endeavor," would turn away once and for all from himself; he would no longer have *self-consciousness*, but, to summarize Bataille's idea, he would merely be a *conscious thing*.

At this point, the two axes of Bataille's thought converge, the analysis of the individual interior experience and the analysis of historical human experience. In effect, only the prospect of *unbounded* production and accumulation in a world that contains nothing other than man (no "divine") can give rise to a "consciousness" which, not recognizing itself in it and not submitting to it, envisages having "*nothing as its object*" (1967 [1949], p. 248). It is just such a consciousness that attains the atheological experience of non-knowing. In fact, at the end of the *Théorie de la religion* and of *La Part maudite*, the dissolution of knowledge and of sense, as the "intimate operation" of a consciousness that has reached the extreme of "absolute knowledge," is paralleled with the real *destruction* (uncontrolled, during war, or deliberate, during economic crises) of the excesses of a world production given up to infinite growth. In both cases, maximal accumulation is violently reversed into total "loss." In both cases as well the same problem arises, which is that of how the human subject can relate to destructive violence, without being destroyed itself. This is what is at stake in a *sovereign existence*, on the scale of *what is*, not in the sense of the absolutely "perfect" Being of metaphysics, but in the sense of the *incomplete*, of the "*open* heart of the worlds" (1954 [1947], p. 243, our emphasis), never within-self or for-self, but always "*outside of self*": an existence on the scale of the Universe *at play*.

## The universal game and the sovereign existence

As in Hegel, the *experience of consciousness* in Bataille emerges from a universal and irrepressible movement which is only revealed to consciousness at the end of the *historical* unfolding of all its experiential possibilities. With Hegel, this movement is the *evolution of the Spirit*, which ends with the lifting of the opposition between subject and object. In the world that he has produced and where he knows himself in the end to be "at home," the Hegelian subject is totally "satisfied." With Bataille, in contrast, the movement to which consciousness ultimately relates is the *excess energy in the Universe* (see Bataille 1967a [1949]). This is a violent movement that nothing depletes, that no restriction is able to contain, immanent to each individual thing and requiring, in the end, that each thing exceeds its own limits. Bataille sees proof of it in the fact that all "beings" and all "systems" – whether they be physical or social – *communicate* with other beings, other systems, through "gaps," "tears," or "breaches" (see Bataille 1961 [1944]). Even if they first use that communication to preserve or develop their *identity*, they end up reaching an absolute limit of "growth" beyond which they have to free or destroy without benefit that part of energy which exceeds their needs or capacities (see Bataille 1967a [1949]). In the same way, in human consciousness, the desire to suppress the separation between subject and object, between individuality and the *totality* of being, is in the end the desire to go beyond all limits – "Being is *nowhere*" (Bataille 1954 [1943], p. 108) – a desire for the *unindividual*. Thus, the movement to which the experience of consciousness is linked is at the same time that "which leads us to our ruin" (*OC*, vol. VIII, p. 536).

Here we touch upon a decisive point in Bataille's work, but one which is a probable source of misunderstandings. If Bataille is in effect fascinated by death and by "degeneration" in general (in a word, by what is "bad"), it is not a sign of nihilism or morbid inhumanity. In fact, just as we cannot "be *human* without recognizing within us the possibility of suffering [and] also of abjectness" (*OC*, vol. XI, p. 266), so living as a *human* being consists not only of *preserving life*, but also of *living it* as fully as possible (Bataille 1957b, p. 139), by embracing its prodigal movement of unlimited *consuming* until we "get as close as is bearable to death" (Bataille 1961 [1944], p. 128). And when adding emphatically: "if necessary, even by dying," or when he stresses, elsewhere, that *eroticism* is an "approval of life even in death" (1957a, p. 17), Bataille is only pointing to an extreme risk which is not necessarily "tragic." Death is tragic for the "dying-self," in that it is locked in the illusion of *self* (Bataille 1954 [1943], p. 95). In contrast, in the "indifference to any future" (*OC*, vol. VIII, p. 536), the drawing near of death can correspond to a separation from the "serious" world of discontinuous beings shrunk back on their identity; in this way, a man who imagines death "enters into the free play of worlds" (*OC*, vol. VI, p. 303). But if he dies, he no longer participates in the game as a player, rather he has become a simple toy.

It is therefore a matter of *communicating* with the free Universe, "the world of stars, wind and volcanoes" (Bataille 1954 [1947], p. 255), beyond the "official world" (p. 224) of acts, objects, and knowledge where "reason" is entrenched, deployed, and dominates. Not that this "real" world should be abandoned in favor of the irruption of the irrational and injustice. On the contrary, in the "active sphere" of the *external* world, dominated as it is by productive *operations*, reason and equity are necessary conditions if man is not to be subordinated to the order of things: the suppression of the *object* in favor of the *subject* is required by the "clearest" *self*-consciousness, which can no longer be diverted from itself; it is located *after* the presupposed victory of the "slave" over the "master" (in line with the dialectic of the "opposed self-consciousnesses" in Hegel) and it should never be allowed to destroy men themselves (Bataille 1973, p. 137). However, only a "Copernican reversal" of "morality" would be able to lift the historical "curse" of wars and economic waste and subordinate the development of growth to the *universal* principle of loss. In the framework of a "general economy" on a global scale, this would mean concretely that a national economy's surpluses (overabundance always occurs somewhere in the world) would be freely given up to a poor nation. (In *La Part maudite*, Bataille examines the Marshall plan after the Second World War, which provided aid to European countries, as an instance of this.)

Ideally, an individual would be able not only to eat according to his needs, but, beyond this, to *consume* "infinitely the objects that are produced" (Bataille 1973, p. 137) until he is able to free himself from them, all his temporal efforts becoming "nothing." This moment is properly the *instant*. And this is unquestionably "futile"

(p. 135), such as the drinking of alcohol or the "little death" of erotic pleasure. But it is in the instant that "pure happiness" (*OC*, vol. XII, p. 478) is found. It is in futility, in "useless negativity" (a claim expressed (Bataille 1961 [1944], p. 170) in a letter to Kojève), that it is possible to *open up to the totality* of what is – as in the "love of a mortal being" (*OC*, vol. VIII, pp. 496–503), which is seemingly such a "singular concern," compared for example with the State and its *reason*, and yet is that through which an individual may exceed his limits, fuse with a transitory being and "immediately, silently be given back to the universe."

The "happiness" that Bataille evokes is uncertain; it is beyond any "calculation" and given only in the instant. There remains still the imperative to adapt to whatever might occur, even as a "catastrophe": sovereign" availability to the world, beyond the concern for subordinate tasks, which does not demand a "will to power" but only a "will to chance."

## Writings

### Books

Bataille, G.: *Madame Edwarda* (under the pseudonym of Pierre Angélique) (Paris, 1941); 2nd edn ("Préface de G. Bataille") (Paris: Pauvert, 1956).

——: *Somme athéologique*, vol. I: *L'expérience intérieure* (1943), revised and corrected, followed by *Méthode de méditation* (1947) and *Post-scriptum 1953* (Paris: Gallimard, 1954).

——: *Somme athéologique*, vol. II: *Le coupable* (1944), revised and corrected, followed by *L'Alleluiah* (Paris: Gallimard, 1961).

——: *Sur Nietzsche, volonté de chance* (Paris: Gallimard, 1945a).

——: *Mémorandum* (maxims and texts of Nietzsche collected and presented by G. Bataille) (Paris: Gallimard, 1945b).

——: *La Haine de la poésie* (Paris, 1947); reissued under the title *L'Impossible: Histoire de rats*, followed by *Dianus* and *L'Orestie* (Paris: Éditions de Minuit, 1962).

——: *La Part maudite* [1949: *Essai d'économie générale*, vol. I, *La consumation*] preceded by *La notion de dépense* (1933) (Paris: Éditions de Minuit, 1967a).

——: *L'Abbé C* (Paris: Éditions de Minuit, 1950).

——: *La Peinture préhistorique. Lascaux ou la naissance de l'art* (Geneva: Skira, 1955).

——: *Manet* (Geneva: Skira, 1955).

——: *L'érotisme* (Paris: Éditions de Minuit, 1957a).

——: *La Littérature et le mal* (Paris: Gallimard, 1957b).

——: *Le Bleu du ciel* (Paris: Pauvert, 1957c).

——: *Les Larmes d'Éros* (Paris: 1961); 2nd edn, with the addition of unedited letters (Paris: Pauvert, 1971).

——: *Histoire de l'oeil* (under the pseudonym of Lord Auch) (Paris: Pauvert, 1967b).

——: *Oeuvres Complètes*, 12 volumes (Paris: Gallimard, 1970–88).

——: *Théorie de la religion* (Paris: Gallimard, 1973).

### Articles

Bataille, G.: "Nietzsche et les fascistes," *Acéphale*, 2 (1937), pp. 3–19, 17–21.

——: "Le souverain," *Botteghe Oscure*, VI (Rome, 1950), pp. 23–38.

——: "Le non-savoir," *Botteghe Oscure*, XI (Rome, 1953), pp. 18–30.

————: "Hegel, la mort et le sacrifice," *Deucalion*, 5 (1955), pp. 21–43.

————: "Hegel, l'homme at l'histoire," *Monde nouveau paru*, 96 (1956), pp. 21–3; 98 (1956), pp. 1–14.

————: "La souveraineté," *Monde nouveau paru*, 101 (1956), pp. 15–30; 102 (1956), pp. 24–36; 103 (1956), pp. 14–29.

————: "Le pur bonheur," *Botteghe Oscure*, xx (Rome, 1958), pp. 20–30.

————: "Conférences sur le non-savoir," *Tel Quel*, 10 (1962), pp. 3–20.

## References and further reading

Boldt-Irons, L. A. (ed.): *On Bataille: On Critical Essays*, tr. L. A. Boldt-Irons (Albany, NY: State University of New York Press, 1995).

Chapsal, M.: "Georges Bataille," *L'Express*, 510 (March 1961), pp. 34–6.

Derrida, J.: "Un hégélianisme sans réserve," *L'arc*, 32 (1967), pp. 24–44.

Foucault, M.: "Préface à la transgression," *Critique*, 195–6 (1963), pp. 751–69.

Gasché, R.: *System und Metaphorik in der Philosophie von Georges Bataille* (Berne: Verlag Peter Lang, 1978).

Habermas, J.: "The French path to postmodernity: Bataille between eroticism and general economics," *New German Critique*, 33 (1984), pp. 79–102.

Hawley, D.: *Bibliographie annotée de la critique sur Georges Bataille de 1929 à 1975* (Geneva: Slatkine, 1976).

Marmande, F.: *Georges Bataille politique* (Presses Universitaires de Lyon, 1985).

Perniola, M.: *Georges Bataille e il negativo* (Milan: Feltrinelli, 1977).

Richman, M.: *Reading Georges Bataille. Beyond the Gift* (Baltimore/London: Johns Hopkins University Press, 1982).

Sartre, J.-P.: "Un nouveau mystique," *Cahiers du Sud*, 260 (1943), reprinted in *Situations I* (Paris: Gallimard, 1947), pp. 133–74.

Sasso, R.: *Georges Bataille: le système du non-savoir. Une ontologie du jeu* (Paris: Éditions de Minuit, 1978).

Surya, M.: *Georges Bataille. La Mort à l'oeuvre* (Pairs: Séguier/Birr, 1987).

# 25

# Blanchot

## PAUL DAVIES

Why Blanchot for philosophy?

As a philosopher, why read Blanchot?

I had imagined this article beginning quite straightforwardly, if somewhat hyperbolically, with the following assertion and answer: The critical essays of Maurice Blanchot constitute one of the twentieth century's profoundest and most significant philosophical reflections on literature and literary language. This is, after all, not only what I believe to be the case but also an assertion and a belief whose plausibility this article would like to demonstrate. What makes it impossible simply to begin in this fashion is the manner in which such an opening seems to require that the conceptions of literature, of philosophy, and of the relations and tensions between them be fixed in advance. If Blanchot's writing is, to an arguably interesting degree, marginal to and deliberately other than philosophy, then our account of it would seem to require an account of that marginality and its significance. To consider Blanchot in relation to philosophy is to find oneself in danger of being faced with two unsatisfactory and constricting ways of proceeding, although neither is obviously wrong.

To speak of the critical *essays* is already to limit ourselves, not unproblematically, to only one part of Blanchot's work, namely that part made up, in the main, of the six volumes of essays published between 1945 and 1970: *Faux pas, La Part du feu (The Work of Fire), L'Espace littéraire (The Space of Literature), Le Livre à venir, L'Entretien infini (The Infinite Conversation)*, and *L'Amitié*. We would be wise then to keep in mind the context established by Blanchot's own development away from the specifically indicated distinctions between fictional and non-fictional works and towards the unclassifiable "fragmentary" works such as *Le Pas au-delà (The Step (Not) Beyond)* and *L'Écriture du désastre (The Writing of the Disaster)*, works which bring to the fore a series of devices Blanchot has introduced in his reworking and reorganizing of the essays comprising *L'Entretien infini*. It is these later works, with their cryptic but deliberate references to the philosophical texts of NIETZSCHE (see Article 11), HEGEL (Article 6), HEIDEGGER (Article 18), and LEVINAS (Article 20) and their highly stylized interventions into the contemporary philosophical reception of such texts, which are the primary focus for the recent interest in Blanchot, and yet the context that best protects their status as interestingly and importantly marginal is nothing but the development towards them. There is a sense of Blanchot's project or itinerary which, in situating the otherwise perhaps generically and thematically unsituatable "fragmentary" works, also demands that discussion of *any* of Blanchot's writings be referred to these later works and to their context. This gesture enhances and ensures Blanchot's status as a solitary and *literary* figure, but in so doing, it also forgets that so much of what has concerned him over the years has been the very idea of literary projects, itineraries, and *apprentissages* and the difficulty of letting them stand as contexts.

To characterize the essays which will concern us here as *critical* and as *philosophically so* is to beg one of the questions with which they are increasingly concerned, namely the question as to what in literature itself – if there is a literature *itself* – either warrants or makes possible that type of thinking about it we call "criticism." Blanchot's worrying over what it is that literary language tells us about language as such and his insisting that this inquiry and its implications remain foreign to the various undertakings of criticism never suffice to turn his project into a strictly or recognizably philosophical one. Of primary importance here is not the distinction between literary criticism and philosophy, with Blanchot's writing somehow being won over for and by the latter, but rather what it is in those things we call works of literature which turns or returns even the most disarming of philosophical treatments of them into criticism. It is as much the literary critical assumptions of philosophy as it is the philosophical assumptions of criticism. "Philosophy" and "philosophical" have a wide scope, stretching to Heidegger's, for Blanchot, laudable attempt to think an encounter with poetry and poetic language in which the philosophical and critical assumptions about language founder on an awareness of a change in the essence or nature of language itself, an awareness and a change ostensibly brought about by the poem. If, in his reading of Hölderlin, as Blanchot suggests, Heidegger opens philosophy to the space of literature,[1] that opening does not help to secure a new encounter between poetizing and thinking, but rather, as an opening onto the space of literature, can only be returned constantly to the philosophizing criticism from which it stemmed. If Blanchot's thinking would also effect a certain disengagement from criticism it is bound to the same frustration and performative contradiction, a reading of what criticism cannot read, and, so performed, it is returned to criticism but to criticism now thought in and from this turning as the *impossibility* of criticism. Later, when it is no longer a matter of essays critical or otherwise, Blanchot will sometimes write of the gift the poem brings to thought, a gift thinking is unable to accept, a ruinous or disastrous gift.[2] Because the books or volumes in which one finds these utterances allow them no context, not even the anti-context of being a fragment – in one such formulation it is precisely the "fragment" that is said to be the gift – the reader turns perhaps inevitably to the twofold context alluded to above: to the project which brings Blanchot to this sort of book and to the climate in which literature, poetry, the work, or the poem is deemed not only to matter to philosophy but to matter terribly, as though above everything else.

For some, a defining feature of recent "continental" philosophy is the status it accords the question of literature and literary language, a status not dissimilar to that reserved elsewhere and by others for science. And it is therefore, some suspect, less a matter of the problem posed to, say, a philosophical account of language or meaning by the existence of fictional and poetic statements than it is a matter of such statements serving as an ideal, as something to be emulated, and so as something which increasingly undermines the attempt to provide any purely philosophical account of language or meaning at all. A certain sort of philosophy is thus deemed to aspire to the condition of poetry or literature as elsewhere and in another guise it aspires to the condition of science, and, in effect, to claim that such an aspiration rests on philosophy's being somehow continuous with poetry or literature as elsewhere it is held to be continuous with science. This latter claim also entails that, in the case of poetry or literature as in the case of science, the philosophical realization of this continuity dictates how philosophy is henceforth to conceive of itself, its tasks, and its future. If with respect to science there appears to be no intrinsic difficulty in formulating the thesis and in envisaging how a philosophy convinced of the truth of the thesis could both argue for it and proceed from it, this is not clearly so for poetry or literature, where continuity and the promise of a genuinely poetic or literary philosophy would seem to risk the jettisoning of method, of argument, and of the requirements and responsibilities proper to both. And it could quite easily be thought to lead to the production of texts and to a style of writing which simply cannot be recognized as philosophy by those less confident that such an aspiration is advisable or even intelligible. Ironically these critics might well be quite content with such texts were they to be simply presented as literary and were their author's assertion that whatever is going on in them is no longer philosophy to be taken as a straightforward biographical or institutional fact. The problem arises from the refusal to leave it at this, from the author's still holding that in some sense philosophy is no longer possible and that an encounter with literature or poetry, freed from the assumptions which traditionally define the relations between philosophy and literature or poetry, is able either to justify and to demonstrate this impossibility (and here one might be tempted to insert the name of DERRIDA – Article 50) or to provide the means for a "post-philosophical" or poetic thinking (and here the name might be that of HEIDEGGER – Article 18).

An obvious and perfectly feasible move would be to retrieve Heidegger and Derrida from such a summary. To show how the notion of aspiration and the presumption of continuity fail to do justice to the manner in which literature or poetry becomes an issue for them. Yet the rescue could never be complete, for, in different ways, they do want to endorse the drastic consequences for philosophy of an encounter with a writing or language from which it has almost always sought to keep its distance and against which it has frequently defined itself. And these consequences do raise urgent and unsettling questions concerning the responsibilities and requirements of a thinking whose traditional definition no longer sustains or directs it but which nevertheless must continue.

A careful and sympathetic reader will quickly see what is inadequate in the various summaries of Derrida and Heidegger provided by commentators such as Rorty and Habermas. He or she will be able to point out that, again in different ways, Heidegger's and Derrida's texts on poetry or literature and on the end or the closure of philosophy do not simply exempt themselves from the criteria traditionally attendant upon philosophical writing and argument. To the extent that there is exemption there is also a philosophical discussion, albeit sometimes implicit, of those criteria to be called into question. He or she will also be able to show how Heidegger, in always binding "poetic thinking" to an ambiguous *not yet* and so to the promise of a future on which we must learn to wait without that future's being given to us as the object of expectation, is also always bound critically to the philosophy which we can, on his terms, *no longer* unproblematically endorse. We cannot then easily apply the name "poetic thinking" to Heidegger's own work, not even to that part of his work in which he introduces the name. With Derrida, our friendly reader will perhaps wish to distinguish the more philosophical texts and essays from the more literary ones, treating the latter as of the order of experiments, attempts at developing an encounter between philosophy and literature but not for the sake of a new genre or a synthesis, nor for the sake of a writing that could somehow do without the more philosophical arguments and readings. More subtly, avoiding any overt use of this unsatisfactory distinction, he or she will indicate what in the formally less philosophical works already prevents their subsumption under a new genre or synthesis, for example the challenge (the always philosophical challenge) to *formal* or generic identification as such.

A partial, although not unviolent, retrieving of Heidegger and Derrida for philosophy is thus always possible and indeed sometimes necessary, but, in its violence, what it leaves unsaid is just the extent to which, like the poetic and literary works and language which so intrigue them, they do want to have produced a writing which disturbs philosophy and in which philosophy can be seen or heard to be disturbed, and a part of that disturbance will be the minimal sense in which that writing's proximity to philosophy can only be registered in and by philosophy as *not quite* or *no longer* philosophy. The danger or temptation here is that everything that was supposed to attest to the significance of literature and poetry, their importance despite a history of attempted disavowals for and from philosophy, tends once again to a reduction of literature and poetry, a reduction to just this debate, this interminable indicting and undermining of a tradition: philosophy, metaphysics, the thought which cannot receive the gift it is now nonetheless supposed to think is a gift.

It is hard not to see Blanchot's work as an example of just such a writing, just such a disturbance, and so as an argument for and a product of the debate which calls for such writing and disturbance; so exemplary in fact that it can seem impossible to think of Blanchot's work in relation to philosophy except within the parameters of this debate. Either we refer to Blanchot's project, itself determined as a literary affair, or we refer that project to the debate, affirming the relentless effect literature has on philosophy. In this latter context, a retrieval of Blanchot for philosophy will produce a text and an argument closely aligned with Derrida's, and this is for some the best way of interpreting both Blanchot's critical project (as on the way to deconstruction) and his "fragmentary" works (exemplary marginal writings). The poem, a fragmentary gift to thought that thinking cannot receive, and so a ruinous gift, something which resists each and any interpretation or reading, even one that would reify it as the unreceivable: here, surely, we have a quintessential Blanchot*ian* reflection, one that prohibits any theoretical appropriation of it, characterizing a type of writing whose relentless remarking of what in literature remains alien to the critical philosophical or theoretical endeavor also removes itself from the domains of each. How to respond? Admiration or despair; any commentary or counterstatement falls foul of the simple phrase itself. Even to say paradox here will not suffice; for paradox too is a figure and its writing a genre, a type of utterance with which one knows one cannot live in theory but which this knowledge nonetheless accepts, and so lives with, as a challenge to the theory. If it is true that only a logician cannot live with a paradox it is surely equally true that only a logician can live with a paradox. Anything we (we philosophers) say here will fall short of the matter, and the phrase itself gains currency to the extent that it resists these sayings, bequeathing us an interminable and infuriating non-dialogue where if a certain "other" and "unknowable" are reputedly at stake it seems set to be the most predictable of returns, and exchange to infinity.

But why should we have begun to take seriously a statement (a gift to thought that thinking cannot receive) whose reduction to a simple and logically inadequate paradoxicality is only refused us by appeal to some sort of decree? If one has to stop somewhere, here one searches in vain for a reason as to why we need ever have begun. And so, why as a philosopher begin to read Blanchot? Already one knows how the interminable debate is to continue. *As* a philosopher one cannot read, just that. To read as a philosopher is either a contradiction in terms or an indication that "as a philosopher" can only denote one of the ways in which one reads, a way which is judged to have been called into question by this sort of text. However subtly evasive and however knowing about their inability to work as contributions to a debate, Blanchot's texts seem to have won for themselves an extraordinary invulnerability. How can this not be the last word, theirs and ours?

In what follows I want to look at one of the essays from *La Part du feu* (*The Work of Fire*), an essay entitled "The Language of Fiction," in an attempt to reconsider and to resituate this thematics of failure and inability which underpins the use of terms such as "passivity" and "fragmentary." To ask whether Blanchot's contention that poetic and literary language is essentially impoverished does not merit a more deliberate and, dare one say it, traditional philosophical commentary and appreciation. The first two sentences can be read as implicitly touching on issues and objections concerning the privileging of poetry both in the history of the philosophy of art and in Hegel's and Heidegger's responses to that history. This is not, however, to be our focus.

> It is generally acknowledged that the words of a poem do not play the same role or maintain (*entretenir*) the same relationships as those of ordinary language. But a narrative written in the simplest prose already suggests an important change in the nature of language. (p. 74)

For Blanchot, talk of a change in the nature of language cannot be restricted to a consideration solely of poetry or poetic language. Such change is already under way in the most familiar of narratives and fictions. This is not to say that Blanchot encourages the collapsing or blurring of distinctions between poetry and narrative fiction, rather that such distinctions are not to be sustained either by appealing to the poetic possibilities of language or by arguing that these possibilities and the possibility of poetry itself disclose the inherent richness of language, a richness, and so a resource, that philosophy is prone to overlook or denigrate. Nothing simply follows from the fact of there being poetry. Likewise, nothing simply follows from philosophy's traditional unease with poetic language, nor from its frequent attempts to exclude consideration of such language from a theory of meaning or truth. Already at work in the essays of *The Work of Fire* is the thought that the essence of literary and poetic language has everything to do with what it cannot achieve, with its commitment to an absence allowing of no philosophical or conceptual recuperation; and if, to begin with, the distinction between poetic and other literary language is not to be upheld, even to the extent of letting Mallarmé's account of poetic naming ("I say: a flower") encompass every fictional utterance ("I say: X", where X is fictional), the book, in the closing pages of "Literature and the Right to Death," will end with an attempt to reconsider the differences between poetry and prose.

Blanchot contrasts a reading of the sentence "The head clerk called" as a memo from my secretary with a reading of the same sentence in Kafka's novel *The Castle*. With the former, everything is in place and even if there may be ambiguity or uncertainty here, as in a mistake or misunderstanding, it is received against an unambiguous and certain background. I know what it is to receive this sort of message. I know as an employee. The message works because the context in which it circulates and of which it is always able to remind and reassure me is inexhaustible and inexhaustibly real. "My knowledge is, in a way, infinite." With the latter,

> I am not only infinitely ignorant of all that is happening in the world being evoked, but this ignorance is part of the nature of that world, from the moment when, as an object of a narrative, it is presented as an unreal world, with which I come into contact by reading, not by my ability to live. There is nothing poorer than such a universe. What is this head clerk? Even if he were described to me in detail, as he later is, even if I entered perfectly into the whole mechanism of the Castle's administration, I would still be more or less aware of the little that I know, for this poverty is the essence of fiction, which is to make present to me that which makes it unreal; it is accessible to reading alone, inaccessible to my existence.   (p. 75)

The language in and of my everyday existence is used up by that existence; and any theory of that language will both contain an account of this use, a theory of signs and signification, and contribute to an account of this existence, a general and (in the broadest sense) hermeneutic ontology for and from which there is always understanding. Although Blanchot frequently alludes to an Hegelian account of naming and meaning, at least proposing that names acquire their meanings by virtue of a dialectics of presence and absence, appearance and disappearance, and although the references here to everyday existence bring to mind a quasi-instrumentalist account of language as we perhaps initially find it in *Being and Time*, it is important to note that Blanchot deliberately does not outline a specific theory of (everyday or ordinary) language, preferring to leave us with a description with which virtually any theory can be made consistent, the important element

309

being language's (the word's) propensity to disappear before that to which a theory would append it: a thing, a referent, a meaning, a context of use. Here the reality embraces both real and ideal entities, and the contrast is between that language which can and that which cannot be theorized, between a language one can and a language (the language of fiction) one cannot speak. But this is to move too quickly.

In both sentences or both occurrences of the sentence, "the head clerk" serves as a name. In the memo, to serve as a name is, Blanchot says, to serve as a label and thus as something which disappears in its being appended to what it labels. To think of the name in the memo, to wonder about it as a name, is to bring to mind what need not be brought to mind in the usual course of reading a memo, that is the fact that the name can be described as a label. But to think of the name in the novel, to wonder about it as a name, is to run up against a difficulty. In the novel, the name cannot acquire its meaning from being a label but rather exists "as a verbal entity." It is the verbality of the name which makes the word present as a name in a way names are not present in their everyday use. A certain linguistic Platonism holds true in our dealings with everyday language, for it is a matter, to an extent, of communicating as though without words, of making oneself understood without drawing attention to the means by which we do so. In fiction, the name "the head clerk" cannot make the head clerk present. Not simply because there is no head clerk, it might happen that I look up from the memo puzzled because there is no head clerk, but rather that even when I know that, in the novel, there is a head clerk what I know is wholly dependent upon this name "the head clerk." Without this and all the other names and sentences that tell of the world of the Castle and of K's attempts to do business with it, I would know nothing of that world, it being nothing apart from those names and sentences. In so far as the names and sentences of fiction are everything, they cannot function as names and sentences do in a world where their successful operation requires them to be virtually nothing. And if in fiction they are everything, there is a sense in which they cannot do or disclose anything. Language appears, is present, in literature, and, when I am gripped by a story, I am gripped by nothing but language.

> We like to say of a reading that it holds us; the expression answers to (the radical transformation language undergoes in the story): the reader is in fact held by the things of fiction that he grasps, given by the words; like their own characteristics, he holds on to them, with the feeling of being enclosed, captive, feverishly withdrawn from the world, to the point of experiencing language as the key to a universe of bewitchment and fascination where nothing of what he lives is found. (p. 78)

When language appears, as it does in fiction, the world disappears.

But it is not always or only a matter of being lost in a story. Fictions surely have a use too, an account of which would not only yield a theory of fiction but also, in binding fictional discourse to a function or goal, would return our talk of fiction to talk of the world. Note that this theory of fiction would however not be a theory of the language of fiction. Rather, it would stipulate that the question of the use of that

310

language take precedence over the question of language itself. Blanchot concedes that our dealings with stories are not always to be described in terms of fascination. The unreal world of the fiction, that of which the language tells, is often thought of as itself possessing or representing a meaning. Blanchot suggests three ways in which this further meaning – a meaning proper to the story rather than to any of its components – is understood and theorized. The terms Blanchot adopts here carry so much critical and philosophical baggage, and more so now than they did 50 years ago, that the ease with which they are re-introduced by me may seem embarrassing. Nevertheless they serve a purpose and advance the argument. First, *allegory*, which enables us to think of the story in relation to an idea: the presence of the idea, the success of the allegory, is won at the expense of the disappearance of the story, a disappearance which reunites the language of the story with the language of the world. Secondly, *myth*, which, unlike allegory, is not to be construed in terms of a sign and signification: here it is more a matter of "an actual presence between the beings of fiction and their meaning" (p. 83). The story does not disappear but, in its appearance, is deemed meaningful. The meaning of the story is nothing apart from the story but it is the story considered as a thing in the world. Here, we might say, the ignorance which attaches to fictionality, the nothing I can really be said to know about the world of the story, acquires a positive value. As mythic, the story makes a certain sort of thinking possible, a thinking with stories, with fiction, and – given the deliberate refusal to sustain an uncritical or simply generic distinction – a poetic thinking. "[L]iterature can create an experience that, illusory or not, appears as a means of discovery and an effort not to express what one knows but to experience what one does not know" (p. 83). As an allegory, the story is subordinated to the idea it is said to signify. As a myth, the story itself functions as a tool. In each guise, fiction is accommodated in and by a theory: in the first instance, a theory of signs, a theory of meaning; in the second instance, an ontology. But Blanchot's third term, he wants to claim, cannot be so accommodated.

A *symbol* is not an allegory. In Blanchot's words "its task is not to signify a particular idea by a determined fiction: the symbolic meaning can only be a global meaning" (p. 83). Not a meaning which returns the story to the world but "the meaning of the world in its entirety." Not a meaning which returns the language of fiction to the language of existence but "the meaning of existence in its entirety." In this third moment, there is no determinate meaning or idea whose sign the story can become. The story persists in and with the sense of its meaning more than it says, of there being more to it than the characters, descriptions, and events it recounts, but it is a surplus that no particular meaning can satisfy. As such, the story although still inscribed within talk of meaning can never be said to signify *this* or *that*. In reading a story we can have the sense that everything is meaningful and that everything means something, but that nothing in particular means anything. Thought in terms of this total meaning, that is thought in terms of the symbol, fiction would seem to find its finest justification, namely as an attempt to justify the world and existence by binding them to their meaning. If fiction is more than what appears on the page, the surplus intensifies the unreality of fiction, making of it the

311

fiction of another meaning, a greater and further meaning, a meaning beyond all regional and particular meanings. In its third guise, fiction is always looking to disappear, but the meaning before which it would disappear is so vague and so abstract it can never be given. The disappearance for which a symbolic literature waits is thus indefinitely postponed and logically unrealizable. On Blanchot's reading, the notion of the symbol contains an impossible or contradictory demand. It instructs the reader to look elsewhere when there is nowhere else to look and to understand something more when there is nothing more to understand.

With a precision and an awareness of a proximity to Hegel that will come to the fore in "Literature and the Right to Death" and *The Space of Literature*, Blanchot's choice of the words "symbol" and "symbolic" intentionally evoke and repeat Hegel's use of the term as a name for one of the three forms of art. The only name that is not an historical category, it indicates the beginnings of art, a beginning bound to fail because in the symbol the spiritual and material components can never be reconciled. The symbolic work, in always having to point away from itself, is never able to grasp itself as a complete entity, and the impossibility of closure here prevents even the most basic grasp of what art is as an activity and an historical reality. Without the symbol and the symbolic there will not have been art (fine [beautiful] art) in the sense required by aesthetics and recognized by history, but as the symbol and the symbolic, the work can never cohere as the work *of* art and so can neither occur historically nor be thematized by a philosophy of art.[3] Although the direct reference is to Hegel's *Aesthetics*, the implications of Blanchot's appropriation of the term (the symbol, the symbolic) touches just as much on the treatment of death in the *Phenomenology*. Blanchot wants to retrieve these thoughts of the failure of the symbolic and the impossibility of closure from the Hegelian narrative in which the dilemma or contradiction embodied by them is superseded. He wants to confront this Hegelianism with an art which continues and must continue to fail. For Hegel, the abstraction of the thought of a meaning to and beyond existence must give way to the thought of the absence of such a meaning and such a beyond, the thought of an existence whose limit is death. This facing up to the impossibility of a beyond does not go unrewarded and the thinking capable of it derives from that thought not a meaning beyond death but the meaning *of* death, death as meaningful.

Blanchot encourages us to compare this recuperation of meaning from out of its negation, the slow step of the Hegelian advance, with a reading of the example of Kafka and the treatment of the impossibility of death in Kafka's sometimes symbolic fiction. If Hegel would take us from the thought of a beyond and an impossible transcendence, first to the denial of that beyond and an awareness of its impossibility, and secondly, to the thought of a genuine progression, a reading of Kafka will only ever take us from the thought of that fiction in relation to a meaning which lies beyond it, first to a realization of the impossibility of that beyond, and secondly, back to the fiction itself and to what it says about death and the interminable; "There is no actual death in Kafka, or, more exactly, there is never an end" (p. 87).

A whole variety of topics and trajectories opens up or ought to open up here, amongst them the idea of the impossibility of death and the theme of the interminable, Blanchot's inspired recollection of the "bad infinite." Blanchot's relations with

Hegel and Kafka, explicitly introduced and formulated for the first time in *The Work of Fire*, are from now on to inform all his writing. Crucially, it is Kafka's name which provides the insight and accompanies the thought that to write is to move from the first to the third person, the thesis *The Space of Literature* is subsequently said to have demonstrated, and it is Kafka who is said to teach us that the narrative voice is neutral, *le neutre* being one of the key terms in the complex vocabulary Blanchot develops in and beyond *The Infinite Conversation*. In *The Writing of the Disaster*, Blanchot writes of "what Kafka gives us – the gift we do not receive," which gift is "a sort of battle (*combat*) through literature for literature" (p. 141). But if this discussion of fictional language as symbolic already begins to instruct us as to how to read this later formulation it also takes us to the heart of the question as to how philosophy and a philosophical account of language are to deal with the fictionality of fiction.

Concerning Kafka and his exemplary novel, Blanchot writes:

> One can certainly interpret the odyssey of K. One can recognise in him the being who left his homeland, as one leaves existence, and who, with the very means that he used to live, tries to get himself accepted by death. K. was called, and it is quite true that death seems a call; but it is also true that to answer this call is to betray it, to make something real and true of death. All his efforts to reach the Castle are marked with this contradiction: if he strives, struggles, desires, he reveals always more existence; while if he remains passive, he misses what he aims for, death being death only when one makes it one's own . . .   (p. 82)

K's curious exile between the village and the Castle and between a past life and a future in the service of the Castle, an exile provoked by his being called into that service, is endless. Nothing can terminate it, or rather, what could terminate it (death, final access to the Castle) is never allowed to become a possibility for K. Well, then, let us make of this endless quest for meaningful death or meaningful employment something representative, an image, perhaps, "of the unhappiness of existence that cannot be grasped as existence because it cannot be found as the end of existence." Let Kafka's story stand for a certain existential predicament. Indeed it seems to demand this sort of interpretation. It is this demand, the demand on the reader that reading be conflated with existing, which so puzzles Blanchot and which he spends so long trying to unpack. For the content of Kafka's novel prohibits our thinking of it as either allegory or myth and yet it is as allegory or myth that we think of it when we assume that it produces or stands in a relation to something, some *thing* it represents or which it serves as an image. It is not simply or solely that a fiction that would tell of the endlessness of a quest for meaning cannot tell of it in the manner of an allegory or myth, rather that the endlessness is, of necessity, a literary affair, a fiction. What we have is a symbol in which the symbolic is symbolized, a fiction in which the fictionality of fiction comes to the fore. Any attempt at likening K's condition to ours, detecting in it the fictionalizing and aestheticizing of the quest that is a life, forgets the fictionality of K and his condition and so presents as a determinate meaning what can never be so determined.

> So one must plunge the interpretation back into the heart of the story, lose it there and lose it from view, and grasp again the movement of fiction whose details assert only themselves. The inn, the peasants with their stubborn, frustrated faces, the iced light of the snow, Klamm's pince-nez, the pools of beer in which Frieda and K. roll – that is what matters, that is what one must experience to enter into the life of the symbol. (p. 83)

The novel which tells of K's attenuated efforts to find significance in some of these details would seem to tempt the reader at many points to identify his predicament as reader with K's, and even to resist this temptation is perhaps to find in the subsequent disillusion a further point of contact. We, *like K,* are frustrated, etc. But to speak of K's "predicament," or "condition," as though it were a means of lifting something from this story so as to diagnose it or set it to work diagnostically, is already to say too much. K is frustrated as much by his inability to be frustrated as he is by his inability to get through or to receive an answer. The predicament or condition is a life in which no predicament or condition is established, and very quickly, almost from the first, there is little that is quest-like about K's "quest." The novel itself tells against the inclination to introduce or to fall back upon such descriptions as "frustration," "predicament," "condition," "quest," each of which, insofar as it is applicable to the novel, is exacerbated by its being, in the novel, endlessly unproductive and unproductive above all of a diagnosable frustration, predicament, condition, and quest. Kafka has left us with the strangest of phenomena, an unfinished book which closes in on itself and only speaks to and of itself, but *symbolically.* This is no theoretically or aesthetically comforting turn (in)to the autonomy or self-sufficiency of the literary work. In the terms in which this essay of Blanchot's puts it, to begin reading Kafka's fiction and to ask about its status, its being, as fiction is never to be able to have done either with it or with that question, just as to treat the symbolic as symbolic is to be confined to an experience of fiction which never enables one to reunite the language of fiction with the language of the world. If the symbol would attempt just such a reconciliation and in the most impressive fashion, it is, as Blanchot and Hegel both aver, bound to fail. Blanchot however adds that in order to move away from this failure, judging it to be inessential to art and to history, one needs to criticize it for being something it isn't and something it never claimed to be, as though, for example, it were a fiction that thought, along with so many of its philosophical readers, that it was something other than a fiction (an allegory, a myth, a tool, a "useful" fiction) rather than a fiction that could be read as demonstrating . . . – and yet what verb could ever suffice here, this being virtually the whole issue, and will not Blanchot's scrutiny always be directed onto each and any instance or candidate ("demonstrates," "shows," "expresses," etc.) and onto the phenomenology of the work it carries with it? – . . . not "demonstrating," then, but a fiction that could be read *so as to let us* say something about how fiction *as* fiction has always sought unsuccessfully to be something other than fiction. And in this failure Blanchot will begin to detect a clue as to what it is that separates literary language from any other, a clue as to the essence of fiction, the literary *thing* itself.

To conclude, albeit far too succinctly – each of the concluding paragraphs would require at the very least its own separate paper and argument.

There are perhaps two main ways in which poetry and literature, poetic and literary language, become an issue for contemporary philosophy. On the one hand, as a problem posed to the attempt to develop a logical theory of truth or meaning, we might expect to encounter questions as to the status of fictional names and entities, of expressions seemingly with sense but without reference and so without truth value. Here too fictions might be likened to, and accepted as analogous with, a sort of counterfactual reasoning, and the topic of fiction aligned with that of possible worlds. It is interesting that, whatever the particular focus, Blanchot's account of allegory would nevertheless serve to encompass them all. To the extent that an account of fiction is to be given in and by a theory of meaning or implied by a definition of meaning, the language of fiction is restored to the language of the world, restored either as a particular way of using the language of the world or in its being, like that language reducible or subordinatable to a theory of ideal entities (meanings, propositions).

On the other hand, for a philosophy committed to the view that such theorizing mistakenly ascribes a primary and foundational reality to the theoretical entity, poetic and fictional discourse can stand as evidence of a pre-logical capacity in language just as a renewed ontology can provide access to the pre-theoretical world of meaningful activity. We have already noted Blanchot's response to the view which sees in poetry both a possibility for a thought no longer uncritically in thrall to logic and evidence of the unfathomable richness of language. Note that such a view would also have to tie in with what Blanchot says about myth. Blanchot in this early essay not only shows how philosophy in ostensibly addressing fiction employs a twofold account of fiction, as allegory and as myth, which enables it to keep the question of fiction as such at bay, but also produces a reading of Kafka in which that question, now construed as a question of the symbol, is experienced as unavoidable.

## Notes

1   Or *almost* suggests? See "The 'sacred' speech of Hölderlin," in *The Work of Fire*; and P. Davies, "A linear narrative?" in *Philosopher's Poets*, ed. D. Wood. For a revised and extended account see chapter 1 of P. Davies, *Experience and Distance: Essays on Blanchot and Levinas* (forthcoming).

2   A reflection on the impossibility of the gift runs throughout *The Writing of the Disaster*. See, in particular, "Parole de fragment," in *L'Endurance de la pensée*.

3   It would be interesting in this connection to contrast Blanchot's appropriation of the term "symbol," and the partial commentary on Hegel it implies, with Paul de Man's reading of the term in his essay "Sign and symbol in Hegel's *Aesthetics*" (*Critical Inquiry*, 8, Summer 1982) and with his reworking of the term "allegory" both in that essay and elsewhere. Given what is to be said about the distinction between existing and reading, that is, Blanchot's distinction, and what has been said about our reluctance simply to present Blanchot's essays as stages on the way to deconstructive reading, it should be clear just how fruitful and intriguing a comparative study of Blanchot and de Man might be.

## Writings

Blanchot, M.: *The Gaze of Orpheus*, tr. L. Davis (Barrytown, NY: Station Hill Press, 1981).

——: *The Siren's Song*, ed. G. Josipovici, tr. S. Rabinovitch (Brighton: Harvester, 1982).

——: *The Space of Literature*, tr. A. Smock (Lincoln, NB: University of Nebraska Press, 1982).

——: *The Writing of the Disaster*, tr. A. Smock (Lincoln, NB: University of Nebraska Press, 1986).

——: *The Step (Not) Beyond*, tr. L. Nelson (New York: SUNY Press, 1992).

——: *The Infinite Conversation*, tr. S. Hanson (Minneapolis, MN: University of Minnesota Press, 1993).

——: *The Blanchot Reader*, ed. M. Holland (Oxford: Blackwell, 1995).

——: *The Work of Fire* (Berkeley, CA: Stanford University Press, 1995).

## References and further reading

Davies, P.: "A fine risk: reading Blanchot reading Levinas." In *Re-Reading Levinas*, ed. R. Bernasconi and S. Critchley (Bloomington, IN: Indiana University Press, 1991).

Derrida, J.: "Living on: border lines." In *Deconstruction and Criticism*, ed. H. Bloom (New York: Continuum, 1979).

——: "The law of genre." In *Acts of Literature*, ed. D. Attridge (London: Routledge, 1992).

Gill, C.(ed.): *Blanchot and the Demand of Writing* (London: Routledge, 1996).

Levinas, E.: *On Maurice Blanchot*, together with *Proper Names* (London: Athlone, 1996).

Warminski, A: "Dreadful reading: Blanchot on Hegel." In *Readings in Interpretation* (Minneapolis, MN: University of Minnesota Press, 1987).

# PART V

# RELIGION WITHOUT THE LIMITS OF REASON

# 26

# Rosenzweig

## PAUL MENDES-FLOHR

Franz Rosenzweig (1886–1929) was a German-Jewish philosopher who became the focus of a renaissance of Jewish religious life and thought in Weimar Germany. Born into a highly assimilated Jewish family in Cassel, Germany, Rosenzweig affirmed Jewish religious faith in the midst of a philosophical and existential crisis. As a student, he was initially drawn to the neo-Hegelianism popular in German academic circles during the first decade of the twentieth century. Although he would write his doctoral dissertation on Hegel – later published with the support of the Heidelberg Academy of Sciences, *Hegel und der Staat* (1920, 2 vols) – Rosenzweig slowly lost his conviction that the dialectical providence of history would assure the ultimate convergence of truth and existence. Already in the autumn of 1910, when he was completing his dissertation under the supervision of Friedrich Meinecke, he questioned Hegel's ascription of an ontological status to history. History is not the unfolding of Being, he wrote to a friend, rather it is but the discrete acts of men. "We see God in every ethical event, but not in one complete Whole, not in history." Indeed, history, which takes shape in the phenomenal world, cannot serve as a vessel for divinity. "Every human act becomes sinful as it enters history"; although the actors may have intended otherwise, the morality of an act is neutralized by the material world of necessity. We are hence, Rosenzweig reasoned, left with only one possible conclusion: God redeems humanity not through history but – "es bleibt nicht anders übrig" – through religion (*Briefe*, vol. 1, pp. 111–13).

This was not a statement of faith, however. It was a philosophical proposition, a logical deduction. Rosenzweig would adopt religious faith only three years later. This decision was made within the context of a circle of friends who from similar premises had already taken the step toward religious faith by embracing a passionate Christianity. Unlike his friends (who also happened to be of Jewish provenance), Rosenzweig wanted to enter the Church not as a pagan but as a Jew, as a conscious, if not a believing Jew. Thus while preparing for baptism, he waited several months for the occasion of the Jewish high holidays, in which he would participate before his conversion. Utterly dissatisfied with the New Year's services of his parents' liberal synagogue in Cassel, he decided to go to Berlin and attend a traditional synagogue for the Day of Atonement. Emerging from the day-long fast and prayer, he reversed his decision. He wrote to a friend who was to serve as his godfather at the baptismal font: "I must tell you something that will grieve you and may at first appear incomprehensible to you. After prolonged, and I believe thorough self-examination, I have reversed my decision. Conversion no longer seems necessary to me, and, therefore, being what I am, no longer possible, I will remain a Jew" (*Briefe*, vol. 1, pp. 132f). It was not necessary, as he and his friends had assumed, to go beyond the synagogue to find the possibility of a living faith, which they had defined as *Offenbarungsglaube*, an affirmation of divine revelation as an historical fact and existential possibility. Rosenzweig had discovered that Judaism was not a spiritually desiccated religion, for as he had apparently witnessed on that Day of Atonement, it – at least in its traditional form – still allowed for genuine expressions of faith.

Scholars debate whether or not this observation was prompted by an actual religious experience. Significantly, even if he had had such an experience, Rosenzweig never evoked it as the basis of his religious philosophy. Indeed, his magnum opus, *The Star of Redemption* (*Der Stern der Erlösung*, 1921), makes no appeal to personal religious experience. Rather he presents faith as a specific cognitive orientation shared by a given liturgical community – the Church and the Synagogue – and articulated through the biblical categories of Creation, Revelation, and Redemption. Rosenzweig places faith so understood into a strategic alliance with philosophy – philosophy as conceived by German Idealism modified by a realization of the existential reality of each and every individual. Thus, as a philosophical project, *The Star* – written in the trenches of World War I – has as its central task to establish a new relationship between faith and reason, which would respect the distinctive integrity of each while acknowledging their mutual dependency.

God's truth, Rosenzweig accordingly declares in *The Star*, "wants to be entreated with both hands. It will not deny itself to him who calls upon it with the double prayer of the believer and the disbeliever" (Rosenzweig 1970 [1921], p. 297). The contrasting perspectives of the theologian and the philosopher, he contended, must "unite," and fraternally conjoin their endeavors to illuminate truth. This envisioned cooperation between theology and philosophy will lead to a radically new conception of theological and philosophical activity, to what Rosenzweig hailed as a "new theological rationalism" (p. 104). Thus, the alliance of these formerly antagonistic disciplines will generate a new type of thinker, "situated between theology and philosophy" (p. 106). God's truth, according to Rosenzweig, is disclosed to the individual who embodies within himself the graced tension between belief and disbelief. For "it is the same man, disbelieving child of the world and believing child of God in one, who comes with dual pleas and must stand with dual thanks before Him who gives of his wisdom" (p. 297).

This union of faith and reason emerges from Rosenzweig's conviction that theology and philosophy do not just complement one another but have, in fact, an intrinsic need for one another. "The theologian whom philosophy requires for the sake of its scientific status is himself a theologian who requires philosophy for the sake of his integrity" (p. 106). This cooperation, Rosenzweig avers, is objectively and dialectically necessary, and it serves to break the circle of distrust that has prevailed in Western culture between theology and philosophy in which, at best, either of the two was assigned an ancillary role in the service of the other – and at worst, one regarded the other with indifference and even contempt.

Rosenzweig acknowledges that in the past an occasional "truce" of sorts existed

320

between "the two hostile powers" (p. 6). With Tertullian the truth of revelation was reverentially held to be inaccessible to philosophy: *credo quia absurdum*; and with Anselm philosophy lent the ultimate confirmation to the claims of revelation: *credo ut intelligam*. Against Tertullian's assumed incommensurability of faith and knowledge, philosophy's pride rebelled, unwilling to "bear the thought" (ibid.), as Rosenzweig puts it, of a door it couldn't unlock. And faith, refusing to accept the decree that it was but one truth among others, would rebel against what it deemed to be Anselm's cavalier reconciliation of the claims of revelation and reason. In modern times, Hegel's promise to resolve the conflict also proved abortive. What Hegel proposed, Rosenzweig succinctly remarks, "was neither separation nor concord, but an intimate relationship" (ibid.) – a relationship to be borne by what Hegel perceived to be a fundamental homology between the law of thought, governed by philosophy, and the law of being initially assigned by divine revelation to the care of faith. As philosophy evolves with what Hegel asserted to be a dialectical necessity, however, it subsumes and ever refines the revealed teachings of religious faith. With the completion of history's dialectical journey, the law of thought and the law of being – the truths of Reason and Revelation – are now, so taught Hegel, nestled in the mature bosom of philosophy, "the truth content of faith" has been absorbed or more precisely *"aufgehoben"* into reason (p. 104). But, as Rosenzweig observes with reference to the existential protest of Kierkegaard, Hegel's solution also proved illusory. From the vantage point of the anguished consciousness of his finitude, Kierkegaard contested Hegel's "inclusion" of revelation in the All – or Universal Truth – of philosophy. Kierkegaard insisted, according to Rosenzweig, that genuine religious faith registers the individual's existential need for redemption and God's love, and that hence faith cannot accept Hegel's view that philosophy "fulfills what was promised in revelation" (p. 7). Rosenzweig elaborates Kierkegaard's protest, and in fact reverses Hegel's claim, boldly contending that divine revelation is the fulfillment of the promise of philosophy. In appealing to an image somewhat suprising for one who wished to reaffirm the dignity of Judaism, Rosenzweig states this proposition epigrammatically: "Philosophy is the Old Testament of theology" (p. 108). Philosophy adumbrates, or more correctly, prophesies faith – experience celebrated by theology.

Rosenzweig's call for a new relationship between philosophy and theology is based on an analysis of the historical situation of theology and philosophy, respectively. The development of philosophy and theology, as Rosenzweig understands it, has led them both to a cul-de-sac from which they could emerge only with the assistance of each other. Grounded in an assumed homology of reason and being, philosophy has logically exhausted its possibilities with Hegel's panlogism. To philosophize *post Hegel mortuum*, the philosopher is dialectically compelled to find an Archimedian footing outside of the "cognitive All," which knew no contingent, autonomous facts. This vantage point beyond the imperious purview of reason is found when the philosopher "in the utter singularity of his individuality . . . [steps] out of the world which knew itself as the conceivable world, out of the All of philosophy" (p. 10). But the *Standspunkts-Philosophen* – as Rosenzweig calls this new, bold breed – perforce court the danger of unmitigated subjectivism which

321

would permit them only to utter aphorisms, implicitly denying their vocation as philosophers to obtain a systematic, coherent knowledge of reality. Similarly, since the early nineteenth century, theology – inspired by the likes of Friedrich Schleiermacher and Albrecht Ritschl – has steadily retreated inward, seeking sanctuary in the personal experience of God and His will. Concomitant with this turn inward, Rosenzweig observed, is an abandonment of the objective authority of faith embodied in tradition and doctrine.

Ensconced in the realm of inner experience, theology like philosophy suffers from subjectivity; it is bereft of a compelling and objective reference to truth. Thus for the sake of the "integrity" of its founding experience, theology requires philosophy, to which Rosenzweig assigns the "task" of restoring the *auctoritas* of religious faith. Hence, "what was for philosophy a demand in the interest of objectivity, will turn out to be a demand in the interest of subjectivity for theology" (p. 106). Subjective religious experience – celebrated by Ritschl as "revelation" – is but self-authenticating and hence cognitively vacuous; to have the authority of truth it requires an objective, ontic status. The requisite objectivity, however, cannot be attained by negating the subjective "point of departure," which is now shared by both theology and philosophy. Indeed, to remain beholden to subjectivity and, at the same time, attain objectivity is the challenge faced by both. But neither theology nor philosophy has the "resources" to attain this objectivity on its own.

For philosophy, Rosenzweig holds, the "bridge" between subjectivity, which it is to jealously maintain, and "the lucid clarity of infinite objectivity" is provided by the "theological concept of revelation" (p. 106). To be sure, this proposition entails a particular conception of revelation. For Rosenzweig it is a grievous distortion to regard revelation as purely a subjective, inner experience. Properly understood, he maintains, revelation is anchored in the concept – and faith experience – of Creation, the world at large in which God's providential Presence is manifest. "Creation in the full gravity of its substantiality has to be placed once more next to the experience of revelation" (p. 103). Testifying as it does to God's active relation to the facts of existence, Creation is the *arche* – the first principle – to which philosophers should direct their inquiry. "And precisely creation is now the gate through which philosophy enters into the house of theology" (ibid.)

The concept of creation, however, has been virtually banished from modern theology. Embarrassed by what Rosenzweig characterizes as a superficial view of natural law and science, "enlightened" theologians self-consciously placed a shroud of silence on the concept of creation, thereby relinquishing theology's claim to the objective world of fact and knowledge. By reconstructing the concept of creation philosophy restores to theology its epistemological patrimony and authority. Formerly, as noted, the authority of religious faith was constituted by tradition, the vessel of teachings and lore that bear witness to the founding "miracles" of the faith. As a cognate concept of creation, the concept of miracle likewise conflicts with modern sensibility and is accordingly ignored by the theologians of the era. Citing Goethe's maxim that "miracle is the favorite child of belief (Goethe, *Faust*, Pt 1, "Night"), Rosenzweig ironically asks whether genuine faith can exist without an affirmation of the concept of miracle (see Rosenzweig 1970 [1921], pp. 93–7).

Philosophy as understood by Rosenzweig discloses the miraculous dimension of existence *qua* creation; that is, it discerns in existence "signs" pointing to God's providential relation to all the discrete "factualities" of existence – the world and man. This operation of philosophy is the focus of Book One of *The Star*, in which Rosenzweig reconstructs our conception of existence based on a method derived from the positive philosophy of the late Schelling and Hermann Cohen's "Theory of Sources." *In nuce*, following Schelling he denies the identity of reason and being, and rejects the monistic thrust of classical philosophy by which the All of being – the universal truth of being – was subject to reason's commanding laws. From Schelling, Rosenzweig inherited the demand to preserve the priority of being over existence. The ultimate dimensions of the three basic "factualities" or "elements" of existence – the world, man, and God – that elude the grip of reason, Rosenzweig identifies by the prefix "meta," and accordingly speaks of the meta-logical, the meta-ethical, and the meta-physical. Denoting priority, "meta" underscores the fact that the essential, "hidden" dimensions of the world, man, and God cannot be subdued by reason and, *a fortiori*, neither can they be reduced to a rationalized conception of any of the other elements. Sundered from a monistic view of existence, the elements, in their essential dimension, seemingly remain isolated from each other.

At this juncture, Rosenzweig raises a paradox that will serve as the epistemological leitmotif at the heart of his philosophical meditations: While thought cannot comprehend the elements in their meta-dimensional reality, experience (*Erfahrung*) does. While the meta-dimensional reality of the elements – God, man, and the world – are not mediated by reason, they are accessible to experience and what Rosenzweig calls "sound common understanding" (*gesunder Menschenverstand*) (see Rosenzweig 1964) What we seek, Rosenzweig defiantly declares, "does not first require thought in order to be" (Rosenzweig 1970 [1921], p. 20). Put differently, "a 'real Nought' corresponds to the Nought of our [rational] knowledge" (p. 88). Although they elude reason, the Noughts of experience are real, they are not subjective fantasies; they are anchored in reality. Again echoing Schelling, Rosenzweig contends that these Noughts are ontologically "occult powers that are at work inside God, world and man before God, world and man are ever revealed" (ibid.) Hidden from knowledge, these occult, meta-dimensional powers nonetheless strive to be.

Rosenzweig now borrowed from Hermann Cohen what he regarded to be the radical methodological assumption – more radical, he noted, than Cohen himself suspected – that thought *per se* is not *the* source or principle providing existence with unity, with an inner coherence; thought rather achieves a unity *with* existence through what Cohen had called "correlation." Unity between thought and the irrefragable multiplicity of existence, according to Cohen, can only be obtained by acknowledging that the multiple facts of the phenomenal world are real. Cohen insisted that thought must begin with the given data of the world, and it does so by "negating" what is to be explained. This negation, however, is not to be construed as *nihil negativum*, a negating negation. Rather Cohen conceived of this negation as pushing the sense data back to nothingness in order to arrive at their "origin," or

323

pre-phenomenal, noumenal state. But this nothingness is not absolute nothing, for as we learn from infinitessimal calculus, zero is an infinite quantity. Indeed, as calculus teaches us, zero "spontaneously" generates positive numbers (or the phenomenally existent). The noumenal world, which by definition is beyond the net of reason, is the source or origin of the phenomenal order that does come under the tutelage of reason. Rosenzweig regarded this insight as constituting a radical break with Idealism, for with his "theory of origins," Cohen "took his stand in most decided opposition precisely to Hegel's founding of logic on the concept of Being, and thereby in turn to the whole philosophy into whose inheritance Hegel had come" (p. 25). Hence, "for the first time a philosopher who still considered himself an 'Idealist' . . . recognized and acknowledged that what confronted reasoning when it set out in order 'purely to create' was not Being but – Nought" (ibid.). That is, Cohen identified the Nought as that which cannot be known by reason, namely, the "meta" – dimensional reality of the elements which despite their imperviousness to reason are nonetheless encountered in experience.

Cohen's theory of origins also disclosed for Rosenzweig the dynamic of this encounter. In contradistinction to the "static" logic of "the old thinking" that had hitherto dominated philosophy, the "new thinking" inaugurated *inter alia* by Cohen is "dynamic." Moving from Nought to Aught, from nothing to something, and back again, there is a continuous movement of negation and affirmation, hiddenness and revelation, near and far. By virtue of this dynamic, thought – now guided not by the law of identity between reason and being, but by mathematical logic – and being are "correlated," a relation is established between thought and the "noumenal" world. So conceived, philosophy thus concurs with experience, or rather, as Rosenzweig emphasizes, "anticipates" experience. Thus, in contradistinction to Kant, for Rosenzweig *Erfahrung* is not confined to the phenomenal world. In consonance with this understanding of *Erfahrung*, Rosenzweig also ascribes a unique status to two decisive categories in the lexicon of idealism: *Sein* (being) is for him coterminous with the phenomenal realm – and thus, indeed, subject to the tutelage of reason – whereas *Dasein* (existence) denotes for him the fuller range of reality experienced by humans, although, to be sure, this experience lies beyond the epistemological grasp of reason.

The "anticipated" experience of a relation between the elemental factualities of existence – which, again, for Rosenzweig are God, man, and the world – is manifest in the life of faith. In the vocabulary of faith this threefold relation is known as Creation (that is, the relation obtaining between God and the world), revelation (the relation between God and man), and redemption (the relation, quickened by revelation, between man and the world). It may be said that the elements reach out of their "nothingness" to reveal themselves and to establish a relation with one another.

Philosophy, as pursued in Part One of *The Star*, then anticipates "the contents of faith," or more precisely, it establishes the "foundation" bearing the "preconditions" of the life of faith (p. 108). This foundation, Rosenzweig further illuminates by assigning each vector of the dynamic disclosed by Cohen's theory of origins with an arch-word (*Urwort*): "yea," "nea" and "and" – the latter conjunction denoting

324

the relation between the thinking mind and the "non-knowable" otherness of the elements of reality. These arch-words, Rosenzweig contends, constitute the silent, inaudible logical structure of language. Being mute they are but the language of logic, the "foundation and preconditions" of real speech; they are "the soundless realm of the Faustian Mothers," and thus bespeak "no more than the ideational possibilities" of real language.

> Real language, however, is the language of the terrestrial world. The language of logic is the prognostication of this real language of grammar. Reasoning is mute in each individual by himself, yet common to all, and thereby the basis of speaking which is common to all. What is mute in reasoning becomes audible in speech. But reasoning is not speaking, that is, it is not "silent" speaking but rather a speech prior to speaking, the secret foundation of speaking. Its arch-words are not real words but rather the promise of the real word.   (p. 109)

In the relation between the silent "logic of language and its grammar," its audible expression as a real language, Rosenzweig discerns, by analogy, the "link" between creation and revelation (ibid.).

Rosenzweig identifies the world disclosed by philosophy as the proto-cosmos, the world prior to its full illumination by the faith experience. This proto-cosmos, he suggests, may also be regarded as the world of creation – the world in which the relation between it and God remains mute because it has yet to be touched by the divine revelation to man that would render the relation manifest and artic-ulate. For although creation precedes revelation, our theological consciousness is born only with revelation. In retrospect, so to speak, the logic of the proto-cosmos serves to "predict" the unfolding drama of the "real world" of experience, a world rendered "visible" and "articulate" in faith. "Revelation is 'foreseen' in creation" (p. 108).

In discerning the "signs" of a relation between the basic factualities or elements of existence – God, the world, and man – philosophy serves a "prophetic" role of anticipating the "contents" of theology, the relation of Creation experienced in faith. In illuminating the miracle of creation pulsating in existence, philosophy thus restores the *auctoritas* of the faith experience of revelation. Once again miracle becomes the favorite child of faith.

Philosophy, however, only anticipates the experience of faith, the contents of theology. Only experience (*Erfahrung*) provides the necessary confirmation and verification (*Bewährung*) of philosophy's "prophecy." This seemingly circular argu-ment – the philosophical anticipation of the faith experience being subject to veri-fication by that experience – opens Rosenzweig to the charge of an arbitrariness indicative of a personal theological bias. This charge can only be properly evaluated when one considers that Rosenzweig's envisioned cooperation between philosophy and theology is a crucial building-block in the construction of a "system of philos-ophy," which he deemed *The Star of Redemption* to be. One must therefore recognize his system's special character. Crucial is the system's epistemological point of departure, namely, Rosenzweig's assumption of the non-identity of reason and existence. In contrast to the tradition extending "from Ionia to Jena," from the pre-

325

Socratics to Hegel, he argues that rather than reality conforming to the precepts of reason, thought must acknowledge that existence is prior to and unyieldingly independent of reason.

This calls for a New Thinking, which Rosenzweig introduces in Book Two of *The Star*. Epistemologically the New Thinking is grounded in the existential logic of speech, of the ordinary speech of genuine conversation which accepts – with what Schelling called "ecstatic" wonder – the unfolding facts of reality. Speech – speaking to someone who "has not merely ears . . . but also a mouth" ("Das neue Denken" (1925), in Rosenzweig, *Zweistromland*, p. 152) – may be said to be revelatory. Indeed, Rosenzweig regards speech as "the organon of revelation." Broadly defined, revelation thus becomes the overarching fact of experience. Divine revelation is now also rendered credible. Its confirmation and validation as a fact, however, is not individual and happenstance. Nowhere, as already noted, does Rosenzweig evoke a personal experience of revelation. The confirmed factuality of divine revelation is rather to be furnished by the religious congregation, which in its liturgical life proleptically experiences God's revelatory love.

The experience of revelation, Rosenzweig argues in Book Three of *The Star*, is not the privileged grace enjoyed by a blessed few but a universal promise, a promise as Rosenzweig understands it that is to be realized at the end of time – or more correctly, beyond time – in the moment of ultimate redemption. This promise gains the force of a concrete ontological possibility by virtue of the praying congregation, specifically the Synagogue and the Church. These spiritual "configurations" (*Gestalten*), which as Rosenzweig emphasizes are objective sociological entities, engender a "hyper-cosmos," anticipating the Kingdom to Come in which all of humanity will be graced by the Presence of God and will witness as a community the meeting of time and eternity.

One may accordingly speak of Rosenzweig's system as a System of Revelation. Upon the scaffold of this system Rosenzweig projects his vision of a new covenant between theology and philosophy. The philosophical cogency of this covenant ultimately lies in the testimony of the praying congregation and its proleptic experience of the *eschaton* in which the universal reality of God's revelatory love is manifest. The proleptic power of the liturgical community thus provides the ontological claims of revelation – and the system in general – with a dramatic verification. Rosenzweig, of course, realized that this type of verification was not genuinely philosophical. Indeed, his system hinges on a novel criterion of verification:

> Unlike the truth of the philosophers, which is not allowed to know anything but itself, this truth must be truth for someone. If it is to be one truth, it can be one only for the One, God. And that is why our truth must of necessity be manifold, and why "the" truth must be converted into "our" truth. Thus truth ceases to be what "is" true and becomes a verity that wants to be verified, realized in active life. This becomes the fundamental concept of this new theory of knowledge. . . . [It] leads over those [scientific, rational] truths for which a man is willing to pay, on to those that he cannot verify save at the cost of his life, and finally to those that cannot be verified until generations upon generations have given up their lives to that end. ("Das neue Denken," p. 159)

Perhaps it was this "Messianic theory of knowledge" (ibid.), which evokes the theme of martyrdom, that Rosenzweig had in mind when he said that although *The Star of Redemption* was a system of philosophy – and, he insisted, not a philosophy of religion or of Judaism – that it was nonetheless somehow also a Jewish book.

## Writings

Rosenzweig, F.: *Hegel und der Staat* (Hegel and the State), 2 vols (Munich/Berlin, 1920; Aalen: Scientia Verlag, 1982).

——: *Der Stern der Erlösung* (Frankfurt am Main, 1921; The Hague: Martinus Nijhoff, 1976; Frankfurt am Main: Bibliothek Suhrkamp, 1988); tr. William W. Hallo, *The Star of Redemption* (New York: Notre Dame Press, 1970).

——: *Der Mensch und seine Werk, Gesammelte Schriften* (The Hague: Martinus Nijhoff, 1979–83), 4 Sections, 6 vols (Section: *Briefe und Tagebücher* (Correspondence and Diaries), vol. 1, 1900–1918; vol. 2, 1918–1929, eds Rachel Rosenzweig and Edith Rosenzweig-Scheinmann with the cooperation of Bernhard Casper; Section 2: *Der Stern Erlösung*, ed. Reinhold Mayer; Section 3: *Zweistromland. Kleinere Schriften zu Glauben und Denken*, eds Reinhold and Annemarie Mayer (Land of Two Rivers: Shorter Writings on Faith and Thought); Section 4: *Sprachdenken im Übersetzen*, vol. 1, *Hymnen und Gedichte des Jehuda Halevi* (Speech Thinking in Translation, The Hymns and Poetry of Jehuda Halevi), ed. Rafael N. Rosenzweig; vol. 2, *Arbeitspapiere zur Verdeutschung der Schrift* (Working Papers on the German Rendering of the Scriptures), ed. Rachel Bat-Adam.

——: *Das Buchlein vom gesunden und kranken Menschenverstand*, ed. and intro. by Nahum N. Glatzer (Düsseldorf, 1964; Frankfurt am Main: Judischer Verlag, 1992); tr. T. Luckman, *Understanding the Sick and Healthy: A View of the World, Man, and God* (New York: Noonday Press, 1953).

## References and further reading

Anckaert, L. and B. Casper (eds): *Franz Rosenzweig: A Primary and Secondary Bibliography* (Leuven: Bibliothek van der Faculteit van de Godeleerdheid van de K. V. Leuven, 1990). (This comprehensive review of, by, and on Rosenzweig contains 936 items.)

Cohen, R. A.: *Elevations: Height of the Good in Rosenzweig and Levinas* (Chicago, IL: University of Chicago Press, 1994).

Freund, E.: *Die Existenzphilosophie Franz Rosenzweigs* (Leipzig, 1933; Hamburg: Felix Meiner, 1959); tr. Stephen L. Weinstein and Robert Israel, ed. P. Mendes-Flohr, *Franz Rosenzweig's Philosophy of Existence: An Analysis of the Star of Redemption* (The Hague: Martinus Nijhoff, 1979).

Gibbs. R., *Correlations in Rosenzweig and Levinas* (Princeton, NJ: Princeton University Press, 1992). (Exploring the affinities between Rosenzweig and the contemporary French philosopher Emmanuel Levinas, this work seeks to show how their thought can be used to correlate traditional ethical themes of Judaism with the postmodern critique of classical philosophical reason.)

Glatzer, N. N.: *Franz Rosenzweig: His Life and Thought* (New York: Schocken Books, 1953, 1961). (This volume contains extensive excerpts from Rosenzweig's correspondence, diaries, and writings.)

Mendes-Flohr, P. (ed.): *The Philosophy of Franz Rosenzweig* (Hanover/London: University Press of New England and Brandeis University Press, 1988). (This is a collection of twelve essays by scholars from America, Europe, and Israel who examine various critical issues in Rosenzweig's philosophical and religious writings.)

Moses, S.: *Système et Révélation. La philosophie de Franz Rosenzweig*, Preface by Emmanuel Levinas (Paris: Éditions du Seuil, 1982); tr. C. Tihanyi, *System and Revelation. The Philosophy of Franz Rosenzweig* (Detroit: Wayne State University Press, 1992). (This is the most comprehensive statement of Rosenzweig's philosophy, analyzing both his relationship to Idealism, particularly Hegel and Schelling, while highlighting its relevance for postmodern thought.)

# 27

# Buber

MAURICE FRIEDMAN

Martin Buber (1878–1965) is best known for his philosophy of dialogue, or the "I–Thou relationship," especially as expressed in his classic *I and Thou* (Buber 1958). He is also known as a philosopher of religion, but he is not a theologian. Perhaps above all he is a philosophical anthropologist – one concerned for the wholeness and uniqueness of the human. Certainly his two basic words – I–Thou (the relationship of mutuality, directness, presence, and openness) and I–It (the subject–object relation of knowing and using) – provide us with no metaphysics or world-view that can be understood apart from philosophical anthropology.

## Philosophical influences

According to his own testimony, Buber's philosophical education was based primarily on a thorough reading of Plato, Greek being his favorite language. In addition Buber tells of two catastrophic events connected with philosophy. One came when at the age of fourteen he found himself close to suicide through a compulsion to imagine time and space either as finite or as infinite – both of which left him with a world that had become uncanny and absurd. He found philosophical freedom through reading Kant's *Prolegomena to Any Future Metaphysics*, which told him that space and time were forms of our sensory perception. In the second event philosophy itself was the catastrophe, namely the seduction of the seventeen-year-old by Nietzsche's *Thus Spoke Zarathustra*, which "replaced the manifest mystery of the uniqueness of all happening" by the "pseudo-mystery" of the eternal return of the same (Schilpp and Friedman 1967, pp. 11–13). Because of this seduction Buber came only years later to what he regarded as the true step beyond Kant, namely the recognition that we are in "eternity" – that incomprehensible reality "which sends forth time out of itself and sets us in that relationship to it that we call existence" – *and* that we can meet it in our meeting with what is facing us.

Ludwig FEUERBACH (see Article 7) and Søren KIERKEGAARD (Article 9) were a part of Buber's existence from his student days. Feuerbach made essential the I–Thou relationship between man and man, Kierkegaard that between man and God. Buber put the two together through his insistence that in every finite Thou (art and nature as well as our fellows) we meet the "eternal Thou." Two professors who influenced Buber were Wilhelm DILTHEY (Article 37), whose phenomenology leaves room for the unique in a way Husserl's does not, and Georg Simmel, who moved in the direction of the relational.

During and after World War I a number of dialogical thinkers arose who had no influence on Buber and who were largely independent of one another – Ferdinand Ebner, Franz ROSENZWEIG (Article 26), Gabriel MARCEL (Article 28), and Karl JASPERS (Article 17), to name the most important (see Buber 1965, Afterword). Buber himself was a major influence on the French philosopher Emmanuel Levinas, and he has had a great impact upon any number of philosophers of religion, theologians, educators, psychologists and psychotherapists, social philosophers, socialists, political scientists, and even economists and city planners (see Friedman 1996).

## Ontology

Because it possesses no smooth continuity, the experience of the "sphere of the between" has been annexed to the soul and to the world, so that what happens to an individual can be distributed between outer and inner impressions. But when two individuals "happen" to each other, there is an essential remainder which reaches out beyond the special sphere of each. In an essential relation two persons participate in each other's lives not merely psychologically, as images or feelings, but ontologically as a manifest, if not continuous, reality of the between.

Despite Martin Heidegger's famous watchword "*Dasein ist Mitsein*" ("To exist is to be together with others"), in his ontology human existence takes place primarily in the relation between the individual person and Being *per se* and only secondarily and correlatively in the relationship between person and person. Heidegger's interpretation of Heraclitus's *logos* as the speechless Word through which man brings Being to unconcealment contrasts in the strongest possible fashion with Buber's interpretation of it as the "speech-with-meaning" through which persons build together the common cosmos of the Essential We. From Buber's standpoint Heidegger's claim that one can relate directly to Being as the unique, not-to-be-outstripped potentiality of the nonrelational person means taking one's stand in the realm of monologue and turning one's back on the life of dialogue (Friedman 1988–9).

## Philosophical anthropology

In *The Knowledge of Man*, the last and decisive stage of his philosophical anthropology, Buber found it necessary to deepen the ontology of the between by discovering the two basic movements from which the twofold principle of human life (I–Thou and I–It) is derived. The first of these movements Buber calls the "primal setting at a distance," the second "entering into relation." The first movement is the presupposition for the second; for we can enter into relation only with being that has been set at a distance from us and thereby has become an independent opposite. Only through this act of setting at a distance do we have a "world" – an unbroken continuum which includes not merely all that we and others know and experience, but all that is knowable now and in the future. That "synthesizing apperception" through which being is perceived as a whole and as a unity takes place not only through setting at a distance, but also through entering into relation. The great

330

phenomena on the side of distancing are preponderantly universal, those on the side of relating preponderantly personal. "Distance provides the human situation; relation provides man's becoming in that situation" (Buber 1988b, ch. 2).

In human life together, it is the fact that one human being sets another at a distance and makes the other independent that enables the one to enter into relation, as an individual self, with those like oneself. Through this "interhuman" relation, we confirm one another, becoming a self with the other. The inmost growth of the self is not induced by our relation to ourselves, "as people like to suppose today," but by the confirmation in which one person knows herself to be "made present" in her uniqueness by the other. "Self-realization" is not the *goal* but the *by-product*. The goal is completing distance by relation, and relation here means cooperation, genuine dialogue, and mutual confirmation.

Buber distinguishes the "interhuman" from the "social" in general. The "social" includes the I–It relation as well as the I–Thou; many interpersonal relations are really characterized by one person's treating the other as an object to be known and used; most are a mixture of I–Thou and I–It. The unfolding of the sphere of the between Buber calls the "dialogical." The psychological, that which happens within the soul of each, is only the secret accompaniment to the dialogue. "Individuation is only the indispensable personal stamp of all realization of human existence," writes Buber. "The self as such is not ultimately the essential, but the meaning of human existence given in creation again and again fulfills itself as self" (Buber 1988b, pp. 74ff).

We have in common with every thing the ability to become an object of observation, writes Buber, but it is the privilege of man, through the hidden action of his being, to be able to impose an insurmountable limit to his objectification. Only as a partner can the person be perceived as an existing wholeness. To become aware of a person means to perceive her wholeness as person defined by spirit: to perceive the dynamic center which stamps on all her utterances, actions, and attitudes the recognizable sign of uniqueness. Such an awareness is impossible if, and so long as, the other is for me the detached object of my observation; for she will not thus yield her wholeness and its center. It is possible only when she becomes present for me.

The essential problematic of the sphere of the between, writes Buber, is the duality of being and seeming. The person dominated by being gives herself to the other spontaneously without thinking about the image of herself awakened in the beholder. The seeming person, in contrast, is primarily concerned with what the other thinks of her, and produces a look calculated to make herself appear "spontaneous," "sincere," or whatever she thinks will win the other's approval. This seeming destroys the authenticity of the life between one human being and another and thus the authenticity of human existence in general. The tendency toward seeming originates in our need for confirmation and in our desire to be confirmed falsely rather than not to be confirmed at all. To give in to this tendency is our real cowardice, writes Buber; to withstand it is our real courage.

Mutual confirmation is essential to becoming a self – a person who realizes her uniqueness precisely through her relation to other selves whose distance from her is completed by her distance from them. True confirmation means that I confirm

331

my partner as this existing being even while I oppose her. I legitimize her over against me as the one with whom I have to do in real dialogue. This mutual confirmation is most fully realized in what Buber calls "making present," an event which happens partially wherever human beings come together, but in its essential structure only rarely.

Making the other present means to "imagine the real," to imagine quite concretely what another person is wishing, feeling, perceiving, and thinking. This is no empathy or intuitive perception, but a bold swinging into the other which demands the intensest action of one's being in order to make the other present in her wholeness, unity, and uniqueness. One can do this only as a partner, standing in a common situation with the other, and even then one's address to the other may remain unanswered and the dialogue may die in seed (Buber 1988b, ch. 3).

## Philosophical accounting

Buber says of himself that he stood under the duty to insert his experiences into "the human inheritance of thought" and that to do so he had "to make an It out of that which was experienced in I–Thou and as I–Thou." Reason can function as a trustworthy elaborator in communicating this kind of experience, for "this elaboration is of necessity a philosophical, and that means a logicizing task." But reason may not properly sacrifice to consistency anything of the reality to which it points. The corrective office of reason is incontestable in setting right incongruities of one's own perception with what is common to one's fellows. "But it cannot replace the smallest perception of something particular and unique with its gigantic structure of general concepts." (Rome and Rome 1964, pp. 48f, 53ff).

Though the I–Thou is not in the first instance bound by the logic of I–It, Buber says of his task of communication: "I am bound to the philosophical method, indeed to a dialectic that has become unavoidable with the beginning of philosophical thinking." Thinking Buber sees as "a noetic movement from a personal meeting to a factual knowledge-structure." In this meeting I–Thou and I–It cooperate in the human construction and reconstruction of a "world" accessible to human thought (Rome and Rome 1964, p. 57; and Buber 1988b, ch. 4). "Every essential knowledge is in its origin contact with an existing being and in its completion possession of an enduring concept." The original investigator discovers only in contacts with unique, concrete reality. He must from time to time radically relinquish this contact in order to attain general insights and exact formulae, "but at the beginning of the way he is ever again led by the genius of meetings until it can deliver him to the reliable spirit of objectification" (Rome and Rome 1964, p. 40).

In the end Buber's venture into the philosophizing of It is for the sake of pointing us back to the reality of the Thou that had too little been seen. "Being was not to be treated, but solely the human twofold relationship to being." The philosophizing had to be essentially an anthropological one directed to the question of how man is possible. Thus could emerge a compact structure but not one that joined everything together or went beyond Buber's own experience, which was naturally limited but not for all that "subjective" (Schilpp and Friedman 1967, pp. 689–93).

332

## Epistemology

The I–Thou relation is a direct knowing which gives one neither knowledge about the Thou facing one nor about oneself as an objective entity apart from this relationship. It is "the genuinely reciprocal meeting in the fullness of life between one active existence and another." Although this dialogical knowing is direct, it is not entirely unmediated. The directness of the relationship is established not only through the mediation of the senses, e.g. the concrete meeting of real living persons, but also through the mediation of the "word," i.e. the mediation of those technical means and those fields such as language, music, art, and ritual, which enable human beings ever again to enter into relation with what faces them. The "word" may be identified with subject–object, or I–It, knowledge while it remains indirect and symbolic, but it is itself the channel and expression of I–Thou knowing when it is taken up into real dialogue.

Subject–object, or I–It, knowledge is ultimately the socially objectivized and elaborated product of the real meeting which takes place between the human being and her Thou in the realms of nature, social relations, and art. It is only when this objectivized character of subject–object knowledge is forgotten or remains undiscovered (as is often the case) that I–It knowledge ceases to point back toward the reality of direct dialogical knowing and becomes instead an obstruction to it.

When this has taken place, the true nature of knowledge as communication – as the "word" which results from the relation of two or more separate existing beings – is forgotten. "Words" are taken to be entities independent of the dialogue between person and person and the meeting between man and nature, and they are understood either as expressions of universal ideas existing in themselves or as nominative designations for entirely objective empirical reality. The latter way of seeing words attempts to separate the object from the knowing subject, to reduce words to sheer denotation, and to relegate all "connotations" and all that is not "empirically verifiable" to subjective emotion or "poetic truth." The former retains the true symbolic character of the word as something more than a conventional sign and as something which does refer to a true order of being, but it misunderstands the nature of the symbol as giving indirect knowledge of an object rather than as communicating the relation between one existing being and another. A symbol is not a concrete medium for the knowledge of some universal if not directly knowable reality – though this is the way in which most writers on symbolism have treated it. It is instead a mythical or conceptual representation of a concrete reality met in the actual present. Only when it becomes abstract and universalized is that meeting forgotten.

One enters the I–Thou as a whole being in the present whereas I–It is always entered as a partial being after the present has become past. What takes place in the present is ordered through the abstracting function of I–It into the world of categories – of space and time, cause and effect. We usually think of the I–It categories as reality itself, but they are actually merely the symbolic representation of what has become. The attempt of logical positivism to relegate ethics, religion, and poetry to subjective emotion without real knowledge value acts as if there were no present reality until that reality has become past and can be dealt with in our thought categories. It also means that it abstracts the knowing subject from one's existence as a person in relation to other persons and then attempts to establish an "objective" impersonal knowledge abstracted from even that knowing subject.

The contrast between the presentness of I–Thou and the pastness of I–It also provides us with a key to the most misunderstood part of Buber's I–Thou philosophy – his assertion of the I–Thou relationship with nature. In the presentness of meeting are included all those things which we see in their uniqueness and for their own selves, and not as already filtered through our mental categories for purposes of knowledge or use. In this presentness it is no longer true that the existing beings facing us cannot in some sense move to meet us as we them. We can feel the impact of their active reality even though we cannot know them as they are in themselves or describe that impact apart from our relation to it. Although natural things do not have the continuity, the independence, or the living consciousness and consciousness of self which make up the human person, or the "I," they can, nonetheless, "say" something to us and become our Thou. This view alone allows to non-human existing beings their true "otherness" as something more than the passive objects of our thought categories and the passive tools of our will to use (see Friedman 1976, ch. 19).

Henri Bergson too distinguishes between two types of knowing, which he calls intellectual and intuitive. But Bergson claims that the thinker, by discerning the process of duration within himself, is able to intuit the absolute reality in other things. To Buber, in contrast, intuition does not set aside the duality between the beholder and what is beheld. Intellect holds us apart from the world which it helps us use; instinct joins us with the world but not as persons; intuition binds us as persons to the world, affording an intimate glimpse into hidden depths, but does not make us one with it (Buber 1990b, pp. 81–6).

Through the presentness and concreteness of the meeting with the "other," Buber avoids the pitfalls of Descartes, who abstracts the subject into isolated consciousness; of the idealist, who removes reality into the knowing subject, and of Kant, who asserts that we cannot know reality but only the categories of our thought. To Kant's statement that we can only know of the $x$ that it is, Buber adds "and that the existent meets us." This is a powerful knowing, Buber claims, "for in all the world of the senses there is not one trait that does not stem from meetings, that does not stem from the co-working of the $x$ in the meeting."

Our relation to nature is founded on numberless connections between movements to something and perceptions of something. Even the images of fantasy draw their material from this foundation. That to which we move and which we perceive is always sensible. The sense world itself arises out of the intercourse of being and being, and this does not mean between the human person and his sense object but between the person and an "$x$" that we cannot know as it is in itself. The multiplicity that shoots up to us from each unrealizable connection in the $x$-world enters into a formed unity with which my senses work together in close association to produce the wholly sensible correspondence that now stands in its place as a being in nature, its existence dependent on us. "Vision is figurating faithfulness to the unknown and does its work in co-operation with it" – faithfulness not to the appearance but to the inaccessible being with which we associate.

Even the meeting of the artist and the world is an encounter between the being of the artist and the being of the $x$. All human beings deepen perception into vision through making the figure manifest, but only the artist is "full of figure." Only the artist fashions the sense world anew through his figuration in vision and in work – not through trying to penetrate behind the world of the senses, but through completing its form to the perfect work of figuration. The perception of all human generations is, as figuration, only preliminary and the sense world that it produces only a stage: "Perception draws out of the being the world that we need; only vision and, in its wake, art transcends need and makes the superfluous into the necessary."

In the course of becoming human there arise "two constituent factors of the human person closely bound to each other: dissatisfaction with being limited to needs, and longing for perfected relation." It is the artist in whom these two factors come together most strongly and whose meetings with $x$ are of an intensity peculiar to him. The artist does not portray or remold the form but drives it into its perfection in its fully figured reality, "and the whole optical, the whole acoustical fields become refashioned ever anew." Art, to Buber, is the work and witness of the relation between the *substantia humana* and the *substantia rerum*, the realm of the "between" which has become a form (Buber 1988a, ch. 7).

## Ethics

Buber finds the ethical "only there where the human person confronts himself with his own potentiality and distinguishes and decides in this confrontation without asking anything other than what is [intrinsically] right and what is wrong in this his own situation." The truest source for the critical flame that distinguishes and decides is "the individual's awareness of what he 'really' is, of what in his unique and nonrepeatable created existence he is intended to be" (Buber 1988a, pp. 95ff). This is what Buber calls "personal direction." Direction is apprehended through one's inner awareness of what one is meant to be, for it is this that enables one to make a genuine decision. Yet this process is reciprocal, for in transforming and directing one's undirected energies, one comes to recognize ever more clearly what one is meant to be. One discovers the mystery waiting for one not in oneself but in the encounter with what one meets. Although the one direction of the hour toward God changes time and again by concretion, each moment's new direction is *the* direction if reality is met in lived concreteness (Buber 1980).

Buber's ethics, therefore, is neither moral autonomy nor moral heteronomy but a freedom that means freedom *to* respond and a responsibility that means both address from without and free response from within. "The idea of responsibility is to be brought back from the province of specialized ethics, of an 'ought' that swings free in the air, into that of lived life" (Buber 1965, pp. 16ff). The unique claim of the situation and our unique response to it with the resources that we have are both

335

integral to Buber's ethics. We can give direction to our "evil urge" and turn to the good in such a way as to unify impulse and will.

"No responsible person remains a stranger to norms," writes Buber, "but the command inherent in a genuine norm never becomes a maxim and the fulfilment of it never a habit." Rather the command remains latent in one as a basic attitude or life stance until it is evoked by a concrete situation which one could not have anticipated. Even the most universal norm must be recognized in unique situations in which one is aware of oneself as the "Thou" that is addressed and commanded (Buber 1965, p. 114). "I have never doubted the absolute validity of the command, 'Honor thy father and thy mother,'" Buber writes in his reply to a critic who accuses him of moral relativism. "But he who says to me that one, in fact, knows always and under all circumstances, what 'to honor' means . . . does not know what he is talking about." The "eternal values" must be expounded with one's own life (Schilpp and Friedman 1967, p. 720). A truly ethical action cannot well up out of one's inner goodness or fellow feeling but must arise in the meeting with otherness in which one imagines the real and makes the other present in her wholeness and uniqueness. Ethical action is neither altruism nor impartial objectivity but the binding of decision and action in the "between" – the relation of I and Thou.

One cannot do evil with the whole soul, for to do evil one must hold down forcibly the forces in one striving against it. One can only do good with the whole person, but not in isolation: "the wholeness of the soul is to be authenticated just in the brokenness of the human situations."

Buber's good cannot be referred back to any Platonic universals or impersonal order of the cosmos, nor can it be founded in any utilitarian or pragmatic general system of utility or justice. It grows instead out of the actual present concreteness of the unique direction which one realizes in the meeting with the everyday. One cannot demand or expect that the moral person will always "love" others. Even Jesus, Buber points out, loved only the loose, lovable sinners and not the self-righteous ones, but he stood in genuine dialogue with the latter as with the former.

## Philosophy of religion

Martin Buber declared not only that he knew of no cogent proof of God's existence but also that he would reject it if it existed. "I have no metaphysics on which to establish my faith," writes Buber, and adds that when he speaks of an event as having ontological significance it is to distinguish this reality from a purely psychological happening. If Buber posited no metaphysical thesis, neither did he posit a theological one. Theology means a teaching *about* God, even if it is only a negative one. Though Buber cannot leave out of consideration the fact that the human being lives over against God, he cannot include God himself at any point in his explanation. I know nothing of a "double truth," writes Buber. "My philosophy . . . does not serve a series of revealed propositions . . . but an experienced, a perceived attitude that it has been established to make communicable." (Schilpp and Friedman 1967, pp. 690ff).

The "eternal Thou" for Buber does not mean the traditional God of the philosophers, metaphysicians, and theologians – the God whose existence could be proved and whose nature and attributes could be described. He wishes rather to show us the road on which we can meet God, whom we can never know as he is in himself apart from our relation to him. "God," says Buber in *I and Thou*, "is the Being that is directly, most nearly, and lastingly, facing us, that may properly only be addressed and not expressed." God *is* not a person, yet in relationship with us God *becomes* one, so to speak, to love and be loved, to know and be known by us (Buber 1958, pp. 134–6; Buber 1988a, pp. 96ff). This is the paradox of the God who remains unlimited and yet enters into direct relation with us. This paradox sets Buber in contrast to traditional metaphysics, which demands the choice between an absolute that is not in relation to the world and a God who is in relation and therefore less than absolute. (Schilpp and Friedman 1967, p. 717).

God is the "Absolute Person" who is met whenever we meet our fellows, nature, or art as "Thou." God is the "eternal Thou" who cannot become an "It." The true God can never be an object of our thought, not even the "Absolute" object from which all others derive. Buber rejects any notion of a supernature or the supernatural in favor of the God who is above both nature and spirit yet bears and permeates them. "Meet the world with the fullness of your being," writes Buber, "and you shall meet Him."

Faith is binding oneself in relationship "with an undemonstrable and unprovable, yet even so, in relationship, knowable Being, from whom all meaning comes." The religious essence of every religion is found in "the certainty that the meaning of existence is open and accessible in the actual lived concrete, not above the struggle with reality but in it." This meaning must be authenticated by one's own commitment and response. Religious reality begins "when our existence between birth and death becomes incomprehensible and uncanny, when all security is shattered through . . . the essential mystery" (Buber 1988a, pp. 36–8).

Human truth is participation in Being, writes Buber, not conformity between a proposition and that to which the proposition refers. It cannot claim universal validity, yet it can be exemplified and symbolized in the true life-relationships of the human person. Buber's "eternal Thou" is best understood as "eternally Thou" – the Thou met ever again in the reality of the present. "According to my insight of faith," writes Buber, "God is before as well as after time; he encompasses time and he manifests himself in it" (Rome and Rome 1964, p. 87).

The attempt to fix God in an image prevents God from hiding and revealing himself ever anew in the concrete situation. The religious reality of the meeting with God knows no image of God, nothing comprehensible as object. "It knows only the Presence of the Present One." Every symbol of God, whether image or idea, crude or subtle, means turning the Thou into an It. Yet God suffers that one look at him through these necessarily untrue images – until they swell themselves up and obstruct the way to God by claiming to be the reality itself rather than just a pointer to it. At this point the philosopher's criticism of the image that no longer does justice to God enables the religious person to set forth across the God-deprived reality to a new meeting with the nameless Meeter (Buber 1988a, pp. 45ff).

Revelation, religious knowledge, means mutual contact and communication rather than a detached observation of an object. The "signs of address" that we become aware of when we meet the world are neither objective signs capable of interpretation nor subjective projections of human values, but the address that comes from the unique present when you recognize that *you* are the person addressed. What we can know of God when we are addressed by these signs of life is never accessible apart from that address. Yet from a succession of such "moment Gods" there may arise for us with a single identity "the Lord of the Voice." Each new Thou renews in all presentness the past experiences of Thou, so that the moments of the past and the moment of the present become simultaneously present and joined in living unity. "In the infinite language of events and situations, eternally changing, but plain to the truly attentive, transcendence speaks to our hearts at the essential moments of personal life" (Buber 1968, p. 216).

Revelation, to Buber, is our meeting with God's presence rather than information about God's essence. The word that results from this meeting is human in its meaning and form yet witnesses to the Being that stimulated it. Revelation is not written text but speaking Voice, speaking in the present moment and for the concrete present situation. Buber does not mean by the "eternal Thou" "God." Rather "God" means the "eternal Thou" – the reality of the "between." "Revelation seizes the human elements that are at hand and recasts them: it is the *pure shape of the meeting*" (Buber 1990a, p. 135).

## Writings

Buber, M.: *I and Thou*, 2nd edn, with Postscript by Author added, tr. R. G. Smith (New York: Charles Scribner's Sons, 1958).

———: *Between Man and Man*, tr. R. G. Smith, with Afterword: "The History of the Dialogical Principle," tr. M. S. Friedman (New York: Macmillan, 1965).

———: *A Believing Humanism: Gleanings*, tr. with Introduction and Explanatory Comments by M. S. Friedman (New York: Simon & Schuster, 1967).

———: *On Judaism*, ed. N. N. Glatzer (New York: Schocken Books, 1968).

———: *Good and Evil: Two Interpretations* (New York: Macmillan, 1980).

———: *Eclipse of God: Studies in the Relation between Religion and Philosophy*, tr. M. S. Friedman et al., Introduction by Robert M. Seltzer (Atlantic Highlands, NJ: Humanities Press International, 1988a).

———: *The Knowledge of Man: A Philosophy of the Interhuman*, ed. with Introductory Essay (Ch. 1) by M. S. Friedman, tr. M. S. Friedman and R. G. Smith (Atlantic Highlands, NJ: Humanities Press International, 1988b).

———: *Pointing the Way: Collected Essays*, ed. and tr. M. S. Friedman (Atlantic Highlands, NJ: Humanities Press International, 1990).

## References and further reading

Friedman, M. S.: *Martin Buber: The Life of Dialogue*, 3rd edn with new Preface and Bibliography (Chicago, IL: University of Chicago Press, 1976).

———: *The Confirmation of Otherness: In Family, Community, and Society* (New York: Pilgrim Press, 1983).

——: *Martin Buber and the Eternal* (New York: Human Sciences Press, 1986).

——: *Martin Buber's Life and Work: The Early Years, 1878–1923* (New York: E. P. Dutton, 1982).

——: *Martin Buber's Life and Work: The Middle Years, 1923–1945* (New York: E. P. Dutton, 1983).

——: *Martin Buber's Life and Work: The Later Years, 1945–1965* (New York: E. P. Dutton, 1984).

——: "Intersubjectivity in Husserl, Sartre, Heidegger, and Buber," *Review of Existential Psychology & Psychiatry*, 21, Nos 1, 2, and 3 (1988–9), pp. 63–80.

——: *The Worlds of Existentialism: A Critical Reader*, 2nd edn, with new updated Preface, ed. with Introductions and Conclusion by M. S. Friedman (Atlantic Highlands, NJ: Humanities Press International, 1991).

——: *Encounter on the Narrow Ridge: A Life of Martin Buber* (New York: Paragon House, 1991; paperback 1993).

——(ed.): *Martin Buber and the Human Sciences* (Albany, NY: SUNY, 1996).

Rome, S. and Rome, B. (eds): *Philosophical Interrogations* (New York: Holt, Rinehart & Winston, 1964), "Martin Buber" section, pp. 13–117, conducted, ed., and Buber's responses tr. by M. S. Friedman.

Schilpp, P. A. and Friedman, M. S. (eds): *The Philosophy of Martin Buber*, volume of *The Library of Living Philosophers* (LaSalle, IL: Open Court, 1967; Cambridge: Cambridge University Press, 1967).

# 28

# Marcel

## PHILIP STRATTON-LAKE

Marcel was probably the first modern, French existentialist. Nevertheless, outside of France he is the least well known. His account of human existence is distinctive in that it gives a central place to hope. His account of hope draws on many other notions in his philosophy, such as participation, the "I–thou" relation, availability, and having, and is hence largely unintelligible unless these concepts are understood. So although we shall come to focus on his account of hope it will be helpful first to give an overview of the central concepts of Marcel's existentialism.

## The mystery of being

The guiding thread of Marcel's philosophy is his concern to show the impossibility of thinking of being objectively – that is, as some object for a cognitive subject. This impossibility constitutes what Marcel calls the mystery of being. Being is a mystery in the twofold sense that it cannot be demonstrated and that its nature is unknowable. In the first respect Marcel follows KANT (1929 [1781], pp. 500ff) and KIERKE-GAARD (1985 [1844], pp. 40–3) (see Articles 2 and 9) in claiming that one cannot argue *to* existence, but must always argue *from* it. Being cannot be demonstrated, it can only be alluded to. The second aspect of the mystery of being is its inexhaustibility. Whatever being means, its "essence" cannot be reduced to a catalog of facts. Its nature can only be known negatively as the overflowing of any such inventory. The mystery of being leaves only two possibilities: skepticism or realism. Marcel opts for the realist position both because he considers skepticism to be incoherent and because he holds that existence is a datum which is beyond all doubt.

## Participation

This realist position is supported by the notion of intentionality. Like Brentano and HUSSERL (see Article 15) before him Marcel held that all mental states are intentional: their object is not consciousness itself, but something other than consciousness. He thus held that the subject has direct contact with existence and the existent world through feeling and sensation.

Marcel does not conceive of sensation on the empiricist model as the reception of sense data from objects distinct from the perceiving self, but describes sensation as a form of *participation* in being. It is, he says, "the immediate participation of what we normally call the subject in a surrounding world from which no veritable

340

frontier separates it" (Marcel 1952 [1927], pp. 331–2). The concept of participation is central to Marcel's philosophy and is intended to convey the thought that subjects cannot be understood individualistically as isolated egos and that the world cannot be understood as something opposed to subjectivity. Rather, the subject must be understood primarily in terms of its involvements (participation) in the world and with others.

He holds that an atomistic conception of the self and the world is merely the result of a distorted view generated by objective thinking. By adopting the standpoint of objectivity one relates to being as a spectator, rather than as a participator, and hence conceives of oneself as external to, and as detached from it. But precisely for this reason the standpoint of the participator cannot adequately be grasped from the standpoint of the spectator. So although we naturally adopt this standpoint when we reflect, by doing so we inevitably frustrate the purpose of such reflection, which is to come to understand better ourselves and the world in which we live. Marcel later qualified this view (Marcel 1950 [1951], pp. 121–2), but never abandoned the claim that objective thinking distorts the way things really are. Objective reflection, therefore, gives rise to the need for a different type of reflection which restores the integrity that objectivity has sundered. It is such "secondary reflection" which Marcel aims to provide.

## The I–thou relation

The most significant development of the notion of participation in Marcel's thought is the "I–thou" relation. When I enter into this relation I do not regard the other person objectively, from a third-person, detached perspective, but regard myself as intimately involved with her. This involvement entails that I do not think of her as some determinate set of properties or characteristics, which can be subsumed under general concepts without remainder, but that I encounter her *as other* (Marcel 1949 [1935], p. 104). To relate to the other as other is to encounter her in her uniqueness, in her "nonreducible being." A relation to the other as other is the authentic form of this relation, but it is not the only form it can take. One may relate to one's *idea* of the other. The idea of the other is a conception of her merely as related to me in some way, either as within my horizon of intelligibility – in which case I relate only to a representation, not to the other herself – or as a mere instrument for my use.

Although for the most part Marcel describes the "I–thou" relation in terms of inter-personal relations, it is clear that he does not limit it in this way. The distinction between "*thou*," on the one hand, and "*it*" or "*her*," on the other is not a distinction between persons and things, but a distinction between different ways of relating to other beings, be they things or persons (see Cain 1963, p. 38). Other beings are only "thou" for me in so far as I no longer conceive of myself as a spectator in the world and think of myself as a participator in it.

Marcel describes God as the *absolute* Thou. This is because God is a being to whom we can never relate objectively, but *only* as a thou. A detached, impersonal relation to God is no relation to God at all. "A God for whom my belief were of no interest would not be God but a mere entity of metaphysics" (Marcel 1952 [1927], p. 154). Furthermore, my relation to God as Thou can never just be a relation to God. Because of His unique characteristic of all-inclusiveness my relation to Him as Thou is at the same time a relation to all other beings as thou. It is, as Marcel describes it, an act of communion in being.

## The self and its body

Incarnation is the basic condition of human existence. Objective thinking not only distorts the way in which I conceive of the world and others, but distorts this basic mode of being. As long as I conceive of myself as relating to foreign objects or things in an alien world it is perfectly natural to conceive of my body as mediating these relations. To conceive of my body in this way is to conceive of it as an instrument. But, Marcel claims, this conception is quite implausible. First, my body is not merely some thing which I utilize, but is the *condition* of my using anything at all. As such it cannot itself be used by me. Secondly, conceiving of my body as an instrument does not do justice to my consciousness of my body. I am conscious of my body not merely as something I make use of, but as something *I am*, whereas when I conceive of it as an instrument I conceive of it as a mere thing, i.e. as something alien to me.

While Marcel insists that the self is not something detached from its body, he wants to avoid a complete identification of these two terms. To conceive of myself as nothing more than my body is, he claims, the crudest form of materialism. This leads to a certain tension in Marcel's account of the relation of the self with its body, since he wants to avoid both the Scylla of distinctness and the Charybdis of absolute identity. At times he tries to resolve this tension by abandoning the idea that one is *related* to one's body at all, but Marcel never quite solved this problem.

## Having and self-obsession

In the 1930s Marcel described the basic distinctions elaborated in "Existence and Objectivity" and the *Metaphysical Journal* in terms of *being and having*. One can relate to oneself and the world either as possessor and possessed or in an existential relation of availability. The relation of having is not so much characterized by material possessions, as by a certain self-obsession. Cut off from the other, and the ontological security which the other can bestow by the act of recognition, the subject seeks to give to herself ontological weight by accumulating possessions, and by attempting to identify with these. But this possessive relation is a dialectical one in which the subject becomes the victim of her possessions (Marcel 1949 [1935], p. 163). She is always in fear of losing the things she has, and since she identifies with these, she is always in fear of losing herself. Just as the master becomes subordinated to the slave in Hegel's master–slave dialectic, so the possessor becomes enslaved by her possessions. This relation leads inevitably to despair because in the end my own death will take everything from me.

Although having is characterized by self-obsession, it still implies a (repressed) relation to others. Having, Marcel writes, is intricately related to showing. To have something is to be able to show it. Marcel's favorite example of this is that of having a secret. On the one hand, this is only a secret because I keep it from others, but at the same time it is only a secret because I could *reveal* it to others (Marcel 1949 [1935], p. 160). We can only express ourselves in terms of having when we are moving on a level implying reference to others, but at the same time having denies this reference, replacing the other with the subject's idea of the other.

## Being and availability

In contrast to having, which is characterized by anxious self-obsession, being is characterized as a state of openness which Marcel calls *disponibilité* (availability or disposability). Availability is not meant to imply a certain emptiness, as in the case of an available dwelling (*local disponible*), but means "an aptitude to give oneself to anything which offers, and to bind oneself by the gift" (Marcel 1951 [1945], p. 23). This handing oneself over should not be understood as a state of indifference to one's destiny or character. In availability we not only *undergo* whatever fate offers, but *make* whatever is given our own "by somehow recreating it from within" (Marcel 1949 [1935], p. 117). This "recreation from within" is the active aspect of availability. Marcel is not clear in what sense this appropriation is creative, but he probably has in mind the fact that the circumstances, or fate with which one identifies in availability always underdetermine the *way* in which they can be incorporated into the self, and this underdetermination leaves room for interpretation, judgment, and creativity.

## Hope

The most distinctive characteristic of Marcel's existentialism is the centrality he gives to hope. Nietzsche and Camus were highly suspicious of hope. Nietzsche speaks approvingly of the Greeks when he notes that they "differed from us in their evaluation of hope: they felt it to be blind and deceitful [*Tückisch*]" (Nietzsche 1982 [1881], p. 40). Camus also talks disparagingly about great hopes which transcend life in such a way as to refine it and give it a meaning, but ultimately to *betray* it (Camus 1955 [1942], p. 15). Marcel, however, claimed that hope neither deceives nor betrays one, but rather is the condition of the integrity of the subject and of a genuine communion with the world and others.

Marcel is concerned not with hopes which are constituted by trivial desires and external reasons (calculations of objective possibility), but with hope the ground of which has its roots in the very depths of what one is. Such hope is always oriented towards a longing for deliverance, or salvation, and is never constituted by a calculation of possibilities in the way that more trivial hopes are.

Significant hope is always situated, is always bound up with *my* situation. More precisely, such hope is always bound up with a particular type of situation, namely that of trial, or captivity. What is distinctive about this captivity is not that it implies a restriction on our freedom of movement or of action, but that it implies "the impossibility . . . *of rising to a certain fullness of life, which may be in the realms of*

343

*sensation or even of thought in the strict sense of the word"* (Marcel 1951 [1945], p. 30). Captivity is not a trial which only the unlucky must suffer, but is part of the human condition itself, since this condition is constituted by limitations on all sides. Hope constitutes one (but not the only) way in which the subject can respond to this condition. For this reason there is no hope without the temptation to despair.

To despair is to capitulate before one's captivity and to capitulate is literally to go to pieces under one's sentence.

> It is at bottom to renounce the idea of remaining oneself, it is to be fascinated by the idea of one's own destruction to the point of anticipating this very destruction itself. (Marcel 1951 [1945], pp. 37–8)

Despair is a form of destructive self-obsession and is hence the end-point of the dialectic of having. If hope is understood as the act by which the temptation to despair is victoriously overcome it can be understood as the means by which I keep myself together, hold onto myself and onto my integrity. But how does hope function in this way?

It is tempting to reply that one holds onto oneself by holding onto some specific hope, perhaps for some miracle cure, or for liberation, or perhaps by making the securing of one's own integrity the object of one's hope. But Marcel claims that although hope tends to latch on to specific objects, genuine hope always transcends such determination and hence always survives disappointment. Fundamental hope "tends inevitably to transcend the particular objects to which it at first seems to be attached" (Marcel 1951 [1945], p. 32). Consequently the subject does not hold onto herself by pinning everything on the realization of some desired object. Absolute hope is not hope *for* something or other but hope *in* a certain creative process which is being itself. Understood in this way, to hope is to abandon oneself in absolute confidence (absolute availability) in such a way as to transcend all possible disappointment. As he puts it in *Being and Having*, "to hope is to put one's trust in reality" (Marcel 1949 [1935], p. 74). Hope then is for Marcel the paradigm case of availability, of being open to the creative process which is reality, and actively identifying oneself with this process.

Marcel is at pains to distinguish this attitude from that of optimism. The optimist is detached from the world; he stands back far enough to be certain that the tensions and contradictions of the world dissolve (Marcel 1951 [1945], p. 34). The standpoint of the optimist is the standpoint of the spectator. Someone who lives life in hope, on the other hand, is not someone who is detached in this way, but someone who is *involved* and *participating* in the creative process of being. Furthermore, there is no room for hope in the optimist's world, since the optimist's certainty that things will get better, or will ultimately be for the best, makes hope inappropriate, for there is no hope where there is certainty. It does not make sense to hope for something I know I shall receive. Marcel goes so far as to say that hope is opposed even to the notion of calculating probabilities (Marcel 1949 [1935], p. 79).

Marcel considers the most adequate characterization of hope to be: "I hope in thee for us" (Marcel 1951 [1945], p. 60). It is a hope in thee, because to hope is to place one's trust in the other. It is to hope for us, because the subject of hope is not the isolated ego, but the subject which is open, or available to whatever is given. Since the subject is not one who thinks of herself as opposed to others, one's hope – which is always ultimately for salvation – is not for *me*, but for *us*.

Marcel believes that the only thing which can justify such hope is God. Only the absolute Thou can guarantee the union which binds the "thou" and "us" in absolute hope. Such hope is hence inseparable from a faith which is equally unconditional. Hope, therefore, presupposes a leap of faith, a complete freedom from will and knowledge, that is, from the shackles of having in all its forms. Marcel is not unaware of the difficulties of such emancipation, but is quite explicit that these difficulties mean that absolute hope "must remain the privilege of a very small number of chosen souls" (Marcel 1951 [1945], p. 61).

Marcel's philosophy has been largely ignored by philosophers, despite the fact that he was probably the first modern French existentialist. Even theologians such as Moltman and Peukert who give a central place to hope, make no reference to him. There may be some justification for this. His often fragmented and evocative style of writing makes it difficult to get a clear picture of his particular brand of existentialism. His *Metaphysical Journal* and *Being and Having* read more like *notes* for a book rather than the finished product (which is indeed all the *Metaphysical Journal* was intended to be). Furthermore, there are many unresolved tensions in Marcel's work, for example, between the identity and difference of the individual and her body, or between the absolute confidence and the humility of hope. But for just this reason his work is highly suggestive and rich. He at least leaves us with a clear understanding of the problem of the relation, or bond between the self and its body, and, unlike conceptions of hope as a desire plus a belief about possibility, his account enables us to make sense of the notion of hope *as a virtue*. For these reasons alone his work deserves more consideration than it has received.

## Writings

Marcel, G.: *Journal métaphysique* (Paris, 1927); tr. B. Wall, *Metaphysical Journal* (London: Rockliff, 1952).

——: *Être et avoir* (Paris, 1935); tr. K. Farrer, *Being and Having* (Westminster: Dacre, 1949).

——: *Homo Viator: Prolégomènes à une métaphysique de l'espérance* (Paris, 1945); tr. E. Craufurd, *Homo Viator: Introduction to a Metaphysic of Hope* (London: Victor Gollancz, 1951).

——: *Le Mystère de l'être*, vol. I: *Réflexion et mystère* (Paris, 1951); tr. G. S. Fraser, *The Mystery of Being*, vol. I: *Reflection and Mystery* (London: Harvill, 1950).

## References and further reading

Anderson, T. C.: "The nature of the human self according to Gabriel Marcel," *Philosophy Today*, 29 (1985), pp. 273–83.

Blackham, H. J.: *Six Existentialist Thinkers* (London: Routledge & Kegan Paul, 1951), ch. 4.

Cain, S.: *Gabriel Marcel* (London: Bowes & Bowes, 1963).

Camus, A.: *Le Mythe de Sisyphe* (1942); tr. J. O'Brien, *The Myth of Sysiphus* (London: Penguin, 1955).

Gallagher, K.: *The Philosophy of Gabriel Marcel* (New York: Fordham University Press, 1962).

Gibbs, R. B.: "Substitution: Marcel and Levinas," *Philosophical Theology*, 4 (1989), pp. 171–85.

Godfrey, J. J.: *A Philosophy of Human Hope* (Dordrecht: Martinus Nijhoff, 1987).

Hammond, J.: "Gabriel Marcel's philosophy of human nature," *Dialogue*, 35 (1) (1992), pp. 1–5.

Kant, I.: *Kritik Der Reinen Vernunft* (1781); tr. N. Kemp-Smith, *Critique of Pure Reason* (Basingstoke: Macmillan, 1929).

Kierkegaard, S.: *Philosophiske Smuler eller En Smule Philosophi* (1844); tr. H. V. Hong and E. H. Hong, *Philosophical Fragments* (Princeton, NJ: Princeton University Press, 1985).

Koenig, T. R.: *Human Existence and Philosophical Experience* (Malabar: Krieger, 1985).

Michaud, T. A.: "Secondary reflection and Marcelian anthropology," *Philosophy Today*, 34 (3) (1990), pp. 222–8.

Nietzsche, F.: *Morgenröte* (1881); tr. R. J. Hollingdale, *Daybreak: Thoughts on the Prejudices of Morality* (Cambridge: Cambridge University Press, 1982).

Ricoeur, P.: *Gabriel Marcel et Karl Jaspers: Philosophie du mystère et philosophie du paradox* (Paris: Éditions du Temps Présent, 1947).

——: "La pensée de Gabriel Marcel," *Bulletin de la Société Française de Philosophie*, 78 (1984), pp. 3–63.

Schilpp, P. A. and Hahn, L. E. (eds): *The Philosophy of Gabriel Marcel* (LaSalle, IL: Open Court, 1984).

PART VI

# THREE GENERATIONS OF CRITICAL THEORY

# 29

# Benjamin

REBECCA COMAY

## Marxist rabbi

Philosopher, theologian, philologist, urban sociologist, literary critic, collector, archivist, essayist, memoirist, children's author, allegorist, media theorist, hashish connoisseur, closet surrealist, theorist of fascism, professional melancholic – it is by now habitual to begin any account of Walter Benjamin's work with an inventory of the grafts and incongruities traversing his tangled maze of writings. First known through his rather fraught association with Gershom Scholem and Theodor Adorno (who were effectively responsible for the posthumous dissemination of his corpus); sometime ally and interlocutor of Brecht, Kracauer, Bloch, and Buber; refugee in the Paris of Bataille and company during the 1930s: Benjamin exerts today a fascination all the more striking for its untimeliness. Adopted as spiritual soulmate and precursor of almost every major trend in contemporary Continental thought – from cultural studies to deconstruction, from psychoanalysis to new historicism, from critical theory à la Frankfurt school to poststructural linguistics, from molecular politics to death-of-God theology, from radical geography to phantomology, from film theory to Heideggerean hermeneutics, from Foucaultian micrology to cyberpunk aesthetics – he epitomizes that unclassifiable swirl of intellectual impulses we have come to associate with the peregrinations of Weimar culture.

The ironies of the story are forceful. Virtually ignored in his own lifetime, an intellectual star in ours; ostracized by his own university, a minor academic industry today; self-confessed bungler, success story of our times: the whole thing poses the familiar paradoxes of the *qui perd gagne*. His belated canonization smacks inevitably of the historicism he disavowed. Over and above the conventional aporia of just what it would mean to a strike a success whose only possible measure could be its own failure to be inscribed within the continuum of tradition, even one summarized as loosely as "continental" – Nietzsche stands in this respect as ultimate precursor – the question of Benjamin's "actuality" today (to use his own highly charged term) exerts its own specific pressures on thought. His protectors brandish at potential disciples a scary reading-list of prerequisites – thorough mastery of Hegel, Marx, Leibniz, Goethe, Kant, Humboldt, Hölderlin, Baader, Hamann, French symbolism, German Romanticism, Talmud, Lurianic kabbalah, surrealism, Weimar film theory, architectural modernism, Parisian town-planning, Kafka, Proust,

Weber, Lukács, Cassirer, Bloch, Simmel, Fourier, Bachofen, Klages, Jung, Russian anarchism, Blanqui, Dostoevsky, Brecht, Luxembourg, Sorel, Carl Schmitt, Karl Kraus, German and Spanish Baroque drama, and so on – a smokescreen which does predictably little to dispel the fog or to demystify what is equally conveniently dismissed as "cult" or fashion.

Benjamin himself famously summarized his own record as "a series of small-scale victories and large-scale defeats." His various agonies – from professional suicide to final overdose – have become the delicious stuff of melodrama. Obsessed with ruins, from the abjections of Baroque theatre to the urban detritus of surrealism, from the shattered vessels of kabbalistic theology to the fragmented body of the Brechtian *gestus*, from the symbolist cadaver to the lucubrations of the fascist death state, he was eventually to throw his own work, life, and epoch onto the mounting pile of rubble. His notoriously hermetic *Habilitationsschrift* on German Baroque tragic drama was rejected by the University of Frankfurt on grounds of "unintelligibility." A major Goethe study commissioned by the Moscow *Encyclopaedia* was rejected. His life project, the so-called *Passagenwerk*, a vast assemblage of quotations charting the cultural terrain of Baudelaire's Paris, composed over more than a decade of grinding exile, remained incomplete and uncompleteable. His late theoretical interventions were subject to censorship and economic sanction. Adorno and Horkheimer were infamously to refuse publication of his 1938 essay on nineteenth-century Paris in their *Zeitschrift für Sozialforschung*, the official journal of the by-then exiled Frankfurt Institute for Social Research, the so-called Frankfurt School, of which he was a fellow-traveler (although never an official member), and on whose moral support and somewhat paltry stipend he by then depended. With the exception of his doctoral dissertation on German Romanticism, an early monograph on Goethe's *Wahlverwandtschaften* (hailed by Hoffmansthal as one of the masterpieces of modern criticism) and a collection of aphorisms (*One-Way Street*), his corpus is confined to essays, fragments, and an immense proliferation of posthumous notes, quotes and sketches, recently assembled by the painstaking labors of his German editors. In this kaleidoscopic montage, whose method can be characterized as surrealist no less than Proustian, one can glimpse the remnants of a by-now vanished epoch.

Benjamin's life and thought are framed by the double trauma of the two world wars. From the start an assimilated German Jew, by the end a disenchanted Marxist, he was to register the contradictions besetting an entire generation. He was to characterize his earliest childhood milieu as a "mausoleum." Bound to a familial environment he was destined to repudiate, dependent on institutions which were inevitably to exclude him, drawn to a religious tradition to which his connection was at best tenuous, his work epitomizes the precarious situation of the Jewish European intellectual between the wars. This is pure Kafka territory. The pressure of an unlived life – Adorno's memorable phrase – was to afflict his entire corpus. From his earliest preoccupation with the literary afterlife (Schlegel's conception of the structural incompletion of every work and thus the immanent necessity of critique as supplement or *Ergänzung*) through to his impossible requiem to the

350

unmourned dead (the posthumous "Theses on the philosophy of history"), his thought was driven by the paradoxical demand for a redemption that could only arrive too late.

Between his birth in 1892 (into a well-off Jewish Berlin family of antiquarians and carpet-dealers) and his premature death in 1940 (fleeing Nazi-occupied France at zero hour), he was to experience the repeated shattering of modern Europe. He observed the bankruptcy of the bourgeois culture of the Wilhelmine epoch, the collapse of Weimar liberal democracy, and beyond that and above all the failure of every effort of the revolutionary left – the workers' parties of Germany, Hungary, Spain, France, and eventually Russia – to counter the rising tide of fascism as it spead through Europe. If in his mind such a crisis was eventually to resonate with the grand desolations defining three centuries of modernity – from Lutheran melancholia to Baudelairean spleen, from the Thirty Years War through the post-Napoleonic class wars in France and elsewhere – this is out of no comparativist nostalgia (nor its depressive obverse), but rather registers the groundless hope which fastens precisely on the repetition of missed opportunities and as such draws its very energy from past defeat.

"Hope in the past" (a late formula) spells the simultaneous promise and imperative exerted on the present through its shocklike encounter with the repressed possibilities of the past. Affinities with the structure of involuntary memory in Proust (whom Benjamin translated), symbolic correspondence in Baudelaire (ditto), Messianic belatedness in Kafka (with whom he greatly identified), ritual repentance in Judaism (about which he professed ignorance), eternal return in Nietzsche (about whom he remained singularly ambivalent), ecstatic temporality in Heidegger (whom he detested), abreaction of trauma in Freud (whom he read patchily), memory of the immemorial in Levinas and Blanchot (whom he preceded), have all been justly noted. Photographic technology (again, pure Proust, premonitions of Barthes) was eventually to supply at once the model and the leading metaphor of this logic of *Nachträglichkeit* or deferred action. What distinguishes Benjamin's version from any of these models is a specific emphasis on history as the essential locus of redemption: history here indicates the site of a loss all the more irreparable for being tied to class oppression. More specifically still: it is neither theory nor therapy but politics of a peculiar sort which will ignite the spark or create the constellation (two of Benjamin's most persistent metaphors of illumination) between past and present. The Messianic restoration of a fallen nature becomes here inseparable from the elimination of class oppression.

Redemption, then, is unthinkable without revolution. And this in turn means precisely the repetition of a past never quite present to itself insofar as it was already blocked or fractured by its own self-betrayal of its most essential promise. If "the origin is the goal" (one of Benjamin's favorite citations by Karl Kraus), any retrieval would be founded on the impossibility of every restitution or return and thus on the ultimate dislocation of the very concept of the originary. The spectacle of a world in ruins enables neither the consoling vision of a restored paradise nor the equally reassuring fantasy of a fresh start under the modernist rubric of the *tabula rasa*. If

351

thought is thus marked by an essential belatedness or anachrony, this invites neither the grey-on-grey retrospection of the owl of Minerva (Hegel's crepuscular metaphor for philosophy) nor permits the imaginary projection of a new beginning. The pressure of dead generations becomes not an obstacle to revolution (as both Hegel and Marx for complementary reasons suggested) but indeed its most essential stimulus. The impossibility of burying the dead, of successful or completed mourning, becomes the very necessity of class insurrection. The "Jewish" imperative to remember past sufferings turns into the "Marxist" imperative to eliminate present ones – but so too, equally, and this is the twist, the converse. Theology and politics start to merge. Benjamin thereby at once consummates the enlightenment project of secularization or disenchantment and subjects it to its most sustained interrogation.

## Theological/political

This is something other than the *reconciliation* of theology and politics along, for example, rationalist lines. Such a reconciliation typically involves the secularization of religious eschatology as the continuous amelioration of the human race: the heaven-on-earth projected by enlightenment humanism. Benjamin's synthesis must thus specifically be distinguished, on the one hand, from every theodicy of progress in the wake of Kant and Hegel – from the *Eighteenth Brumaire* to the Second International – that is, from the belief in history as the site of the immanent unfolding of human freedom. And it must be distinguished, on the other hand, from the contemporary efforts of Haskalah (enlightenment) Judaism in the wake of Moses Mendelssohn – Hermann Cohen and Leo Baeck here stand as immediate foils and precursors – to find in Judaism the universal "religion of reason" announcing the progressive fulfillment of the infinite task.

By Benjamin's day such a reconciliation could well assume a variety of guises. It was to inspire the historicist agendas of Ranke, Troeltsch, or Ritschl, together with their academic offshoots in German *Geisteswissenschaften*. (Gadamer's critique of historicism would here be entirely pertinent, even if his proposed alternative of fused horizons would be for Benjamin equally suspect.) It was to inspire the positivist historiography of the *Wissenschaft des Judentums* – the so-called "science" of Judaism, represented by Geiger, Zunz, and Graetz – whose mandate in the wake of the Jewish emancipation under Joseph II would reach the point of identifying the Messianic imperative with the needs of the modern European state. (In a related move, Hermann Cohen was by 1915/16 to salute the German war effort as the essential "preparation for perpetual peace.") It was to inspire the political theology of the Catholic crown jurist (and anti-Semite) Carl Schmitt, who was to legitimate the domination of the omnipotent sovereign as the secularized figure of the divine. And, on yet another front altogether, it was to inspire the confidence of every evolutionary Marxism (Benjamin will ultimately stretch the rubric to extend from Social Democracy to the Comintern): underlying the optimism which would find comfort in the "ideal of liberated grandchildren" – what has come to be called the "Marxist humanism" of a Fromm or a Kolakowski could equally be appended –

Benjamin detects the desperate opportunism which would crave accommodation with the status quo.

Benjamin refuses every such sublimation of the theological impulse – on both theological and political grounds. If the elision of the gap between the theological and the political typically leads to either bad theology (theocracy) or bad politics (progress) – or both – it will be the task of Benjamin's Messianic politics to displace that initial opposition by sharpening it until each pole comes to reflect the other at the point of its most pronounced antithesis. In a letter of 1926 to Gershom Scholem, Benjamin refuses to "concede any essential difference" between the order of religion and the order of politics, while at the same time rejecting any possible "mediation" (*Vermittlung*) between them. The Heraclitean image is introduced elsewhere of a bow arched to maximum tension. According to this logic (which persists in calling itself dialectical), thought is to proceed "ruthlessly and radically" in a "paradoxical reversal" which moves "from one extreme to another."

According to the early "Theological–Political Fragment" (1921), "nothing historical can relate itself on its own account to anything Messianic." The image is introduced here of two "arrows" or forces reciprocally intensifying each other at the point of their most abrupt opposition. Redemption is "not the goal but the end of history." An absolute caesura explodes the homogeneous stream of time such that profane history finds its consummation in its arrest or "Messianic cessation." Hölderlin's remarks on tragedy are here decisive; Sorel's reflections on violence no less so. But if, during the course of his life, Benjamin finds a similar caesura theorized by writers as disparate as Schlegel, Proust, Brecht, or Baudelaire (Leibniz, Kant and even Plato all figure equally), it is ultimately the apocalyptic strands in both Judaism and Marxism which become for Benjamin essential.

The former includes sources ranging from the Talmud to Franz Rosenzweig: crucial here is the insistence on a cataclysmic rupture between the profane order of history (*olam hazeh*) and the "world to come" (*olam haba*). The Mosaic prohibition of graven images – the so-called *Bilderverbot* – here extends to a restriction within the prophetic tradition which would problematize every discursive determination of the end. The latter crystallizes in Marx's critique of utopian socialism. The famous refusal to "write recipes for the cookshops of the future" (afterword to *Capital*) is precisely the refusal to determine redemption (the "realm of freedom") according to the categories of the present day (the "realm of necessity"). Messianism, on the one hand; revolution, on the other: the issue in either case is to maintain the critical gap or discontinuity between finite being and the absolute.

Religion and politics thus come eventually to coincide at the moment of their most extreme incongruity. The tension between the two poles is marked as internal to each. To sharpen the distinction between the two spheres is ultimately to maintain in each an explosive tension between immanence and transcendence. Messianic theology is secularized precisely to the extent that the very opposition between the historical and the eternal is inscribed as essentially intra-historical, and in this way reinflected as the Marxist opposition between prehistory and history. The whirlpool which swallows up the stream of becoming (an early image of Benjamin's) ruptures history precisely by returning it to an origin paradoxically

353

marked as being at once restored and essentially irretrievable because "imperfect" or "incomplete." Such a structure of impossible restitution – it is tempting to revert here to the finite repetition of a Heidegger – announces the limits both of every politics of compensation and of the theological otherworldliness which inevitably (according to Nietzsche) underpins this.

By the end of his life Benjamin insists, in defiance of every teleology of progress, that we restore to the concept of the classless society its "true Messianic face." Tellingly, Benjamin's image for the transition from religion to politics (and vice versa) is *not* one of simple enlightenment, not the elimination of the numinous or occult by way of pure illumination or critique, but rather that of an invisible stain or residue resisting the perfect legibility of thought. "My thought relates to theology as a blotting paper to ink. It is completely saturated with it. If it were up to the blotting paper, though, nothing of what was written would remain." The most perfect absorption of theology would imply its persistence precisely as unsublatable remainder. A late, enigmatic image (perhaps Benjamin's most famous) compares theology to a wizened dwarf haunting the infernal machine of progress. If the ghost which drives the machine simultaneously arrests its movement – this is the essential force of Benjamin's oxymoronic formula "dialectic at a standstill" – the image points equally to a remnant all the more recalcitrant for being concealed within the apparatus, whose effectiveness presupposes its most intense entanglement with what opposes it.

This cannot imply, then, a nostalgic "hunger for wholeness" (Peter Gay's characterization of a certain reactionary strand of Weimar anti-modernism), or a return-to-religion along, say, Schelerian or Buberian lines. Benjamin will sharply attack the latter for its "agricultural tendency" (read: Zionism) and its vitalist, communitarian turn. One of his earliest polemics (see his partially published correspondence of 1912 with Ludwig Strauss) is directed against any revivalist effort – whether nationalist, cultural, or "personal" – to retrieve an immediacy of "Jewish" *Erlebnis* untrammeled by the exigencies of modern enlightenment or critique. Similar misgivings will be expressed regarding the Buber–Rosenzweig translation effort to recreate in a breathy German the "original" *Ursprache* of the Hebrew Bible (Benjamin's suspicions more or less coincide here with those expressed more forcibly by Siegfried Kracauer). Even Bloch's "system of theoretical Messianism" (*Geist der Utopie*) will be found in the end guilty of a comparable naturalism or essentialism.

In this sense, the persistent thrust of Benjamin's effort will be to rescue the critical power of transcendence from every nostalgic otherworldliness (which would include its obverse, simple immanence). This would be to redeem the very notion of "redemption" from every ideology of consolation. Nietzsche is never distant here. Everything Benjamin writes in this sense can be read under the rubric of this paradoxical modernity. Such a rubric organizes Benjamin's work both long before and long after the self-announced conversion or "turn" (*Wendung*) to Marxism.

This is the essential thrust of the concept of the "holy-sober" (*heilignüchtern*) which the young Benjamin takes over from Hölderlin. By 1919, such an oxymoron will be grafted onto Schlegel's and Novalis's prismatic idea of "prose," and invoked to rescue early Romanticism from the steamy abstractions of *Sturm und Drang* mysticism (not to mention its later Catholic revisions and perversions), together with its later-day mutations in the reactionary *Lebensphilosophie* of contemporary Weimar. (See *Der Begriff der Kunstkritik in der deutschen Romantik*, Benjamin's successfully completed doctoral dissertation for the University of Bern.) Soon after, the disenchantments of Baroque allegory will be rehabilitated against the mythic plenitude of the idealist symbol. The redemption of the phenomena – Benjamin idiosyncratically looks to Plato for confirmation here – is to be thought not beyond but through the fragmented rubble of a profane or "fallen" world stripped of all grace or immanent transfiguration, as exemplified by the corpse scenes and extravaganzas of suffering, decay, and *vanitas* characteristic of so much seventeenth-century German drama. (See Benjamin's *Der Ursprung des deutschen Trauerspiels*, the famous fiasco of 1925, eventually published in 1928.)

The politics of the modernist avant-garde is thus established essentially as a theology. Such an uneasy conjuncture and series of impossible conjunctions – metaphysics and materialism, Messianism and historicity, sacred and profane, tradition and modernity – continues to mutate and circulate throughout Benjamin's later corpus. Nowhere more so than where it is a question of confronting the final avatar of a reified theology in the various art-religions of his day. In 1929 the surrealist venture of Breton and Aragon was revisited under the paradoxical rubric of "profane illumination." To "arch the bow between Breton and Le Corbusier" is precisely to overcome every abstract opposition, including those proposed by the surrealists themselves, between inspiration and technique, rationality and myth (and so on), and as such to perfect the "dialectical optic" that comes to "perceive the everyday as impenetrable, the impenetrable as everyday."

Every aesthetic ideology would thereby topple. This is the essential force of Benjamin's allegorical rescue of Goethe (against the sacralizing monumentalism of German classicism), Proust (against the consoling platitudes of the book-as-cathedral), Kafka (against the salvationist hagiography of Max Brod), and Baudelaire (against the pieties of *l'art pour l'art*), and will receive its most extreme and programmatic expression in the championing of Brechtian theatre and of the avant-garde mass media. In "The work of art in the age of its technical reproducibility" (a late, influential essay, surely his most controversial), Benjamin locates in film the decisive shattering of a tradition hobbled by the "cult" of aesthetic immanence or purity – the authoritarian myth of singular, irreproducible originality or authorship: the fascist *Führerkult* is never distant here – and as such a release of art's hitherto oppressive because parochial or restricted power. As the most disenchanted and public art form (Benjamin's eyes are open here: this is, yes indeed, 1936, the year of Leni Riefensthal), film comes to epitomize the modern project of profane illumination, and as such completes the Baroque paradox of redemption in ruination.

From here, the prolific analyses of the trivial ephemera of late nineteenth-century Paris – shopwindow displays, arcades, interior decorating, boulevards, fashion, and so on (it is the seemingly infinite neutrality of the "and so on" which calls most of all for interpretation here) – at once the signature of a rigidly commodified universe and the very cipher of utopian fulfillment. From the reading of the extant urban text (Marx's "social hieroglyph") emerges not only the demystification or critical unmasking of social relations of domination but equally the prefiguration (but by no means the prediction) of a redeemed or classless society. (See the massive, unfinished, as yet untranslated, posthumously baptized *Passagenwerk*, a "work" – purists dutifully correct the title to *Passagenarbeit* – that was to assume Mallarméan proportions as Benjamin struggled against all odds to provide the "philosopher's stone" which would transform the rubble of a world of lifeless artefacts into a "dialectical image" of redemption. The seemingly stupid optimism of the project was eventually to elicit Adorno's most extreme disapproval.)

In this respect there is perfect consistency from the early to the late agendas.

## Early/late

To be sure, there is an obvious difference – Benjamin himself announces nothing less than "total revolution" – between Benjamin's early, "metaphysical" (his own label) writings and the overtly politicized essays, manifestos and social commentaries of the 1930s. Dramatic changes in historical circumstances (the collapse of bourgeois German society after the First World War, inflation, mass unemployment, racism, the rising nightmare of European fascism) no less than institutional conditions (Benjamin's eviction from mandarin academic culture following the débâcle of his failed *Habilitationsschrift* and – following the withdrawal of his father's financial support – his forced "proletarianization" as freelance journalist) and indeed personal ones (divorce, poverty, exile, internment) would indeed go a long way to account for the multiple shifts, by now well documented, in topic, tone, and tactic.

It has become conventional to date the break to 1924/5. This is the year in which Benjamin (in the following order but no necessary connection) discovers Lukàcs, falls in love, is ejected from Frankfurt University. From this point on, under increasingly precarious circumstances, he ekes out a living publishing literary reviews in German feuilletons and newspapers: first in Berlin, then, following Hitler's 1933 takeover, in exile in Paris where, despite fitful efforts to emigrate, torn between the seemingly impossible alternatives of Jerusalem, New York, and Moscow (some read in such a dilemma the essential aporia of Benjamin's entire life), he remains until his famous suicide. (Fleeing occupied France, apprehended by the Gestapo at the Spanish border without the proper transit documents, Benjamin took an overdose of morphine in September 1940.) The most vivid account of this harrowing last period remains Benjamin's own recently translated *Correspondence* as well as his exchange of letters with Scholem.

Such a break can be represented in a variety of fashions: a shift in venue (and, accordingly, style) from academic to journalistic channels; a shift in taste from the canon of *Germanistik* (Kant, Leibniz, Goethe, German Romanticism, seventeenth-century Baroque drama) to the avant-garde of Weimar, Moscow, and Paris (Dada, surrealism, agit-prop, Brecht, constructivism, Russian film, the architectural modernism of Le Corbusier, Loos or Scheerbart); a shift in focus from fundamental questions of epistemology and metaphysics (the status of critique or criticism, monadology, the nature of "pure" language, the metaphysics of the fragment) to recognizable questions of politics and sociology (analyses of fascism, consumer culture, the impact on the public sphere of changing conditions of capitalist production); an apparent shift in allegiance from "high" or élite literary culture to "mass" visual and tactile culture (film, architecture, technology, the everyday artifacts of modern metropolitan existence) as the essential locus of meaning and redemption; a shift in temperament from a vaguely militant romantic or libertarian anarchism (linked variously to the influences of Dostoevsky, Bakunin, Sorel, Gustav Landauer) – this will not preclude, notoriously, a fascination with Carl Schmitt – to a severe, at times deliberately "vulgar," Marxism (although never of a card-carrying kind) forged through association with Brecht – *plumpes Denken* – and by way of a sustained (if somewhat strained) reading of Marx's chapter on commodity fetishism, as processed through a selective reading of Georg Lukàcs; and, finally, a shift in voice from the dissertation mode and metaphysical pronouncement to the somewhat unclassifiable *melange* of aphorisms, manifestos, autobiographical memoirs, hashish impressions, city portraits and travel journals (including the *Moscow Diary*, Benjamin's memoir of his somewhat miserable visit to his lover, Asja Lacis, in the Soviet Union during the winter of 1926/7), which together constitute a significant portion of the output from the last period of Benjamin's life.

The precise significance of such a shift is, of course, open to interpretation. Whether one chooses to read in Benjamin's official "turn" to Marxism a self-betrayal of his earlier idealism (Scholem, spectacularly, was to accuse him of intellectual suicide), or rather to celebrate here a salutary self-awakening or maturation, it is undeniable that there are profound tensions both between and within the earlier and the later corpus. Periodizing readings (beginning with Adorno) have tended to dissipate or regulate this tension by proposing bifurcations which conveniently split the differences as antithetical polarities charted along a developmental trajectory. Some, no less conveniently, reconstruct a dialectical waltz from (abstract) Messianism through (vulgar) Marxism to a triumphant synthesis of Messianic materialism (the crucial text usually invoked here is the "Theses on the philosophy of history," Benjamin's posthumous testament of 1940). The lovable portrait is circulated of a schizophrenic Benjamin torn helplessly between the claims of competing friends (Scholem, Brecht, Adorno), traditions (Judaism, Marxism), disciplines (philosophy, theology, politics, literature), and even places (Berlin, Moscow, Paris, Jerusalem) – a portrait strangely comforting in that it securely relegates to influence or ambivalence what would otherwise present an unbearable and explosive pressure. No less reassuring in this context is the myth of the dithering romantic outsider – solitaire, free-thinker, eclectic ragpicker – easily domesticated as the curse and luxury of the free-floating intellectual. (Benjamin himself had a snarl-word for this class-based abstraction: left-wing melancholy.)

## Afterlives

Already within his own lifetime Benjamin's thought had become a minefield. Accusations – these are from his *friends* – ranging from "Jewish fascism" (Brecht) to "wide-eyed positivism" (Adorno) eventually led him to compare his predicament, as he remarked to Scholem (one no less quick to draw fire), to that of someone pinned between the jaws of a crocodile. Too theological, not theological enough – the symmetrical litanies of reproaches refuse precisely the uneasy dialectic upon which Benjamin never stopped insisting. Brecht found the "mysticism" creepy. Scholem accused him of writing "communist credos." Adorno, who alone appreciated the drive for synthesis (while forever doubting Benjamin's own capacity to articulate it) suspected an unwholesome blend of superstition and empiricism, and was to detect in Benjamin's attachment to the scraps of actually existing culture (a particularly acrimonious exchange concerns, among other things, the utopian potential of Mickey Mouse) the servility of one who would assume "an all too intimate footing with the *Weltgeist*." Underpinning the well-known debates over the revolutionary possibilities of mass media culture – debates which are as much about the possibility of revolutionary mass politics in the age of advanced capitalism as about the specific potentials of the new media – one can detect a tension which strikes at the very heart of both the political and the theological traditions. In the struggle between Benjamin and Adorno one can overhear echoes of the agonies chronically afflicting Marxism. The conflict between Luxembourg and Lenin might stand here as exemplary. The political antinomy of spontaneism and avant-gardism can be rendered equally as a theological one: idolatry and otherworldiness would in this case represent, respectively, the twin abstractions of myopic immanence and untethered transcendence.

Residues of the classic debates of the 1930s have from the outset informed the reception and dissemination of Benjmain's corpus. Complementary suspicions of idealism and positivism have typically split the readership. The relevant opposition is here perhaps not so much between "left-wing" and "right-wing" interpretations (on the model of the famous post-Hegelian aftermath of the 1840s) as between competing tendencies within the Marxist (and post-Marxist) traditions. It would be overly simple to characterize this in terms of the weary opposition between formalism and historicism. If the general trajectory of Benjamin reception has tended to move in waves, from a neo-Brechtian emphasis during the 1960s and 1970s (inspired by the student movement, energized by the new surge in media and communication studies, catalyzed by outrage over Adorno's alleged suppression of the political texts in his posthumous editions of Benjamin's writings, disseminated by magazines such as *Screen* and *Alternative*) to the seemingly more "transcendental" perspective of the 1980s (under the impact of Derrida and de Man, one can witness a growing preoccupation with questions of allegory and language, a privileging of Benjamin's early works, an insistence on "close reading," and an apparent retreat from the immediately politicized concerns of the New Left heyday), it is becoming clear, at least in hindsight, what the price might be of insisting too strenuously on such a dichotomy.

It would be boring and wrongheaded to divide up the terrain between the "Sartrean goats and the Valéryan sheep" – Adorno's famous formula for the collusive stand-off between engagement and aestheticism, between the politically correct and the high priests of culture, between a triumphant pragmatism and a sacralizing otherworldliness. If, during the frenzy of cultural studies, the anti-progressivist impulse of Benjamin's project was typically overlooked or underplayed (or, in another context altogether, repudiated, for example by Habermas) – no doubt unwittingly feeding into the official optimism accompanying postwar reconstruction efforts both in Germany and elsewhere – it would be premature to characterize the "deconstructive" readings that were to follow as inherently quiescent or disengaged. In any case, such a seeming disengagement would have (at least in theory) sprung less from a lingering attachment to a comforting theologoumenon (whether God, presence, meaning, or "art" as such) than from a knowing obliqueness occasioned by the very anti-instrumentalism on which Benjamin himself most emphatically insisted: hence the familiar, Heideggerean-inspired "step back" from the question of politics to the question of the political, from history to historicity, from technology to the nature of *Technik*, from Messianism to Messianicity ("*le méssianisme désertique*"), and so on. That being said: the impossibility of invoking such terms as politics or religion as if they were self-evident is by now self-evident.

The relevant debate may prove to be not so much between "political" and "theological" readings of Benjamin, but rather over the question of what it might possibly mean – today – to speak directly of either politics or theology, or indeed, therefore, of their *Auseinandersetzung*. The legacy of German fascism means, among other things, that both Marxism and Judaism must henceforth mean something rather different than anything Benjamin could have possibly envisaged. To make this painfully obvious observation is by no means to assume the antiquarian neutrality of the latecomer. That the "revolution" has by now (this is 1996) assumed the withered, "ugly" appearance Benjamin once attributed to theology after the death of God; that the generalized disenchantment proclaimed by Nietzsche (Hegel, Marx, Weber, etc.) might now take a form unimaginable in 1940 – none of this should of itself mean abandoning either politics or religion to the junkheap of historicism. It does, however, require reconsidering just what these terms might signify today. And as such it underscores the peculiarity of Benjamin's own fascination for us now.

That the losses registered by Benjamin have become to a real extent our gain – the shock of his defeats our norm, his melancholia our mourning work, his allegory our symbol, his rubble heap our monument – is on the one hand already anticipated by the logic of neutralization or capitalization (in every sense) he himself most vigorously theorized: "Not even the dead are safe from the enemy if he wins." On the other hand, it poses some rather specific demands on thought.

## Writings

Benjamin, Walter: *Gesammelte Schriften*, ed. Rolf Tiedemann and Hermann Schweppenhäuser, 7 vols to date (Frankfurt: Suhrkamp, 1980–91). This critical edition of Benjamin's corpus includes most of the relevant variants, notes, sketches, and correspondence.

——: *Briefe*, ed. Gershom Scholem and Theodor W. Adorno (Frankfurt: Suhrkamp, 1978). Useful to consult on general correspondence as well as on the specific correspondence with Scholem and with Adorno.

Benjamin, Walter and Scholem, Gershom: *Briefwechsel, 1933–1940*, ed. Gershom Scholem (Frankfurt: Suhrkamp, 1980).

Adorno, Theodor W. and Benjamin Walter: *Briefwechsel, 1928–1940*, ed. Henri Lonitz (Frankfurt: Suhrkamp, 1995).

A comprehensive translation of the major works, organized in chronological order, is currently in preparation at Harvard University Press. (The first volume, soon to be published, will include Benjamin's previously untranslated essay on Goethe's *Wahlverwandtschaften*, the previously untranslated doctoral dissertation on German Romanticism, and a retranslation of the *Habilitationsschrift* on Baroque *Trauerspiel*.)

See also *The Correspondence of Walter Benjamin, 1910–1940*, tr. Manfred R. Jacobson and Evelyn M. Jacobson (Chicago, IL: University of Chicago Press, 1994) and *The Correspondence of Walter Benjamin and Gershom Scholem, 1932–1940*, tr. Gary Smith and André Lefevere (New York: Schocken, 1989).

## References and further reading

Adorno, T.: "Walter Benjamin." In *Prisms*, tr. Samuel and Shierry Weber (Cambridge, MA: MIT Press, 1981).

——: "Introduction to Benjamin's *Schriften*." In *Notes to Literature*, tr. Shierry Weber Nicholsen (New York: Columbia University Press, 1992).

Benjamin, Andrew and Osborne, Peter (eds): *Walter Benjamin's Philosophy: Destruction and Experience* (London: Routledge, 1994).

Buck-Morss, Susan: *The Dialectics of Seeing: Walter Benjamin and the Arcades Project* (Cambridge, MA: MIT Press, 1989).

Cohen, Margaret: *Profane Illumination: Walter Benjamin and the Paris of Surrealist Revolution* (Berkeley, CA: University of California Press, 1993).

Derrida, Jacques: "Des Tours de Babel." In Joseph F. Graham (ed.), *Difference in Translation* (Ithaca NY: Cornell University Press, 1985).

——: "Force of Law: The 'Mystical Foundation of Authority.'" In Drucilla Cornell, Michel Rosenfeld, and David Gray Carlson (eds): *Deconstruction and the Possibility of Justice* (London: Routledge, 1992).

Eagleton, Terry: *Walter Benjamin, or Towards a Revolutionary Criticism* (London: Verso, 1982).

Jennings, M.: *Dialectical Images: Walter Benjamin's Theory of Literary Criticism* (Ithaca, NY: Cornell University Press, 1987).

McCole, John: *Walter Benjamin and the Antinomies of Tradition* (Ithaca, NY: Cornell University Press, 1993).

Nägele, Rainer: *Theater, Theory, Speculation: Walter Benjamin and the Scenes of Modernity* (Baltimore, MD: Johns Hopkins University Press, 1991).

Pensky, Max: *Melancholy Dialectics* (Amherst, MA: University of Massachussets Press, 1993).

Scholem, Gershom: *Walter Benjamin: The Story of a Friendship* (London: Faber & Faber, 1982). Smith, by. (ed.): *On Walter Benjamin* (Cambridge, MA: MIT Press, 1988).

——: *Thinking through Benjamin* (Chicago, IL: University of Chicago Press, 1989).

Wohlfarth, Irving: "On the Messianic structure of Benjamin's last reflections," *Glyph*, 3 (1978).

Wolin, R.: *Walter Benjamin: An Aesthetic of Redemption* (New York: Columbia University Press, 1982; rpt. Berkeley, CA: University of California Press, 1994).

See also the special journal issues on Benjamin: *New German Critique*, 17 (1979); 34 (1985); 39 (1986); 48 (1989); *Studies in Romanticism*, 31 (1992); *New Formations*, 20 (1993).

# 30

# Horkheimer

GUNZELIN SCHMID NOERR

Critical theory, as developed by Max Horkheimer during the 1930s, is not a self-sufficient academic philosophy remote from life, but is connected with individual, everyday experiences and an interest in the abolition of social injustice. Consequently, its tenets cannot be dissociated either from the substance of those experiences, or from the *tissue* of their derivation. Their truth remains bound to constellations of social reality. Bearing this in mind, we may distinguish "Critical Theory" from two opposite forms of philosophical and scientific self-understanding. One of these regards itself as independent of such constellations. The other acknowledges them, but reduces this understanding to a general perception of correspondences between mind and matter. In contrast, Critical Theory traces the dependence of consciousness on social existence with the aim of abolishing that dependence. It thus, on the one hand, represents critical unrest *vis-à-vis* all putative first and last certainties, *vis-à-vis* metaphysics and ontology, *vis-à-vis* all thinking that has forgotten its own contingency. On the other hand, it retains the emphatic concept of truth of its philosophical tradition, and thus avoids disintegrating into an indecisive relativism in which everything would be equally true or equally false.

In so doing it adopts an attitude critical of ideology that was already introduced into philosophy and sociological theory by Hegel and Marx, but turns it against idealistic systematic thinking as well as the dogmatic rigidity of post-Marxist materialism and academic sociological relativism. It retains the authentic concept of ideology as a false consciousness which has become transparent. Criticism of ideology, consequently, is not a question of a correct attitude being brought to bear on analysis from outside, but arises from unreserved reference to the analyzed material. The unity of the criticism can be inferred from the variety of its objects, the forms taken by bourgeois society. Its general purpose consists in maintaining the authority and purpose of a reason which is not instrumentally diminished, in the face of a condition of blindness diagnosed as universal.

This attitude had driven Horkheimer, of Jewish extraction, Professor of Social Philosophy and Director of the Institute of Social Research in Frankfurt am Main, into exile in New York by way of Geneva and Paris at the very beginning of the period of National Socialist rule. Having pursued philosophical and sociological studies in America with his colleagues from the Institute for a decade, he finally saw himself confronted with the most ominous political constellations of the century. This was the time when Fascism reigned victorious, arising everywhere, both inside and outside Germany, spreading its policies and military might throughout the world. There seemed no realistic basis anywhere anymore at the level of concrete politics, on which the hope of a better future and the establishment of a more rational social order could be founded. Even more ominously, the political and military opponents of Fascism – Western monopolistic capitalism and Eastern bureaucratic socialism – seemed to be only different paths towards the same goal: unrelenting domination of the individual by the collective, abrogation of the subject.

Such considerations led Horkheimer to radicalize further the critique of reason he had so far formulated, extending it to the philosophy of history. In the winter of 1941/2 he wrote an essay entitled "Vernunft und Selbsterhaltung," which first appeared as "The End of Reason" in the final number of the last, English-language volume of the journal *Zeitschrift für Sozialforschung*, of which he was editor. In this article Horkheimer sees the end of reason not solely in its defeat from outside by modern barbarism, but rather as the result of a process of disintegration immanent within it, a process of which Fascist despotism itself is only a symptom. Since the classical period of Western thought – since ancient Greece – reason was regarded as an organ through which the eternal order of being was recognized. As opposed to this, the European Enlightenment tended to reduce reason to a mere means of controlling outer and inner nature for the purpose of social welfare. Whether in the guise of the Protestant ethic, that of its opposite number – the Catholic religious orders of the Counter-Reformation – or finally that of the early civil mass movements, matters always finally came down to internalization of the new order, with individuals sacrificed to the imperative of domination, which could no longer be questioned. The contemporary crisis in the global development of control over nature is reached with the replacement of competitive capitalism by monopolistic capitalism and with its consequences: the establishment of the authoritarian state, the decay of linguistic communication in industrialized culture, the disappearance of a secure family-based childhood, the extinguishing of the subversive element in sexuality, the end of the sovereign ego. The latter had once been able to pass off the principle of its self-preservation as autonomy, but that pretence has now disappeared. In an ironic sense one could say, following Horkheimer, that for this modern form of domination, heteronomy has become functional: "self-preservation has lost its subject."

Ever since the first enlightened and enlightening thinking attacked fear and superstition, critical reason, as Horkheimer shows, has been unremitting in demystifying the world and destroying conceptual fetishes. In the end, however, it suspects itself of being such a fetish, turns upon itself, together with middle-class progressive ideas of liberty, equality, and fraternity, and the concept of the human being in which it had been embedded. However, the paradox of reason disclaiming itself is concealed in modern positivist science, embodying, as it does an ethic of skepticism and a manipulative mass culture by virtue of the fact that the emphatic claim of reason has been withdrawn. Reason regresses to that utilitarian instrumental principle of self-preservation to which it once owed its birth from animal instincts. As the optimal economic fulfillment of aims set by the interests of

363

domination, reduced to the coordination of means, reason blinds itself to its true claim to call reality by its name.

To a great extent, traditional philosophy – Horkheimer insists – has merely rehearsed and reconstructed, as abstract self-criticism, what actually occurred in the course of history. Theoretical dichotomies and aporias have their historic practical origins and solutions. This is the principal feature of his materialistic argument concerning development and contradictions in the history of philosophy and science. Purely argumentative solutions are not to be expected here, for the ideological criticism of fragmented and instrumental reason confers upon it a power rooted in society, in view of which all adherence to the traditional claims of philosophy to justify values must appear weak or extravagant – at the very least an artificial renaissance of metaphysics. Positivism and modern ontology, as Horkheimer insists in his book *The Eclipse of Reason* (1947), are the two main currents of contemporary thought; although they seem to oppose each other, actually they are related beneath the surface. Whether as a belief in science or as various forms of modern superstition they both influence ordinary consciousness through techniques of mass manipulation used in the culture industry. They reinforce the power of the status quo, by destroying any basis for rationally transcending it.

At the beginning of the 1940s it was scarcely possible for Critical Theory, no longer nurturing illusions about the chances of rational enlightenment, to hold firmly to the prospect of the realization of such an idea. The link between critical sociological theory and the practical transformation of society seemed to be disintegrating. However, for all the social aspirations of the theory, Horkheimer had always been opposed to organizational commitment in the party political sense. This attitude of intellectual aloofness and independence can be traced back to its earliest political expressions at the time when he was a young manager in his father's cotton mill in Stuttgart, a reserve soldier during the First World War, and a student during the subsequent period of the November Revolution in Munich and the creation of a "Räterepublic" there. In the factory, he experienced the conditions under which the workers lived and worked, which were destructive of the personality, and he saw himself, with all his longing for truth and justice, as a beneficiary of exploitation. In Munich, he saw political movements, their spontaneity, their struggle and their defeat. They seemed to refer to forces in society which promised to remove individual contradictions.

He takes up these experiences again theoretically in the volume of aphorisms entitled *Dämmerung: Notizen in Deutschland* (Twilight: notes in Germany), which reflects the collapse of the Weimar Republic and a less than confident hope that destructive social conditions may be overcome. It is no coincidence that the title is reminiscent of Nietzsche, who is to be counted among the theoretical antecedents of Critical Theory, together with the great anti-academics of the nineteenth and the early twentieth century (Schopenhauer, Marx, and Freud) and finally with (and against) the great academics of German philosophy (Kant and Hegel). In this work, Horkheimer offers a new kind of analysis of capitalism: he is concerned with the moral attitudes, characteristics, wishes and hopes resulting from or protesting against economic and social structures. The critical and at the same time synthetic force of this analysis derives from the idea – situated in the philosophical tradition of Kant, Hegel, and Marx – of a rationally organized humanity, whose chances he measures by the state of political, economic, and social development. He uses aphoristic methods to describe the general by means of the particular, the analysis of which as false indirectly shows the outline of what is true. In so far as this procedure remains characteristic of Critical Theory as a whole, *Dämmerung* may be regarded as its early form. During the period that followed, Horkheimer's conviction that truth is to be thought of only in negative terms comes to the fore ever more strongly: he believes that the concept of what is human can be revealed only by the concrete evidence of what is inhuman. The idea of the historical progress of the species is stripped of any justifying function. Happiness would not be happiness without the memory of past – and therefore ever irremovable – suffering endured on the way. Horkheimer's materialism is, as he says, a "melancholy science." Henceforward, Critical Theory's claim to truth was to be that it acknowledged this reality without illusions.

When *Dämmerung* appeared in Zurich in 1934, it reflected a world which had already disappeared. The Nazis had taken over the Frankfurt Institute building, and Horkheimer and his circle had been in exile since the beginning of 1933. The Institute's empirical study of the conscious and unconscious attitudes of German blue-collar and white-collar workers had been a contributary factor in this exile. Its first results had confirmed the fear of the sociologists working at the Institute that no effective resistance was to be expected in Germany to the threatened seizure of power by the Nazis. From 1934 onwards Horkheimer was director of the International Institute of Social Research in New York, which was associated with Columbia University.

The concept which defined the work of the Institute was developed by Horkheimer as early as 1931, in his inaugural lecture as professor and director of the Frankfurt Institute. In it he takes up the philosophical interpretation of the sciences introduced by Kant and Hegel, but at the same time says that criticism of the false claims to independence of positivist empirical thought and of metaphysical construction can no longer be defended in purely philosophical terms. From this he derives the conclusion (programmatic for further studies) of an interdisciplinary, philosophically guided sociology. The *Zeitschrift für Sozialforschung* in particular became the forum for a group of researchers who felt committed to Horkheimer's idea of a comprehensive theory of the course of history. Among them were the philosophers Herbert Marcuse and Theodor W. Adorno, the latter also a musicologist; the psychoanalyst Erich Fromm; the philosopher and literary critic Walter Benjamin; the literary sociologist Leo Löwenthal; Friedrich Pollock, Henryk Grossmann, and Karl-August Wittfogel, economists and sociologists; and the political scientists Franz Neumann and Otto Kirchheimer. Without Horkheimer's power to integrate disparate ideas and personalities, this unusual consortium of researchers would hardly have united and continued to exist as a group.

Horkheimer published the essays which were to be the foundation of his later fame as the *spiritus rector* of Critical Theory in the *Zeitschrift für Sozialforschung* (1932–42). The term "Critical Theory" first appears in the programmatically central essay *Traditionelle und kritische Theorie* ("Traditional and Critical Theory"), which appeared in 1937. In it, Horkheimer outlines a method of research repudiating the subsumptive logic of empirical and analytic explanations and their epistemological objectivism. In rejecting a methodology of the social sciences biased strongly towards natural science he is concerned to demonstrate the mutual influence of facts on theories and of theories back on the realm of facts, an influence determined not only academically but also socially. This bilateral context of research into the life-world is not to be realized solely by means of a materialistic constitutional theory, but is to become practical through seeking a rationally justified modification of irrational reality. Horkheimer here seeks a new relationship between the social sciences and philosophy. In so doing, he aims neither at mere differentiation between the two, nor at their mere unification, but at the epistemological conditions of an emancipatory appropriation of the "traditional" scientific method of cognition.

The essay is thus the positive counterpart to the critique of positivism previously made in the 1937 essay *Der neueste Angriff auf die Metaphysik* ("The latest attack on metaphysics"), written chiefly with reference to the contemporary physicalism of the Vienna Circle. Horkheimer here describes positivism as the equation of science and cognition in general. To him, it means that "knowledge" excludes a critical theory of society because of its own criteria of meaning. A critique of positivism does not mean the denial or wholesale rejection of empirical science, but a philosophical analysis of the boundaries which this imposes upon cognition. Horkheimer traces current empirical claims and methods, particularly of psychology and sociology, back to an interest in calculating the conditions of self-preservation and maximizing them, contrasting with this a way of thinking – dialectical thinking – that takes account of the social conditions of such a calculation itself, and restructures experience with the aim of collectively changing those conditions.

Horkheimer's philosophical project can be described as the reformulation of a critical materialism of social practice. According to him, the idealistic attempt at a conclusive grasp of existence seeks the metaphysical comfort of being beyond one's own mortality, at least in thought. By way of contrast, philosophical materialism is based on the recognition of the finality of death, as well as the endeavor to combat it in reality. Consequently, a need to transcend death lies at the heart of attempts to improve reality. Recognizing death without illusions – even in the face of efforts to deny it – and at the same time objecting to the avoidable threat of it, are the two inseparable sides of materialism. Materialism is opposed not only by the various manifestations of idealism, which transfigure misery, but also by the sciences, which have *de facto* contributed much towards displaying suffering and death in all their naked lack of meaning. But in the guise of an abstract methodology, as the ideology of scientism, they also are nourished by the illusion of the autonomous mind and thus by a spurious metaphysical need for comfort. In contrast, materialism is insight, without comfort and without illusion, into the impossibility of making reparation for past injustice. In the face of the vast indifference of natural history, which in the final result brings the most felicitous of social conditions to an end, historical consciousness is the one fragile and transient place where a memory

366

of human suffering is passed on from generation to generation. Materialism unites indignation at the pointlessly restricted life of the majority of humankind with experience of the irrecoverable nature of happiness.

Most of Horkheimer's essays of this period – among them, for instance, *Materialismus und Moral* ("Materialism and morality," 1933); *Bemerkungen zur philosophischen Anthropologie* ("Remarks on Philosophical Anthropology," 1935); *Egoismus und Freiheitsbewegung* ("Egoism and the Freedom Movement," 1936); *Montaigne und die Funktion der Skepsis* ("Montaigne and the Function of Scepticism," 1938) – revolve around the concept of history and around sociological interpretations of philosophical problems. Western history is reconstructed in a negatively anthropological manner, in terms of the rise and fall of the bourgeois character. Unlike the obligatory historical optimism of the Marxists, Horkheimer's diagnosis is a pessimistic one, which sees the Enlightenment ideals of liberty and solidarity being replaced by a technocratically managed egalitarianism. As opposed to Marx and the Enlightenment, he insists on a dialectical structure in the concepts of freedom and equality. But his movement away from Marx was, at first, tentative, and remained so for a long time. Only in the later aphorisms and essays of the 1960s does he criticize Marx explicitly for identifying reason in society with an effective command over nature. In the end, he says, the realm of freedom – thought by Marx to be the aim of social progress – turns out to be a realm of totalitarian expediency and domination.

Since the 1940s, and assuming these premises for its philosophy of history, Critical Theory sees itself less than ever as the self-reflection of a social movement. The alternatives of the 1920s and 1930s – revolution or a relapse into barbarism – seem at first to have been resolved on the side of the latter. A passage at the end of the *Dialektik der Aufklärung* ("Dialectic of Enlightenment"), written with Adorno, runs apocalyptically thus: "If there is anyone today to whom we can pass the responsibility for the message, we bequeath it not to the 'masses', and not to the individual (who is powerless), but to an imaginary witness – lest it perish with us." In relation to contemporary experience, this book is an attempt at philosophical proof that Nazi terrorism was not a chance accident in Western history, but was rooted deeply in the basic features of the process of civilization. Consequently, Horkheimer sees the destruction of the traditional bourgeois world founded on a dialectic of control of external nature, internal nature, and society. He traces the Enlightenment, which differentiated between these areas, back to its mythical roots. Since these beginnings, liberation from the constraints of external nature has succeeded only when a new domination of a "second nature" has been interposed. The repression of internal natural drives and social domination are already expressed in mythical images of the world; myth itself is understood as an early form of enlightenment, one against which the latter turns. Fascism and the culture industry, finally, are manifestations of the return of repressed nature. In the interests of a progressive rationalization of instrumental reason which takes its guidance from the model of the domination over nature, and which serves that domination, enlightenment thinking is continually undermining itself, until it becomes the new mythology of a resurrected barbaric state of nature, and turns into violence. The book *Dialektik der Aufklärung* begins: "In the most general sense of progressive thought, the Enlightenment has always aimed at liberating men from fear and establishing their sovereignty. Yet the fully enlightened earth radiates disaster triumphant."

The *Dialektik der Aufklärung* and the *Eclipse of Reason*, which appeared at the same time, 1947, also remained systematic reference points for the postwar development of Critical Theory. Only a few years after writing his radical critique of science, morality, and culture conforming to patterns of domination, Horkheimer in fact went back to Germany to rebuild the Frankfurt Institute, with Pollock and Adorno. He was active in the 1950s and 1960s in the university, in the organization of research, in public life, and in cultural politics. This transition from radical non-acceptance to the practice of "small steps" will seem illogical only if one fails to see that Horkheimer, while radically turning enlightenment to self-enlightenment, never succumbs to the paradoxes of later critics of progress who identify reason *in itself* with domination, at the same time using rational arguments to criticize it. "The method of negation," he writes at the end of *The Eclipse of Reason*, "the denunciation of everything that mutilates mankind and impedes its free development, rest on confidence in man."

The *Dialektik der Aufklärung*, too, cannot be fully understood unless one considers the empirical research projects being undertaken at the same time under Horkheimer's general direction: in particular, the extensive studies of authoritarianism, anti-Semitism and prejudice (*Studies in Prejudice*, 5 vols, New York, 1949–50). The connection between sociological empirical science and interpretation in terms of historical philosophy is not, for Critical Theory, something external, but arises both from the limitations of every mere statement of fact and from the self-criticism of the philosophical concept. For the late Horkheimer of the postwar period, the critical claim of philosophy takes the shape of a "longing for *das ganz Andere*." All thinking that concentrates on reality, not just scientific thinking, is subject to this verdict. Here Critical Theory, in imitation of Kantian criticism and agnosticism, approaches a kind of negative theology which remains aware of the transcendence of the world in the claims it makes. As with this negative theology, Horkheimer insists on the memory of what is lost, the practice of what is possible, and the merely regulative idea of what is good. Practical endeavors are intended, if not to refute the prognosis of theoretical pessimism, at least to mitigate or delay its fulfillment.

Horkheimer perhaps affected the thinking of the twentieth century more through his personal influence than through his writings. If he succeeded not only in being academically influential but in expressing the spirit of the times, as Hegel saw the task of philosophy, that fact may be traced back principally to his outstanding influence as a teacher, stimulating and coordinating work, and as a speaker and a conversationalist. His role may be compared with that of Diderot among the French Encyclopaedists. There are some revealing parallels between the Encyclopaedists, who mark the breakthrough of the later Enlightenment, and the Critical Theorists who diagnose its end. Both formulate an encyclopaedic aim, simultaneously rejecting systematic thinking. Both link the rationalization of the various areas of life and of the sciences with an empiricalization of rationalist claims. In

368

both ways of thinking, we can observe the interplay of revolutionary boldness and pre-censoring adaptation to adverse political events. In both, criticism is bound to a past order – conservatism and the will towards progress are curiously intertwined.

Horkheimer inaugurated a new and unique type of philosophical and historical investigation of the social significance of daily attitudes as well as theoretical concepts. At the same time, he did not hypostasize his own categories of criticism as unhistorical abstractions. In this, he set new standards for the self-reflection of philosophy and the sciences. The continuing reflection and criticism of specialized knowledge in relation to the requirements of life as philosophically interpreted and tested, to the social conditions of injustice and suffering, and to the possibility of changing them, remain the vital task of such a critical theory.

## Writings

Horkheimer, Max: *Gesammelte Schriften und Briefwechsel*, vols 1–19, ed. Alfred Schmidt and Gunzelin Schmid Noerr (Frankfurt am Main: S. Fischer, 1985–96).

## References and further reading

Hartmann, Frank: *Max Horkheimers materialistischer Skeptizismus. Frühe Motive der Kritischen Theorie* (Frankfurt am Main: Campus, 1990).

Hese, Heidrun: *Vernunft und Selbstbehauptung: Kritische Theorie als Kritik der neuzeitlichen Rationalität* (Frankfurt am Main: Fischer Taschenbuch, 1984).

Jay, Martin: *The Dialectical Imagination: A History of the Frankfurt School and the Institute of Social Research, 1923–1950* (Boston, MA: Little, Brown, 1973).

Reijen, Willem van: *Horkheimer zur Einführung*, 2nd edn. (Hamburg: Junius, 1987).

Rosen, Zvi: *Max Horkheimer* (Munich: C. H. Beck, 1995).

Schmid Noerr, Gunzelin: *Das Eingedenken der Natur im Subjekt* (Darmstadt: Wissenschaftliche Buchgesellschaft, 1990).

——: *Gesten aus Begriffen. Konstellationen der Kritischen Theorie* (Frankfurt am Main: Fischer Taschenbuch, 1997).

Schmidt, Alfred: *Die Kritische Theorie als Geschichtsphilosophie* (Munich: Carl Hanser, 1976).

Wiggershaus, Rolf: *Die Frankfurter Schule* (Munich: Carl Hanser, 1986).

# 31

# Adorno

## HAUKE BRUNKHORST

Theodor W. Adorno (1903–69) grew up in Frankfurt. His father was a wine merchant, his mother a singer. The political culture of his parents' home was liberal and cosmopolitan and their life-style was bourgeois through and through. Adorno himself later compared his own childhood and youth to the development of a "hothouse plant." This key phrase from his *Minima Moralia*, a collection of aphorisms written in America during World War II and concerning how to lead a right life in a wrong one, allows autobiography to merge with a reflection of the fate of infant prodigies, such as Adorno himself, during the socialization process. Such prodigies "trouble the natural order, and malicious health revels in the danger that threatens them, while society distrusts them as the visible negation of the equation of success with effort" (Adorno 1969a, p. 17).

Adorno may fairly be described as having been born in easy circumstances: unearned good fortune came his way easily and apparently without any effort on his own part – he was not disfigured and distorted by toiling in the sweat of his brow. To him, this element of ease and playful ephemerality, of coincidental chance, was a constituent part of the true Utopia of good luck, the Utopia of a "cloudless day." The "idea of the absolute," he was to write later, is not the eternal, but is temporal and ever transitory, "ephemeral . . . as the bouquet of wine" (Adorno 1981, p. 72). The evil world, with its conceptual efforts and a laborious struggle for existence, broke into the artificial life of the hothouse plant at a late date, from outside. Adorno himself was always able to say, plausibly, that he had a happy childhood which helped all the talents latent in him to break through rapidly.

Adorno's deeply ambivalent relationship with the institutions of modern ethical life was nourished by the experiences of his childhood and family background. To counter the unitarian power of thought and of the normative that trains people to be "disciplinary individuals" (to quote Foucault), making them functioning particles of the bourgeois system of things, Adorno wished to exert the rebellious power of the "non-identical," the anarchic feelings and impulses that constantly elude integration. The "extremely delicate and subtle stratum" (interwoven with the memory of the private happiness of childhood) of what cannot be objectified, the spontaneous and involuntary which cannot be organized or institutionalized, and which Adorno later called the non-identical, requires an institutional framework, a "fixing to organization" (in the words of Hegel). The nature of a completely societal-ized person can enjoy its rights only where there is institutional alienation. The *Dialektik der Aufklärung*, written by Adorno and Max HORKHEIMER (see Article 30) in exile in California in 1944, with the collaboration of Leo Löwenthal and Adorno's wife Gretel, expressly emphasizes that *all* pleasure in human life is the product and consequence of that alienation. And Adorno says in the *Minima Moralia*: "It sometimes appears as if the family, that unfortunate germ cell of society, were also the preservative germ cell of an uncompromising will towards other people" (Adorno 1969a, p. 17). "Individuality," he wrote in the 1960s, "is the product of [social] pressure as well as the energy centre for resistance to this pressure" (Adorno 1966, p. 278).

Consequently, the Fascism that drove Adorno and his friends from Germany in 1933, eventually bringing them into exile in New York by way of Switzerland, England and France, and then to the west coast of America, meant far more to him than the totalitarian variants of repressive class domination and the suppression of instincts. He saw the historical singularity of the "approaching collectivist order" not so much in the intertwining of bourgeois institutions and exploitation as in the totalizing of domination, exploitation, and suppression *by means of* the repressive levelling out of all the ambivalences peculiar to the institutions of the bourgeois order. Although Adorno once said a bourgeois was virtually a Nazi, he meant it only in the sense that the Nazi was created only by the liquidation of the bourgeois: "The approaching collectivist order is an insult to those without class: in the bourgeois it also liquidates the Utopia that was once nourished by maternal love" (Adorno 1969a, p. 16).

At the age of fifteen, Adorno met the editor of the *Frankfurter Zeitung*, Siegfried Kracauer, who was fourteen years older than he was and who quickly became his intellectual and philosophical mentor. Saturday after Saturday the two of them read Kant's *Critique of Pure Reason* together. These readings, and indeed his meeting with Kracauer, left deep philosophical traces on Adorno's work. It is scarcely exaggerating to say that the *Critique of Pure Reason* was more important than any other book for Adorno's intellectual development. The idea of negative dialectics which is Adorno's most original contribution to philosophy owes much to Kant's antinomial teaching, which is in no hurry to cover up contradictions, but keeps them open and allows thought to swing back and forth between opposing extremes. A dialectic which is a "movement between extremes" (Jay 1984, p. 250), passing "right through the extremes" (Adorno 1969b, pp. 19, 29) without synthesis or a centre, is not solely of philosophical significance for Adorno; it is also the basic idea of his aesthetic constructivism and of an ethical theory of a well-spent life (cf. Schweppenhauser 1993).

Very early on Adorno, as an intellectual, adopted an attitude towards conservative cultural criticism of rationality and enlightenment similar to that of his friend Siegfried Kracauer. He takes over Kracauer's formula, developed in a critique of the "active circle" of the "conservative revolution" in the 1920s, to the effect that capitalism rationalized not too much but too little. "Ideals which the intellect has not tasted and enjoyed are useless natural products," wrote Kracauer in the 1920s (1984, p. 366), and later Adorno would lose no opportunity of entering the fray against a soupy mixture of "warmed-up eternal truths" of the kind taught in grammar schools (Adorno 1967, p. 9).

371

In his last year at school he was reading LUKÁC's *Theorie des Romans* (see Article 40) and BLOCH's *Geist der Utopie* (see Article 32), books which fascinated him more than anything else either author had written. Together with the *Critique of Pure Reason*, they are at the roots of his thinking. While preparing for his doctoral examination, Adorno met Horkheimer and his friend Pollock, who were then living in a hotel in Königstein near Frankfurt. "They are both Communists," he wrote on July 16, 1924 to Leo Löwenthal, with whom he had been friends for some time, "and we had long, passionate conversations about the materialistic concept of history, conversations in which we confessed a great deal to each other" (Löwenthal 1980, p. 248). This was the beginning of a life-long friendship with Horkheimer. They wrote the *Dialektik der Aufklärung* together, and with that book behind them they became the outstanding figures of the so-called Frankfurt School in the 1950s and 1960s when they returned from exile to the Federal Republic of Germany. When they spoke of "Critical theory" they meant thinking of the negative as developed by the two of them.

In 1923 Adorno met BENJAMIN (see Article 29), and the two men quickly became friends. The dark and mysterious work of Benjamin, who was eleven years the elder, is an important key to Adorno's thinking. Although he owed Benjamin not only his micrological method but above all the idea of a negative dialectic – the basic features of which he first set out in his inaugural lecture of May 7, 1931, and which he continued tenaciously elaborating all his life – Adorno was to season Benjamin's "dialectic at a standstill" with the salt of Hegelian dynamics. Benjamin's posthumously published theses concerning the history of philosophy and his program of an aporetically ambivalent "control of the control of nature" also became important themes for the *Dialektik der Aufklärung*. However, Adorno distanced himself both from the all too obviously theological impulses of his meditative friend, and from his over-ardent revolutionary hopes for the utopian and explosive potential of the new mass art. Instead of leaving a "theological and political" fragment behind at his death, like Benjamin, Adorno left a fragment of a work on aesthetic theory, a fact which indicates the distance he maintained from both politics and theology. Less of a decisionist than Benjamin, Adorno remained on the comparatively safe path of German idealism with his claim in the *Negative Dialektik*, not a modest claim but by comparison with Benjamin a conventional one, to "have thought out logically to the end what dialectic means" (Wiggershaus 1988, p. 37).

Finally, then, Adorno remained on a path which integrated central themes from the work of his two very different travelling companions, Horkheimer and Benjamin: the enlightenment idea of a *consciousness-arousing* critique, and the aesthetic and theological idea of a *redemptive* critique.

At first the study of philosophy was only a sideline for Adorno. His real domain in the early 1920s was music criticism and musical aesthetics, and his intention was to become a composer. He wrote about a hundred pieces on music between 1921 and 1931, mostly music criticism for the radio. By the end of this period Adorno was a stern and much feared music critic who ardently supported the Schönberg school. At the beginning of 1925 he went to Vienna as a pupil of Alban Berg to train as a composer and concert pianist. "Everything Schönbergian is sacred," he wrote to

Kracauer on March 8, adding, in a rather threatening manner, "apart from that, only Mahler is any good among contemporary composers, and anyone who says otherwise will be crushed." In the journal *Die Musik* he raises Schönberg's authority to the realms of the absolute: "It is not seemly for anyone to criticize Schönberg's works today; they contain the truth" (Wiggershans 1986, p. 88).

Despite his fascination with the irrational, evoked by Schönberg, the early Adorno, who was far more successful as critic than composer, remained entirely rationalistic in his attempts to define an aesthetic of the New Music. That, of course, has to do with the fascination itself, for what fascinated Adorno so much was something rational. Schönberg's twelve-tone technique was organized in a wholly constructive way, and as such it stood, in Adorno's eyes, for the crucial progress from nature and immediacy to a technically mediated art in the "process of the rationalization of European music." To him, it was no less than the demythologizing of that music: "The material has become clearer and freer, and is removed for ever from the mythical conditions of number as they control the harmonic series and tonal harmonics" (Adorno 1974, p. 180).

After his studies, Adorno set out with great energy on two careers at once: as philosopher and as musician. By the middle of the 1920s both his careers had suffered setbacks. Adorno had to abandon his dream of being a composer, and he gained his qualifications as a university lecturer only at the second attempt. In 1933 he was among the first to be forbidden to pursue his profession. After trying unsuccessfully to make his way as a journalist and piano teacher, he went to England in 1934 to continue studying at Oxford, where he met Gilbert Ryle among others, although Ryle's thinking had no influence on him. After a last visit to Frankfurt in 1937 he fled to New York, became one of the group working at Horkheimer's Institute for Social Research, and initially took charge of the musical side of the Radio Research Project directed by Paul Lazarsfeld.

His experiences of exile were varied and ambivalent; the most outstanding but also the most one-sided and controversial document to come out of this period was the theory of the culture industry developed in the *Dialektik der Aufklärung* and in many monographs. The group's thesis is that in the age of Hollywood and television, enlightenment threatens to turn to mass deception. Kant's definition of art as "purposiveness without a purpose," as described in a polemical formulation in this work, written throughout in a mood of black irony, has long since become "lack of purpose for any purpose": the instrumental annihilation of any point in life. However, the thesis clings to the *difference* between enlightenment and mass deception, so that it can denounce the culture industry as a betrayal of the original intentions of the Enlightenment. It is thus consciousness-arousing critique, but does not do justice to Benjamin's own critique of the cinema, jazz, and light entertainment, which came down on their side.

The America of his exile always remained alien to Adorno; the distancing from old Europe which he inflexibly maintained caused him to see the dark side of America's brilliant progress even more clearly. Once back in Europe, however, he began to see the old continent through American eyes, and the alienating sense of distance acquired in exile far away now made the barbarism of retarded conditions at home all the more glaring. When the Frankfurt School returned to Frankfurt, the newly opened Institute for Social Research was its avant-garde, and Adorno neglected few opportunities to emphasize that point in the 1950s, demonstrating the superiority of progressive statistical methods and analytical techniques of enquiry to the old humanistic belief in the revelatory power of comprehension.

It was a long time before Adorno became a full professor in Germany. The post to which he was finally appointed in 1957 was disparagingly described in official jargon as a "reparations chair." Adorno and Horkheimer were exposed to the uncivilized anti-Semitic hostility of their colleagues. Adorno was never to be appointed to a "normal" professorship at a German university. At the time Horkheimer noted bitterly: "The majority of Germans who sympathized with National Socialism are better off today than those who kept aloof from Fascism" (Horkheimer 1974, p. 178).

In 1959 Adorno became Director of the Institute, succeeding Horkheimer, and after 1965 he was twice elected chairman of the *Deutsche Gesellschaft für Soziologie*. The famous dispute over positivism which followed became a matter of cultural politics, and the sociological congress of 1968 in Frankfurt, which Adorno opened with a brilliant paper on the question "Late capitalism or industrial society?," was already caught up in the violent cultural revolutionary storms of the time.

Adorno's influence grew in the 1960s, communicating by no means unsuccessfully with the mass culture he criticized with increasing vehemence, a culture that oppressed him as critic even as it waited avidly for his next radio piece. He was active in the journalism, the lecture halls, and even sometimes on the television screens of the young Federal Republic.

Adorno died of a heart attack on August 8, 1969, while on holiday in the Valais canton of Switzerland, shortly before completing his *Ästhetische Theorie*. In the pieces he wrote with increasing frequency as he grew older, on the occasion of the round-number birthdays or deaths of his close friends, Adorno regularly inveighed not only against the idea of a gerontocracy, which he hated, but against the secret alliance of metaphysics and death. Writing to celebrate Max Horkheimer's 70th birthday, he recalls Kant's idea of the immortality without which nothing good can be conceived. It gives us the "power to resist the dilapidations of nature . . . which is at one with our sympathy for oppressed nature" (Adorno 1978, p. 164). On the death of Siegfried Kracauer, the friend of his youth, he noted: "The one thing that this thoughtful life did not reflect in itself, truly its blind spot, was death. Its hastening towards him now makes final what he, of his own intent, opposed: all that is final. The fact that this most individual of men had to die is an indictment of the universal" (ibid., p. 196).

That last quotation brings together the main themes of Adorno's negative dialectic: emphasis on the self-reflecting, conscious life; a condemnation, criticizing metaphysics, of all that is final and of speculative systems of thought; and the plea for the "open" and "experimental" which Adorno all his life put in opposition against the "closed society" (Popper) of the Hegelian "forced reconciliation" between the individual consciousness with the collective whole. The "non-identical," a *leitmotiv* of his thinking, is the individual factor which eludes subsumption under general

374

concepts and norms, and Adorno sees the fact of its denial and "savaging" as a forceful indictment of the existing state of things. Albrecht Wellmer has aptly called Adorno an "advocate of the non-identical." The "non-identical" is the *individual* which can never be wholly grasped by description in general terms. It can only be re-described again and again. The "context of blindness" of which Adorno speaks refers to that *blindness of the subject* which erroneously believes itself to be in possession of absolute truth, able to give a *conclusive* description and account of the individual, which Adorno sometimes calls, with Hegel and Husserl, the *thing itself.* Adorno also uses the term *identitarian thinking* for the blindness of a merely "subjective reason," centered on the perspective of the ego and confined to a one-sided projection. In so far as it marks a "collective consciousness" (Durkheim) or even wide areas of "Western rationalism" (Weber), Adorno calls it a "context of blindness." Claims to absolute or "conclusive" knowledge are presumptions on the part of a human reason unaware of its own limitations, for reason itself is the reason of mortal, individual, naturally imperfect beings. In this respect, human reason is always *non*-identical with itself when it thinks it has recognized absolute truth and "the whole." It is never entirely transparent to itself, since *our* reason is itself something individual, the product of a process of individualization. Conclusively identitarian thinking deceives itself about itself and its own history. However, what eludes the identitarian self-knowledge of reason is the factor whereby reason itself remains an opaque, non-transparent piece of "nature." Consequently, Adorno understands the dialectic of enlightenment as a "mindfulness of nature in the subject" which should recall to our reason the cognitively suppressed "pre-history of subjectivity."

Such feats of memory, however, do not by any means lead back to the "dull absence of antithesis" (Hegel) of natural individuality. "The illusion of taking direct hold of the many" by simply abandoning reason, knowledge, and the reflective power of identitarian thinking, writes Adorno in the *Negative Dialektik*, "would be a mimetic regression . . . into mythology, into the horror of the diffuse (Adorno 1966, p. 160). Even worse than the blindness of identitarian thinking would be regression into the barbarism of a dull absence of antithesis. Consequently, we can escape the forgetfulness of our thinking and the blindness of our reason (Adorno often speaks of the "Utopia of having escaped") only by trying to make visible – by methods of the constructive rationality of identitarian thinking – what those methods themselves make dark, hidden, and forgotten: the elusive individuality of our naturally imperfect mortal being. Adorno does not, therefore, require us to abjure reflection, but to undertake a *second reflection*; not to return to the unmediated and undivided, but to continue the mediations and differentiations of thought to a *second immediacy*; in the same way, he does not call for romantic silencing of the affirmative art that transfigures and glorifies what exists, but for the bold construction of a *second musical language* which can be acquired only by *more* technique, by perfect command of the material, and is not to be had, for instance, at the cheap price of pre-technical expressivity.

Adorno developed these philosophical ideas quite early, and none of his early writings has been as influential as his inaugural lecture of 1931 on the *Actuality of*

*Philosophy*. It was preceded by the paper he intended to submit, but did not, as his qualifying thesis to become a lecturer, and which was published only posthumously, as the *Concept of the Unconscious in Transcendental Psychology*, and also by the thesis published in 1931 on *Kierkegaard's Construction of the Aesthetic*, which owes much to Kracauer and Benjamin.

While Adorno sees the *actuality of philosophy* in a certain practice of *thinking*, at the same time he distinguishes it sharply from scientific *explanation*. As interpretation, philosophy is a *second reflection*, but as such it remains dependent on the first or scientific explanation. It is no less experimental and constructive than that explanation, operates with "models" and keeps designing new "experimental arrangements." It does not fall back on original forces, but only on knowledge, reflection, and identitarian thinking which long ago separated and analyzed "pre-found" reality into its "elements." *Meaning* always begins with the *difference* (Hegel's "division") between identity and non-identity, reflection and object. What is finally revealed, "with cogent evidence," as the truth is *solely* the result of an experimental and operational practice which takes from pre-found reality all that it arranges for experiment. The *essay* is therefore literally (in the sense of being an "attempt") the form for philosophical interpretation. This idea is reflected decades later in Adorno's essay on the *Essay as Form*, which he prefaces to his *Noten zur Literatur* of 1958.

Adorno's understanding of freedom is oriented by the experiences of the aesthetic moderns. It coincides with neither negative freedom from tyranny nor with positive freedom to realize a reasonable plan of life. Adorno's model of freedom aims instead for conscious and intentional self-exposure even to the contingency of situations one can neither command nor control. Aesthetic experiences, according to Adorno, are obtained only when we abandon ourselves to the impulses that overpower us as we hear a concert or read a book. In our experimental relationship to our own world we are neither mere copies of pre-given patterns (as was, for instance, the case with the traditional storyteller) nor are we cast in the part of one who (like the ideal author of the classic bourgeois novel) has the whole story under his control. Rather, we expose ourselves to the dialogue of contradictory modes of language, or voluntarily let ourselves be carried away by the "flowing stream of notes themselves" (Hegel). What Hegel saw as the loss of any freedom on the part of the subject is interpreted by Adorno as an opportunity to gain freedom: as freedom from the subject's compulsion to control and preserve itself. The subject reveals a new dimension of freedom in the very fact that it abandons itself to conflicting impulses and exposes itself to a diversity of situations which cannot in principle be controlled (cf. Menke 1993, p. 228). This understanding of freedom is related to John Stuart Mill's in *On Liberty* as well as to that of Nietzsche, Derrida, or Rorty. The freedom to experiment with oneself and the "linguistic" material of the world makes new forms of existence possible, so that we need no longer make our way through life as mere "copies" (Rorty) but are in a position to lead a non-conformist and "different life" from that of other people (Mill 1972, p. 137). Adorno describes this as a "sudden" and "explosive" breakthrough of "materialization," and this is the attitude the essay adopts towards reality.

376

The essayistic technique of writing which distinguishes Adorno's work even in his major systematic texts strives to rule out any idea of a "second world beyond, to be revealed by analysis of the apparent world," for that idea is the core of subjectivist projection of an absolute truth on to the outside world. Rather, the truth never reveals itself to us except as the result of our own practice. It must "amalgamate" to form a *new* arrangement of *pre-found* elements, which then precisely *matches* our problems and internal "mysteries" like the *correct* "combination of numbers" on the "lock of a well-guarded safe-deposit box" (Adorno 1966, p. 165).

"Anyone who would explain matters," says Adorno early as his inaugural lecture, "by seeking a world in itself behind the phenomenal world, a world on which it is built and which supports it, is behaving like one who would seek in the mystery the image of a Being behind it which reflects the mystery." This is the old Platonic method, which Adorno rejects. For the "task of philosophy is not to explore hidden and present intentions of reality, but to interpret intentionless reality by raising those questions whose cogent formulation is the task of science by virtue of the construction of figures . . . from isolated elements of reality; it is a task to which philosophy always remains bound, since its power to cast light cannot be kindled except by those hard questions" (Adorno 1974, p. 335).

We find Adorno, then, related in this to both American pragmatism and the early Heidegger, replacing the Platonic relation between the original picture and its image, with its theory of the correspondence of truth, by a pragmatic theory of truth supported by the relation between action and experience. Mimesis, the basic concept of Adorno's anthropology and aesthetics, is not a mere *imitation* of reality or the ideas lying behind it (as in Plato and Aristotle); instead, it is expressive *assimilation* to something which eludes the subject or threatens to overpower it. Whatever one may think of Adorno's emphatic concept of aesthetic truth, it is at least far from the idea of a "mirror of nature" (Rorty). Works of art are themselves a form of real behavior, and they thus become a "second reality, reacting to the first" (Adorno 1971, p. 425). "The unique nature of music," says Adorno in his posthumously published fragments on *Beethoven*, lies in the fact that it is "not an image, does not stand *for* another reality, but is a reality *sui generis*" (Adorno 1993, p. 235).

While in exile in England, Adorno completed a major study of HUSSERL (see Article 15) which appeared in 1956 under the title *Zur Metakritik der Erkenntnistheorie* in which he clearly rejected all original philosophical claims to final justification.

During his period at the New York Institute under the direction of Horkheimer, Adorno worked principally on studies of the culture industry and the social psychology of prejudice. In the 1940s one side of these studies, the one dealing with the culture industry, led to the *Dialektik der Aufklärung* (1947), and the other to the great study on the authoritarian personality which instantly made the Frankfurt School famous in its professional field.

In Adorno's work as an empirical sociologist, which he himself always regarded as an important corrective to philosophical speculation, the centre of interest is the mechanism of the subject-centered projection of objective truths into the strange and alienated world of others (races, peoples, minorities, outsiders, intellectuals, etc.). "Anti-Semitism," as the *Dialektik der Aufklärung* sums up the result of the Institute's socio-psychological researches in a chapter written with Leo Löwenthal, "is based on false projection. . . . If mimesis makes itself resemble its environment, then false projection makes the environment resemble it" (Horkheimer and Adorno 1947, p. 220). The false projections of the anti-Semite are interpreted by Horkheimer and Adorno as an extreme case of identitarian thinking. While they see in "true mimesis" a decentralizing achievement of the strong ego, false projection brings one's own ego to the center of the world with exclusive force, so that the world becomes the "powerless or all-powerful idea of what is projected on it" (p. 224). In this the racist resembles the complementary figures of these who suffer from delusions of grandeur or of persecution. "The consistency of what is always the same becomes a surrogate for omnipotence. It is as if the snake, who told Adam and Eve that they would be as God, had kept its promise in the character of the paranoiac, who creates everything in his own image" (ibid.).

Adorno completed work on the *Dialektik der Aufklärung* and his *Minima Moralia* at the end of the war. Both books offer an extremely gloomy diagnosis of the times. The hope of the 1930s for science and enlightenment seems to have disappeared without trace. However, appearances are deceptive. In fact, in both works Adorno was concerned to support the idea of enlightenment without idealistic illusions or metaphysical hopes, even under conditions which seemed almost to exclude any realization of its rational approach. To understand the books correctly we must bear in mind Adorno's method of using the essay form, and read them as philosophical interpretation, model, and experimental arrangement. They are then revealed in their dual function as a *diagnosis of the times* and as a radical *experiment in ideas*, endeavoring to explore the extreme case of enlightenment achieved under the conditions of its opposite. Whereas the *Dialektik der Aufklärung* is concerned with the historical and social condition of the reason brought to bear on it, a condition in which theory threatens to be absorbed into technique, practice into universal availability and art into industry, the interest of the *Minima Moralia* is directly practical: its aphorisms draw up an ethic of damaged life. The question is how a right way of life is possible in the damaged conditions of modern times, and the answer runs, apodictically: "There is no right life in the wrong life." That does not, however, exclude the possibility of *acting* rightly; the thesis initially confirms only that there can be no right life *as a whole* in the wrong life. This again does not imply, as Nietzsche said, that everything is permissible. It is perfectly possible to judge whether any individual action is right or wrong, moreover, the attitudes and characteristics of people in modern times, the various aspects, and all the separate factors making up their experience of life, are open to moral evaluation. Furthermore, Adorno's thesis states only that *no right life* is possible in the extreme case of a wholly wrong one. This does not mean, on the one hand, that even in such a case a life which is *not wrong* is inconceivable. For applied to our state of morality the *double negative* is by no means the same as the *single affirmative* (this fundamental logical insight of Hegel's was always a guideline to Adorno). On the other hand, the *Mimima Moralia* are "Reflections from a damaged life," as the subtitle tells us, and yet again, a damaged life is *not the same as* a wholly wrong one. The same holds good of such much-quoted aphorisms as "The whole is the untrue." That again does not mean there is no truth in the world, that there are no true statements or right actions. This aphorism, directed against Hegel, states only that truth cannot be expressed by society or history as a whole. The point is therefore primarily critical of metaphysics, but it is as far from a totalizing critique of reason, such as is characteristic of Nietzsche, Heidegger, or Foucault, as it is from metaphysics of the old, transfiguring type.

The criticism of metaphysics in the *Negative Dialektik* is constructive, not destructive. It aims to liberate its truth while toppling it. It "shows solidarity for metaphysics at the moment of its fall." But it does not wish to set up a new metaphysics or rehabilitate an old one: "It aims at the absolute, but a broken and indirect one," without any claim to "what is conclusively total" (Adorno 1981 [1958], pp. 573, 570).

In 1949 Adorno published a book written between 1940 and 1948, which he himself wished to be seen as his own contribution to the theme of the dialectics of enlightenment; this was the *Philosophie der neuen Musik*. Despite its still pessimistic and negative mood, there is a notable difference between it and the *Dialektik der Aufklärung*. The new book postulates throughout an open dialectic between progress and regression, and is able to separate the productive antinomies of progress from the destructive contradictions of regression, although it remains well aware of the dangerous interweaving of the two directions of movement. All progress in modern life is, as Adorno shows from the examples of Schönberg and Stravinsky, threatened *both* by technocratic materialization *and* by the heterogeneity of natural immediacy. However, it is not only endangered but empowered by *both* threats. The *grand one-sidedness of identitarian thinking* and the *grand uncertainty* of the non-identical, the individual, of organic pleasure and the diffuse urges of instinct both involve the chance of genuine progess, of liberation from narrow and repressive circumstances.

Adorno's posthumously published and voluminous fragment provides an "aesthetic theory" to go with his "musical monographs" on Wagner, Mahler, and Berg, and to the *Noten zur Literatur*. It confirms Adorno's as probably the "most important aesthetic of this century, a period rich in the production of art but rather poor in its theory." His *Ästhetische Theorie* is concerned with the "law of movement" of modern art, which Adorno thinks he has seen in the breaking of the autonomy of a constructivist spirit of form and a sensuously mimetic expressive shape. Abstraction, reflection, and formalistic intellectualization loosen all conventional bonds with the sensuous and expressive aspect of art. Both extremes run diametrically away from each other, yet belong together – for instance, in Schönberg with the expressive "musical style of freedom" of his early period around 1910, and his technically perfected twelve-tone music of the 1920s; *intellectualization* makes *de-intellectualization* possible. This is the law of movement of cultural modernity, aiming to explain its dynamic, which contains both risk and potential. Modernism in art and culture causes the "explosion of metaphysical meaning," along with the emancipation of the subject. The explosion which makes "anti-traditionalistic energy . . . an engulfing Maelstrom" (Adorno 1971, p. 41) destroys metaphysics

379

and liberates its fragile meaning, which is *both* futile and elevated, at least at those fortunate moments when we are not wasting our lives (Wellmer 1997).

Proper understanding of the *Ästhetische Theorie* was impeded in the period immediately after its publication by the assumption that it was a conservative retreat to the concept of the work of art, and to the moderns who had by now become classics themselves. Adorno's criticism of the overblown political claims of the more recent avant-garde, however, was fundamentally misunderstood. After all, long before this Adorno himself had noted the "ageing of the New Music." Moreover, he always adopted an experimental and open attitude, sometimes even a vacillating one, towards whatever was the latest development. In his famous lecture on non-formal music, he himself calls for a departure from the one-sided constructivism of the Schönbergian school, and in a lecture on "Art and the Arts" delivered in the early 1960s which attracted far too little attention, right at the beginning of the great new departure, he traced the profound accord between the "most recent movement" and his own aesthetics. He emphasizes the tendency to overstep boundaries, speaks of a reciprocal "fraying" of art, life, and the arts, and explains it as a subversive crossing of borders arising from within the arts themselves and validating its own language. "Fraying" and the overstepping of boundaries are not movements aiming at a whole: they do not seek to establish a new *Gesamtkunstwerk* ("total art work"), or to shape life as a work of art, as in Fascist and Stalinist myth. Instead, they are concerned with those partial and always unique infringements of borders which do not destroy the autonomy of the aesthetic (Adorno 1967; Eichel 1993).

In the same context Adorno also corrects his criticism of HEIDEGGER (see Article 18), making it clear that his own concept of the aesthetic "material" which is constantly presenting the mind of the interpreter with new riddles, and turning interpretation into a process that cannot be concluded, is related to Heidegger's concept in his essay on art, as is the emphasis on the "linguistic character of all art" (Adorno 1967). Just as Adorno sees the work of art as the right place for experimental freedom owing its existence to the antagonism of construction and mimesis, rationality and material, sensuous language and non-sensuous natural things, all in strict artistic and methodical arrangement, so Heidegger too defines the work of art as a "struggle" between the comprehensible, always meaningful "world" and the closed, de-intellectualized, silent "earth" which, Adorno would have said, holds the "natural material" from which the world of works is made.

Despite this considerable agreement with Heidegger (and many deconstructionists) on Adorno's part, he is no linguistic idealist. He does not believe that the power of works of art to reveal the world necessarily and unarguably validates a higher truth of being, wholly unavailable to ordinary mortals and their everyday language, a truth in whose light alone we see individual things as what they are. For him, consequently, the "dispute" between "world" and "earth," between meaningful language and the speechless silence of things, a dispute which the works settle in themselves, is not an inescapable fact of existence, remote from practical life and the dispute of "human beings speaking and acting among themselves" (Marx). Adorno's last word is: "There is no being without beings" ("*Kein Sein ohne Seiendes*").

# Writings

Adorno, T. W.: *Negativ Dialektik* (Frankfurt: Suhrkamp, 1966).

——: *Ohne Leitbild* (Frankfurt: Suhrkamp, 1967).

——: *Minima Moralia* (Frankfurt: Suhrkamp, 1969a).

——: *Nervenpunkte der Neuen Musik* (Reinbek: Rowohlt, 1969b).

——: *Ästhetische Theorie* (Frankfurt: Suhrkamp, 1971).

——: "Realition und Fortschritt." In *Adorno/Krenelz: Briefwechsel* (Frankfurt: Suhrkamp, 1974).

——: *Vermischle Schriften – I*, vol. 20 of *Gesammelte Schriften* (Frankfurt: Suhrkamp, 1978).

——: *Noten zur Literatur* (1958; Frankfurt: Suhrkamp, 1981).

——: *Beethoven* (Frankfurt: Suhrkamp, 1993).

Horkheimer, M. and Adorno, T. W.: *Dialektik der Aufklärung* (Amsterdam, 1947).

# References and further reading

Eichel, C.: *Vom Ermatten der Avantgarde zur vernetzung der Kunste* (Frankfurt: Suhrkamp, 1993).

Jay, M.: *Marxism and Totality* (Cambridge: Cambridge University Press, 1984).

Kracauer, S.: "Mimimalforderungen an die Intellektuellen." In Stark, M. (ed.), *Deutsche Intellektuelle, 1910–1933* (Heidelberg, 1984).

Löwenthal, Leo: *Mitmachen wollte ich nie* (Frankfurt: Suhrkamp, 1980).

Menke, C.: "Liberalismus in konflikt." In Brumlik, M. and Brunkhorst, H. (eds): *Gemeinschaft und Gerechtigkeit* (Frankfurt: Fischer, 1993).

Mill, J. S.: *On Liberty*, in *Utilitarianism* (London, 1972).

Schweppenhauser, G.: *Ethik nach Auschwitz: Adorno Negative Moralphilosophie* (Hamburg, 1993).

Wellmer, A.: *Adorno: Die Moderne und das Erhabene* (1997).

Wiggershaus, R.: *Die Frankfurter Schule* (Munich: Hansa, 1986).

——: *Adorno* (Munich: Beck, 1988).

# 32

# Bloch

HANS-DIETER BAHR

The common thread that links the thinking of Ernst Bloch (1885–1977) to "Critical theory" is Bloch's Marx-oriented criticism of society. Epistemological and ethical criticism move on the same plane of discourse. A conditioned dialectic is to mediate the break between theory and practice made by Kant's critique of metaphysics. However, Bloch disputes the claim of Hegel's dialectic to have completed that mediation, a mediation as a consequence of which not only do history and actual events as suffered and experienced comprehend themselves, but so does the suffering itself. However, whatever meaning is imputed to the latter, there is no such thing as suffering that comprehends itself, for it is inherent in real suffering that in addition it suffers from its incomprehensibility and urgently wishes for its sublation.

However, Bloch resists the tendency of "Critical theory" to turn philosophy into social criticism. Paradoxically, he develops a metaphysic of history in which the "superstructure" is determined as the "basis" of the future so that at the same time it will keep destroying it.

In his thinking, the term "Utopia" – taken from Thomas More – does not merely undertake the negative function of criticism; those ideals which are constantly aiming at their possible realization are described as "utopian." We therefore have a situation in discourse which no longer perfectly matches dialectic. On the one hand, the "Utopia" is supposed to take over the critical function of a "determinate negation" and the speculative function of syntheses capable of anticipation, but, on the other, it is supposed to be able to break with any kind of determination purely in order to open up new possibilities. However, that openness contains, as it were, its final absolution; surviving the "death of God" (Habermas 1971), "Utopia" is free of him. The openness occurs not as an original principle, but as ever recurrent. In this, however, it does not constitute any sequence or historical development in itself. Rather, it fragments all genealogy and allows the emergence of mysterious events, "real ciphers" and indistinct fragments of wishes. However, such *Spuren* ("Traces" 1918) coming from nowhere and going nowhere (Mayer 1965) never condense into an inescapable fate or a tragic dilemma. Instead, Bloch classifies them hierarchically above ever-extensible claims to complete wish-fulfillment and world-fulfillment – suffusing the Judaeo-Christian tradition in an "anti-Greek" and yet pagan manner (Lyotard 1976). Impelled by latent lack, utopian openness thus equally abruptly becomes a closed "darkness of the experienced moment." However, unlike despair closing in, and unlike fear or confidence which are certain of the end or the future, the "comprehended activity of an affect of expectation," i.e. hope, persists in the uncertainty of utopian openness (Bloch, *Das Prinzip Hoffnung*, 1957).

Here, a series of cleavages in Bloch's thinking becomes evident. Utopia, as a "function," is finally supposed to disappear in the identity of completely realized fulfillment, instead of "traveling endlessly" or regulating a never-ending idea. From this, we see that Bloch expects nothing but a history of acquisition in a process of the total eradication of what is foreign (Bahr 1994). Nor did he escape the tendency to mythologize violence as a "midwife" (Bloch, *Thomas Münzer*, 1922), a tendency found in anti-liberal currents in philosophy as well as in other fields, especially in Germany. By way of contrast, however, Utopia is also supposed to undertake the function of liberating man and nature, a function that cannot be fulfilled and become absolutely present if it is also, when all has been realized, supposed to keep open the possibility itself as a state of "being like Utopia." But Utopia is also evident in the function of a nihilistic possibility, since that liberty could also prove to be absolute emptiness and nothing. Where Bloch felt that the utopian openness eludes its functionalization in the play of possibilities, he spoke of a "question that cannot be constructed" (*Geist der Utopie*, 1918).

Even if they rejected his "chiliastic socialism," his readers were impressed by Bloch's expressionist, dithyrambic style (Hesse 1935). He was far-sighted enough to analyze the emergent National Socialism, from 1924 onwards, as a critique of a Marxism hostile to the imagination, although he believed as firmly as his friends Lukács and Benjamin that Marxism could be regenerated (*Erbschaft dieser Zeit*, 1925). On his return from exile in the USA he taught philosophy in Leipzig from 1949 until the time when he was banned from teaching and publishing in the GDR, on the grounds that he "led the young astray" by his "revisionism and mysticism." After the building of the Berlin Wall he moved to Tübingen. Although his thinking on theology was to prove highly influential, it did not bring about any decisive changes in philosophical argument. This may be partly due to the fact that he addressed most of his philosophical contemporaries polemically rather than sympathetically. Above all, however, Bloch displayed little patience with phenomenological, hermeneutic, and other studies. He was regarded by the New Left as an iconoclast who shattered the dogmatic pattern of base and superstructure, promoting not only the criticism of mass culture as a media industry but also the design of subcultures. With the decline of the New Left the term "Utopia" swiftly regained that aura of intoxicating yet inspiring ideals which had surrounded it since Goethe, since Engels, since Mannheim, and which Bloch himself criticized as "utopianism." Since the collapse of Soviet Communism, "Utopia" has once again been equated with those "unrealizable ideals" which merely lead to despotic regimes if put into practice. In view of neo-nationalist xenophobia, ecological catastrophes, possible apocalyptic disaster in the fields of nuclear energy and gene technology, even the open possibilities seem to be closing. Why did attempts at thinking along lines of "utopian openness" prove so weak?

The term *topia* was used in ancient Rome for gardens and accounts of them. The coinage "u-topia" (for *ou* + *topos*) as used by More not only declares the not-being

(*ou*) of a place which is simultaneously an imaginary good place (*ou* used enclitical-
ly for *eu*), but also implies the *where* (*ou*) of these places, an elsewhere. However, no
light is cast on the problem of the space opened by such utopian places, to which
one cannot keep returning as if it were real: partly because the open space was
accused of being "empty," partly because it was given the status of the problem of
freedom in the metaphysics of will, and partly because it was shifted to a "horizon,"
as in phenomenology. Above all, however, the space itself was interpreted in temporal metaphysical terms as an omnipresent place, never-ending or ending only
*n*-dimensionally. A certain understanding of temporality was inscribed in this
"space," which can be absent only as nothing. In this omnipresent space–time,
everything emerging and decaying, everything constant and recurrent, is subjected to an irreversible sequence which repeats only itself (qua subject) as identical.
That which is actually in being is thus defined as re-presentation. Bloch initially
remains bound to this tradition. For however much the content of ideals, of pre-
appearance in art, and of material possibilities may change, their own not-yet-
being – through which they tend towards realization – already has been. Here
Bloch does not escape what he himself deplored as a basic feature of philosophy to
date: the assumption that a re-presenting "anamnesis" precedes what has been and
what has already become. Through the ideal, something unreal can be grasped in
every reality, and can be anticipated as having been realized even if it is not yet
possible for it to take concrete shape. However, as Bloch rejects the dogma of
"necessary developmental laws" he must, as it were, express the future perfect of
this future state of having become in the subjunctive: "it may have become." The
possibility opened up, however, is not just imperatively pervaded by the weight of
suffering, so that it seems as if the removal of that suffering could never reach a
state of equilibrium without lapsing into indifference. Rather, Bloch formulates an
imperative of enjoyment through which every happiness capable of being experienced can be exceeded by a "melancholy of fulfillment." In this Faustian motif, the
assumed "incomprehensibility" of experienced happiness becomes paradoxical evidence of its absence, which as yet is not experienced.

However, in the obvious pleasure taken in a style overflowing with metonymy
and metaphor, Bloch demonstrates an aesthetic suspension of desire which – in
Kant's terms – brings a double surplus into play: on the one hand there is a "more
desire" which exceeds the "synthesis of self-awareness" by allowing enjoyment to
take part in a *sensus communis*; on the other, a "more thinking" which does not lag
behind logical understanding but exceeds it in the play of its possibilities. The
literary nature of his thought shows symptomatically in his extremely extended use
of the term "category," which thus takes on the function of what Aristotle described
as rhetorical *topoi*. As desire always exceeds the perception of reality and its comprehension in argument, the aesthetic surplus becomes the most significant factor
in Bloch's beliefs.

But what else does the term "utopia" mean in an aesthetically communicable
dialectic of lack and surplus? In 1961 ADORNO (Article 31) remarked that Bloch was
inclined to bury Utopia by functionalizing it. In view of the lack of prospects for
realizing a good that cannot yet be imagined, Adorno prefers to hold that its still

undetermined negativity is perceived. However, this does not adequately present the theme of the difference between utopian openness and possibility.

"Utopia," in Bloch's discourse, marks the incision through which the emergence of an *episteme* can first be noted. But unlike the "origin" this incision neither proceeds analytically to separation and synthetically to connection, nor does it form the denominator of a fracture through which the probability of events can be described. "Utopia" describes the openness through which an episteme finds the way to its "end" whereby it is exposed to an open space. However, this finality does not determine whether the episteme forms limited *topoi* or continues on its way unlimited, as discourse. Where Bloch attaches importance to this difference, to avoid identifying "Utopia" with the absolute – Hegel's God – he distances it from an unrealized and as if still latent subject, through which possibilities can be closed or opened. In that case, however, Utopia must be denied any function of truth. It neither reveals nor conceals that which is in being or that which is not. "Utopia" then denotes an ateleological finality through which truth itself is exposed to an open space. However much this openness may be pervaded by what is not clear and cannot be interpreted, by the play of "allegorical" allusions and ambiguities or by "symbolical" meanings, Utopia can only be indicated. But Bloch, too, constantly shrinks from the "death of God" whereby utopian openness is experienced and interpreted only as the remaining emptiness. He therefore replaces the "transcending without transcendence" which he had demanded by a strong faith whereby he aims to convince himself of possibilities.

But here "possibility" itself becomes a problem for him. He initially understands it as a latent indeterminacy which distinguishes both material events and the formation of ideals themselves. Yet, however reality and ideals may ferment, certain "tendencies" in them oppose chaos. The inclinations and disinclinations of drive-tendencies can be represented in ideals and operate in action, for or against, by means of "conceptualized hope." That, however, does not avert possible chaos. Bloch will not refer to a God opposing entropic tendencies by a counter-tropic tendency, as if they were creations from outside, any more than he will refer to systems emerging and declining merely by chance. He therefore has to introduce a "subjective factor" whereby aims are to some extent definable as "free," and in accordance with which possibilities are determined, thus realizing a "*novum*," something that has never before existed. However, if determination is only "according to possibility" (*kata to dynaton*), then one is assuming a passively material substrate formed solely from outside. But there is no idea of matter which in itself is indifferent at the basis of the Marxist postulate of a "naturalization of mankind through the humanization of nature." However, as humanity itself proceeded from nature, the possibility of free self-realization must be already present in the material (*to dynamei on*). Yet this would make it conceivable that a cosmically creative material may be realized not only through humanity but also independently of it (*Das Materialismusproblem*, 1972). Critics of this transhuman natural teleology who prefer to see the subject of self-realization limited solely to humanity neglect to ask from what metaphysical viewpoint we may say, with Bloch, that a self-liberating, self-realizing subject is itself not yet liberated and not yet realized.

On the one hand, Bloch offers a moral condemnation of possible nonsense only as "bad fullness" which eludes all further ability to assume meaning, and, on the other, of what can be only formally conceived of as "bad openness." He guesses at the dilemma in which he would find himself if he were to accept "possibility" as a category of a determinable alternative. If he did, one could conceive of the impossibility whereby, conversely, the possibility that reality can always be different would be defined as a necessity. But it would then be impossible to anticipate a complete self-realization in which all possibilities would not be fully exhausted. Such a total presence would be "too much good," like that perfect epiphany which even in myth was conceivable only as total absence, the death of mortals. The prospect of an alternative – all or nothing, total success or failure – thus turns out to be the greatest illusion of hope itself. Where Bloch suppresses utopian openness he is simply suffering from an apparently endless deferment of decisions, i.e. from a game in which "teleology" and self-realization are as indeterminately possible or impossible as chance itself (*tyche*). However, when he recovers openness he is able to set "human dignity" against this totalitarian tendency of wish-fulfillment (*Naturrecht*, 1961) and does so hoping that the conflict between unjust and just violence can be resolved. He then feels that one cannot satisfy oneself with utopian openness as a constant possibility.

This conflict initially caused him to overlook, in Stalinism, what he could not help observing in National Socialism: the possibility of nihilism beginning to realize itself politically.

In suspecting that use of the term "nothing" can also condemn what is open as nothing but absolute emptiness, Bloch even sought to define death and nothing as "extremely counter-utopian utopian categories." But here he risked blunting concern for the memory of the annihilated victim. He separates death not just from dying but also from the conscious self-being of our own transience (Levinas 1976). If, as Bloch says, a subjective substance which has not yet come into being cannot pass away either, then it can no longer be understood as becoming or as coming into being – unless as some divine stimulus arousing it from outside. Then those desires for death and annihilation which are realized as "empty mania" must appear correspondingly "diabolical" (*Tübinger Einleitung*, 1970). In view of the death-dealing violence exerted by paranoiac phantasms in the twentieth century, Bloch's belief in that "Faustian dialectic" which in the last resort works only for good by annihilating evil was bound to be shaken. There now emerges, however, the possible reversal of a direction of wishes which Bloch had so far perceived as being almost exclusively the conservative and reactionary preserve of rulers: it can be good not to realize what has not yet come into being, and to preserve that which has. However, this was not the only way in which Bloch disturbed the image of linear progress. He had seen that National Socialism did not just produce ideologies whose sole purpose was to disguise the political and economic interests of the ruling classes: it also showed the continuing operation of "archetypes" which had been formed in past societies. These archetypes, however, operated not only as patterns of now unconscious behaviour, but through them were all unfulfilled wishes of the past transferred to the present. As anticipations now out of their time, they could manifest themselves all the more violently the less appropriate they were to a reality already tearing itself apart in social conflict. If archetypal desires exceed the present as uncritical myths, they are aiming at its annihilation, if in an only abstract way. We can go beyond Bloch's interpretation and complete it by saying that while terrorism itself seeks to annihilate the traces of its process of annihilation – as if thereafter what had been annihilated were never to have existed – it is proceeding to the actual destruction of history. Bloch is sometimes inclined to interpret nihilism simply as "anti-Utopia" when he fails to see that utopian openness is not in itself a guarantee that closed possibilities will open.

With this archetypal future inherited from the past, Bloch does not just shatter the idea of a generally communicating "contemporaneity," in so far as this is determined by real interests of a communal nature or otherwise. The "non-contemporaneity" of ideals and their manifestations causes the decline of a pattern of progress imagining that it is unified in a linear image of succession. We thus see a scene of fragments, topical dispersion, and surreal montages, a scene which no longer matches the hierarchic scheme of Bloch's designs for hope. Conversely, that hierarchy itself may be seen as an archetypal ideal which sometimes lets its philosophical thinking appear at an inappropriate time – in curious contrast to its "avant-garde" aspect.

While retaining the general mode of Marxist thinking, Bloch went beyond it in becoming involved with those daydreams which may appear superstitious, cheap, banal, and shabby – daydreams and accounts of them which had not just been thought unworthy of any philosophical discussion of ideas but were frequently condemned as mere "proletarian lack of culture." Certainly, Bloch is sometimes rather like the alchemist seeking the philosopher's stone in what is invisible, condemned, and proscribed – that is to say in remnants of unofficial cultures making their way to the forefront. But in surveying fairy-tales and sentimental stories, fairs and country taverns, shooting galleries and ghost trains, provincial revues and sensational literature, he points up oddities and ciphers which do not just circulate in the depths below the "great meanings" nor anticipate them as future meanings, but surge up and over them. In this very overflow, the right of the individual and its "polyphony" can be perceived, preserved from those impatient excesses which abandon it as worthless. Such a right is also demonstrated by Bloch's own style: he uses metaphors which not only press forward to greater meaning but express their own feeling for reality and resolve plays of confusion (Bense 1956), often in magnificent pleonastically exaggerated impressions which risk becoming obsolete even before they are capable of forming a concept. Anacoluthic words often stand like statuary gestures in a paratactically arranged garden of ideas – the tropes of a "topia."

In his last work, *Experimentum Mundi* (1975), Bloch attempted to define the utopian function of propositions themselves. He formulated it as: "S (subject) is not yet P (predicate)." In conjunction with Peircean semiotics this "not yet" could be regarded as iconic representation corresponding on the part of the interpretant to the rheme as an unsatisfied sign in need of completion (Kübler 1975). But how, then, can the familiar antinomies be avoided? Bloch's assertion about an open form

387

of assertion ("$S$ is not yet $P$") is not only itself a completely indexical (dicentric) sentence, but may also be regarded universally as a "symbolic argument" as long as the circumstances themselves have not yet found their fully realized truth. Does this not mean that Bloch has already caught the bird he thinks he can approach? The implicit distinction between meta-language and object-language merely represents a return to Hegel's metaphysics of language: the resurrected divinity of language is evident in the fact that nothing seems able to elude the dialectical logos of predictability as long as logic endlessly attributes to itself the function of teleologically opening up possibilities. But as long as a suppressed impossibility is also at work, as a necessary negation of possibility, a utopian openness of language cannot even be described. However, utopian openness of language need not be condemned as "inexpressible;" it is not a lack of language but its supplement, since language does not cease to fail to come to speech.

A complete edition of the works of Ernst Bloch was published between 1959 and 1978 by Suhrkamp (Frankfurt am Main). This complete edition included: vol. 1: *Spuren*; vol. 2: *Thomas Münzer als Theologe der Revolution*; vol. 3: *Geist der Utopie*; vol. 4: *Erbschaft dieser Zeit*; vol. 5: *Das Prinzip Hoffnung*; vol. 6: *Naturrecht und menschliche Würde*; vol. 7: *Das Materialismusproblem, seine Geschichte und Substanz*; vol. 13: *Tübinger Einleitung in die Philosophie*; vol. 15: *Experimentum Mundi: Frage, Kategorien des Herausbringens, Praxis*.

## References and further reading

Adorno, T. W.: "Blochs Spuren." In: *Noten zur Literatur*, vol. II (Frankfurt: Suhrkamp, 1961).

Bahr, Hans-Dieter: *Die Sprache des Gastes: Eine Metaethik* (Leipzig: Reclam, 1994).

Bense, Max: "Ernst Blochs Prosa und die neue Seinsthematik" (1956). In: *Materialien zu Ernst Blochs "Prinzip Hoffnung,"* ed. Burghart Schmidt (Frankfurt: Suhrkamp, 1978).

Habermas, Jürgen, "Ernst Bloch. Ein marxistischer Schelling." In: *Philosophisch-Politische Profile* (Frankfurt: Suhrkamp, 1971).

Hesse, Hermann: "Ernst Bloch's *Erbschaft dieser Zeit*" (1935). In: *Ernst Blochs Wirkung. Ein Arbeitsbuch zum 90. Geburtstag* (Frankfurt: Suhrkamp, 1975).

Kübler, Renate: "Die Metapher als Argument. Semiotische Bestimmung der Bloch'schen Sprache." In: *Ernst Blochs Wirkung. Ein Arbeitsbuch zum 90. Geburtstag* (Frankfurt: Suhrkamp, 1975).

Levinas, Emmanuel: "Sur la mort dans la pensée de Ernst Bloch." In: *Utopie-Marxisme selon Ernst Bloch*, ed. Gérard Roulet (Paris, 1976).

Lyotard, Jean-François: "Puissances des traces, ou Contribution de Ernst Bloch à une histoire païenne." In: *Mélanges Ernst Bloch* (Paris: Payot, 1976).

Mayer, Hans: "Ernst Blochs poetische Sendung. Anmerkungen zu dem Buch *Spuren*." In: *Ernst Bloch zu ehren. Beiträge zu seinem Werk*, ed. Siegfried Unseld (Frankfurt: Suhrkamp, 1965).

# 33

# Marcuse

## DOUGLAS KELLNER

Herbert Marcuse gained world renown during the 1960s as a philosopher, social theorist, and political activist, celebrated in the media as the "father of the New Left." University professor and author of many books and articles, Marcuse won notoriety when he was perceived as both an influence on and defender of the "New Left" in the United States and Europe. His theory of "one-dimensional" society provided critical perspectives on contemporary capitalist and state communist societies, and his notion of "the great refusal" won him renown as a theorist of revolutionary change and "liberation from the affluent society." Consequently, he became one of the most influential intellectuals in the United States during the 1960s and early 1970s. However, ultimately, it may be his contributions to philosophy that are most significant, and in this article I shall attempt to specify Marcuse's contributions to contemporary philosophy and his place in the narrative of Continental philosophy.

## Heidegger, Marxism, and philosophy

Marcuse was born in 1898 in Berlin and, after serving with the German army in World War I, went to Freiburg to pursue his studies. After receiving his doctorate in literature in 1922, and following a short career as a bookseller in Berlin, he returned to Freiburg in 1928 to study philosophy with Martin HEIDEGGER (see Article 18), then one of the most influential thinkers in Germany. Marcuse's first published article in 1928 attempted a synthesis of the philosophical perspectives of phenomenology, existentialism, and Marxism, a synthesis which decades later would be carried out again by various "existential" and "phenomenological" Marxists, such as Jean-Paul SARTRE (see Article 21) and Maurice MERLEAU-PONTY (see Article 23), as well as American students and intellectuals in the New Left.

Marcuse argued that much Marxist thought had degenerated into a rigid orthodoxy and thus needed concrete lived and "phenomenological" experience to revivify the theory; at the same time, Marcuse believed that Marxism neglected the problem of the individual, and throughout his life he was concerned with individual liberation and well-being in addition to social transformation and the possibilities of a transition from capitalism to socialism.

Marcuse continued to maintain throughout his life that Heidegger was the greatest teacher and thinker that he had ever encountered. The Marcuse archives contain a full set of his lecture notes from the late 1920s until he left Freiburg in

1933, and these document the intensity of his interest in Heidegger's philosophy and his devotion to his lectures. Yet Marcuse was highly dismayed over Heidegger's political affiliations with national socialism and after completing a "Habilitations dissertation" – *Hegel's Ontology and the Theory of Historicity* – he decided to leave Freiburg in 1933 to join the *Institut für Sozialforschung* (Institute for Social Research) which was located in Frankfurt, but which would soon open branch offices at Geneva and then at Columbia University, both of which Marcuse would join.

His study *Hegel's Ontology and the Theory of Historicity* (1932) contributed to the Hegel renaissance that was taking place in Europe by stressing the importance of Hegel's ontology of life and history, as well as his idealist theory of spirit and his dialectics. Moreover, Marcuse published the first major review in 1933 of Marx's just published *Economic and Philosophical Manuscripts of 1844*; the review anticipated the tendency to revise interpretations of Marxism from the standpoint of the works of the early Marx. These works revealed Marcuse to be an astute student of Germany philosophy and he began to emerge as one of the most promising theorists of his generation.

## Critical theory of society

As a member of the Institute for Social Research, Marcuse soon became deeply involved in their interdisciplinary projects which included working out a model for critical social theory, developing a theory of the new stage of state and monopoly capitalism, articulating the relationships between philosophy, social theory, and cultural criticism, and providing a systematic analysis and critique of German fascism. Marcuse deeply identified with the "Critical theory" of the Institute and throughout his life was close to Max HORKHEIMER (see Article 30), T. W. ADORNO (see Article 31), and others in the Institute's inner circle.

In 1934, Marcuse – a German Jew and radical – fled from Nazism and emigrated to the United States where he lived for the rest of his life. The Institute for Social Research was granted offices and an academic affiliation with Columbia University, where Marcuse worked during the 1930s and early 1940s. His first major work in English, *Reason and Revolution* (1941), traced the genesis of the ideas of HEGEL (see Article 6), MARX (Article 8), and modern social theory. It demonstrated the similarities between Hegel and Marx, and introduced many English-speaking readers to the Hegelian–Marxian tradition of dialectical thinking and social analysis. The text continues to be one of the best introductions to Hegel and Marx and one of the best analyses of the categories and methods of dialectical thinking.

In 1941, Marcuse joined the OSS (Office of Secret Services) and then worked in the State Department, becoming the head of the Central European bureau by the end of World War II. After serving in the US government from 1941 through the early 1950s, which Marcuse always claimed was motivated by a desire to struggle against fascism, he returned to intellectual work and published *Eros and Civilization* in 1955 which attempted an audacious synthesis of Marx and Freud and sketched the outlines of a non-repressive society. While Freud argued in *Civilization and its Discontents* that civilization inevitably involved repression and suffering, Marcuse argued that other elements in Freud's theory suggested that the unconscious contained evidence of an instinctual drive towards happiness and freedom. This evidence is articulated, Marcuse suggests, in daydreams, works of art, philosophy, and other cultural products. Based on this reading of Freud and study of an emancipatory tradition of philosophy and culture, Marcuse sketched the outlines of a non-repressive civilization which would involve libidinal and non-alienated labor, play, free and open sexuality, and production of a society and culture which would further freedom and happiness. His vision of liberation anticipated many of the values of the 1960s counterculture and helped Marcuse to become a major intellectual and political influence during that decade.

Marcuse argued that the current organization of society produced "surplus repression" by imposing socially unnecessary labor, unnecessary restrictions on sexuality, and a social system organized around profit and exploitation. In light of the diminution of scarcity and prospects for increased abundance, Marcuse called for the end of repression and creation of a new society. His radical critique of existing society and its values, and his call for a non-repressive civilization, elicited a dispute with his former colleague Erich Fromm who accused him of "nihilism" (towards existing values and society) and irresponsible hedonism. Marcuse had earlier attacked Fromm for excessive "conformity" and "idealism" and repeated these charges in the polemical debates over his work following the publication of *Eros and Civilization* which heatedly discussed Marcuse's use of Freud, his critique of existing civilization, and his proposals for an alternative organization of society and culture.

In 1958, Marcuse accepted a tenured position at Brandeis University and became one of the most popular and influential members of its faculty. During his period of government work, Marcuse had been a specialist in fascism and communism and he published a critical study of the Soviet Union in 1958 (*Soviet Marxism*) which broke the taboo in his circles against speaking critically of the USSR and Soviet communism. While attempting to develop a many-sided analysis of the USSR, Marcuse focused his critique on Soviet bureaucracy, culture, values, and the differences between the Marxian theory and the Soviet version of Marxism. Distancing himself from those who interpreted Soviet communism as a bureaucratic system incapable of reform and democratization, Marcuse pointed to potential "liberalizing trends" which countered the Stalinist bureaucracy, which indeed eventually materialized in the 1980s under Gorbachev.

Next, Marcuse published a wide-ranging critique of both advanced capitalist and communist societies in *One-Dimensional Man* (1964). This book theorized the decline of revolutionary potential in capitalist societies and the development of new forms of social control. Marcuse argued that "advanced industrial society" created false needs which integrated individuals into the existing system of production and consumption. Mass media and culture, advertising, industrial management, and contemporary modes of thought all reproduced the existing system and attempt to eliminate negativity, critique, and opposition. The result was a "one-dimensional" universe of thought and behavior in which the very aptitude and ability for critical thinking and oppositional behavior was withering away.

Not only had capitalism integrated the working class – the source of potential revolutionary opposition – but new techniques of stabilization through state policies and new forms of social control had been developed. Thus Marcuse questioned two of the fundamental postulates of orthodox Marxism: the revolutionary proletariat and the inevitability of capitalist crisis. In contrast with the more extravagant demands of orthodox Marxism, Marcuse championed non-integrated forces of minorities, outsiders, and radical intelligentsia and attempted to nourish oppositional thought and behavior through promoting radical thinking and opposition.

*One-Dimensional Man* was severely criticized by orthodox Marxists and theorists of various political and theoretical commitments. Despite its pessimism, it influenced many in the New Left as it articulated their growing dissatisfaction with both capitalist societies and Soviet communist societies. Moreover, Marcuse himself continued to defend demands for revolutionary change and defended the new, emerging forces of radical opposition, thus winning him the hatred of establishment forces and the respect of the new radicals.

## The New Left and radical politics

*One-Dimensional Man* was followed by a series of books and articles which articulated New Left politics and critiques of capitalist societies: "Repressive Tolerance" (1965), *An Essay on Liberation* (1969), and *Counterrevolution and Revolt* (1972). "Repressive Tolerance" attacked liberalism and those who refused to take a stand during the controversies of the 1960s. It won Marcuse the reputation of being an intransigent radical and ideologue for the Left. *An Essay on Liberation* celebrated all of the existing liberation movements from the Viet Cong to the hippies and exhilarated many radicals while further alienating establishment academics and those who opposed the movements of the 1960s. *Counterrevolution and Revolt*, by contrast, articulates the new realism that was setting in during the early 1970s when it was becoming clear that the most extravagant hopes of the 1960s were being dashed by a turn to the right and "counterrevolution" against the 1960s.

In 1965, Brandeis refused to renew his teaching contract and Marcuse soon after accepted a position at the University of California at La Jolla where he remained until his retirement in the 1970s. During this period – of his greatest influence – Marcuse also published many articles and gave lectures and advice to student radicals all over the world. He traveled widely and his work was often discussed in the mass media, becoming one of the few American intellectuals to gain such attention. Never surrendering his revolutionary vision and commitments, Marcuse continued to his death to defend the Marxian theory and libertarian socialism. A charismatic teacher, Marcuse's students began to gain influential academic positions and to promote his ideas, making him a major force in US intellectual life.

Marcuse also dedicated much of his work to aesthetics and his final book, *The Aesthetic Dimension* (1978), briefly summarizes his defense of the emancipatory potential of aesthetic form in so-called "high culture." Marcuse thought that the best of the bourgeois tradition of art contained powerful indictments of bourgeois society and emancipatory visions of a better society. Thus he attempted to defend the importance of great art for the project of emancipation and argued that cultural revolution was an indispensable part of revolutionary politics.

Marcuse's work in philosophy and social theory generated fierce controversy and polemics, and most studies of his work are highly tendentious and frequently sectarian. Although much of the controversy involved his critiques of contemporary capitalist societies and defense of radical social change, in retrospect Marcuse left behind a complex and many-sided body of work comparable to the legacies of Ernst BLOCH (see Article 32), Georg LUKÁCS (Article 40), T. W. ADORNO (Article 31), and Walter BENJAMIN (Article 29).

## Marcuse's legacy

Since his death in 1979, Herbert Marcuse's influence has been steadily waning. The extent to which his work has been ignored in progressive circles is curious, as Marcuse was one of the most influential radical theorists of the day during the 1960s and his work continued to be a topic of interest and controversy during the 1970s. While the waning of the revolutionary movements with which he was involved helps explain Marcuse's eclipse in popularity, the lack of new texts and publication has also contributed. For while there have been a large number of new translations of works by Benjamin, Adorno, and Habermas during the past decade, few new publications of untranslated or uncollected material by Marcuse have appeared, although there have been a steady stream of books on Marcuse (see the References and Further Writings section below). In addition, while there has been great interest in the writings of FOUCAULT (see Article 49), DERRIDA (Article 50), BAUDRILLARD (Article 53), LYOTARD (Article 52), and other French "postmodern," or "poststructuralist," theorists, Marcuse did not fit into the fashionable debates concerning modern and postmodern thought. Unlike Adorno, Marcuse did not anticipate the postmodern attacks on reason and his dialectics were not "negative." Rather, he subscribed to the project of reconstructing reason and of positing utopian alternatives to the existing society – a dialectical imagination that has fallen out of favor in an era that rejects totalizing thought and grand visions of liberation and social reconstruction.

The neglect of Marcuse may be altered through the publication of a wealth of material, much of it unpublished and unknown, that is found in the Herbert Marcuse archives in the Stadtsbibliothek in Frankfurt. During the summers of 1989 and 1991, and the fall of 1990, I went through the archival material and was astonished at the number of valuable unpublished texts. The Marcuse archive is a treasure house and plans are developing to publish many volumes of this material. Some extremely interesting manuscripts from the 1940s on war, technology, and totalitarianism, and some unpublished book manuscripts, articles, and lectures from the 1960s and 1970s may lead to a Marcuse renaissance, or at least reawaken interest in his work (see Marcuse 1997).

Such a return to Marcuse is plausible, first, because he addresses issues that continue to be of relevance to contemporary theory and politics, and the unpublished manuscripts contain much material pertinent to contemporary concerns which could provide the basis for a rebirth of interest in Marcuse's thought (for examples of the contemporary relevance of Marcuse, see the studies in Bokina and Lukes 1994). Secondly, Marcuse provides comprehensive philosophical perspectives on domination and liberation, a powerful method and framework for analyzing contemporary society, and a vision of liberation that is richer than classical Marxism, other versions of Critical theory, and current versions of postmodern theory.

Indeed, Marcuse presents rich philosophical perspectives on human beings and their relationship to nature and society, as well as substantive social theory and radical politics. In retrospect, Marcuse's vision of liberation – of the full development of the individual in a non-repressive society – distinguishes his work, together with sharp critique of existing forms of domination and oppression, and he emerges in this narrative as a philosopher of forces of domination and liberation. Primarily a philosopher, Marcuse's work lacked the sustained empirical analysis in some versions of Marxist theory and the detailed conceptual analysis found in many versions of political theory. Yet he constantly showed how science, technology, and theory itself had a political dimension and produced a solid body of ideological and political analysis of many of the dominant forms of society, culture, and thought during the turbulent era in which he lived, and he constantly struggled for a better world.

Thus, I believe that Marcuse overcomes the limitations of many current varieties of philosophy and social theory and that his writings provide a viable starting-point for theoretical and political concerns of the present age. In particular, his articulations of philosophy with social theory, cultural criticism, and radical politics seem an enduring legacy. While mainstream academic divisions of labor isolate philosophy from other disciplines – and other disciplines from philosophy – Marcuse and the critical theorists provide philosophy with an important function within social theory and cultural criticism and develop philosophical perspectives in interaction with concrete analyses of society, politics, and culture in the present age. This dialectical approach thus assigns philosophy continued functions in the theoretical discourses of our era.

In addition, Marcuse emerges as a sharp, even prescient, social analyst. He was one of the first on the left who both developed a sharp critique of Soviet Marxism and yet foresaw the liberalizing trends in the Soviet Union (Marcuse 1958). After the uprisings in Poland and Hungary in 1956 were ruthlessly suppressed, many speculated that Khrushchev would have to roll back his program of de-Stalinization and crack down further. Marcuse, however, differed, writing in 1958:

> The Eastern European events were likely to slow down and perhaps even reverse de-Stalinization in some fields; particularly in international strategy, a considerable "hardening" has been apparent. However, if our analysis is correct, the fundamental trend will continue and reassert itself throughout such reversals. With respect to internal Soviet developments, this means at present continuation of "collective leadership," decline in the power of the secret police, decentralization, legal reforms, relaxation in censorship, liberalization in cultural life. (Marcuse 1958, p. 174)

In part as a response to the collapse of Communism and in part as a result of new technological and economic conditions, the capitalist system has been undergoing disorganization and reorganization. Marcuse's loyalty to Marxism always led him to analyze new conditions within capitalist societies that had emerged since Marx. Social theory today can thus build on this Marcusean tradition in developing critical theories of contemporary society grounded in analyses of the transformations of capitalism and emergence of a new global economic world system. For Marcuse, social theory was integrally historical and must conceptualize the salient phenomena of the present age and changes from previous social formations. While the postmodern theories of Baudrillard and Lyotard claim to postulate a rupture in history, they fail to analyze the key constituents of the changes going on, with Baudrillard even declaring the "end of political economy." Marcuse, by contrast, always attempted to analyze the changing configurations of capitalism and to relate social and cultural changes to changes in the economy.

Moreover, Marcuse always paid special attention to the important role of technology in organizing contemporary societies, and with the emergence of new technologies in our time the Marcusean emphasis on the relationship between technology, the economy, culture, and everyday life is especially important. Marcuse also paid attention to new forms of culture and the ways that culture provided both instruments of manipulation and liberation. The proliferation of new media technologies and cultural forms in recent years also demands a Marcusean perspective to capture both their potentialities for progressive social change and the possibilities of more streamlined forms of social domination. While postmodern theories also describe new technologies, Marcuse always related the economy to culture and technology, seeing both emancipatory and dominating potentials, while theorists like Baudrillard are one-dimensional, often falling prey to technological determinism and views of society and culture that fail to see positive and emancipatory potentials.

Finally, while versions of postmodern theory, such as Baudrillard's, have renounced radical politics, Marcuse always attempted to link his critical theory with the most radical political movements of the day and to thus politicize his philosophy and social theory. Thus, I am suggesting that Marcuse's thought continues to provide important resources and stimulus for radical theory and politics in the present age. Marcuse himself was open to new theoretical and political currents, yet remained loyal to those theories which he believed provided inspiration and substance for the tasks of the present age. Consequently, as we confront the theoretical and political problems of the day, I believe that the works of Herbert Marcuse provide important resources for our current situation and that a Marcusean renaissance could help inspire new theories and politics for the contemporary era, providing Continental philosophy with new impulses and tasks.

## Writings

Marcuse, Herbert: *Negations* (Boston, MA: Beacon Press, 1968).
——: *Reason and Revolution* (New York: Oxford University Press, 1941; repr. Boston, MA: Beacon Press, 1960).

395

————: *Eros and Civilization* (Boston, MA: Beacon Press, 1955).

————: *Soviet Marxism* (New York: Columbia University Press 1958; 2nd edn, 1988).

————: *One-Dimensional Man* (Boston, MA: Beacon Press, 1964; 2nd edn, 1991).

————: *An Essay on Liberation* (Boston, MA: Beacon Press, 1969).

————: *Counterrevolution and Revolt* (Boston, MA: Beacon Press, 1972).

————: *Studies in Critical Philosophy* (Boston, MA: Beacon Press, 1973).

————: *The Aesthetic Dimension* (Boston, MA: Beacon Press, 1978).

————: *Technology, War and Fascism*, ed. Douglas Kellner (London: Routledge, 1997).

## References and further reading

Alford, C. Fred: *Science and the Revenge of Nature: Marcuse and Habermas* (Gainesville, FL: University of Florida Press, 1985).

Bokina, John, and Lukes, Timothy J. (eds): *Marcuse: New Perspectives* (Lawrence, KS: University of Kansas Press, 1994).

Institut für Sozialforschung: *Kritik und Utopie im Werk von Herbert Marcuse* (Frankfurt: Suhrkamp, 1992).

Kellner, Douglas: *Herbert Marcuse and the Crisis of Marxism* (London and Berkeley, CA: Macmillan and University of California Press, 1984).

Lukes, Timothy J.: *The Flight into Inwardness: An Exposition and Critique of Herbert Marcurse's Theory of Liberative Aesthetics* (Cranbury, NJ: Associated University Presses, 1986).

Pippin, Robert et al. (eds.): *Marcuse, Critical Theory and the Promise of Utopia* (South Hadley, MA: Bergin & Garvey, 1988).

# 34

# Habermas

## THOMAS McCARTHY

Jürgen Habermas was born in Düsseldorf in 1929 and raised in Gummersbach. After receiving his *Abitur* in 1949, he studied philosophy, history, psychology, literature, and economics at the universities of Göttingen, Zurich, and Bonn, where he submitted a dissertation on Schelling, "Das Absolute und die Geschichte," in 1954. From 1956 to 1959 he was Theodor Adorno's assistant at the Institute for Social Research in Frankfurt. After habilitating at Marburg University in 1961 with *The Structural Transformation of the Public Sphere*, he taught philosophy and sociology at the universities of Heidelberg and Frankfurt, where he was a professor of philosophy until his retirement in 1994.

Habermas's life and work were deeply influenced by the traumatic events of his youth under National Socialism. From the time of his involvement with the German student movement in the 1960s, he has been one of Germany's most prominent public intellectuals, speaking out on a wide array of issues, from violations of civil liberties and attempts to "historicize" the Holocaust to immigration policy and the manner of German reunification. Habermas's scholarly writings, which aspire to a comprehensive critical theory of contemporary society, range across many of the humanities and social sciences. In that respect, among others, they may be understood as renewing the interdisciplinary research project launched by Max HORKHEIMER (see Article 30) and his associates in the early 1930s. That original program of what later came to be called the "Frankfurt School" had, in turn, been understood as a renewal of Marxism. An updated Marxism had to take account of the altered realities of advanced capitalism and to integrate areas of inquiry neglected by traditional Marxism (such as political theory, cultural studies, and social psychology). From a philosophical perspective, it was a continuation of MARX's *Aufhebung* (see Article 8) of philosophy in social theory and practice. Linking philosophy to history and the human sciences in a kind of "philosophically oriented social theory," Critical Theory undertook a sociohistorical, practically oriented critique of reason and of its claimed realizations. While dominant forms of reason were often distorted in the interests of dominant classes, Critical Theory did not simply negate them but, through illuminating their geneses and functions, transformed them and enlisted them in the struggle for a better world. This insistence on the "truth content" of the "bourgeois ideals" of freedom, truth, and justice, the refusal to abandon them as mere ideology, was severely tested by the horrors of World War II, National Socialism, fascism, and Stalinism. Early in the 1940s, in their collaborative reflections on the "Dialectic of Enlightenment," Horkheimer and

ADORNO (see Article 31) painted a more pessimistic picture of the history of reason. Keying on a tendency that Max Weber had emphasized, the relentless spread of purposive-rational or "instrumental" rationality, they now saw rationalization processes as the core of a domination that had spread to all areas of life and, in the process, had immobilized potential subjects of social change. In this "totally administered society," with what MARCUSE (see Article 33) later called its "one-dimensional men," Critical Theory could at most reveal the unreason at the heart of what passed for reason, without offering any positive account of its own.

Habermas's work since the 1960s could be viewed as an attempt to avoid this impasse by introducing into Critical Theory a fundamental shift of paradigms from the philosophy of the subject to the theory of communication, and from means–ends rationality to communicative rationality. His early and influential *The Structural Transformation of the Public Sphere* (1962) was a historical, sociological, and philosophical account of the emergence and transformation of a liberal public sphere in which the activity of the state was to be monitored and directed by the informed, critical, public discourse of the governed. Examining the preconditions, structures, functions, ideologies, and tensions of this central domain of modern society, Habermas noted the contradiction between its constitutive catalogue of "basic rights of man" and its *de facto* restriction to certain classes of men. And he traced the conflicts this occasioned as, with the further development of capitalism, the public expanded to include groups that were systematically disadvantaged by the workings of the market. The consequent interlinking of state and society in the late nineteenth and twentieth centuries meant the end of the liberal public sphere. The public sphere of social-welfare-state democracies is rather a field of competition among conflicting interests, in which organizations representing diverse constituencies negotiate and compromise among themselves and with government officials, while excluding the public from their proceedings. Public opinion is, to be sure, taken into account, but not in the form of unrestricted public discussion. Its character and function are indicated rather by the terms in which it is addressed: "public opinion research," "publicity," "public relations work," and so forth. The press and broadcast media serve less as organs of public information and debate than as technologies for managing consensus and promoting consumer culture.

While the historical structures of the liberal public sphere reflected the particular constellations of interests underlying it, the idea it claimed to embody, the idea of legitimating political activity through rational public debate and reasoned public agreement, remains central to democratic theory. But can an effectively functioning public sphere be instituted and maintained under the very different socioeconomic, cultural, and political conditions of the present? Is democracy really possible? Habermas returned to these themes three decades later in *Between Facts and Norms* (1992), where he again applied the idea of justification by appeal to generally acceptable reasons to the deliberations of free and equal citizens in a constitutional democracy. The primary function of the system of basic rights, he argued, is to secure personal and political autonomy. And the key to the latter is the institutionalization of the public use of reason in the legal–political domain. Ac-

cordingly, his procedural conception of democratic deliberation combines fair ne-
gotiations and pragmatic considerations with ethical and moral discourses under
conditions which warrant the presumption that procedurally correct outcomes will
be ones with which free and equal citizens could reasonably agree. The basic principles of the democratic constitutional state are conceived as a response to the
question of how such conditions of rational deliberation can be effectively institutionalized not only in official governmental bodies but also in unofficial networks of
communication.

Independent public forums, distinct from both the economic system and the state
administration – having their locus rather in voluntary associations, social movements, and other networks and processes of communication in civil society, including the mass media – are for Habermas the basis of popular sovereignty. Ideally, the
"communicative power" generated by the public use of reason in non-governmen-
tal arenas should be translated via legally institutionalized decision-making procedures – for example, electoral and legislative procedures – into the legitimate
administrative power of the state. In this model of a deliberative decentering of
political power, the multiple and multiform arenas for detecting, defining, and
discussing societal problems, and the culturally and politically mobilized publics
who use them, serve as the basis for democratic self-government and thus for
political authority. Not even constitutional principles are exempt from this public
use of reason. Rather, democratic constitutions should be understood as "projects"
that are always open, incomplete, and subject to the ongoing exercise of political
autonomy, as shifting historical circumstances demand. Because public discourse
is ineluctably open and reflexive, our understanding of the principles of justice must
remain so as well. For this reason Habermas limits political theory to reconstructing the conditions and presuppositions of democratic deliberation and leaves all
substantive questions to the public use of reason by participants themselves. Anything beyond that reconstruction should be understood only as a contribution to
public debate and thus as permanently susceptible to all its vicissitudes. Established
law, then, has constantly to be reinterpreted in light of changing needs; and this
may involve collective actors articulating collective experiences of violated integrity. Thus an adequate concept of an abstract system of basic rights with various
constitutional realizations has to accommodate collective "struggles for recognition." As the latter often have to do with basic elements of a society's cultural
self-understanding, traditional patterns of interpretation, and established interpretations of needs, the rational acceptability of proposed laws, policies, and programs
will be a function not only of universal principles but also of particular self-
understandings, that is, of both the "right" and the "good."

One might read Habermas's extensive writings in the three decades between
these two studies of democratic public life as a protracted examination of the cultural, psychological social, and political preconditions for and barriers to its effective
realization. The essays of the early 1960s, a number of which were collected in
*Theory and Practice* (1963), introduced the idea of analyzing society as a historically
developing whole for purposes of enlightening political consciousness and guiding
political practice. At that point, critical social theory was conceived as an "empiri-

cal theory of history with practical intent." The methodology and epistemology behind this approach were elaborated in the later 1960s in *On the Logic of the Social Sciences* (1967) and *Knowledge and Human Interests.* (1968). A principal target of both books was the neopositivist thesis of the unity of scientific method, particularly the claim that the logic of inquiry in the human sciences is basically the same as in the natural sciences.

In his methodological reflections Habermas challenged the existing division of labor between the sciences and the humanities and argued that the differences between them had to be resolved within the human sciences. Starting from an examination of the nature and role of *Verstehen* in social and historical inquiry, he showed that access to symbolically prestructured object domains called for procedures similar in important respects to those developed in the text-interpreting humanities. The "meanings" to which social actors are oriented prominently include the shared meanings constitutive of the sociocultural matrices within which they live and act – inherited traditions and worldviews, values and practices, norms and roles, and so on. Purely objectivistic approaches that neglect these interpretive schemata, through which social action is structured, are doomed to inadequacy. In making that point, Habermas was able to draw on developments in the phenomenological, ethnomethodological, and linguistic traditions and thus to anticipate in all essential respects the subsequent decline of positivism and rise of interpretivism. But he argued just as forcefully against swinging to the opposite extreme of hermeneutic idealism. The reduction of social research to an interpretation of meaning would be an unwarranted sublimation of social processes entirely into subjectively intended and culturally transmitted meanings. But such meanings can conceal and distort as well as reveal and express the social, political, and economic conditions of life. If social research is not to be restricted to excavating and explicating meanings, we must somehow grasp the objective interconnections of social actions, the "meanings" they have beyond those intended by actors or expressed in traditions. We must, in short, study culture in relation to the material conditions of life and their transformation.

With this in mind, Habermas went on to examine functionalist approaches, in particular the structural-functionalism of Talcott Parsons. He argued that Parsons' attempt to conceive the social system as a functional complex of institutions in which cultural patterns are made normatively binding for action did supply important tools for analyzing objective interconnections of action, but it suffered from a short-circuiting of the hermeneutic and critical dimensions of social analysis. A more suggestive model for the historically oriented, critical theory of society with practical intent, to which he aspired, could be found in psychoanalysis, which attempted to reconceptualize and reintegrate interpretive, explanatory, and functionalist motifs in a "theoretically generalized narrative" of self-formative processes. In contrast to normal hermeneutics, the "depth hermeneutics" that Freud developed to deal with "texts" which both expressed and concealed their "author's intentions" relied on theoretical assumptions. Habermas understood psychoanalytic theory as a general interpretive schema of psychodynamic development, whose application to the reconstruction of individual life-histories called for a peculiar combination of interpretive understanding and causal explanation, and whose corroboration depended in the last analysis on the successful continuation of those life-histories. In an analogous way, critical social theory was to provide theoretical-ly generalized, narrative reconstructions of the formative processes of societies, with a view to their successful continuation.

In *Knowledge and Human Interests* Habermas undertook a historical and system-atic study of "the prehistory of modern positivism," in an attempt to free the ideas of reason and rationality from what he regarded as their "scientistic misunder-standing." Tracing the development of the critique of knowledge from Kant through German Idealism to Marx, and its transformation into the methodology of science in early positivism, he elaborated his own position in critical encounters with three classic but flawed attempts to overcome positivism from within method-ological reflection: Peirce's reflections on natural science, DILTHEY's on historical and cultural inquiry (see Article 37), and FREUD's on self-reflection (see Article 12). In each case he uncovered the roots of a certain type of knowledge in a basic aspect of human life; and he argued generally for an internal connection between structures of knowledge and "anthropologically deep-seated" human interests. A key feature of this "quasi-transcendental" theory of "cognitive" or "knowledge-guiding" inter-ests was a distinction between the "technical" interest in prediction and control of objectified processes, on the one hand, and the "practical" interest in mutual under-standing and "emancipatory" interest in distortion-free communication with speaking and acting subjects, on the other hand. Although the problematic and frame of reference of *Knowledge and Human Interests* were new, its idea of a "mate-rialistically transformed phenomenology" (in HEGEL's sense – see Article 6) worked with essentially the same combination of empirical and philosophical, systematic and historical, theoretical and practical elements as could be found in his *On the Logic of the Social Sciences*. As an attempt to reconstruct the formative process of the human species, phenomenological self-reflection was meant to expand the practi-cal self-understanding of social groups. Critical of ideology, it analyzed the develop-ment of the forms of the manifestation of consciousness in relation to constellations of power and from the standpoint of an ideal of social arrangement based on undistorted public communication.

The work of the 1970s focused on the notions of communication, communica-tive action, communicative competence, undistorted communication, and the like that were presupposed at every point in Habermas's developing conception of crit-ical social theory. The ground level of this research program consisted of a general account of communication in natural languages, a "universal pragmatics," as he called it. The idea behind it was that not only phonetic, syntactic, and semantic features of sentences but also certain pragmatic features of utterances – of lan-guage-in-use or speech – admit of rational reconstruction in universal terms. "Communicative competence" must be regarded as including not only the ability to produce and understand grammatical sentences but also the ability to establish and understand the connections to the world through which situated speech becomes possible. The act of utterance places sentences in relation to the "external world" of objects and events, the "internal world" of a speaker's own experiences, and a "social world" of shared normative expectations. From this pragmatic perspective, it becomes clear that mutual understanding in language involves raising and recognizing a variety of "validity claims" – claims to the truth of assertions in relation to the external world, to the rightness of actions in relation to a shared social world, and to the sincerity of expressions of the speaker's own intentions, feelings, desires, and the like. Naturally, claims of these sorts can be contested and criticized. One way of settling disputed claims, weighing reasons pro and con, appealing to no force but the force of the better argument, has since Socrates been regarded as fundamental to the idea of rationality, and is by Habermas as well. In respect to assertions, this approach issues in a "discourse theory of truth," which traces truth's internal connection to processes of discursive argumentation or justification, and thence to the rational acceptability of assertions under ideal conditions (the "ideal speech situation"). But Habermas expends considerably more energy in developing a discourse theory of justice.

"Discourse ethics" is a reconstruction of Immanuel KANT's idea of practical reason (see Article 2) which turns on a reformulation of his categorical imperative: rather than prescribing to others norms that I can will be to be universal laws, I must submit norms to others for purposes of discursively testing their putative universality: "Only those norms may claim to be valid that could meet with the approval of all those affected in their capacity as participants in practical discourse" (Habermas 1990 [1983], p. 66). Normative validity, construed as rational acceptability, is thus tied to argumentation processes governed by a principle of universalization: "For a norm to be valid, the consequences and side effects of its general observance for the satisfaction of each person's particular interests must be acceptable to all" (ibid., p. 197). Furthermore, by requiring that perspective-taking be general and reciprocal, discourse ethics builds a moment of empathy or "ideal role-taking" into the procedure of practical argumentation.

Like Kant, Habermas distinguishes the types of practical reasoning and the corresponding types of "ought" connected with questions concerning what is pragmatically expedient, ethically prudent, or morally right. Calculations of rational choice furnish recommendations relevant to the pursuit of contingent purposes in the light of given preferences. When serious questions of value arise, deliberation on who one is and wants to be yields insight into the good life. If issues of justice are involved, fair and impartial consideration of conflicting interests is required to judge what is right or just. And, again like Kant, Habermas regards questions of the last type, rather than specifically ethical questions, to be the proper domain of theory. (Thus discourse ethics might properly be called "discourse morality.") This is not to deny that ethical discourse is rational or that it exhibits general structures of its own; but the irreducible pluralism of modern life means that questions of self-understanding, self-realization, and the good life do not admit of universal answers. In Habermas's view, that does not preclude a general theory of a narrower sort, namely a theory of justice. Accordingly, the aim of his discourse ethics is solely to reconstruct the moral point of view from which questions of right can be fairly and impartially adjudicated.

By linking discourse ethics to the theory of communicative action, Habermas means to show that our basic moral intuitions are rooted in something deeper and more universal than particularities of our tradition, namely in the intuitive grasp of the normative presuppositions of social interaction possessed by competent social actors in any society. Members of our species become individuals in and through being socialized into networks of reciprocal social relations. The mutual vulnerability that this interdependence brings with it calls for guarantees of mutual consideration to preserve both the integrity of individual persons and the web of their interpersonal relations. In discourse ethics, respect for the individual is built into the freedom of each participant in discourse to accept or reject the reasons offered as justifications for norms, and concern for the common good into the requirement that each participant take into account the needs, interests, and feelings of all others affected by the norm in question. Hence the actual practice of moral discourse depends on forms of socialization and social reproduction that foster the requisite capacities and motivation.

Habermas's theory of socialization, the second level of his research program of the 1970s, centers around a developmental account of the acquisition of communicative competence in which the idea of an autonomous self is freed from its idealist presuppositions. He sketches a multidimensional model of self-formation as an interdependent process of linguistic, cognitive, and interpersonal development: the ego develops in and through the integration of "inner nature" into the structures of language, thought, and action. Here, too, Habermas has focused most of his energy on the moral domain. Adapting Kohlberg's hierarchical schema for the ability of making moral judgments, he places it in a larger action–theoretical framework by coordinating stages of that ability with a revised version of Selman's schema for stages in the development of interactive competence. In this way, Kohlberg's notion of a "postconventional" moral consciousness gets translated into the terms of Habermas's theory of communicative action, precisely as the level of communicative competence required for discourse ethics.

To be sure, the acquisition of universal, "species-wide" competences concerns only the structural side of self-formative processes; the other side comprises affect and motive formation. Unless subjects are able to express their needs adequately in available patterns, development may be pathologically deformed. Thus a general theory of self-formation would have to combine an account of the interdependent development of cognitive, linguistic, interactive, and moral development with an account of affective and motivational development. This would also make it possible to analyze the frequent discrepancies between moral judgment and moral action.

As noted above, the exercise of communicative competence depends not only on forms of socialization but also on forms of sociocultural reproduction. The third level of Habermas's research program in the 1970s was a "reconstruction of historical materialism" that gave as much weight to developments in the sphere of social integration as to those in the economic sphere. It turned on the thesis that the rationalization of communicative-interactional structures has a different logic than the rationalization of productive forces and relations. Employing structural comparisons to the ontogenetic developmental processes he had analyzed in the framework of his theory of communicative competence, he focused his studies of "social evolution" on the history of law and morality. The explanatory schema he proposed rested on a distinction between the *logic* of development of normative structures and the *dynamics* of their development: whether new structural formations arise, and if so, when and where, depends on empirical learning processes and contingent boundary conditions. The results of learning processes find their way into cultural traditions and comprise a kind of cognitive potential that can be drawn upon in social movements when unsolvable system problems require a transformation of basic forms of social integration. But whether the institutional embodiment of culturally available structures of rationality actually takes place is not merely a developmental-logical matter. Indeed, with reference to the transformation of contemporary society, it is a practical, political matter.

Habermas's critical theory does not exhaust itself in a reconstruction of historical materialism; its ultimate aim remains an historically oriented, practically engaged analysis of *contemporary* society – that is, a reconstruction of the critique of capitalism. His main contribution to that task in the 1970s was *Legitimation Crisis* (1973). The crux of his argument was that legitimation problems arise in developed capitalist societies as the result of a fundamental conflict built into their very structure, a conflict between the social-welfare responsibilities of mass democracies and the functional conditions of their capitalist economies. The state is forced to deal with the dysfunctional side-effects of economic processes under highly restrictive conditions, balancing a policy of economic stability against a policy of social reform in a world economy that increasingly limits its latitude for action. To the extent that it fails to keep these side-effects within acceptable bounds, manifestations of delegitimation appear: for example, economic instability, sharpened struggles over distribution, the breakdown of reform politics, the disintegration of motivational patterns essential for the reproduction of capitalist society, and the spread of dysfunctional patterns. Attempts to deal with these problems through conscious manipulation are faced with systematic limits, for the cultural system is particularly resistant to administrative control. The effect of administrative intervention into economically conditioned crisis tendencies is a heightened pressure for legitimation, which arises not only from the need to secure acceptance of increased activity in new spheres but also from the unavoidable side-effects of that activity. And it cannot be relieved by an "administrative production of meaning," for the state cannot effectively control social integration or "plan ideology."

The groundwork of the 1970s culminated in Habermas's monumental *The Theory of Communicative Action* (1981). He argued there that, because social cooperation requires the goal-directed actions of disparate individuals to be linguistically coordinated, "communicative rationality" is no less basic to social life than means–ends rationality. This intersubjectivist approach to reason imbues the conceptual framework and normative foundations of his critical theory of contemporary society. For one thing, it directs attention to the broader sociocultural contexts of individual goal-directed actions; thus the idea of the "lifeworld" (*Lebenswelt*) – the taken-for-granted, indeterminate, and inexhaustible background of all our activities – is introduced as an essential dimension of communicative interaction. For

404

another, in the course of social and cultural rationalization, the use of reasons or grounds to gain intersubjective recognition for validity claims takes an increasingly reflective turn in certain domains. Modes of argumentation are differentiated and discursive institutions established that permit sustained, organized discussions of specific types of validity claims – and that makes learning processes possible in such areas as science and technology, law and morality. This means, Habermas argues, that cultural and social changes often evince features that have to be grasped in terms of the differentiation, development, and institutionalization of various dimensions of communicative reason. From this perspective, the selectivity of capitalist modernization becomes evident.

Habermas maintains that many of the problems and dilemmas of modernity are rooted in a one-dimensional rationalization of culture and society, the failure to develop and institutionalize in a balanced way the various, complementary potentialities of communicative reason. Forms of instrumental rationality have achieved a cultural and institutional dominance, while moral and political forms have atrophied. Developing a two-level concept of society that seeks to combine the usually competing paradigms of "lifeworld" and "system," he explains this in terms of the growing "colonization of the lifeworld" by forces emanating from the economy and the state. Subsystems in which instrumental rationality is embodied increasingly dominate other areas of life and transform them in their own image and likeness. Systemic mechanisms such as money and power drive communicative forms of social integration and symbolic reproduction out of domains in which they cannot be replaced. The phenomena that Weber pointed to in his vision of an "iron cage" and that Marxists such as LUKÁCS (see Article 40) analyzed in terms of "reification" arise, in this view, from an incessant "monetarizing" and "bureaucratizing" of lifeworld relations, their conversion over to the control of market and administrative mechanisms. This relentless undermining of the communicative infrastructures of society can be contained, Habermas argues, only by a countervailing expansion of the areas of life coordinated by communication and, in particular, by the subordination of economic and administrative subsystems to decisions arrived at in open, critical, public debate. Thus the antidote to colonization is democratization, and the key to democratization is effectively functioning cultural and political public spheres.

What separates this critique of modernity from the welter of counter-enlightenment critiques during the last two centuries is Habermas's unflinching defense of enlightenment rationality, a defense that is, to be sure, itself informed by a critique of rationalist pretensions and by an insistence on the unfinished character of the project of enlightenment. Redeeming the failed promise of a life informed by reason means, on this analysis, simultaneously redeeming the failed promise of democracy.

## Writings

Habermas, J.: *The Structural Transformation of the Public Sphere* (1962), tr. T. Burger and F. Lawrence (Cambridge, MA: MIT Press, 1989).

405

——: *Theory and Practice* (1963), tr. J. Viertel (Boston, MA: Beacon Press, 1973).

——: *On the Logic of the Social Sciences* (1967), tr. S. Nicholsen and J. Stark (Cambridge, MA: MIT Press, 1988).

——: *Knowledge and Human Interests* (1968), tr. J. Shapiro (Boston, MA: Beacon Press, 1971).

——: *Legitimation Crisis* (1973), tr. T. McCarthy (Boston, MA: Beacon Press, 1975).

——: *Communication and the Evolution of Society* (1976), tr. T. McCarthy (Boston, MA: Beacon Press, 1979).

——: *The Theory of Communicative Action* (1981), 2 vols, tr. T. McCarthy (Boston, MA: Beacon Press, 1984).

——: *Moral Consciousness and Communicative Action* (1983), tr. C. Lenhardt and S. Nicholsen (Cambridge, MA: MIT Press, 1990).

——: *The Philosophical Discourse of Modernity* (1985), tr. F. Lawrence (Cambridge, MA: MIT Press, 1987).

——: *Justification and Application: Remarks on Discourse Ethics* (1991), tr. C. Cronin (Cambridge, MA: MIT Press, 1993).

——: *Between Facts and Norms: Contributions to a Discourse Theory of Law and Democracy* (1992), tr. W. Rehg (Cambridge, MA: MIT Press, 1995).

## References and further reading

Baynes, K.: *The Normative Grounds of Social Criticism* (Albany, NY: SUNY Press, 1992).

Benhabib, S.: *Critique, Norm, and Utopia* (New York: Columbia University Press, 1986).

Bernstein, R. (ed.): *Habermas and Modernity* (Cambridge, MA: MIT Press, 1985).

Calhoun, C. (ed.): *Habermas and the Public Sphere* (Cambridge, MA: MIT Press, 1992).

Cooke, M.: *Language and Reason: A Study of Habermas's Pragmatics* (Cambridge, MA: MIT Press, 1994).

Dews, P. (ed.): *Autonomy and Solidarity: Interviews with Jürgen Habermas* (London: Verso, 1986).

Geuss, R.: *The Idea of a Critical Theory* (Cambridge: Cambridge University Press, 1981).

Günther, L.: *The Sense of Appropriateness* (1988), tr. J. Farrell (Albany, NY: SUNY Press, 1993).

Holub, R.: *Jürgen Habermas: Critic in the Public Sphere* (London: Routledge, 1991).

Honneth, A. and Joas, H. (eds.): *Communicative Action* (1986), tr. J. Gaines and D. Jones (Cambridge, MA: MIT Press, 1991).

Hoy, D. and McCarthy, T.: *Critical Theory* (Oxford: Basil Blackwell, 1994).

Ingram, D.: *Habermas and the Dialectic of Reason* (New Haven, CT: Yale University Press, 1987).

McCarthy, T.: *The Critical Theory of Jürgen Habermas* (Cambridge, MA: MIT Press, 1978).

Rasmussen, D.: *Reading Habermas* (Oxford: Basil Blackwell, 1990).

Rehg, W.: *Insight and Solidarity: The Discourse Ethics of Jürgen Habermas* (Berkeley, CA: University of California Press, 1994).

Thompson, J. and Held, D. (eds.): *Habermas: Critical Debates* (London: Macmillan, 1982).

Wellmer, A.: *Critical Theory of Society* (1969), tr. J. Cumming (New York: Seabury, 1971).

White, S.: *The Recent Work of Jürgen Habermas* (Cambridge: Cambridge University Press, 1988).

——(ed.): *The Cambridge Companion to Habermas* (Cambridge: Cambridge University Press, 1995).

# 35

# Third generation critical theory

## MAX PENSKY

A "third generation" of critical theory can no longer be said to be composed of anything as cohesive and unified as a "school." Critical theory today continues across a much more diverse spectrum of different philosophical approaches, influences, and questions. Its adherents are no longer united by national, geographical, or even linguistic ties, and do not necessarily even share the basic commitment to radical political change that characterized first generation critical theory. How, then, ought one to characterize the spectrum of philosophers, social and political theorists, and literary critics who could be said to make up a "third generation" of the Frankfurt School?

Describing the "third generation" of critical theorists should start with two prefatory comments – one the observation of a strange sort of historical irony, the other an obvious fact. First the irony: when HORKHEIMER (see Article 30) laid the foundations of a critical theory of society, he did so in explicit contrast to "traditional" theory, and with this contrast Horkheimer meant, among other things, that critical theory was to differ from previous, traditional theories by its unwillingness *itself* to become yet another form of theoretical tradition. In Horkheimer's sense, Critical theory was to be envisioned as an interdisciplinary cooperative enterprise, in which an interlocking constellation of various theoretical–critical interventions in modern culture would coalesce to form a basis for organized oppositional political action. Thus the social context of theory itself, its dependence on bourgeois institutions that nurture theoretical thinking while simultaneously subverting any internal connection between theory and emancipatory action, was itself to be subverted by a new *kind* of theory: one of the main tasks of "first generation" or "classical" critical theory was to liquidate the tradition of theory *within* theory itself.

Hence the irony that, insofar as we speak about a second and now a third generation of critical theory, we are in some sense always talking about the extent to which classical critical theory failed to realize its ambitious project. The very continuity of critical theory – its success in becoming one among many competing traditions within Continental philosophy – is also the measure of the defeat of its founding intentions, and its accommodation with the very context – "philosophy" – whose purpose it was to transform radically, a recognition that THEODOR ADORNO (see Article 31) aphoristically expressed when he said, at the opening of his *Negative Dialectics* (1973), that "[p]hilosophy, which once seemed obsolete, lives on because the moment to realize it was missed." As third generation critical theorists situate themselves within a tradition, then, they do so with the constant need to respond

407

*critically and dialectically* to their own heritage; a fact whose paradoxical aspect serves surprisingly well to characterize the unique traits of the "Frankfurt School" that survive into a third generation.

The obvious fact previously mentioned pertains to the "second" generation of critical theory; that is, to the work of Jürgen HABERMAS (see Article 34). Habermas's work provides the irreducible context for the entire question of the third generation of critical theory. Within the current tradition of critical theory, Habermas's refashioning of the initial orientations of the Frankfurt School dominates. Habermas recast the theoretical underpinnings of critical theory by moving it from a paradigm of the isolated subject to one of intersubjectivity; and from a paradigm of consciousness to one of language and communication. He introduced a fundamental distinction between strategic and communicative rationality in order to address the theoretical failure of the first generation of critical theory: its inability either to ground itself adequately in a theory of domination-free rationality, or to convince itself that such a self-grounding was neither necessary nor desirable.

Habermas definitively rejected much of what constituted the distinctiveness of first generation critical theory: its status as a form of "Western Marxism;" its political radicalism, its self-understanding as extramural, intransigently oppositional and in "permanent exile," as Martin Jay (1973) puts it. Equally significantly, Habermas rejects classical critical theory's characteristic dark mood, what Peter Sloterdijk (1987) has called its "a priori pain," along with its increasingly pessimistic diagnoses of contemporary Western society, its growing hopelessness in the face of what it took to be the complete hegemony of political and cultural domination, typified in the project, in Horkheimer and Adorno's *Dialectic of Enlightenment* (1944), to trace domination back phylogenetically to the prehistory of the human species, and logically to the very form of conceptual thought itself. Rejecting classical critical theory's radical politics and radical pessimism, Habermas also rejects the increasingly large role that was played by aesthetics in classical critical theory, particularly in the late work of Adorno.

The relation of third generation critical theory to Habermas's grand synthesis is both a source of continuity and a spur towards new directions. In some cases, sympathetic readings of Habermas lead back to renewed appraisals of the first generation of critical theory as well. In other cases, more extensive disagreements with Habermas's work provide the basis for reformulating some of the fundamental questions of "classical" critical theory: is bourgeois democracy worth defending? Is late capitalism capable of being "domesticated" into a *relatively* domination-free mode of material and cultural reproduction, or must it inherently oppress in order to survive? Can an emancipatory and critical dimension of rationality be theoretically reconstructed and defended?

Classical critical theory would tend to answer the first two of these questions negatively, while the third question led Adorno to the aporetic project of a "theory" of reason and *mimesis*. Habermas would answer positively on all counts, provided that the theoretical reconstruction of the emancipatory capacity of reason was humble enough to understand reason in the weak sense of intersubjectively shared communicative competencies, and provided that social "emancipation" is understood simply as the capacity of actors to take steps to reduce the extent of non-essential, non-communicative impediments to public processes and institutions of mutual understanding. Third generation critical theory, too, defines itself – within and against its own tradition – in how it takes up these kinds of questions. It might be defined by the manner in which it elaborates a critical position *between* its two basic sources: classical critical theory on the one hand, and Habermas on the other.

This working definition of third generation critical theory should be accompanied by a cautionary note, for the temptation to see an undialectical either/or between overly pessimistic classical critical theory and overly optimistic Habermasian critical theory is a false alternative. Critical theory must remain sensitive to the dialectical tension *between* its alternative formations. Taking a critical perspective towards both of its major traditional sources, third generation critical theory is naturally better equipped to investigate some of the grounds of this tension, and to reflect upon the possibilities open to critical thought *beyond* the alternatives of classical critical theory and Habermas's theory of communicative action. Engaging in their own philosophical heritage thus provides the tools for criticizing it and, perhaps, moving beyond it.

This characteristic dialectic is evident in the many third generation critical theorists who have based their work on historical and theoretical reconstructions of the tradition of critical theory itself: for example, Martin Jay's history of the Frankfurt School, *The Dialectical Imagination* (1973), set the tone for much of his later work on the concept of totality and on Adorno's work; Thomas McCarthy's influential study *The Critical Theory of Jürgen Habermas* (1978) introduced Habermas's work to an English-language audience and situated it in relation to his predecessors; Seyla Benhabib's *Critique, Norm, and Utopia* (1986) studied the theoretical foundations of critical theory in Hegel's action theories, and showed how subject–object and subject–subject relations in the Hegelian philosophy structured the development of critical theory all the way to Habermas's work.

Friendly criticisms by students of Habermas often open new insights into his relation with classical critical theory. In particular, Albrecht Wellmer (1991) has pointed out the unsatisfactory treatment of art and aesthetic experience in Habermas's *Theory of Communicative Action*, and has argued in a number of works that a re-appropriation of the aesthetic theory of Adorno could provide a valuable expansion of Habermas's project, which for Wellmer is fundamentally sound. Axel Honneth, perhaps Habermas's most prominent student, has more recently branched off from Habermas's discourse ethic towards a theory of the moral grammar of social conflict in which a re-appropriation and redescription of the Hegelian notion of recognition, coupled with a critical philosophy of psychology, serves as the basis for a new, critical understanding of the bases of possible social solidarity, a key moral concept for Habermas and for third generation critical theory as well.

Explorations of the relations between Habermas and classical critical theory have merged, in many third generation critical theorists, with another and equally philosophically relevant project: delineating the relationships – philosophical, cultural, political, and otherwise – between the tradition of critical theory and what is loosely and unsatisfactorily referred to as "postmodern" or more narrowly "post-structuralist" philosophy, a term meant to include the predominantly French appropriations of NIETZSCHE and HEIDEGGER (in such figures as FOUCAULT, DELEUZE, LYOTARD, and BAUDRILLARD – see Articles 11, 18, 49, 51–3) as well as the philosophical and literary practice of deconstruction (DERRIDA – see Article 50). Many clear affinities exist between this realm of contemporary Continental philosophy and critical theory in all its forms: both share a rejection of traditional philosophy and a critique of the metaphysical tradition; a project of tracing the effects of power relationships both in current social institutions and practices as well as in texts; a paradigm-shift from subject to intersubjectivity, from certainty to indeterminacy, and from consciousness to language, and a keen interest in developing alternatives to standard conceptions of rationality.

Habermas, however, has forcefully rejected any common ground between his own project and that of the French post-structuralists. In his work *The Philosophical Discourse of Modernity*, Habermas famously grouped Horkheimer and Adorno together with the key figures of the postmodern tradition: NIETZSCHE, HEIDEGGER, BATAILLE (see Article 24), FOUCAULT, and DERRIDA; a rejection of any internal connection between reason and emancipation links all these figures, for Habermas, in an essentially anti-modern, anti-Enlightenment mood. In calling for a clean break between classical critical theory and himself, Habermas insisted that a theory of rationality, however weak, was necessary to prevent normative criticism of existing institutions and practices from lapsing into groundless and discrete critical episodes, or a "performative contradiction" where a critical intervention cannot exempt itself from the same pervasive structures of power and domination it attacks. In the wake of this rejection, and of the enormous influence of recent French philosophy, third generation critical theory has justifiably taken up the question of its relation both to classical critical theory and to Habermas. Much work has supported Habermas's basic assertion of a subterranean political conservatism within the postmodern philosophical scene – for example, Thomas McCarthy's *Ideals and Illusions* (1991) and Richard Bernstein's *The New Constellation* (1992). Other works, such as Axel Honneth's *Critique of Power* (1991), comparing Habermas and Foucault, or Peter Dews's *Logics of Disintegration: Post-structuralist Thought and the Claims of Critical Theory* (1987) on the more general problem of the critical resources of contemporary French thought, or Albrecht Wellmer's collection of essays, *The Persistence of Modernity* (1991), offer case-studies of critical theory's insistence on dialectical thinking. Other third generation critical theorists seek to find common ground between critical theory and post-structuralism in the commonalities of intellectual heritage and philosophical mission: Fred Dallmayr, for example, has devoted numerous books to the exploration of the shared terrain between the Frankfurt School and the heirs of Heidegger (see Dallmayr 1991).

What is the future of critical theory? Classical critical theory lives on as a legitimate object of academic study, as offering a valuable resource of descriptive terms for concrete phenomena of social injustice, and as a sort of philosophical antidote towards too much faith in the meliorative capacities of advanced democratic societies. Habermasian analysis will continue to influence various research programs and critical reinterpretations of social and political phenomena across academic and scientific disciplines. Third generation critical theory has been most fruitful in strengthening Habermasian sorts of analyses *through* critical re-examinations of classical critical theory. Critical theory's future rests in the continuation of this sort of work, particularly in areas in which Continental philosophy has, for some time, been shown to be less than ideally suited: moral philosophy and interdisciplinary projects between philosophy and the empirical social sciences.

Third generation critical theory holds promise for the "rediscovery" of moral theory in contemporary Continental philosophy. The recognition of the need for moral philosophy, with the simultaneous rejection of any traditional philosophical elements of a moral *theory*, have launched much of contemporary Continental philosophy in an often awkward search for the "bases" of its own moral self-understanding. By insisting on the inherently political dimension of moral philosophizing, and by emphasizing the moral dimension of the critique of existing structures of domination, critical theory radicalizes moral philosophy. By insisting also on the project of a moral *theory* – insisting, in other words, that reason not be left out of the picture in moral philosophy – critical theory provides a helpful corrective against a tendency to blur distinctions between moral questioning and aesthetic performance that besets much of contemporary Continental philosophy. Critical feminism is one area in which third generation critical theorists have had much to contribute: Seyla Benhabib, Nancy Fraser, and Drucilla Cornell figure prominently among the many theorists developing a politically incisive form of feminist theory that appropriates the best features of critical theory. In the quest for a critical theory that can also appropriate the best of the moral consciousness of French thought, Central and South American political theorists such as Enrique Dussel are developing political analyses that combine elements of Habermas's and Karl-Otto Apel's discourse ethic with the work of Emmanuel LEVINAS (see Article 20).

In the philosophy of the social sciences, a number of third generation critical theorists have been deeply influenced by the basic questions of a critical theory of society, and have developed diverse critical perspectives on modern mass democracy and Western political culture. Sociologists and political theorists such as Claus Offe, Andrew Arato, Jean Cohen, Anthony Giddens, Stephen Lukes, while perhaps not directly "heirs" of the Frankfurt School, demonstrate well how critical sociology continues to take up such questions.

To summarize and conclude: "third generation critical theory" cannot be taken as a simple or undialectical continuation of the "tradition" of critical theory, insofar as the "tradition" of the Frankfurt School itself resides, if anywhere, in its rigorous commitment to the principle that all intellectual traditions are always available for criticism, and that criticism, in turn, is a practice of rational insight in the interest of real human emancipation. For this reason, the best work of the eclectic band of

411

philosophers, theorists, and sociologists referred to collectively here as a "third generation" consists in creatively and continuously challenging the reception and re-interpretation of the Frankfurt School itself. This means, between "classical" critical theory and Habermas, the legacy of the Frankfurt School lives on in the spirit of critical and dialectical thinking, and in the commitment to the theoretical elaboration of the affinity between reason and emancipation.

## Writings

Benhabib, Seyla: *Critique, Norm, and Utopia: A Study of the Foundations of Critical Theory* (New York: Columbia University Press, 1986).

——: *Situating the Self: Gender, Community, and Postmodernism in Contemporary Ethics* (New York: Routledge, 1992).

Bernstein, Richard: *The New Constellation: The Ethical–Political Horizons of Modernity/ Postmodernity* (Cambridge, MA: MIT Press, 1992).

Cornell, Drucilla: *Beyond Accommodation: Ethical Feminism, Deconstruction, and the Law* (New York: Routledge, 1991).

——: *Feminism as Critique: on the Politics of Gender* (Minneapolis, MN: University of Minnesota Press, 1987).

Dallmayr, Fred: *Between Frankfurt and Freiburg: Toward a Critical Ontology* (Amherst, MA: University of Massachusetts Press, 1991).

Dews, Peter: *Logics of Disintegration: Post-structuralist Thought and the Claims of Critical Theory* (London: Verso, 1987).

Dussel, Enrique: *The Philosophy of Liberation* (Maryknoll, NY: Orbis Press, 1985).

Fraser, Nancy: *Unruly Practices: Power, Discourse and Gender in Contemporary Social Theory* (Minneapolis, MN: University of Minnesota Press, 1989).

Honneth, Axel: *Critique of Power: Reflective Stages in a Critical Social Theory* (Cambridge, MA: MIT Press, 1991).

——: *Kampf um Anerkennung: Zur moralischen Grammatik sozialer Konflikte* (The struggle for recognition: on the moral grammar of social conflicts) (Frankfurt: Suhrkamp, 1992).

Jay, Martin: *The Dialectical Imagination: A History of the Frankfurt School and the Institute of Social Research, 1923–1950* (Boston, MA: Little, Brown, 1973).

McCarthy, Thomas: *The Critical Theory of Jürgen Habermas* (Cambridge, MA: MIT Press, 1978).

——: *Ideals and Illusions: Reconstruction and Deconstruction in Contemporary Critical Theory* (Cambridge, MA: MIT Press, 1991).

Wellmer, Albrecht: *The Persistence of Modernity: Essays on Aesthetics, Ethics, and Postmodernism* (Cambridge, MA: MIT Press, 1991).

## References and further readings

Adorno, Theodor: *Negative Dialectics* (New York: Continuum Press, 1973).

Dubiel, Helmut: "Domination or emancipation? The debate over the heritage of critical theory." In Axel Honneth, Thomas McCarthy, Claus Offe, and Albrecht Wellmer (eds): *Cultural–Political Interventions in the Unfinished Project of Enlightenment* (Cambridge, MA: MIT Press, 1992), pp. 3–16.

Habermas, Jürgen: *The Philosophical Discourse of Modernity* (Cambridge, MA: MIT Press, 1987).

Horkheimer, Max: "Traditional and critical theory." In *Critical Theory: Selected Essays* (New York: Seabury Press, 1972), pp. 188–243.

Sloterdijk, Peter: *Critique of Cynical Reason* (Minneapolis, MN: University of Minnesota Press, 1987).

PART VII

# HERMENEUTICS

# 36

# Schleiermacher

## BEN VEDDER

Without suggesting that Kant is responsible for the rise of hermeneutical philosophy, there are some developments in his philosophy which are important in relation to hermeneutics. Kant made the distinction between things-in-themselves and phenomena or appearances (see Article 2, KANT). The world we know depends on a conceptual projection of categories of our mind; we do not have access to the things-in-themselves, but only to interpretations of things such as they appear to us, after they have been edited by the understanding. This domestication of rationality led to the fideism of Jacobi: if reason can not bring us to reality, the only instance that can give us any sense of an objective and real world is faith with a kind of "knowledge" which is higher than our rational knowledge. In his early *On Religion: Speeches to its Cultured Despisers* (1799) Friedrich Schleiermacher (1768–1834) followed Jacobi in denying the pretensions of rational knowledge and determined religious sentiment to be a source of "knowledge" which transcends rational understanding (Vedder 1994). This background of Schleiermacher's hermeneutics is important to acknowledge. Therefore in this essay I will emphasize the fragility of hermeneutical knowledge for Schleiermacher. First I shall explain the hermeneutics of Schleiermacher; then I shall examine the relation between hermeneutics and dialectics.

## Hermeneutics

First a short sketch of Schleiermacher's hermeneutics (Kimmerle 1977, pp. 175–214). All understanding of foreign speaking belongs to the domain of hermeneutics. This means that hermeneutics is not the exclusive domain of the explanation of the Bible in theology or the explanation of the Classics in the study of literature. The complete domain of speaking and language belongs to hermeneutics. Therefore the principles of hermeneutics can be used in the complete domain of language and not only in the domain of the Classics and the Bible. Hermeneutics is as universal as language.

The first requirement for hermeneutics is something strange that has to be understood. In contrast with this there has to be something common or communal with the object to be explained; otherwise one cannot get any knowledge about the strange and foreign. If something is completely strange, explanation is not possible. But if something is completely clear, explanation is superfluous. In that case reading and hearing a text would be sufficient to understand it. With this addition hermeneutics is extended to all such places within language where, in the expression of thoughts, something is strange or incomprehensible for a listener or a reader. This can only be demystified when at least something is understood between the listener and the speaker, when there is a certain confidence between them.

Hermeneutics for Schleiermacher has to do also with ordinary speaking and writing, not only with classical or theological writings. For Schleiermacher conversation is the model par excellence for hermeneutics, even for the hermeneutics of written language. Hermeneutics is situated in the conversation (Kimmerle 1977, p. 181). Hermeneutical operations predominate when one tries to connect the thoughts of a fellow speaker. With this he defines hermeneutics as a connection of thoughts. It is not necessary for the language of the conversation to be a foreign language, for in using the same language there can be moments of misunderstanding. Hermeneutics belongs to language and culture as such, not only to a certain part of it. Schleiermacher's preference for spoken language arises from the idea that in a conversation there is a manifestation of a series of thoughts which express one's life. This relation of each thought with the whole of life is not seen in written language. Every utterance is surrounded by its entire living context.

Schleiermacher divides hermeneutics into two areas: one studies language and history (grammatical or historical hermeneutics), the other studies language as an expression of a personal life (psychological or technical hermeneutics). In these areas he tries to develop the specific kind of certainty which is attainable. The kind of certainty needed to reconstruct the original thoughts of an author is characterized by Schleiermacher as a "divinatory" certainty. One can prove that in certain connections a word has this specific meaning, but there are many texts and speeches about which one can say very little with certainty. This uncertainty is given both in grammatical and in psychological hermeneutics. In this case the translator or the listener has to guess, or to conjecture, the meaning of the text in this particular place, which is defined by the historical situation of the author, from which he gets his individual method of combination and connection of words. Therefore, in this area claiming is something different from proving, and the divinatory certainty is opposed to a demonstrative certainty.

Mostly divinatory certainty is related to psychological hermeneutics. Nevertheless, Schleiermacher expects of the interpreter, both in historical/grammatical hermeneutics and in psychological/technical hermeneutics, a good skill and knowledge. But in psychological hermeneutics he does not expect an equal skill from every practitioner. On this level one understands one's friends better than others.

The division into grammatical and psychological hermeneutics is not the same as the division into demonstrative and divinatory certainty. In both areas demonstrative and divinatory certainty appear. The former is characterized by comparing, the latter by guessing or divining. There has to be a cooperation between the comparative and the divinatory method. The former method dominates in grammatical and historical hermeneutics, the latter method dominates in psychological

418

hermeneutics. In the comparative method the interpreter will bring the known and the familiar near to the unknown and strange. So he will confine the unknown to narrower borders. But this comparing does not completely exhaust the explanation; also the divinatory method is necessary. After all an author or a speaker can deviate from grammatical rules or his usual opinions. Using the divinatory strategy the interpreter tries to reach the individuality of the other. The divinatory method is important because thinking is never without words. The fact that thinking (universal) occurs in words (historical) makes it necessary to use both methods, as I will explain later.

This relationship between thinking and words is a circular relationship, one of mutual implication. To explain this, Schleiermacher refers to the situation of a child that is learning to speak. Children do not possess language, but seek to obtain it. Nor do they know the activity of thinking, because there is no thinking without words. The question now is on which side they will start. They do not have any point of comparison. When they have obtained some words they can, by comparing, quickly master a lot of words. Still the question is: how do they acquire the first one? This first fixation, according to Schleiermacher, is a divinatory movement. They guess or conjecture. This happens at the beginning. Thus the human mind shows itself to be a through-and-through conjectural and guessing being. Words or thinking, one cannot say which is the first. The first step is a jump or a leap and never can we decipher the guessing which results from this.

After all, we live continually in this situation, on a smaller and lower scale. Starting from common knowledge, something remains strange and foreign in the language of the other. We will always have uncertainties, to which we must react with the same divinatory "knowledge." Again and again the mind has to find its way because everyone in his own and particular being is the not-being (*Nichtsein*) of the others. In this respect misunderstanding will never disappear. This means, according to Schleiermacher, that language hinders a complete understanding of the other, and therefore we need a *Kunstlehre des Verstehens*.

Nevertheless every word can only be understood when it is understood as a part of a whole. Every chapter has to be understood within the work as a whole. Everywhere one has to know the whole, from which one can understand the particular. Against this background one always has great uncertainties. One draws provisional conclusions, which emerge from a preliminary orientation towards the extended whole which raises new questions. This circular inference from part to whole can stop at a certain moment. At the end there is presumably complete illumination, and everything is understood in its own place. Schleiermacher describes this moment of full enlightenment as something sudden, just like the moment of the first fixation of word and thought.

As long as we have not caught the whole of the meaning of a text we need a guessing anticipation. For this we benefit from a foreword and an introduction, but very practically, also turning over the leaves of a book or first reading the last chapter can be useful. Every anticipation of the whole is incomplete until hermeneutics is no longer needed. But catching the whole of meaning transcends hermeneutics; it approaches religious insight. In hermeneutics every solution always

419

again appears as an approach. For it is almost impossible to replace the divinatory knowledge with a demonstrative or comparative knowledge. This holds for both grammatical and psychological hermeneutics. The divinatory moment is the moment at which an interpreter tries to comprehend the individual creative act of an author.

## Hermeneutics and dialectics

In the next part of this essay I outline Schleiermacher's vision of dialectics, to give broader insight into Schleiermacher's hermeneutics. Like hermeneutics, dialectics is situated in conversation. In conversation I learn to express or put into language my thoughts on something. Dialectics is the theory of expressing and ordering thoughts, not as a kind of rhetoric but as a skill to put into words the real meaning of something (Odebrecht 1988, p. 5). Hermeneutics is its opposite; in hermeneutics words are restored to thoughts (Rieger 1988). This we have seen in Schleiermacher's explanation of hermeneutics. Therefore hermeneutics is not only a philological discipline; it is also a philosophical discipline in which one reconstructs thoughts about something. In this respect dialectics and hermeneutics are both part of conversation and reciprocally related to each other as a philosophical discipline.

A conversation is advanced by trying to unify differences between persons, languages, and historical situations. The move from differences to unity and truth with respect to the subject is the motive of conversation. Difference of language and possible unity in thought make dialogue possible. But these differences are also the reason why in the area of dialectic there is no absolute knowledge. There is only a finite, partial, and provisional knowledge, because every finite knowledge is always a start for a new dialectical explanation, because another proposal can always be made with respect to the subject of the conversation. The dialogical character of knowing does not allow a definite answer or solution. There exists an unremovable relativity, in the sense that everything is related to another thing. Nevertheless, this does not lead to skepticism because conversation is only meaningful if the ideal of complete knowledge remains attainable.

The contrast, the opposite, the position of the other is constitutive of the process of thinking. Without this tension thinking would not develop. The conflict is always related to the truth of something, i.e. in the last analysis to being, with which thinking is concerned. The first object of thinking is formally defined as being; in thinking this being in the first instance is empty. It gets its provisional determination from conversation about it (Odebrecht 1988, p. 23). Thinking has a pre-understanding of the identity of being which has to be proved and formed in the conversation.

Because thinking never reaches the absolute identity of the opposites, and always moves between identity and difference, knowing has an invincible provisionality. This is because thinking is always formed in an individual and historical way; for every concept is formulated in language. In this way, to every universality adheres the individuality of historical speaking. This dependence of the concept on

420

the assertion is the reason why no concept embodies an absolute knowledge. It is always finite and provisional.

Therefore knowing always has a hypothetical character: it is a proposal in relation to the question it concerns. The hypothesis which approaches identity arises from inventing (divination) (Odebrecht 1988, pp. 75, 327). This happens by fantasy. Fantasy is led by feeling, because feeling is the place of unity of the subject. According to Schleiermacher feeling is the entrance to the unity of the world, not thinking or willing.

The medium of thinking is language. In language there is a relation to the universal and the individual. Language is a system of differences and distinctions. But this system of differences is always ordered in an individual way. In this respect all languages are irrational in relation to each other. As far as a language is individual it is not compatible with another language. Translating is only possible by using common or communal thinking, for thinking is universal, as far as it exists in communal language.

Therefore language is also universal; otherwise we would not understand each other. But every announcement about objects is a permanent continuation of the experiment to determine if all men construct their ideas in an identical way (Odebrecht 1988, p. 373). Language makes distinctions, individualizes and, at the same time, universalizes, as far as there is a common language. In so far as there is a common language, language is the expression of thinking. Thinking becomes clearer and more complete in language (Odebrecht 1988, p. 127). In a certain way thinking and speaking (*Rede*) are the same. But the difference between them is that thinking is concerned with universality and identity, while speaking always takes place in an individual language. This problem cannot be solved by a universal language, because it will always be individual and historical (Odebrecht 1988, p. 16).

We are able to be conscious of this relativity and provisionality of knowledge (Odebrecht 1988, p. 327). The permanent partial character of our knowledge in dialectics reinforces the possibility of misunderstanding in hermeneutics. The incapacity to reach complete knowledge by thinking requires clear rules in understanding someone. Through these rules the individual is fixed and his borders are delimited. Because of this, hermeneutics is motivated by the common uncertainty about the individual and the permanent possibility of misunderstanding. Therefore the individual can only be comprehended approximately (Odebrecht 1988, p. 378).

Strictly speaking, hermeneutics is concerned with texts. In this way hermeneutics and dialectics also apply to texts. Schleiermacher does not distinguish very strictly between spoken and written language. Texts are a result of thinking formulated in words. Therefore dialectics is not only a theory of conversation, but also a theory of the constitution of a text. In that case a text is the object of a dialectical process in which the opposites of the conversation are removed. But the text is also a result of an individual language. The universality of thinking acquires an empirical individual form in the text. But the process of thinking again happens as a conflict between opposite proposals. The solution of this conflict in the conversation results in a common knowledge, which will be formulated in the text. In a text the truth of other texts is united, but also every judgment is historical (Rieger 1988, p. 286).

So, the meaning of a text is highly determined by the individuality of a text. Nevertheless, the meaning of a text is also created by the interpretation. Interpretation already occurs in the constitution of the text. One cannot think correctly without aiming to be understood. Thinking becomes common and complete if it is communicable (Odebrecht 1988, p. 126). In that case one can speak of "knowledge" (ibid., p. 90). Therefore the writer has to ask how he will be interpreted. The other, the reader, the interpreter is already there in the constitution of the text. Schleiermacher writes (as a predecessor of GADAMER, see Article 38) in his *Dialektik*: "The more a text is dialogic, the more complete it is" (Odebrecht 1988, pp. 53–4). In this way constitution and interpretation of a text are dependent on each other. Interpretation is uniting, not separating; it is inquiring about identity, not about differences. But constitution leads to the differences in the text, interpretation to the identity of meaning in the text. In this way constitution and interpretation of a text are woven into each other. The constitution is also interpretative and the interpretation is also constitutive. But it is the insuperable individuality which both motivates one to seek an identity of meaning, and prevents it.

Dialectics and hermeneutics are related as text-construction and text-interpretation. The arts of speaking and understanding imply each other. Speaking is the external side of thinking; in this way hermeneutics is, connected to the art of thinking, a philosophical discipline. The philosophical character of hermeneutics is based on the fact that it – like dialectics – produces provisional knowledge developed in conversation. They are related like listening (hermeneutics) and speaking (dialectics).

This interaction happens in a historical process as a movement from the universal to the individual and from the individual to the universal. The movement from thinking to speaking is related to dialectics, that from speaking to thinking to hermeneutics. These two do not only complement each other, they need each other. Dialectics needs hermeneutics, because the identity of knowledge can never be found without the analysis of the language which it has to unify. On the other hand, hermeneutics needs dialectics because language and text can only be understood if there is an identity to be discovered in it; otherwise language would not be open to understanding.

In this way we see that dialectics is hermeneutical and that hermeneutics is dialectical. In other words, the circle between thinking and speaking is repeated in the circle between dialectics and hermeneutics. Against this background Schleiermacher distinguishes between two kinds of thinking, one that starts from the identity of all thinking subjects and another that starts from the differences between them (Odebrecht 1988, p. 165). Through dialectics every kind of knowledge dissolves into individual differences. Hermeneutics is aware of this and raises dialectics to a new universality. It is aware that every sort of knowledge has the character of individuality and historicity, because it has to apply to a text which is historical.

The critical function of hermeneutics guards dialectics from an untimely or illusory identity. Hermeneutics argues in favor of the unresolvability of the differences, the individual and the non-understandable (Odebrecht 1988, p. 170). The hermeneutical and dialectical process in conversation are therefore constitutive of the meaning of knowledge, because they show that an absolute identity is not available. It is only possible approximately; there is always a remnant that is not understood.

A text is understood if its irreducible (or insuperable) individuality, its partial non-understandability is recognized. In this sense hermeneutics is a correction of dialectics, which constantly aims at the unity of the conversation. Dialectics takes place within the ideal of a universal identity of the same, but disintegrates unwillingly into the individual irrationality. Hermeneutics presupposes these individual differences. "We have to understand the individual difference, with this we stay in our task, namely the striving for knowledge" (Odebrecht 1988, p. 378). Hermeneutics points out the fictional character of a solution to the conflict through its attention to the individual differences.

Hermeneutics relates dialectics to history and thus makes knowledge more complete. It allows plurality and difference. By emphasizing the dialogical structure of our knowledge, Schleiermacher opens the way to a broader insight into the world. Through dialogue we can go beyond the limits of our selves and attain a relative universality. We learn to see things from different points of view. We can find traces of this in Gadamer's hermeneutics, in the project of a "*Diskursethik*" in HABERMAS (see Article 34) and in the notion of narrative in RICOEUR (see Article 39).

## Writings

Schleiermacher, F. D. E.: "On the concept of hermeneutics, with reference to F. A. Wolf's Instruction and Ast's Textbook." Published in: Friedrich Schleiermacher, *Hermeneutics: The Handwritten Manuscripts*, ed. Heinz Kimmerle, tr. James Duke and Jack Fortsman (Missoula, MT: Scholars Press, 1977). Cited as Kimmerle 1977. This is the only text which Schleiermacher himself published on the subject of hermeneutics during his life. The original German edition is: Fr. D. E. Schleiermacher, *Hermeneutik: Nach den Handschriften* (Heidelberg, 1959).

——: *Dialektik*, ed. Rudolf Odebrecht (Darmstadt: Wissenschaftliche Buchgesellschaft, 1988). Cited as Odebrecht 1988.

——: *On Religion: Speeches to its Cultured Despisers* (1799), intro., tr., and notes by Richard Crouter (Cambridge: Cambridge University Press, 1988).

## References and further reading

Blackwell, Albert L.: *Schleiermacher's Early Philosophy of Life: Determinism, Freedom and Phantasy* (Chico, CA: Scholars Press, 1982).

Forstman, Jack: *A Romantic Triangle: Schleiermacher and Early German Romanticism* (Missoula, MT: Scholars Press, 1977).

Hinze, Bradford E.: *Narrating History, Developing Doctrine: Friedrich Schleiermacher and Johann Sebastian Drey* (Atlanta: Scholars Press, 1933).

423

Maraldo, John C.: *Der hermeneutische Zirkel: Untersuchungen zu Schleiermacher, Dilthey und Heidegger* (The Hermeneutic Circle, inquiries into Schleiermacher, Dilthey and Heidegger) (Freiburg: Alber, 1974).

Palmer, Richard E.: *Hermeneutics: Interpretation Theory in Schleiermacher, Dilthey, Heidegger and Gadamer* (Evanston, IL: Northwestern University Press, 1969).

Rieger, Reinhold: *Interpretation und Wissen, Zur philosophischen begründung der Hermeneutik bei Friedrich Schleiermacher und ihrem geschichtlichen Hintergrund* (Interpretation and knowledge: on the philosophical foundation of hermeneutics in Schleiermacher and its historical background) (Berlin, New York: De Gruyter, 1988).

Tice, Terrence N.: *Schleiermacher Bibliography (1784–1984)* (Princeton, NJ: Princeton Theological Seminary, 1985).

Vedder, Ben: "Schleiermacher's idea of Hermeneutics and the feeling of absolute dependence." In: *Epoche*, 2(1) (Spring 1994).

# 37

# Dilthey

## RUDOLF A. MAKKREEL

The place of Wilhelm Dilthey (1833–1911) in the history of hermeneutics has been subject to considerable misinterpretation. He is rightly regarded as having expanded the scope of hermeneutics by adding human actions to the kinds of texts that can be interpreted, but is wrongly dismissed as having overlooked the full significance of this move. His distinction between understanding and explanation has been stereotyped as a mere methodological distinction relevant for his theory of the human sciences. His reflections on interpretation have been relegated to the domain of traditional philological hermeneutics and excluded from philosophical hermeneutics. Heidegger's ontical–ontological distinction has been used to drive a wedge between the two and place Dilthey on the ontical side of a divide that cannot be fully justified. On the basis of newly available writings, a more adequate account dealing with the philosophical content of Dilthey's hermeneutic contributions can now be given.

When Dilthey relates his own views on understanding and interpretation to traditional hermeneutics, he notes a gradual process whereby theological constraints have been replaced by philological, historical, and philosophical considerations. Dilthey is not unwilling to discuss philological issues, but places them in a philosophical context. For instance, in commenting on August Boeckh's view that philology is the knowledge of the products of the human spirit, Dilthey claims that he was wrong to conceive these products as themselves a kind of knowledge. Boeckh did so when he proceeded to define philology as *Erkenntnis des Erkannten*: knowledge of past knowledge. Dilthey refuses to intellectualize interpretation in this way by reducing it to methodological recognition, and instead regards it as a process of coming to know. What we come to know through interpreting the products of the human spirit is the full scope of psychic and historical life.

Dilthey developed a descriptive psychology which would allow us to understand more than intellectual processes. The full range of consciousness must encompass emotional and volitional processes, not only as supplements to our cognitive activities, but also as implicated in them. Psychic life cannot be abstracted from its historical context, for there is no pre-existing subject that grounds consciousness. The self is acquired in terms of a temporal process whereby a nexus of consciousness is differentiated into inner and outer processes. Dilthey shows in his *Introduction to the Human Sciences* (1883) that the idea of a self is meaningful only as a correlate of a world that resists felt impulses. As much as the individual subject develops a kind of self-sufficiency, it always remains a point of intersection for the many social and cultural systems in which it participates. When Dilthey says that ultimately understanding has something singular as its goal, he means not only individual subjects, but also the specific historical systems that provide their context. His final position as articulated in the *Formation of the Historical World in the Human Sciences* (1910) is that the initial framework of interpretation must always be "objective spirit." With this term, adopted from Hegel, Dilthey designates the whole range of human objectifications, whether they be expressions meant to communicate or deeds meant to influence.

Objective spirit is at once the embodiment of human thought and action, as well as the medium within which they occur. This is the framework of communal meaning to which elementary understanding is oriented. When this does not sufficiently clarify the meaning of a text, higher understanding oriented toward more specific historical, social, or cultural systems is required. Thus puzzling passages in a play by Shakespeare may not be understandable until they are referred to dramatic conventions of Elizabethan England, or to events or practices of the time. Only after we have exhausted what these appropriate public contexts can do to clarify the meaning of these passages, would Dilthey recommend turning to the subjective context of Shakespeare's psychic life.

In 1887 Dilthey thought it desirable to relive or reproduce the author's state of mind, but subsequently he rejected this as unfeasible. Instead, he comes to speak of re-experiencing the meaning of a text whereby disinterested structural analogues of personal responses are created. Like Kant and Schleiermacher before him, Dilthey's hermeneutic maxim is to understand authors better than they understood themselves, not exactly as they understood themselves. To be sure, for each of these three thinkers this maxim has a somewhat different significance. For Kant it involves the conceptual clarification of the language used by an author, for Schleiermacher it means psychological clarification. The latter is rooted in the Romantic assumption that the work of an artist stems from an unconscious seminal decision which must be made conscious. Dilthey in turn worries that Schleiermacher's idea of an underlying seminal decision imposes an unjustified unifying explanative schema on interpretation. He wants to leave open the possibility of external influences on a work of art. For Dilthey, interpreters have the opportunity to understand a work of art better than its creator if they can gain some distance, especially historical distance. Thus in retrospect it is possible to better understand the relation of artists to their historical context and thus arrive at an evaluation of the overall meaning of their work.

The appeal to authorial intention is most obviously present in Schleiermacher's theory of seminal decisions, but it is also involved when Kant claims that because Plato "has not sufficiently determined his concept, he has sometimes spoken, or even thought, in opposition to his own intention" (Kant 1965, A314/B370). Authorial intention is similarly implicit in Kant's theory of authentic interpretation as developed in response to the problem of theodicy. Kant asserts that "all theodicy should really be the interpretation [*Auslegung*] of nature insofar as God manifests the *intention of his will* through it" (Kant 1923, p. 264). Originally, an authentic theodicy might seem to rest exclusively on the authority of God's self-interpretation

426

as the author of the world. But Kant insists that insofar as we conceive God rationally as a moral and wise Being, it is "*through our reason itself* that God becomes the interpreter of his will as proclaimed in his creation" (Kant 1923, p. 264). Authentic moral interpretations reconcile divine and human volitional perspectives through the intersubjective medium of practical reason, just as reflective aesthetic judgments reconcile the feelings of self and others by reference to a *sensus communis* (see Makkreel 1990, pp. 141–8).

Whereas Kant appealed to the idea of interpretation primarily to round off certain systematic aspects of his philosophy which would have been left abstract by the determinations of the regulative use of theoretical reason, Dilthey shows in his early prize-essay *Schleiermacher's Hermeneutic System in Relation to Earlier Protestant Hermeneutics* (1860) how thoroughly the Romantic idea of reconstructing a creative act was rooted in idealistic philosophy. Dilthey criticizes the philosophical base of Schleiermacher's hermeneutics as a dialectic of concepts that attempt to explain historical outcomes by manipulating static and timeless concepts. What would have been more appropriate, according to Dilthey, is a hermeneutics based on a philosophy oriented to the formation of judgments. Such a philosophy relates concepts, not to each other, but to the actual particulars of historical life. Only such a judgment-oriented philosophy can provide an understanding of historical change (Dilthey 1996, p. 709).

The philosophical character of Dilthey's hermeneutics can be related in a general way to Kant's theory of reflective judgment, where the mediation of particulars and universals is not for the sake of the extension and application of the latter, but for the felt appreciation of the individuality of the former. A reflective judgment as developed in Kant's third *Critique* is a comparative evaluation made by a subject participating in a community – even if only indirectly. Such judgments, whether aesthetic or teleological, presuppose a being situated in the world, and can be contrasted to the absolute but solitary stance of determinant judgment as defined in the first two Critiques.

In an 1867 lecture on intuition and understanding, Dilthey suggests that in a moral and aesthetic community I can "understand everything." Yet he goes on to say that a "human being who understood everything, would not be human" (Dilthey 1996, p. 100). Since to understand something for Dilthey is to grasp its individuality, there will always be a limit to what can be understood. To understand everything would be to lose one's own individuality. Unlike explanation, understanding is never just a matter of abstract thought. Instead, it requires the imagination to exhibit the universal in the particular, the whole in the part. We can discern the remnants of older intuition theories when Dilthey defines the hermeneutic task as understanding "the whole of a text . . . in a flash-like instant" (Dilthey 1996, p. 231). However, understanding is basically an inference from analogy which proceeds from particular to particular. This means that an initial reading cannot yet produce understanding: "it only gives a general idea; we must then understand the particularity [of the work]" (ibid.). To understand a text is not merely to grasp the general meanings of its words, nor merely to imaginatively reactivate the particular sense it had for its author, but to activate that concrete sense that it can have in

427

relation to my present experience (see ibid., p. 233). Here understanding becomes a function of criticism and considers relevance as well as meaning.

One of the interesting features of this lecture is the way the discussion of hermeneutics leads into that of history. This relation between hermeneutics and historical consciousness leads Dilthey to broaden hermeneutics from the science of interpreting texts to the science of interpreting all historical objectifications. But more than that, it allows us to conceive the relation between hermeneutics and history as moving from the mere philological art of interpreting meaning to the philosophical theory of judging truth. The theory of history (*Historik*) is a crucial link, for through it "a sense for truth was first cultivated" (Dilthey 1996, p. 234).

"The Rise of Hermeneutics" (1900) goes back earlier than the Protestant background used in the Schleiermacher prize-essay to the exegetical and rhetorical views of the Greeks and allows us to distinguish two general hermeneutic approaches, the first rooted in the linguistic considerations found in Aristotle's *Rhetoric* and *Poetics*, the other in the spiritual concerns of Platonic and Stoic philosophy. Aristotle's contribution to hermeneutics lies in his ability to organize our understanding of texts through the analysis of plot structures and linguistic means. The Aristotelian approach to the metaphorical use of language is to see it as a modification of a literal use by means of a kind of transference. Although Dilthey himself adheres to the Vichian view that poetic meaning is more original than literal meaning, he finds Aristotle's approach to metaphor attractive in that it allows us to intuit similarity in dissimilars. Whereas Aristotle points to a continuity between literal and figurative meaning, the Platonic and Stoic approaches separate them as the sensuous versus the spiritual. Although allegorical interpretations can be ingenious in overcoming anomalies and contradictions in a text by appealing to higher spiritual senses, they do not resolve these problems in ways that promote historical understanding. For Dilthey the linguistic-grammatical approach provides the kind of interpretation that can be more readily allied with historical inquiry.

Dilthey notes in the Addenda to the "Rise of Hermeneutics" that the history of hermeneutics has been an episodic one. This is because hermeneutics "receives attention only when there is a great historical movement, which makes it urgent that singular prehistorical phenomena be understood scientifically. But then the interest in hermeneutics wanes again" (Dilthey 1996, p. 252). Because hermeneutics had already accomplished its goal of codifying the philological rules necessary for historical understanding in the work of Boeckh and Droysen, Dilthey found the interest in hermeneutics to be declining. In order to revive hermeneutics, Dilthey broadened the scope of understanding to encompass what is distinctive of all the operations of the human sciences. Hermeneutics then no longer provides merely the material rules for understanding human objectifications, but is also the formal theory of what makes understanding in the human sciences possible. "If understanding is basic for the human sciences," writes Dilthey, then "the epistemological, logical and methodological analysis of understanding is one of the main tasks for the foundation of the human sciences. The importance of this task only becomes fully apparent when one makes explicit the difficulties contained in the nature of understanding with reference to the practice of a universally valid science" (ibid., pp. 252–3).

Because these difficulties constitute aporias or impasses, a long-term interest in hermeneutics now seems assured. The first aporia formulated by Dilthey states that each of us is "enclosed, as it were, within his own consciousness" (ibid., p. 253). Clearly Dilthey does not share the Rankean ideal of self-effacement when it comes to understanding others. The optimal condition for understanding others is the supposition that the same basic psychic properties and activities are to be found in all individuals. It is more realistic to assume that they are possessed in varying degrees of intensity, producing structural variations. Dilthey's motto "transposition is transformation" (ibid., p. 253) indicates that the possibility of understanding others by transposing myself requires a structural self-transformation.

Dilthey's second aporia involves the familiar hermeneutical circle between parts and wholes and the paradox that one must already have a preliminary sense of the whole before one can truly understand it on the basis of the parts. The third aporia points out that a psychic state is not understood from within, but on the basis of "the external stimuli that aroused it." As a consequence, "milieu is indispensable for understanding" (ibid., p. 253). Since understanding involves all kinds of external factors, Dilthey admits that "when pushed to its limits, understanding is not different from explanation, insofar as the latter is possible in this domain" (ibid.). Having first distinguished understanding and explanation, he now sees them as eventually converging.

This projection of an ultimate convergence between understanding and explanation can be imagined in two different ways. The first or weaker version of convergence merely acknowledges that the full understanding of human life must also take into account the explanation of the external contextual factors involved. Here explanation can continue to mean what it normally means for Dilthey: the derivation of particular instances from the general causal laws found in the natural sciences. However, it is also possible that Dilthey is conceiving a more limited mode of explanation. Then explanation would be the process of bringing what we know about the external contextual factors to bear on the inner processes to be understood. This is what is suggested when Dilthey goes on to write: "There, where general insights are consciously and methodically applied in order to bring what is singular to comprehensive knowledge, the expression 'explanation' finds its proper place in the knowledge of the singular. It is only justified insofar as we remain aware that we can never allow what is singular to be fully submerged by what is universal" (Dilthey 1996, p. 257).

Gadamer's characterization of Dilthey's hermeneutics as primarily a traditional or technical inquiry into the methodological status of understanding in the human sciences can now be corrected. Dilthey contributed more than that by discussing the aporias of both understanding and explanation. The recently published full version of the *Introduction to the Human Sciences* makes it clear that he was concerned with what the natural and human sciences share epistemologically as well as with what differentiates them (Dilthey 1989, pp. 407, 431). But more importantly, Dilthey shows why the conceptual knowledge (*Erkenntnis*) arrived at in the

429

human sciences cannot, like that of the natural sciences, abstract from the immediate knowledge (*Wissen*) of life that already exists at the level of prescientific experience. Both kinds of science take their departure from the "facticity" (Dilthey 1958, p. 287) of the world, but whereas the natural sciences seek to focus on the way things behave independently of our human involvement, the human sciences take account of this very involvement. The interpretive understanding of social and cultural practices obtained in the human sciences must therefore be related back to the basic forms of the pre-understanding of life already found in simple consciousness and rudimentary linguistic categories. By also inquiring into these general conditions that make understanding possible, Dilthey is certainly examining hermeneutics philosophically.

Otto Bollnow has proposed a linguistic distinction between philosophical hermeneutics and hermeneutical philosophy, where the former involves doing hermeneutics in light of philosophical insights and the latter involves doing philosophy in light of hermeneutical insights (Bollnow 1984, pp. 49f). In terms of that distinction, the exploration into the conditions of understanding and interpretation, whether it is done on the basis of epistemic and reflective considerations, as in Dilthey, or existentially, as in parts of Heidegger's *Being and Time*, counts as philosophical hermeneutics. And Gadamer's own characterization of his *Truth and Method* as a philosophical hermeneutics can be questioned, for it is really more a hermeneutical philosophy which recognizes that concerning certain ultimate questions we can obtain merely interpretive, not definitive, solutions.

One version of hermeneutical philosophy is the perspectivalism of Nietzsche, according to which there are no facts, only interpretations. Dilthey confronts the perspectival nature of philosophy in his *Weltanschauungslehre*. Thus whereas his examination of the conditions that make understanding and explanation in the sciences possible can be considered part of philosophical hermeneutics, his separate analysis of world-views and of their three incommensurable types can be seen as part of hermeneutical philosophy. World-views intimate an overall sense of life, which transcends the specific meanings and truths made available by the sciences, but is already implicit in reflection on everyday experience. World-views are articulated in great literature, in religions, and finally in philosophical systems where they receive a conceptual formulation that allows them to be typed as either a form of naturalism, of idealism of freedom, or of objective idealism. Each of these metaphysical types of world-view is a reflective interpretation of reality respectively emphasizing either our cognitive capacities, our volitional ends, or what is felt to be valuable. Despite being totalistic, these types of world-view cannot attain absolute knowledge according to Dilthey. They aim at an impossible synthesis of the perspectives of the natural and the human sciences that cannot in principle be reconciled. Our interpretations of the meaning of everyday and historical life will thus always be left with certain insoluble riddles that prevent us from conceptualizing the ultimate sense of life.

In his 1925 Kassel lectures on "Wilhelm Dilthey's Work and the Present Struggle for a Historical World-View," Heidegger is not concerned with Dilthey's world-view typology and his reflections on the limits of our metaphysical interpretations.

430

Instead, he looks to Dilthey for the beginnings of a historical world-view which locates historicity as the source of our factical existence. He claims that Dilthey's ultimate interest lay not in historical methodology, but in "historical Being (*geschichtlichen Sein*)" (Heidegger 1993, p. 157). "He has shown and stressed that the basic character of life is its being-historical (*Geschichtlich-Sein*)" (ibid., p. 173). What Dilthey did not go on to ask according to Heidegger was what being-historical means, namely, its rootedness in time. Heidegger was prevented from knowing, by the fact that much of Dilthey's work was still unpublished in 1925, that Dilthey did explore the nature of time in relation to his reflections on the meaning of history. But what is of greater import is that Heidegger regards the historical world-view not as a reflective response to the riddles left unsolved by the sciences (Dilthey's sense of world-view), but as a fundamental ontological stance that grounds our very existence. The historical world-view is as much constitutive of all understanding as it is regulative of any and all perspectival interpretations. Heidegger no longer separates philosophical hermeneutics from hermeneutical philosophy, although the two can still be distinguished. Another way to consider his stance is to see constitutive questions about understanding and regulative questions about interpretation as equiprimordial.

Like Dilthey, Heidegger felt more affinity with Aristotle than with Plato, for in Aristotle's thought the factical and ideational are not as much in danger of moving apart. Ontology is not a matter of isolating pure beingness, but understanding the relation of Being to actual beings. Just as Dilthey was suspicious of Platonizing or allegorical interpretations that isolate a pure spiritual meaning, and preferred the kind of symbolic meaning that could illuminate historical change, Heidegger wants to show that the Being that human beings try to understand is nothing transcendent but the very time that constitutes their own existence.

Although Dilthey and Heidegger would agree that the ontical and ontological dimensions of philosophy are inseparable, they would differ about the relative stress each should be given. This difference can be nicely illustrated by their respective ways of conceiving the relation between life and death. Although Dilthey's philosophy exhibits the meaning of life primarily on the basis of ordinary ontical lived experiences, it also reflects on our awareness of death and other metaphysical mysteries. Death which seems to impinge from without is, however, to be understood as the inherent corruptibility of life itself. Heidegger by contrast gives death ontological priority in that only when we are able to anticipate our own death do we become able to understand the meaning of our life. As much as such a projection of nothingness serves to focus our appreciation of life, it cannot for Dilthey be the horizon of our understanding of it. Dilthey's hermeneutics is radically immanent in requiring us to understand life out of life itself.

## Writings

Dilthey, Wilhelm: *Gesammelte Schriften*, vol. VII (Göttingen: Vandenhoeck & Ruprecht, 1958).
——: *Selected Works*, vol. 1: *Introduction to the Human Sciences* (1989), vol. 4: *Hermeneutics*

431

*and the Study of History* (1996), vol. 5: *Poetry and Experience* (1985); eds Rudolf A. Makkreel and Frithjof Rodi (Princeton, NJ: Princeton University Press).

## References and further reading

Bollnow, Otto: "Festrede zu Wilhelm Diltheys 150. Geburtstag," *Dilthey Jahrbuch*, 2 (1984).

Ermarth, Michael: "Objectivity and relativity in Dilthey's theory of understanding," *Dilthey and Phenomenology* (Washington, DC: Center for Advanced Research in Phenomenology & University Press of America, 1987).

Heidegger, Martin: "Wilhelm Diltheys Forschungsarbeit und der gegenwärtige Kampf um eine historische Weltanschauung," *Dilthey Jahrbuch*, 8 (1993).

Kant, Immanuel: *Critique of Pure Reason*, tr. Norman Kemp Smith (New York: St Martin's Press, 1965).

Kant, Immanuel: "Über das Mißlingen aller philosophischen Versuche in der Theodicee," *Gesammelte Schriften*, vol. 8 (Berlin and Leipzig: Walter de Gruyter, 1923).

Makkreel, Rudolf A.: *Imagination and Interpretation in Kant: The Hermeneutical Import of the "Critique of Judgment"* (Chicago, IL: University of Chicago Press, 1990).

——: *Dilthey: Philosopher of the Human Studies* (Princeton, NJ: Princeton University Press, 1992).

Rodi, Frithjof: "Dilthey's concept of 'Structure' within the context of nineteenth-century science and philosophy," *Dilthey and Phenomenology* (Washington, DC: Center for Advanced Research in Phenomenology & University Press of America, 1987).

# 38

# Gadamer

DENNIS J. SCHMIDT

Any determination of Hans-Georg Gadamer's place in Continental philosophy needs to begin by noting that his contribution to that tradition is associated with the style of philosophizing designated as "hermeneutics." But while a presentation of Gadamer's thought is well-advised to begin with a discussion of his conception of hermeneutics, it must not end with that theme. In fact, what is perhaps most notable about Gadamer's work is both its historical and disciplinary breadth as well as the wide range of issues that it addresses. That engagement with the history of philosophy and such a diverse collection of issues is itself a reflection of the project of hermeneutics as Gadamer has developed it: not a "method," Gadamer's hermeneutics is more aptly described as the effort to solicit the experience of limits harbored by all experience, and to demonstrate that this experience of finitude is not restricted only to some forms of experience. So one turns to his body of work and finds significant texts on ancient Greek philosophy and literature, all forms of art, translation, questions of contemporary culture and politics, theology, as well as issues in medicine and health. Just as one finds a remarkable pluralization of the fields in which Gadamer's hermeneutics can take root, so too one finds a similar situation with respect to the formative influences upon Gadamer's thought: while he is most frequently associated with the name of his teacher, HEIDEGGER (Article 18), it is clear that Plato, Aristotle, Augustine, Hölderlin, KANT (Article 2), HEGEL (Article 6), DILTHEY (Article 37), HUSSERL (Article 15), Rilke, and Celan need to be understood as providing many of the decisive impulses for Gadamer's own original philosophic contributions.

So as one begins to ask just what it is that the name of Gadamer signals for contemporary thought one immediately notices that his work and long career have drawn inspiration from, and given inspiration to, an uncommonly diverse set of philosophical experiences. One notices as well that such an openness to diversity, and the almost ethical sensitivity to limits that is the corollary of such genuine openness and that is the Kantian element in Gadamer's thought, are the hallmarks of Gadamer's work generally. In the end, one finds that this deep fidelity to openness is reflected as well in the form of Gadamer's own texts: there is no system to be found, no method to be "applied," no effort to say the final word, no authorization of expertise, only the deep conviction that the law of interpretation is to be found in the details of each experience and in the belief that no matter how sedimented a tradition might become it is never resistant to unfolding itself and disclosing something new. Indexed always to openness, Gadamer's hermeneutics is especially attentive to the possibility of posing questions. So potent is the logic of the question in hermeneutic theory that it might easily take as its motto the line from e.e. cummings that says "Always the more beautiful answer who asks a more beautiful question."[1]

Gadamer's best known work, and perhaps the basic work of hermeneutic theory, is *Wahrheit und Methode* (1960), but his essays and interviews might, in the modesty of their claims to authority and their persistent effort to open rather than close issues, be more typical of what Gadamer's name has come to represent in the contemporary philosophical world. The context for situating Gadamer's philosophical contributions is perhaps best provided by some of his autobiographical works, works in which the hermeneutic temperament is clearly evident.

## On Gadamer's life and the context of his work

Among Gadamer's texts are two that are fundamentally autobiographical. The first, *Philosophische Lehrjahre* (*Philosophical Apprenticeships*, 1985 [1977]), speaks chiefly about his education and early years as a professor of philosophy. The second is Gadamer's essay for the *Library of Living Philosophers* (1996) in which he speaks mostly of his intellectual itinerary after the publication of *Wahrheit und Methode* (*Truth and Method*, 1975). Together they give some insight into the formative intellectual and cultural influences active in his life. From them one also gleans something of Gadamer's life. But what is perhaps most interesting about these texts is the manner, the extraordinary reticence, with which Gadamer reveals himself to his readers. The motto of *Philosophische Lehrjahre*, the line from Bacon that once served as the epigram for Kant's *Critique of Pure Reason*, "*de nobis ipsis silemus*" ("of ourselves we remain silent"), announces that reticence from the outset. The self-portrait of Gadamer that emerges is one reflected through the portraits that he draws of his friends, surroundings, and times. Though he only occasionally speaks of himself, a clear sense of who he is comes through: above all one discovers that his philosophical temperament is thoroughly dialogical. One sees in that style something of Gadamer's understanding of hermeneutics in actions; namely, that the truth of a matter emerges only insofar as we are, as he puts it echoing Hölderlin, "in a conversation."

Born in 1900 in Breslau, Germany, Gadamer has lived through the rapid and dramatic transformations in the conditions of life that belong to the twentieth century. In his *Philosophische Lehrjahre* he speaks of his memories of the introduction of the electric light, the telephone, the Zeppelin, and the automobile. He also speaks of the catastrophe of the two world wars and the Holocaust. Elsewhere he speaks of more recent alterations in global politics and of the technological innovations, and technological threats, to be found at the end of this century. Having experienced these cultural revolutions, Gadamer's work is notable for its continuing efforts to comprehend those revolutions philosophically.

The beginnings of, and dominant influence upon, Gadamer's philosophic itinerary must be traced back to his early work with his teachers Heidegger, Nicolai Hartmann, and Paul Natorp. Trained in the then new movement of "phenomenology" and encouraged by Heidegger to pose questions about "the end of metaphysics," Gadamer's interests were none the less mostly to be found in Greek philosophy. Gadamer's first book, *Platos dialektische Ethik* (*Plato's Dialectical Ethics*) (1931), is the result of that interest. That early involvement with Greek thought was to prove to be the most enduring focal point of his work (this is borne out by the fact that, despite the range of his writings, three of the ten volumes of his collected works are devoted to Greek philosophy). In the pre-Socratics, especially Heraclitus, Gadamer found a manner of thinking and speaking that was not overwhelmed by the conceptual potentials of language. In Plato, he found a rich resource for thinking through the logic of question and answer that is decisive for the elaboration of hermeneutics. In Aristotle, especially the *Ethics*, Gadamer found a model for thinking the riddle of finite knowing understood as coupled with the notion of tradition. Steeped in Heidegger's and Husserl's revolutionary phenomenology, posing questions about the end of the tradition of Western philosophizing, Gadamer's work – like Hegel's – centered itself on the origins of that tradition and raised new questions about the nature of traditions and their transformation.

Such a wedding of impulses and interests, German and Greek, revolutionary and traditional, make it difficult to classify Gadamer's thought according to the dominant philosophical taxonomies of the present age (taxonomies that Gadamer's own work has helped call into question). But it becomes all the more difficult to align Gadamer with any specific philosophical movement once one acknowledges the role that art and literature have played in his work. Always alert to the riddle of language and always calling attention to the limits of what can be said, Gadamer has turned to art and poetic language as part of his effort to open traditional philosophizing to the limits of what can be said in its conceptual language. The "clue" that art supplies philosophy, a clue to the limits of philosophy itself with regard to truth, is, according to Gadamer, first systematically exposed by Kant in his *Critique of Judgment*. In this appeal to (and critique of) Kant's analysis of aesthetic experience, Gadamer's hermeneutics of experience begins to set itself apart from Heidegger's early "hermeneutics of facticity" which served as its initial model.

So, while the impetus that Gadamer took from Heidegger needs to be the starting point for any understanding of Gadamer's own philosophic contribution, it should be clear that his contribution should not be defined simply as emerging in the wake of Heidegger. It was, in fact, not until 1960, the time of the publication of *Truth and Method*, almost four decades after his first encounter with Heidegger. That is a striking period of silence, a period during which Gadamer found the requisite distance from Heidegger. By the time of the publication of his *Heidegger's Ways* (1983) Gadamer's debt to, and distance from, Heidegger could be taken. But it is also clear that Gadamer's thought cannot only be approached by referring to its intellectual antecedents. His lifetime, especially the formative years of his twenties to early forties, was powerfully defined by the disasters of war and the atrocities of National Socialism. Those experiences help shape Gadamer's unique philosophic sensibility rendering that sensibility uncommonly sensitive to the force and effective life of history and the life of peoples.

# Elements of Gadamer's philosophical hermeneutics

Despite the title of his major work, *Truth and Method*, which might give the mislead-ing impression that it promises a method that will expose truth, Gadamer never develops his philosophical hermeneutics as a philosophical method. Quite the con-trary: a fundamental argument of that text is that no method can ever be sufficient for the disclosure of truth and that truth belongs so essentially to history that it can never be disclosed fully. The question that animates hermeneutics is clearly not the question of method that motivates Descartes and serves as the leading question in the development of modernity. One sees this point reflected in *Truth and Method* in Gadamer's opening criticisms of the dominance of the model of the natural and mathematical sciences in reflection about human affairs. One also finds these themes addressed in *Reason in the Age of Science* (1976) where the excessive claims of Enlightenment conceptions of reason, and the assertions of authority character-istic of modern science, are analyzed in light of the limits of both reason and science that hermeneutic theory exposes. Against this progressive scientization, and its demand for certitude and perfectibility, Gadamer argues that reflection about hu-man affairs is best understood according to the problematic of judgment where "judgment" is best understood with reference to Aristotle's conception of *phronesis* in the *Nichomachean Ethics* and to what Kant designates as reflective judgment as opposed to determinate judgment.

According to Kant, in determinate judgment we have a universal, a concept, which we only need to apply to a particular case. Such judgments are in need only of rules for their application (though, as Gadamer points out, there are no rules for the application of rules). In reflective judgment on the other hand we are confront-ed with a particular case for which no universal law is adequate. No method, no rules, no question of application is possible since here we are confronted by a particular case that exceeds any prior conceptualization. "Its ideal is rather to understand the phenomenon itself in its unique and historical concreteness. How-ever much general experience is involved, the aim is not to confirm and expand these general experiences" (Gadamer 1975, p. 6). In his analysis of such judg-ments, Kant, like Gadamer, turns to the judgment of taste, the claim that something is beautiful. Pointing out that no law of taste can be given, that beauty is not able to be determined by a concept but always only in the individual case, but arguing that taste none the less lays a claim to universality, Kant contends that aesthetic judgment can be taken as a model for every judgment that lays claim to truth. Gadamer makes a similar claim in the first part of *Truth and Method* but adds to this interpretative model the situation found in juridical judgment as well. In the court of law, the task of the judge is, especially in those cases lacking sufficient precedent, illustrative of the problematic of judgment that is so central to the full elaboration of hermeneutic theory. What makes the problems of judgment so elemental to hermeneutic theory is that in them the finite nature of human understanding is most powerfully evident. The limits of rationality become active thereby producing the situation of judgment; consequently, in the problematic of judgment the finite character of all understanding is congealed. In the hermeneutic theory of judgment it is the failure of any possible methodology and the limits of conceptuality that become visible.

But Gadamer argues that the hermeneutic situation is not restricted to the special problems of aesthetic experience, jurisprudence and (as will be added later in the text) translation. Rather, his contention is that hermeneutic theory has a universal sway. That is why Gadamer suggests that such examples of the hermeneutics of experience are not isolated modes of experience, but represent the essence of experience itself. That is not to say that hermeneutics is a theory of absolute knowing such as one finds in Hegel. The Hegelian dialectic is simultaneously redeemed and hampered by hermeneutics (and in this Gadamer's views resemble Adorno's position in *Negative Dialectics*). Gadamer's debate with Jürgen Habermas, which was mostly carried on in the 1970s, seeks to refine this point of the universal claim of hermeneutics. Gadamer's point in that debate and elsewhere is that the finitude which undermines every possible claim to absolute knowing which is disclosed in hermeneutic theory is universal. To say that finitude itself is the universal disclosed hermeneutically is to say that no absolute is possible, and that no consensus in the conversation we are having can ever be final. Furthermore, according to Gadamer, "if one takes this finiteness seriously, then one must also take the reality of history seriously" (Gadamer 1975, p. xxiii). History becomes the memento of the finitude of human experience generally. The epigram to *Truth and Method*, a poem by Rilke, refers to this significance of history: "Catch only what you've thrown yourself, all / is mere skill and little gain; / but when you're suddenly the catcher of a ball / thrown by an eternal partner / with accurate and measured swing / towards you, to your centre, in an arch / from the great bridge building of God: / why catching then becomes a power – / not your, a world's."

When Gadamer formulates the topic of history more precisely and so demonstrates how it is that tradition poses a central problem for any theory of hermeneutics, it also becomes evident that the element of history, the medium wherein its effective life is transmitted, is language. The logic of the mediation in history, a logic which Hegel interpreted as the logic of negation, is, for Gadamer, to be thought as the logic of language itself. History and the question of traditions are not only preserved in texts that are handed down through time, but are themselves best interpreted according to the logic of textuality itself. Gadamer's recent debate with Jacques Derrida, and the efforts of both to draw the fine line that distinguishes hermeneutics and deconstruction as two of the inheritors of Heidegger's work, centers in part around their different understandings of the nature of textuality.[2] Gadamer clarifies his views on these matters most explicitly in "Text and Interpretation" (1981). There he reaffirms his lifelong commitment to the view that history and human affairs are best understood as a "conversation" in which the struggle is for understanding between the participants in that conversation.

Gadamer's discussions of the notions of tradition and of conversation , which come together in his notion of the "fusion of horizons," should not be mistaken as suggesting either that Gadamer is giving philosophical credence to the idea of a canonical tradition, nor that he is suggesting that the "fusion" of horizons is progressive. The sense of finitude active in Gadamer's thought is simply too active to permit such suggestions. The task of tradition, which is the concretion of human finitude, is to engage the openness of history and to illuminate the way in which traditions form and deform themselves as part and parcel of the same process of "fusion." Tradition, understood hermeneutically, becomes an infinite task, a task that Gadamer investigates when he addresses the notion of "*Bildung*."[3] This is one of the points at which Gadamer's deep affiliation with Greek thought comes into play in a decisive manner. Gadamer's discussions of the rigors of openness that define the logics of tradition and of "*Bildung*" draw their inspiration from the openness exhibited by the logic of question and answer in the Platonic dialogues, and from the responsiveness to context that is so crucial in Aristotle's ethical thought.

It is not arbitrary that the dialogue becomes a model for understanding history, nor is it the only privileged textual model for the hermeneutic unfolding of history. Having argued that language is the medium for the event of history, Gadamer further argues that the most pronounced form of the self-presence of language is to be found in the literary text, but most especially in the poetic text. The reason for this claim is simple: in literature generally, and poetry most of all, language itself comes to presence. No matter what it might have as its topic – love, death, plums, or a river – poetry is always language that is about language, language at the point of its greatest reflexivity. That is why poems inevitably exhibit such a strong hermetic quality, and why they are so difficult to understand. In them language folds back upon itself and arrives at the point of its greatest density. This condensed experience of language in the poem, the experience of language as language, is akin to the experience of finitude that is found in history. Gadamer makes this link between poetry and history one of the topics in his interpretation of the poet Paul Celan in *Wer bin Ich und Wer bist Du?* (*Who Am I and Who Are You?*) (1973). The choice of Celan as the poet to whom Gadamer turns in order to raise questions about the kinship of language and history, as well as the finitude specific to language and the horizon of communicability it opens, is quite deliberate and aims to engage questions of memory and the possibility of ethical life. While not "simply" a poet of the Holocaust, Celan is a poet for whom the catastrophe of German history is decisive. Gadamer's turn to Celan as a poet of uncommon significance for the elaboration of philosophical hermeneutics acknowledges that the question of history cannot be asked unless it is posed as an ethical and political question. He also tacitly answers Theodor Adorno's haunting question – whether poetry is possible after Auschwitz – by suggesting that perhaps poetry is most adept at the task of thinking after Auschwitz.

Like Heidegger, Gadamer finds the experience of language in the poem to be a preeminent form of the experience of finitude. Both argue that the capacity of language to simultaneously reveal and conceal, to transmit and to close off, is decisive for every experience and for the possibility of truth. Both also argue that the density of language in the poem sharpens the experience of finitude that language bears. Gadamer underscores this fundamentality of language when he declares that "Being which can be understood is language" (Gadamer 1975, p. 432) and when he devotes the final section of *Truth and Method* to the significance of language for hermeneutics suggesting that language is the medium of hermeneutic experience. Like Heidegger, Gadamer finds Friedrich Hölderlin to be a poet of precisely this experience of language in the poem. But Heidegger finds this experience sheltering a secret kinship binding language and death, a bond which leads Heidegger to speak of human being as the mortal life that belongs to a "fourfold" consisting also of the heavens, earth, and gods. Gadamer, on the other hand, finds that the force of finitude felt here is much less extreme, but no less elemental. So, it is not the limits of life, it is not death, that becomes the focus of his turn to poetic language, but the limits of language itself that win Gadamer's attentions. Translation then, most of all the final impossibility of translation becomes the supreme form of the hermeneutic experience of language.[4] Here Hölderlin's text on, and practice of, translation serve as a touchstone for Gadamer. Less evident, but equally influential for understanding Gadamer's views on translation, is the important piece "Die Aufgabe des Übersetzers" (1922) by BENJAMIN (see Article 29).

For Gadamer, the poem fulfills itself in the ideal of untranslatability, in the particularity that is almost carnal that language in the poem discloses. That aspect of poetic language, namely its particularity, its "thisness," makes such an experience of language especially well suited to exhibiting the attachment of hermeneutic theory to particularities that escape capture by the law of conceptuality. The so-called "quarrel" between philosophy and poetry which Plato already calls "ancient," and which he knew to be at bottom a political quarrel,[5] can be interpreted in this light: poetry, by naming that which is unnameable by the language of the concept, becomes a memento of the limits of philosophic speaking and thinking. This is the "threat" of poetic speech to the juridical claim to authority and universality asserted by the conceptual, eidetic, language of philosophy. Gadamer's hermeneutics is situated at this limit of philosophy and is dedicated to probing the possibilities harbored in the experience of such limits. The sense of the limits, or the "end," of philosophy that one discovers in Gadamer's work is thus distinctive even though there are undeniable resonances with the discussions of the end of philosophy found in Hegel, as well as those found in Heidegger and which were such an inspiration to Gadamer during his own student years.

What most distinguishes Gadamer's part in this discourse about the end of philosophy – a theme that might be fairly described as the touchstone problematic for contemporary philosophy – is that his sense of the end of philosophy is coupled with an uncompromised sense of the centrifugal force of history. The limits of speech and thought exist in tension with the logic of history that is perpetually surpassing the limits of the given. This means that Gadamer's conception of the end of philosophy lacks some of the "radicality" that one finds in Heidegger, Nietzsche, or Hegel, each of whom finds the end of philosophy to be signal of a radically new beginning. While not as mitigated in its radicality, as one finds for instance in a view such as Rorty's conception of an ongoing "conversation," Gadamer's sense of the finitude of experience that belongs to language is clearly separated from Heidegger's by virtue of Gadamer's willingness to grant that language not only brands experience as finite, but, simultaneously, opens its transcendent possibilities.

439

Gadamer is quite aware of his apparent separation from Heidegger, and even introduces *Truth and Method* by highlighting the importance of this question of the nature of human finitude for both of them: "I shall not deny, however, that within the universal context of these elements of understanding I have emphasized the element of assimilation of what is past and handed down. Heidegger also, like many of my critics, would probably feel the lack of an ultimate radicality in the drawing of conclusions. . . . But it seems to me that the onesidedness of hermeneutic universalism has the truth of a corrective" (Gadamer 1975, p. xxv). This question of how the experience of limits is to be understood philosophically is also the question that sits between Gadamer and Derrida. Again, Gadamer is aware of this difference when he writes that "Derrida finds my speaking about a lived context and the fundamental place of living dialogue especially problematical" ("Reply to Jacques Derrida," in Michelfelder and Palmer 1989, p. 56). Like Ricoeur, Gadamer argues that the "rupture" characterizing finite experience does not signal a radical, a fundamental, breach between all that belongs to experience. In other words, there is no final break, or divide, that separates people, peoples, and times such that solitude is the ultimate sense of finite experience; rather, the ruptures that are indeed the truth of finite life themselves belong to the process of "fusion" itself (with the caveat that fusion is never to be understood as signaling something like a Hegelian absolute, but as always itself contemporaneous with what one might call the equally hermeneutically significant process of "fission").

This is perhaps Gadamer's most distinctive contribution to contemporary philosophizing. Namely, the manner in which he has acknowledged, even advanced, the truth of the finitude of experience that Heidegger has exposed beginning with the analytic of *Dasein* in *Being and Time*, and the manner in which Gadamer has demonstrated that such a truth does not permanently disrupt the possibility of solidarity and of true communication. The experience of limits, thought hermeneutically, does not bring thinking to the point of an unliftable aporia; rather, it is precisely the experience of limits, the most radical experience of finite life, that instructs us about that which cannot be understood from within our own particularity. Gadamer puts the point thus: "Of course we encounter limits again and again; we speak past each other and are even at cross-purposes with ourselves. But in my opinion we could not do this at all if we had not travelled a long way together, perhaps without even acknowledging it to ourselves. All human solidarity, all social stability, presupposes this. . . . The experience of limits that we encounter in our life with others – is it not this alone that conditions our experience and is presupposed in all the common interests bearing us along" (Michelfelder and Palmer 1989, p. 57).

Recent years have seen Gadamer's work turn more to asking about the possibilities for the discourse among finite, historical beings. In particular, his concern is about the chances for a better form of solidarity in these times of great transformation, transformations mostly determined by the logic of technology. In a text such as *The Heritage of Europe* (1989) Gadamer, who was born at the turn of this century of enormous, sometimes monstrous, change, turns his attention to the question of having a future. The question, as he poses it from out of the framework of philosophical hermeneutics and its attentiveness to the finite life, is one which understands the question of the future as intimately bound to the enigma of having a history. It is the question of the future of a conversation that we do not control, a question very much attuned to the unpredictability of the dialogue which so fascinated Plato and which was, for Plato, decisive in his understanding of social life.

When Gadamer takes up the question of culture and the future in these recent works he does so not with the intentions of a prophet, but as someone alert to the still unreleased emancipatory potentials of the past and as engaged in the effort to advance the conversation that can be had on the basis of such potentials. When he does this, when he takes up such questions he does not turn to science and technology in order to ask about the possibility of a future ready for the possibilities of solidarity. For Gadamer, it is not the promise of the economies of reason defined by the horizons of scientific reason and method and technological claims to calculability that summon thinking today. Rather, it is to the promise of the work of art, to what cannot be said in the language of philosophy, that he looks. In the work of art, in that field of experience where there can be no expertise, no authority, and where there is the infinite openness of interpretation, he finds an avenue of promise. In the end, then, Gadamer's philosophical hermeneutics, while true to its roots in Heidegger's destruction of metaphysics and analytic of finite experience, also stands as the reminder that such experience is itself the signal of something larger than that which sits within the limits of the present. This sense of something greater than that which can be thought or said in the present, this sense of history, this sensitivity to the kindred sense communicated in the experience of the work of art, is one of the original elements of Gadamer's contribution to contemporary philosophizing. Enlisted in the project of philosophizing that Heidegger inaugurates, profoundly engaged in the questions of tradition, informed by his deep understanding of Greek thought, Gadamer's philosophical hermeneutics struggles to open and widen the possibilities of thinking today beyond those determined by philosophic conceptualization. It is a struggle to carry on the conversation of philosophy and, at the same time, to move it beyond itself into a future.

## Notes

1  e.e. cummings, *Complete Poems: 1913–1962* (New York: Harcourt Brace Jovanovich, 1968), p. 462.

2  See Gadamer's recent essay "Hermeneutik auf der Spur," in Gadamer, *Gesammelte Werke*, vol. 10 (1994).

3  The usual translation of "*Bildung*" is "culture," but for Gadamer it also refers to the process of education and cultivation. His sense of the notion is much closer to the Greek sense of *paeidia* that is Plato's concern in the *Republic* than it is to the enlightenment concern with cultivation. See *Truth and Method*, Part 1, section 1, for a more precise definition of this important term.

4  On these points see Heidegger's *On the Way to Language*. See also his *Hölderlins Hymne "Der Ister"* where Heidegger writes "Tell me what you think of translation, and I will tell you who you are."

5  See Gadamer's "Plato und die Dichter" (1934) where Gadamer discusses the significance of the political context of Plato's critique of mimetic praxis. That text, composed

during the period of the Nazi rise to power in Germany, can be read as formulating a covert critique of that political situation.

## Writings

Gadamer, Hans-Georg: *Truth and Method* (New York: Seabury Press, 1975).

——: *Philosophical Hermeneutics*, ed. David E. Linge (Berkeley: University of California Press, 1976).

——: *Reason in the Age of Science* (Cambridge, MA: MIT Press, 1981).

——: *Philosophical Apprenticeships* (Cambridge, MA: MIT Press, 1985).

——: *The Relevance of the Beautiful and Other Essays*, ed. Robert Bernasconi (Cambridge: Cambridge University Press, 1986).

——: *Literature and Philosophy in Dialogue* (Albany, NY: State University of New York Press, 1994).

## References and further reading

Michelfelder, Diane, and Richard E. Palmer (eds): *Dialogue and Deconstruction: The Gadamer–Derrida Encounter* (Albany, NY: SUNY Press, 1989).

Warnke, Georgia: *Gadamer: Hermenetics, Tradition, and Reason* (Stanford, CA: Stanford University Press, 1987).

# 39

# Ricoeur

### RICHARD KEARNEY

Paul Ricoeur is one of the most significant hermeneutic thinkers of the twentieth century. Born in Valence, France, in 1931, he taught as professor of philosophy at the universities of Strasbourg, Paris, and Chicago, and also served as director for the Center of Phenomenology and Hermeneutics in Paris. Together with HEIDEGGER (Article 18) and GADAMER (Article 38), Ricoeur developed a philosophy based on the view that existence is itself a mode of interpretation (*hermeneia*). Or, as the hermeneutic maxim goes: Life interprets itself. But where Heidegger concentrated directly on a fundamental ontology of interpretation, Ricoeur advances what he calls the "long route" of multiple hermeneutic detours. This brought him into dialogue with the human sciences, where philosophy discovers its limits in what is outside of philosophy, in those border exchanges where meaning traverses the various signs and disciplines in which being is interpreted by human understanding. He challenged Heidegger's view that being is accessible through the "short route" of existence understanding itself through its ownmost possibilities, maintaining instead that it is always mediated through an endless process of interpretations – cultural, religious, political, historical, and scientific. Hence Ricoeur's basic definition of hermeneutics as the "art of deciphering *indirect* meaning." A definition he explains as follows:

> Philosophy remains hermeneutics, that is, a reading of the hidden meaning inside the text of the apparent meaning. It is the task of hermeneutics to show that existence arrives at expression, at meaning, and at reflection only through the continual exegesis of all the significations that come to light in the world of culture. Existence becomes a self only by appropriating this meaning which first resides "outside," in works, institutions and cultural monuments in which the life of the spirit is objectified.   (Ricoeur 1969)

One of the main targets of Ricoeur's hermeneutics is the idealist view that the self is transparent to itself. In his early works – *The Voluntary and the Involuntary* (1950) and *The Symbolism of Evil* (1960) – Ricoeur explodes the pretensions of the cogito to be self-founding and self-knowing. He insists that the shortest route from self to self is through the other. Or to put it in Ricoeur's felicitous formula: "to say self is not to say I." For hermeneutics the self is much more than an autonomous subject or transcendental ego: it is always "self-as-another," a *soi* that passes beyond the illusory confines of the *moi* and discovers its meaning in and through the linguistic mediations of signs and symbols, stories and ideologies, metaphors and myths. The self returns to itself after numerous hermeneutic detours through the language of others, to find itself enlarged and enriched by the journey. The Cartesian model of the cogito as "master and possessor" of meaning is radically subverted. "Interpretation is interpretation *by* language before it is interpretation *of* language" (Ricoeur 1969).

We thus find Ricoeur endeavoring to steer a course beyond the rationalism of Descartes and KANT (Article 2), on the one hand, and the transcendental idealism of HUSSERL (Article 15), on the other. (Ricoeur actually began a translation of Husserl's *Ideas* during his captivity in a German prisoner-of-war camp in the early 1940s which was published in 1950.) Advocating a move beyond the early phenomenology of Husserl in the direction of hermeneutics, Ricoeur writes: "It remains that the early Husserl reconstituted a new idealism, close to the neo-Kantianism he fought: the reduction of the thesis of the world is actually a reduction of the question of being to the question of the sense of being; the sense of being, in turn, is reduced to a simple correlate of the subjective modes of intention" (Ricoeur 1969).

Where Husserl located meaning in the subject's intuition of the "things themselves," Ricoeur follows the hermeneutic dictum that intuition is always a matter of interpretation. This implies that things are always given to us *indirectly* through a detour of signs, but it does not entail an espousal of existentialist irrationalism. The interpretation (*hermeneia*) of indirect meaning invites us to think more, not to abandon speculative thought altogether. And nowhere is this more evident than in the challenge posed by symbolic meaning. By symbols Ricoeur understands all expressions of double meaning, wherein a primary meaning refers beyond itself to a second meaning which is never given directly. This second or surplus meaning provokes interpretation.

> The symbol invites: I do not posit the meaning, the symbol gives it; but what it gives is something for thought, something to think about. First the giving, then the positing; the phrase suggests, therefore, both that all has already been said in enigma and yet that it is necessary ever to begin and re-begin everything in the dimension of thought. It is this articulation of thought . . . in the realm of symbols that I would like to intercept and understand.   (Ricoeur 1978)

Ricoeur's first application of his hermeneutic agenda is to be found in *The Symbolism of Evil* (1960). Here the human experience of guilt, finitude, and fallibility – as limits to our consciousness – finds expression in the encounter with the enigma of evil. And so we witness a vast hermeneutic detour via the avowals of fault inscribed in the symbols of the major Western traditions – Greek, Hebraic, and Babylonian. By interpreting the primary symbols of stain, guilt, and sin, the secondary symbols of wandering, decline, fall, and blindness, and the tertiary symbols of the servile will, Ricoeur develops a hermeneutics of double meaning.

But Ricoeur's hermeneutics is by no means confined to hermeneutics of symbol and myth. In a debate with Freudian psychoanalysis in the 1960s – *Freud and Philosophy: An Essay on Interpretation* (1965) – he was to discover a "semantics of desire" where unconscious drives challenged the primacy of reflective conscious-

444

ness, exposing hermeneutics to a *conflict* of interpretations. This conflict centered on three fundamental, often competing, approaches: (1) an *archaeological* hermeneutic disclosing an unconscious origin of meaning prior to the conscious ego (Freud); (2) a *teleological* hermeneutic pointing forward to a goal of meaning beyond the conscious ego (Hegel); and (3) an *eschatological* hermeneutic testifying to a transcendent or sacred dimension of meaning before the beginning and after the end (Eliade). In each case, the putative sovereignty of consciousness found itself in question, exposed to dimensions of meaning outside of itself.

An additional challenge was posed by Ricoeur's encounter with structuralism and the sciences of language (Greimas and Benveniste). Here again the primacy of subjective will is challenged by the discovery of hidden structures of language which operate *involuntarily*, behind our backs. The hermeneutic field was thus enlarged by the encounter with structuralist linguistics, enabling Ricoeur to amplify his model of hermeneutic phenomenology by incorporating language as an unconscious system of structures deeper than the intentional subject. It prompted an extension of his project.

> It appeared that the linguistic dimension of all symbolism had not been made the object of a distinct and systematic treatment in my earlier works, in spite of the fact that the detour via symbols had, since *The Symbolism of Evil*, taken the form of a detour of reflection on the self via an investigation of the mediating *signs* of this reflection. It is upon this terrain of the investigation of language that I encountered a new challenge, that of French structuralism, which eliminated any reference to a speaking subject from its analysis of signifying systems. I thus discovered a convergence between the structuralist critique originating from linguistics and the psychoanalytic critique originating from Freud, a convergence in what I called collectively the *semiological challenge*. (Ricoeur 1981)

This semiological challenge motivated a turn in Ricoeur's hermeneutics towards the model of the text. Where the earlier hermeneutics of symbols was limited to expressions of double intention, the later hermeneutics of texts extended interpretation to all phenomena of a textual order, including narratives (*Time and Narrative*, 1983–5) and ideologies (*Lectures on Ideology and Utopia*, 1986). This opened a new hermeneutic dialogue with the human and social sciences, encapsulated in Ricoeur's maxim: "to explain more is to understand better"(*Expliquer plus c'est comprendre mieux*). Here the traditional bias of hermeneutic philosophy against "explanation" (*erklären*) and in favor of "understanding" (*verstehen*) – running from Schleiermacher and Dilthey through Heidegger and Gadamer – was redressed. Moving from "speech" (the immediate dialogue of speaker and listener) to "text" (mediated discourse), Ricoeur acknowledges the alterity and distantiation of meaning as essential dimensions of the hermeneutic dialectic. (These dimensions were largely distrusted by Romantic-existential hermeneutics as symptoms of scientific objectivism.) So doing, Ricoeur endorses a positive hermeneutic conversation with the sciences – a conversation which has existed in almost all great philosophies: Plato with geometry, Descartes with algebra, Kant with physics, Bergson with biology, etc. In the interpretation of texts, scientific "explanation" and phenomenological "understanding" converse and converge. Philosophy thus opens itself once again to a productive dialogue with its other.

But if the semiological challenge restores hermeneutics to the model of the text, it does not in any sense enclose it in some prison house of language. On the contrary, the hermeneutic dialectic advanced by Ricoeur is one which passes through the detour of the text in the name of something beyond it – which he calls the "matter of the text." Here we encounter the ontological horizon of world-meaning opened up by the text. "It was then necessary to expand the hermeneutic project . . . to the dimensions of the problem posed by the passage from the structure immanent in every text to its extra-linguistic aim (*visée*) – the aim or reference which I sometimes designate by other related terms: the matter of the text, the world of the text, the being brought to language by the text" (Ricoeur 1981).

This ultimate aim or reference – to a world not merely represented by the text but disclosed by the text – brings us beyond epistemology to ontology. Thus, the ultimate horizon of Ricoeur's work remains, from beginning to end, the horizon of being which signals to us obliquely and incompletely, a promised land but never an occupied one, a truncated ontology – provisional, tentative, exploratory. This limitation on the pretensions of speculative reason represents, for Ricoeur, a renunciation of Hegel and all other versions of systematic closure. The interpretation of being is always something begun, never finally completed.

The implications of Ricoeur's privileging of the text as a model of interpretation are radical. Meaning is no longer construed as an essence to be intuited (Husserl) nor a transcendental condition of possibility to be reflected upon (Kant). The text breaks the circuit of internal reflection and exposes us to intersubjective horizons of language and history. Meaning involves *someone saying something to someone about something*. This requires us to pay attention to the particular contexts and presuppositions of each speaker and each reader. "It is with this selective function of context that interpretation, in the most primitive sense of the word, is connected. Interpretation is the process by which, in the interplay of question and answer, the interlocutors collectively determine the contextual values which structure their conversation" (Ricoeur 1969). Interpretation thus explodes the confines of the timeless reflective subject and discloses us as language-using beings in a world with others.

The hermeneutic model of the text reveals complexities of meaning beyond the *face-à-face* of spoken dialogue. It goes beyond the direct reference of two interlocutors co-present to one another in an immediately identifiable situation "here and now." It involves a "long" intersubjective detour through the sedimented horizons of history and tradition. "The 'short' intersubjective relation (of two speakers in conversation) is intertwined, in the interior of the historical connection, with various 'long' intersubjective relations, mediated by diverse institutions, social roles and collectivities (groups, nations, cultural traditions etc). The long intersubjective relations are sustained by an historical tradition, of which dialogue is only a segment" (Ricoeur 1969). Hermeneutic explication coincides with the broadest historical and cultural connections.

The mediating function of the text becomes exemplary in this context. The extension of meaning beyond the original reference of spoken utterance is analogous to the written text where meaning survives the absence of the original author and addressee. The meaning of the text enjoys a certain autonomy with respect to the author's original intention, the auditor's original reception and the *vis-à-vis* reference of the initial situation of speech. Hermeneutic interpretation produces a "second order reference" *in front of the text*, soliciting a series of multiple, and often conflicting, readings.

Interpretation discloses a hermeneutic circle of historical intersubjectivity, precluding the idealist claim to occupy an "idealist Standpoint." To interpret meaning is, for Ricoeur, to arrive in the middle of an exchange which has already begun and in which we seek to orient ourselves in order to make some new sense of it. His hermeneutic wager is that our self-comprehension will be enhanced rather than diminished by our traversal of the circle. The more we explain outer meanings, the more we understand our inner meaning. Ricoeur accordingly renounces both the Husserlian pretension to a transcendental foundation and the Hegelian claim to absolute knowledge. "The key hypothesis of hermeneutic philosophy is that interpretation is an open process which no single vision can conclude" (Ricoeur 1969). It entails a belonging to meaning in and through distance. Hermeneutics may thus be understood as the endeavor to render near what is far – temporally, geographically, scientifically, culturally – by reappropriating those meanings that have been "distantiated" from our consciousness. Once again, the textual paradigm proves exemplary. By exposing myself to the textual horizons of "other" or "alien" meanings, I transcend the familiar limits of subjective consciousness, opening myself to possible new worlds of meaning. If subjectivity continues to exist for hermeneutics it is as that "self-as-another" which, Ricoeur argues, is only attained after the intersubjective detour of interpretation. Hermeneutic subjectivity is not that which initiates understanding but that which terminates it. But this terminal act does not presume to rejoin the so-called "original" subject (*moi*) which intends meaning. On the contrary, it *responds* to the proposal of meaning which the matter of the text unfolds.

This retrieval of selfhood, at the far end of the hermeneutic circle, is the counterpart of the distantiation which establishes the second-order reference of the text beyond the first-order reference (of original author, situation, and addressee). Ricoeur's notion of appropriation, far from signaling a triumphalist return of the sovereign ego, offers a way of understanding oneself *in front of the text*. It is a question of exchanging the *moi*, master of itself, for the *soi*, disciple of the text. For this reason, Ricoeur's hermeneutics may be said to serve as a critique of both *egology* (the view that the self is origin of itself) and *ideology* (the view that understanding is a matter of false-consciousness).

Ricoeur reveals, furthermore, how the working of the text is itself a process of *semantic innovation*. In the case of the symbol, this involves a crossing of intentionalities at the level of the *word*. In the case of metaphor, it involves a production of new meaning at the level of the *sentence*. Whereas in the case of narrative, it takes the form of an emplotment (*mise-en-intrigue*) which synthesizes heterogeneous temporal elements at the level of *language* as a whole. This last is what Ricoeur names

447

"configuration." And like symbol and metaphor before it, he relates it to the sche-matizing function of the productive imagination. "Emplotment engenders a mixed intelligibility between what has been called the point, theme or thought of a story (its intellectual component) and the intuitive presentation of circumstances, char-acters, episodes, and changes of fortune that make up the denouement. In this way we may speak of a schematism of the narrative function" (Ricoeur 1983).

This schematizing role of narrative operates a dialectic between the hermeneutic demands of *tradition* and *innovation*. Each supplements the other. Tradition needs innovation in order to sustain itself as a living transmission of meaning capable of being reactivated in its inaugural moments. While innovation needs tradition in order to make sense as a form of expression governed by rules. Even in its deviant or transgressive guises, it is a matter of "rule-governed deformation." The *nouveau roman* and *anti-roman* presuppose the *roman*. Once again, Ricoeur reminds us that we are part of a hermeneutic circle of distantiation and belonging, of novelty and familiarity, of far and near. "The possibility of deviation is inscribed in the relation between sedimented paradigms and actual works," writes Ricoeur. "Short of the extreme case of schism, it is just the opposite of servile application. Rule governed deformation constituted the axis around which the various changes of paradigm through application are arranged. It is this variety of applications that confers a history on the productive imagination and that, in counterpoint to sedimentation, makes a narrative tradition possible" (Ricoeur 1983).

This dialectic of innovation and tradition involves not just writing but reading. We pass accordingly from what Ricoeur calls "configuration" to "refiguration." From the text to the reader who acts in a world. Hence the title of Ricoeur's volume *Du texte à l'action* (1986). Written narrative requires the reader for its completion. Or to put it in Ricoeur's terms, emplotment is a joint work of text and reader. It is the reader who accompanies the interplay of the innovation and sedimentation of paradigms, schematizes emplotment, plays with narrative constraints and gaps, refigures what the author configures and defigures. This recreative labor signals, in the last analysis, a "refiguring of the world of action under the sign of the plot."

Plots are not, of course, confined to texts signed by individual authors. They are also to be found at the level of what Ricoeur calls the *social imaginary* – that body of collective stories, histories, and ideologies which inform our modes of social and political action. "Social imagination," as Ricoeur puts it, "is constitutive of social reality itself" (Ricoeur 1986). He examines this phenomenon under the dialectical headings of ideology and utopia. While ideology tends to promote collective images which "integrate" a community around a shared identity, utopian images work in the opposite direction of novelty, rupture and discontinuity. The social imagination serves both an ideological role of identification and a utopian role of disruption. The former preserves and conserves; the latter projects alternatives. Thus one of the central functions of hermeneutics identified by Ricoeur is the critical interrogation of the socio-political *imaginaire* which governs any given society and motivates its citizens. In relation to society, no less than in relation to the text, Ricoeur promotes a dialectical balance between belonging and distance. Ideology as a symbolic con-firmation of the past and utopia as a symbolic opening towards the future are complementary. Cut off from one another, they run the risk of pathological extremes: ideology imprisoning us in reactionary conservatism, utopia sacrificing us to a schizophrenic image of an abstract future without the conditions for its realization.

In this regard, Ricoeur manages to combine a Gadamerian respect for tradition with a Habermasian critique of ideology. The risk for Gadamer is innocent obedience to the authority of inherited prejudice; the risk for Habermas is obliviousness to the truth that critique is also a tradition – one which, as Ricoeur points out, reaches back to the Greek narratives of Socratic questioning and the biblical narratives of exodus and resurrection (Ricoeur 1981). The danger is severing our utopian horizon of expectation from the ideological horizon of past and present. One of the most urgent hermeneutic tasks today, says Ricoeur, is to reconcile these two faces of the social imaginary, reanimating tradition and realizing utopia.

This dialectic of critique and innovation is, of course, an exemplification of Ricoeur's canonical play between a hermeneutics of *suspicion* and *affirmation*. Suspicion takes the form of a critique of false consciousness by the three "masters of suspicion" – Freud, Marx, and Nietzsche. By contrast, the hermeneutics of affirmation emphasizes our *desire to be* open to an irreducible "surplus of meaning" (*surcroît de sens*). The former, Ricoeur argues, is a necessary critical prelude to the latter. We can only recover and reaffirm our ontological *desire to be* in a "second naïveté" by first interrogating ourselves as we exist *outside of ourselves*. Hence the crucial importance of Freud's disclosure of unconscious desire, Nietzsche's genealogy of will-to-power, and Marx's critique of false consciousness. All three recognized that meaning, far from being transparent to itself, is an enigmatic process which conceals at the same time as it reveals. Hence the need for a hermeneutics of suspicion which demystifies our illusions, permitting us to decipher the masked workings of desire, will, and interest. Hermeneutic doubt reminds us once again that consciousness (individual or social) is a relation of concealing and revealing which calls for a specific interpretation. "The task of hermeneutics," as Ricoeur puts it, "has always been to read a text and to distinguish the true sense from the apparent sense, to search for the sense under the sense . . . uncovering what was covered, unveiling what was veiled, removing the mask" (Ricoeur 1978).

That is not the only task of hermeneutics, however. Once divested of illusions, we often find ourselves faced with a remainder of ontological meaning which exists beyond the self and invites the affirmation of our desire-to-be. But the "promised land" of ontological affirmation is at best a hope which the interpreter, like Moses, "can only glimpse before dying" (Ricoeur 1969). That is why hermeneutic truth takes the form of a wager, never a possession. Because we are finite beings, our understanding always remains within the historical limits of the hermeneutic circle. The myth of absolute reason is resisted in favor of a plurality of detours and debates. "It is because absolute knowledge is impossible," states Ricoeur, "that the conflict of interpretations is insurmountable" (Ricoeur 1981). This explains Ricoeur's characteristic willingness to open his hermeneutic phenomenology to a critical debate with such ostensible rivals as structuralism, psychoanalysis, analytic philosophy, political theory, sociology, theology, and the sciences of language.

Here as elsewhere his hermeneutic maxim prevails – the shortest route from self to self is through the other.

The ontological surplus of meaning is, for Ricoeur, ultimately an invitation to create. This theme of creation runs from Ricoeur's first hermeneutic studies on symbolism to the later studies of "narrative identity" in *Time and Narrative* and *Oneself as Another* (1990). "My single problem since beginning my reflections has been creativity," concedes Ricoeur in a 1981 interview with the French journal *Esprit*, founded by his friend, Emmanuel Mounier. "I considered it from the point of view of individual psychology in my first works on the will, and then at the cultural level with the study on symbolisms. My research on narrative places me precisely at the heart of this social and cultural creativity, since telling a story . . . is the most permanent act of societies. In telling their own stories, cultures create themselves" (Ricoeur 1981). But poetics for Ricoeur cannot be removed from ethics. It is always a question of moving back and forth between text and action. That is why it is no accident that Ricoeur's hermeneutic studies of narrative identity in *Oneself as Another* lead directly to what he calls his "little ethics" – a discussion of how cultures seek to realize the Aristotelian goal of a "good life with and for others in just institutions." This is a task which the Greeks identified with the conjunction of practical wisdom (*phronesis*) and creative action (*poiesis*). Ricoeur's hermeneutics represents, I believe, one of the most significant contemporary realizations of this most ancient of philosophical tasks.

## Writings

Ricoeur, P.: *History and Truth* (1955), tr. C. Kelbley (Evanston, IL: Northwestern University Press, 1965).

——: *The Symbolism of Evil* (1960), tr. E. Buchanan (New York: Harper & Row, 1967).

——: *Fallible Man* (1960), tr. C. Kelbley (Chicago, IL: Henry Regnery, 1965).

——: *Freud and Philosophy: An Essay on Interpretation* (1965), tr. D. Savage (New Haven, CT: Yale University Press, 1970).

——: *The Conflict of Interpretations: Essays in Hermeneutics* (1969), tr. W. Domingo et al., ed. D. Ihde (Evanston, IL: Northwestern University Press, 1974).

——: *The Philosophy of Paul Ricoeur: An Anthology of his Work* (Boston, MA: Beacon Press, 1978).

——: *Hermeneneutics and the Human Sciences*, ed. and tr. J. B. Thompson (Cambridge: Cambridge University Press, 1981).

——: *The Rule of Metaphor* (1975), tr. R. Czeny, K. McLaughlin and J. Costello (Toronto: University of Toronto Press, 1977).

——: *Time and Narrative* (1983–5), tr. K. McLaughlin and D. Pellaner, 3 vols (Chicago: University of Chicago Press, 1984–6).

## References and further reading

Clark, S.: *Paul Ricoeur* (London: Routledge, 1990).

Ihde, D.: *Hermeneutic Phenomenology: The Philosophy of Paul Ricoeur* (Evanston, IL: Northwestern University Press, 1971).

Kemp, P., and Rasmussen, D. (eds): *The Narrative Path: The Later Works of Paul Ricoeur* (Cambridge, MA: MIT Press, 1989).

Reagan, C. (ed.): *Studies in the Philosophy of Paul Ricoeur* (Athens, OH: Ohio University Press, 1979).

Thompson, J. B.: *Critical Hermeneutics: A Study in the Thought of Paul Ricoeur and Jürgen Habermas* (Cambridge: Cambridge University Press, 1981).

Van Den Hengel, J. W.: *The Home of Meaning: The Hermeneutics of the Subject of Paul Ricoeur* (Washington, DC: University Press of America, 1982).

Vam Leeuwen, T. M.: *The Surplus of Meaning: Ontology and Eschatology in the Philosophy of Paul Ricoeur* (Amsterdam: Rodopi, 1981).

# PART VIII

# CONTINENTAL POLITICAL PHILOSOPHY

# 40

# Lukács

GYORGY  MARKUS

One of the leading representatives of a "Western" Marxism, György (Georg) Lukács was born in 1885 in Budapest. He joined the Communist Party of Hungary in 1918. During the short-lived Hungarian Commune of 1919 he was responsible for the cultural policy of the revolutionary regime. After its collapse he lived in emigration in Vienna, Berlin, and Moscow. Following the condemnation of his political views by the Comintern in 1928 he withdrew from direct participation in politics. He returned to Hungary in 1945. A new wave of official attacks in 1949 resulted in his renewed retreat from political activity. During the Hungarian revolution of 1956 he was minister of culture in the government of Imre Nagy. First interned in Romania, he worked then in the situation of an internal emigration and banishment in Hungary till 1967, when he was allowed to return to public cultural life. He died in 1971.

Before his Marxist turn of 1918 Lukács' theoretical activity was directed at the problems of literature and aesthetics. Questions concerning the contemporary situation and general significance of art were, however, posed by him within the broader context of cultural crisis: the impossibility, at least under conditions of modernity, of forming a common/communal understanding of the world without which there can be no genuine communication between the individuals, and the related impossibility of endowing their life with a unique and unified sense. In some writings of this period – especially *Soul and Form* (1910) and the unfinished, only posthumously published *Heidelberg Philosophy of Art* (1912–14) – this situation was characterized in existential terms as the constitutive inauthenticity of everyday life, with its uneliminable accidentality, ambiguity, and conventionality. It is only the work of art which – due to the power of aesthetic form – can confer a stable meaning upon the material of life, but it simultaneously transforms this material into a self-enclosed, ideal meaning-complex, a harmonious totality elevated over and insulated from life. Aesthetic experience, therefore, can offer only a momentary escape and satisfaction, it leaves the chaos of ordinary life unredeemed.

Simultaneously, however, in other works of the same period (*History of Development of the Modern Drama*, 1911, and *The Theory of Novel*, 1916) the crisis of culture was analyzed by Lukács as a particular historical phenomenon connected with the spread of a functional division of labor and its associated commodity economy that transformed the humanly created social world into a "second nature" of blind facticity. In these contexts some works of art – especially the novels of Dostoevsky

455

– appeared as expressions of the human impulse and utopian hope to overcome this state of "ultimate fallenness."

The Marxist turn of Lukács meant to conceive this goal of radical transcendence as a historical-collective task. His first writings of Marxist inspiration (*Tactics and Ethics*, 1919) were addressed to the central problem of the revolutionary period: the legitimacy of violence. They still to a large extent retained that dualist framework which characterized his pre-Marxist works. The historical necessity of violence, as the only way to break the power of the existing exploitative order, was sharply counterposed to the universally valid moral imperative never to treat another person as a mere means, for whatever ends. Only if all those who exercise violence do so in the full consciousness of its ethical impermissibility, taking it upon themselves as a historically inevitable "sin," is violence legitimate, and only then can it lead to the creation of a society in which the morally right way of life becomes the effective norm of everyday conduct.

The effort to overcome this dualism, with its utopian – from the viewpoint of a mass movement – consequences, dominated Lukács' theoretical activity in the early 1920s. Its result is the volume of essays *History and Class-Consciousness* (1923), the founding text of "Western" Marxism, offering a radically new way of understanding the philosophical sense and significance of Marx's thought.

Marxism is for Lukács primarily the theory of the historical creation and determination of forms of objectivity and the corresponding forms of subjective consciousness. It understands history not simply as a sequence of social structures, but as a change in the underlying practical and theoretical relations between the subject and the object. In this sense Marx gave an answer to the problem central to German Classical Idealism: how is an independent and intersubjective world of objects created in, and by, the activity of the subjects? This question, conceived by Kant as an epistemological one, was transformed already by Hegel into a practical-historical problem. But since he could not comprehend the making of history otherwise than as a process of unconscious rationality, his solution – the conception of Absolute Spirit – remained still a piece of philosophical mythology. Only Marx, by discovering the social agent who can consciously form history and thereby itself, the proletariat as the subject-object of history, could find the key to the riddle of German Idealism in the materialist theory of human practice as the process of the self-formation of subjectivity through the productive creation of a world of social objectivity.

The main topic of *History and Class-Consciousness* was, however, the characterization of contemporary capitalism understood as a specific form of social objectivity and its correlated forms of subjectivity: the theory of *reification*. It represented a philosophical generalization of the Marxian conception of commodity fetishism which connected it up with Weber's critique of goal-rationality.

Reification is both an objective and subjective phenomenon. From the side of objectivity it means the transformation of the humanly created world into a "second nature" governed by its own laws, the laws of the market, independent of the will and consciousness of the human agents. This simultaneously involves the elimination of the qualitative and individual characteristics of all the products of human activity, making them interchangeable commodities, together with the liquidation of the individual character of the process of their making: labor becoming an abstract activity. Subjectively, this implies the fragmentation and depersonalization of the individual as the ultimate source of conscious rationality. The exercise of reason becomes equated with the successful performance of purely formal operations, allowing the calculative prediction of the behavior of its object through the decomposition of this latter into abstract and manipulable elements. In its entirety the reified subject–object relation manifests itself in the ever-growing formal rationalization of every separated, specialized sphere and institutional unit of social life and the complete accidentality of their global interaction. Under such conditions, both what is irreducibly individual and the totality appear as untranscendable limits of reason, as bearers of an incomprehensible irrationality.

Reification pervades all walks of social life and penetrates the consciousness of all individuals. The immediate, "empirical" consciousness of a wage-worker is no less reified than that of the capitalist. True, the long-term interests of the proletariat do not bind it to this system, its cognitive possibilities ("imputed consciousness") in principle allow it to comprehend the social totality as something produced by its own activity and therefore transcendable. But in what way can the workers, in their collectivity, raise themselves from the standpoint of reified immediacy to the practical acquisition of "imputed consciousness"?

Lukács answers this question with the postulation of a long process of mediation as a practical learning process in which the proletariat, on the basis of the experiences of its struggle initially governed by its system-immanent, empirical interests, step by step penetrates through the veil of reification. The immanent possibility of such a mediation is warranted by the way the individual worker is constituted as subject. Under conditions of modernity all individuals are socially posited as free subjects of autonomous choices – this is what distinguishes capitalism from systems of slavery and serfdom. For the individual bourgeois there still remain areas of activity (the roles of the "rational" entrepreneur and the "free" consumer) with which it can identify itself as subject. For the worker, however, no sphere of activity is open which could appear as that of the exercise of autonomous subjectivity: the pseudo-activity of calculative rationalization is performed not by, but upon him or her. The self-consciousness of the worker is therefore characterized by an internal contradiction between his/her actual life experience as a mere object controlled by external forces and the consciousness of an empty and purely potential subjectivity. It is this contradiction which – reproduced at ever higher levels in a collective practice – drives proletarian self-consciousness on the path of mediation.

In *History and Class-Consciousness* Lukács makes a strenuous effort to indicate at least the principal stages of such a potential social learning-process, but his argument remains not only fragmentary, it clearly fails. Thus, especially in the concluding essays of the volume, he replaces the originally declared solution with another one: he transforms the "imputed self-consciousness" of the proletariat from a cognitive possibility into an empirical reality which, as it were, from outside directs the class on its way toward the "standpoint of totality." This objective embodiment of the imputed consciousness is the Party of a Bolshevik type basing its activity on the knowledge of the objective tendencies of historical development. With this his general conception of history also acquires openly Hegelian, teleological features that function as historio-philosophical guarantees of the transcendability of capitalist society.

Though *History and Class-Consciousness* in its ultimate conclusions philosophically legitimated the Leninist theory of the party, its interpretation of Marxism as the philosophy of radical praxis so deeply challenged its scientistic understanding, prevalent not only in Social Democracy, but also in the evolving Soviet Marxism as well, that the book evoked an immediate official condemnation. When, a few years later, this was followed by an equally sharp rejection of Lukács' political views, he retreated from the minefield of philosophy. During the following three decades he was primarily active as a literary critic and theorist of literature. The main accomplishments of this period – his theory of literary realism and its negative supplement, the critique of aesthetic modernism as a phenomenon of "decadence" – reflected a partly conscious, partly unconscious adaptation to the pervasive spirit of Stalinism. At the same time they reaffirmed the values of Enlightenment humanism and represented a defense of the autonomy of art against the predominant tendencies of its crude politicization.

During this time Lukács dealt with explicitly philosophical problematics only in historical contexts. *The Young Hegel* (written in the late 1930s, but first published after the war) in some respects continued the theoretical line of *History and Class-Consciousness*, by emphasizing the centrality of alienation for Marx as the vital link connecting his dialectic with Hegel's. At the same time its sympathetic reconstruction of Hegel's own evolution from his youthful radicalism to his mature, resigned acceptance of historical reality may perhaps be regarded as Lukács' own apologia. In *The Destruction of Reason* (1954) he attempted to uncover the spiritual roots of Nazism in the specific characteristics of German cultural development. While the book aimed at the resurrection of the "other" German tradition, that of Enlightenment rationalism and plebeian democracy, its blanket identification of "irrationalism" with proto-Fascism, and the indiscriminately wide and vague character of the former charge made some of its critical analyses (e.g. of Nietzsche, Max Weber, etc.) strikingly one-sided. Among all the writings of Lukács, this work is the most thoroughly influenced by doctrinal Stalinism.

It was only after 1956 that Lukács returned to philosophy proper. *The Specificity of the Aesthetical* (1963) presented the generalization and philosophical justification of the basic principles of his literary criticism in the form of an elaborate aesthetic theory. Departing from the concept of aesthetic mimesis, he systematically outlined the categorial structure pertaining to the authentic work of art. At the same time the book reconstructed the process of genesis of the aesthetic appropriation and representation of reality out of everday life and thinking, the ultimate ground of all higher objectifying activities, as a process of differentiation in which the various, relatively autonomous forms and spheres of cultural productivity gradually emerge. In this way Lukács outlined a general theory of "ideal," cultural objectivations, explicating the particular place and function of art in its relation to science, religion, law, and morality. Aesthetic mimesis as the artistic modeling of reality is characterized by its anthropomorphizing character, always relating its object to the human subject as a species-being. Through this, art fulfills a defetishizing, potentially emancipatory function, and makes possible the cathartic transformation of recipient subjectivity towards human universality.

Lukács died before he could undertake the revisions he considered necessary on the manuscript of his last work, *The Ontology of Social Being* (published posthumously in 1976). In it he aspired to raise again and to answer anew the problems central to *History and Class-Consciousness*: the questions about reification/alienation and the possibilities of overcoming it. The overall aim of the work consisted in the systematic explication of the categories characterizing the socio-historical form of human existence as an irreducible ontological sphere, a *sui generis* way of being. The fundamental category of this analysis was that of labor as teleological activity and the most elemental, determining form of social action. By laboring the human individual realizes – within pre-given, causally determined conditions and depending on the scope of his/her knowledge of causal connections – consciously intended ends which effectuate further chains of (partly foreseen, partly unforeseen) causal consequences. This unity of causal determination and conscious finality, which pertains already to labor, confers upon social existence its basic characteristic: historicity. The intrinsically historical character of the human way of being means that individuals and their collectivities always act in a field of – more narrowly or broadly circumscribed, but always real – possibilities, within a range of personal and social alternatives. They are not only determined objects of anonymous social forces, but also subjects, to some degree always capable of forming their lives and, collectively, of influencing the course of history.

This already sets up Lukács' answer to the problem of alienation which is discussed in this work almost exclusively from the viewpoint of the life-possibilities of the individual. Labor represents the unity of objectivation (production of an object of social utility) and externalization (realization of conscious ends through the activation of subjective abilities). Under definite historico-social circumstances these two aspects of the process of labor become, however, sharply divorced from, and opposed to, each other. Alienation implies a situation in which the requirements of social reproduction to be fulfilled in the activity of the individual are antagonistically opposed to the possibility of his/her self-expression, the self-realization of personality. Alienation, however, as Lukács underlines in a polemics directed against Heidegger as well as Adorno, never is, nor can be, total. The individual as an "answering" being always acts within some scope of alternatives. Of course, he/she can simply accept, without any distancing, his/her social place and function, merely enacting the interests determined by them. Then (as an ideal case) he/she is a mere particular, a social being solely in the sense of a socially determined being, a species being in-itself. But primarily the great forms of cultural objectivations, representing the historical consciousness and self-consciousness of humanity, allow the individual to acquire a relation, both distanced and active, to his/her social position and its demands, to form – within some scope of social possibilities – his/her life, by overcoming mere particularity and raising him/herself to the standpoint of species being for-itself. In this context Lukács emphasizes not

459

only the relative independence of "ideologies," but first of all the fact that genuine, epochal ideologies are not mere reflexes of preset social interests, but forms of ideal objectivations that bring the principal alternatives of an age to awareness and allow their conflict to be consciously fought out and to be transformed into intentional life-choices. In this sense Lukács' last work ends with a particular answer to the question which he passionately raised at the very beginning of his theoretical activity: the problem of the function of culture in contemporary life.

## References and further reading

Arato, A. and Breines, P.: *The Young Lukács and the Origin of Western Marxism* (New York: Seabury Press, 1979).

Dannemann, R. (ed.): *Georg Lukács – Jenseits der Polemiken* (Frankfurt: Sendler, 1986).

Goldmann, L.: *Lukács and Heidegger: Towards a New Philosophy* (London: Routledge, 1977).

Heller, A. (ed.): *Lukács Revalued* (Oxford: Blackwell, 1983).

Jung, W.: *Georg Lukács* (Stuttgart: Metzler, 1989).

Kadarkay, A.: *Georg Lukács: Life, Thought and Politics* (Oxford: Blackwell, 1991).

Löwy, M.: *Georg Lukács: From Romanticism to Bolshevism* (London: New Left Books, 1979).

Merleau-Ponty, M.: *Adventures of the Dialectics* (Evanston, IL: Northwestern University Press, 1972).

Mészáros, I.: *Lukács' Concept of the Dialectic* (London: Merlin, 1972).

# 41

# Gramsci

## ERNESTO LACLAU

Born in 1891 in Sardinia, Gramsci studied in Turin and in 1919 founded, together with Palmiro Togliatti, the *Ordine Nuovo*, a journal which tried to give expression to the aims of the council movement, which developed during those years in the industrial cities of northern Italy. In 1921 he was a founding member of the Italian Communist Party and, after the fall of the ultra-leftist leadership headed by Bordiga, became in 1924 the Party's general secretary. Imprisoned by the Fascist regime in 1926, he spent the rest of his life in jail. He was freed in 1937, a few days before his death.

The importance of Gramsci as a political thinker lies in his reformulation of a socialist strategy centered around the concept of "hegemony," but the philosophical significance of the latter should be found in the changes in the basic presuppositions of Marxism that it brought about. The meaning of his intervention has to be seen against the background of the deadlock reached by Marxist thought in the first decade of the century. Thomas Masaryk had spoken of a "crisis of Marxism." This crisis was the result of the dissolution of the intimate imbrication between theory and practice that had characterized the early phases of social democracy in Europe. For Marxism, the overthrow of capitalism was going to be the result of an exclusively proletarian revolution, the possibility of the latter depending on the increasing simplification of the social structure under capitalism. This social transformation was going to be the direct expression of the economic contradictions of capitalism, which inexorably led to the dissolution of the middle classes and the peasantry and the transformation of the whole of the population into a vast proletarian mass. In those circumstances, the only possible strategy was to concentrate on the organization of the working class and to wait until the "necessary laws of history" did the rest. So, the correctness of the strategy entirely depended on the correctness of the theory. This blend of theory and strategy had found philosophical expression in Engels' *Anti-Dühring*, the most popular *Vulgata* of Marxist thought at the end of the century, which attempted an uneasy combination of Hegelianism and Darwinism.

The "crisis of Marxism" was mainly shown in the dissolution of this strict imbrication between theory and strategy. After the long crisis of capitalism, which lasted from 1873 to 1896, the subsequent economic recovery shook the hope of any imminent collapse of the system. At the same time, new social problems arose: those posed by the intermediate social strata which, far from disappearing, were expanding and required a differentiated political expression; and the tensions within the working class, whose internal fragmentation was only too visible on the eve of World War I. Between the *Endziel* (the final aim) of the movement and the political tasks of the present, an increasing gap was developing. How to fill it? Three main solutions were attempted – the third one being the immediate prelude to Gramsci's intervention. The first was the solution of Marxist orthodoxy, best represented by Kautsky and Plekhanov: the laws of capitalism were in full operation and the economic recovery could only be a temporary phenomenon. The working class had to avoid any kind of alliance with bourgeois forces and to prepare itself for the coming final showdown. As this showdown, however, did not announce itself in any obvious way in the empirical reality of the present, the whole strategy depended, even more than in the past, on the soundness of its philosophical foundation. This foundation was provided by what Plekhanov called, coining a new term, "dialectical materialism." The second tendency – Bernstein revisionism – radically questioned the "necessary laws of capitalism" as formulated by Marx. The world did not advance towards an increasing simplification of the social structure and, consequently, not towards a proletarian revolution either. Social forces and initiatives were bound to be increasingly fragmented. In those circumstances, advance towards a socialist society was only possible on the basis of a series of ethico-political initiatives brought together by the principle of *Entwicklung*, the tendency of humanity to move towards higher forms of social organization. The principle of unification, which could not be found in an objective history, was going to be provided by a Kantian ethical imperative. The third tendency – represented by Sorel and the tradition of revolutionary syndicalism – fully accepted Bernstein's critique of Marx's "objective laws of capitalism," but attempted to preserve the revolutionary vocation of the working class. Given, however, that this revolutionary role was no longer adjudicated by an objective structure – at the level of the social structure there is, for Sorel, only mélange – it could only result from a subjective will, from a conscious attempt at overcoming the objective tendencies towards disintegration and integration into the system. The condition for the formation of such a subjective will was, for Sorel, violence, or struggle which constantly reconstituted a proletarian identity opposed to bourgeois decadence; and the necessary requirement of such a struggle was a "myth" which galvanized around itself the proletarian energies. This myth was, for Sorel, the "general strike," conceived not so much as an actual future event, but as a horizon giving tendential unity to a succession of initiatives in the class war. What is important from the perspective of Gramsci's approach is that he found in Sorel a notion of collective wills which were not conceived as homogeneous identities, resulting from underlying necessary laws, but as contingent and pragmatically constructed social aggregations. Both Bergson's vitalism and James's pragmatism had an important influence in the shaping of Sorel's philosophical outlook.

But if these broad currents within Marxism give us the basic parameters to establish the meaning of Gramsci's intervention, its immediate antecedent, as far as his mature approach – that to be found in the *Prison Notebooks* – is concerned, is Leninism and the whole experience of the Russian revolution. The latter had taken place, against the expectation of Marxist orthodoxy, in a backward country. The democratic revolution against feudalism, which had taken place in western Europe under bourgeois leadership, was in Russia – given the structural weaknesses of the local bourgeoisie – the result of a popular uprising led by the working class of St Petersburg. This created a breach with the classical economistic and deterministic tendencies within Marxism: political initiative was going beyond the rigid stageism of the Second International's strategy. Gramsci saluted the new revolution in an article entitled "The revolution against *Capital*." This involved an autonomization of the political – and of the strategic calculation – *vis-à-vis* the dictates of the economic "base." This new relationship, by which a social class took up the tasks which in a "normal" development would have corresponded to another class, was what the Russian revolutionists called "hegemony." And, together with this subversion of classical stageism, came a new logic of political agreements between social actors: the notion of "class alliance" – which in the Russian case was that between workers and peasants – was the cornerstone of Lenin's strategic thinking. If Leninist political practice was thus subverting Marxist basic categories, this subversion was not, however, translated to the theoretical level but led, on the contrary, to a reaffirmation of Marxist orthodoxy. This paradox is to be explained by the exceptional character that, in the eyes of the Russian revolutionists, their revolution had: the Russian revolution was seen just as the prelude of the German one, which would take place according to the postulates of the Marxist canon. It was going to be Gramsci's task to delve into the theoretical implications of Leninist practice – transforming, in many ways, the latter – and to produce a series of new theoretical concepts which amounted to a complete reformulation of Marxism.

Given the fragmentary nature of the *Prison Notebooks*, it is not advisable to make a presentation of Gramsci's approach *selon l'ordre des raisons* – giving it a systematic architectonics which is not warranted by the texts themselves. A better way of proceeding is to concentrate on his main categories, one by one, and to see their mutual overdetermination and the systemative coherence which derives from the latter. I shall follow this procedure.

## Intellectual and moral leadership

This concept, which had been used (as intellectual and moral *reform*) by Sorel – who, in turn, had taken it from Ernest Renan – represents a key displacement in Gramsci's problematic *vis-à-vis* Leninism. In Lenin's conception, the notion of class alliances presupposed that the identities of the forces entering into the alliance were external to the alliance as such. "Class alliance" was conceived as a zero-sum game in which separate groups, each with its own identity and aims, establish some pact with other groups for a limited period of time and with perfectly delimited objectives ("to strike together and to march separately"). The alliance cannot change in the least the identity of the forces entering into it. There is a strict separation between the terrain in which the identities of the social agents are constituted and that in which they politically compete and negotiate. It is the very possibility that this process of negotiation can "contaminate" the identity of diffuse social forces that makes imperative the presence of the "vanguard" party, which is beyond the possibility of such a contamination. So, the leadership of a hegemonic alliance can only

463

be conceived as *political* leadership, leaving unchanged the social identity of the political agents. As a result, politics does not play any substantial role in the constitution of social identities. Gramsci, on the contrary, speaks of *intellectual and moral* leadership. Now, in the latter, the led *identify* themselves, to some extent, with the leading group; so, the political process (the alliance) changes the identity of the forces participating in it. The political is not only a level in which the social is represented, but also one in which the social is, somehow, constituted. This begins the subversion of the Marxist notion of social totality, and the blurring of the line separating base from superstructure.

## Collective will

Sorel had questioned the essentialist logic governing the constitution of social identities in classical Marxism, but not the identification of the revolutionary agency with the working class. Lenin, for his part, had thought of a broader revolutionary agency, resulting from class alliances, but the "molecular" composition of that alliance – the classes as undeconstructible atoms – was still conceived in the traditional Marxist way. Gramsci is going to go beyond both limitations: he will retain from Sorel the notion of agencies as constituted through non-objective, pragmatic aggregations, and from Lenin the idea of agencies broader than particular classes. This operation is crystallized in his notion of "collective wills." A collective will is the precipitate of a plurality of demands, political initiatives, traditions and cultural institutions, whose always-precarious unity is the result of the fusion of these heterogeneous elements into global images constituting a "popular religion" (the link with the Sorelian "myths" is clear). These "collective wills" can be conceived as "classes," but in that case classes are no longer structural locations – they result from bringing together a set of dispersed elements with no objective underlying logic – and are not predestined to coalesce with each other. The level of strategic displacements is no longer the reflection of a ground different from itself, but is the very terrain in which social identities are constituted.

## Historical bloc

This idea of "collective will" was clearly incompatible with the traditional Marxist notion of social totality, centered around the base/superstructure distinction. The distinctive feature of the latter was that the necessary laws of the infrastructure integrated a social formation (and constituted, in that way, a social totality). This vision does not need to be cast in an economistic-mechanistic formulation: it can, on the contrary, expand and sophisticate the system of mediations that link the base to the superstructure, as in Lukács, but in any case these mediations are seen as *necessary*, and the ultimate impetus for social transformation is conceived as proceeding from economic class locations within the social totality. For Gramsci, on the contrary, whatever unity a social formation can have proceeds from the constitution of collective wills and, given that the latter result from contingent hegemonic articulations, they cannot be the expression of any necessary underlying unity different from themselves. The unity of the collective will is, in that sense, a contingent "ideological" unity, but the ideological is no longer conceived as "super-structural" but as the very terrain of constitution of social relations. A social totality thus unified through collective wills is what Gramsci called an "historical bloc."

## Organic intellectual

If the notion of ideology is enlarged to the point of becoming identified with the articulating logic governing the construction of social relations (which is close to what later would be called "discourse"), the function of the intellectual had to be expanded in a parallel way. The classical notion of "intellectuals" had attributed to the latter a mere contemplative function or a function of "knowledge." This was understandable as far as social reality was conceived as constituted through neces-sary laws, independent of the will of men. But if the degree of unity which a social formation can have is the result of contingent articulatory interventions, the intel-lectual function becomes eminently practical. Anybody constructing an articula-tion of social elements whose configuration was not predetermined by the elements in themselves, considered in isolation, can be considered as an intellectual. A union organizer, for instance, would be considered as an intellectual in the Gramscian sense. The agents of this creative/articulatory activity, which vastly expands the intellectual function, are called by Gramsci *organic intellectuals*, as distinguished from the *traditional* ones.

## War of position

The classical strategic vision of Marxism turned around one central moment: that of the seizure of power, the axial time signaling the transition from one type of society to another. The duality, war of position/war of movement, was grounded on the primacy of the second over the first. Power was a *given* object to be seized. Both the separated identities of the two conflicting forces and the externality of these identities *vis-à-vis* their strategic moves, were the basic presuppositions of this type of political calculation. Gramsci is going to reverse this primacy: for him it is the war of position which shows, through its internal workings, the logic of the political. If the "collective wills" are the actual historical agents, and if their unity and consti-tution proceed through contingent and pragmatic reaggregations, each strategic move changes also the identity of the social forces in conflict. It is not that fully-fledged social agents *choose* strategies, but, rather, that strategies *constitute* the identities of those agents. In that sense, the war of movement is just an internal moment of a war of position. Two important conclusions follow from this reversal. The first is that strategic movements do not *express* something that society *already* is but, instead, they are the primary level in the constitution of social relations. The political – conceived, of course, in a widened sense – is the primary ontological level in which the social is formed. The second conclusion is that power is not something one can "seize." Gramsci does not speak of the "seizure of State power" but of the "becoming State" of the working class. Against all forms of political vanguardism

465

he sees social movement as part of a mass process which changes the fundamental configurations of society. The State is for him – in a way which is closer to Hegel than to Marx – the moment of universalization of the community but, against Hegel, he does not see this moment of universalization as a particular instance within social totality, but as a configuration active in the totality of social relations. There is thus a double process of socialization of the universal (political) instance and of politicization of society. The result is his enlarged conception of the State – seen by him as an "integral State."

## Hegemony

All the theoretical displacements previously mentioned coalesce around a category which is the central innovation of Gramsci's vision of politics: the category of "hegemony." As in all the preceding cases, hegemony is part of a basic opposition: that between "corporative class" and "hegemonic class." A class is corporative as far as its aims are particularistic and never transcend its own limited interests. It is, on the contrary, hegemonic when it transforms its own aims into those of the community as a whole. There is a universalistic dimension in a hegemonic class which is absent from a purely corporative one. What is the ontological possibility of a hegemonic relation? According to Gramsci, everything depends on: (1) the presence of an unfulfilled task whose achievement is not *necessarily* linked to the objectives of any particular group; (2) the ability of a particular group to transform its own objectives in the historical means of fulfilling that task. For instance, the objective of national unity had been an unfulfilled but recurrent aim of the Italian people since the Renaissance, and the contemporary obstacles to its achievement – the so-called Vatican and Mezzogiorno questions – had only underscored even more its need. It was only if the working class became an authentic national class, if it presented its own objective – socialism – as the historical vehicle which made possible the achievement of national unity, that it had any prospect of success as a hegemonic class, in such a deeply fragmented society as Italy. While the increasing centrality of the working class objectives was for classical Marxism the result of objective movements of the infrastructure – leading to a progressive polarization of society – it was for Gramsci the result of a hegemonic articulation at the political (in the widened sense) level. As we see, all the political dimensions previously mentioned coalesce around this notion of hegemonic articulation: the political and moral leadership is possible because those unfulfilled aims do not essentially belong to any particular group but require, in order to be fulfilled, the agency of some particular social force; the agency of historical transformation, being itself the result of this piecemeal contingent reaggregation of partial aims and demands, does not overlap with the interest of any *particular* group but is rather a collective will whose frontiers and contents are always susceptible of subversion and redefinition; being the type of unity that a hegemonic articulation brings to social life, essentially precarious and threatened, it can never aspire to the solid determination of a ground but only to the transient unification of a historical bloc; the cement of such historical bloc, being only provided by contingent discursive practices, requires the

466

intervention of the agents of those practices – the organic intellectuals; finally, as any ultimate ground is excluded, there is no revolutionary chasm at the level of power which can have, in itself and by itself, the dignity of a radical foundation: there are only movements of frontiers which perpetuate *sine die* the war of position (even the seizure of political power is one more movement in that process of frontier displacement).

The ensemble of these strategic displacements *vis-à-vis* the classical Marxist paradigm could have not taken place without producing, at the same time, a rethinking of the relationship between theory and practice. It is here that the main contributions of Gramsci to philosophy (within the Marxist tradition) are to be found. Two major developments should be indicated:

(1)   Following his critique and deconstruction of the function of the intellectual (as indicated above) Gramsci necessarily had to blur the frontiers separating philosophy (or theory, in general) from other forms of social discursivity. The way this blurring took place was through a multiplication of the instances through which collective imaginaries – conceived as totalizing ones – take shape. "Philosophy" is seen by him as the highest order in which a totalizing task, which starts with "common sense" and "religion" (or "ideology") is achieved. Two misapprehensions should be avoided at this point. The first is to conceive this progressive totalization in "sociologistic" terms, i.e., as the *expression* of the world-view of an *already* constituted group. On the contrary, each of those three levels is, for Gramsci, a primary terrain in which the very unity of the group takes shape. In his words: "This problem is that of preserving the ideological unity of the entire bloc which that ideology serves to cement and to unify" (Gramsci 1971, p. 328).

The second mistake would be to conceive that totalizing moment as expressing an a priori coherent *Weltanschauung* – and the use by Gramsci of the expression "conception of the world" could easily lead to this misapprehension. However, being the "conception of the world," for Gramsci, the ideological crystalization which results from and, at the same time, makes possible the constitution of a collective will, it cannot have any a priori transcendental unity – it is rather the result of this open-ended interplay between an incomplete totalizing function (grounding the transient unity of a group) and the threat to the latter by the centrifugal tendencies inherent in any war of position. What is implicit here is that Philosophy realizes itself as far as it dissolves itself as a separate activity into a plurality of discourses cementing the unity of a "historical bloc."

(2)   To characterize his whole theoretical approach, Gramsci spoke of "absolute historicism." This has been frequently given a teleological reading, especially in the Italian context, where it was only too easy to locate Gramsci's thought within an intellectual continuum leading from Labriola to Croce. Althusser also condemned Gramsci's historicism by linking it to Lukács' teleologism. This is not only a misreading, but attributes to Gramsci exactly the position from which he is trying to disassociate himself. What Gramsci understands by "absolute historicism" is the fact that there is no a priori historical teleology, that the contingent unity of dispersed elements which is associated with categories such as "historical bloc," "collective will," and "hegemony" is the only type of historical unity to be found,

467

and that it cannot be traced to any deeper kind of ontological or transcendental grounding.

With hindsight, of course, many of Gramsci's deconstructive gropings look rather ambiguous and half-hearted. Why, for instance, after having shown the complex and heterogeneous nature of the collective wills and of the operating of hegemonic grounding, does he insist that only the fundamental *classes* of society can fulfill hegemonic roles? In many respects it looks as if the innovative theoretical avenues that he is opening, find a stumbling block in his attachment to a vision of history and society still deeply anchored in the classical Marxist paradigm. But it is certain – also with hindsight – that his theoretical intervention represents the most advanced attempt, in the interwar period, to move in the direction of a post-Marxism able to deal with the fragmented and incomplete character of social identities in the contemporary world.

## Writings

The critical edition in Italian of Gramsci's prison writings is *Quaderni del carcere*, 4 vols (Torino: Einaudi, 1975), edition prepared by Valentino Gerratana.

In English we have: *Selections from the Prison Notebooks* (London: Lawrence & Wishart, 1971); *Selections from Political Writings (1910–1920)* (London: Lawrence and Wishart, 1977); *Selections from Political Writings (1921–1926)* (London: Lawrence & Wishart, 1978); *Letters from Prison* (New York: Harper & Row, 1973).

## References and further reading

Adamson, Walter L.: *Hegemony and Revolution: a Study of Antonio Gramsci's Political and Cultural Theory* (Berkeley, CA: University of California Press, 1980).

Buci-Glucksmann, Christine: *Gramsci et l'Etat: pour une théorie matérialiste de la philosophie* (Paris: Fayard, 1975).

Cammet, John McKay: *Antonio Gramsci and the Origins of Italian Communism* (Stanford, CA: University of California Press, 1967).

Davidson, Alastair: *Antonio Gramsci: Towards an Intellectual Biography* (London: Merlin, 1977).

Mouffe, Chantal (ed.): *Gramsci and Marxist Theory* (London, Routledge, 1979).

# 42

# Schmitt

## G. L. ULMEN

Celebrated and castigated as the "Hobbes of the twentieth century" and even a modern Machiavelli, Carl Schmitt (1888–1984) is undoubtedly the most controversial legal and political theorist of the twentieth century. He greatly influenced the thinking of such political scientists and political philosophers as Hans J. Morgenthau, Franz Neumann, Otto Kirchheimer, Leo Strauss, and Julien Freund. But Schmitt always spoke and wrote as a jurist. He grounded his thinking in jurisprudence and was the teacher in the wider sense of such jurists as Ernst-Wolfgang Böckenförde and Ernst-Rudolf Huber.

As a jurist, Schmitt found himself in a problematic situation between theology and technicity, between jurists of theology (canonists) and jurists of secular law (legal positivists). From the standpoint of the existential struggle of jurisprudence, he was a "theologian of jurisprudence" in the sense that he attempted to hold the ground of an authoritative instance in an age of total secularization. On the one hand, he celebrated the liberation of jurisprudence from theology and its development as an independent vocation; on the other, he opposed the complete elimination of the bounds of nature and the consequent human compulsion to total power and total planning. On the one hand, he celebrated the sovereign state as a specific accomplishment of occidental rationalism; on the other, he opposed the positivistic legalization of law attending unchained technicism. Once state legality became the functional mode of a state bureaucracy, he sought a radical grounding of law in the vocation of jurisprudence – in its historical roots and common precedents.

If the relation between jurisprudence and theology was often conflictual, the relation between jurisprudence and philosophy was no less problematic, although for different reasons. In his testament – his lecture on "The Plight of European Jurisprudence" – Schmitt privileged jurisprudence at the expense of philosophy. This lecture was scheduled to be published in a *Festschrift* celebrating the 60th birthday of his friend, Johannes Popitz, on December 2, 1944. Years later Schmitt wrote:

> Popitz was of the opinion that concepts of person, reciprocity, and numerous other such concepts are of purely philosophical origin, and that there can be no jurisprudence without reference to philosophy. A prime example for him was the influence of Greek philosophy on Roman jurisprudence. I found just the opposite to be the case – that jurisprudence was able to free itself from the blind alley of the general concepts of every philosophy. In my view, Socrates, Plato and Aristotle were primarily teachers of

law and not what one today calls philosophers. Of course, by this and the term jurisprudence I do not mean something equivalent to the present division of faculties with their examinations and assistants. The philosophy of law is for me not the application of a given philosophical system to juridical questions but the development of concrete concepts derived from the immanence of a concrete legal and social order.  (1958, p. 427)

As early as 1914, in *Der Wert des Staates und die Bedeutung des Einzelnen*, Schmitt undertook a critique of the "spirit of the age," which, he understood in terms of its tendency to codification, calculation, and subsumption – as an essentially anti-individualistic age owing to its emphasis on money economy and technology, its attitude of skepticism, and its belief in the exact sciences. The antithesis of law and state was only an example of a general antithesis of immediacy and mediation, for which he found a parallel in HEGEL's *Phenomenology of Mind* (see Article 6). This was an age in which the individual knew no other law than that mediated by the state. Whether or not the antithesis between law and state could or should be overcome was not his problem or concern, only the concrete situation.

Schmitt's emphasis was on the *concrete situation* and on *concrete concepts*. In one of his most seminal works, *Political Theology*, he wrote: "All significant concepts of the modern theory of the state are secularized theological concepts, not only because of their historical development . . . but also because of their systematic structure" (1985 [1922], p. 36). As Schmitt saw it, a sociology of juridical concepts was necessary to the understanding of the sociology of *sovereignty*, which became a central concern of his life. He stressed the systematic analogy between theological and juridical concepts precisely because "a sociology of juridical concepts presupposes a consistent and radical ideology" (1985 [1922], p. 42). He was careful to specify in this context that the sociology of concepts he had in mind transcends juridical conceptualization oriented to immediate practical interest. It is *radical* because it presupposes that the metaphysical image of a particular epoch has the same structure as that immediately apprehended as the form of its political organization. In the modern theory of the state, the form was transferred from the subjective to the objective. This was in part the reason for Schmitt's lapidary assertion: "Sovereign is he who decides on the state of exception" (1985 [1922], p. 5). In his view, it is precisely the exception that makes the *subject* of sovereignty relevant. A decision on the exception is for Schmitt a decision in the true sense, because in his view: the norm proves nothing; the exception proves everything.

Even as he rejected Kant's definition of law as distinct from ethics, which left unanswered the most important questions, particularly those concerning the justification of legal force, Schmitt rejected the neo-Kantian conception of form. Since legal form is governed by a legal idea, and because a legal idea cannot realize itself, "it needs a particular organization and form before it can be translated into reality" (1985 [1922], p. 28). This was true also of the translation of a general legal norm into positive law and of the application of it juridically or administratively. Since most jurists of Schmitt's day spoke the language of legal positivism, and philosophers tended to follow the language of jurists, Schmitt demonstrated how the word

*Gesetz* (law, as opposed to *Recht*, right) tended to mislead the discussion of *nomos*. As in "The Plight of European Jurisprudence," so in his last great work, *Der Nomos der Erde*, Schmitt's concern is with "the existential question of jurisprudence itself, which today will be eroded between theology and technicity if the basis of its present character is not maintained in a way that is both conceptually clear and historically correct" (1974 [1950], p. 6). He begins with corollaries of *nomos*, the most important being that the original meaning of *Recht* is order and orientation: originally, all law was land-bound; it was constitutive of the order of life in general and the orientation to a specific location. In the wider sense, *nomos* embraces the appropriation of land, the distribution of property, and the production of goods for the sustenance of life.

After decades of misuse of the legality of the centralized *Gesetzesstaat* (a perversion of the liberal *Rechtsstaat*), the concept of legitimacy appeared to be the only corrective. The more centralized this type of state authority becomes, the more intense the compulsion to make laws whose hyper-formality is matched by their lack of content. Schmitt employed a specific understanding of *nomos* as an antidote to this positivistic understanding of *Recht* – the law of the *Gesetzesstaat*. Already with Plato, *nomos* acquired the meaning of a *schedon* – a mere rule. Plato's *nomoi* exhibit the utopian character of modern laws: they have little to do with fortuitous *nomoi* and even less with politics. But Schmitt found something of the original relation between order and orientation in Aristotle, meaning that *nomos* is still a component of a concrete spatial dimension. Aristotle claimed that *nomos* is antithetical to *psephisma* and other designations having only the character of decrees. Unlike in modern ideologies of the rule of law, Aristotle's *nomos* recognizes a common principle and is consistent with the fair division of property. By contraposing *nomos* and *physis*, the Sophists contributed to the destruction of the original meaning of *nomos*, which was thereby reduced from a fact of life (*Sein*) to a prescribed ought (*Sollen*). It thus became indistinguishable from *psephisma* and other designations for arbitrary prescriptions.

In terms of the history of jurisprudence, Schmitt found his distinctive place in linking the historical, the sociological, and the political spheres, whereas the majority of sociological jurists of his time did not take the state into account. In most instances, these jurists subscribed to something akin to Hans Kelsen's "pure" theory of law, which was unconcerned with the state and sovereignty because these were not juridical but political questions. Of course, it was not only economic and social but also political conditions that gave rise to the sociological movement in law. Not only was the capitalist economic system expanding and consolidating, the political structures of Western society were undergoing significant changes owing to the extension of political democracy to the masses. Not only did many claims of the working class require institutionalization through legislation, social and political struggles were increasingly focused on claims for the enactment or repeal of legislation. But the pattern and work of the courts did not change as significantly as did the perception among jurists of the actual or potential claims upon the legal system, which necessitated a revaluation of law and its institutions. Particularly meaningful for Schmitt was the fact that these changes brought the state and its

471

institutions into even greater prominence at a time when the distinction between state and society was disappearing.

As long as the state was a clear and unequivocal entity confronting non-political groups and affairs – as long as the state possessed the monopoly of politics – general definitions of the political were understandable and justifiable. But in Schmitt's arguably most controversial and seminal work, *The Concept of the Political*, he asserted that "the equation state = politics becomes erroneous and deceptive at exactly the moment when state and society penetrate each other. What had been up to that point affairs of state become thereby social matters and, vice-versa, what had been purely social matters become affairs of state" (1976 [1927/32], p. 22), which is necessarily true in any democratically organized unit. Democracy eliminated all the typical distinctions and depoliticizations characteristic of the liberal nineteenth century, such as those between state and economy, state and culture, etc. Already after 1848, the qualitative distinction between state and society lost its previous clarity, and by the early twentieth century it was clear to Schmitt that "the political must therefore rest on its own ultimate distinctions, to which all action with a specifically political meaning can be traced." He concluded: "The specific political distinction to which political actions and motives can be reduced is that between friend and enemy" (1976 [1927/32], p. 26).

Schmitt's assertion of the political was polemically directed at the "negation of the political" he found inherent in liberalism and individualism. Whereas liberalism systematically "evades or ignores state and politics" and typically "moves between ethics (intellect) and economics (trade)," individualism "leads necessarily to the distrust of all political forces and forms of state and government but never produces a positive theory of politics" (p. 70). Inherent in Schmitt's critique is the polemical assertion that liberalism destroys democracy even as democracy destroys liberalism. The result: "The state turns into society: on the ethical-intellectual side into an ideological humanitarian conception of humanity, and on the other, into an economic-technical system of production and trade" (p. 72). Both philosophically and politically, the logic of liberalism – *classical* liberalism – not only recognized the autonomy of different spheres but drove them toward specialization and even isolation, the most important example being the validity of legal norms and economic laws. Schmitt insisted that there is no escape from the logic of the political. Even though it appeared that economics was becoming the destiny of the world, he said that what had occurred was that economics had become political and thereby the destiny.

Schmitt considered one of the failures of his life that he had not pursued "the great theme of the deeper relation between Savigny and Hegel" because "this struggle concerning the relation of jurisprudence and philosophy almost always ends in a dialogue concerning the relation between Savigny and Hegel" (1973 [1958], pp. 427–8). Both were subject to "political simplifications," whereby Savigny was the reactionary and Hegel the revolutionary: "Thus Hegel the philosopher doubtless plays the favorable role in terms of his contemporary actuality" (1973 [1958], p. 429). Simultaneously, Schmitt attempted to enlist Hegel in the cause of jurisprudence and to establish the "contemporary actuality" of Savigny. He had failed to respond to the arguments of the leading Hegelian legal philosophers of his time, Julius Binder and Karl Larenz, and it was too late – in the 1950s – to make up for this "great omission." He did, however, indicate an answer, which first took the form of a defense of Savigny against Hegel and then found them brothers under the skin, so to speak. "Hegel appears to claim for philosophy everything scientific or scholarly in jurisprudence and to ignore the subalternate technicism and formal-ism of jurists and their faculty" (1973 [1958], p. 428). Schmitt was not concerned with the struggle of faculties *per se* but with a "deeper relation," which was not exhausted by the antithesis of reactionary and revolutionary. He saw this antithe-sis much more in light of the question of legality and legitimacy.

Schmitt contended that the closed system of legality of the parliamentary-legislative state had developed its own system of justification, and that the meaning and task of "legality" was directed against the "legitimacy" not only of monarchs but of any higher authority or ruling body. It was in this sense that he understood Max Weber's assertions that "this legality can pass for legitimacy" and that "the most familiar contemporary form of legitimacy is the belief in legality" (Weber 1978, vol. I, p. 39), whereby both legitimacy and legality are reduced to a "common concept of legitimacy" (1968 [1932], pp. 13–14). This is also why he found Kirch-heimer's formulation correct, namely that the legitimacy of parliamentary democ-racy "resides only in its legality," and that today "the bounds of law are equated with legitimacy" (1968 [1932], p. 14). Not only did the distinction between legality and legitimacy become artificial, the terms became so loose that "legal" came to mean something "purely formal," which is why Schmitt saw the collapse of the system of legality expressed "in a formalism and functionalism devoid of either a subject or a relation" (p. 14). He thus traced the course of a dual transformation – of legitimacy into legality and of legality into legislation, which is at once a "shoddy legality" and a "lightning legality." This "legalitarian" dilemma had even more serious political consequences. The legal holding of political power – state power – created a "super legality" Schmitt characterized as "political surplus-value" (1987 [1978], p. 74). Not only did this purely functional legality create the possibility of Hitler and Nazism, but also of a "legal" world revolution, communist or any other.

Schmitt's critique of the instrumentalization of law is perhaps his greatest contri-bution to legal theory and political thought. As he observed, the term *Rechtsstaat* "arose in Germany shortly before 1848, in the critical period in which an unprob-lematic legal sphere split into legality and legitimacy – a distinction that today can only be denied by artificial means" (1990 [1943/4], p. 58n.). France, the land of the legists, was the premier and best example of a positivistic legalization of right into a state codification of law. This centralized *Gesetzesstaat* not only replaced the *Rechtsstaat* but precluded a *Rechtsstand*, such as obtained in England, which, as Schmitt said, "is social, professional and, in its specific legal basis, an 'estate' and not a 'state'" (ibid., p. 59). The historical counter-concept to this non-state legal fraternity was the continental *Gesetzesstaat*, wherein there could be no *Rechtsstand* or even *Gesetzesstand* because the judge is a state official applying state law and is thus not only other than, but opposed to, a non-state "free" jurist in civil society. Savigny attempted to make jurisprudence an essential source and a guardian of right, i.e. to develop a conception of jurisprudence as the agent and defender of law – the core of a true *Rechtsstand*. This goal foundered both in and on the nineteenth century, because such a legal fraternity was incompatible and even antithetical to a *Gesetzesstaat*.

Schmitt had to admit that Hegel's state was not a *Rechtsstaat* but already a *Gesetzesstaat*, and that its jurists were no longer an autonomous estate but a state bureaucracy. He thus had his task cut out for him, which was to reconstitute the vocation of jurisprudence as a *Rechtsstand* – not by giving the English precedent a German (or better: European) accent, but by finding a German (European) precedent in Savigny and a German (European) partner in Hegel. On the surface, Schmitt appears to be one with the German Romantics, who looked back nostalgically to the *historical* – absolutist – legitimacy that had been replaced by the *revolutionary* legality of the French Revolution. But Schmitt was no Romantic. He had something else in mind, namely to enlist Hegel in the struggle against legal positivism. He needed Hegel to bridge the gap with both philosophy and modernity, which in the nineteenth century had become increasingly wider owing to Hegel's enlistment in Marxism – in revolutionary as opposed to historical legitimacy.

Hegel justified codification even as he acknowledged that it resulted in an "antinomy" or contradiction, which necessarily arises when fixed principles are applied to particular cases, and that it was historically "incomplete." His argument against Savigny and all opponents of codification was that civil rights can only be guaranteed by civil codes. Nevertheless, Schmitt argued that a new situation was already present in 1830, when legality and legitimacy were separated and became antithetical. Although Hegel stood on the side of the French Revolution when he opposed Savigny, Schmitt said the new situation "could well be grasped with Hegelian categories" (1973 [1958], p. 429). In order to enlist Hegel in his cause, Schmitt also had to argue that Hegel's opposition to Savigny had been transformed into "a completely different dialectic" (p. 429) during the nineteenth century – the Marxist dialectic. But he had in mind the "deeper relation" between Savigny and Hegel, by which he meant that both were true *katechonten* (restrainers) of "open atheism" in Germany. The term "open atheism" is a euphemism for the Enlightenment, which is clear from Schmitt's assertion that there is "no justification for making Hegel into an absolute accelerator whose negation is nothing more than movement and whose movement is nothing more than negation" (p. 429).

Schmitt believed that every movement, be it Romantic or revolutionary, is based, first, on a characteristic attitude toward the world, and, second, on a specific (if not always conscious) idea of ultimate authority. The development from the seventeenth to the nineteenth century led to entirely new ideas of God and the absolute. The transcendent God – the highest and most certain reality of traditional metaphysics – was eliminated, initiating a philosophical controversy over who or what would or should assume the function of the absolute – the ultimate point of legitimation. In place of God appeared two mundane realities which "carried through to a new ontology without waiting for the conclusion of the epistemological discussion" (1986 [1919], pp. 58–9). Although both were irrational in terms of rationalist philosophy, these demiurges appeared to be objective and self-evident in their supra-individual validity and thus came to dominate thought: humanity, the revolutionary; history, the conservative. Hegel synthesized them and thereby took the step that inevitably dethroned the traditional God of metaphysics. The people, rationalized into the state, and the *Weltgeist* (world spirit), developing historically, were thereby united, but in such a way that Savigny's *Volksgeist* (spirit of the people) functioned only as an instrument of the *Weltgeist*. Both empirically and psychologically, said Schmitt, the latitude of the *Volksgeist* was broad enough for Hegelianism to have both a revolutionary and a historical tendency, which he characterized respectively as the Promethean and the Epimethean. He argued that the intellectual bearings of both Savigny and Hegel were akin to the spirit of Prometheus' brother, Epimetheus (who did not revolt against Zeus), even though Hegel was able "to recognize, appreciate and comprehend the Promethean direction of his age" (1973 [1958], pp. 428–9).

The most important question for Schmitt was whether Savigny or Hegel was the stronger *katechon*, and in view of this question Schmitt said it was possible that Nietzsche's rage "was directed to the right address, namely Hegel, because Savigny recognized only the voluntary accelerators and could only become somewhat irritated with involuntary accelerators" (1973 [1958], p. 429). Whereas Savigny had restrained the "total functionalization" of law into legality and legislation, Hegel had restrained the abstract universalism of the Enlightenment, which *itself* lays down the law and accomplishes not a particular but a universal task. Hegel certainly had no quarrel with the Enlightenment's program of the disenchantment of the world, which he himself brought to completion. The problem was with the Enlightenment's misguided rationalism or, more specifically, with its absolutization of reason. True freedom, as Hegel saw it, could only be found in the laws and customs of a concrete community – the state – in which the free self-conscious individual can find himself. Not for this reason alone did Schmitt find in Hegel a *katechon*, but also in that Hegel did not make the conscious result of the whole process of negation into an absolute, as Marx would have it, but in fact opposed this process. Hegel thus fits more easily into Schmitt's conservative guise than into Marx's revolutionary guise.

In considering Savigny a paradigm of the first step away from the positive legality of the *Gesetzesstaat*, Schmitt was not calling for any movement "Back to Savigny," which was the slogan (spoken or unspoken) of all reactionary tendencies and parties: "A historical truth is true only *once*. The concept of the historical is itself subject to transformations and reinterpretations; its realizations in various areas of intellectual life take many forms" (1990 [1943/4], p. 59). On this score, he left no doubt: "At issue today is not some reactionary retreat but rather the apprehension of a wealth of new knowledge which can become fruitful for jurisprudence and which must be acquired and used creatively. In view of this task, let the dead positivism of the 19th century bury its dead" (ibid., p. 60). In the same vein, especially because of the political implications, Schmitt would say today: let the dead legalism of the twentieth century bury its dead.

# Writings

Schmitt, C.: *Der Wert des Staates und die Bedeutung des Einzelnen* (Tübingen: J. C. B. Mohr [Paul Siebeck], 1914).

——: *Political Romanticism* (1919), tr. Guy Oakes (Cambridge, MA: MIT Press, 1986).

——: *Die Diktatur: Von den Anfängen des modernen Souveränitätsgedankens bis zum proletarischen Klassenkampf* (1919), 4th edn (Berlin: Duncker & Humblot, 1978).

——: *Roman Catholicism and Political Form* (1923), tr. with an Intro. and Notes by G. L. Ulmen (Westport, CT: Greenwood Press, 1996).

——: *The Crisis of Parliamentary Democracy* (1923), tr. Ellen Kennedy (Cambridge MA, and London: MIT Press, 1985).

——: *Verfassungslehre* (1928), 5th edn (Berlin: Duncker & Humblot, 1970).

——: *The Leviathan in the State Theory of Thomas Hobbes: Meaning and Failure of a Political Symbol* (1938), tr. George Schwab and Erna Hilfstein, Foreword and Intro. by George Schwab (Westport, CT: Greenwood Press, 1996).

——: *Positionen und Begriffe im Kampf mit Weimar – Genf Versailles 1923–1939* (1940), 2nd edn (Berlin: Duncker & Humblot, 1988).

——: *Der Nomos der Erde im Völkerrecht des Jus Publicum Europaeum* (1950), 2nd (Berlin: Duncker & Humblot, 1974).

——: "Die Lage der europäischen Rechtswissenschaft" (1943/44), in Carl Schmitt, *Verfassungsrechtliche Aufsätze*, pp. 386–426; appended notes, pp. 427–9; "The Plight of European Jurisprudence," tr. by G. L. Ulmen, in *Telos*, no. 83 (Spring 1990), pp. 35–70.

——: "Die legale Weltrevolution: Politischer Mehrwert als Prämie auf juridische Legalität," in *Der Staat*, no. 3 (1978), pp. 321–39; "The Legal World Revolution," tr. by G. L. Ulmen in *Telos*, no. 72 (Summer 1987), pp. 73–89.

——: *Legalität und Legitimität* (1932), 2nd edn (Berlin: Duncker & Humblot, 1968).

——: "Nehmen/Teilen/Weiden: Ein Versuch, die Grundfragen jeder Sozial- und Wirtschaftsordnung vom Nomos her richtig zu stellen" (1953), republished in Schmitt, *Verfassungsrechtliche Aufsätze aus den Jahren 1924–1954: Materialen zu einer Verfassungslehre* (1958), 2nd edn (Berlin: Duncker & Humblot, 1973), pp. 489–501; "Appropriation/distribution/production: toward a proper formulation of basic questions of any social and economic order (1953)," tr. G. L. Ulmen, in *Telos*, no. 95 (Spring 1993), pp. 52–64.

——: "Nomos – Nahme – Name," in *Der beständige Aufbruch: Festschrift für Erich Przywara*, ed. Siegfried Behn (Nuremberg: Glock und Litz Verlag, 1957), pp. 99–105.

——: *Political Theology: Four Chapters on the Concept of Sovereignty* (1922), tr. George Schwab (Cambridge MA, and London: MIT Press, 1985).

——: *The Concept of the Political* (1927/31), tr. with Notes and Intro. George Schwab (New Brunswick: Rutgers University Press, 1976).

——: "The constitutional theory of federation (1928)," tr. G. L. Ulmen, in *Telos*, no. 91 (Spring 1992), pp. 26–56.

# References and further reading

Bendersky, Joseph: *Carl Schmitt: Theorist for the Reich* (Princeton, NJ: Princeton University Press, 1983).

Freund, Julien: *L'Essence du politique* (Paris: Éditions Sirey, 1965).

Gottfried, Paul: *Carl Schmitt: Politics and Theory* (Westport CT, and London: Greenwood Press, 1990).

Picccone, Paul, and Ulmen G. L.: "Schmitt's 'Testament' and the future of Europe," in *Telos*, no. 83 (Spring 1990), pp. 3–34.

Quaritsch, Helmut (ed.): *Complexio Oppositorum: Über Carl Schmitt* (Berlin: Duncker & Humblot, 1988).

Schwab, George: *The Challenge of the Exception: An Introduction to the Political Ideas of Carl Schmitt between 1921 and 1936* (1970), 2nd edn (Westport, CT: Greenwood Press, 1989).

Taubes, Jacob (ed.): *Der Fürst dieser Welt: Carl Schmitt und die Folgen* (Paderborn, Vienna, and Munich: Wilhelm Fink Verlag/Verlag Ferdinand Schöningh, 1983).

Ulmen, G. L.: "The concept of *Nomos*: introduction to Schmitt's 'Appropriation/Distribution/Production,'" in *Telos*, no. 95 (Spring 1993), pp. 39–51.

——: *Politischer Mehrwert: Eine Studie über Max Weber und Carl Schmitt* (Weinheim: Acta Humaniora, 1992).

——: "Schmitt and federalism: introduction to 'The Constitutional Theory of Federation,'" in *Telos*, no. 91 (Spring 1992), pp. 16–25.

Weber, Max: *Economy and Society: An Outline of Interpretive Sociology*, ed. Guenther Roth and Claus Wittich (Berkeley, CA: University of California Press, 1978), vol. I.

*Telos*, Special Issue, "Carl Schmitt: Enemy or Foe?," no. 72 (Summer 1987).

# 43

# Arendt

## ROBERT BERNASCONI

Hannah Arendt was born in 1906 into an East Prussian Jewish family. In 1933 she fled the Nazi regime and after brief stays in Prague and Geneva she found a temporary home in Paris. In 1941 she succeeded in gaining entry to the United States, where after ten years she became a citizen. Arendt had short-term positions at a number of universities, but was most closely identified with the New School for Social Research in New York, where she was professor of Political Philosophy at the time of her death in 1975. Much of her most important work attempted either to address the anti-Semitism that had forced her to leave Europe or to celebrate the political ideals of the United States that had enabled her to find refuge there. In the course of exploring these issues she presented a synoptic view of the Western tradition of political thought from the time of the early Greeks to her own day.

Although Hannah Arendt's writings often gave rise to controversy, the most bitter dispute was occasioned by her 1963 report on Eichmann's trial, *Eichmann in Jerusalem*, which popularized the provocative phrase "the banality of evil." Nevertheless, even her most theoretical works were widely denounced by those who were puzzled by what they considered her lack of scientific method. If some of these responses themselves now seem exaggerated, it is in large measure because there is a deeper appreciation of the way in which her thought belongs in the context of the philosophy of existence. Arendt was a student of HEIDEGGER (see Article 18) for the academic year 1924–5; after a semester with HUSSERL (see Article 15) in Freiburg, she went to Heidelberg where she worked with JASPERS (see Article 17) and completed her dissertation on Augustine's concept of love in 1929. Arendt never wavered in her admiration for Jaspers, who figured prominently in her book *Men in Dark Times*, whereas, by contrast, her relation to Heidegger's thought was at the very least complicated by his involvement with National Socialism. Nevertheless, her intellectual debt to Heidegger was the greater. She generously repaid her debt to both men by working strenuously to secure an audience in the United States for their works.

Arendt's first major work after World War II was *The Origin of Totalitarianism*, in which she attempted to understand why and how the West had been brought to the breaking-point. Her own experience as a refugee was reflected in her assessment that the fate of stateless peoples in the twentieth century had shown "the hopeless idealism" of the very phrase "human rights" (Arendt 1967 [1951], p. 269). The Rights of Man, far from being "inalienable," in the sense of independent of all governments, proved vacuous as soon as human beings found themselves deprived of the only institutions that were able to guarantee them (Arendt 1967 [1951], pp. 292–3). Although Arendt looked to the nineteenth century to find the roots of totalitarianism in anti-Semitism and imperialism, she insisted that totalitarianism represented a unique danger in which, in her famous phrase, "human nature as such is at stake" (Arendt 1967 [1951], p. 459). Eric Voeglin challenged the formulation on the grounds that a change of nature is a contradiction in terms, but in her defense of it, Arendt made clear that she was relying on the idea that the essence of being human was existence, albeit she colored that teaching by focusing specifically on the contribution of political freedom to human reality.

*The Human Condition* (1958) can quite properly be considered a broadening of these early reflections, insofar as she now identified the conformism of mass society as what threatened humanity in its plurality. She also traced this development back to the Greek philosophers, insofar as they did not always succeed in their theoretical works in keeping separate labor, work, and action, although the Greeks generally regarded these activities as distinct. Action was what the Greeks valued most. Through action one discloses *who* one is, but its unpredictability and fragility makes it possible to place a higher valuation on work, insofar as its products are more lasting and provide for that measure of permanence that is necessary for there to be a world at all. Labor, which in modernity has often been confused with work, is, by contrast, directed to meeting the biological necessities of life. The distance separating action and labor was crucially important for the Greeks because it served as the basis for separating the public realm of politics, which was the space of action, freedom, and speech, from the private realm of the household, which was dedicated to satisfying one's needs. Whereas the participants in politics addressed each other at the level of equality, the household realm was hierarchical with women and slaves playing a subordinate role.

One of Arendt's most important claims in *The Human Condition* was that in modernity the distinction between the private and the public had become confused by virtue of what she called the rise of the social. This phenomenon was illustrated by the fact that economic considerations, which on her understanding belonged properly to the household sphere, came to dominate politics. Whether Arendt's apparently historical account of these distinctions is indeed supported by the historical evidence, or whether it is better regarded as a kind of fiction in the service of clarifying conceptual distinctions, is still debated. However, two things are clear.

First, Arendt recognized a tradition of political thought that began in Greece and sought to get behind it to certain basic experiences that had been covered over by that tradition, much as Heidegger had done in his destructuring of the tradition of a history of ontology which was equally focused on Greece. Indeed, her focus on action and work, or *praxis* and *poiesis*, reflected concerns that were already operative in Heidegger's lectures at the time she was his student. Another example of the same process can be found in the essay "What is Freedom?" in the collection *Between Past and Future*. Arendt argued there that the philosophers had distorted the concept of freedom when they transposed it from the political realm, to which it belonged, to the interior realm, a process completed by Augustine when he posed the problem of freedom as a problem of the free will. Similarly, in "What is Authority?" from the same collection of essays, Arendt took up the classic issue of authority and deprived it of its self-evidence, in part on the grounds that it was a Latin term which had no clear equivalent in Greek thought. This is a gesture familiar to readers of Heidegger, who are used to the strategy of scrutinizing concepts by locating them within the context of the founding experiences of Greek thought.

Secondly, Arendt sometimes gave to these distinctions a normative role that went beyond the merely descriptive. It was as if she considered a return to the Greek conception of politics to be an imperative within politics and not just an intellectual exercise. Arendt resisted the agenda of contemporary politics with its focus on economic and social issues. She did not consider these issues to be appropriate subjects for action or debate, which is what, in her conception, politics should involve. The results of this decision were already apparent in her commentary on the civil rights movement of the 1950s in "Reflections on Little Rock," where she argued that it was racial legislation, and not discrimination and social segregation, that constituted the perpetuation of the original crime of the United States and was, therefore, the appropriate target in the battle for civil rights. Needless to say, Arendt's conviction that this was a proper context in which to insist that the largely ignored distinction between the political and the social should determine the selection of remedies provoked controversy. However, it should be emphasized that Arendt did not always understand the appeal to the Greek paradigm in this way. Her point was more frequently that the fundamental experiences underlying the Greek experience of politics still governed the contemporary conception and practice of politics, and that it was still possible to find illumination in the distinctions in which those experiences had been secured for subsequent generations.

The full force of Arendt's use of Greek distinctions for a discussion of modern politics was not apparent until 1963 when, in *On Revolution*, she argued for the superiority of the American Revolution over the French Revolution on the grounds that the Founding Fathers of the United States respected the distinction between the social and the political that was ignored in France. Arendt's explanation was that poverty did not present the problem in America that it did in Europe. This is not the place to determine the accuracy of this claim or to decide what would follow if, in the context of modern society, social issues were suddenly to be withdrawn from political debate: perhaps issues of social justice would be placed beyond debate and finally given their due, as Arendt seemed to think, or perhaps it would mean that it would no longer be possible to secure the economic resources to address those issues, as her critics feared. Arendt's point in *On Revolution* was that freedom, not pity, should dominate politics. This was, on her analysis, what the Founding Fathers of America had succeeded in doing, when they turned back both to Roman antiquity and to the Biblical covenant in order to find a way of making sense of a beginning that transcended whatever preceded it. Of course, Arendt recognized the paradox that in order to start something new, one ended up in a sense self-consciously repeating what had already been done in the classic foundation legends of the West. Nevertheless, the United States did have the additional advantage for Arendt of being built on the strength of mutual pledges. Because totalitarianism in Germany had broken the *consensus iuris* by which a people is constituted without establishing a new consensus, Arendt had every reason to remember how in her adopted country the strength of the Republic depended on both the faithful memory of its founding and respect for its Constitution. It was the strength of her commitment to the Constitution, combined with her appreciation of plurality, that made her article on "Civil Disobedience" in the volume of her essays collected in 1972 under the title *Crises of the Republic* a particularly fine example of her writing. Her characteristic strategy when faced with a new problem was less to argue a case than to try to orient her readers by locating signposts wherever she could find them in the classics of philosophical and political thought, in history, and even in poetry.

Arendt was still left with the task of identifying resources with which to promote plurality and combat the dangers of mass society, particularly totalitarianism. Her study of Eichmann had shown that his thoughtlessness, his "inability to think," had contributed to his capacity to act as an instrument of evil. As a result she began to focus on thinking as a possible, if unlikely, safeguard. What made thinking an unlikely recourse in the face of the moral and political collapse to which she had personally been a witness was the fact that withdrawal from the world of human affairs was a condition of thinking. Nevertheless, in the 1971 essay "Thinking and Moral Considerations," which was later incorporated in the first volume of *The Life of the Mind*, Arendt further explored the possibility that non-thought and evil were connected. She did not rely on the apparent resemblance between the lack of identity within consciousness and the duality of conscience, because she doubted the political efficacy of conscience. Instead, she focused on the distinction between thinking and knowing that can be found in the later Heidegger, but which also corresponded to the Kantian distinction of *Vernunft* from *Verstand*. It was difficult to keep the two distinct, in both theory and practice. Although thinking was said to be an examination that did not produce results, it was still easy to turn this non-result into a result, just as Alcibiades and Critias perverted the thinking of Socrates into license and cynicism. Nevertheless, what was important to Arendt was that thinking could also liberate the capacity for judging particulars. In the general run of things this too would be of little political significance, except, as Arendt said, referring to what Jaspers called "boundary situations," in those "rare moments when the chips are down" and "the stakes are on the table" (Arendt 1978, vol. 1, pp. 192–3). When she died Arendt was still working on this account of judgment. It would have formed the third part of *The Life of the Mind*, but what she would have said can at best only be reconstructed through her *Lectures on Kant's Political Philosophy* that draw heavily on Kant's *Critique of Judgment*. Nor did Arendt ever seem to resolve the question of why Heidegger, who along with Socrates was her main source for our knowledge of thinking, was so singularly inept at judging.

The two volumes of *The Life of the Mind* that were published were devoted to thinking and willing respectively. Arendt sought to discover the experiences underlying what she called "the metaphysical fallacies" and the discovery of the will. These were not conventional philosophical explorations. She was in a sense running counter to philosophy. Just as thinking is an activity contrary to the human

481

condition, so philosophers seem to have been reluctant to allow for radical novelty and unpredictability, which, as Arendt emphasized, characterize action, as opposed to work. Although in this late work Arendt examined the writings of the philosophers for what they had to say about freedom, which they tended to conceive in terms of the will of the solitary individual, she remained committed, as she had been in "What is Freedom?," to what she had learned from the agents of history. Freedom belongs to the sphere of human plurality, where action is inspired by principles, rather than being guided by motives, and power is a relation that springs up between people acting together in concert, rather than being something that belongs to each individual as such.

When in *The Life of the Mind* Arendt described as a dismantling of metaphysics her attempt to find in such metaphysical fallacies as the two-world theory a clue to the nature of thinking (1978, vol. 1, pp. 211–12), she was inviting her readers to think of her work as a continuation of Heidegger's destructuring of philosophy. This is not to suggest that she did not find fault with Heidegger on many points and at very different levels, from his personal involvement with National Socialism to his focus on solitude, for which she found an antidote in Jaspers. But it is with reference to Heidegger's overcoming of metaphysics that one can best understand Arendt's tendency to address alternative political theories in terms of the tradition in which she situated them, rather than on their own terms. This does not sit well with adherents of those theories, whether they are liberals, Marxists, or conservatives. Nevertheless, if one takes seriously her claim that the advent of totalitarianism was an event that none of our inherited concepts can fathom, then her claim about the need to look beyond that tradition makes sense. Furthermore, it was from Heidegger that she learned that it was not necessary to look so much outside the tradition as behind it to Greek experiences overlooked by the philosophers. Of course, there was nothing in Heidegger that would have encouraged her to find a model for political action in the founding of the United States. However, to the extent that Arendt followed this model, with its emphasis on political freedom, consent, and plurality, she provided Continental philosophy with a way of addressing issues in political philosophy that seemed to be a genuine alternative to the Marxism that had tended to dominate political thought within Continental philosophy. It is perhaps for this reason that, as Marxists faced the crisis of coming to terms with the post-Soviet bloc world, and as Heideggerians sought to distance themselves from his politics, interest in Arendt's work soared to new levels, far beyond anything that she had known in her lifetime.

## Writings

Arendt, H.: *The Human Condition* (Chicago, IL: University of Chicago Press, 1958).
——: "Reflections on Little Rock," *Dissent*, 6 (1959), pp. 45–56.
——: *Between Past and Future* (New York: Viking Press, 1961; London: Faber & Faber, 1961).
——: *On Revolution* (New York: Viking Press, 1963; London: Faber & Faber, 1963).
——: *The Origin of Totalitarianism* (New York: 1951); rev. edn (London: George Allen & Unwin, 1967).

——: *Crises of the Republic* (New York: Harcourt, Brace & World, 1972).
——: *The Life of the Mind* (New York: Harcourt Brace Jovanovich, 1978).
——: *Lectures on Kant's Political Philosophy* (Chicago, IL: University of Chicago Press, 1982).

## References and further reading

Bernasconi, Robert: "The Double Face of the Political and the Social: Hannah Arendt and America's Racial Divisions," *Research in Phenomenology*, 26 (1996), pp. 3–24.
Bernstein, Richard J.: *Philosophical Profiles* (Cambridge: Polity Press, 1986), pp. 221–59.
——: *Hannah Arendt and the Jewish Question* (Cambridge, MA: MIT Press, 1996).
Canovan, Margaret: *Hannah Arendt: A Reinterpretation of her Political Thought* (Cambridge: Cambridge University Press, 1992).
Hinchman, Lewis, and Hinchman, Sandra: "In Heidegger's shadow: Hannah Arendt's phenomenological humanism," *Review of Politics*, 46 (1984), 183–211.
Hinchman, Lewis, and Hinchman, Sandra (eds): *Hannah Arendt: Critical Essays* (Albany NY: State University of New York Press, 1994).
Kateb, George: *Hannah Arendt: Politics, Conscience, Evil* (Totowa NJ: Rowman & Allanheld, 1984).
Taminiaux, Jacques: *La Fille du Thrace et le penseur professionel: Arendt et Heidegger* (Paris: Payot, 1992).
Voeglin, E.: "The origins of totalitarianism," *Review of Politics*, 15 (1953), pp. 68–85. [Includes Arendt's response to Voeglin.]
Young-Bruehl, Elisabeth: *Hannah Arendt: For Love of the World* (New Haven, CT: Yale University Press, 1982).

# 44

# Lefort

BERNARD FLYNN

This essay will present an outline of the concept of the *empty place* which plays a central role in the political philosophy of Claude Lefort. The notion of the place of the political in contemporary political theory might serve as a point of demarcation by which one can indicate Lefort's relation to, and his distance from, various strands of modern political discourse. I shall begin by evoking two "ideal types," and referring to actual theories only insofar as they illustrate these two types. For lack of better terms let us call them communitarianism and liberalism.

Communitarianism founds the political on some form of pre-existing, prepolitical community; it can be either a common history or language, or a shared substantive conception of the "good life" – the habitation, in a thick sense, of a common place. All such communities are limited and historically situated. Liberalism, on the other hand, seeks the intelligibility of the political in a purely formal characteristic shared by all men; it can be either the fact of human equality before God, the fear of death, the sovereignty over one's own body, or the ability to enter into communicative behavior. All of these subtypes can be viewed, in one sense or another, as variants of the theory of the social contract. Moreover, these two broad types cannot be distinguished by using the axis of left and right. There are right- and left-wing variants of each. Neither I, nor Lefort, claims that this particular set of binary oppositions, namely right/left, is alone in not being subject to a deconstructive reading.

The virtue of the first type of theory, communitarianism, is that it is historically situated. It has historical content. It embeds the political in a thick network of practices and symbols, in a historical form of life. However, its notorious vice is a characteristic hostility towards democracy, whose claims of universality and equality are viewed as leveling, ahistorical, destructive of community, and producing a generalized anomie – an emptying of all sense of place, both in its spiritual and geographical sense. (Jacques Taminiaux once told us that, on the occasion of his last seminar, Heidegger remarked that "Tourism should be forbidden.")

The habitual virtue of liberal theories is their assertions of human equality and dignity. But their recurring aporia is that in a secular society, where an appeal to equality before God is not adequate, they are unable to demonstrate a foundation for the equality and universality that they claim. Characteristically their claims to universality are undermined by showing that there are unavowed historical presuppostions which subtend and thus problematize them; for example, Marx contests the alleged universality of the Rights of Man by relating them to the historically specific figure of the bourgeoisie. Others have argued that Habermas's conception of the universal structures of communication is based on an idealization of a historically specific institutional employment of language. Both communitarianism and liberalism search for the *real* conditions which transform a plurality of people and an expanse of land into a society with some form of identity. In a certain sense they are both forms of positivist thought.

By *positivism*, taken in a very broad sense, I mean any form of nominalism which simply characterizes the intelligible as an invention of the mind, or of language, or of scientific procedure, etc. Thus the intelligible is based on the factual, the world is the sum of everything that is the case. In general, it can be said that Lefort's position incorporates a whole tradition of anti-positivism stemming from Kant through phenomenology, and in particular MERLEAU-PONTY's gestaltist critique of positivism (see Article 23) in *The Structure of Behavior* and *Phenomenology of Perception*. Lefort elaborates a critique of the "scientific point of view" in the social sciences in his article "The Permanence of the Theologico-Political?" (1988, pp. 213–56). In its social science variant, positivism contends that modern society divides itself into different spheres: the economic, the juridical, the technical, and so forth. Each sphere becomes the object of a specific science. Knowledge of the whole is effected by a synthesis of the various sciences and, correlatively, of the various independent spheres of society. Lefort argues that such a procedure denies any prior knowledge of the whole, without which knowledge of the various spheres would be impossible. The allegedly independent spheres are always already seen *as* spheres of the same society. In a manner analogous to Merleau-Ponty's contention – that the analytic decomposition of the peceived object into sensations and its reconstruction by the "laws of association," or judgment, presupposes a prior knowledge of the perceived object, and that the object serves as the guiding thread of its own reconstruction – Lefort claims that there is a flesh of the social into which "facts," as well as the subject who knows them, are intertwined. According to him, the attempt to disengage independent spheres of intelligibility is motivated by the epistemological desire to disengage the knower from the known in order to confront it as an object. He elaborates upon a remark of Merleau-Ponty that "Being is not in front of us but around us." In his article "The Question of Democracy," he writes: "The corollary of the desire to objectify is the positioning of a subject capable of performing intellectual operations which owe nothing to its involvement in social life" (1988, p. 12). At this point Lefort's thought joins the contemporary critique of the subject.

According to him, the question of social identity is not pursued on the level of a real determination, but rather on the level of representation. However, it is not a representation that remains at a distance from what it *re*-presents, rather it is a representation which is constituted by what it represents. A society without a representation of itself is unthinkable. He refers this quasi-representation, which is constitutive of society's self-identity, to the synthesis that the body effects on itself in the thought of Merleau-Ponty. In *Phenomenology of Perception*, he spoke of a "body schema." On the societal level, Lefort speaks of a "*mise-en-scène*." This is not a picture, or an image, any more than the body schema is; rather it is a synthesis, or

485

more properly speaking, an intertwining of the visible and the invisible. It is a quasi-representation by which a society unifies its dispersion in both space and time.

The figure of the God-man, Christ, is for Lefort a central figure of the *mise-en-scène* by which pre-modern European societies constituted their political identity. He finds in Kantorowicz's *The King's Two Bodies: A Study in Medieval Political Theology*, an interrogation of the figure of the God-man which was not undertaken by modern philosophy. I shall briefly summarize the use to which Lefort puts Kantorowicz's analysis. The double nature of Christ, human and divine, serves as an *imago* through which the European monarchy was constituted. As Christ was both human and divine, likewise the Church constituted a mystical body, both visible and invisible, with the Pope as a figure of mediation between the temporal and the eternal, between the faithful and Christ. The secularization of this notion issues in the figure of the kingdom, the realm, unified as a quasi-mystical body with the king as its head, and in like manner, as a mediation between God and men. In virtue of this role of mediator, the king has two bodies: body of nature; and body of grace. His body is the point of intersection between the visible and the invisible.

The king represents at the same time the unity of the realm, and the intersection with the divine through which the operations of power have their legitimacy. The unity thus constituted transcends the level of events, particular occurrences, and engenders a unity and identity in depth by which the living are put into relation to the dead and to the future. This unity is projected on the body of the king. According to Lefort, the figure of the king's body as overcoming both spatial and temporal dispersion, and as the focal point of the Divine origin of legitimacy, is not simply a "mystification" concealing the process of the extraction of surplus value, or masking the operations of power. Rather it constitutes the social space within which class conflicts can operate, and within which one can distinguish between the legitimate and the illegitimate uses of power. The king as mediator between the body politic and the Divine is not a theory; thus it is neither true nor false. Rather it opens the space in which one can distinguish between the true and the false in social and political discourse.

In pre-modernity, there is an intertwining of the religious and the political. Concerning religion, Lefort writes:

> What philosophy discovers in religion is a mode of portraying or dramatizing the relations that human beings establish with something that goes beyond empirical time and the space within which they establish relations with one another. This work of the imagination stages [*met en scène*] a different time, a different space. Any attempt to reduce it to being simply a product of human activity is doomed. . . . Once we recognize that humanity opens on to itself by being held in an opening it does not create, we have to accept that the change in religion is not to be read simply as a sign that the divine is a human invention, but as a sign of the deciphering of the divine or, beneath the appearance of the divine, of the excess of *being* over *appearance*. (1988, p. 223)

For Lefort religion, in our secular age, does not consist of a compendium of curious beliefs that unenlightened men were once credulous enough to entertain. Rather, according to him, this view attests to the vanity of perceiving the social and the political fields as purely and simply a product of human invention. That is to say, his position offers a critique of humanism. The root of man is not, as Marx wrote, man himself, but – interpreted under the divine – is "an excess of being over appearance," a power of revelation which philosophy cannot surpass. Religion poses, in its own way, the non-identity of society with itself, the *écart* which defers society's identity with itself. As the immanence of the body with itself is, in the thought of Merleau-Ponty, perpetually deferred, likewise the immanence of the body politic is, according to Lefort, also deferred and submitted to a non-identity with itself – a difference from itself, an irreducible alterity. Religion "dramatizes" the Other. Religious discourse orchestrates a problematic of difference. Lefort borrows a term from the psychoanalytical writings of Lacan – the notion of the *symbolic*. Concerning this notion, he writes in the review *Psychanalystes* in an issue devoted to *Le Mythe de l'Un dans le Fantasme et dans la Réalité Politique*, "When we speak of symbolic organization, symbolic constitution, we seek to disclose beyond practices, beyond relations, beyond institutions which arise from factual givens, either natural or historical, an ensemble of articulations which are not *deducible* from nature or from history, but which order the apprehension of that which presents itself as real" (1983, p. 42).

Consider now the new dimension of political existence that emerges with modernity. Speaking of the symbolic order that characterizes pre-modernity, Lefort writes:

> This symbolic [*dispositif symbolique*] has the peculiar characteristic of being able to secure the conditions of occultation without which could arise the question of an opposition between the imaginary and the real. Indeed, the real turns out to be determinable only in so far as it is assumed to be already determined, by virtue of an utterance which, mythical or religious, attests to a knowledge whose basis cannot be brought into play by the actual process of knowledge, by technical inventiveness or by the interpretation of the *visible*. (1986, p. 198)

Religious discourse fixes social determinations as natural and dissimulates "social division in the representation of a division which is massively affirmed – in the representation, that is, of another world, of a materialized invisible" (1986, p. 198). The religious, or the mythical, representations are not ideological, rather they are efficacious. In a pre-modern society the social divisions – the articulation of Law, Power, and Knowledge – are determined from *another place*. The point of mediation between society and this other place is the body of the king. The body of the sovereign marks the place in which the social body, the body politic, is incarnated. The king is the point of mediation between the sensible world and the supersensible world; the place from which the social institution is marked as determin*able* only insofar as it is already determin*ed*.

The regicide enacted by the French Revolution constituted an erosion of all guarantees of certainty for the social division. The disappearance of the supersensible guarantee of the social institution institutes a new *dispositif symbolique* in which

487

the place of social identity becomes an empty place. This place is not empty in the absolute sense, as my office is empty of alligators, but rather it is empty on the horizon of a moment in which this place was once occupied. This event contains certain latencies. Lefort analyzes both Democracy and Totalitarianism as latencies within this new *dispositif symbolique*. The event which presides over both of them is the disappearance of the image of the king as guarantor of social identity, as mediator between *the visible and the invisible*. The place of social identity is symbolically an empty place; this remains the symbolic dimension of the social. This place, symbolically empty, constitutes a new form of legitimacy without identity.

Recalling that for Lefort, religion is "grafted on a more original experience," I shall describe the new manner of experiencing the world and the social that happens with the onset of modern democracy. Speaking of this democracy Lefort writes, "This shaping [*mise en forme*] testifies to a new determination-figuration of *the place of power*" (1988, pp. 224–5). As we have seen, the place of power in the *Ancien Régime* is *another place*. In its modern form this other place does not disappear; it remains an empty place. Modern society maintains an exteriority from itself; this exteriority from itself is what permits it to have a quasi-reflection on itself. Note that Lefort is not doing transcendental reflection; it is what Merleau-Ponty called "hyper-reflection." The difference is striking and important: his reflection does not lead to a system of categories that are unconditional, as with Kant, but rather to a particular symbolic dispositive which is itself contingent and generated by history. For Lefort, the characteristic mis-recognition of this new configuration is the following: once having noted the disappearance of this discourse on "another place," one then concludes that society is intelligible radically in terms of itself. Which is to say that a society is intelligible in terms of the *real*. To evoke and paraphrase the famous formula of Feuerbach: having ceased being lovers of God, to become lovers of men; having ceased being theologians to become anthropologists. This is the gesture that initiates positivism on the level of political theory. After this it is simply a question of which real process will be given causal efficacity: forces and relations of production; tendency toward functional equilibrium; technological progress; etc.

One of the merits of Lefort's political philosophy is to recognize that even with the disappearance of "another place," modern society continues to manifest an exteriority of society with itself, assuring it of a quasi-representation of itself. But he writes:

> We must of course be careful not to project this externality on to the real; if we did so it would no longer have any meaning for society. It would be more accurate to say that power makes a gesture towards something *outside*, and that it defines itself in terms of an outside. Whatever its form, it always refers to the same enigma: that of an internal-external articulation, of a division which institutes a common space, of a break which establishes relations, of a movement of the externalization of the social which goes hand in hand with its internalization. (1988, p. 225)

To say that the social no longer exists in function of its relationship to something else is not to say that it is identical with itself. Rather it is a form of society which maintains in its own particular way the divergence (*écart*) of the symbolic and the real. This place emptied of the figure of the Other is the place in which the distinction between the symbolic and the real is maintained. Modern society effaces the *figure* but not the *dimension of the Other*. This dimension of the Other cannot be materialized, or incarnated, in a determined figure of the Other. It remains radically indefinite. The source of legitimacy in a democratic regime is *the people*, but the people remains indeterminate.

In this democratic regime, unlike the pre-modern regime, there is no distinct figuration of the Other; correlatively there is no figure which incarnates the One. This radical indeterminacy of the people is a central tenet of Lefort's conception of modern democracy. The democratic regime is defined by the legitimacy of division and conflict. The democratic form of society, by eliminating the reference to *another place*, opens a space proper to the political. According to Lefort, the identity of the people remains latent; it is dependent on the discourse which expresses it. There is no one who is a priori certified to speak in the name of the people. Each one does speak in the name of the people, but each is *legitimately* contradicted by others who, with as much right, also evoke the name of the people.

I can now consider the latencies that Lefort finds linked to this symbolic dispositive. He understands democracy as the disincarnation of society; "there is no power linked to a body" (1986, p. 303). The symbolic place of society's identity with itself remains empty. In a democratic society, this place can only be occupied temporarily and through procedural rules that legitimate opposition and contestation. There is an irreducible exteriority of power from itself; its center does not coincide with a point of mediation which would link it to a supersensible domain, to another place. The exercise of power and its legitimacy are inextricably intertwined. Lefort writes:

> There is no law that can be fixed, whose articles cannot be contested, whose foundations are not susceptible of being called into question. . . . There is no representation of a center and of the contours of society: unity cannot now efface social division. Democracy inaugurates the experience of an ungraspable, uncontrollable society in which the people will be said to be sovereign, of course, but whose identity will constantly be open to question, whose identity will remain latent. (1986, pp. 303–4)

Modern democratic society is radically historical.

Democracy exists within the indices of a certain contradiction. Its legitimacy arises from the people, but because the people are radically plural – since there is no body, no king, that incarnates social identity – the legitimacy of democratic power is threatened in two respects, from two directions. Since legitimacy arises from the people and inasmuch as the people have no unified representation, the one who exercises power – insofar as he/she is a particular person – faces the threat of the cancelation of his/her symbolic legitimacy and of being denounced as a usurper, as one who rules in the name of the people but who in fact serves personal or private interests. In short, the democratic leader risks falling from the symbolic into partic-

489

ularity, into the real, thereby exposing him/herself to contempt – something Machiavelli judged more dangerous than hatred. Legitimacy must continuously be re-established through discourse; however, when such discursive validation fails, the state is perceived as the "executive committee of the ruling class." This possible loss of symbolic legitimacy is endemic to democracy because of the indeterminate and divided nature of the people. It is in terms of this structured possibility of the erosion of legitimacy that Lefort views the possibility of the emergence of the totalitarian state. He writes:

> With totalitarianism an apparatus is set up which tends to stave off this threat, which tends to weld power and society back together again, to efface all signs of social division, to banish the indetermination that haunts the democratic experience. But this attempt, as I have suggested, itself draws on a democratic source, developing and fully affirming the idea of the People-as-One, the idea of society as such, bearing the knowledge of itself, transparent to itself and homogeneous, the idea of mass opinion, sovereign and normative, the idea of the tutelary state.   (1986, p. 305)

With totalitarianism there is a re-emergence of the body, the social body as the incarnation of the society with itself. The social division is foreclosed on the level of the symbolic; and thus division, opposition, is viewed as emanating from the outside – from Jews, cosmopolitans, foreign agents, mad people, etc. The foreclosure of difference and division on the level of the symbolic gives rise to the phantasm of the body of the People-as-One on the level of the imagination. This phantasm of the One-Undivided-People is incarnated in the State, the Party, the Führer, the Egocrat, in a place in which there is a condensation of power, law, and knowledge. This phantasmatic image of the People-as-One annuls the very notion of social heterogeneity; legitimate antagonism of interests is rendered impossible, and thus those who announce the factual conflicts of interests are denounced as enemies of the people.

In the totalitarian regime all references to transcendence are suspended. In democracy there is a disentangling of the symbolic order and the divine; and since there is no body of the king to represent the point of mediation between the human and the divine, there is a disincarnation of society. At the same time, modern democratic society maintains a gap between the real and the symbolic in the place left empty by the disappearance of the king. Whereas in totalitarian society there is an attempt to abolish the symbolic order altogether, and replace it by an imaginary representation of the unity of society with itself through the body of the Führer or the Egocrat.

Totalitarianism, born as it is from the dissolution of symbolic legitimacy, wishes to annul all aspects of the indeterminate. Out of the fear engendered by society's perception of itself as fragmented (*morcelée*) ". . . we see the development of the fantasy of the People-as-One, the beginning of a quest for a substantial identity, for a social body which is welded to its head, for an incarnated power, for a State delivered from division" (1988, p. 20). Totalitarianism wishes to abolish the Other. Through the imaginary identification with the image of the People-as-One, totali-

490

tarianism would foreclose the symbolic order and with it the dimension of the Other. For Lefort the project of democracy is to retain the place, but not the figure, of the Other.

## Writings by Lefort in English

Lefort, C.: *The Political Forms of Modern Society: Bureaucracy, Democracy, Totalitarianism*, ed. John Thompson (Cambridge, MA.: MIT Press, 1986).
——: *Democracy and Political Theory*, tr. David Macey (Cambridge: Polity Press, 1988).
——: "Machiavelli: history, politics, discourse." In *The State of Theory* (New York: Columbia University Press, 1990), pp. 113–24.

## Writings by Lefort in French

Lefort, C.: *Éléments d'une critique de la bureaucratie* (Genève: Droz, 1971).
——: *Le Travail de l'oeuvre Machiavel* (Paris: Gallimard, 1972).
——: *Un Homme en trop: Reflections sur l'Archipel du Goulag* (Paris: Seuil, 1976).
——: *Les Formes de l'histoire: Essais d'anthropologie politique* (Paris: Gallimard, 1978).
——: *Sur une colonne absente: Écrits autour de Merleau-Ponty* (Paris: Gallimard, 1978).
Mouchard, C.: "Claude Lefort: une pensée politique," *Critique*, Decembre (1980), pp. 1111–23.
——: *L'Invention démocratique: Les limites de la domination totalitaire* (Paris: Fayard, 1981).
——: *Le Mythe de l'Un dans le fantasme et dans la réalité politique, Psychanalystes*, 9 (1983).
——: *Essais sur le politique, XIX–XX siècles* (Paris: Seuil, 1986).
Lefort, C.: "La Révolution comme religion nouvelle." In *The French Revolution and the Creation of Modern Political Culture* (Oxford: Pergamon Press, 1989), pp. 391–9.
——: "La dissolution des repères et l'enjeu démocratique." In *L'Humain à l'image de Dieu* (Genève: Labor et Fides, 1989), pp. 89–108.
——: "Renaissance de la démocratie," *Pouvoirs, Revue Française d'études constitutionnelles et politiques*, 52 (1990), pp. 5–22.
——: "La liberté à l'ère du relativisme." In *Les Usages de la liberté*, Rencontres internationales de Genève (Editions de la Baconnière, 1990).
——: Édition de *La Monarchie* de Dante accompagnée d'une introduction (Paris: Belin, 1993), pp. 1–72.
——: *Écrire: A l'épreuve du politique* (Paris: Calmann-Levy, 1992).

## References and further reading

Chene, Janine: "Penser le politique," in *Ethique et Philosophie Politique* (Paris: Editions Odile Jacob, 1988), pp. 134–48.
Flynn, Bernard: "Lefort: the flesh of the political." In *Political Philosophy at the Closure of Metaphysics* (London: Humanities Press, 1992), pp. 164–203.
Habib, Claude, and Claude Mouchard (eds): *La Démocratie a l'oeuvre: Autour de Claude Lefort* (Paris: Éditions Esprit, 1993).
Kantorowicz, Ernst: *The King's Two Bodies: A Study in Medieval Political Theology* (Princeton, NJ: Princeton University Press, 1957).

# 45

# Castoriadis*

## FABIO CIARAMELLI

"Being is *what requires creation of us* for us to experience it," wrote Maurice Merleau-Ponty in *The Visible and the Invisible* (1968 [1964], p. 197; emphasis in the original).

The vigorous claim that *creation*, in an ontologically weighty sense, is not simply required or summoned forth by Being but constitutive of its very occurrence, forms the originality and the common denominator of Cornelius Castoriadis's political, psychoanalytical, and philosophical contribution to contemporary thought.

Having arrived in France at a young age in 1945 (he was born in Constantinople in 1992 and soon moved to Athens), Castoriadis has in effect, and almost always simultaneously, been a politi-cal activist, a revolutionary theorist, and an econo-mist, to become later on, at the beginning of the 1970s, a psychoanalyst. Although "smitten" early on by the questions of philosophy, he at first led a life of political activity and reflection without becoming directly involved in philosophy, properly speaking. It was at this time that he wrote his texts for *Socialisme ou Barbarie* (1949–65), which were later reprinted in the eight volumes of the Éditions 10/18 collection (1973–9) and then partially translated in the three volumes of his *Political and Social Writings* (1988a [1946–55] and 1988b [1955–60], 1993 [1961–79]). Since then, his initial preoccupation with the "revolutionary question, the question of the self-transformation of society" (1997a [1981], p. 312) has led to a general renewal of the problems of philosophy. Here we shall attempt to elucidate this problematic by looking at the capital theme of creation.

The point of departure for Castoriadis's philosophical reflection is the observation that a profound analogy exists between the questions and tasks with which politics, as the goal of social autonomy, is confronted and those with which psycho-analysis is confronted in its effort to foster individual autonomy. Castoriadis proposes to reflect on politics and psychoanalysis together in attempting to offer a new account of the irreducible tension that exists between the properly singular dimension of the human being and the collective dimension, which is at once social and historical. This irreducible tension may be said to provide the texture for the concrete existence of the *individual*, so long as one takes care not to reproduce the abstraction (denounced, already, by Marx) whereby one separates and opposes individual and society (1984 [1978], pp. 38–9). The individual is never anything but a *social individual*, an individual socialized in and through the social institutions

*Translated by David Ames Curtis.

as they each time are given. The irreducibility or the tension is not, therefore, between the individual and the society but between the "monadic core" of the *singular psyche* and the collective field of the *social-historical*. The social individual is the outcome of the process by which a given society socializes the singular psyche, a process that never succeeds in abolishing the polarity between psyche and society or in resolving the former into the latter. "Starting with the psyche, . . . the instituted society each time makes the individuals – which, as such, can henceforth only make the society which has made them" (1991 [1988], p. 146). Whence comes, then, society's alteration, its historicity? It is thanks, precisely, to the irreducibility of the *radical imagination* of the singular psyche to the social individual that the latter is not limited to being a factor in the reproduction of instituted society but is just as much a vector of its alteration. This implies, at the same time, that, in virtue of the ongoing work of "*instituting* society" within "*instituted* society" (1987 [1964–5], p. 112), the social field is irreducible to its each time instituted historical figure.

The central place Castoriadis accords to the *creative* dimension of this psyche/ society polarity, which culminates in social individuals, is the basis for his philosophical reflection on politics and on psychoanalytic practice.

(1)   As concerns politics, it should be recalled that, as both activist and theoretician, Castoriadis criticized from the outset and in a radical way Russian "bureaucratic totalitarianism" in the name of the political project of the *self-transformation of society*. The basic content of this project is the deployment of the autonomous activity of individuals and social groups, and its goal is for society to achieve effective self-government. It is starting from this critique and from this project – which did not enjoy majority support when the European Left was fascinated by the myth of the USSR but which also was in the minority after the collapse of "Marxism," when this same Left discovered, in an equally a-critical manner, the virtues of "free-market" economic liberalism – that he arrived at the idea that *human history is creation*, creation in the full sense of the term, ontological genesis: the surging forth and positing of unprecedented and irreducible forms of social and collective life.

In Castoriadis, the break with Marxism has become the basis for a political-theoretical itinerary that is incomparable to the itineraries of so many former Marxists who have come to sing the praises of contemporary Western society and "free-market" liberal capitalism, which supposedly furnish the conditions for the only sort of democracy possible – "really existing democracy," one might say in memory of Leonid Brezhnev's defense of "really existing socialism." Quite to the contrary, in Castoriadis the critique of bureaucratic totalitarianism has repercussions for the analysis of Western societies and permits one to discover another form of bureaucratic *alienation* in the alienation of individuals to the *instituted imaginary*, the imaginary of a pseudorational mastery of reality, the imaginary of unlimited economic growth, the imaginary of the enslavement of human life to economics "as central (and, in fact, *unique*) value" (1997a [1989], p. 416).

Marxism reached this point because it shared the dominant tendency of the modern capitalist imaginary, namely, humanity's alienation from its own works. In contemporary society, this alienation takes on the features of bureaucratic pseudorationalization, which is at once a political and an economic phenomenon expressive of "the most deep-seated tendencies of modern capitalist production. . . . In the main, the division of contemporary societies . . . into classes no longer corresponds to the division between owners and nonowners, but instead to the much more deep-seated division, which is much more difficult to eliminate, between *directors* and *executants*," order-givers and order-takers (1974 [1957], p. 386).

On this basis, one can discern the genuine and intrinsic contradiction in the process of bureaucratization. Contemporary society "is contradictory in the same way a neurotic individual is so: it can try to carry out its intentions only through acts that constantly thwart these same intentions" (1988b [1961], p. 259). Whether this contradiction is manifested at the level of production, of politics, or of culture, the institutions of contemporary society are designed explicitly to *distance* citizens from public affairs, to persuade them that they are incapable of involving themselves in such affairs, while complaining at the very same time about citizens' passivity and apathy and appealing to them to participate. In brief, contemporary society pursues the chimera of individuals "who always can be found simultaneously at the height of enthusiasm and in the depths of passivity" (1988a [1972], p. 19).

Thenceforth, as Castoriadis wrote in 1964, "If the term *barbarism* has a meaning today, it is neither fascism nor poverty nor a return to the Stone Age. It is precisely this 'air-conditioned nightmare,' consumption for the sake of consumption in private life, organization for the sake of organization in collective life, as well as their corollaries: privatization, withdrawal, and apathy as regards matters shared in common, and dehumanization of social relationships" (1993 [1964], pp. 46–7).

The present phase seems to be characterized by the increasingly passive acceptance of the autonomization of the imaginary of *limitless development* (1991 [1974–6], pp. 176–218). "At the same time that the rage for 'power,' the fetishism for a 'rational mastery,' waxes triumphant, the other great imaginary signification of Greco-Western history – that of autonomy, notably in its political manifestations – seems to be suffering an eclipse. The present crisis of humanity is a crisis of politics in the grand sense" (1991 [1987], p. 274), a crisis of the democratic *ethos*, a crisis of praxis.

What emerges from all the foregoing, therefore, is a substantive conception of politics as *praxis*, and consequently its irreducibility to any concretization of an Absolute Knowledge or to any sort of technique. "We term praxis that doing in which the other or others are intended as autonomous beings considered as the essential agents of the development of their own autonomy" (1987 [1964–5], p. 75). Political praxis breaks free from its degeneration into bureaucratic technique to the extent that it aims at the autonomy of society, at the overcoming of its alienation, that is to say, at the explicit self-institution of society.

(2) The "instauration" or originary establishment of autonomy, the overcoming of instituted heteronomy, implies an alteration of the conformism characteristic of the institution. Indeed, "there always is in institutions a central, strong, and effec-

tive element of, as well as instruments for, self-perpetuation (what we would call in psychoanalysis repetition), and the main one of these instruments is . . . the fabrication of conformable individuals" (1997b [1981], pp. 131–2), of individuals who can only reproduce the social imaginary, such as it is instituted, by internalizing the significations of which this imaginary is the vehicle. The institution of this *closure* of the individual who lives in repetition, implies the enslavement of the individual's subjective imagination to the instituted imaginary. This is the social-historical side of the psychoanalytic process of repression (1997b [1987], p. 264), and it culminates in a repression/mutilation of the creative power of the individual psychical imagination (1986 [1979], pp. 259–60).

Now, in as much as it aims at overcoming repetition while assisting the individual to become the subject of autonomous activity, psychoanalysis belongs fully to the emancipatory project of democracy and philosophy. "But, unless we are to enter into an endless repetition, the contents and objects of this activity . . . must be supplied by the soul's radical imagination. This is the source of the contribution of the individual to social-historical creation" (1997b [1987], p. 133). The above-mentioned irreducibility of psyche to society is what makes such a contribution possible. But this contribution on the part of the individual becomes a genuine and effective contribution to collective creation, and therefore something other than reverie, velleity, delirium, "only to the extent that it is taken up again on the social level," and "the conditions for its being taken up in this way . . . extend infinitely beyond what can be provided by the individual imagination" (1987 [1975], p. 264). These conditions depend on a self-alteration of the social-historical, which is the work of the *radical instituting imaginary*. Such self-alteration is possible, precisely to the extent that the social is not reduced to the institution but always goes infinitely beyond it (1987 [1964–5], pp. 111–12). The social as it is instituted is always, so to speak, worked upon by the social in its capacity as instituting, and the social *is* only in its permanent self-altering of itself. Consequently, its being escapes the identitary ontology of determinacy: in its essential temporality, in its historicity, it is not something determined, but instead incessant surging forth of other determinations. This is why societies that are *heteronomous* institute themselves in and through the *denial* of their historicity (see 1987 [1975], p. 186).

This indetermination of the being of the social-historical is the positive condition for its dynamic creativity, namely, for its ontological self-transformation. This ontological self-transformation does not come to it from the outside but instead from within itself, from its own imaginary roots, which constitute the prime moment of its instability, the source of its incessant self-alteration.

The social-historical is radically instituting because it creates its own figures in opening itself up to the contribution of the imaginary and, notably, in making it possible for "the singular social individual to have, in return, an independent action on society" (1991 [1988], p. 146). This action is possible only if the *anonymous collective* escapes identitary determinacy and nourishes itself on the creative contribution of the psyche's radical imagination. But such action is exceedingly rare in societies where instituted heteronomy reigns, since it is precisely these societies that intend to ignore (and that tend – without ever completely succeeding – to

495

abolish) the self-alteration of the social sphere. In heteronomous societies, conse-quently, "the only *ascertainable* ways in which the singular psyche can manifest itself are transgression and pathology" (ibid.).

The aim of individual autonomy is therefore to be defined as the "passage of the psyche and the heteronomous social individual to reflective and deliberative subjectivity," and it thereby implies "the elucidation of *two* different modes of sub-limation" (1997a, p. 381). There is, indeed, a "radical difference between the sublimation that leads up to an imaginary social object and the sublimation that goes beyond it" (1984 [1968], p. 39).

Despite his uncertainties on this score, what Freud was trying to think under the title of "sublimation" is the process by which the psyche comes to be socialized. The change in goal and in the object of the drive – the change that, in Freudian terms, constitutes sublimation – presupposes the social institution. 'The object of sublima-tion, an imaginary object or nonobject, is essentially social" (1984 [1968], p. 38; cf. 1987 [1975], pp. 311–20). The socialization of the psyche is the process by means of which the latter is led to cathect social objects, to satisfy its own demand for meaning in and through collective significations, which are furnished by insti-tuted society. In its tendency toward self-perpetuation, instituted society represses the individual imagination of the psyche as well as its creative role; as for psycho-analysis, it aims, precisely, at "go[ing] beyond repetition" (1997a [1988], p. 271) through the liberation of the immense creative potential of this subjective imagina-tion. "The practical essence of psychoanalytic treatment lies in this rediscovery by the individual of himself as partial origin of his history, his undergoing gratuitously the experience of making himself, which at the time was not recognized for what it was, and becoming once again origin of possibilities, as having had a history which was history and not fatality" (1984 [1968], p. 26). In this sense, psychoanalysis is not an exclusively regressive undertaking, but a "practico-poietic activity" (1984 [1968], p. 34; 1984 [1977], p. 59) which goes back to the origin only in as much as it posits and discovers this origin as *creation* (1984 [1968], pp. 25–6).

(3)   In order to elucidate the ontological implications of human creativity – whether it be at the level of the singular psyche or at the level of the social-historical – we must now broach the question of their *mode of being*. The inherited categories of thought reveal here their complete inadequacy, inasmuch as they are posited as "transregional" (1984 [1973], pp. 217–20), whereas "being is always only the being of beings, and . . . each region of beings unveils another sense of: being" (1987 [1975], p. 183). Now, within the stratified totality of *what is*, the human domain represents a specific type of being – irreducible to other regions or strata of reality – and its mode of being is *the imaginary*.

The kind of imaginary about which Castoriadis is speaking is not image *of*. "It is the unceasing and essentially *undetermined* (social-historical and psychical) cre-ation of figures/forms/images, on the basis of which alone there can ever be a question *of* 'something.' What we call 'reality' and 'rationality' are its works" (1987 [1975], p. 3). The element common to the psyche and the social-historical – which are otherwise irreducible, the one to the other – is that "for both, there is and there has to be *nonfunctional meaning*" (1997a, p. 37a). This nonfunctionality of

496

meaning created by the imaginary is decisive, as it allows us to recognize the dividing line between the human and the nonhuman. "We must postulate that a break in the psychical evolution of the animal world occurs when human beings appear," and it is by virtue of that break that "the human psychical world becomes *afunctional*. Hegel said that man is a sick animal. We must say much more than that: man is a mad animal, radically unfit for life. 'Whence' – not as 'cause,' but as condition of what is – the creation of society" (1997b [1988], p. 262). The a-functional character of the human psychism manifests itself in the rupture of the instinctual regulations of animal behavior and bases itself on the autonomization of the imagination and on the domination of representational pleasure over organ pleasure. "As we know from Freud, from psychoanalytical practice, and from everyday life," man is a being who is capable of forming "representations according to [his] desires" (1982, p. 5).

"[O]riginally," wrote Freud, "the mere existence of a [re]presentation [*Vorstellung*] was a guarantee of the reality of the [re]presented" (1961 [1925], p. 237). On this originary level, all desires are not simply fulfillable but always already fulfilled (1987 [1975], p. 296). The recognition that there is a reality shared by all, a regulated reality that does not obey the desires of the psyche, is imposed upon the psyche by the institution, for the psyche, in its originary monadic core, is "autistic" libido (1987 [1975], p. 293): at the outset, all of its psychical energy can cathect nothing other than this total unity that is the subject itself, before the emergence of separation and differentiation. It is only through its inclusion in the world that the psyche is led to exit from its monadic core and to recognize the unfulfillable character of "this desire, master of all desires, of total unification, of the abolition of difference and of distance. . . . If the unconscious is unaware of time and contradiction [as Freud said], this is also because, crouched in the darkest part of this cave, the monster of unifying madness reigns there as lord and master" (1987 [1975], p. 298).

One must recognize in the "uncanniness" of this abyssal ground of the human being – which is never fully mastered by the social-historical institution – the "first matrix of meaning, the operating-operated schema of bringing into relation [*mise en relation*] or connection. . . . It is here that the subject once was 'in person' the prototype for the connection it will always continue to search for, against all odds" (1987 [1975], p. 299). In its originary identity, which is unaware of and abolishes all difference, in the autistic identification of totalitarian and solipsistic inclusion (1987 [1975], pp. 294, 296–7), the self coincides with the whole and being is immediately meaning. The protomeaning of the solipsistic psyche "realizes by itself, just where meaning obviously cannot yet exist, total meaning, universal and unbroken bringing into relation" (1987 [1975], p. 299) – which will be continued in the theoretico-speculative phantasm of achieving a complete explanation of everything in terms of absolute identitary determination.

The matrix of meaning is therefore the "senseless character" of this "indestructible holding-together, aiming at itself and grounded on itself, the unlimited source of pleasure of which nothing is lacking and which leaves nothing to be desired" (1987 [1975], p. 294). The inclusion of the psyche in the world implies the break-up of its monadic "state," a veritable loss of self or a scission of this total self. Nevertheless, and despite all repression, it is the aim of this primal and forever lost satisfaction "that continues to reign in the fullest, rawest, most savage and intractable manner over the unconscious processes" (1987 [1975], p. 297).

Here, too, we find the birthplace of the "rational" requirement of *reductio ad unitatem* that governs the logic of inherited thought and that corresponds to the identitary dimension of reality, grasped as a functional set of distinct and well-defined terms. "It is not hard to recognize one of the origins of reason in this madness of inclusion-expansion, of plurality as unity, of the ultimate 'simplicity' of the given" (1987 [1975], p. 299).

The break-up of the psyche's monadic and solipsistic universe is the mark of its accession to reality. The demand for meaning – which constitutes the psyche's radical demand (1992, p. 87) – remains, but now its satisfaction is assured by the supply of another kind of meaning than the protomeaning of the psychical monad, namely, by a diurnal, waking, public meaning – the meaning the institution furnishes it under the form of *social imaginary significations*.

These significations, however, are not to be understood, either, as purely functional responses to the necessities of the survival of the species. "The gulf which separates the necessities of man as biological species from the needs of man as historical being is dug by the human imaginary" (1984 [1973], p. 241).

The imaginary dimension is thus irreducible to the functionality of the identitary dimension. The latter is an indispensable instrument of the social institution, but it is derivative. The institution of society is obviously made up of a host of particular institutions that form and function as a coherent whole, but their unity exceeds all functionality (1987 [1964–5], pp. 115–17). This unity of the total or overall institution of society is, therefore, the unity and the internal cohesion of the immensely complex fabric of the *magma* of social imaginary significations (1987 [1975], pp. 340–4) that orient and direct the entire life of society and of the individuals who make it up.

It is here that we encounter, in its form, the principal question raised by the contemporary age. "Due to the fact that its imaginary significations (progress, growth, material well-being, 'rational' mastery) are wearing out, society today is less and less capable of furnishing meaning" (1986 [1983], p. 102). And as we have seen, on the radical level individuals cannot fabricate their own meaning for themselves. The crisis of today's society is therefore a crisis of meaning, which includes a veritable collapse of society's self-representation. Having become autonomized, the imaginary of this society reproduces itself inertly. "Present society does not want itself as society, it endures itself"; "the typical contemporary man acts as if he were *submitting* to society," without cherishing any longer any project in relation to his society, neither that of its transformation nor even that of its preservation/reproduction. He no longer accepts social relations; he feels caught in them and he reproduces them only insofar as he cannot do otherwise. Contemporary society becomes for him an "odious chore" (1997a [1982], p. 263).

(4)  In what sense, then, does all the preceding relaunch the question of philosophy, with its eminently political import? It is relaunched precisely by way of giving

498

a new impetus to the question of creation. It is this question, in its properly ontological breadth, that must now be examined.

It is, in effect, the very Being of what is that could not even be without creation. Being is not Meaning or Ground of Meaning: Being is Chaos, Abyss, Groundlessness; it is indeterminate. But this absence of determinateness is not mere privation: Being is creation, emergence of other determinations, of new forms (*eidē*) of what is. Being requires creation of us, as Merleau-Ponty said. But this requirement is not due solely to a transcendental reason (creation is not only condition for the possibility of our experience); it also is a requirement for a more radical and originary ontological reason: Being is itself creation.

"If being is not creation, then there is no time" (1997a [1981], p. 308), therefore no emergence of radical otherness, or "alterity." In turn, "Time either is nothing or is creation" (1997b [1981], p. 3). Without creation, being would be reduced to the stability of the identical and time would be only identitary time, the time of indefinite repetition of what is; it would be only an ontologically supernumerary spatial dimension (see 1987 [1975], p. 200; 1997a [1981], p. 308). For time to be grasped in its ontological thickness, for it not to be reduced to the needs of marking and measure (1987 [1975], p. 190), for it to be conceived as genuine time, irreducible to space, the time of shattering apart, of emergence, of ontological genesis, of the surging forth of radical alterity, it has to be conceived as creation. In this sense, "creation, being, and time go together" (1986, p. 8).

Let us try to elucidate this ontological point. Contrary to what the inherited ontology maintains, Being is not determinacy, stability, or system; it is not some thing, a subsistent being, *ousia*, congealed into its thematic positing in a present. Being is not *theme*, placed before a gaze that inspects its stable or passing determination, where the movement or process of becoming would coagulate – since, in order to affect Being, becoming would none the less remain ontologically inferior to the accomplished plenitude of its exercise of being. It is this very exercise, it is the very work of Being itself that is permanent self-alteration, explosion of its present, wrenching of its passing identity, distortion of the *theme* in which it places itself or coagulates itself when congealed into a present, an unfolding that escapes *system* and *synthesis*, and this is so precisely because the very work of Being produces itself as a permanent surging forth of alterity. Thus is there emergence or self-engenderment of the radical Other, a self-alteration of Being which explodes its gathering into presence – and which thereby makes its essential temporality unfold under the form of originary temporalization. But it is also the self-alteration of the Same, in which its modifications, its avatars, its new figures are produced as types or forms, as *eidē* that could not be deduced, produced, or composed on the basis of what was already there. The new form is ontologically new, precisely because it is *created*: it emerges as *other*. Radical, ontological alterity is irreducible to diversity or difference, that is, to a different arrangement of the same: properly speaking, the different is not the Other of the Same; it shares the same time, its form proves to be reducible to that of the Same. The radical Other supposes a discontinuity of time, an ontological heterogeneity: its alterity is not spatial, but temporal (1987 [1975], pp. 194–201).

Time is the other name for Being only if Being is grasped as "Chaos with a nonregular stratification" (1997b [1981], p. 3). This Chaos includes "a radical incompleteness of every determination *between* strata of Being/being [*être/étant*]" (1997b [1986], p. 353). It therefore must be said that Being is not simply "in" Time, but that it *is* "through" Time. "In essence, being is time" (1997b [1981], p. 3). "Or Being is essentially to-be" (1997b [1986 addition to 1981], p. 3).

Creation is therefore ontological genesis producing itself in, through, and as Being/Time. "The *present*, the *nun*, is here explosion, split, rupture – the rupture of what is as such. This present exists as originating . . . as the surging forth of onto-logical genesis. What is contained *in* this present is not contained *there*, for it is burst asunder as a determined 'place' in which something determined could simply stand. . . . Social-historical time – time that *is* the social-historical itself – allows us to apprehend the most pregnant, the most striking form of this time" (1987 [1975], p. 201).

And yet, the social-historical is instituted as the denial of time and of alterity, a denial that functions as a psychical compensation (1987 [1975], pp. 213–14). With the aid of such compensation, heteronomous society offers to socialized indi-viduals the means for them to defend themselves against the vertigo of the Abyss of Being. Each human bears this Abyss within himself, in the innermost depths of his psyche. The work of the social institution, what is so appropriately called socializa-tion, consists in occulting it and covering it up.

Ontological genesis is therefore radical creation in as much as it is "this faculty of making be, of bringing out of itself modes of being, determinations, and laws that will henceforth be that self's laws, determinations, modes of being. . . . But what is this 'self' that makes itself be, without 'yet' being a determinate something, but which *is going* to *determine* itself thus and not otherwise? This is what I call the Groundless, the Chaos, the Abyss of the (singular or collective) human being" (1997a [1989], p. 404).

There is, therefore, radical creation in which the new form is irreducible to the one that is already there and is impossible to compose on the basis of the previous form. But this is creation of self, self-creation, in which the self that makes itself be without "yet" being determined – the Chaos of Being – remains as an unfathomable point of origin that prevents this same creation from being conceived as presuppo-sitionless linear advance. "*Creation presupposes itself*" (1991 [1983], p. 94; cf. 1987 [1975], p. 249) and it is impossible to exit from this primitive and originary circle (see my own text in the Busino volume, 1989, pp. 87–104).

The being of what is is not to be thought of as a determinate stability but as an ever-recommencing event or occurrence, with irregular stratification, that unceas-ingly entails its own modification, its transfiguration, the possibility of being other-wise. This verbality [*verbalité*] of being is its originary temporality, a temporality that should not be envisaged as a fall into time or as an imitation of the eternal but as the very unfolding of the essence of being. Being is Time, precisely because the essence of Being is nothing other than the laying out of its temporal work, the surging forth of new forms or figures of what is, the self-engendering of the Other starting from the Same, without this incessant self-alteration presupposing any inalterable ground or foundation.

This ontological genesis in and through Time, which is itself the self-creation of Being in its discontinuity and in its ruptures, is not sayable or accessible in itself. It is out of the question that one might approach it at its initial or ultimate origin, for every approach already presupposes it. It would be illusory to want to inspect it or contemplate it panoramically from the outside. We can only speak about it after the fact. And the "after the fact" is, here, originary.

That does not mean only that this circularity – the impossibility of getting away from the "after the fact" – precludes any "God's-eye view" (*pensée de survol*), obliges us to abandon all privileging of the theoretico-speculative attitude, and confers upon the hermeneutic circle a derivative and second-order status. It implies, above all, a recognition of an originary circularity of creation in itself, of ontological temporality in its *kath' auto*, independent of our inability to grasp it speculatively. It should even be said that this inability of ours depends above all on the circular status of ontological genesis, on the fact that it presupposes itself.

All of what is, in its fact of being and its mode of being, is time – that is to say, the surging forth of radical alterity, self-alteration, self-engenderment, and therefore self-creation. It thereby presupposes this *autos*, this "self" that makes itself be in being and in becoming, without "yet" being what it is going to be, but in being "already" that on the basis of which it is going to self-alter itself.

This *autos* is the very Abyss of Being from which the human emerges. It emerges from this Abyss in creating meaning, in creating itself as instance of meaning, source of significations. Being does not have meaning, it is that "place" alone in which a meaning can be created. Humanity, in creating the institution, the *form* of the institution, creates itself as humanity (1991 [1988], p. 64). This creation finds conditions and limits outside itself, but these conditions and these limits do not *determine* it.

As a matter of fact, the existence of the institution signifies that we are already in the instituted, that the institution is originary, that one cannot go back beyond it in order to create it as if this creation did not presuppose anything. Humanity creates itself as humanity and as *this* humanity, but one could not impute this creation to a collective Subject that would precede its own work. Here, the identitary logic of attribution is irrelevant. The originary, unfathomable Groundlessness is the Other of Reason, the Other of radical alterity, yet it is also strangely familiar, for it is this Groundlessness that – in its incessant alteration, and in its innumerable avatars – haunts the abyss of the psyche and constitutes the source for its both creative and destructive power.

Here, we are touching upon the intractable aporia of the origin, the radical self-presupposition of the origin, which constitutes the ultimate limit of every ontological elucidation and of every political project. This ineliminable self-presupposition does not "explain" anything, in the sense that the before would explain the after or would allow one to deduce it. But this self-presupposition does allow us, in the most acute and striking manner, to posit the philosophical project as the project of putting oneself into question. The sole possible foundation for this project is self-foundation and its sole possible limitation is self-limitation.

Philosophy interrogates the abyss of being and, in its unlimited questioning of the instituted, it aims at the instauration of a new relation to this abyss from which the institution emerges, a relation as free and lucid as possible. To stand up straight and face the abyss (1997b [1978–80], p. 324), to border on it without denying it, to become capable of living at the edge of the Abyss (1997b [1987], p. 136), such is the project of philosophy. Its import is eminently political in character, inasmuch as all of the foregoing implies that the Abyss or the Groundlessness of Being is not lived as a curse but as an incessant appeal to human creativity.

## Writings

Castoriadis, C.: "Bilan, perspectives, tâches," *Socialisme ou Barbarie*, 21 (March 1957); reprinted in *L'Expérience du mouvement ouvrier*, vol. 1: *Comment lutter* (Paris: Editions 10/18, 1974).

——: "Interview with Cornelius Castoriadis," in *Psych-Critique*, 2 (1982), pp. 3–8.

——: *Les Carrefours du labyrinthe* (Paris: Seuil, 1978); tr. Martin H. Ryle and Kate Soper, *Crossroads in the Labyrinth* (Brighton: Harvester, 1984).

——: *Domaines de l'homme: Les Carrefours du labyrinthe II* (Paris: Seuil, 1986). [Some of these writings have appeared in English as Castoriadis 1991, 1993, 1997a, and 1997b]

——: *L'Institution imaginaire de la société* (Paris: Seuil, 1975); tr. Kathleen Blamey, *The Imaginary Institution of Society* (Oxford: Polity, and Cambridge, MA: MIT, 1987). (The first half of this book consists of "Marxism and Revolutionary Theory," which was published in the final issues of *Socialisme ou Barbarie*, 36–40 [1964–5]. Excerpts from both parts appear in 1997a.)

——: *Political and Social Writings*, tr. David Ames Curtis, vol. 1: *1946–1955: From the Critique of Bureaucracy to the Positive Content of Socialism* (Minneapolis, MN: University of Minnesota Press, 1988a).

——: *Political and Social Writings*, tr. David Ames Curtis, vol. 2: *1955–1960: From the Workers' Struggle Against Bureaucracy to Revolution in the Age of Modern Capitalism* (Minneapolis, MN: University of Minnesota Press, 1988b).

——: *Philosophy, Politics, Autonomy*, ed. David Ames Curtis (New York: Oxford, 1991).

——: "Passion and knowledge," *Diogenes*, 160, Winter (1992), pp. 75–93.

——: *Political and Social Writings*, tr. David Ames Curtis, vol. 3: *1961–1979: Recommencing the Revolution: From Socialism to the Autonomous Society* (Minneapolis, MN: University of Minnesota Press, 1993).

——: *The Castoriadis Reader*, ed. David Ames Curtis (Oxford: Blackwell Publishers, 1997a).

——: *World in Fragments*, tr. David Ames Curtis (Stanford: Stanford Unversily Press, 1997b).

## References and secondary sources consulted

Busino, Giovanni (ed.): *Autonomie et auto-transformation de la society: La philosophie militante de Cornelius Castoriadis* (Geneva and Paris: Droz, 1989). (This volume previously appeared in vol. 28 of the *Revue Européenne des Sciences Soliales*, 86 (1989). It includes discussions of Castoriadis's work by Giovanni Busino, Edgar Morin, Pierre Vidal-Naquet, Eugène

Enriquez, Kan Eguchi, Attilio Mangano, Vincent Descombes, Fabio Ciaramelli, Mihály Vajda, J. M. Bernstein, Francis Guibal, Bernhard Waldenfels, Agnes Heller, Hans Joas, Axel Honneth, Hans G. Furth, Joel Whitebook, Jean-Pierre Dupuy, Philippe Raynaud, Andrew Arato, David Ames Curtis, Johann P. Arnason, Luc Ferry, Evelyne Pisier, Sergio Zorrilla, Jean-Pierre Siméon, Ferenc Fehér, Sunil Khilnani, Hugues Poltier, and Gérald Berthoud, in addition to Castoriadis's response, "Done and to be done", translated in 1997b.)

Freud, Sigmund: *Die Verneinung* (1925), in *Gesammelte Werke*, vol. 14; tr. James Strachey, *Negation*, in *Standard Edition* (London: Hogarth, 1961), vol. 19, p. 237.

Habermas, Jürgen: "Excursus on Castoriadis," in *The Philosophical Discourse of Modernity*, tr. Frederick Lawrence (Oxford: Polity, 1987), pp. 318–35.

Merleau-Ponty, Maurice: *The Visible and the Invisible* (1964), tr. Alphonso Lingis (Evanston, IL: Northwestern University Press, 1968).

Reitter, Karl: "Perspectiven der Freud-Rezeption," in Cornelius Castoriadis, Agnes Heller, et al., *Die Institutionen des Imaginären: zur Philosophie von C. Castoriadis* (Berlin: Turia und Kant, 1991), pp. 103–29.

## Further readings in English

Arnason, Johann: "Culture and imaginary significations," *Thesis Eleven*, 22 (1989), pp. 25–45.

Curtis, David Ames: "Cornelus Castoriadis," in *Social Theory: A Guide to Central Thinkers*, ed. Peter Beilharz (North Sydney: Allen & Unwin, 1992), pp. 46–53.

Curtis, David Ames (ed.): *Thesis Eleven*, 49 (May 1997). (This special issue devoted to Castoriadis on the occasion of his 75th birthday includes texts by Vassilis Lambropoulos, Stathis Gourgouris, Fabio Ciaramelli, and Stephen Hastings-King, as well as two new texts by Castoriadis.)

Hirsh, Arthur: "Castoriadis and *Socialisme ou Barbarie*," in *The French New Left: An Intellectual History from Sartre to Gorz* (Boston, MA: South End Press, 1981), pp. 108–37.

Howard, Dick: "Introduction to Castoriadis," *Telos*, 23 (Spring 1975), pp. 117–31.

——: "Ontology and the political project" and "Cornelius Castoriadis: ontology as political," in *The Marxian Legacy*, 2nd edn (Minneapolis, MN: University of Minnesota Press; London: Macmillan, 1988), pp. 224–63 and 365–71.

Rundell, John: "From the shores of reason to the horizon of meaning," *Thesis Eleven*, 22 (1989), pp. 5–24.

Singer, Brian: "The early Castoriadis: socialism, barbarism and the bureaucratic thread," *Canadian Journal of Political and Social Theory*, 3 (Fall 1979), pp. 35–56.

——: "The later Castoriadis: institutions under interrogation," *Canadian Journal of Political and Social Theory*, 4 (Winter 1980), pp. 75–101.

Thompson, John B.: "Ideology and the social imaginary: an appraisal of Castoriadis and Lefort," *Studies in the Theory of Ideology* (Cambridge: Polity Press, 1984), pp. 16–41.

Whitebook, Joel: *Perversion and Utopia: A Study in Psychoanalysis and Critical Theory* (Cambridge, MA: MIT Press, 1995), see in particular the index.

# PART IX

# STRUCTURALISM AND AFTER

# 46

# Lévi-Strauss*

## MARCEL HÉNAFF

Structuralism was the major intellectual concern of French philosophy during the 1960s and 1970s. Elsewhere it was not, except in circles influenced by French thought. Lévi-Strauss seemed to embody this theoretical trend; actually, he was simply its most outstanding figure. That situation was a strange one, in several respects: Lévi-Strauss was not the initiator of structuralism as such, nor did he aim to cause any upheaval in the field of philosophy. But it is undeniable that most of the thinkers who were (often wrongly and against their will) deemed to be structuralists, or post-structuralists, or neo-structuralists, such as DERRIDA (see Article 50), ALTHUSSER (Article 48), FOUCAULT (Article 49), DELEUZE (Article 51), Serres, LYOTARD (Article 52), Barthes, LACAN (Article 47), Marin, entertained a special relationship with structural linguistics and with Lévi-Strauss's anthropology. This is what needs to be understood. Thus the following sets of questions will be addressed: (1) Why, and because of what methodological requirements, did Lévi-Strauss seek explanatory models for *some* anthropological problems in structural linguistics? (2) How and why did this choice made by Lévi-Strauss have a decisive influence upon some of the major philosophers in France at that time? What were the fruits, and what were the limits and misunderstandings of the structuralist inspiration, particularly in its anthropological version, in philosophy. In other words, what assessment can be made today of the relationships between philosophy and Lévi-Strauss's anthropology?

In fact, these questions unite two domains which we aim to distinguish: that of the method – structural analysis – and that of the structuralist paradigm. The first of these domains is epistemological; the second is philosophical in the stricter sense.

## Anthropology, linguistics, and the structural model

Lévi-Strauss performed a methodological revolution in the field of anthropology by importing models of analysis that had been developed in structural linguistics, which is to say by the first non-historical linguistics. Credit for this new linguistics should probably be given to Saussure; even if others (such as Troubetskoï in Russia and Bloomfield in the United States) independently developed its premises; Saussure's explicit heirs were linguists such as Jakobson, Karcevsky, Hjemslev, Ben-

*Translated by Jean-Louis Morhange.

véniste, and Martinet. The methodological revolution performed by structural linguistics can be summarized in the following manner: first, it precisely specified its object, namely language as a system of forms, as opposed to speech as an individual act; next, it determined minimal units, or basic components (such as phonemes or morphemes) that constitute the formal system of any language; then, it posited that the relationship between these components is a systematic one, and that their values are reciprocal and differential; finally, by choosing to regard language as a form rather than as a substance, it required that only the synchronic level be considered, which is to say the system of their relationships rather than their historical genesis (which however does not exclude their logical genesis).

## The phonological model

At the time Lévi-Strauss was writing *The Elementary Structures of Kinship* (between 1940 and 1949), following his encounter and discussion with Jakobson, he became convinced that *the same model* that had been developed to account for certain linguistic data, particularly in phonological systems, could also account for data related to kinship. This project may seem to be a strange one; in fact, it was merely the transfer of a model. Indeed, Troubetskoï's phonology, Lévi-Strauss noted, deserved credit for being based upon the following: (1) it studied phenomena beyond their conscious aspect; (2) it demonstrated that a term is relevant only in its relation with other terms; (3) it presupposed that all these relationships constitute a system; and (4) it was able to determine laws. Such principles might be taken for granted in the natural sciences. However, they constituted significant advances in the sciences of the mind: "for the first time, a social science is able to formulate necessary relationships" (1963 [1955], p. 33).

To be able to import the model of structural analysis from linguistics and apply it to systems of kinship, it was both sufficient and necessary that these systems meet similar requirements: that they be constituted by basic terms, that the values of these terms be determined by their reciprocal relationships, that all these relationships constitute a system, that these systems be self-regulated, independent from the level of explicit consciousness. "The problem can therefore be formulated as follows: Although they belong to *another order of reality*, kinship phenomena are *of the same type* as linguistic phenomena. Can the sociologist, by using a method that is analogous *in form* (if not in content) to the method used in structural linguistics, achieve the same kind of progress in his own science as that which has taken place in linguistics?" (1963 [1955], p. 34; Lévi-Strauss's italics). What was the advantage of importing this model? Instead of considering certain facts as the products of an obscure and most often unverifiable history, it allowed them to be made intelligible by resorting to a structural hypothesis. For instance, instead of assuming that the prohibition of incest was the remnant of ancient and extinct practices (according to Durkheim, it referred to an old interdiction concerning menstrual blood, that had been extended to the clan's blood), Lévi-Strauss showed that the reason for this interdiction is still relevant, and that it lies in the law of reciprocity, which is to say in the practices of gift/countergift that are the most universal form of recognition between groups, and of which the gift of a wife made by one group to another constitutes the most accomplished form. The prohibition of incest is not a moral one, and it does not apply to every social actor; it implies in essence that a father or a brother may not keep a daughter or a sister for himself, but must let her enter into the movement of reciprocity with other groups. The prohibition of incest is nothing more than the universal fact of exogamic union. The structural hypothesis allowed Lévi-Strauss to shed light upon this old enigma which anthopologists had finally declared to be unsolvable and therefore uninteresting. The validity of this hypothesis is crosschecked by its potential to solve a related enigma: that of the preferential marriage between cross-cousins (chidren of the mother's brother or of the father's sister), and of the prohibition of marriage between parallel cousins (chidren of the father's brother or of the mother's sister); in the first case, there is a potential relation of reciprocity, therefore of exogamy, because the cousins belong to different groups; in the second case, there is none, because they belong to the same groups. The two sets of cousins are biologically identical; it is the logic of reciprocity that favors a union in one case and prohibits it as incestuous in the other.

In the same way, structural analysis illuminated the complex systems of (positive or negative) attitudes in the relations between maternal uncle and nephew, father and son, brother and sister, husband and wife; to be more precise, Lévi-Strauss used a set of cases to demonstrate that these relations make up pairs of implication. Thus, if the relationship between maternal uncle and nephew is a conflicting one, that between father and son is a trustful one; if in the same case the relation between brother and sister is subject to a strict taboo, conversely the relationship between husband and wife tends to be one of tenderness. Other cases show a symmetrical reversal of all of these attitudes. In short, there clearly is recurrence of situations, which is to say structure and constancy in relations, which is to say a structuring law. Here is how Lévi-Strauss summed up his results: "the relation between maternal uncle and nephew is to that between brother and sister as the relation between father and son is to that between husband and wife. Thus if we know one pair of relations, it is always possible to infer the other" (1963 [1955], p. 42).

There is no doubt that the structural approach made it possible to understand what remained unintelligible in the systems of kinship, to discover a logic where only the remnants of a lost history had been seen. The results are equally impressive in other fields: systems of classification and myth analysis. Let us consider the case of "totemism." This term was coined (at the end of the eighteenth century) to refer to what was assumed to be relationships of identification between a group or an individual and an eponymous animal (or plant). As long as researchers strove to understand these relationships in mystical or psychological terms, they always came up against this question: why was a particular animal or plant chosen, rather than any other one? Lévi-Strauss showed in an illuminating way that totemic figures (animals, objects, plants, etc.) were above all terms in a system of classification, and, most importantly, that these classifications were not random (and therefore were based not only upon general differences but most often upon differences bearing on very specific details). Thus, in this field as well, the phonological model provided great inspiration in that it made it comprehensible that the value of terms is relational, and refers to differences, oppositions, or symmetries. The correct explanation can be neither genealogical nor functionalist nor psychological; it is of a logical nature, even if that logic bears upon tangible features (this is what Lévi-Strauss called "la pensée sauvage"). As we shall see, the same line of argument could be applied to the analysis of myths.

With the results obtained so far, it is already possible to clarify the following questions: can structural analysis be applied to any object in the social sciences or the sciences of the mind? In other words, what is its range of relevance? To what concept of structure does Lévi-Strauss's anthropology refer? Is it relevant to talk of a structuralist philosophy?

## The range of relevance of structural analysis

Can structural analysis be applied to any object in which differential features or pertinent oppositions can be discovered? This technique might become trivial if, regarding texts or works of art, it amounted to selecting among a set of markers those that best fit the project. It would always be possible, then, to locate in the object what one wishes to find in it. It would be tempting to leave aside what does not fit the project. The result would be a reduction of the object to benefit the method, rather than a better understanding of it for its own sake.

Such a method is not that of the linguists or the anthopologists who use structural analysis, which consists in a particular perspective on some objects of knowledge, and only on objects of a certain type. This was implied by a remark made by Lévi-Strauss: "Any society at all is therefore comparable to a universe in which only discrete masses are highly structured" (in *Introduction to the Work of Marcel Manss*, p. 18). Such would be the case of facts of kinship, "since the notion of structure has found its chief application in that field and since anthopologists have generally chosen to express their theoretical views also in that connection" (1963 [1955], p. 279). Based upon his further research, he could have added systems of classification and narrative traditions such as myths and tales. It can thus be assumed that other aspects of social reality are less receptive to the structural approach, precisely because they are less structured. Lévi-Strauss could therefore have applied to the notion of *structure* the same remark that he made about that of *function*: to say that, in a society, there is structure, is a truism; to say that everything in a society is structured is an absurdity (cf. ibid., p. 13). It was to this same limitation that Lévi-Strauss referred, to counter certain critics who "assume that the structural method, when applied to anthropology, is aimed at acquiring an exhaustive knowledge of societies. This is patently absurd. We simply wish to derive constants that are found at various times and in various places from an empirical richness and diversity that will always transcend our efforts at observation and description" (ibid., p. 82). The same thing should be said of the homology between culture and language: "the conclusion which seems to me the most likely is that some kind of correlation exists between certain things on certain levels, and our main task is to determine what these things are and what these levels are" (ibid., p. 79).

Structural analysis can thus only be applied to objects in which there is a sufficient degree of internal motivation (as opposed to arbitrariness): "I am quite prepared to accept that, within the whole of human activities, some levels can be structured, and some cannot. I choose classes of phenomena, types of societies, where the method is profitable" (in Bellour 1978, p. 49). This essential clarification made by Lévi-Strauss has often been neglected by some of his disciples and ignored by his critics. It shows very clearly the range of relevance, and consequently the limitations, of the structural approach.

Several important conclusions can immediately be drawn from these considerations. The first is that if the structural method is adequate to some objects and not to others, its use cannot be generalized. Thus it is well known that, in linguistics, it is very successful when applied to phonology, but much less to syntax and lexicon; that, in narratology, it is very fruitful when applied to the analysis of tales, myths, and folk traditions in general, but that it can only be applied to a certain level or certain aspects of novels or historical narratives, and is inadvisable for objects in which probabilistic factors prevail over crystalline organization and diachrony over synchrony.

The second conclusion is of a theoretical order: it is hard to see, considering these limitations in the range of the method, how one could have claimed to develop a "structuralist philosophy." If it amounted to hypothesizing a universal and all-encompassing structuration, it would be nothing more than hyper-rationalism. That is indeed the position that was mistakenly attributed to Lévi-Strauss, while the limits that he had explicitly assigned to the range of application of his method were ignored. That he restricted himself to the study of objects taken from peoples without writing, which is to say highly-structured objects (such as kinship, totemic classifications, rituals, and myths) does not allow one to assume that he aimed to subject all other data to these models.

## The concept of structure

This method requires that one agree on what the concept of structure means. It is important to clarify this point: this notion has been used in such a vague and unreliable way that it is not surprising so many people have been given this label for little or no reason.

When Jakobson, Benvéniste, Lévi-Strauss, and a few others, started to use this term, they were dealing with several fairly different heritages concerning its definition. They clearly distanced themselves from some of these, while claiming some others. Let us summarize them.

First of all, there is a common use of the term, that refers to two models: the first is an architectural one (and, historically, it is indeed "the first": *structura* designates in Latin the frame of a building), it provides the foundation for the constructivist idea of interdependence between parts and whole; the second is biological, and it refers to the idea of organic unity between components. It is this double inspiration, in addition to the growing influence of *Gestalttheorie*, that French philosophers could find in Lalande's classic, *Vocabulaire technique et critique de la philosophie*:

511

"A structure is a whole made up of interdependent phenomena, such that each one depends upon the others, and can be what it is only in and through its relationship with them" (Presses Universitaires de France, 1926; reissue 1983, "Structure"). This definition is not wrong, but it is not specific; it could just as well apply to any form of organization, and does not distinguish between what can be empirically observed and what is reconstructed through reasoning. Therefore, it defines very general and minimal conditions of existence of a structure: namely, systematicity. It can even be said that it defines the concept of system rather than that of structure. If these terms are equivalent, why talk of structuralism?

Lévi-Strauss, for instance, at the time when he was writing his work on kinship, had to deal with two very precise conceptions of the notion of structure: one of these, the concept of "social structure" developed by Anglo-Saxon anthropologists, was already the accepted one within his field; the other, which he had recently come upon, came from linguistics (notably through Jakobson's teaching, which led him to read Saussure and Troubetskoï). There was no link between these two conceptions, if not for the term itself. The originality of Lévi-Strauss's approach was to set up this link, or rather to pose the problems in a way that would lead him to completely rethink the anthropological concept of structure, based on what structural linguistics provided him.

One of the first researchers who made a constant and specific use of the notion of structure in anthropology was Alfred Radcliffe-Brown. He described his position in a 1940 article, "On Social Structure" (*Journal of the Royal Anthropological Institute*, vol. 71). According to him, social structure must be understood as the whole of empirically observable social relations, organized as a system. Lévi-Strauss wondered what it meant to resort to the notion of structure in the analysis of social facts, what specific advantages it provided over other approaches. If the social structure were in fact nothing more than the totality of the social relations that can be noticed in a given society, it would mean that the structure could be reached through empirical observation alone. In this case, the phrase *social structure* would merely be a synonym for *social organization*. It would provide no theoretical profit. One would only perform an inventory of relations, which would certainly supply a good description of an organism, but without reaching what makes it intelligible, which is not directly accessible to observation but, as in any science, can only be reached through conceptual elaboration. Lévi-Strauss stated his position in these terms: "The term 'social structure' has nothing to do with empirical reality but with models which are built up after it" (1963 [1955], p. 279). This social structure should not be confused with the social relations which are only "the raw materials out of which the models making up the social structure are built, while social structure can, by no means, be reduced to the ensemble of the social relations to be described in a given society" (ibid., p. 279).

Before specifying what Lévi-Strauss means by "building models," we must recall what his perspective owes to linguistics. It was through Jakobson's teaching and through interaction with him (in New York, from 1941) that Lévi-Strauss became acquainted with this discipline. It was precisely Jakobson who (with N. Troubetskoï and S. Karcevsky) had introduced this term in linguistics as early as 1928; it gained acceptance the next year in the manifesto of the Circle of Prague, in which the group's indebtedness to Saussure was explicitly acknowledged. They tended to substitute the notion of structure for the Saussurean notion of system. In fact, both notions kept their relevance. System is asynchronic totality when the structure *of* language is considered. But as far as structures *within* language are concerned, the term designates sets of invariant relations between terms (as was shown in phonology); when it has been proven that these relations recur, one can then talk of a law of structure.

Such is, in a few words, the linguistic notion of structure to which Lévi-Strauss referred: he was interested mostly in its second aspect, which allowed him to consider the structure as a model. This conception itself had been elaborated first in mathematics, notably in France by the Bourbaki group, which defined structure as a form of constant relations between terms in certain determined axiomatic conditions, independent of the sets in which these terms are found.

This mathematical conception of structure is that which Michel Serres referred to when he wrote: "On a given cultural content, be it God, table or bowl, an analysis *is structural* (and *is structural only*) when it presents this content as a model" (Serres 1968, p. 32). The notion of model is indeed central to a precise understanding of Lévi-Strauss's structuralism. What made his position original was the way he corrected the British or American sociological and anthropological approach with the method inspired by structural linguistics. It was the mathematical conception of the notion of model that constituted the major feature of this reconsideration, the objective of which he thus defined: "The object of social-structure studies is to understand social relations with the aid of models" (1963 [1955], p. 289). That definition pinpoints what is at the heart of the opposition between Lévi-Strauss and the theoreticians who identify social structure with the sum of the social relationships that can be empirically observed: "social relations consist of the raw materials out of which the models making up the social structure are built" (ibid., p. 279). If the model is a theoretical artifact, and if it makes the structure manifest, it is because the latter is not visible. While being "real," the structure is not a given, in that it cannot be immediately experienced.

Access to the structure must therefore be mediated by *models* (such as the avuncular model that accounts for the exogamic alliance and the prohibition of incest, or the model of the atom of kinship that formalizes the relationships between names and attitudes, or the canonical pattern of the myth). Bringing models to the fore does not, however, lead to formalism. For in this case, unlike in mathematics, the model does not imply indifference toward content. Serres's statement is therefore relevant to structure in mathematics, but in no way to the social sciences. Why? Because structure is not a general form that could be applied to any kind of content (as Propp believed, indicated by his concept of morphology, or as Greimas did later, with his semiotic square). Lévi-Strauss wrote: "*Form* is defined by opposition to material that is other than itself. But *structure* has no distinct content; it is content itself, apprehended in a logical organization conceived as property of the real" (1976 [1973], p. 115).

Let us bring this first approach to a conclusion: the method of structural analysis is valid for certain objects and for those only. Any attempt to use it beyond its range of relevance is not only reductionist but also completely inappropriate. Lévi-Strauss himself explicitly said so over and over. It is surprising that he would have been so poorly understood. The blame probably goes to a few epigones who, in other disciplines (semiology of texts, of film, of the visual arts, etc.) used the structural method in a sometimes vague and often inappropriate manner, thus fueling philosophical misunderstandings of Lévi-Strauss's theoretical undertaking, which they often claimed to follow.

So much for the structural *method*; it can be said that, within its range of relevance, it has proven its epistemological legitimacy through the novelty and the quality of its results.

The question of the structuralist *paradigm* is altogether different.

## Structuralism and philosophy

No philosophy can be derived from the method of structural analysis (which is to say that there is no world in which this analysis could be applied everywhere). Yet there certainly is a structuralist paradigm. This paradigm can be understood as a generalization of the model of language as Saussure defined it by opposing it to speech (*parole*). Can such a generalization be found in Lévi-Strauss's work? Undoubtedly, as can be seen in more than one place in his work, such as this excerpt from *A World on the Wane* on Caduveo art: "The ensemble of a people's customs has always its particular style; they form into systems. I am convinced that the number of these systems is not unlimited and that human societies, like individual human beings (at play, in their dreams, or in moments of delirium), never create *absolutely*; all they can do is to choose certain combinations from a repertory of ideas which it should be possible to reconstitute" (1961 [1955], p. 160); Lévi-Strauss even believed it possible to establish a sort of "periodic table of chemical elements of these combinations" (ibid., p. 160). Such a repertory is the exact analogue of the language system: limited in its terms, unlimited in its combinations. There is something very Leibnizian in this relation between possibilities and their actualizations. This is why, rather than following Ricoeur in defining Lévi-Strauss's position as a "Kantianism without a transcendental subject," it would be more appropriate to define it as a Leibnizianism without divine understanding.

For Lévi-Strauss, this conception of an ideal repertory is inseparable from a theory of the *human mind*. Several reasons led him to resort to this notion. The first was a matter of principle. Let us call it the postulate of universality. We are forced, he explained, to assume that, as long as humankind has existed as a species, its intellectual abilities have been essentially the same everywhere: abilities to speak, reason, communicate, adapt, act upon its environment, invent tools, produce narratives and forms, develop a social organization. In short, the mental apparatus is identical and can be found throughout the diversity of cultural expressions. And it is precisely this identity of potential that makes it possible for us to understand forms and cultures that are extremely distant in space and time. We must draw the conclusion that cultural relativism's positions are philosophically weak, and above all contradictory.

This principle-based reason for assuming a universality of the human mind must be supplemented with grounds founded on empirical observation. Anthropologists have noticed that identical solutions to certain (technical, artistic, organizational) problems can be found in areas and periods so distant from each other that diffusionist hypotheses (though acceptable in some cases) are not scientifically credible. For instance, Lévi-Strauss noticed a surprising similarity in the decorative solutions applied to convex surfaces (such as faces or vases) that were developed in fourth-century BC China as well as among present-day New Zealand's Maoris or Brazil's Caduveos. In a completely different field, one can only be struck not only by the universality of the prohibition of incest but also by the close similarity of all related institutions, such as the privileged part played by the maternal uncle, or the preferential marriage between cross-cousins, or the prohibition of marriage between parallel cousins. Many similar examples could easily be found in a variety of fields. These close formal similarities, which are brought to the fore by structural analyses, call for the hypothesis of an identical ability to respond to comparable problems. Lévi-Strauss wrote: "From my point of view, it might just as well be a case of structural similarity between societies that have made related choices from the spectrum of institutional possibilities, whose range is probably not unlimited" (1963 [1955], p. 133). To use Chomskyan terms, it could be said that an identical apparatus of competence becomes apparent through the diversity of performances. This is precisely what Lévi-Strauss means by the human mind: both universal abilities specific to humankind and evidence of these abilities in the form of structures, or constant relationships, revealed by empirical expressions (institutions, attitudes, visual forms, techniques, narratives, representations, etc.).

This human mind to which Lévi-Strauss refers is not, therefore, an idealist chimera or a notion designed in order to generalize his hypotheses. Edmund Leach ("The Legitimacy of Salomon") was thus mistaken when he criticized Lévi-Strauss for using this concept of mind either as a "ghost in the machine" – in Gilbert Ryle's words – or as a new version of the Hegelian *Geist*. In fact, once again the relevant model is that of language: on the one side, the system of basic elements, on the other, the unique expressions of speech.

Resorting to the model of language implies another very important consequence: namely, that the operations under consideration do not belong to the realm of consciousness. The systems of difference and oppositions in language, like those of alliance in the domain of kinship, or of variants in mythical narratives, are not the outcome of an explicit design, but arise from rational regulations whose logic becomes apparent to researchers only in retrospect. This non-conscious character is evidence for their objectivity and confers upon them, as Troubetskoï asserted about phonology, the status of phenomena analogous to those of the natural sciences.

The unconscious under consideration here has no relationship with that described by Freud – which is according to him the product of an original repression – but merely designates the level of operations that generate an order independent

515

of the conscious subject. This objective and autonomous order (rules of language, of kinship, narrative systems, etc.) constitutes a system of the formal conditions of meaning.

Such are the conditions that structuralism constantly emphasized. Such is the thesis which had a lasting influence upon French philosophy in the 1960s and 1970s. This explains the fast and general break with phenomenology that occurred at the time when it seemed in a position to establish its dominance everywhere under the powerful influence of SARTRE (see Article 21) and above all of MERLEAU-PONTY (Article 23). The latter defined language, in an important chapter of *La Phénoménologie de la perception*, as the act of individual speech that takes up and reorients in its enunciation the heritage of the language. In his early work Merleau-Ponty neglected the contributions of structural linguistics. RICOEUR (see Article 39), who at that time played a major part in introducing and translating HUSSERL (Article 15), perfectly understood and analyzed the theoretical deficiency tied to this ne-glect; he noted that: "The fact that the notion of language as an autonomous system is not taken into consideration weighs heavily on this phenomenology of speech" (Ricoeur 1974, p. 249), and further, that "it is through and by means of a linguistics of language that a phenomenology of speech is possible today" (Ricoeur 1974, p. 251). In short, not only is there an already-said before I start to speak; there are also formal conditions of language without which my speech could not be identified, communicated, or understood.

If this discovery of linguistics was truly the central event for French philosophy, it is because it took its place in the series of dis-appropriations of the traditional field of philosophy, following those operated by MARX (see Article 8) upon history and FREUD (Article 12) upon the subject. However, if the discovery of this indebtedness had amounted to introducing the science of language into the philosophy of lan-guage, there would not have been a structuralist trend. But something else hap-pened: the paradigm mentioned above was adopted; this can be described as structuralist and is dominated by the following axiom: meaning is generated by the interplay of the differences between signs, independent of the speaking subject. Understood literally, this statement amounted to giving equal value to meaning and to the formal conditions of its generation. It unquestionably established domin-ion of the semiotic over the semantic. Many works in fields such as literature, the visual arts, music, etc., have been marked by this excess. Semiology (that of Grei-mas for instance) has probably represented the hardest tendency in the structural-ist trend. Lévi-Strauss may have believed that such excesses had no bearing upon him, inasmuch as his theoretical program, modeled on that of linguistics, was not to bring out meanings but only to highlight the formative elements of the systems he studied and to reveal the structural relationships that existed between these elements. But it was unavoidable that the necessity of interpreting would lead him to go beyond this program and to lay himself open to criticism. The structuralist axiom should therefore be corrected in the following manner: meaning, realized in the act of the speaking subject, is generated, at the level of the formal conditions of its emergence, by the interplay of differences between signs.

Post-phenomenological French philosophy took this statement seriously, and was marked by it. It grounds such concepts as Derrida's *écriture*, Deleuze's *évène-ment pré-personnel*, Lyotard's *figural*, Foucault's *ordre discursif*, Lacan's *symbolique*, Barthes's and Marin's *texte*. None of these authors were, strictly speaking, structuralists, nor did they claim to be (and Lévi-Strauss himself denied that they were). But it is unquestionable that all of them are indebted to Saussure's linguistics, and more specifically to Lévi-Strauss's anthropology, for having raised the question of meaning in a new way.

## Writings

Lévi-Strauss, C.: *Les Structures élémentaires de la parenté* (Paris: Presses Universitaires de France, 1949); English translation: *The Elementary Structures of Kinship*, tr. J. Bell, J. von Sturmer, and R. Needham (Boston, MA: Beacon Press, 1969).

——: *Tristes tropiques* (Paris: Plon, 1955); English translation: *A World on the Wane*, tr. John Russell, London: Hutchinson, 1961).

——: *Anthropologie structurale* (Paris: Plon, 1955); English translation: *Structural Anthropology*, vol. I, tr. C. Jacobson and B. Graundfest Schoepf (New York: Basic Books, 1963).

——: *Le Totémisme aujourd'hui* (Paris: Presses Universitaires de France, 1962); English translation: *Totemism*, tr. Rodney Needham (Boston, MA: Beacon Press, 1963).

——: *La Pensée sauvage* (Paris: Plon, 1962); English translation: *The Savage Mind* (Chicago, IL: University of Chicago Press, 1966).

——: *Mythologiques – I: Le cru et le cuit* (Paris: Plon, 1964); English translation: *The Raw and the Cooked*, tr. John and Doreen Weightman (New York: Harper and Row, 1969).

——: *Mythologique – II: Du miel aux cendres* (Paris: Plon, 1967); English translation: *From Honey to Ashes*, tr. John and Doreen Weightman (London: Cape, 1973).

——: *Mythologiques – III: L'Origine des manières de table* (Paris: Plon, 1968); English translation: *Origin of Table Manners*, tr. John and Doreen Weightman (London: Cape, 1978).

——: *Mythologiques – IV: L'Homme nu* (Paris: Plon, 1971); English translation: *The Naked Man*, tr. John and Doreen Weightman (New York: Harper and Row, 1981).

——: *Anthropologie structurale deux* (Paris: Plon, 1973); English translation: *Structural Anthropology*, vol. II, tr. M. Layton (New York: Basic Books, 1976).

——: *Le Regard éloigné* (Paris: Plon, 1983); English translation: *The View from Afar*, tr. J. Neugroschel and Ph. Hoss (New York: Basic Books, 1985).

——: *La Potière jalouse* (Paris: Plon, 1985); English translation: *The Jealous Potter*, tr. Benedicte Chorier (Chicago: University of Chicago Press, 1988).

——: *Histoire de Lynx* (Paris, Plon, 1991); English translation: *The Story of Lynx* (Chicago: University of Chicago Press, 1995).

——: *Introduction to the Work of Marcel Manss*, tr. Felicity Barker (London: Routledge & Kegan Paul, 1987).

## References and further reading

Badcock, C. R.: *Lévi-Stauss: Structuralism and Sociological Theory* (London: Hutchinson, 1975).

Bellour, Raymond: *Le livre des autres* (1978).

Hénaff, Marcel: *Claude Lévi-Strauss* (Paris: Belfond, 1991).

Leach, Edmund: "The legitimacy of Salomon," *Archives europeenes de Sociologie*, VIII (1968).

——: *Claude Lévi-Strauss* (New York: Viking Press, 1970).

Ricouer, Paul: "The question of the subject," tr. Kathleen McLaughlin. In *The Conflict of Interpretations: Essays in Hermenentics*, ed. Don Ihde (Evanston, IL: Northwestern University Press, 1974).

Serres, Michel: *La Communication* (Paris: Minuit, 1968).

Sperber, Dan: *Le Structuralisme en Anthropologie* (Paris: Seuil, 1973).

# 47

# Lacan

## WILLIAM J. RICHARDSON

The oft-proclaimed "return to Freud" of Jacques Lacan (1901–81) was a return to what he took to be the great creative insight of Freud, insight into the way that language works in the vagaries of unconscious human experience. In Lacan's own formula, "the unconscious is structured like a language" (1977, p. 234). One way to grasp this may be by reflecting on the familiar anecdote recounted by Freud, himself, in *The Psychopathology of Everyday Life* (1960 [1901], pp. 8–11). Freud recounts how he had met on a train a well-educated young man of Jewish descent who, while decrying the anti-Semitism by which he had been victimized, tries to cite the line from Virgil's *Aeneid* in which Dido calls for vengeance upon Aeneas, "*Exoriare . . .*" – tries, indeed, but fails. Asked for help, Freud quotes the line exactly: "*Exoriar[e] ALIQUIS nostris ex ossibus ultor*" (*Aeneid* 4:625, literally: "Let someone (*aliquis*) arise from my bones as an avenger!"). Recalling Freud's claim that such words are never forgotten without a reason, the young man asks Freud to help him understand the reason for drawing a blank. Freud agrees, insisting on the fundamental rule of psychoanalysis: to say "candidly and uncritically" whatever comes to mind as he concentrates on the forgotten word.

Dividing *aliquis* into *a* and *liquis*, the young man soon associated to *Reliquien* (relics), liquefying, fluidity, fluid, etc. Subsequently, there are allusions to certain saints of the Church (such as Simon, Augustine, Benedict), and the text continues:

> "Now it's St. *Januarius* and the miracle of his blood that comes into mind – my thoughts seem to be running on mechanically."
>
> "Just a moment: St. *Januarius* and St. Augustine both have to do with the calendar. Won't you remind me about the miracle of his blood?"
>
> "Surely you must have heard of that? They keep the blood of St Januarius in a phial inside a church in Naples, and on a particular holy day it miraculously *liquefies*. The people attach great importance to this miracle and get very excited if it's delayed, as happened once at a time when the French were occupying the town. So the general in command – or have I got it wrong? Was it Garibaldi? – took the reverend gentleman aside and gave him to understand, with an unmistakable gesture towards the soldiers posted outside, that he *hoped* the miracle would take place very soon. And in fact it did take place. . . ."
>
> "Well, go on. Why do you pause?"
>
> "Well, something *has* come into my mind . . . but it's too intimate to pass on. . . . Besides, I don't see any connection, or any necessity for saying it."

"You can leave the connection to me. Of course I can't force you to talk about something that you find distasteful; but then you mustn't insist on learning from me how you came to forget your *aliquis*."

"Really? Is that what you think? Well then, I've suddenly thought of a lady from whom I might easily hear a piece of news that would be very awkward for both of us."

"That her periods have stopped?"

"How would you guess that?"

"That's not difficult any longer; you've prepared the way sufficiently. Think of the *calendar of the saints, the blood that starts to flow on a particular day, the disturbance when the event fails to take place, the open threats that the miracle must be vouchsafed, or else.* . . . In fact you've made use of the miracle of St. Januarius to manufacture a brilliant allusion to women's periods." (1960 [1901], pp. 10–11)

So far the anecdote. It comes from the early Freud, to be sure, but is all the more revealing for that. The full flush of Freud's genius is most evident, Lacan claims, in the analysis of wordplay in the early works, chiefly in: *The Interpretation of Dreams* (1953 [1900]), *The Psychopathology of Everyday Life* (1960 [1901]) where this anecdote is found, and *Jokes and their Relation to the Unconscious* (1905). If Freud resorted to nineteenth-century physics as a model for his theoretical speculation (his "metapsychology"), this was the only paradigm he knew that would make his experience appear intellectually respectable to his scientific peers. The twentieth century has offered another scientific paradigm, however, that is much more congenial to the original insight into the processes of language: the science of linguistics. One can conceive of Lacan's entire enterprise as an attempt to return to Freud's original experience of how language functions in the "talking cure"and reinterpret it according to the more congenial scientific model of structural linguistics.

To be sure, this was not the initial thrust of his ambition when his career began in 1932. In fact, the general parameters of Lacan's odyssey become clear only with the help of the distinction made formally for the first time only in 1953 between "imaginary," "symbolic," and "real" – terms to which I shall return below. In retrospect it becomes clear that in the 21 preceding years he had been preoccupied largely by the function of images in psychic structures, i.e. by what is subsequently considered the "imaginary." By 1953, however, he had discovered Lévi-Strauss, and from then on the structures (and structuring) of language in the psychoanalytic process became paramount in his thought. Accordingly, the focus of attention shifted to the "symbolic" and its effect on the imaginary. This emphasis lasted until the early 1960s, when Lacan became more and more concerned with an attempt to formalize his thinking by a turn to mathematizing and topology. Soon it focused on the role of the "real" in this topology, i.e. what is not representable by either imaginary or symbolic. With the 1970s, one may say, at least in a general way, that his principal concern was to think all three registers together in their mutual complementarity with the help of a model called the "Borromean knot." Let this suffice for general orientation. Now in more detail:

Born in 1901 of an upper-middle-class family, Lacan trained as a psychiatrist, and in 1932 published his doctoral dissertation, *On Paranoid Psychosis in Its Relationship to Personality*, an exhaustive case study of the role of social milieu in the development of psychosis. This left him with a double interest: in the role of milieu on the one hand and of image on the other in the formation of personality. In 1938, he addressed the first issue in an article on the family in de Monzie's *Encyclopédie française*, entitled "Family complexes in the formation of the individual"; more significant for the later work were his reflections on the role of image in the formation of the ego itself. He first addressed the issue at the Fourteenth International Psycho-analytical Congress in Marienbad in 1936, but his classic formulation of the problem comes from a second, much revised presentation at the Sixteenth International Psycho-analytical Congress in Zurich, 1949, entitled "The Mirror Stage as Formative of the Function of the 'I' as Revealed in Psychoanalytic Experience" (1977, pp. 1–7).

The nub of the matter is that Lacan recognized in Freud a certain ambiguity in his conception of the ego. In the essay "On Narcissism: An Introduction" (1957 [1914], pp. 78–9), Freud considers the ego to be an object of narcissistic love rather than the subject's internal world as a whole, while from 1920 on, and particularly in 1923, the ego is thought of as an agency of adaptation that manages the tensions between id and superego when faced with the challenge of "reality." Lacan champions the first interpretation. With support from the experimental work of such researchers as Charlotte Bühler (1927) and Henri Wallon (1949 [1934]) he argues that the human infant comes into the world as a bundle of impulses in total disarray and experiences itself as a unity only when it discovers itself as reflected in the unity of an other, as if in a mirror – whether this other be an actual mirror reflection or simply the mothering one herself taken as a whole. Normally this phenomenon takes place somewhere between the age of 6 and 18 months. Since the unifying image is external to the infant, its unity is an alienated one and inevitably both distorted and distorting. None the less, it serves as an image of idealized totality, an armor-like structure that grounds the mechanisms of defense. Such an ego remains essentially an image and, as such, precisely the paradigm for what Lacan calls the "imaginary" dimension of the inchoate subject, essentially a bi-polar, one-to-one relationship such as between reflecting and reflected. In the case of Freud's travel companion (he deserves a name: let him be called "Adam"), the narcissistic injury triggered by the signs of anti-Semitism would have been an offense to such an "imaginary" ego, i.e. ego-as-image.

As already mentioned, Lacan awoke to the importance of language in its relation to the unconscious with the discovery of the work of Claude Lévi-Strauss in the early 1950s. Two essays seem to have been especially influential: "The Effectiveness of Symbols" (Lévi-Strauss 1949) and "Language and the Analysis of Social Laws" (Lévi-Strauss 1951). In the author's quest for a satisfactory methodology for cultural anthropology that would render it genuinely scientific, he had turned to structural linguistics, pioneered by the Swiss linguist, Ferdinand de Saussure, for a model. Here was a "social" science whose method dealt with data that resulted from long statistical runs, admitted of rigorous mathematical instruments and reduced the influence of the observer on the data under scrutiny to minimum. By adopting a comparable method for cultural anthropology, Lévi-Strauss was able to speak of an unconscious structure of human intercourse that was reducible to a function,

521

"the symbolic function, which no doubt is specifically human, and which is carried out according to the same laws among all men, and actually corresponds to the aggregate of these laws" (1949, pp. 202–3). This postulate permits the question, then: "can we conclude that all forms of social life are substantially of the same nature – that is, do they consist of systems of behavior that represent the projection, on the level of conscious and socialized thought, of universal laws which regulate the unconscious activities of the mind?" (1951, pp. 58–9). Lacan's answer was, of course, "yes," and he asks rhetorically in turn: "Isn't it striking that Lévi-Strauss, in suggesting the implication of the structures of language which regulate marriage ties and kinship, is already conquering the very terrain in which Freud situates the unconscious?" (1977, p. 73).

With Lévi-Strauss's work as stimulus, Lacan went directly to Saussure and took from him chiefly: the distinction between language as structure (closed system of signs governed by the laws of diacritical opposition) and speech as act; the distinction within a linguistic sign between speech sound (signifier) and mental representation (signified); and the arbitrary nature of the relationship between signifier and signified (there is no intrinsic necessity binding the sound "blood" to its corresponding mental image – *sang*, *Blut*, or *sanguis* would do as well).

Furthermore, while Saussure writes the relationship between signifier and signified in the form of an arithmetic fraction, where the signified is located on top of the separating bar and signifier on the bottom (s/S), Lacan reverses this form of inscription by writing it: S/s. This suggests two elements of his conception that are not to be found in Saussure: a primacy that is to be attributed to the signifier over the signified; a blockage to be seen in the bar separating signifier and signified as if the bar were a barrier to immediate signification of any one-to-one relationship between signifier and signified. Rather, any given signifier refers not to any corresponding signified but to another signifier in a sequence or "chain" of signifiers that Lacan describes as being "like rings of a necklace that is a ring in another necklace made of rings" (1977, pp. 153). That is why "we can say that it is in the chain of the signifiers that the meaning 'insists' but that none of its elements 'consists' in the signification of which it is at the moment capable. We are forced, then, to accept the notion of an incessant sliding of the signified under the signifier" (1977, pp. 153–4).

More specifically, in Freud's anecdote we see how the forgotten word *aliquis*, taken as a starting-point for free association, soon leads to other signifiers ("liquefying," "liquid," "fluidity," "relics," etc.) by a kind of contiguity (whether of sound, meaning, or etymology) along what the linguists call an "axis of combination," which Lacan, following Jakobson and the early rhetoricians (Jakobson 1956, pp. 63–75) call "metonymy." The meaning of the chain does not "consist" in any one element but rather "insists" in the whole exchange and is discerned retroactively when Freud punctuates the discourse with his decisive question concerning the cessation of periods. From another point of view, the symptom in question (the forgetting of *aliquis*) serves as a replacement, a kind of signifier *in absentia*, for the unconscious anxiety over the possibility of unwelcome news. In that sense it may be situated along what linguists call an "axis of substitution" and plays the role of what rhetoricians have always called "metaphor." If the phenomenon may be spoken of in terms of "metonymy" and "metaphor" in this way, then it follows an essentially linguistic paradigm. Lacan, following the inspiration of Roman Jakobson but developing it in his own way, makes much of this homology, arguing that the laws of the unconscious that govern dream-formation (laws of displacement and condensation) follow the same pattern as the functions of metonymy and metaphor.

For Lacan, such laws pertain to the symbolic function itself, the dynamic pattern that governs the entire signifying system. This function does not operate in the abstract but rather is woven into the entire fabric of human history. For Adam, such a fabric would include the cultural myths of his race, his ethnic style, the particularity of his ancestral lineage, the personal and social milieu of his immediate family (e.g. the full scope of his Jewishness from the birth of Abraham down to his own circumcision) – in short, the universal discourse that preceded him and into which he had been born. Moreover, the universality and ineluctability of this fabric constitute it as law, in fact *the* law, and since all law proceeds from a lawgiver characteristically thought of as father of the law, Lacan speaks of the law of symbolic functioning as *the* Law of *the* Father (sometimes as the "name"/"no" [nom/non] of the Father) – not of the actual father in the flesh, of course, but of the Dead Father as Freud postulates him in the hypothesized myth of *Totem and Taboo* (1913).

It was to the elaboration of this conception of the symbolic order and its relevance to clinical practice that Lacan devoted his energies through the 1950s, with frequent referral to the Freudian text. In the early 1960s, beginning with Seminar IX, *Identification* (1962), there was a shift in focus, partly because he became more and more interested in formalizing his speculation with the help of mathematical and topological models, partly because in doing so he began to emphasize the third component of psychic structure (beyond imaginary and symbolic), i.e. the "real." Essentially, the real is not "reality" in the normal sense of the word, for this is already patterned by imaginary and symbolic representations; rather, it is "the impossible," i.e. impossible to represent – by either images of the imaginary or signifiers of the symbolic. It is experienced most dramatically in psychic trauma but may be thought of more tranquilly as the unknown domain where reside the still-to-be-discovered secrets of science. In any case, what jutted into the flow of Adam's discourse and jolted him into forgetting *aliquis*, this would have been the real.

With the 1970s, at least from the seminar of 1972–3, *Encore*, on and until he stopped teaching in 1980, Lacan tried to think imaginary, symbolic, and real together in their mutuality. The knot is a unity of three spheres, or "holes," in which each sphere operates in such complete complementarity with the others that if one is destroyed, the entire knot disintegrates.

With this much to indicate the fundamental parameters of Lacan's thought, the way in which Lacan's thought matured, let us explore more in detail how the infant passes from the first imaginary identification with its own image in/through the mother to full-fledged subjectivity. Initially, the infant enjoys an imaginary symbiosis with the mother (homologous with what it once enjoyed in the womb) according to which the mother is both its Other and its All. Eventually, this dyadic bond is ruptured as the child begins to exercise its capacity for speech. This is what Lacan sees to be the significance of the experience Freud describes in the game that he observes his grandson playing with a spool of thread (1955 [1920], pp. 14–15). For Freud, the o-o-o and a-a-a suggest *fort* ("away") and *da* ("here") – an effort to control in play fashion the mother's absence and presence, i.e. to deal with its own libidinal needs. For Lacan, they represent the infant's first effort to articulate phonemes, i.e. to enter actively into the symbolic order, to which it has been exposed passively (at least indirectly) since its first moment of gestation. The *fort/da* experience initiates a "splitting" in the infant (to use a Freudian term in a non-Freudian way) by which part remains conscious and another part becomes completely submitted to the Other of the symbolic order, i.e. of the unconscious, to be thought of now as a place, or field, or "treasury" of signifiers. It is the unconscious in this sense that Lacan speaks of as "subject," the "subject of the unconscious." This splitting of the subject corresponds for Lacan to what Freud postulates under the guise of "primary repression."

The division of the subject (written $) finds expression in the distinction made between the speaking subject and the spoken subject. The spoken subject (*sujet de l'énoncé*: "subject of the statement") is the conscious "I" to which the speaker himself refers (e.g. "*I*'ve suddenly thought of a lady from whom *I* might easily hear . . ."); the speaking subject (*sujet de l'énonciation*: "subject of the affirmation") is the "I" that recedes from the statement in the very act of making it, that slips underneath the succession of signifiers and is suspended from them, that does the forgetting as distinct from the (spoken) "I" that suffers it. Let this suggest how Lacan understands the subject as an "effect of the signifier," where the signifier (as opposed to a sign, which represents something for someone) must be understood as "represent[ing] a subject for another signifier" (1966a, p. 840). It is the signifier that determines the subject, then, more profoundly than any element that could be called psychological:

> The displacement of the signifier determines the subjects in their acts, in their destiny, in their refusals, in their blindnesses, in their end and in their fate, their innate gifts and social acquisitions notwithstanding, without regard for character or sex. . . . Willingly or not, everything that might be considered the stuff of psychology, kit and caboodle, will follow the path of the signifier. (1958 [1955], p. 60)

The signifier in question here is the signifying system as such, the chain within chains of signifiers from which the subject is suspended, governed by the law of the Father. What happens then? Recall that the rupture of the bond with the mother is a cutting off from her, and in that sense a form of "castration" – imaginary, to be sure – and proper to girls as well as boys. The result is a terrible loss for the infant – an emptiness, a lack, a want-to-be (*manque-à-être*) reunited with the mother. This want(-ing) of the mother is what Lacan understands by desire. He distinguishes it clearly from need, on the one hand, a purely physical exigency (e.g. for food) that can be adequately alleviated, and from demand, on the other, which, even if it pertains to the satisfaction of a need, includes with it articulation in language. The latter implies some other to whom the demand is addressed, hence the presence, or being, of that other that, as such, exceeds the mere satisfaction of need. Lacan refers to this presence/being of the other as "love" and insists that demand, beyond appeal for satisfaction, is always a request for love. Be that as it may, desire differs from both need and demand, occupying a kind of virtual space between them. Once the subject is divided the desire of the subject must pursue the endless quest for its lost object in metonymic fashion through the defiles of the symbolic system, governed as this is by the law of the Father.

To be sure, this quest is doomed to failure, for the original psychic fusion of the infant with the mother was never anything more than an imaginary fullness – as an "object" it was always already lost. And yet, it is this irretrievably lost object that remains "cause" of the subject's desire which subsequently is instantiated in more proximate objects that are represented for the subject in fantasies, i.e. images that are taken up into signifying functions through which the subject plays out the various scenarios of its desire. Fantasies, then, are the *mise-en-scène* of desire.

The infant's desire to retrieve the lost fusion with the mother Lacan conceives in Hegelian terms as the desire to be recognized as the desired of its desired (the mother). Now for Lacan (taking his cue from Freud), the signifier *par excellence* of desire is the phallus, which, as signifier, must be differentiated now from the male sexual organ (penis). In this sense, then, the infant would desire to *be* the phallus for the mother. Alas, this is impossible. For the father (with phallus) is there, at the very least the symbolic father as law, in this case as law against incest:

> It is to the extent that the function of the pleasure principle is to make man always search for what he has to find again, but which he will never attain, that one reaches the essence, namely that sphere or relationship which is known as the law of the prohibition of incest. (1992 [1959–60], p. 68)

The law against incest, then, that interdicts the infant's being the phallus for the mother is not some moral injunction but a structural, not to say ontological, fact – the radical impossibility of its ever retrieving the always already lost object that causes desire.

How the Oedipal drama actually unfolds for the infant, i.e. how it comes to forgo its desire to *be* the mother's phallus and settle for the condition of "having" (or "not having") it – and even, in having it, to renounce any pretense to master it; or, to put the matter differently, how the infant learns to accept its indigenous want, i.e. finitude, with the consequence that the same law (of the Father), which prohibits indulging the child's want to be the mother's phallus, is the law that henceforth mediates this want through the exigencies of linguistic structures through which desire must express itself (i.e. the symbolic order) – all this demands fuller orchestration than is possible here. Let it suffice to say that the full orchestration of acceptance by the subject of this radical limitation is what Lacan means by castration on the symbolic level and sometimes refers to in Heideggerian terms as Being-unto-death.

In this context one should say a word about a notion that finds its roots in Freud but that has been thematized by Lacan and made his own: *jouissance*. The closest English equivalent would be "enjoyment," but this could be very misleading and it seems better to leave the term untranslated. Its radical sense may be gained from its etymology: it has roots in the *joy* of the courtly poets for whom it meant full sexual satisfaction; it has roots, too, in an ancient juridical sense of "enjoyment" as the right to profit, say, from property without title to ownership. Lacan uses the term to translate Freud's use of *Genuss* as distinct from *Lust* ("pleasure") as this appears in the famous essay of 1920, *Beyond the Pleasure Principle*, where Freud reflects upon the motivation for such phenomena as repetition compulsions, war neuroses, negative therapeutic reactions, etc., that cannot be explained by a "pleasure principle" that explains pleasure as a reduction of tension in some energistic sense. To account for the appeal of such phenomena, one must postulate a gratification in the subject of another order completely, beyond the scope of sheer thermodynamics. This for Lacan is the order of language, and the gratification, which never loses a connotation of some sexual delectation, he calls *jouissance*. In terms of pleasure, *jouissance* is always interdicted, not because it is forbidden by some censor but because it is woven into ("inter-") the texture of language ("-diction") through the mediation of which, as the Other of the symbolic order, desire pursues its lost object. As *jouissance* is beyond pleasure, so, too, it may be beyond pain – or at least may include pain (e.g. sadomasochism). One may get a sense of its relation to language, perhaps, best by returning to the experience of *fort/da*. This phenomenon is presented as an example of the repetition compulsion, hence as beyond the scope of the pleasure principle. The gratification of the child would seem to come not from the mimetic game as such – at least, so I understand Lacan – but precisely through its conjunction with the inchoative language of the phonemes. Such is the nature of *jouissance*.

The import of all this is far-reaching. Let it suffice here to mention only one direction opened up by Lacan late in his career that may be worth further exploration. If *jouissance* is a correlative of the order of language, and if the phallus is the signifier *par excellence* of that order ("intended to designate as a whole the effects of the signified, in that the signifier conditions them by its presence as a signifier" [1977, p. 285), then all *jouissance* would seem to be necessarily "phallic" in nature, whatever that might mean. In fact, however, in the 1972–3 seminar entitled *Encore*, Lacan, with the help of some first-order logic of his own invention, suggests the possibility of a *jouissance* that is other than phallic to which Woman has a privileged access. How such a notion might affect the way psychoanalysis addresses the issue of "what a woman wants" is a question that cannot be explored further here.

By way of summary, one may ask: how would Lacan proceed with the analysis itself, if some Adam (or Parisian cab-driver), impressed by a display of Lacan's virtuosity, asked to be analyzed? Normally, analysis begins with the request for relief from a certain suffering that the analysand supposes is caused by a constellation of factors that determine his existence in some way unknown to him and which Lacan, following Freud, calls the "unconscious." This unconscious, in so far as it is conceived as a subject that is Other than the conscious one, is presumed to possess a kind of knowledge that includes within its scope this constellation of determining factors. It is this knowledge that is presumed to belong to the subject of the unconscious (to the Other as Lacan conceives it) that the prospective analysand seeks to understand, and the analyst, in accepting such a client into analysis, agrees to occupy the place of the subject of the unconscious with all of its presumed knowledge.

Transference, of course, does its work. Lacan conceives of transference as a relation between two human beings that includes the real component of both subjects but takes place in both an imaginary and a symbolic mode. In the imaginary mode, transference is the dyadic relationship between the ego of the analysand and the ego of the analyst, principally on the level of affect, which is often expressed in conventional terms as a "repetition, a new edition of an old object [i.e. interpersonal] relationship" (Greenson 1967, p. 152). In the symbolic mode, however, transference consists in the relationship between the analysand as subject of speech and the analyst as holding the place of the Other of the unconscious, attending to the discourse of the Other as it comes to pass in the analysand and echoing it back to the analysand so that he/she may hear it too. The task of the analyst is to avoid being trapped in the imaginary transference, to acknowledge it as inevitable but to transcend it whenever, wherever, and however possible in order to transpose the relationship to the register of language, where alone the effective work of the analysis is done. Thus the task of "making the unconscious conscious" has a different sense for Lacan than in the classic Freudian formula: *Wo Es war soll Ich werden.* Here it means: "Where It (*Es*) [i.e. the Other of language] was, there I (*Ich*) [as subject through which language speaks, distinct from its objectivating representation in the image called "ego"] must come to be [aware of It speaking in me]." Likewise, if all goes well, the analysand comes to appreciate the meaning of his/her own desire as desire of the Other, and that the cause of this desire is an object that has been lost in some primordial way, never to be found again.

At the end of analysis, then, the analysand learns how to deal with the knowledge originally attributed to the unconscious, but the process is no more gratifying for that. In effect, the end of analysis brings with it a sense of loss, and with that an experience of mourning: mourning, first of all, for the analyst himself, who, having taken the place of unconscious knowledge, becomes no longer necessary, henceforth superfluous and useless, so much rubbish (*déchet*) in Lacan's terminology; mourning, too, for the object that causes desire, recognized now as lost forever; mourning, finally, over the inevitable castration, painful and definitive, that the end of analysis implies. The end of analysis according to Lacan, then, comports a profound desolation: one's being (*être*) has become a "dys-being" (*désêtre*) (Lacan 1968, p. 25), and all the losses that have been endured constitute a complete "destitution" of the subject.

But it is also a moment of truth, and of whatever freedom truth of this sort can bring. Is it worth what it cost? Only the analysand can say. But it is to Lacan's credit that at least he never promised more than he could deliver:

Psychoanalysis may accompany the patient to the ecstatic limit of the *"Thou art that,"* in which is revealed to him the cipher of his mortal destiny, but it is not in our mere power as practitioners to bring him to that point where the real journey begins. (1977, p. 7)

## Writings

Lacan, J.: *De la psychose paranoïaque dans ses rapports avec la personnalité* [*On Paranoid Psychosis in Its Relationship with Personality*] (1932) (Paris: Seuil, 1975).

——: "La Famille" (1938). In: *Encyclopédie française*, vol. I (*La vie mentale*), ed. A. de Monzie (Paris: Librairie Larousse, 1984).

——: *The Language of the Self: The Function of Language in Psychoanalysis* (1953), tr. A. Wilden (Baltimore: Johns Hopkins, 1968).

——: *The Seminar of Jacques Lacan*, Book I: *Freud's Papers on Technique* (1953–4), ed. J.-A. Miller; tr. J. Forrester (New York: Norton, 1988).

——: *The Seminar of Jacques Lacan*, Book II: *The Ego in Freud's Theory and in the Technique of Psychoanalysis* (1954–5), ed. J.-A. Miller; tr. S. Tomaselli; notes J. Forrester (New York: Norton, 1988).

——: "Seminar on 'The Purloined Letter'" (1955), tr. J. Mehlman, in: Muller, J. and Richardson, W., *The Purloined Poe: Lacan, Derrida & Psychoanalytic Reading* (Baltimore, MD: Johns Hopkins, 1988), pp. 28–54.

——: *The Seminar of Jacques Lacan*, Book III: *The Psychoses* (1955–6), ed. J.-A. Miller; tr. R. Grigg (New York: Norton, 1993).

——: *The Seminar of Jacques Lacan*, Book VII: *The Ethics of Psychoanalysis* (1959–60), ed. J.-A. Miller, tr. D. Porter (New York: Norton, 1992).

——: *The Four Fundamental Concepts of Psycho-analysis*, (1964), ed. J.-A. Miller; tr. A. Sheridan (New York: Norton, 1977).

——: *Écrits* (Paris: Seuil, 1966a).

——: *Écrits: A Selection* (1966b), tr. A. Sheridan (New York: Norton, 1977).

——[1968]: "Proposition du 9 Octobre 1967 sur le pschanalyst de l'École," *Scilicet*, 1 (1968), pp. 14–30.

——: *Encore* (1972–3), ed. J.-A. Miller (Paris: Seuil, 1975).

——: *Télévision: A Challenge to the Psychoanalytic Establishment* (1973), ed. J.-A. Miller (New York: Norton, 1990).

General bibliographies:

Dor, J.: *Bibliographie des travaux de Jacques Lacan* [*Bibliography of the Works of Jacques Lacan*] (Paris: InterEditions, 1983).

Clark, M.: *Jacques Lacan: An Annotated Bibliography* (New York: Garland, 1988).

## References and further reading

Bühler, C. *Soziologische und psychologische Studien über das erste Lebensjahr* (Jena: Fischer, 1927).

Freud, S. [1900]: *The Interpretation of Dreams*. Standard Edition, 4 & 5 (London: Hogarth Press, 1953).

——[1901]: *The Psychopathology of Everyday Life*. Standard Edition, 6 (London: Hogarth Press, 1960).

———[1905]: *Jokes and their Relation to the Unconscious, Standard Edition*, 8 (London: Hogarth Press, 1960).

———[1913]: *Totem and Taboo. Standard Edition*, 13:1–162 (London: Hogarth Press, 1953).

———[1914]: "On narcissism: an introduction," *Standard Edition*, 14:67–102 (London: Hogarth Press, 1957).

———[1920]: "Beyond the pleasure principle," *Standard Edition*, 18:7–64 (London: Hogarth Press, 1955).

———[1923]: "The Ego and the Id," *Standard Edition*, 19:12–66 (London: Hogarth Press, 1961).

Greenson, R.: *The Technique and Practice of Psychoanalysis* (New York: International Universities Press, 1967).

Jakobson, R.: "Two aspects of language and two types of aphasic disturbances," *Fundamentals of Language* (The Hague: Mouton, 1956), pp. 53–87.

Lévi-Straus, C.: "The effectiveness of symbols" (1949). In *Structural Anthropology*, tr. C. Jacobson and B. Schoepf (New York: Basic Books, 1963), pp. 186–205.

———[1951]: "Language and the analysis of social laws," in *Structural Anthropology*, tr. C. Jacobson and B. Schoepf (New York: Basic Books, 1963), pp. 55–66.

Wallon, H.: *Les Origines du caractère chez l'enfant: Les Préludes du sentiment de personnalité*, 2nd edn (Paris: Presses Universitaires de France, 1949).

# 48

# Althusser

## JACQUES RANCIÈRE

Althusser's entire theoretical undertaking has one objective and can be summarized in a single paradox. The objective is defined in 1965 in the opening lines of *Pour Marx*: "the *research* into Marx's *philosophical* thought, which is indispensable if we are to emerge from the theoretical impasse that history has left us in" (Althusser 1965, p. 11). The paradox is recalled in his lecture on "La Transformation de la Philosophie": "Marxist philosophy exists, and yet it was not produced as philosophy" (Althusser 1994, p. 149).

In the beginning, then, there is "history," which the cautious militant communist is reluctant to name overtly: the transformation of the great Soviet hope into a police state, the submission of the European communist parties to the interests of this state; the elimination of revolutionary political debate and of theoretical Marxist debate, exemplified during the Cold War by the "Lyssenkist" episode. Althusser's objective was at this stage to find in Marx's own thinking the principle of a theoretical understanding of Marxism's aberrations. For him, such an understanding could not be found in the critical Marxist traditions that already existed. These were *theoretically* compromised in the misguided course followed by the Soviet Union. Indeed, social-democracy had molded the economic and evolutionist vision which had dominated Soviet development. And, for its part, the leftist tradition had established the belief in the omnipotence of the subjective will which had served as its complement or corrective. Both were rooted in the idealistic vision of *Aufklärung*, of a history dedicated to the realization of the human subject's essential goals. And there was little point expecting that more would come from the generous attempts to reactivate the humanism latent in the texts of the young Marx. In presupposing the existence of a human essence that will be realized in history, humanism retreats, on the one hand, into the bourgeois politico-philosophical tradition and leads, on the other, to all the aberrations of revolutionary subjectivism. Marx's political thought can only allow an understanding of these aberrations if it is made free from any subject, any origin, or any end of history.

Hence the importance assumed by the question of the young Marx and by an understanding of the break realized in *The German Ideology* with his "old philosophical conscience." All the previous corrections of Marxism favored the young Marx's thought as a vital source that fed into the scientific undertaking of *Capital* as well as into the construction of workers' parties and the workers' International. In the essays collected in *Pour Marx*, Althusser adopts the opposite approach. He wants to increase the scope of the break: it is a break with the philosophy of the

530

subject in the two forms it assumed for the young Marx: Feuerbach's theory of the alienation of the human essence and the Hegelian theory of history as the realization of Spirit. Historically, this constitutes an epistemological break similar to that of Galileo, the foundation stone of modern physical science. Just as Galileo and Descartes had done for the natural sciences, so Marx rids history of the obstacle of final causes, even if they were human and no longer divine. But he also rids history of the subjection to a unified principle of causality. Althusser encapsulates this emancipation in the notion of overdetermination, a notion whose conceptual construction is a good illustration of the characteristic detour taken by Althusser's thought, as well as the problems that this creates. Althusser wants to emphasize the Marxist assertion of the reversal and placing back on its feet of Hegelian dialectics. However, a reversed Hegelian dialectics, which puts the real instead of the Idea in the causal position, would preserve the core of Hegelian idealism: the expressive conception of the simple totality, driven by a principle that is expressed in each of its manifestations and by an idea of contradiction as an internal scission of the principle into its opposing aspects. The true "reversal" of dialectics therefore consists in the modification of its elements and the way they interrelate. This is the meaning of the notion of overdetermination (*surdetermination*). A social totality is never driven or destroyed by the basic contradiction alone, the opposition between productive forces and the relations of production. It is a complex whole in which the principal contradiction is always specified by the forms of the superstructure (State, dominant ideology, religion, organized political movements, etc.) and by the historical situation. It is this specific difference in the Marxist contradiction that is revealed by the Leninist political decision founded upon the understanding of the "present moment." Unlike the Marxist vulgate, this brings to the fore overdetermination, the condensation of contradictions that in 1917 made of an economically "backward" Russia the weak link where the imperialist chain could break.

This analysis of overdetermination is a model of Althusserian displacement. In order to formulate the specific difference of the Marxist theory of history, Althusser borrows a notion from Freud (overdetermination) and a concrete demonstration from Lenin. We need to return to Marx's own thought if we are to get communist practice out of its impasse. But Marx's own thought is not to be found in Marx's texts, it is only to be found in a practical state in Leninist political action. However, at this point the displacement appears to constitute a vicious circle. Lenin *practiced* the Marxist science of historical materialism. But he did not formulate the principle of scientificity. So, the theoretical principle of Leninist action must be sought once again from the Marxist texts. *Lire le Capital* is devoted to this task: examine Marx's scientific work in order to bring out its philosophy, inquire into its scientificity. This examination is necessary because the author of *Capital* never suggests, as a thesis, a theory for his own scientific work. In order to question the text we will therefore need to conduct a "symptomatic" reading of it in order to uncover the formula of the work of transformation that Marx's science, like all science, provides. Scientific practice shares a structure with any practice which, with the aid of instruments, transforms a raw material into products: it operates already-existing "generalities" – those of the previous science – upon the raw material in order to produce with the aid of concepts, new knowledge, new generalities. The scientific work of *Capital* is a work of production in two senses: it constructs notions and relations which were missing from political economy in order to account satisfactorily for its objects. But to "produce," in the etymological sense of the word, is also to "bring forward," to make apparent what was latent. The work of Marxist science is to make apparent, for example, notions such as labor power, the value of labor power, and profit which a classical economy could not recognize even though it witnessed the effects of them. Not that it failed to see them through lack of attention. Rather, they were its own invisible side: they constituted questions which, had they been asked, would have caused the system to disintegrate, even though it did identify objects and problems in the system. "Marx's philosophy," then, is the work that brings out the invisible side of the old science, the absent cause – necessarily absent – of its errors. Truth, according to Spinoza, is *index sui et falsi*: it cannot have criteria, it carries its own mark, the mark of its difference. In its Althusserian version, this formula can be stated as follows: science is the science of itself inasmuch as it is the science of its opposite, ideology.

The distinctive quality of what has inappropriately been called Althusserian "theoreticism" is the way in which he linked two theses about ideology. Firstly, ideology is the system of imaginary relations that individuals have with their conditions of existence. Secondly, ideology is the opposite of science. This elaboration can only be understood at the core of the Althusserian paradox. If the particular thinking of Marxist science is never actually formulated by itself, it must be grasped in its efforts to produce the difference of science with its other, ideology. The Marxist science of capital is of the way in which the science of the means of production eludes the agents and the "supports" of the relations of production because they are under the illusion that they conduct these relations. It is the science of the inevitable way in which this science has eluded those classical economists who have constantly played hide the thimble with an invisible cause. For Althusser, to decode the work of science is also to decode the way in which *Capital*, in revealing the unseen of the classical economy, produces a critique in actuality of the humanist problematization of the economy which is characteristic of the young Marx.

Thus the ordinary illusion of the agents of capitalist production, the errors of classical political economy, and the impasses of the young Marx's humanism stem from the same principle of illusion which is the core of ideology: the subject's illusion in which the law of the subject-free process of capitalist production – such as it is perceived by the subject-free process of scientific production – is accomplished and dissimulated. Marx's "own" thought, revealed by Althusser, links the Bachelardian theme of the epistemological break between science and its prehistory with, on the one hand, the Freudian theory of the unconscious revised by Lacan and, on the other hand, Foucault's analysis of "man" as a historically dated and perishable product of the new *episteme*, articulated in relation to the new positivities of language, work, and life. Althusserian Marxism, with its notion of the subject-free process and its radical opposition to all humanism, is at the heart of the ambiguous configuration known in the 1960s by the name of structuralism. Many critics have underlined the paradoxes of this "real" Marxism which constantly had to take the opposite view to Marx's explicit ideas in order to bring his texts into line with the theoretical tendencies of the time. But it is more interesting to situate the problem at the level of the intimate paradox of "Marx's philosophical thought" such as it was investigated by Althusser.

In effect, Althusser did not simply undergo the influence of structuralism as something that was "in the air" at the time. He ranked among its most important creators. For Lévi-Strauss, structuralism was a new paradigm for the "social sciences." In establishing a link between this linguistic paradigm in anthropology and both the Lacanian redevelopment of the theory of the unconscious and the Foucauldian archaeology of knowledge-power, Althusser, more than any other, made structuralism a *philosophical* paradigm: the paradigm of a philosophical alternative to the philosophies of the subject, capable of fleshing out the Marxist "epistemological break." But what is more, the structuralist paradigm of unconscious rationality resolved the paradox of "latent philosophy." It facilitated the treatment of Marx's text in turn as a scientific text, as philosophical practice included within scientific practice and as a manifestation of the lack of self-awareness that affects any practice. On the negative side, it established a vicious circle that became never-ending: the rationality of the truth that Lenin "practiced" needed to be sought out in the same way that Marx revealed the unseen of the classical economy as well as the necessity of this invisibility. But the rationality that Marx put into operation was in turn subjected to the law of ideological capture that affects any practice: in the same way that Adam Smith had failed to notice the "labor power" which was "literally staring him in the face," Marx inevitably failed to be aware of the concept of rationality that he "produced" and "practiced" when revealing the unseen, in other words failed to see his "own" philosophy. And so the question arose of how the general theory of discourses conceived by Althusser in order to express the truth practiced and unseen by Marx could claim to stop the process of the infinite regression. In short, two different ideas were mixed together: first, a philosophy that is "practiced" and that is not in the form of an auto-explanation and, second, a philosophy that is a science of science, a discourse that brings out the principle of the scientificity of science. In bringing together these two ideas, Althusser's thought locked itself into the alternative between the universal illusion that affects any practice of production and the miracle that shields science or the science of science from a universal misrecognition (*méconnaissance*). At the same time, it was not the relation of "theory" to "practice" that was made indeterminable as has been claimed, but rather the relation of the practice of scientific production to political practice.

The turning point in Althusser's thought between 1968 and 1972 consisted in the dissociation of these two ideas. In *Lénine et la philosophie*, as in *Philosophie et philosophie spontanée des savants*, Althusser explicitly abandons any attempt to assimilate "Marxist philosophy" to a science of science or to a theory of scientificity. Once more, it is the Leninist "practice" of the decision which provides him with a model. *Materialism and empiriocriticism* is not a "philosophy of Marxist materialism"; it constitutes a materialist practice that is entirely new, a practice of intervention which no longer aims to express the scientificity of science but to establish a

533

boundary between the ideas (materialist) that serve science and the ideas (idealist) that exploit it. Philosophical *categories* are neither the determinations of the scientific object nor are they conceptualizations of its scientificity. They are the simple operators of this drawing of a boundary. The philosophy "practiced" by Lenin does not have to explain itself to the idea of a philosophy as science of science or of thought as pure thought. On the contrary, it suggests a new idea of philosophy, that is, a new idea of what philosophy has unceasingly done since Plato: a double representation of politics in relation to the sciences, and of the sciences in relation to politics; a political alignment or an act of class struggle within theory. Consequently, far from practicing a philosophy that was still unaware of itself, Lenin's Marxism eliminated the denial of its own practice that philosophy had always operated by proclaiming itself the science of science or the thought of thought.

In this way Althusser solves the paradox of the science of Marxist science at the same time as he replies to the accusation of "theoreticism" by asserting the political dependency of philosophy. But it can be asked whether this political "radicalization" of philosophy as an arm of class struggle does not lead Althusser back into the confusion that his whole theoretical undertaking had attempted to dissipate. The difference between this form of political alignment and that of the historical forms of the submission of Marxist philosophy to party politics remains unclear. No doubt Althusser manages, in asserting the empty nature of philosophical categories, to preserve philosophy from all identification with political content disguised as a scientistic thesis. On the other hand, the political act of philosophy is thrown back to categories of political struggle that remain uncriticized. The complexities of the political treatment of overdetermined contradiction are thrown back to the eternity of a class struggle that is reflected in the eternity of the opposition between materialism and idealism. This eternalized process appears to translate the perpetual oscillation of Althusserian political philosophy between two poles: a Platonic pole of knowledge, which alone can liberate, and a political pole of "alignment" which again consigns philosophy to its status as ideology.

This oscillation is evident again in the development of the concept which seems to complete the self-criticism of "theoreticism," that of the ideological apparatus of the State. In the text "Idéologie et appareils idéologiques d'État," Althusser sets out to give a materialist face and a political foundation to a theory of ideology that tended to confuse ideology with the other of Science. Ideology is not simply a misrecognition which stands in opposition to science, it is produced by the apparatus of power in the context of a struggle. This materialist and political specification of the concept thus seems to complete the political radicalization of the theory for which the thesis of political alignment provided evidence. But this apparent complementarity hides a new tension: among the apparatuses which produce and reproduce the ideologies of subservience, Althusser places political parties, including "workers' parties." The latter seem then to lose any privilege they might have had in the class struggle, supported by philosophy, and take their place among the instruments that reproduce class domination. This signifies also that the materialization of ideology once more turns ideology into machinery which irremediably traps any subject. Borrowing the analysis of the mirror stage from Lacanian

534

psychoanalysis, Althusser twists its meaning in order to understand it as providing an entire theory of the subject. Thus he identifies political subjection with the subjection to the very idea of the subject. Every subject is caught in subjection as soon as it recognizes its image and answers to its name. The theoretical "leftism" of the theory of ideological interpellation returns once more to a Platonism which connects the human order of birth to the descent into illusion and makes salvation depend solely on the miracle of science or of decision.

Althusser's last texts testify to a desire to break out of the circle by developing a philosophy "for" Marxism and no longer one specific to Marx. This research is expressed in the notion of random materialism. The materialist philosopher is described as a traveler who catches the train on the move, who "registers sequences of random encounters" and derives from these encounters some general constants "of which the 'variations' can account for the singularity of the cases under consideration and therefore produce both knowledge of a 'clinical' sort and ideological, political and social effects" (Althusser 1994, pp. 64–5). The series of encounters which Marxism consists of can then be interpreted in the light of a materialist tradition whose heroes are Epicurus, the thinker of emptiness and of the *clinamen* which leaves aside all origin, Machiavelli, the thinker of the "present moment" and of the decision in the emptiness, and Heidegger, the thinker of *es gibt* and of the critique of the principle of reason. This materialism which is more dreamt-about than constructed is still in line with the Althusserian oscillation: it is a philosophy for Marxism but also a radical critique of all philosophy, the beginning of an "objective knowledge of philosophy's mode of being," which raises the question of the branch of knowledge to which this belongs. In *Pour Marx*, Althusser had denounced the initial illusion of the young communists of his generation who identified Marxist knowledge with the "end of philosophy." His last texts demonstrate a persistent tension between a discourse of philosophy and a discourse on philosophy which positions his Marxism once more among the problematics developed by other French philosophers of his generation from Nietzsche or Heidegger. This oscillation over the Marxist status of philosophy stems from a deeper paradox in Althusser's approach: this thinker who never gave up wanting a philosophy *for* politics was constantly held up by his reluctance to call into question the categories of politics itself.

## Writings

Althusser, Louis: *Montesquieu; La politique et l'histoire* (Paris: PUF, 1964).
——: *Pour Marx* (Paris: François Maspero, 1965).
——: *Lénine et la philosophie* (Paris: François Maspero, 1969).
——: *Positions* (Paris: Editions sociales, 1976).
——: *Sur la philosophie* (Paris: Gallimard, 1994).

## References and further reading

Balibar, Etienne: *Écrits pour Althusser* (Paris: La Découverte, 1991).
Benton, Ted: *The Rise and Fall of Structural Marxism: Althusser and his Influence* (London: Macmillan, 1984).

Elliot, Gregory: *Althusser: The Detour of Theory* (London: Verso, 1987).

Giacometti, Maria, et al.: *La Cognizione della crisi, Saggi sul marxismo di Louis Althusser* (Milano: Franco Angeli, 1986).

Kaplan, Ann, and Sprinker, Michael (eds): *The Althusserian Legacy* (London: Verso, 1993).

Karsz, Saül: *Théorie et politique: Louis Althusser* (Paris: Fayard, 1973).

Lazarus, Sylvain (ed.): *Politique et philosophie dans L'oeúvre de Louis Althusser* (Paris: PUF, 1993).

Moulier-Boutang Yann: *Althusser: une biographie* (Paris: Flammarion, 1992).

Pogliani, Filippo: *L'ideologia e la sua critica: dopo Marx e Althusser* (Milano: Franco Angeli, 1985).

Rancière, Jacques: *La leçon d'Althusser* (Paris: Gallimard, 1974).

——(with Macherey, P., Balibar, E., and Establet, R.): *Lire le Capital* (Paris: François Maspero, 1969).

# 49

# Foucault

## PAUL PATTON

Michel Foucault (1926–84) invented a new practice of philosophy. His books trace the emergence of some of the concepts, institutions, and techniques of government which delineate the peculiar shape of modern European culture. They include a history of madness, an account of the birth of clinical medicine at the end of the eighteenth century, an archaeology of the modern sciences of language, life, and labor, a genealogy of the modern form of punishment, and fragments of a history of sexuality. These are all historical studies by virtue of the kinds of claim advanced and the documentary evidence adduced to illustrate and support them, but they do not conform to established rules of historiographical method and often invent new objects of historical research. The title chosen by Foucault for the chair he occupied at the Collège de France provides a clue to the distinctive nature of his research: professor of the history of systems of thought. By "thought" he means firstly the forms of theoretical and conceptual reflection developed within philosophy and the human sciences. His early work deals with the history of psychopathology and clinical medicine in a manner which owes much to the approach of French philosopher-historians of science such as Bachelard and Canguilhem. However, by "thought" Foucault also means the forms of rationality embedded in the everyday practice of administrators, doctors, priests, and private individuals, and expressed in technical manuals, projects for institutional reform, and the writings of moralists. His work on madness, criminal punishment, and sexuality exposes the historical singularity of forms of experience which involve thought in both of these senses. The history of systems of thought thus defines an approach to the workings of a culture rather than a specific level within a given culture.

While the exhumation of particular systems of thought requires historical research, the demonstration of their historical character is a matter for philosophical criticism. Foucault's conception of philosophy as critical history of thought is indebted to both Kant and Nietzsche: it involves analysis of the conditions of possibility of particular systems of thought, but in contrast to Kantian criticism it is not concerned with their epistemic status as knowledge, nor does it assume unique a priori conditions of knowledge. Rather, it assumes only the fact that certain statements are made and that these function as knowledge within a given period. Foucault seeks to uncover the historical a priori conditions of what passed for knowledge in empirical domains such as language, political economy, and criminal anthropology. The critical force of this "archaeological" history emerges in its relation to present social movements. Foucault's historical studies are intended to assist the criticism of systems of thought and practices informed by them. They are indirect responses to questions such as the following: what else could we do with criminals but imprison and attempt to rehabilitate them? How can we understand the social relations between the sexes other than as the product of natural differences? How could we regulate our sexual behavior other than by discovering and accepting the truth about our desire? Such criticism, Foucault suggests, "does not mark out impassable boundaries or describe closed systems; it brings to light transformable singularities" (Foucault 1984c, p. 335).

Foucault identified the philosophical tradition within which he worked as that which extends from Kant through Hegel, Marx, and Nietzsche to contemporary critical and post-structural theorists. This tradition does not look for universal or timeless structures of knowledge, language, or moral action, but for ways of characterizing the present as a particular moment in history and for paths beyond it. The conception of history and the fundamental elements of the corresponding "ontology of the present" vary from one member of this tradition to the next (Foucault 1986). For Nietzsche, different forms of society and types of human being are to be understood as successive cultural manifestations of will to power. Only in *The Birth of Tragedy* is there an implicit teleology which haunts the succession of forms of thought, namely the impending re-emergence of the tragic experience of existence which had been subsumed by Greek rationalism and Christianity. While Foucault drew upon this historical model and this Romantic sensibility in his history of madness, his later work implies a less prophetic conception of criticism. He remains skeptical with regard to all forms of teleology and all anthropological universals.

*Folie et déraison: Histoire de la folie à l'âge classique*, Foucault's major thesis for the Doctorat d'Etat, was published in 1961. Although it has since been influential in the development of an entire sub-discipline devoted to the history of madness, and widely criticized for its historical shortcomings, only a heavily abridged version of the original 600-page work has hitherto been translated into English. In its complete version, *Histoire de la folie* weaves together several interconnected narratives in the attempt to delineate the European experience of madness between the end of the Middle Ages and the early part of the nineteenth century. A primary concern is to provide a critical history of the origins of modern psychiatry. A second aim is to provide a political and economic account of the circumstances under which the mad began to be confined. Foucault argues that what distinguished the treatment of the mad during this period was the confinement of those who previously were allowed or forced to circulate freely within society. Madness during this period was embedded within a broader category of "unreason." Not only were those who would later be identified as mentally ill confined: so too were beggars, free thinkers, offenders against sexual morality, and other indigent elements of the population. At the end of the eighteenth century, this category dissolved, once more specialized treatments were applied to the poor, criminals, and the mentally ill.

A third and more general aim is to bring to light one of the fundamental principles of exclusion within modern thought. Early modern European culture harbored an ambivalence toward madness: it represented the dark, inexplicable underside of human existence, associated with death but also with a privileged relation to the truth. On the other hand, because it was the result of all-too-human error, foolishness, or pride, madness was an ever-present threat to human reason. However, in both guises, madness was widely represented in the literature and painting of the period, whether in Shakespeare's *King Lear* or the paintings of Bosch, Breughel and Dürer. By contrast, the classical age saw this cultural dialogue replaced by the silent opposition between reason and unreason. Ultimately, Foucault writes, "the language of psychiatry, which is a monologue of reason about madness, could be established only on the basis of such a silence. I have not tried to write the history of that language, but rather the archaeology of that silence" (Foucault 1965 [1961], pp. x–xi).

Perhaps the most controversial dimension of Foucault's history is the parallel he draws between institutional confinement and the absence of intellectual dialogue between reason and madness. Commenting on Descartes' dismissal of the possibility of madness as a ground of error at the beginning of his *Meditations*, Foucault suggests that his intellectual gesture parallels the social and institutional exclusion of the unreasoning elements of the population. These remarks became the focus of a critical review of *Histoire de la folie* by Derrida, to which Foucault later replied (Derrida 1978 [1964]; Foucault 1979 [1972]). Derrida challenges Foucault's reading of Descartes, arguing that madness is not simply excluded from Descartes' conception of the rational subject, but that the hypothesis of the evil demon amounts to a kind of total madness to which the fundamental certainty of the thinking subject nevertheless remains immune. Secondly, Derrida denounces the aspiration to presence implied by Foucault's allusions to the possibility of an unmediated experience of madness, of the kind which is occasionally glimpsed in the work of artists such as Goya or writers such as Nietzsche and Artaud. Foucault later dissociates himself from any ambition to write a history of "madness itself" (Foucault 1972 [1969], p. 47). Nevertheless, this exchange became a test site for the relative merits of deconstructive and Foucauldian methods of reading, and gave rise to a considerable secondary literature (see Article 50, DERRIDA; Boyne 1990).

## Truth

Foucault acknowledges a debt to Nietzsche throughout his works, from the preface to the first edition of *Histoire de la folie*, which he described as a work carried out "under the sun of the great Nietzschean enquiry" (Foucault 1965 [1961], p. v), through to the final interview in which he said: "I am simply a Nietzschean, and try as far as possible, on a certain number of issues, to see with the help of Nietzsche's texts" (Foucault 1989, p. 327). However, Foucault was never an uncritical Nietzschean, and different aspects of Nietzsche's work were important to him at different stages of his career: the tragic experience of existence, effective history, genealogy, and the concept of power were all at times identified as significant influences. Perhaps the single common Nietzschean element which runs though all his work is the kind of historical philosophizing whose advent Nietzsche announced in *Human, All Too Human* and which seeks an explanation of phenomena in terms of their worldly origins. Nietzsche advances the hypothesis that the greatest triumph of historical philosophy will one day be "a history of the genesis of thought," by which he means a natural history of that "realm of ideas" which defines "the world" for human beings (Nietzsche 1986, p. 18). Similarly, in his inaugural lecture at the Collège de France, Foucault described his project as that of analyzing the various forms of truth throughout European history: a morphology and a critical history of the Western will to truth (Foucault 1984a, pp. 130–1).

By "will to truth," he means all those forms of thought which purport to represent reality and which are sufficiently complex to allow for the distinction between true and false statements. The morphological task is undertaken by the "archaeologies" of knowledge which remain an important aspect of all Foucault's work. For example, one element of the project outlined in *The History of Sexuality*, vol. I was the specification of the form of modern knowledge of sex. Foucault argues that this developed out of religious discourse on sexual behavior which assigned a privileged role to confession, and that a number of theoretical postulates and transformations in the form of such confessional discourse were necessary before it could be adjusted to the norms of nineteenth-century science (Foucault 1978 [1976], pp. 65–7). Similarly, in his Introduction to *The History of Sexuality*, vol. II, Foucault suggests that his account of the ancient Greek sexual ethics and corresponding conception of the self represents some further fragments towards a history of truth (Foucault 1985 [1984], pp. 6–7). By characterizing particular systems of thought, these archaeological studies seek to specify the conditions which enable the production of particular kinds of truth and falsity. In this sense, it has been argued that Foucault holds an epistemological coherentist view of knowledge (Alcoff 1993).

*The Archaeology of Knowledge* sought to define the precise object of this archaeology in contrast to other approaches to the history of ideas or the sciences, by spelling out Foucault's conception of discourse. Discourse was defined with reference to statements or "things said," where these are understood as events of a very particular kind: at once tied to an historical context of utterance and yet capable of repetition. The regularities between statements, and between statements and non-discursive procedures, together define particular discursive formations such as clinical medicine or the mercantilist discourse on wealth. These regularities include the type of subject-position presupposed by a given type of utterance, the type of theoretical object to which they may refer, and the empirical or institutional domains in relation to which statements are formed. The resulting "rules of formation" which define a given discursive formation provide a rich theoretical apparatus which allowed Foucault to propose detailed analyses of the transformations which such formations may undergo. In many respects, this theory of discourse only systematized the kind of analysis undertaken in Foucault's work prior to 1969. Thus, *Histoire de la folie* argues that it was against the background of the amorphous category of unreason that the concept of mental illness emerged in the nineteenth century. On the one hand, the theory of mental alienation represents a decisive break with the earlier systems of classification which saw various forms of mental aberration as the effects of bodily disorder. On the other hand, the forms of medico-moral treatment practiced within the enlightened asylums maintain certain normative elements of earlier conceptions of madness as a physical and moral disorder.

Foucault's early studies in the history of various empirical sciences stress the historically variable character of that which has been regarded as knowledge. They share several assumptions with post-Kuhnian philosophy of science. For example, they reject the idea of pure observation and insist on the "statemental" character of knowledge. They reject the idea that the history of knowledge is a more or less continuous process of the elimination of error. Instead, these studies point to discontinuities and the sudden emergence of new ways of perceiving and describing natural phenomena, such as took place at the end of the eighteenth century when the medical language of humors was rendered obsolete by an anatomical discourse about bodies and their diseases. *The Order of Things* carries furthest the display of such radical discontinuities in the history of thought, highlighting mutations in the forms of knowledge about language, wealth, and living beings since the end of the sixteenth century. The crucial difference which separated knowledge during the classical period from the nineteenth-century human sciences which followed was the fact that in classical thought there was no place for a concept of man, even while it provided knowledge of such distinctively human activities as speaking and exchanging goods. At the end of this book, Foucault suggested in a phrase which became emblematic of the anti-humanism associated with structuralist thought, that the figure of "man" is destined to disappear "like a face drawn in sand at the edge of the sea" (Foucault 1970 [1966], p. 387). By "man," he meant the peculiar figure which defines the epistemological space in which the nineteenth-century human sciences became possible forms of knowledge: a figure which finds philosophical expression in Kant's dual conception of man as both object of empirical knowledge and transcendental subject of all knowledge.

*The Order of Things* confines itself to describing the underlying conditions of knowledge within the empirical domains mentioned. No attempt is made to account for the transformations which occurred, much less to relate these to social and institutional changes. However, such self-imposed methodological limitations should not be mistaken for a general feature of Foucault's approach to the history of truth. *Histoire de la folie* and *Birth of the Clinic* do suggest correlations between non-discursive events and developments within the sciences. But it is with *Discipline and Punish* that Foucault's distinctive contribution to this question begins to emerge. Here, he rejects the idea that power and knowledge bear only external relations to one another, arguing instead that "power and knowledge directly imply one another; that there is no power relation without the correlative constitution of a field of knowledge, nor any knowledge that does not at the same time presuppose and constitute power relations" (Foucault 1977 [1975], p. 27). His claim is that objects of social scientific inquiry such as delinquency and criminality have not always existed. Rather, their historical conditions of possibility include the institutions and techniques of power deployed in relation to crime during the early part of the nineteenth century. Similarly, *The History of Sexuality*, vol. I, argues that knowledge of "sexuality" developed along with the political regulation of sexual conduct. Foucault illustrates his internal relation thesis by pointing to a series of figures which double as mechanisms of power and techniques for the production of truth: measurement, investigation, examination, and confession correspond respectively to the demonstrable truths of geometry, natural scientific knowledge, the normalizing truth of the human sciences, and the modern knowledge of sexuality. Each embodies a particular type of power and marks an important stage in the history of the Western will to truth. Foucault's comments about the role of inquisitorial techniques are one of the rare occasions on which he refers to the natural sciences in general (Foucault 1977 [1975], p. 226). These comments do not commit him to relativism. His historical epistemology does reject the idea that what passes for truth is independent of social and political forces, but this does not imply that all sciences remain bound to the institutional and political conditions under which they originated. Equally, Foucault rejects the idea that political "interests" have only distorting effects upon what passes for knowledge. The political question with regard to intellectual products, he suggests, "is not error, illusion, alienated consciousness, or ideology; it is truth itself. Hence the importance of Nietzsche" (Gordon 1980, p. 133).

## Power

During the 1970s, Foucault became increasingly preoccupied with the analysis of power. By 1976, with the publication of *The History of Sexuality*, vol. I, he could claim that the point of this project lay in the re-elaboration of the theory of power (Gordon 1980, p. 187). This book included a critique of what he called the "juridico-discursive conception" of power, and a sketch of the methodological principles which informed his own analyses of the strategies of power deployed in relation to sex. As an alternative to traditional questions about the nature, limits, and legitimate exercise of power, Foucault proposed a more concrete and positive approach oriented toward the question of how power is exercised. Initially, the conceptual basis of this new approach took the form of a series of methodological injunctions: power is not a thing but a relation; power relations operate at all levels throughout society and not merely through the apparatuses of the state; power should be analyzed from below; power must be understood in terms of strategies, but without reference to a unique strategist; power is not always repressive but productive; and so on. These injunctions, along with the analyses of discipline and sexuality, contributed to opening up important new perspectives for historical analysis and social theory.

Nevertheless, Foucault was widely criticized for failing to distinguish clearly between different kinds of exercise of power and for failing to provide any normative criteria by which power could either be legitimated or condemned (Fraser 1989 [1981]; Habermas 1987). Such criticisms reflected differences between his concept of power and those current in political theory. One important difference is that he eschews normative issues and proposes a non-evaluative concept of power. A second important difference stems from the fact that he employs a concept of power as capacity, whereas political theory tends to focus upon power in a relational sense: power as exercised over or in concert with others. In *Discipline and Punish* and *The History of Sexuality*, vol. I, Foucault employed a language of bodies and forces in describing the fundamental elements of any power relation. Thus, the object of disciplinary techniques was a body composed of forces, which discipline sought both to enhance and to subjugate with the aim of producing "subjected and prac- tised bodies" (Foucault 1977 [1975], p. 138). In later writings, he defines power in the relational sense as action upon the actions of others. Despite the terminological change, his primary concept of power remains the same: the capacity of a body to perform certain kinds of action.

On this basis, Foucault is able to distinguish different forms of exercise of power. One of the things individual or collective human bodies can do is to act upon each other's actions. Power is exercised by one party *over* another when the actions of A succeed in modifying the field of possible actions of B. This is a normatively neutral concept of power, since it involves no reference to action against the interests of the other party, or indeed to any particular outcome. Further, the exercise of power over others will not always imply effective modification of their actions. Precisely because power is always exercised between subjects of power, each with their own distinct capacities for action, resistance is always possible: "where there is power, there is resistance" (Foucault 1978 [1976], p. 95). For this reason, it is only in exceptional circumstances that A can be sure of achieving a particular desired effect on B. Only when the possibility of effective resistance has been removed does the power relation between two subjects of power become unilateral and one-sided: "A relationship of confrontation reaches its term, its final moment (and the victory of one of the two adversaries) when stable mechanisms replace the free play of antagonistic reactions. Through such mechanisms one can direct, in a fairly con- stant manner and with reasonable certainty, the conduct of others" (Foucault 1983a, p. 225). In such cases, we have something more than the exercise of power over another, namely the establishment of a state of *domination*. In these cases, "the relations of power, instead of being variable and allowing different partners a strat- egy which alters them, find themselves firmly set and congealed" (Foucault 1987, p. 114). Bentham's Panopticon, which Foucault analyzes in *Discipline and Punish*, provides a model of such mechanisms for controlling the conduct of others: the asymmetrical structure of visibility which is the key to its architectural design maps on to the fixed and asymmetrical distribution of power which defines every system of domination.

Foucault is not the first to identify domination with stable and asymmetrical systems of power relations. However, his definition does make it clear that such systems are always secondary results, achieved within or imposed upon a primary field of relations between subjects of power. Moreover, as with the definition of power over others, this concept of domination is non-normative. Domination al- lows more or less predictable control of the actions of others. Beyond that, little is said about the purposes for which such states are established and maintained. States of domination may allow members of a particular social class, caste, or sex to extract benefits from the power of others, but they may also occur in situations where the flow of capacities or benefits is non-extractive. For example, in Hobbes' account of sovereign power, the relationship of domination which obtains between the state and citizens is a condition of maintaining the rule of law. In this case, the purpose of the system of domination is not further extraction but the preservation of the powers of its subjects. Pedagogic relations are another sphere in which a measure of domination may be acceptable, at least during some part of the educational process. Foucault uses this example in order to suggest that the exercise of power over others is not always bad, and states of domination are not always to be avoided (Foucault 1987, p. 129).

Since the exercise of power over others will be an inescapable feature of any society, it makes no sense to recommend liberation from all forms of power. Nonetheless, the fact that a sufficient number of individuals possess a capacity for relatively autonomous self-direction in the use of their powers and capacities ensures that the historical and political present will always include movements of resistance to particular mechanisms of power and forms of domination. While he abjures the traditional critical task of providing legitimation for such movements, Foucault argues that the task of critical thought is to assist such movements for change. His own practice of genealogy seeks to point out the singular, contingent, and therefore surpassable character of those elements of modern social being which are often presented to us as universal, necessary, and inescapable (Foucault 1984b, p. 45).

There is a sense in which the analysis of specific forms and technologies of power may be regarded as pursuing a project analogous to that undertaken in relation to truth: in this case, a morphology and a critical history of the will to power. Much of Foucault's work during the 1970s dealt with techniques of bodily coercion, control, and training that he called "micro-power." However, these by no means exhaust the modern techniques of power over others. At the end of *The History of Sexuality*, vol. I, in contrasting the ancient form of power over death with modern power over life, Foucault points to the political control of population as another pole of this "bio-power." In fact, the seventeenth and eighteenth centuries saw the development of a series of new techniques for the government of populations, and new forms of knowledge such as statistics and political arithmetic which served this end. In subsequent lectures and articles, Foucault proposed to identify different conceptions of the aim, function, and characteristic operations of political government, and to characterize the "forms of rationality" implicit in various discourses on the art of government which appeared in Europe from the sixteenth century onwards. To this end, he points to the development during the eighteenth and nineteenth centuries of mechanisms of security which govern by means of action not upon individuals but upon populations of one kind or another, and traces from Jewish and Greek sources through the Christian Church and into modern government the outlines of a pastoral conception of power, where the objects of government are the individual members of the herd of those governed. While the Church's exercise of this pastoral power has declined since the eighteenth century, Foucault suggests that it has been taken up in a variety of other social institutions such as welfare and medical agencies. These studies suggest the possibility of an historical analysis of different forms of "governmentality" which would also function as a genealogy of the forms of power exercised by the modern state (Foucault 1981; 1983a; Burchell et al. 1991).

## Subjectivity

By the early 1980s, Foucault was able to propose another restatement of the overall objective of his work: the history of the different ways in which human beings have been made particular kinds of subject (Foucault 1983a, p. 209). In *Discipline and Punish* and *The History of Sexuality*, vol. I, he had argued that certain kinds of subject are fabricated by means of particular techniques for the government of others, such as discipline or the policing of children's sexual behavior: "it is one of the prime effects of power that certain bodies, certain gestures, certain discourses, certain desires come to be identified and constituted as individuals" (Gordon 1980, p. 98). The thesis that power creates subjects refers, firstly, to the way in which particular educative, therapeutic, or training procedures are applied to individuals in order to make them into subjects of certain kinds. Secondly, it refers to the manner in which new techniques for examining, training, or controlling individuals, along with their accompanying new forms of knowledge, bring into existence new possibilities for social being. In this sense, neither delinquents nor habitual criminals existed before the penal institutions and criminal anthropologies of the nineteenth century produced them as identifiable modes of social being. Conversely, the advent of new categories and new ways of describing human actions opens up new possibilities for intentional action, since this is always action under a description of some kind. The result is to change what it is possible for individuals to do or to become in a given historical context.

There is a third dimension to the exercise of power in the constitution of subjects, namely the ethical dimension which plays an important role in practices such as confession. Confession was a technique through which the church sought to govern the souls of its flock, but it was also a technique which obliged individuals to give an account of themselves. It thus established a critical and hermeneutic relation of the self to the self in which, Foucault suggests, we might discern one source of the modern concern to understand our true nature by analyzing our desires. In the second and third volumes of *The History of Sexuality*, Foucault shifts his focus on to these techniques of self which enable individuals to act upon themselves and to transform themselves in particular ways: what kinds of relation to the self, what kinds of self-reflection and self-transformation are required in order to make oneself into a moral subject of a certain kind? These volumes also shift the chronological focus, firstly to problems in the sexual ethics of classical Greece and secondly to Greek and Roman literature on the care of the self during the first and second centuries AD.

The hypothesis which informs his study of the Greek ethics of moderation and

545

self-mastery in the use of bodily pleasures is that "there is a whole rich and complex field of historicity in the way the individual is summoned to recognise himself as an ethical subject of sexual conduct" (Foucault 1985 [1984], p. 32). In order to analyze this field, he proposes a novel conception of ethics as the form of the relation of the self to the self practiced within a given style of moral life. There are four aspects to this relation: the part of the self or its actions that is relevant for ethical judgment (ethical substance); the manner in which the self relates to moral rules and obligations (mode of subjection); the kinds of activity undertaken on the self by the self (ethical work); and finally the goal or type of being the self aspires to become (telos). In a given period, change may occur at different rates along some or all of these levels. For example, while ancient Greek and Christian asceticisms may involve similar kinds of ethical work upon the self, the substance, mode of subjection, and the telos of the activity might be different (Foucault 1983b, pp. 237–43). This conception of ethics thus allows for the analysis of continuities and changes in the forms of relation to the self in a manner which parallels the history of transformations in discursive formations proposed in *The Archaeology of Knowledge*.

Foucault's interest in this new field of historicity was positive as well as critical. In interviews, he suggested that contemporary styles of homosexual life might be seen to involve the search for a new ethics in this sense. His cautious advocacy of the Greek practice of an "ethics of existence" might be read as a proposal for a non-universalizable ethics or a different economy of power with respect to our sexual being. This would be different from that of the ancient Greek men for whom self-mastery and moderation was both conditioned by and predicated upon relations of domination over others, but also different from the modern regulation of sexual conduct by means of legal obligations and truths about sexuality. More generally, the problem addressed by Foucault's turn to ethics is not that of formulating the moral norms that accord with our present moral constitution, but rather the Nietzschean problem of suggesting ways in which we might become other than what we are. For Nietzsche, moral interpretations of phenomena are among the most important means by which human beings act upon themselves and others: it is by such means that one can arouse pity in others, or experience one's own actions as cowardice or humility according to whether one lives in the moral culture of ancient Greece or European Christianity. Like Nietzsche, Foucault refuses any form of philosophical anthropology. He rejects the idea that there is a universal human nature, even while supposing the existence of a distinctively human body endowed with particular forces and historically constituted capacities for action and self-interpretation. The systems of knowledge, moral judgment, and government which he studied in relation to such things as mental illness, punishment, and sexuality are important elements of the interpretative framework within which Europeans have acted upon their own actions as well as those of others. In this sense, the thought of which Foucault writes the history may be found in every manner in which individuals speak and behave: "In this sense, thought is understood as the very form of action" (Foucault 1984c, p. 335).

(See Article 2, KANT, Article 11, NIETZSCHE, Article 48, ALTHUSSER, and Article 51, DELEUZE.)

# Writings

Foucault, M.: *Folie et déraison: Histoire de la folie à l'âge classique* (1961), 2nd edn with new preface and appendices titled *Histoire de la folie à l'âge classique* (Paris: Gallimard, 1972); abridged version tr. Richard Howard, *Madness and Civilization* (New York: Pantheon, 1965).

——: *Naissance de la clinique: une archéologie du regard médical* (Paris, 1963), tr. Alan Sheridan, *The Birth of the Clinic* (London: Tavistock, 1973).

——: *Les Mots et les choses: une archéologie des sciences humaines* (Paris, 1966), tr. Alan Sheridan, *The Order of Things: An Archaeology of the Human Sciences* (London: Tavistock, 1970).

——: *L'Archéologie du savoir* (Paris, 1969); tr. Alan Sheridan, *The Archaeology of Knowledge* (London: Tavistock, 1972).

——: *Surveiller et punir: Naissance de la prison* (Paris, 1975), tr. Alan Sheridan, *Discipline and Punish* (London: Allen Lane, Penguin, 1977).

——: *Histoire de la sexualité 1: la volonté de savoir* (Paris, 1976), tr. Robert Hurley, *The History of Sexuality*, vol. I: *An Introduction* (London: Allen Lane, Penguin, 1978).

——: *L'Usage des plaisirs: histoire de la sexualité II* (Paris, 1984), tr. Robert Hurley, *The Use of Pleasure: The History of Sexuality*, vol. 2 (New York: Pantheon, 1985).

——: *Le Souci de soi: histoire de la sexualité III* (Paris, 1984), tr. Robert Hurley, *The Care of the Self: The History of Sexuality*, vol. 3 (New York: Pantheon, 1986).

# References and further reading

Alcoff, Linda: "Foucault as epistemologist," *The Philosophical Forum*, vol. XX, no. 2 (Winter 1993), pp. 95–124.

Armstrong, T. J. (ed.): *Michel Foucault Philosopher* (Hemel Hempstead: Harvester Wheatsheaf, 1992).

Bernauer, J., and Rasmussen, D. (eds): *The Final Foucault* (Cambridge, MA: MIT Press, 1988).

Boyne, Roy: *Foucault and Derrida: The Other Side of Reason* (London: Unwin Hyman, 1990).

Burchell, G., Gordon, C., and Miller, P. (eds): *The Foucault Effect* (Hemel Hempstead: Harvester Wheatsheaf, 1991).

Derrida, J.: "Cogito et l'histoire de la folie," *Revue de métaphysique et de morale*, 3–4 (1964), pp. 460–94; reprinted in Derrida, J.: *Écriture et la différence* (Paris, 1967), tr. Alan Bass, *Writing and Difference* (Chicago, IL: University of Chicago Press, 1978).

Dreyfus, H. L., and Rabinow, P.: *Michel Foucault: Beyond Structuralism and Hermeneutics*, 2nd edn (Chicago, IL: University of Chicago Press, 1983).

Eribon, Didier: *Michel Foucault*, tr. Betsy Wing (Cambridge, MA: Harvard University Press, 1991).

Foucault, M.: "My body, this paper, this fire," tr. G. Bennington, *Oxford Literary Review*, vol. 4, no. 1 (1979).

——: "Omnes et singulatim: towards a criticism of 'political reason.'" In *The Tanner Lectures on Human Values*, ed. S. Macmurrin (New York: Cambridge University Press, 1981), pp. 224–54.

——: "The subject and power," Afterword to Dreyfus and Rabinow (1983a).

——: "On the genealogy of ethics: an overview of work in progress," Second Afterword to Dreyfus and Rabinow (1983b).

———: "The order of discourse" (1971). In Young, R. (ed.): *Untying the Text* (London: Routledge, 1981); reprinted in Shapiro, M. (ed.): *Language and Politics* (Oxford: Blackwell, 1984a).

———: "What is enlightenment?" In Rabinow, P. (ed.): *The Foucault Reader* (1984b).

———: "Preface to The History of Sexuality, Volume II." In Rabinow, P. (ed.) (1984c).

———: "Kant on Enlightenment and Revolution," tr. C. Gordon, *Economy and Society*, 15 (1986), pp. 88–96.

———: "The ethic of care for the self as a practice of freedom," *Philosophy and Social Criticism*, vol. 12, nos 2–3 (Summer 1987).

———: "The return of morality," tr. John Johnston, in Lotringer, S. (ed.) (1989).

Fraser, Nancy: "Foucault on modern power: empirical insights and normative confusions," *Praxis International*; vol. 1, no. 3 (1981); reprinted in *Unruly Practices* (Minneapolis, MN: University of Minnesota Press, 1989), pp. 32–3.

Gordon, C. (ed.): *Michel Foucault: Power/Knowledge* (Brighton: Harvester, 1980).

Gutting, G.: *Michel Foucault's Archaeology of Scientific Reason* (Cambridge: Cambridge University Press, 1989).

———(ed.): *The Cambridge Companion to Foucault* (Cambridge: Cambridge University Press, 1994).

Habermas, Jürgen: *The Philosophical Discourse of Modernity*, tr. Frederick G. Lawrence (Cambridge: Polity, 1987).

Hoy, D. C. (ed.): *Foucault: A Critical Reader* (Oxford: Blackwell, 1986).

Kritzman, L. D. (ed.): *Michel Foucault: Politics, Philosophy, Culture* (London: Routledge, 1988).

Lotringer, S. (ed.): *Foucault Live* (New York: Semiotext(e) Foreign Agents Series, 1989).

Nietzsche, F.: *Human, All Too Human: A Book For Free Spirits*, tr. R.J. Hollingdale (Cambridge: Cambridge University Press, 1986).

Rabinow, P. (ed.): *The Foucault Reader* (New York: Pantheon, 1984).

Still, Arthur, and Velody, Irving (eds): *Rewriting the History of Madness: Studies in Foucault's "Histoire de la folie"* (London: Routledge, 1992).

# 50

# Derrida

GEOFFREY BENNINGTON

It is at least plausibly arguable that Derrida's will have been the most important philosophical contribution (in French, at least) of the last 30 years, in spite of the impassioned argument his work has provoked and still arouses (concretized most recently in the argument over Cambridge University's proposal to award him an honorary degree, but also in a series of other "affairs" and polemics). It is entirely proper that an account of his work should appear in a volume such as this, and yet the philosophically most striking thing about Derrida's work is probably that it is *not* philosophy in any straightforward sense, but its permanent traversal, excess, or outflanking. Derrida has not so much re-defined philosophy (the traditional task of philosophy) as rendered it permanently in-definite. This difficult situation has been the cause of many misunderstandings of Derrida, by both philosophers and non-philosophers, and demands a delicacy of reading which is all but unmanageable, but which goes some way towards explaining the attraction Derrida's work has held for students of literature. It is unhelpful to view Derrida as belonging to any particular philosophical lineage, because his work upsets *all* the concepts that allow us to posit philosophical lineages (he is thus arguably as "close" to Plato or Kant as to Heidegger or Nietzsche), and it is also difficult to discern any obvious lines of development or change in his thinking, which seems to have remained remarkably consistent – though constantly surprising and unpredictable – since the 1960s. But in spite of its undeniable difficulty, Derrida's work is in fact quite susceptible of reasoned exposition *up to a point*, beyond which something "undecidable" begins to happen, as we shall see.

Derrida made his spectacular entry into the field of published philosophy in 1967, bringing out three major books (*De la grammatologie*, *L'Ecriture et la différence*, and *La Voix et le phénomène* – he had earlier published a long, prize-winning intro-duction to his own translation of Husserl's "Origin of Geometry" appendix to the *Crisis* in 1962), and these books lay out most of the premises for Derrida's subse-quent vast output (some 40 books to date, and thousands of pages of unpublished seminar material), although careful study of that subsequent output is necessary for this to be readily perceived (see, too, Derrida's own comments on the 1990 publication of his Master's dissertation from 1953, in which he is surprised to find already much of what was to come over the next 40 years). Derrida is concerned to argue something like this: the self-identifying tradition of Western philosophy ("Western metaphysics," "onto-theology") is, as Heidegger argued, dominated by the value of *presence*. Whatever its perception of the complexities involved, and whatever its doctrinal inclination, metaphysics seeks out some supreme value which is inseparable from this value of presence, whatever particular content it may otherwise be supposed to exhibit. Establishing the excellence of this presence (which can be modulated across a huge variety of inflexions, including – perhaps even most commonly – those of more or less radical absence, of a presence now lost or always yet to come, *arkhe* and/or *telos* in the stories philosophy habitually tells) commits metaphysics to a thinking which makes privileged use of binary, oppositional structures, whereby a positively marked term is defined against a negatively marked one (presence as against absence, the inside as against the outside, the soul as against the body, meaning as against its sign, the spirit as against the letter, the clear as against the obscure, the literal as against the figural, the rational as against the irrational, the serious as against the non-serious, and so on, indefinitely). Even in cases where such oppositions are presented as neutral and descriptive, Derrida argues, they are in fact violently (i.e. dogmatically) hierarchical, the result of an "ethico-theoretical decision," so that, for example, it is assumed without question that meaning is logically prior, and ontologically superior, to its linguistic expression, or that serious literal speech is logically prior, and ontologically superior, to jokes or fiction. What has become famous as "deconstruction" involves less an *operation on* than a *demonstration about* such hierarchized binaries in the history of Western thought, and Derrida has found occasion in that demonstration to examine in some detail most of the established masters of the tradition.

It would have been difficult to predict that Derrida would find an entry point into this immense field by concentrating on the question of *writing*, led there perhaps by his – abandoned – doctoral project on "The ideality of the literary work." Writing, since Plato's *Phaedrus* (the object of a long and brilliant reading in *La Dissémination*, 1972) has had a bad press in the philosophical tradition. If meaning requires expression, says the philosopher, let this be essentially vocal: the spoken word coincides with its sense, disappears as it delivers up its meaning (especially, as Husserl will insist, in my monologue with myself, where the meaningful word need not even depart from my consciousness into the facticity of the world), and attests to the animating presence of the intending, meaning-giving consciousness of the speaker; whereas writing, mere mechanical adjunct to speech, extends the spatial and temporal range of linguistic communication but at the cost of producing a worrying material, worldly *remainder* in the form of *script* or *text* which invites repeated but repeatedly different readings without further corrective ("paternal") intervention from the intentional source (for, as Derrida shows without difficulty, the fact of writing analytically entails – as a "necessary possibility" – the death of the writer (and of any particular reader, for writing generates a potentially endless series of different contexts in which it can be read)). Massively, for a tradition that does not begin with Plato and does not end with Austin or Lacan, the voice is "naturally" privileged over writing as the place where, to use the terminology of Saussure, the signifier seems most transparent or subservient to its signified, which it exists only to relay. Husserl, on whom Derrida spends a great deal of time in these early texts, pursues the essence of what he calls the "expressive" sign into the inner monologue of the transcendental subject, while writing is placed on the side of the merely indicative, the material and empirical, the contingent.

Nowhere does Derrida suggest that this tradition of thinking about writing and its relation to the ideality of meaning is simply *false* (if only because the values of true and false are complicit with what is here under analysis). The interpretative operation carried out on Husserl, Saussure, or Plato (but we shall see that this is not interpretation *stricto sensu* – because interpretation cannot but share the presuppositions about sign and meaning that are here in question – and nor is it an operation, because this is not something that Derrida *does to* the texts he reads) consists, rather, through a constant and grateful, commemorative, recognition of their depth and rigor, in a demonstration ("deconstruction") that first unravels the hierarchization of the speech/writing opposition (and with it that of the oppositions it brings along with it, for one of Derrida's constant claims about metaphysics will have been that pulling at a bit of it brings it all along too, that its concepts are organized in a network of mutually-defining elements in dynamic solidarity, so that this construal of meaning is inseparable from a complex of positions about truth, *mimesis*, but also, say, life, death, sexual difference), and then questions not just the *hierarchy* of the opposition, but its very *oppositionality*. So, for example, Husserl is suspicious of writing because its availability for repeated access in a futurally open series of different contexts, away from the animating intention of its author, separates it from the transcendental "Life" the ideality of whose meaning it is supposed (teleologically) to express, but which it is more likely to betray or mortify: but the most ideal idealities, such as those of geometry, cannot but rest for their ideality (their repeatability as the same in an infinite series of actualizations) on the very graphic inscription that is elsewhere so suspect. But if writing is thus something like the condition of possibility of the very ideality it is also thought to sully (so that, according to a logic constant in Derrida's thinking, the condition of possibility is simultaneously the condition of impossibility of the purity of the phenomenon made possible), then the valorizations implicit in the metaphysical description are radically disturbed, and it is shown to rest on something like a grounding incoherence.

Derrida pursues the deconstruction of speech and writing into its second stage by arguing that not only is writing not simply a secondary adjunct to speech, but that all linguistic signs are, in a certain sense, radically written. The argument goes as follows: the metaphysical description of writing is that it is the (graphic) signifier of a (phonic) signifier, which is the signifier of an (ideal) signified; but it can be shown that all signifiers refer for their meaning only to other signifiers (this part of the argument drawing on the Saussure of the linguistic "system of differences" as against the more traditional Saussure of the sign); if metaphysics wants to call "signifier of signifier" by the name "writing," it had therefore better call all language writing if it wants to be consistent. But this it does not want, for to call all language "writing" in this way upsets its basic axiology, whereby writing *must* take a secondary place with respect to speech. Using the term "writing" (or "archi-writing") in this displaced (and apparently provocative) sense, then, both brings out a certain (repressed) truth of the metaphysical tradition (it is committed in spite of itself to the view that all meaning exhibits the features it none the less tries to limit to writing), and confronts it with its own foundational dogmatism (it flatly denies that this is the case). Metaphysics is thus redescribed as the variable economy of this contradiction.

My present, intended meaning is possible only because language as a system of differences allows its differential identification in terms of a system I inherit and do not dominate (I cannot simply choose the language I speak nor the concepts it provides me with); and its expression is possible only in the perspective of the necessary possibility of its repetition in the absence of my supposedly animating (or at least sub-scribing) intention. Whether actually written or spoken, my utterance functions only in so far as it always might be repeated in my absence (if necessary by mechanical means, but the *possibility* of these is built into language from the start, language has always been such that its mechanical repetition is possible): "in my absence," radicalized, after my death. As you read this, you do not know (and this is an essential ignorance, not merely an empirical one, it is entailed by the structure of writing) whether I am alive or dead, nor, by extension, whether I am serious or not, whether I mean it or not, whether I really wrote it or not. In so far as you are inclined to attribute intentions to me (or to someone) in this respect, you construct them retroactively on the basis of the text read, and the text read functions "mechanically," independently of the intentions you attribute in fact, after the fact, to its supposed author. (This also suggests why subjectivity is an inscribed rather than foundational concept.)

Further, the fact that this text cannot *exhaustively* control the reading you give it (no text can *read itself without remainder*, although philosophy may be the discourse which has tried hardest to do just that, and the Hegelian system the most consistently tried) implies that there is no end to reading, no conceivable horizon of interpretation. Deconstruction is not a form of hermeneutics, however supposedly radical, for just this reason: hermeneutics always proposes a convergent movement towards a unitary meaning (however much it may wish to respect ambiguity on the way), the word of God; deconstruction discerns a dispersive perspective in which there is no (one) meaning. Many readers of Derrida have lost their nerve at this point, fearing a nihilistic consequence which does not in fact follow (others have imagined that Derrida, who spends a lot of time justifying his readings, must here be caught in contradiction). The absence of a unitary horizon of meaning for the process of reading does not commit Derrida to the *recommendation* of meaninglessness, nor does it entail the equivalence in value of all different readings (rather the singularity of each), and indeed demands the most rigorous textual evidence for readings proposed: but it does argue that no one reading will ever be able to claim to have exhausted the textual resources available in the text being read.

This description still suggests too clear a separation between writing and reading: texts (of sufficient complexity – the memory of Gödel's theorem here is not fortuitous) *already* tend to read themselves, to offer up a preferred or "official" reading (often the one assumed by subsequent readers to coincide with the author's intention): so Plato, Rousseau, Husserl, Saussure, and many others (demonstrably) *declare* their preference for speech over writing; but they also manage (demonstrably) to *say* the very opposite too. Derrida's work consists essentially in bringing out the textual resources that question the "official" version. These resources are demonstrably put forward, however discretely, by the texts being read, and are not imported by Derrida, whose place in this process is thereby rendered problematical: it is not that Derrida (actively) deconstructs anything at all, but rather that he shows *metaphysics in deconstruction*. This is not the expression of a preference at all, but a bolder claim, namely that the deconstructive operation of apparent oppositions is the only possible "ground" upon which metaphysics could ever claim to identify itself in the first place.

Derrida can thus be said to *repeat metaphysics differently*. All of his work consists in readings of (usually philosophical) texts carried by the tradition, then shown to upset traditionality as much as they respect it. (Another important strand of readings examines texts which look as though they might escape from metaphysics, only to show points of unthought complicity.) This can look like a problem merely for historians of philosophy (in fact it poses insuperable problems to any history of philosophy, because it renders unanswerable the question "when?" posed of a text), but also involves consequences for "doing" philosophy in general. Effects of identity *in general* (as much in, say, a perceptual field as in a linguistic system, though questions of language and meaning remain paramount in that metaphysics is *logocentric*) are now understood to be generated on the basis of *difference*. Derrida spends a good deal of effort establishing that this differential condition of identity need not give rise to a dialectic in the Hegelian sense: Hegel's famous demonstration in the *Greater Logic* that difference collapses dialectically into identity depends on an *absolutization* of difference which Derrida is at pains to show is unthinkable (difference is intrinsically non-absolutizable, intrinsically finite) and on a prejudgment that difference is answerable to opposition (Hegel is, for example, *already* thinking difference as opposition when arguing that what is different from difference is identity). Difference (radicalized by Derrida's neologism *différance* to bring out both spatial and temporal resonances, identity being an effect of differences from other elements *and* between events of repetition) is the *milieu* in which identities are sketched but never quite achieved (any element being defined only in terms of all the others and all its repetitions, the *trace* of which remains as a sort of constitutive contamination), but never quite lost (*différance* can be thought of as a dispersion, but never an *absolute* dispersion). Identities depend on traces of other identities: but the trace "itself," now the logically prior term, is not answerable to any metaphysical characterization (it is, for example, neither present nor absent, and, as the condition of identity in general, is not itself *identifiable*).

*Différance* is one attempt to name this complex "origin" of space and time and meaning, but there are many other attempts too: dissemination, *pharmakon*, trace, supplement, and many more, drawn from the apparent contingency of the texts of the tradition. A consistent argument for the non-originarity of identity can hardly propose a single name for the "origin" of that non-originarity, whence the open series of names proposed. As consequence of this that has troubled many readers of Derrida is that the apparently transcendental privilege of *différance* (or the trace) cannot be maintained, in so far as differentially defined "identities" can never achieve the stability required of a transcendental realm. In fact, the conjoined thinking of difference and repetition entails that anything like the transcendental is generated as a more or less provisional and unstable effect by a series of partially contingent and essentially singular events, whereby a given text tries to *put up* a transcendental term, and the deconstructive reading registers its inevitable fall back into its contingent textuality. For example, Descartes generates an immortal thinking substance on the back of the finitude of a mortal individual, and looks down on mortality as a contingency from the height thus achieved: but the deconstructive reading shows that that "contingency" is the positive condition of the supposedly transcendental position, its "transcendental" condition. For Derrida, the transcendental itself has a transcendental in what the transcendental calls the empirical or the contingent. This does not mean that the transcendental can simply be debunked in a positivist or empiricist spirit (the gesture of the human sciences), because such a gesture, which would correspond to the *reversal* stage of deconstruction, cannot fail to generate a new transcendental term it is unable to deal with ("experience," "history," "society," "material conditions," and so on, or even "writing"), but that it must be thought as a *movement*, variously described in the texts of the tradition of philosophy, which there is no question of *doing without* (in some fantasy of a purely immanent materiality). This irreducible inscription of "contingency" *in* the transcendental entails, among other things, that philosophical "arguments" cannot be neatly separated from their "expression," for example in a given natural language, or a given more or less idiosyncratic idiom (philosophical texts bear a singular *signature*), nor from the tradition which they bear and contest (the singularity of that signature is constitutively compromised by its intelligibility). In this sense, all philosophy is radically historical (and "geographical"), and there is no doing philosophy that does not engage (even if in the mode of denial) with the history (and geography, including the social and political geography) of philosophy – but philosophy, which cannot help but attempt to reduce that history, can never quite understand this remainder of contingency, this spatio-temporal dispersion, which makes it possible. This configuration has often been called, by Derrida and others, "quasi-transcendental," but this name, and the Kantian reference it involves, has at best a heuristic privilege with respect to many others in the open series of deconstructive events. There is no proper name for deconstruction or its "results," whence the philosophical unease it cannot fail to generate.

This argument, which *limits* the pretensions of philosophy with respect to other disciplines insofar as it posits the inability of philosophy ever to establish itself successfully as uniquely *philosophical*, and therefore opens it to scrutiny by non-philosophical agencies – especially perhaps psychoanalysis), simultaneously *extends* the philosophical domain beyond all definable limits (for these non-philosophical agencies are themselves both shot through with metaphysical values and assumptions and the bearers of a contingency metaphysics cannot quite manage). Many early receptions of Derrida by non-philosophers enthusiastically embraced what could look simply like a critique of philosophical pretension: Derrida seemed to some to make philosophy look like *no more than* a kind of writing, a particular use of language, a literary *genre*, a rhetoric, maybe even a set of essentially psychical operations. But Derrida has also spent a good deal of energy (especially perhaps in *L'Ecriture et la différence* (1967) and the 1972 collection *Marges de la philosophie*) showing how attempts to *reduce* philosophy in this way (anthropologically – Lévi-Strauss; historically – Foucault; poetically – Valéry; linguistically Benveniste; psychoanalytically – Lacan; sociologically – Bourdieu) rely on often naively unquestioned philosophical assumptions. For example, the attempt to reduce philosophy to a set of rhetorical tropes (and essentially metaphors) which have simply forgotten their metaphorical status and which can then be debunked in the name of something like "literature" founders on its need to hold clear of this operation, to place in a transcendental position, just that concept (the concept of metaphor, a *philosophical* concept) which is supposed to achieve the reduction of *all* concepts. Similarly, linguistic reductions of philosophy transcendentalize a (philosophical) concept of language, historical reductions a (philosophical) concept of history, according to a mechanism we can follow Derrida in calling "transcendental contraband." The general form of this argument is that any attempt to claim an *escape* from metaphysics necessarily involves the blind appeal to at least one metaphysical concept which compromises the escape the moment it is claimed.

This situation has led some commentators to assume on Derrida's part, far from an iconoclastic desire to destroy philosophy in the name of "play" (the object of much indignation from philosophers convinced of how very serious they are), a culpable and perhaps reactionary complicity with a metaphysics he is supposed to be denouncing: but Derrida's argument establishes that "complicity with metaphysics" is both unavoidable (traditionality as the positive condition of thinking) and infinitely negotiable once the twin blindnesses of simple subservience and heroic oppositional revolt have been pointed out. The unease that this situation generates is, however, real. It looks as though Derrida has established, through recognizably rational argument, that metaphysical values (grounded in the *Ur*-value of presence) are untenable because of the prior necessity of *différance*; but also as though there is no simple alternative to those values (trying to make *différance* into an alternative value means thinking it in terms of a potential presence again: this is the "libertarian" reception of Derrida). The relationship with metaphysics is endlessly negotiable, as Derrida shows through a series of similar but non-identical encounters with the texts of the tradition, but it is still unclear what motivates these encounters or what dictates the strategy adopted in them. If we know a priori that metaphysics can be neither established nor overcome, what are we trying to achieve in our dealings with it?

This question, which has driven a number of commentators to identify what might appear to be a new stress in Derrida on ethical and political issues (although these questions are raised from his very earliest work in fact) can be given, if only provisionally, a negative and a positive characterization. Negatively, in a spirit of critique which deconstruction never rejects but which cannot in principle exhaust it, deconstruction warns against metaphysical purifications, essentializations, totalizations and transcendentalizations of all sorts. Thus, to take a dramatic example, Heidegger's engagement with Nazism (often thought to be an object of embarrassment to Derrida, whereas his writings on this matter are among his most uncompromisingly critical) can be shown to be related to Heidegger's unthought appeal to a metaphysical value ("spirit"). That this value is shared with eminent opponents of Nazism (Husserl, Valéry) points to deeper grounds of complicity to be considered with the utmost vigilance of thought (rather than quick assurances that Nazism is adequately thought by the values of humanism), and some of Heidegger's later thinking can help with that consideration. Although this demonstration has been greeted with a certain degree of confusion and bad faith, it suggests that deconstruction gives in principle some ethico-political guidance ("avoid uncritical appeals to metaphysical values") without, however, proposing any replacement metaphysical values.

This characterization of deconstruction is, however, still a little misleading. We seem to have reached a position which states that on the one hand complicity with metaphysics is unavoidable, but that complicity with metaphysics is to be avoided as far as possible, without any guidance being given as to that "as far as possible." Some degree of confusion here is itself an object of affirmation for Derrida: deconstruction cannot provide rules for avoiding metaphysics, and never suggests that talk about contingency, writing, undecidability, or dissemination will produce results which are necessarily "better" than talk about necessity, speech, decidability, or univocality (it is quite possible to talk logocentrically about, for example, dissemination, as some enthusiastic followers of Derrida have discovered to their cost). If deconstruction maintains that we are always in a *tension* between the metaphysical and its undoing, it cannot predict a priori what the best adjustment of that tension might be in a given case: although something like equivocality is affirmed as the "ground" of any meaning whatsoever, Derrida nowhere suggests that *more* equivocality is necessarily better than *less*, for example.

What deconstruction can say more "positively" about ethical and political issues does, however, depend on a certain affirmation of the undecidable. The argument goes as follows: for a decision to be worthy of the name, it must be more than the simple determinative subsumption of a case under a rule. Looking up the rule for the case and applying the rule is a matter for administration rather than ethics. Ethics begins where the case does not entirely correspond to any rule, and where the decision has to be taken without subsumption. A decision worthy of its name thus takes place in a situation of radical *indecision* or of undecidability of the case in question in terms of any rules for judging it. The decision must therefore involve a measure of *invention*, and that invention entails both an uncertainty and the affirmative projection of a future. A decision is like a performative which has both to perform and to invent the rules according to which it might, after the event of its performance, be received as "happy." This essential undecidability of the event as it arrives and calls for decision flows from the deconstructive analyses of language and time that we have already summarized. Already in *Of Grammatology*, Derrida announced that a thought of the trace bound together the possibility of meaning, the opening of temporality, and the relation to the other in general. This possibility of ethics in undecidability and inventivity is not itself (yet) ethical or political, but is, beyond good and evil (as Derrida said of writing in 1967) also the impossibility of any ethics's being ethical. But if this opening is not yet itself ethical, it gives both a principle for judging (any ethical or political judgment that closes off this condition of undecidability is *ipso facto* suspect) and a principle for the infinitization of ethics and politics. This infinitization, which takes place each time finitely, is also called justice. For all metaphysical doctrines of ethics and politics close off the undecidable at some point: political and moral philosophies of all colors project teleologies whereby politics and morals are oriented towards their end (in social justice, virtue, transparency, etc.), whereas the deconstructive construal cannot but suspend this teleological thrust (this has made it suspect to many commentators) with its radical appeal to a future (the coming of the undecidable singular event) which will never be a present (this future that is not a future present determining the claim from the earliest work that the future is necessarily monstrous, i.e. formless), although it always happens *now*. This appeal to an irreducibly futural future (the interminably *à-venir* or to-come) suspends deconstruction always this side of any ethical or political *doctrine* or *program*. But Derrida is prepared to link this thinking to that of a democracy which is the ethico-political figure of the never-absolute, never-present dispersion of *différance*. Far from preventing ethico-political decisions of the most concrete and pressing kind, this democracy to-come would be the condition of possibility of all such decisions, and simultaneously the condition of impossibility of any self-righteousness about them.

Deconstruction thus, quite consistently, gives no grounds for any doctrinal ontology, epistemology, or ethics. It is perhaps, then, not surprising that to date no remotely convincing philosophical critique of deconstruction has been forthcoming (the attempts by Searle and Habermas are risibly ill-informed, and other critics have carefully avoided all normal philosophical precautions before issuing unargued condemnations), perhaps because it is simply not susceptible to such a critique. Derrida's work seems to have managed the exploit of being intensely philosophical and yet impervious to any imaginable philosophical refutation. But it is also a mistake (made most notably by Rorty) to assume that Derrida is to be praised in so far as he is doing something simply non-philosophical (story-telling, literary invention), and criticized to the extent that he cannot help himself sometimes getting involved in philosophical argumentation. Derrida's work stands or falls on the rigor of its philosophical argumentation (it claims to pass *right through* philosophy), and demands the most philosophical reading it can be given: that this philosophical reading leads into uncertain zones inaccessible to philosophy as such is part of deconstruction's claim, and the source of the endless irritation it causes philosophers. But if Derrida is right, this irritation cannot be simply attached to the work of one philosopher or his followers: it must be ("always already") inscribed in all the texts of the tradition as the very possibility of philosophy itself. Writing, in Derrida's sense (which is not then different from Plato's sense), is already "in" the *Phaedrus*, the quasi-transcendental is already "in" Kant. In putting his name to his inimitable *oeuvre*, Derrida has also done no more than add a counter-signature to all the others who have given philosophy their ambivalent guarantee. This situation, which Derrida has not invented, is already deconstruction, which is thus unavoidable, however much it may continue to be denied.

## Writings

Derrida, Jacques: *Of Grammatology*, tr. Gayatri Chakravorty Spivak (Baltimore and London: Johns Hopkins University Press, 1967).

——: *Writing and Difference*, tr. Alan Bass (Chicago, IL: University of Chicago Press, 1967).

——: *Dissemination*, tr. Barbara Johnson (Chicago, IL: University of Chicago Press, 1972).

——: *Margins of Philosophy*, tr. Alan Bass (Chicago, IL: University of Chicago Press, 1972).

——: *Speech and Phenomena and Other Essays on Husserl's Theory of Signs*, tr. David B. Allison (Evanston, IL: Northwestern University Press, 1973).

——: *Glas*, tr. John P. Leavey and Richard Rand (Lincoln, NB: University of Nebraska Press, 1974).

——: *The Post Card: From Socrates to Freud and Beyond*, tr. Alan Bass (Chicago, IL: University of Chicago Press, 1980).

——: *Psyche: inventions de l'autre* (Paris: Galilee, 1987).

——: *Given Time*, tr. Peggy Kamuf (Chicago, IL: University of Chicago Press, 1992).

## Further reading

Bennington, Geoffrey (with Jacques Derrida): *Jacques Derrida* (Paris: Seuil, 1991), tr. G. Bennington (Chicago, IL: University of Chicago Press, 1993).

Gasché, Rodolphe: *The Tain of the Mirror* (Cambridge, MA: Harvard University Press, 1986).

Norris, Christopher: *Derrida* (London: Fontana, 1987).

# 51

# Deleuze

## BRIAN MASSUMI

### Concept

The work of Gilles Deleuze (1925–95) spreads over four decades and twenty-four volumes (and counting). The titular subject-matter of his books ranges from topics in Western philosophy to psychoanalysis to literature to cinema to painting to the multiple itself (*A Thousand Plateaus* . . . and counting). The list of single-authored works is intersected by a series of high-profile collaborative projects with Félix Guattari (1930–92). In no two books, solo or duet, does the theoretical vocabulary entirely coincide. Where terms recur, their contours shift. The continual variation in content, voice, and terminology makes a traditional overview impossible.

One response to this difficulty is to periodize: locate a break in Deleuze's work at the time of the French student–worker revolt of May 1968, after which Deleuze, under Guattari's tutelage, descended from the ivory tower to dirty his majestically finger-nailed hands in "practice," with lasting reverberations in his theory. Another response, in reaction to the first, is to scrub under the nails, to purify: drop the name "Guattari," even when referring to jointly authored works, to yield a solitary, professorial voice answering to "Author" or even "Genius," unmarked by the dirty Guattarian business of day-to-day institutional psychotherapy and far-left grass-roots activism. Yet another way is to make generic distinctions within the opus: separate the "high" theory from the "applications." Or make a thematic break: between works dedicated to proper names in the European pantheon (Hume, Leibniz, Spinoza, Kant, Proust, Foucault, Kafka, Francis Bacon) from thematically defined volumes. Or separate layers: set the "political" against the "philosophical," or the "ethical" against the "ontological," as contrasting dimensions of the texts. All of these taxonomic strategies, and others, have been heard. They manage the self-differing of the Deleuzian corpus by division, pinning its still-twitching parts to labels on the academic collecting board. To divide and pin makes it possible for an independent system of judgment to measure the parts and their dissected whole against an extrinsic standard, of truth or utility. This is done, ostensibly, to provide a frame for collective agreement on the value of the work. Dissection for ostensible consensus is called "academic debate."

None of the divisions mentioned above is operative in the texts. Deleuze's own characterization of his work is as unitary as it is unwavering: philosophy, from beginning to end, nothing but philosophy. *What Is Philosophy?*, asks a late volume co-written with Guattari (1994). Neither a discipline nor a genre (or if both, only derivatively). And certainly not a forum for edifying debate. Philosophy is best understood as a self-referential process, to which consensus-seeking public discussion is as inimical as censorship. The process that is philosophy is the creation of concepts, as distinguished from propositions. The proposition is the unit of debate. The combination of words forming the proposition follows established rules. Although the number of possible combinations is infinite, a word recurring in any two combinations is enjoined to remain semantically itself across its successive appearances, just as the syntactic principles of its combination with other words are enjoined to remain unchanged. Self-identical units variously combined according to unvarying rules are independent variables whose congress is regulated by constants. Two or more propositional combinations taken together define a set of possibilities. What they are possibilities for is the designation of a state of things posited as external to the proposition and its enunciation. The proposition and the state of things, and their respective elements, must be in conformity with one another. A noun is to a thing as a proposition is to a state of things; things are to states of things as words are to propositions. There is a grammar of things and a grammar of words that can be mapped on to each other in one-to-one correspondence. Relations between elements on one level mirror the relations obtaining on the other. The system of things and the system of words are in analogy. The discipline of logic is the policing of the analogy, enabler of representation. The job of disciplinary logic is to maintain the conditions under which words and things remain the same across their variations, safeguard the constants according to which propositions are constructed, and judge the appropriateness of the coupling of propositions with states of things. This last task is a matter of assessing the range of possible propositions and choosing the right one in each case, as measured by an accepted standard of correctness. That standard exists on a different plane from the debatable words and the changeable things it polices, unaffected by their variation. The truth is the invariance against which the constancy of variations is measured. It is held up as transcendent to the debate it arbitrates. An old and overworked philosophical divide occurs on the issue of how the correspondence between words and things is founded. Grossly, an empirical approach derives the conformity of our expression to its referents from the order of presentation of things in our experience, from which a corresponding order of thought arises. A transcendental approach sees the presentation of things as conforming to the underlying order of a Subject outside experience, of which particular existing subjects are limited reflections. In the first case, thought is stenciled from ordinary things; in the second, things are stenciled from an extra-ordinary *ur*-thought. In both cases, the foundation *resembles* (*repeats*) what it founds. The proposition formalizes that repeatability.

Independent variable, constant, designation, conformity, correspondence, analogy, representation, possibility, extrinsic standard, transcendence, an opposition between the empirical and the transcendental, resemblance, repetition. This is the inherited fallow ground, the "image of thought," upon which the Deleuzian concept falls. Where it grows is somewhere else again: precisely in a nonconformity of words to things, in their non-relation, in a gap across which something less formed but more forceful and in a sense more real than representation paradoxically passes. A something constitutive of *difference*. The concept is the extreme expression of difference, rather than the moderator of agreement. It is self-referential not because it is different from all else but because it is a difference in itself, taken to its limit, in contrast to nothing external, in comparison to no extrinsic standard distributive of sameness and stable distinction (difference *from*). It is immanence, but not *to* something, as the transcendental subject is immanent *to* particular subjects. Deleuze and Guattari define the concept as a "field" of pure immanence. The field of immanence is composed of variations without constants. Without constants to anchor it, the variation continues. The boundary between one variation and the next is fuzzy. There is no longer an independence of variables, but an inseparability of variations. Since one variation passes indiscernibly into the next, continually, the variations are strangely simultaneous, while remaining differentiated. They are co-present "moments" in a nonlinear time that is also an unbounded space, delineated only by a folding into and out of itself. No thing could withstand the deformation of variations occurring so fast as to pass into simultaneity. No body could exist in the fractality of the self-enfolding field. The components of the variation are not things in extension, in the linear time of succession and the three-dimensional space of juxtaposition; nor are they mappable to extended things in one-to-one correspondence. They are "singularities," understood as bifurcation points: points at which a change in direction occurs, coinciding with a jump in levels (from one potential variation to the next, and to all of them).

Underline "potential." Singularities are the precise points at which all of the variations in (of) the field are co-present, from a certain angle of approach, *in potential*. That co-presence in potential is "*intension*" as opposed to extension. The potential is not a logical possibility, closer to a "virtuality." The difference between a possibility and a virtuality in Deleuze's sense is that a possibility precedes the real to which it is selected to correspond, as from a set of pre-established alternatives. A virtuality *is* real. To reality there is no alternative. Deleuze is nothing if not literal. He considers the field that is the concept to be *absolutely real*. It is absolute in that it is nowhere in the space-time coordinates of extension, and yet it is perspectival, since the variation of the field is ever on the approach, from a certain angle, to a singularity of its own co-presence. It is real, yet incorporeal. What moves along the folding line of continual variation? A "paradoxical point" that is thought in itself, as opposed to immanent to an enlightened subject; "pure thought" that is its own "dark precursor," a movement so fast as to approach itself from every angle at once. The field of immanence is to thought as "phase space" is to matter. Where the field of immanence fuzzes into phase space – in their virtual "zone of indiscernibility" thought and matter meet, as one. Really, literally, not in reflection, in no conformity or correspondence.

We have gone from taxonomy to paradox. This is progress. At least a tentative answer suggests itself to the question of what to do with a work that resists being defined. Take it at its involuted word. If Deleuze is nothing if not literal, then the same goes for a Deleuzian reading. At their word, the texts are not made of propositions, but of concepts. If the texts express a field of variation, the concepts in play are "singularities." The approach to a concept is always from a certain angle and,

561

at the bifurcation point that the variation is always about to reach and has always already just reached, all of the singularities of the work are in immediate proximity, even over period breaks, under topic categories, unimpeded by the order of appearance in time of the actual (extended) texts conveying them. It is not that these divisions are not also real. It is not necessarily that they are untrue or useless. It is more that the conceptual consistency of the work exists elsewhere. Analytic divisions, whether true or in error by any particular standard, are extrinsic, tools of management. However useful they may be in their own framework, their utility befalls the work, impinges upon its field of immanence and ruptures its "unity," which is the "consistency," or continuity, of its intensive movement. Such divisions are fall-out from extension settling back upon and slowing, limiting the movement of the text-borne conceptual field, toward which they are in a relation of transcendence. Limitative slow-down may not only be useful, but downright satisfying. Another way, otherly satisfying, is to follow the conceptual movements more on their own terms. This can only mean mimicking (surrendering to) the "paradoxical" point. There will always be a difference, of course. The reader, however spry, is not infinitely deformable. The approach to a bifurcation point will be in a temporal order of succession, as the angle of the approach will be from a placeable point of view. This is thought encased in an existing body, no longer "pure" and "absolute," but relative to the positional coordinates of extended time and space, actualized in situated speech (internal or external dialogue) or writing. The analytic divisions mentioned earlier pertain to that actual situation more than they do to the work. They are a function of the work's reception. In itself, the work is conceptually unbounded. Its limitation is in its encounter with a qualitatively different order of movement that transcends it. *Its limits are in its actual expression*, its mimicking in extension, its reception: its linear *unfolding*.

## Composition

The same reading encounter that limits the work de-limits the reader. Although the approach is in extension, when it reaches the bifurcation point the intensive movement of the conceptual field and the extensive movement of reading phase into each other. If the reading is not content to pin, that is. If the taxonomic impulse is consciously checked, the extrinsic criteria defining which, of all Deleuzian concepts, is the next logical one to approach disintegrate. The work's singularities resurge, unruptured, along with the infolded totality of their potential variations. These are virtually co-present not only in and to themselves, but *to the reader*. The actual reading process is "contaminated" by, permeated by, supersaturated with the virtuality of the conceptual field, with which it enters into a zone of indiscernibility. Any and every concept in the field presents itself as an equally "possible" next step. Which means that none is "really possible. With consciously applied standards in abeyance, the conditions of possibility for judicious selection are inoperative. There is nothing, objectively (extrinsically), to recommend one selection over another. At each step, an unruly crowd of concepts presses for attention, for actualization, as if under the impulsion of a dynamic all their own. The "choice" is left to chance. "Chance" is not the absence of selection, but rather the intrusion of a different order of selection. The reader's will to judgment dissolves – into her or his circumstances. It is they that decide.

But what are the circumstances, if not the situatedness of the reader, his/her "state" as a thing, as defined by a relative position not only in relation to space-time coordinates, but also relative to the extrinsic standards s/he normally feels compelled to apply in judgment, and those s/he is called upon to submit to as an object of judgment by others? The answer is that the circumstances *are* that situatedness – minus its actuality. The reader is assailed by potential conceptual moves pretending to actualization. Half-thoughts emerge, not clearly distinguished from images, which are not exactly visions, glimpsing as they do sounds and touches as they shade into memories, before disappearing as abruptly as they came, followed by another surge of half-thoughts. The voluntary cessation of conscious judgment has sundered the situation, resulting in a blockage, not by deficit but by overcharge. The reader's learned responses and habits of thought are interrupted, her/his situation misplaced. Any attempt to choose from a familiar position of strength, aided by a return to comforting criteria, founders in confusion, or disappointment in the result, only a shadow of a thought. A painful "crack" opens in the framing of the situation, and through it wafts the reader's potential. For the half-thoughts that are synaesthetic images that are memories are situated responses past, pressing to come again. They are has-beens to-be. Future-pasts. Minus the present, which has been submerged in mistimed tendencies. The present is only half-formed, not yet emerged from the variability, deformability, of the virtual. Minus the actual, plus the virtual. Or both, but not quite: both blurred, in the fuzziness where they recede, or proceed, to their respective limits (each other), into a reciprocal beyonding. The reading process has resolved the reader into an almost-actual, still virtual plane of immanence. The encounter between the reader and the text occurs between two planes of immanence, in the crack, in the space between a paralytic subtraction and a supercharged addition. It does not take place between two formed, positioned, extended things. The totality of the conceptual field of immanence attached to the proper name "Deleuze" is in direct, if fuzzy, contact with the totality of the reader's experiential field of immanence. The "chance" that will decide which concept will fully emerge as actual (spoken, written, in situatable, judgable form), is the reader's circumstances, virtualized, as one field of immanence dopplering into another: circumstance turned happenstance (from situation to event). A new situation, the newly produced speech-act or text, forms as the actual precipitate of the conversion.

The distributions of bifurcation points on the two planes and the patterns of absolute movement that link them may resonate in spots, or clash. What emerges is a product of the *interference* between the planes. Each plane is a complex, chaotic system. The interference registers actually as confusion, which is momentarily dissipated when a language-act precipitates. If the reading is being registered in a writing, a charged turn of phrase will be deposited on the page. This textual precipitate will be irreducible to its propositional value by virtue of being "overdetermined," overly intense, too potentialized, too seething to remain agreeably inside the accepted generic or disciplinary bounds of the writing. This composition-event is "selected" by the complex interaction of the fields, not by a "will" residing on one side and acting upon the other from a position outside it. In that interactive encounter, at that reciprocal limit, the planes have fused into one. The distinction between the two actual formations in play is indiscernible. This is the "unity" of philosophy implied in Deleuze's answer to the question of what it was all about. Philosophy, nothing but philosophy – as a process, as opposed to a thing (genre or discipline). Philosophy-as-process is all "about" generating collective composition-events that mimic a "pure" thought. The process involves a conscious dereliction of conscious choice, a self-unplugging of individual judgment in favor of an intersection of nonconscious planes, a contamination or communication of unconsciouses. The circumstances designated by the proper names in play dissolve into an overlap that is added to, without supplanting, the actual sets of which it is the union.

Turns of phrase embodying the composition-event most fully, most intensely, will stand out in the flow of the actual text produced. They will strike one as rough or idiosyncratic. They will be sticking points, sites of friction or resistance. They may come across as nonsense, or idiosyncrasy, or inspiration. They are "remarkable" points in the lines of the text. They are often incomplete or ungrammatical, as if language were somehow overpowered, twisted out of shape by a force greater than it. "Drunkenness as the triumphant irruption of the plant in us." That's one. Like a formula. The formula is an actualization of the paradoxical point. It breaks the line of development leading up to it. The text stops a moment, then veers off again. Its linear unfolding begins again, in a new direction that was unforeseeable the phrase before, yet suggests multiple potential connections to and from it. The text will interrupt itself, and no sooner reconnect to itself, at each turn with greater complexity and "consistency," understood once again as the co-presence of movements in thought whose to-ing is simultaneously a fro-ing. Deleuze calls this folding in on itself of a linear development a style. Styles involve intensification through conscious dereliction, and feature an unfolding punctuated by infolding. They are "rhizomes." Philosophy as the plant in us. Drunk on water, drunk by dint of sobriety. For the stylistic formulae are most effective under conditions of rarity. They must be punctual. If they come too fast and close, there is nothing to interrupt, no pulsing, no rhythm, no reciprocal limiting, no co-selection, no happenstance, just surging. Disorder out of chaos.

The rhizomatic text is not one without linearities. It is one with linearities that bifurcate infinitely but punctually. Between the bifurcation points, in the approach, pacing them, are linear unfoldings of words functioning propositionally. The nature of the linear stretches define the genre of the writing. Philosophy-as-a-genre is distinguished from fiction, for example, not as uncreative to creative writing, but by the kind and pacing of the linear sequences intervening between creative moments, between bifurcation points into the unforeseen. Philosophy-as-a-genre involves an accumulated knowledge of the propositional content of a disciplinarily defined corpus of past texts and the criteria of judgment they deployed or suspended. Its linear sequencing involves a hyperconsciousness of logical antecedents. Drunk by dint of sobriety: a contamination or communication of unconsciouses interrupting and infolding an excess of consciousness, embracing it as in a "hand-to-hand combat of energies." At least in its original French, Deleuze's writing achieves a kind of learned lucidity that can only be described as a Dionysian sobriety, a lunacy of intensified clarity. The style of the texts co-authored with Guattari is palpably different. They have a denseness, a lushness, that are no doubt fall-out from Guattari's tropism toward a frenetic diversity of charged situations, as a tireless political activist championing the new social movements growing out of May 1968 and professionally as a psychiatrist in an experimental clinic.

## Pragmatics

A formula may be taken up as a technical term that recurs, in continual variation, so as to take on consistency in its own right as a conceptual subfield. The terminological subfield does not cease to belong fully to the larger conceptual field of the work, but is autonomous in the sense of having a logic and a dynamic that do not entirely coincide with those of the work as a whole (it is a fuzzy subset of the work, or one of its "part-objects"). Its autonomy is not its separation from the work, as one whole from another, or as a fragment from the whole. It is its peculiar fissionability. When a concept leaves the orbit of the Deleuzian work to enter another, its subtraction adds in both directions: the receiving work gains a particle that the donating work retains, in addition to gaining a transition-to that is integrated into its own consistency, or pattern of connection. The concept-particle is doubled by a division that changes the energetic properties of both compounds involved, through a process of additive subtraction (which is what every division is, as seen from the side of the virtual; it is only in actuality that there is subtraction, it is only the actual that is subtracted). The Deleuzian work is in a constant state of recursive revision by virtue of its systemic openness. Its composition is ongoing. A case in point is "the body without organs" – "BwO" (another name for the plane of immanence), that most borrowed and most feared of Deleuzo-Guattarian terms. Each appropriation of the "BwO" cannot fail to distort the receiving work, by virtue of the charge of paradox it carries. At the same time, it adds a dimension to the interpretability of Deleuzian work by enabling further unfoldings of one of its intensest points of infolding. It would be a mistake, however, to divide formulaic from non-formulaic terms. The patterns of interference marked by the formulae produce a wave that sweeps backwards and forwards across the text, taking up every word in its wake. Every Deleuzian word is swept up in the actualization of a paradoxical point, all the while retaining in parallel the power to generate new propositions. Composition is making words do double duty in a parallel processing, or superposition, of "pure" thought and situated thought.

A "concept" is constitutionally unstable, in two ways. First, since its internal logic (its consistency) is not exhausted by a propositional logic favoring one-to-one correspondences and ordered successions, the concept will not restrict itself to a linear development. Its overall patterning will be unpredictable. From one book to the next, and even within the same book, a given concept's trajectory will zigzag, sometimes making breathtaking leaps, sometimes falling entirely off the map only

565

to reappear again many years and books later. At each recurrence, the term acti-
vates a different set of potential connections, to itself and to other concepts. The
work of Deleuze is anti-methodological. This is not to say that it is unsystematic. It
is highly systematic, but the meaning of system has changed: from closed to open,
univocal to rhizomatic, simple to complex, clarifying to problematizing. The Deleuzian text is self-problematizing, always confronting the reader with the question of
what it is all about, and what to do with it. The last thing it does is constrain one to
"follow" it in the sense of *believing* in it as a sequential set of verified propositions to
be "applied." It challenges the reader to *do* something with it. It is pragmatic, not
dogmatic. Just as the "Deleuze" conceptual field shades into the "Guattari" conceptual field to compose a plane of immanence that supplements without supplanting
its component fields, readers are challenged to surrender to the happenstance of
their encounter with the work in a way that produces a fourth plane of immanence
precipitating their own composition-events, be they written, spoken, painted, or
performed, in the domain of philosophy, politics, or art. "Deleuze," "Guattari,"
"Deleuze-Guattari," "x". . . . A multiplication of autonomous but absolutely interconnected planes of composition, fissile and fusional by turns. Readers are invited
to fuse with the work in order to carry one or several concepts across their zone of
indiscernibility with it, into new and discernibly different circumstances. The concepts are meant to migrate into and help precipitate new situations. This is the
second way in which the Deleuzian concept is unstable: not only does it tend to leap
into new situations, across generic and disciplinary boundaries; it has an irremedi-
able tendency to convert itself into its propositional other. A concept that has
migrated into a new situation marks that situation, to which or for which it begins
then to refer. It can be placed into correspondence with components of the situation
at hand, or used to designate links between that situation and others. It passes
automatically, imperceptibly, into propositions, which may be used to generate
new truths or utilities. It is recaptured by the systemic closure it took such pains to
open. This is not simply negative, because the integration of a new element modifies
the structure into which it enters. The truth or utility is the reader's, not Deleuze's,
and it is new. The inexorable becoming-other of the Deleuzian concept is one of
the ways in which it is concretely productive of variation. An open system is not
one that sets closure entirely aside as its other, as a closed system purports to do
with openness. An open system is open even to closure. A closed system locally
integrates openness in order to remain the same, as opposed to its other; an open
system integrates closure as one of its local conditions (the condition under which
it effectively becomes other).

In the Deleuzian system, closure and openness are two phases in a single process
bringing self-preservation (capture) and transformation (escape) into close embrace. The process overall is in a constant state of disequilibrium, swinging un-
predictably between its phases, moving toward no discernible end. That is why
"following" the work, in the sense of mimicking it, is a "surrender" on the part of
the reader. The reader is invited to stage an encounter with the work that may
deform him and his situation, perhaps painfully. The reader is placed in a masochist
attitude toward a text threatening to do him violence, to a degree equal to the

seriousness with which he approaches the work. Application is the safe alternative. It makes the propositional moment come first, in order to subsume all possible situations in a systemic closure, rather than allowing closure to precipitate as a by-product or effect that is as unstable as the open system out of which it drops. "Mimicking" the work of Deleuze generates a proliferation of departures from it. Repeating it performs its self-differing. Unless it is concertedly blocked (by attributing the propositions produced to "Deleuze"), the openness of the Deleuzian system is in excess over its closure. There is always a remainder of consistency or variability that cannot pass into propositions and the extended states of things to which they correspond, that overflows situation and signification, toward the renewal of both. This "extra-being" that is pragmatic thought "counteractualizes" the same situations it contributes to actualizing. It is the "sense," as opposed to the signification, of the composition-event. It is possible to mimic but not to designate the sense of a situation. Sense can only be *performed*. And only off balance, as if the performer were about to tip over into a different person or situation, or even on to a different plane. "Cleave things asunder" is a favorite Deleuzian formula. Cleave things asunder, in order to bring out their transformability, their variability. Actualize their virtuality, *as such*, as extra-being. Make each act, each turn of phrase aspire to rejoin a plane of immanence. Make the composition-event a performance of a double transcendence, of the conceptual field by the existential-referential situation, and of the situation by the extra-being of conceptual consistency.

Is not a reciprocal transcendence a mutual immanence? Is not extra-being infra-concrete? Does not extension in itself extend beyond itself, to the precise degree to which it can change? Is not concreteness self-abstracting, to the precise degree to which empirical existence effectively envelops its potential variations? Even a system that was perfectly closed, in the interests of self-preservation and self-sameness, would have an excess that would inexorably transform it. That excess is entropy. Entropic death is the form of transcendence immanent to self-preservation. It is the form under which the event "insists," even in closure. It is the form under which difference returns to haunt the best guarded self-sameness.

## Ethics

An open, dissipative, complexifying dynamic. A closing and conserving anti-dynamic, simplifying unto death. Negentropy, entropy. Evaluate and choose. An opening, digressive, problematizing text. A closing, applicable, resolving text. Evaluate and (let the process) choose. Don't ask what it's all about, unless you want a unitary answer you will then feel called upon to spend pages differentiating. Don't ask what it means, unless you want blockage and debate. Most of all, don't ask whether it is true or useful, or it won't be. But do wonder where it might go, and who or what is doing the choosing. To choose, and to ask Where to? and Which one?, is to practice a Deleuzian ethics. *Provided one fails to reach a final conclusion.* Think about it so hard and so soberly that you unbalance your thinking. Coincide with the paradoxical point of pure thought. Perform locally and precisely, in a way that dizzies a situation by enveloping worlds in it. Make your body the paradoxical

567

point, so as to allow no situation you enter to coincide with itself. This is to practice a Deleuzian ontology. Don't persuade, provoke. Provoke others to repeat to differ, to compose in a way that produces new situations that no sooner gel than dissolve into another consistency. This is to practice a Deleuzian pedagogy of the concept.

## Limit

I surrender. I suppose I have succeeded because I have not only failed to reach a final conclusion, I haven't even begun. "The reader" invoked earlier was not, of course, an ideal reader. The masculine pronoun was reverted to, as a marker of pain, in proximity to masochism, because the reader, in this situation, is me. I had no intention of writing about reading Deleuze's writing and what to do with it. This outcome pains me. My deadline is months past. My word-limit is fast approaching. And still no "results," by the standards I set out for myself beforehand: reader-friendliness; coverage; comparative breadth; no false leads and loose ends; a demonstration of my "expertise" that met these goals yet didn't betray "my" philosophy, or (to be painfully honest) betray *me* as academically inadequate; no silliness. My stomach anticipated this failure with a wrenching I felt for weeks before sitting down to write. An excruciating ache in my jaws bears witness to the grinding tension that wracks my body when I try to write as a "Deleuzian" "about" Deleuze. Or, increasingly, as anything, about anything that I set out conscientiously to write about. I enjoy this, intensely. I enjoy this, to exhaustion. I would leave my home and my job and move to the other end of the earth to have more time to luxuriate in this feeling. I not only would, I did (masochist that I am).

Becoming-Deleuzian, I feel, means liberating the blockage in oneself. To liberate a blockage is to surrender to openness. Under conditions of privilege, a liberatory blockage is a function of possibility. You do interdisciplinary theory? So, you are no longer constrained to observe the generic rules of philosophical writing. You have an academic job? So, you don't have to worry about making ends meet and can concentrate on your work. You left your job? Finally, you are no longer constrained by the disciplinary strictures of tenure and promotion. You're free. Problem is, when you're so "free," there's nothing constraining you to write anything in particular, and no particular reason to write something rather than nothing – there is no reason to *do* something rather than nothing. Correction: no extrinsic constraint and no extrinsic reason. Systems of subjective judgment are ready and waiting and will obligingly provide both. Possibility, after all, is their logical element.

My situation is different from that of many others, for whom blockage has been imposed through poverty or oppression. In such cases, a judgment has already been handed down by the circumstances, and the possibilities it constrains are limited to the extreme. Opposing those circumstances and their limitative reason requires bringing an explicit counter-judgment to bear against the implicit judgment objectified in the situation. It is of no help whatsoever to say that "opposition" is philosophically outdated, in this postmodern and postdialectical world. Where limitation is imposed, opposition is constrained, in both senses of the word: it is necessitated, and limited. It is limited to the precise degree to which it is effective, to the precise degree to which it contours itself to a limitative judgment in order to counter it. So if there is no point in opposing opposition, there is a point in observing its counter-limitations. The greatest of these is that opposition places the opposer on the same moral terrain as the opposed. It sets up a resemblance through contrast (difference-from). The resemblance is the acceptance by the two opposing sides of the mediation of a standard extruding a common medium for battle and debate. The mediating standard is the system of judgment; its medium is possibility, as a logical category tending by right to be an objective condition. Attempts to make explicit the particular judgment objectified in the circumstances, and to make explicit its constraint of possibility, will be resisted by the "majority" (defined not in numerical terms, but as those whose circumstances assign them a surplus of possibility and the means to control it as a medium). In the ensuing battle and debate, judgment is confirmed, even when its particular cast and content are under contention. It is confirmed in form and function. Its form (typically empty) is the Standard: evaluation and comparison according to generally verifiable criteria (the same). Its function (usually unfulfilled) is tendential consensus on rights and recognized possibilities contended for by rival resemblances: difference-from under the protective umbrella of the same (equality). *The form and function of judgment is also that of the majority.* The great power and danger of opposition is that it sets in motion a becoming-major of those upon whom oppressive or marginalizing blockages have been imposed.

As long as imposed blockages remain to be opposed, a becoming-major can and will be pursued. As imposed blockages are overcome through opposition, the minor will become the major incrementally, tending to repeat the oppression with different content by imposing new standards in the name, again, of tendential consensus ("democracy"). It is now this very becoming-major that can and will be blocked, to the extent that the minority retains a memory of its initial conditions. This is where liberatory blockage can find a minoritarian usage. Under conditions of privilege, a liberatory blockage bears on a surplus of possibility inhering in felicitous circumstances. Under opposed conditions of oppression and marginalization, it bears instead on the very becoming-major that wins possibility from those adverse circumstances. Becoming-major and -minor can be superposed and held in tension, in a battle over possibility. Over its form and function. This is the becoming-Deleuzian of politics.

That politics may be said to pertain, in a certain fashion, even to the privileged individual, writing alone. For isn't consciousness itself a form of majority (tendential self-agreement, a democracy of one)? Is not the writer who surrenders to the deforming force of thought engaged in a kind of becoming-minor? Is there not a collectivity involved, in potential (in a tendential contagion of self-dissension)? Suspending conscious judgment while remaining hyperconscious (doubly conscious of the situation and its dereliction), and affirming *as a necessity* what *the process* (as distinguished from the circumstances or situation) decides: these are the minimum conditions for a becoming-Deleuzian. The discomfiture of a certain blockage and breakdown are inherent to that process. They are the part that *converts possibility into virtuality.* Break down and get blocked and you *feel* "it," you *feel*

569

the potential of a pure thought you cannot situate, already here, churning in your stomach and pounding in your aching jaws, but not yet arrived, expressing itself but not yet formulated, pressing, painful. Thought dis-ease. Surrender to it. Carefully, when your situation is such that it will not destroy you.

Necessity is not before, objectified in the situation and the oppressive intention it embodies (nothing is more arbritrary than poverty and abuse). Neither is it outside, in transcendent standards to be striven for (never to be attained). It is neither in imposition nor tendential consensus. It is neither an originating nor regulating foundation. Necessity is an *effect*. It is an effect that comes not before, not outside, but in the middle, a middle that is neither a medium nor a mediation, that is the real indeterminacy of an encounter that is *felt*, felt directly, really felt, as a pounding potential bound up one way or another with pain. That is the foundation. The violence of the foundation is not necessary in the sense of being determined and determining, in the way that judgment and its objectification are: it is determin*able* (a real open-endedness, a virtuality). Determinability, as distinct from determination, is the being of pure thought. It is literal, if nonspecific, *force*. Force is virtuality tending toward an actualization that will extinguish it through effective limitation, by converting it into a *state* of things and a corresponding set of possibilities which, like the imposed, arbitrary determination with which they arise, come before (as a promise, a goal to reach) and lie outside the reach of some (the inevitability of the promise broken; limitative blockage) – and which are in any case pre-cast.

The force of determinability (existential openness) and its conversion (the determination of possibility, as part of a regime of blockage, as a function of closure) are two phases of ontological violence. Force is the "cutting edge" of a plane of immanence as it enters a determinate situation that truthfully and usefully blocks it, and is sundered by it. The blockage into which it is converted (becoming-major) is a measure of the autonomy of the situation *vis-à-vis* the plane of immanence (its possibility). The sundering (becoming-minor as liberatory counter-blockage) is a measure of the autonomy of the plane of immanence *vis-à-vis* the situation (its virtuality). Both autonomies, both freedoms, both violences, are actual necessity. The apparent contradiction between necessity and freedom dissolves in a nondialectical process that is a meeting of reciprocal autonomies and their mutual undoing. There is no final synthesis. The synthesis is at every turn, in the combat of energies from which a *new* situation will again emerge, necessarily, as a precipitate. The "contradiction" is less that than a real tension. The broken line leading from one situation to the next as each in turn is blocked asunder is a linearity added to (superposed with) the circularity of necessity and freedom, major and minor, actual and virtual, in mutual undoing. "Freedom," in the broadest Deleuzian sense, is this undoing, which is asymmetrical even though it is mutual. There is always an overspill, an excess of the virtual over the determined, over the actual and the possibilities it pre-casts. It is this excess that holds final synthesis (the standardized stasis of achieved consensus) at bay and keeps the process rolling. One is free to the extent that one's situations are open. One's situations are open to the extent that one performs the paradoxical point, in surrender and sobriety (ethics). I do not have my freedom or choose it from a set of pre-cast alternatives. I extra-am it. My freedom is selected to be and exceed me by the same process that necessitates the pain of my situation and its unbearability (ethics rolled into an ontology where being is forcible becoming). Again, that process is always collective, requiring a direct communication between at least two planes of immanence designated by the proper names attached to distinct individuals and by the common names attached to the constituencies to which those individuals actually belong, and which they may represent in opposition and provoke to differ in affirmation (ethics and ontology rolled into politics). Deleuzian freedom is immanence to a collective *creative* process necessarily connecting individuals' belongings and unbearabilities to the singularity of their becomings (ethics, ontology, politics, and aesthetics rolled up into one). Deleuzianism as a monist philosophy of the collective expression of singularity.

## Circuit

The being of thought is thought at the limit of itself, at the point where it is blocked. This is the point at which it can be felt, and only felt, remaining as yet unexpressed in actual terms. Unexpressed in actual terms, it is felt as a virtuality. Which is precisely what it is in itself. Except that it isn't, in itself – having entered experience. What isn't, can't be felt. Only thought.

This is just an involuted way of saying that there is a point at which thought and feeling are simultaneously raised to their highest power and are blocked. At this point, they do what only they can do, and roll over into what they are not. The zone of indiscernibility between thought and feeling is the *event*. To be precise, it is the event when considered from the side of the ideal, or pure thought. From the side of the sensible, or the empirical, it is *affect*. Taken from both sides, it is the process whereby intension and extension, the actual and the virtual, the transcendental and the empirical, meet, permeate, and pass into one another. That zone is the mutual limit of ideality and being, where one becomes the other, without resemblance or analogy, with no conformity or correspondence. It is the foundation as dissemblance, as the thought-violence of a vicious circle that is the eternal return of the ever-differing.

## Virtual topic

The topic of this essay is Deleuze's characterization of his philosophy as a "transcendental empiricism." Had the essay been about its topic, it would have explained in no uncertain terms that the "transcendentalism" at play has to do with a reciprocal beyonding, of thought and being, as they become, together, in ontogenetic (creative) tension. There is nothing beyond the reality of that ontogenetic process, nothing "transcendent." The "transcendental," as opposed to the transcendent, refers to the *limit*, the transformation zone where actual faculties, such as conscious thought (pure thought captured and bounded) and individual sensibility, are taken to their highest power, and are blocked. The limit is *of* thought and *of* feeling, but is not *in* them. It is their plane of mutual immanence, where they are *in each*

571

*other.* This plane is not beyond, in the sense of being outside. For if it were outside, it would be relative to an inside. The limit is absolute: no thing can remain outside it. No thing can go beyond it because it beyonds all things. It de-forms them. By the same token, no thing can go beyond it because it beyonds them by *infolding* them. The limit is a deforming *force* no thing can withstand, powerful enough to make a thing what it isn't, to turn it inside out and outside in, to the point that it transcends itself at the extremity of its immanence. This process cannot but be felt, powerfully, totally felt, in effect. The effect is affect, the experience of an encounter with pure thought. This is why the Deleuzian process is as paradoxically empirical as it is transcendental. It is an empiricism in which experience is in ineradicable excess over states of things, and a transcendentalism without a Subject. Effect, affect, excess: an *epiphenomenology of becoming.*

Finally, this essay would have emphasized that its becoming-Deleuzian is not by any stretch the only one. It would have summed itself up in the formula: "repeat to differ."

## Writings

Deleuze, Gilles: *Difference and Repetition,* tr. Paul Patton (New York: Columbia University Press, 1994).

——: *The Logic of Sense,* tr. Mark Lester and Charles Stivale, ed. Constantin Boundas (New York: Columbia University Press, 1990).

Deleuze, Gilles, and Guattari, Félix: *Anti-Oedipus,* vol. 1 of *Capitalism and Schizophrenia,* tr. Robert Hurley, Mark Seem, and Helen R. Lane (Minneapolis, MN: University of Minnesota Press, 1983).

——: *A Thousand Plateaus,* vol. 2 of *Capitalism and Schizophrenia,* tr. Brian Massumi (Minneapolis, MN: University of Minnesota Press, 1987).

——: *What is Philosophy,* tr. Graham Burchell and Hugh Tomlinson (London: Verso, 1994).

## References and further reading

Boundas, Constantin V., and Olkowski, Dorothea (eds): *Gilles Deleuze and the Theater of Philosophy* (New York: Routledge, 1994).

Deleuze, Gilles: *Bergsonism* (New York: Zone Books, 1988).

——: *Critique et clinique* (Paris: Minuit, 1993). (Forthcoming in English translation from University of Minnesota Press.)

——: *Cinema 1: The Movement Image,* tr. Hugh Tomlinson and Barbara Habberjam (Minneapolis, MN: University of Minnesota Press, 1986).

——: *Cinema 2: The Time-Image,* tr. Hugh Tomlinson and Robert Galeta (Minneapolis, MN: University of Minnesota Press, 1989).

——: *Empiricism and Subjectivity: An Essay on Hume's Theory of Human Nature,* tr. Constantin V. Boundas (New York: Columbia University Press, 1991).

——: *Expressionism in Philosophy: Spinoza,* tr. Martin Joughin (New York: Zone Books, 1990).

——: *The Fold: Leibniz and the Baroque,* tr. Tom Conley (Minneapolis, MN: University of Minnesota Press, 1993).

——: *Foucault,* tr. Seán Hand (Minneapolis, MN: University of Minnesota Press, 1986).

——: *Francis Bacon: Logique de la sensation*, 2 vols (Paris: Éditions de la Différence, 1981).

——: *Kant's Critical Philosophy: The Doctrine of the Faculties*, tr. Hugh Tomlinson and Barbara Habberjam (Minneapolis, MN: University of Minnesota Press, 1984).

——: *Nietzsche and Philosophy*, tr. Hugh Tomlinson (New York: Columbia University Press, 1983).

——: *Proust and Signs*, tr. Richard Howard (New York: George Braziller, 1972).

——: *Pourparlers* (Paris: Minuit, 1990). (Forthcoming in English trans. from Columbia University Press.)

——: *Spinoza: Practical Philosophy*, tr. Robert Hurley (San Francisco, CA: City Lights, 1988).

Deleuze, Gilles, and Parnet, Claire: *Dialogues*, tr. Hugh Tomlinson and Barbara Habberjam (New York: Columbia University Press, 1987).

Deleuze, Gilles, and Guattari, Félix: *Kafka: Toward a Minor Literature*, tr. Dana Polan (Minneapolis, MN: University of Minnesota Press, 1986).

Guattari, Félix: *Chaosmosis*, tr. Paul Bains and Julian Pefanis (Bloomington, IN: Indiana University Press, 1995).

Hardt, Michael: *Gilles Deleuze: An Apprenticeship in Philosophy* (Minneapolis, MN: University of Minnesota Press, 1993).

Massumi, Brian: *A User's Guide to Capitalism and Schizophrenia: Deviations from Deleuze and Guattari* (Cambridge, MA: MIT Press, 1992).

# 52

# Lyotard

## JACOB ROGOZINSKI

Jean-François Lyotard was born in 1924. After teaching at the lycée Constantine in Algeria (1950–2), he returned to France and joined the group "Socialism or Barbarism" (*Socialisme ou Barbarie*), which had been founded in 1949 by LEFORT (see Article 44), CASTORIADIS (Article 45), and Trotskyist militants. He then lectured at the Sorbonne and at the University in Nanterre and was involved in setting up the group "Worker Power" (*Pouvoir Ouvrier*) when "Socialism or Barbarism" split in 1964. In Nanterre in 1968, he participated in the activities of the "Movement of 22 March" (*Mouvement du 22 mars*) which was the origin of the student revolt in May. From 1973, he was professor at the University Paris-VIII as well as at different American universities. He succeeded Derrida as president of the International College of Philosophy (*Collège International de Philosophie*) (1984–6).

The unity of Lyotard's work might at first appear difficult to establish. Influenced in the beginning by phenomenology (*La Phénoménologie*, 1954), then by revolutionary Marxism and psychoanalysis (*Dérive à partir de Marx et Freud*, 1973), and afterwards by a "philosophy of desire" which was inspired by the work of DELEUZE (see Article 51), it took Lyotard several years before he developed a really individual set of problems. This was eventually achieved by the "ontology of phrases" developed in *Le Différend* (1984). However, its reception was distorted to a certain extent by the debates and polemics that surrounded the notion of "postmodernity" introduced in *La Condition post-moderne* (1979).

Like many French philosophers of his generation – notably DERRIDA (Article 50), FOUCAULT (Article 49) and LEFORT (Article 44) – Lyotard's starting point was phenomenology. In his first important work, *Discours, figure* (1971), he attempts to move beyond the limitations of HUSSERL (Article 15) and MERLEAU-PONTY (Article 23) by looking to FREUD (Article 12) and the idea of unconscious desire. Since the reduction *to* the perceptible brought about by phenomenology cannot grasp "the enigma of the event," it proves necessary to carry out a reduction *of* the perceptible: to move from the perceptive realm to its "figural" matrix and, in the end, to the "unbounded" urge which according to Freud characterized the "primary processes" of the unconscious. This would facilitate the development of a "figural" aesthetic of "unconstrained," "wild" beauty, as is suggested by modern art. "In making discourse from the unconscious, the energy is left out": by emphasizing the intensities of libidinal energy – the "economic" dimension of Freudian metapsychology – Lyotard opposes the structural conception of the unconscious developed by Lacan, in which it is reduced to a chain of signifiers. This set of concerns – close to the ideas advanced by Deleuze and Guattari in *L'Anti-Oedipe* (1972) – and the "energy" metaphysics which underpin it, finds its most extensive development in *Economie libidinale* (1974), while the task of a "figural" aesthetics is realized through numerous analyses of music, cinema (cf. *Des dispositifs pulsionels*, 1973) and, above all, contemporary painting (Duchamp, Newman, Adami, Monory, etc.).

The year 1975 was a turning point for Lyotard: he abandoned his philosophy of libidinal intensities because it did not allow him to "formulate the problem of injustice," to ponder the legitimacy of narratives or, deeper still, to think through ethical "wrong." Under the influence of Wittgenstein, his research from that point on focused on the analysis of "language games," the multiplicity and incommensurability of which invalidate any claim to unity under the authority of a metalanguage or of a totalizing "great narrative." In order to counter this speculative "terror," representing as it does "absolute injustice," it is necessary to maintain the irreducible plurality of language games, to institute a "justice of multiplicities" which "requires that the singular justice of each game is observed" (*Au juste*, 1979). In *La Condition post-moderne* (1979), this idea is located historically: the modern mechanism of legitimization based on the hegemony of a meta-narrative of emancipation, which has arguably entered an irreversible crisis, is replaced by the postmodern alternative. This is founded upon the plurality of "little narratives," "the atomization of the social into flexible networks of language" which will admit of "paralogy," invention, disagreement.

By "postmodern," we understand that which is no longer modern, that which follows modernity and thereby "goes beyond" it. But this principle of legitimization, according to which that which comes "later" is necessarily "better," is the principle of modernity *par excellence*, the foundation stone of the modern metaphysics of Progress; Lyotard did not fail to see this (cf. *Le Post-moderne expliqué aux enfants*, 1986). In other words, the more *postmodern* one is, the more *modern* one is, precisely because one is "post." The only way to be genuinely *post*modern – that is, irreducible to the modern – would be no longer to be *post*: to renounce all linear chronological periodization, the so-called "postmodern" simply becoming an internal potentiality of the project of modernity.

Therefore, Lyotard logically concluded that the ambiguous notion of "postmodernity" was of secondary importance; henceforth, he stressed the importance of "rewriting modernity," of carrying out its "anamnesis." According to Lyotard, this was neglected by the dominant tendencies of "postmodernism," which were merely "citational" and eclectic, and which he accused of "wasting the inheritance of the avant-garde movements" (cf. *L'Inhumain*, 1988). This perhaps justifies Jencks's remark that Lyotard is not really "postmodern" at all but rather has remained a *late modernist*. On the other hand, it becomes increasingly difficult to understand what differentiates Lyotard's position from that of Habermas, who considers modernity to be an "unfinished project" of which the emancipatory design at last requires realization. However, to Lyotard this "unfinished" quality appears more "tragic" than it does to Habermas: for him it is not a question of a temporary abandonment but rather of an "elimination," an undoubtedly irreparable "break" that the "paradigmatic name" of Auschwitz indicates (cf. "Discussions; ou: Phraser après Auschwitz," 1981; *Le Différend*, 1984; *L'Enthousiasme*, 1986, etc.).

Thus I would suggest that the reception and the appreciation of Lyotard's thought would benefit from being distanced from the debates concerning the (perhaps inconsistent) notion of "postmodernity," and refocused on that fundamental work that Lyotard himself refers to as his "book of philosophy," *Le Différend* (1984). This is the book in which the reflection, begun in 1975, on different narrative modes and on the different types of "language game" is deepened and given its ontological basis. This book stands at the juncture of two major trends in contemporary philosophy, namely the tradition of Anglo-Saxon analytical philosophy, which is influenced by Wittgenstein, and the "continental" philosophical tradition, which is inspired by the phenomenology of Husserl and the ontology of Heidegger. It thus represents one of the first and most convincing attempts to establish a link between these two traditions.

*Le Différend* focuses on the analysis of elementary "language acts" which Lyotard calls "phrases" and on the ways in which they form sequences. The fact that there is such a thing as a phrase is indeed the only presupposition that does not succumb to doubt, since "to doubt that one is phrasing is in any case to phrase." This, however, does not necessitate the position of a transcendental subject as its ultimate condition – as modern metaphysics claims – since the "subject" of a phrase (its addressor) does not exist outside the phrase which presents it. Language, therefore, is not an instrument of communication that functions in order to transmit messages between constituted subjects. Each phrase presents four elements – addressor, addressee, referent and meaning – the mutual arrangement of which forms a "phrasal universe." If "there are as many universes as there are phrases," these universes are none the less constituted according to groups of rules which allow one to distinguish different regimens of phrases, to divide them up into descriptive, ostensive, prescriptive, normative, deliberative, etc. However, this inventory does not permit us to develop a universal syntax. This is a key point in *Le Différend* – shared with the later Wittgenstein as well as Lacan – namely, that "there is no meta-language": no single rule that governs the range of sequences: no "supreme genre" that can state the law of all narrative genres. The fragility of meta-language implies that language is shot through with irreducible discontinuities. No "translation" is possible between two phrases from different regimens: it would be useless, for example, to claim to be able to derive a prescriptive phrase from a descriptive one (an ethical or a political from a factual one). Even more radical is Lyotard's suggestion that no other pre-established rule is able to predict those sequences that are valid, to fill "the chasm of non-being which opens up between phrases." Hence, the canonical idea of *Le Différend*: "To form sequences is necessary: how to form them is contingent."

The heterogeneousness of regimens of phrases exposes language to the "differend," to phrases in dispute. Lyotard labels a conflict that can be expressed within the same discourse regimen a "disagreement" (*litige*), where the "damage" (*dommage*) caused can be repaired by the simple application of a pre-existing rule of judgment. In contrast, the term "differend" is reserved for those conflicts where the opposing parties express themselves within different regimens. As a consequence of the lack both of a common rule and of a judgment whose authority is acceptable to both, the resulting "wrong" (*tort*) cannot be repaired equitably. The wrong is signaled by a silence, which is like an "appeal to unknown phrases," an indication that "something remains to be phrased, which has not yet been so." Thus, the overriding imperative of a phrasal ethics or politics is located in the need to "admit of the differend," to invent a new language and new rules for forming sequences "so that the wrong is able to express itself and the litigant ceases to be a victim." This leaves the question unanswered as to whether it is possible to "repair" a fundamentally radical wrong by phrasing it. It may be the case that under the label "wrong," Lyotard confuses two very different situations; in the first, he uses the term "wrong" to account for the fact that, by choosing a phrase, each sequence wrongs the multiplicity of possible phrases which could have figured instead in the sequence. Such a wrong is based on the insurmountable distance that separates the possible from the real and manifests quite simply the impossibility of "saying everything"; but this is a minor type of wrong. Lyotard fails to distinguish this rigorously enough from the major type of wrong of which the name of Auschwitz – amongst others – is testimony: this type is evidence of a radical interruption that runs the risk of destroying any possibility of sequence formation. The silence surrounding the name of Auschwitz is "the sign that something remains to be phrased," or persists eternally "in suffering," in a silence which is wronged by any narrative or any possible sequence. This radical wrong would not occur in any sequence, but only when there exists a threat to the very possibility of forming a sequence. Whereas the minor wrong only concerns the choice of possible phrases, this one affects the ability-to-phrase itself, the "capacity to speak or to be silent." If the first type can and must be repaired by the invention of new forms of language, the radical wrong remains for its part absolutely irreparable.

This distinction between two forms or two regimens of wrong allows us to reply to Manfred Frank's objection to Lyotard: according to him, *Le Différend* argues that *all* wrongs are irreparable and thus leads – given that each actual phrase causes a wrong to all the other possible sequences – to a generalized agonism in which each phrase enters into conflict with all the others. This would inevitably undermine the possibility of argument and of a minimal consensus reached through argument. However, it is clear that Lyotard does not adopt such a nihilistic and self-destructive position: for him it is the philosopher's particular "responsibility" to "detect disputes" in order to "find the language" which will overcome them and repair the wrong each time this is possible.

Lyotard's position in relation to the paradigm of the "communicative consensus" which is utilized by contemporary German philosophers – HABERMAS (Article 34), Apel, Wellmer, and Frank – must therefore be approached with caution. At a simple level, the controversy that separates Lyotard from these authors seems to be a mere disagreement within the *linguistic turn* of contemporary philosophy. At a deeper level, it must be acknowledged that there exists a real "dispute" between the range of themes that have emerged from the *linguistic turn* and a thought that henceforth devotes its attention to the *unnameable*. In asserting that "the observable social link is made from "strokes" of language" (Lyotard 1979) Lyotard seems to reaffirm the "linking" and unifying function of language, just like those theorists of communicative consensus. However, for the latter language constitutes the social link through a consensual purpose which is principally manifested in the *Diskurs*, in the argumentative usage of language. For Lyotard, it constitutes the social link through *agon*, struggle, dissension. This disallows the reduction of the heterogeneous multiplicity of language games that takes place when priority is given to rational argumentation over other possible games. The disagreement between Habermas and Lyotard stems from their divergent interpretations of Wittgenstein: whereas the German philosopher starts from Wittgenstein's critique of solipsism in order to define an interactional model of language, the Frenchman is more faithful to the radical nature of Wittgenstein's thought, relying on his dismissal of metalanguage and asserting with him the irreducible multiplicity of language acts and the contingency of the sequences they form. However, Lyotard's resistance to the communicative paradigm is also supported by a reference to Kant's *Critique of Judgment*, according to which aesthetic judgment stems from a *concept-free communicability*, which is entirely "sentimental" and indeterminate, and which "eludes the communicative activity . . . that is always presupposed in all conceptual communication" (Lyotard 1988).

However, Lyotard's most recent work is not directed at the analysis of this other mode of communication, but rather at the consideration of an uncommunicable and unpresentable element. Several interests testify to this "unnameable in the secret of names": the "transcendental aesthetic" of the artistic avant-garde that has been analyzed with the Kantian sublime or with Adorno's "negative dialectic"; the "Jews" as emblem of fidelity to the Forgotten; also Heidegger's thinking around the *Ereignis*; and the Freudian conception of *unconscious affect* (cf. *Heidegger et "les juifs,"* 1988). Of all these different subjects, it is above all the last that receives most attention in the most recent writings ("Emma," 1989, and the *Lectures d'enfance,* 1991). The unconscious affect is the unthinkable re-presentation of that which has never been presented as such, the trace of a Forgotten without forgetfulness, which cannot be "forgotten" because it never allowed itself to be graven on a memory, even an unconscious one. Lyotard none the less tries to include the radical strangeness of unconscious affect in the framework of the phrasal pragmatics of *Le Différend*: it appears then as an "affect of phrase" or a "phrase-affect." This is both inarticulable and lacking in discoverable occurrences: it is a zero-phrase which is un-signifying, un-destined, un-referenced and even without an assignable addressor ("pre-egoical"); it is deprived therefore of the four elements that, in *Le Différend*, constituted the universe that any phrase necessarily demonstrates. Consequently, it does not belong to the order of *lexis*, of the articulated phrase, but to the element of the *phone*, of the voice as timbre or tone, a purely "pathic" manifestation without inflexion or diachronic sequencing (cf. "voix: Freud" in *Lectures d'enfance*). However, the recourse to this Aristotelian distinction leaves unanswered the question of the status of this inarticulated voice and of its relation to the system of the language. Here, we are faced with the classic problem of any analysis of the sublime, that is the (perhaps untenable) requirement to present in the very order of presentation that which is unpresentable. It would appear that Lyotard in his most recent works has finally taken note of this difficulty or aporia without really overcoming it.

## Writings

*La Phénomenologie* (Presses Universitaires de France, 1954); English translation: *Phenomenology* (Albany, NY: SUNY Press, 1991).

*Discours, figure* (Klincksieck, 1971); partial translation in *Oxford Literary Review*, 6(1) (1983), pp. 3–34, and *Theatre Journal*, 35(3) (1983), pp. 333–57.

*Dérive à partir de Marx et Freud* (Éditions 10/18, 1973).

*Des Dispositifs pulsionnels* (Editions 10/18, 1973); partial translation in *Telos*, 19 (1974), pp. 127–37, and *Semiotexte*, 3(1) (1978), pp. 44–53.

*Économie libidinale* (Paris: Minuit, 1974); English translation: *The Libidinal Economy* (Bloomington, IN: Indiana University Press, 1992).

*Les Transformateurs Duchamp* (Galilée, 1977); English translation: *Duchamp's Transformers* (Venice, USA: Lapis Press, 1990).

*Au juste* (with J. L. Thébaud) (Bourgois, 1979); English translation: *Just Gaming* (Minneapolis, MN: University of Minnesota Press, 1986).

*La Condition post-moderne* (Paris: Minuit, 1979); English translation: *The Postmodern Condition* (Minneapolis, MN: University of Minnesota Press, 1984).

"Discussions, ou: phraser après Auschwitz," in *Les Fins de l'homme* (Paris: Galilée, 1981).

*Le différend* (Paris Minuit, 1984); English translation: *The Differend: Phrases in Dispute* (Manchester: Manchester University Press, 1988).

*Le Post-moderne expliqué aux enfants* (Paris: Galilée, 1986).

*L'Enthousiasme. La critique kantienne de l'histoire* (Paris: Galilée, 1986).

*Heidegger et "les juifs"* (Paris: Galilée, 1988); English translation: *Heidegger and "the Jews"* (Minneapolis, MN: University of Minnesota Press, 1990).

*L'Inhumain* (Paris: Galilée, 1988); English translation: *Inhuman: Reflections on Time* (Cambridge: Polity Press, 1991).

"Emma," *Nouvelle Revue de Psychanalyse*, 39 (1989).

*Leçons sur l'analytique du sublime* (Paris: Galilée, 1991).

*Lectures d'enfance* (Paris: Galilée, 1991).

*The Lyotard Reader*, ed. A. Benjamin (Oxford: Blackwell, 1989).

## References and Further reading

Bennington, Geoffrey: *Lyotard: Writing the Event* (New York: Columbia University Press, 1988).

Brugger, N., Frandsen, F., and Pirotte, D. (eds): *Lyotard: les déplacements philosophiques* (Bruxelles: De Boeck, 1993).

Carroll, David: *Paraesthetics: Foucault, Lyotard, Derrida* (London and New York: Methuen, 1987).

Frank, Manfred: *Die Grenzen der Verständigung: ein Geistergesprach zwischen Lyotard und Habermas* (Frankfurt: Suhrkamp, 1988).

Guibal, Francis, and Rogozinski, Jacob: *Témoigner du différend*, ed. P. J. Labarrière (Paris: Osiris, 1989).

Jencks, Charles: *What is Post-Modernism?* (London: Academy Editions; New York: St Martin's Press, 1986).

Pefanis, Julian: *Heterology and the Postmodern* (Durham, NC: Duke University Press, 1991).

Readings, Bill: *Introducing Lyotard: Art and Politics* (London and New York; Routledge, 1991).

Wellmer, Albrecht: *Zur Dialektik von Moderne und Postmoderne. Vernunftkritik nach Adorno* (Frankfurt: Suhrkamp, 1985).

Welsch, Wolfgang: *Unsere Postmoderne Moderne* (Acta Humaniora, 1987).

## See the following journal articles which cover the work of Lyotard

"Lyotard," *L'Arc*, 64 (1976).

*La Faculté de juger* (Minuit, 1985).

"J. F. Lyotard: Réécrire la modernité," *Les Cahiers de Philosophie*, 5 (1988).

"J. F. Lyotard," *Denker des 20. Jahrhunderts* (Junghans Verlag, 1989).

"Passages, genres, différends: J. F. Lyotard," *L'Esprit Créateur*, 31(1) (1991).

*Diacritics*, 14(3) (1984).

# 53

# Baudrillard

## MIKE GANE

Jean Baudrillard's apparently diverse *oeuvre* reveals a persistent attempt to think about what he calls the "object" ("that's what I was obsessed with from the start" – 1993a, p. 24). His first book was entitled *Le Système des objets* (1968), and in it he outlined a theory of the "object system". He defined this as the conjunction of the system of commodities and the system of signs: what others have analyzed as the ontological process of reification and alienation became according to Baudrillard a general semiological process which marked the last phase of alienated society. His next book *La Société de consommation* (1970) provided a general account of the affluent society in which consumption, not production, is its dominant mechanism. But by *La Gauche divine* (1985) he thought that even a consumerism characterized by alienation and spectacular consumption had given way to a new glacial, non-spectacular form dominated by information technology and fractal culture (1985, p. 144) in which the significance of the "object" had been radically transformed. Thus Baudrillard's writings seem to chart the evolution of modernity into postmodernity, indeed he has been called "the author of postmodern culture and society" (Kroker and Cook 1988). Although he draws on sociology, his most important philosophical influence is Nietzsche. In 1987 he published a short intellectual autobiography, *L'Autre par lui-même*, perhaps the best short introduction to his work to that date. He claims no longer to adopt the tragic vision entailed in the critique of modernity but rather a melancholy – "let us be stoics" – attitude (1988b, p. 101).

His earliest writings and influences were as a Germanist: he wrote a thesis on Nietzsche; he was the principal translator of the works of Peter Weiss into French; he taught German in a French lycée before taking up a position in sociology at Paris University (Nanterre) in 1966. His early essays are dominated by an effort to develop a critical structuralism of the object system, a project directly influenced by both Henri Lefebvre and Roland Barthes. But his third book, *For A Critique of the Political Economy of the Sign* (originally 1972), and even more *The Mirror of Production* (originally 1973), move decisively to change the basis of his critical position away from that of a traditional class struggle to that of opposing the symbolic order to the semiotic (or simulation) order constituent of contemporary Western culture. The first result of posing this opposition was his study *Symbolic Exchange and Death* (originally 1976), followed by *Seduction* (1979), *Simulacres et Simulation* (1981), *Fatal Strategies* (1983), *The Transparency of Evil* (1990), and *L'Illusion de la fin* (1992). In his intellectual autobiography he suggests that – beginning with *Seduc-*

*tion* (trans. 1990a) – he no longer engages in a critique of modernity from the point of view of symbolic exchange but takes up the position of the object, now a "pure sign" which carries a fatal, objective irony (1988b, p. 90). With the fractal stage, even this effectivity of the sign disappears as he has come to take up the side of the "cosmic order." With great inner consistency his styles of writing changed to embrace the challenge of the symbolic: the poetic (*L'Ange de Stuc*, 1978) and the aphorism and fragment (*Cool Memories*, 1987, and *Cool Memories II*, 1990). It is arguable that his work never finally abandons the idea that symbolic exchange constitutes a superior cultural formation to that of Western rationalism and post-rationalism, or to put it even more strongly, that ultimately the inner structures of Western culture have never been able to escape the dynamic of symbolic exchange (see his critique of Foucault, *Forget Foucault*, 1987) and yet remain incapable of developing a genuinely symbolic superstructure.

Baudrillard's analysis of capitalist society in his first two books was a highly original version of critical theory. Very much against the trend of orthodox Marxism or Althusserianism, he insisted on the decisive novelty of affluence and the way in which consumerism had become the dominant feature of social integration in class-divided societies. Instead of achieving social and class integration through the discipline of work and economic production, the dominant means was now through the activities of consumption, culture, and leisure. He applied Barthes's semiological method to the analysis of objects and combined this with what he called a theory of the "structural law of value." This was an enlargement of Marx's notion of the law of value, or rather Marx's theory was now seen as a particular application of a more general process which could be identified in many distinct spheres of culture. Whereas Barthes's analysis of fashion was essentially formal, Baudrillard's was critical – emphasizing the fact that fashion could invade and restructure any aspect of society, including philosophy, as modular element (the formation of a combinatory system) and as modal temporality (the fashion cycle). Both aspects were seen by Baudrillard as "semiological reductions" – assaults on a vital symbolic culture. In his critique of Marxism he argued that Marx had not really understood this relationship but had merely analyzed the reduction of exchange-value to use-value. In an analysis which has important consequences if correct, use-value was shown to be already produced by semiological culture, which already presupposes utility. Thus Marxism had not been radical enough to escape the logic of capitalist exchange itself. In addition, structuralism, applied in anthropology, naively projected semiotic reason backwards on to primitive societies – an inappropriate method which could at best only end in radical misunderstanding, reinforcing a fundamental contempt for other cultures.

Baudrillard's analysis of symbolic exchange, inspired by Marcel Mauss and Georges Bataille, established the divergence between potlatch and political economy, gift exchange and commodity exchange, seasonal cycles and capital accumulation. At first Baudrillard contrasted the ambivalence of the symbol against the sign. But as his work developed he was able to establish further aspects of symbolic cultures which collectively created a sharp contrast to Western culture: ritual, eternal recurrence, sacrifice, life-death cycle, seduction, reversibility, destiny, and evil. At the most extreme, he argued primitive societies were not societies in that they did not "produce" and did not "consume," in fact did not "exchange." Such concepts, developed in Western philosophy, are dependent on basic notions current within bourgeois society, even and not least the fundamental concept of "mode of production." At this time Baudrillard began to adopt a Nietzschean perspective which regards Western culture as an emergent slave morality of *ressentiment*, plagued by a tragic inversion of values, against which a process of cultural struggle may produce an affirmative transvaluation. The assertion of *amor fati* against *ressentiment* is the theme of Baudrillard's *Fatal Strategies*; the assertion of the principle of seduction against production is the theme of the book *Seduction*, However there seem to be limits to Baudrillard's Nietzscheanism: although he refuses the Christian notion of individual responsibility and subjective guilt, he specifically rejects any possibility of transcending the principle of evil. Indeed he stresses good and evil "transcends us totally" and should be "accepted totally" (*The Transparency of Evil*, 1993b, p. 109). This leads Baudrillard to a fundamental acceptance of Bataille's notion of the accursed share, and links Baudrillard to the central tradition of German moral thought of Goethe and Hölderlin.

*Seduction* is the work that marked the turning point in his writing as far as style and position were concerned. Here the main points of reference are no longer to sociology but to art, philosophy, and literature, to Borges, Kafka, and Kierkegaard. He creates a genealogy for seduction parallel to that established by Walter Benjamin for the work of art: first, a stage of ritual – the anonymity of the artist; second, a stage of individual production of the work of art which carries the mark of individuality and an aesthetic dimension in a system shorn of obligation; and third, the work of art in the period of its mechanical reproducibility. Seduction likewise has its initial ritual phase, based on the relation of the duel. This is followed by an aesthetic phase where the exemplar for Baudrillard is Kierkegaard's seducer (*Diary of a Seducer*) who elaborates an ironic strategy of seduction as an art. This passes into the third "political" form where seduction is maximally dispersed as a social form of solicitation while being deprived of all intensity and content; Baudrillard's formula for this phase is: maximal circulation with minimal intensity. Baudrillard then transposes this into a threefold classification: first, the phase of the duel or dual relation (the object of ritual transformation established by the dominance of the rule); second, the stage of the law, of polarity where the relation is one of dialectic or contract. This passes into a new form where the relation has become a connection determined by the immanence of digitality and models. In this latter phase seduction becomes cool, becomes an ambience.

There is, however, a strong Nietzschean allusion (to "How the 'Real World' at last Became a Myth," *Twilight of the Idols*) in "The Precession of Simulacra" (orig. 1978; for English translation see *Simulacra and Simulation*, 1994), which constitutes Baudrillard's attempt to replace the concept of semiology with notions of simulation first discussed in *Symbolic Exchange and Death* (part 2, "The Orders of Simulacra") and elaborated in *Simulacres et Simulation* (1981). This important discussion is a basis for Baudrillard's own solution to the Marxist problem of ideology and indeed for a periodization of Western culture beyond that established in relation to seduction.

There are a number of orders of Simulacra in this genealogy. The first order dominated European culture from the Renaissance to the eighteenth century, exemplified by the *trompe l'oeil* (the enchanted moment of Simulacra), and the automaton in manufacture, a system of Simulacra corresponding to small craft enterprises. Here simulation entails postulating an original work or object of which the copy is its counterfeit. The poetic work *L'Ange de Stuc*, is an evocation of the ambience of this world (its prose version can be found in *Symbolic Exchange and Death*, pp. 50–3 and in *Seduction* pp. 60–6). Baudrillard also calls it the "natural" stage of Simulacra – corresponding to a stage of use-value.

The second order corresponds to the industrial system and the machine. Here it is mass production which establishes the equivalence of the series. This system is one of reproduction in the absence of any true or natural original from which the series is reproduced. The utopias of this period are promethean – corresponding to the dominant ethos of history, dialectic, progression, revolution. This is the period of the emerging hegemony of science which aims to abolish the world of appearances, to expose and master the real. It is, therefore, for Baudrillard, the "golden age of alienation," of exchange-value and its critique, and later of surrealism in art.

The third order corresponds to the communication revolution, the dominance of codes and the mass media. In this period the key form is genetic reproduction through aleatory commutation. This marks an end to dialectic, history, and revolution. This form of simulation goes beyond any relation of representation; it is that which is always already reproduced. Instead of surrealism in art, here reality itself becomes hyperreal in the aestheticization of reality through sign-value, media, and computer models. These establish "the blind but brilliant ambience of simulacra" (1993d, p. 75). At this stage radicality passes from the alienated subject and installs itself in the objective passion of the object. Here the subject classes adopt a fatal silent strategy of hyperconformity – a new post-revolutionary form of resistance – this time the masses are object.

There is a fourth order which Baudrillard calls the fractal stage, or viral stage, or the "irradiated stage of value"; here value "radiates in all directions, filling in all interstices, without bearing reference to anything whatsoever except by mere contiguity" (in Stearns and Chaloupka 1992, p. 15). This stage also seems to mark the end of the period where the disappearance of things occurs through a finite death or "fatal mode" of return; so here the dominant form is where things are simply and indifferently proliferated and dispersed into the void (1992, p. 12).

This fourth, fractal, stage corresponds to a world dominated by transpolitical forms, the transaesthetic, transeconomic, transproductive, transsexual, etc., and the virtual apocalypse: the virtual economic slump, the virtual (Gulf) war. When culture has rejected all its negative components, it becomes a closed system; it becomes virtual and open to a pathology of the code: to anomaly and metastasis. Unlike the pathologies of earlier stages, to mechanical system failure, or anomie, the new pathology is strangely aestheticized and relates specifically to bodies that have become purged of internal negative principles, they are "virtual bodies" with gravely weakened immune systems.

Baudrillard thus has developed what might be called a general theory of Western social and cultural modernization. This was first offered as a critical theory of capitalist affluence focusing on the system of objects as a form of social alienation. The basis of criticism shifted to symbolic exchange from which were elaborated a series of polarities: sign-symbol, production-seduction, etc. The focus shifted again to examining the transition from history to the features of the societies dominated by third- and fourth-order simulation: here Baudrillard found not a principle of critique, of negation as such, but a principle of evil (carried by the object), and an "unprecedented pathology." In charting this scenario of the genealogy of resistance and opposition, class struggle was clearly located in the promethean phase of production and bourgeois revolution, the hot explosive phase of historical dialectic. The phase dominated by the code turns cultural evolution into an implosive mode: critical opposition to the code, like all negativity, even the proletariat itself, is simply absorbed into the cultural system and neutralized. It is as if, he suggests, the only revolutionary class had been the bourgeoisie which, in establishing bourgeois society, in effect ushered in a post-alienated and classless society, but one quite unlike that envisaged by Marx.

Yet the way in which "the culture of the West" developed is by no means uniform. The clearest difference is between Europe and America. America, he argues, seems to have missed the whole experience of the second order of simulation, to have passed directly from the eighteenth to the twentieth century. Its culture is always already hyperreal, and Baudrillard always insists it is a contradiction of an achieved utopia. American culture therefore knows no internal dissidence or deep irony. The positive banality of American culture, however, is always mythic, permanently dreamlike in character. European culture anticipates reality by imagining it; American culture – and this is its defining characteristic – refuses this order. That is why European culture struggles to adapt to modernity, while America lives it extravagantly. Europe has never become modern (a thesis Latour has developed without acknowledging its Baudrillardian source); it conserves its high culture. America produced no such articulation. Disneyland is a pure expression of this logic, and as such struggles to survive in Europe where it is semiotically inauthentic. Baudrillard's basic image for American culture is that of the desert, and in exchange for the beauty of the desert it would be good to sacrifice a woman. If the image of such a sacrifice seems bizarre or even gratuitous, it is consistent with the logic of symbolic exchange which continues to haunt this essay. But it should not obscure the fact that *America* along with *Cool Memories* seems to open the door to a positive comparative analysis of cultures. Much of the comparison so far initiated in his writing is between France and America, but there are striking references to the specificity of the symbolic strength of Italian, Mexican, and Japanese cultures. It is perhaps against this background that Baudrillard's essays on the Gulf War should be read. His writing strives to capture the specificity of Islamic cultures, the singularity of the Iranian revolution, and the symbolic *fatwa* against Rushdie. With Saddam Hussein's strategy, however, the use of hostages has lost its symbolic

585

power while his calculated practices have become complicit with those of the West. The war in its Western experience was virtual, entirely displaced now into media images and simulation of war: for Baudrillard in fact a war can no longer take place in the West – except virtually – since third- and fourth-order simulations dominate cultural forms.

Western culture cannot tolerate the very alterity of other cultures. Humanism, the doctrine of universal human rights with its assumption of human equality, like evangelical Christianity, seeks to form the world after its own image and thus reduces radical otherness to domesticated "differences." The result is the imperialist process of the homogenization of world culture: the worldwide assult on symbolic cultures. This process also paradoxically creates a new racism and sexism, phenomena which belong strictly to a culture which cannot tolerate radical alterity. In developing his theories, Baudrillard adopts the position of the radical other, that which is "more other than other," the object conceived as as "strange attractor," that which permits an escape from alienation but only into absolute exoticism. From this position the media-dominated culture of the West can appear as the "ecstasy of communication." In fact this formulation may well be too condensed fully to grasp Baudrillard's latest writings. These suggest that the age of the struggle for human rights itself belonged to the period of the alienation of the subject and to the period in which subjective criticism could be effective and have some meaning. We have passed from the alienated individual to a new postmodern individualism, a form he theorizes as an unprecedented structure of autoservitude. His writings on this subject seem among his most brilliant, and yet involve the most difficult changes of position in his work. His astonishing thesis is that "at all events, it is better to be controlled by someone other than by oneself. Better to be oppressed, exploited, persecuted and manipulated by someone other than by oneself," in what he calls the declination of wills (1993b, p. 167). But the logic of this reversal is taken to its extreme conclusion: "the entire movement for liberation and emancipation, in as much as it is predicated on a demand for greater autonomy – or, in other words, on a more complete introjection of all forms of control and constraint under the banner of freedom – is a regression" (p. 167). He advocates a new ethic "founded on the transmission of foreignness" (1993b, p. 168).

In conclusion, two observations. The first is that one of the most remarkable aspects of this work is the development of a general conception of a primitive, or better, primal culture – what he has called the order of "symbolic exchange." Initially this order is essentially ambivalent, and impossible to frame within a structural semiological matrix without disfiguring it entirely. Gradually this seeming "ambivalence" was given greater and greater definition involving ideas of seduction, fate, reversible time, and death. On the other hand, Western culture became the object of a number of brilliant genealogical studies organized around the four stages of simulation. Baudrillard has claimed his position changed so that from *Seduction* (1979) he abandoned as nostalgic the idea that there could ever be a return to the symbolic order, and from that moment he embraced the destiny of the object. However, it seems apparent that he could never let go of his nostalgia for this "lost object" (1988b, p. 80) even though at the same time he embraces the most

586

extreme positions of hyper- or postmodernity. This makes his writing both more conservative and more radical than any other cultural critic.

Secondly, his position on the latest phase of simulation, the fractal phase, does seem to mark a considerable shift in his relation to Nietzsche, for here the "very possibility of the Eternal Return is becoming precarious: that marvellous perspective presupposes that things unfold in a necessary predestined order, the sense of which lies beyond them. There is nothing like that today; things merely disperse in a randomness that leads nowhere. Today's Eternal Return is that of the infinitely small, the fractal, the obsessive repetition of things on a microscopic and inhuman scale. It is not the exaltation of a will, nor the sovereign affirmation of an event, nor its consecration by an immutable sign – such as Nietzsche's thought – but the viral recurrence of microprocesses" (*America*, pp. 72–3). And according to the thesis of the accursed share, anything that purges evil in its own structures signs its own death warrant (1993b, p. 106).

## Writings

Baudrillard Jean: *Le Système des objets* (Paris: Denoel, 1968).
——: *La Société de consommation* (Paris: Gallimard, 1970).
——: *For a Critique of the Political Economy of the Sign* (St Louis: Telos, 1972, 1981).
——: *Symbolic Exchange and Death* (London: Sage, 1976, 1993d).
——: *The Mirror of Production* (St Louis: Telos, 1973, 1975).
——: *Forget Foucault* (New York: Semiotext(e), 1977, 1987).
——: *Seduction* (London: Macmillan, 1979, tr. 1990a).
——: *Simulations* (New York: Semiotext(e), 1981, 1983); *Simulacra and Simulations* (Ann Arbor, MI: University of Michigan, 1994).
——: *Fatal Strategies* (London: Pluto, 1983, 1990).
——: *La Gauche divine* (Paris: Grasset, 1985).
——: *America* (London: Verso, 1986, 1988a).
——: *Cool Memories* (London: Verso, 1987, 1990).
——: *The Ecstasy of Communication* (New York: Semiotext(e), 1987).
——: *Jean Baudrillard: Selected Writings*, ed. M. Poster (Cambridge: Polity, 1988a).
——: *The Transparency of Evil* (London: Verso, 1990, 1993b).
——: *Revenge of the Crystal: Selected Writings*, ed. F. Foss and J. Pefanis (London: Pluto, 1990).
——: *Cool Memories II* (Paris: Galilée, 1990).
——: *L'Illusion de la fin* (Paris: Galilée, 1992).
——: *Baudrillard Live: Selected Interviews*, ed. M. Gane (London: Routledge, 1993a).

## Further reading

Gane, M.: *Baudrillard: Critical and Fatal Theory* (London: Routledge, 1991).
——: *Baudrillard's Bestiary: Baudrillard and Culture*, (London: Routledge, 1991).
Kellner, D.: *Jean Baudrillard: From Marxism to Postmodernism and Beyond* (Cambridge: Polity, 1989).
Kroker, A. and Cook, D. (eds): *The Postmodern Scene* (London: Macmillan, 1988).
Stearns, W. and Chaloupka, W. (eds): *Jean Baudrillard* (London: Macmillan, 1992).

# 54

# Irigaray

## TINA CHANTER

A practicing psychoanalyst, Luce Irigaray is also a linguist and a philosopher. Irigaray's earliest book, *Le Language des déments* (1973), is a study of language and various forms of mental disturbance. It was out of her experience of psychoanalysis, both as analysand and analyst (see 1977, p. 62), that in 1974 Irigaray came to publish *Speculum of the Other Woman*, a book which takes as its trajectory, however, the history of Western philosophy from Plato to HEGEL (see Article 6). In her reinterpretation of the Western philosophical tradition Irigaray identifies and excavates the repressed feminine that she sees as having been systematically sublimated by a logic of representation that functioned according to a monolithic economy geared towards masculinity. Her view is that "all Western discourse presents a certain isomorphism with the masculine sex: the privilege of unity, form of the self, of the visible, of the specularisable, of the erection" which "does not correspond to the female sex: there is not 'a' female sex" (1977, p. 64). Hence the title of her 1977 work *This Sex Which is Not One*, which can be read either as "the (female) sex that does not count as such within the masculine economy of the visible," or as "the (female) sex that is not singular, but multiple" (see Jardine and Menke, 1991, p. 64).

Several of Irigaray's shorter books published in the 1970s and 1980s, such as her 1979 *Et l'une ne bouge pas sans l'autre* ("And one doesn't stir without the other"), and her 1983 *La Croyance même* ("Belief itself"), have been reprinted as essays in later collections, or translated in English-language journals. *The Irigaray Reader*, edited by Margaret Whitford, provides a useful selection of Irigaray's work (1991). Of her most recent works, *Thinking the Difference: For a Peaceful Revolution* (1994), and *Je, Tu, Nous: Toward a Culture of Difference* (1993), are the most overtly political, while *Sexes and Genealogies* (trans. 1993) focuses more upon psychoanalysis. Irigaray's major philosophical texts are *Speculum of the Other Woman* and *An Ethics of Sexual Difference*. She has also written books on HEIDEGGER (1983) and NIETZSCHE (trans. 1991) (see Articles 18 and 11).

*Speculum* begins with a long essay on FREUD (see Article 12), has as its centerpiece an essay on Descartes, and culminates with a major essay on Plato. Its textual organization reflects – or mirrors, like a speculum – the female morphology that Irigaray is trying to retrieve. Using Descartes as her pivot, like most of her contemporaries, but reversing the order of the tradition, Irigaray also turns its assumptions inside-out. As Moi observes, the book

588

is shaped like a hollow surface on the model of the speculum/vagina. At the centre, the section entitled *"Spéculum"* is framed by the two massive sections on Freud and Plato respectively; it is as if the more fragmentary middle section sinks between the solid, upright volumes of the master thinkers.   (Moi 1985, p. 130)

*An Ethics of Sexual Difference* includes essays on Plato, Aristotle, MERLEAU-PONTY (see Article 23), and LEVINAS (see Article 20). Although HEIDEGGER's and DERRIDA's names are not explicitly mentioned (see Articles 18 and 50), the influence of their ways of questioning and reading can be felt throughout. For example, Irigaray's reading of Aristotle's treatise on place in the *Physics* echoes Derrida's (1972) and Heidegger's (1978) readings of Aristotle's treatise on time, while her deliberate overturning of the Heideggerian privileging of time over space in the phrase "space-time" not only reverses Heidegger's formulation "time-space" (1978), but also responds to Derrida's questioning of the metaphysics of presence. While Irigaray has written essays which address Derrida's work directly *"Le (v)iol de la lettre"* (1985), and "Belief Itself" (1993c) – the latter also deals with psychoanalytic themes – for the most part his influence on her work is less thematic. Like all the male theoreticians whose work Irigaray uses, she both learns from Derrida, and maintains her distance from him. The stance that she adopts towards her male contemporaries could be read as a strategic reversal of Socrates' report of Diotima's views on love in Plato's *Symposium* (see 1993a, pp. 20–33). Irigaray turns the tables on male philosophers, invoking them, using them for inspiration, and at the same time creating a *"disruptive excess"* (1985b, p. 78) in the very texts that she reads so closely.

In 1985 the English-speaking world was introduced to Luce Irigaray's work with the translation of *This Sex Which Is Not One*, a collection of essays and interviews, and *Speculum of the Other Woman*, a philosophical study which, in addition to chapters on Freud, Descartes, and Plato, discusses figures such as Plotinus and Hegel. It was not long before many of her readers became disenchanted with Irigaray's alleged "essentialist" tendency (e.g. Plaza 1978), a disenchantment that can only be fully explained against the background of the prevailing conception of feminism in Anglo-American circles. One might argue that the short shrift that Irigaray initially received from her readers was due to the select availability of texts in translation, or to the fact that her work was initially taken up largely by literary critics who were not as conversant with the Continental tradition as philosophers might have been, and who therefore failed to appreciate the nuances of her work. There may be some truth to both suggestions, but neither tells the whole story.

It is true that the limited availability of Irigaray's works has colored her reception amongst her English readers, and that her work has had a more positive impact in much of continental Europe. In Italy, for example, Irigaray has forged strong connections with feminist groups and with the Italian Communist Party. It is also the case that the first substantial responses to Irigaray emanated from French and Literature departments, rather than Philosophy departments (see, for example, Gallop 1982). Even the first monograph to appear in the English language on Irigaray was written by a lecturer in French (Whitford 1992), and concentrates more upon the psychoanalytic aspects of Irigaray's work than on the philosophical.

Whitford's comprehensive study has the virtue of arguing lucidly and persuasively against the view, well established by 1992, that Irigaray was an essentialist.

In order to appreciate how and why Irigaray came to occupy the position of an essentialist in what might be called the cultural imaginary of feminist consciousness in the Anglo-American world, a brief account of dominant trends in recent feminist thinking is required. Dating from the suffragette movement, feminism has been construed for the most part in terms of equality between the sexes. The discourse of equal rights tends to appeal implicitly to an allegedly sex-neutral ideal towards which women aspired. In order to argue for equity in job opportunity, equal pay for equal work, and the like, feminists typically demanded the same opportunities that society traditionally afforded men, without questioning what assumptions were being harnessed in the ostensibly neutral ideals which they strove to obtain for women. Insofar as feminists uncritically adopted apparently egalitarian values, which had been fostered in individualist, post-industrialist capitalist societies, they failed to question the Enlightenment ideals which lay behind these values. And insofar as feminists aspired to be like men, they failed to appreciate that the differences between the sexes may not merely be a sign of what had to be changed, but rather a much more complex set of phenomena which, though undoubtedly loaded with cultural baggage, also contained some more positive possibilities for feminist change.

To the extent that feminism was a matter of eliminating whatever differences pertained between the sexes, in the service of obtaining equal treatment in socio-economic and political spheres, the question of sexual difference was shelved for the moment. The disparity between women and men could be rectified, the assumption was, by improving women's situation so that it approximated to men's. Such "improvement" – even if it could be fully implemented – leaves a host of questions unanswered. Not the least of these include: Is there anything about women's position that gives them critical purchase on the current social order, from which not only women but also society as a whole might benefit? If there are values that are specific to women's traditional ways of caring, mothering, and being involved with others, is there a way of envisaging a society in which such values play an important role, while no longer being prescribed for women with the effect of precluding them from successfully or easily conforming to more masculine-identified roles?

One of the most powerful barriers that stood in the way of pursuing such questions was the fear that feminism would lose the ground on which it had fought its initial battles. The whole point of feminism was to stress that differences between the sexes were incidental, while stressing similarities allowed feminists to lobby for equality. What remains to be asked is whether such strategies are limited in what they can achieve by unspoken constraints. Two such constraints concern, first, the way in which equality is understood as positing an ideal of sameness between the sexes, and second the idea that whatever change is achieved in the name of a feminism construed as a struggle for equal rights, assumes as an underlying premise the superiority of masculine-identified values. I shall explain the first with reference to the sex/gender distinction, and the second with reference to Derrida's reworking of the Hegelian master–slave relation.

An important distinction that feminists used to articulate the need to gain equality for women was that between sex and gender. In order to improve women's situations feminists emphasized the similarities between men and women, and tended to play down the differences between them. The potential for change became strongly associated with arguing for the priority of gender roles over sexual identity. Standard arguments ran along the lines that, given the opportunity, women could achieve just as much as men in, for example, the professions. What held them back were cultural, social, political, and economic barriers, which could be removed. Whether one was female or male became unimportant, what mattered was realizing that gender roles could be reconfigured – a reconfiguration that was played out as the belief that women could learn to do what men had already succeeded in doing. In other words, sex came to be equated with the natural differences between men and women, and gender with their potential similarities. To emphasize sexual difference, as Irigaray did, seemed to risk falling back into, or at least opening the door to, once again defining women by their "natures," a definition that feminism had worked hard to overcome by suggesting that it was culture and not nature that defined women's roles. Hence Irigaray's insistence upon raising the question of sexual difference was read as a danger sign, as if she were trying to ground women's identities in their bodies, and embrace essentialism. In fact, far from naively appealing to the body as a ground, or unchanging essence of womanhood, Irigaray indicates the limitations of a feminist discourse that focuses upon gender roles to the exclusion of sex. Her point is not to deflect attention away from the need to change society – indeed, such change is one of her major concerns – her view is rather that such change will not go far enough so long as women's differences from men are not taken seriously. Like Judith Butler (1993), Irigaray sees the need to examine gender in relation to, and not in exclusion from, sex.

In Derridean terms, the hierarchy between masculine and feminine is accepted, rather than being overturned or even brought into question as a viable model for construing relations between the sexes. Efforts are directed towards compensating women for injustices suffered in the past, by means of affording them the opportunities that men have traditionally taken for granted. Two possibilities ensue. Either some women gain positions of power, and become the peers of men, at the expense of other women. Or women gain power at the expense of men, in which case the hierarchy of power relations is reversed, but not fundamentally changed. Those who occupy the positions of power will have changed, but the positions themselves will not have been put into question.

Irigaray challenges the idea that the Hegelian master–slave dialectic (1993a, p. 10; 1994, p. 6) that underlies this hierarchical conception of relations between the sexes provides an adequate or appropriate way of construing sexual difference. She insists on the centrality of the question of sexual difference. One of the consequences of such insistence is the refusal to accept as neutral or as universally valid the

591

values that are inculcated by a predominantly patriarchal society. Philosophically, an important influence on Irigaray's formulation of the question of sexual difference as the question of our epoch is Heidegger's way of raising the question of Being (Irigaray 1993a, p. 5).

Just as Heidegger sought to bring to the surface a question that, he argued, had long been covered over by the metaphysical tradition so that it no longer made sense to philosophers, so Irigaray seeks to point to an unthought and neglected issue. While sexual difference, in one sense, is taken for granted by feminist discourse (just like Heidegger's Being is taken for granted as the soil on which metaphysics flourishes), in another sense, it remains unacknowledged and unarticulated. So long as sexual difference is merely a symptom of what has to be changed, feminism has not yet properly confronted the question.

To extend the parallel between Heidegger's questioning of Being, and Irigaray's questioning of sexual difference one step further, one could usefully juxtapose Heidegger's ontological difference with Irigaray's sexual difference. For Heidegger, Being was eclipsed in the metaphysical tradition by beings, so that it became impossible, from the Greeks on, to intelligibly raise the question of Being as such. For Irigaray, if the position of women has been at issue at all, women have always been understood as the counterpart of men, that is in terms of their deficiency compared to men, as not-men (1993b, p. 20). Recall, for example, Aristotle, for whom women's deliberative faculty is not as developed as men's, and who assumed menstrual blood was semen that was not fully concocted. According to Freud, the little girl was a "little man" (1985a, p. 25). By emphasizing the similarities between the sexes, and playing down the differences, feminism not only closes off the question of sexual difference before it has been thoroughly articulated, it also accepts the terms of the debate. It assumes, in other words, that women must, if they want to be taken seriously, become equal to (read the same as) men. It also prejudges the standards according to which women should become equal to men – and these standards, although they might present themselves as, and be taken as, neutral, will in fact be invariably masculine. As long as women attempt to match up to, or to be as good as, men, there is no interrogation of the values or ideology that determine what it means to be considered equal to men. There is, similarly, a failure to raise the question of what it means to be a man, and what it means for women to aspire to the ideal of equality with men. There is, in short, no way of asking the question: what does it mean to be a woman? The question of sexual difference is not yet posed – so long as feminism contents itself with representing women as if they were like men.

Irigaray is interested in exploring the differences between men and women, rather than insisting that they are fundamentally the same. As part of her project she is engaged in distinguishing between the apparent neutrality of discourse and the systematic bias towards masculinity that in fact informs that discourse at every turn. If women have typically been construed as the other of men, then the way to effect any fundamental change in women's position is not, in her view, to insist that women are basically the same as men. If woman has no other, having always been the other of men, there is a sense in which women's subordination to men can be understood in terms of their objectification. Women have become the objects of desire, the mirror of the other, without having developed a sense of their own subjectivity. What this implies, for Irigaray, is that the relation between subjects and objects has to be rethought (Jardine and Menke, 1991, pp. 101–3; Irigaray 1994, p. 26).

While there is no exact parallel between the question of Being, as Heidegger conceives it, and Irigaray's questioning of sexual difference, there are certain structural similarities. For example, there is a sense in which women's objectification can be explained in terms of their being reduced to beings – women adopt the position of things or objects, rather than having any sense of their own projects and goals, rather than having their being as an issue. The question of Being could only be asked by assuming that Being was in fact a being. Just as, for Heidegger, the relation of Being is inseparable from beings but is not, for all that, indistinguishable from beings, so what it means to be a woman cannot ultimately be thought in abstraction from what it means to be a man, but neither is being a woman reducible to the similarity or differences between the sexes. The occlusion that sexual difference has suffered at the hands of feminist struggles for equality echoes the suppression of the question of Being by metaphysicians. The urgency with which Irigaray infuses her question gains its impetus from the danger that she sees in the question of sexual difference being put to rest by the discourse of feminism itself, before it has even been articulated as such. Feminism, insofar as it encourages the elimination of femininity in favor of masculinity, has a vested interest in making sure that the question of sexual difference is marginalized, in the same way that metaphysics became invested in reducing Being to beings, according to a schema that privileged presence and is ultimately still trapped in a Cartesian view of reality.

The question of what it means to be, or to become, a woman is one that has never been raised on its own terms. It has only ever been posed in terms of how like men women are, or how far they fall short of being men. To that extent, what it means to be a woman was never at issue, only their comparative status to men was in question. By the same token, what it means for a woman to be a subject is an issue that has yet to be decided. Since, as we have been taught by post-structuralism, subjectivity – implicated in illusions about self-mastery – is precariously situated nowadays, women's negotiation of how to be or become a subject is fraught with difficulties. Not only do women have to find access to a subjectivity that is their own, they also have to contend with the fact that it is far from certain that subjectivity – at least in its traditional guises – is an altogether desirable thing. Thus there is a need for a variegated approach to the question of subjectivity. Irigaray thinks that so long as patriarchal relations go unchallenged the possibilities for women's representation of themselves as subjects remain limited to the adoption of the masculine, which "they believe to be a neutral position" (1993b, p. 21). Coupled with her warning against the destruction of subjectivity (Jardine and Menke 1991, p. 103), this view reflects the difficulty of women's situation, in which we must be wary of doing away with subjectivity before we have ever truly attained it (see 1985b, p. 84).

Irigaray's belief in the need for women to work at producing and carving out for themselves their own subjectivities finds its corollary in her views on language. Although Irigaray has always been interested in language – she was trained as a linguist – it is only in the last few years that she has pursued a systematic analysis of language with a view to shedding light on sexual difference. In *Sexes et genres à travers les langues: éléments de communication sexuée*, Irigaray and her collaborators present the results of their research. In *Thinking the Difference* (1994), Irigaray summarizes some of this research and its conclusions (see also Irigaray 1993b). Through a comparison of the French, Italian, and English languages, based upon language tests that were administered to students, Irigaray argues that women rarely refer to women – either themselves or other women – as the subject of speech, while men often "designate themselves or other men as subjects of a sentence" (1994, p. 46).

Irigaray's theoretical approach cannot be reduced to one discipline, just as the figures who have influenced her are multiple. This multiplicity is a deliberate strategy on her part. Irigaray enumerates several different approaches in her work (1985b, pp. 74–8).

The best-known of Irigaray's strategies is that of "mimicry,"in which "One must assume the feminine role deliberately." Which means "already to convert a form of subordination into an affirmation, and thus to begin to thwart it" (1985b, p. 76). Thus, in a discussion of Plato's cave allegory, for example, Irigaray points out that the "cave itself is speculum, den of reflection" (1985a, p. 285), and asks "Is this to say that the entry into philosophy would not require man to inquire about his own doubling, in appearances?" (1985a, p. 288). By reproducing Plato's discourse, Irigaray at the same time undermines his conclusions by drawing attention to the mirroring, the doubling, that must take place in order for Plato to resolve the many into the one, the illusions into the Idea. By revisiting, replaying, repeating incessantly the structure of Platonic dialogue, Irigaray exposes the gaps and fissures in the economy of Plato's allegorical tale about coming to know what is. *The Republic* as a whole, of course, is merely a phantom, a city in words, an ideal phantasy, and its status is not lost on Irigaray, who borrows Plato's strategy even as she demonstrates its limitations and exclusions. Mimicking Plato's methods, Irigaray at the same time subverts his ends.

Irigaray sees a need "to interrogate *the conditions under which systematicity itself is possible*" (Irigaray 1985b, p. 74). This involves pointing out how "each philosopher, beginning with those whose names define some age in the history of philosophy" is implicated in "the break with material contiguity . . . how the system is put together, how the specular economy works" (Irigaray 1985b, p. 75). Thus, in *An Ethics of Sexual Difference*, for example, Irigaray presents a reading of Aristotle's discussion of place, asking why it is that women, who have always provided places for others, in the role of mother – as incubator, receptacle, container, and in the role of sexual partner – as receiver, retainer, vessel, do not have a place of their own. Is there, Irigaray wants to know, a place of place, in the case of woman? "As for woman, she is place. . . . If she is to be able to contain, to envelop, she must have her own envelope" (Irigaray 1993a, p. 35). If woman is to be thought, then her place must be thought, and the places that others can provide her must be thought.

594

Insofar as woman has provided the matter for which men have provided the form, the basic relations between form and matter, substance and subject, transcendence and immanence need to be refigured (Irigaray 1985b, p. 74). As Irigaray says "Mother-matter-nature must go on forever nourishing speculation" (1985a, p. 77).

Hegel is another philosopher who could be said to be exemplary of his era, and whose understanding of ethical life Irigaray subjects to critical interpretation. Focusing upon Hegel's reading of Sophocles' tragedy *Antigone*, Irigaray makes Hegel "render up" and "give back" what he owes the feminine (Irigaray 1985b, p. 74). For "Antigone, the antiwoman, is still a production of a culture that has been written by men alone" (Irigaray 1993, pp. 118–19). Antigone is of particular interest to Irigaray, who often draws upon the figure of Antigone, both in her teaching (see 1985b, p. 167) and in her writing, "Because she is neither master nor slave": she "upsets the order of the dialectic" (Irigaray 1993, p. 119). As such, Antigone becomes a figure of a non-Hegelian mediation, a mediation that does not synthesize, but respects alterity (see Irigaray 1993, pp. 20–1). Antigone also enacts for Irigaray one of the laws – that of maternal identification – that has typically been subordinated by tradition to those laws of the public sphere that take precedence. Engaged in a struggle over the interpretation of law, Creon represents the order of the *polis*, while Antigone stands for the ties of blood kinship that bind her to Polynices irrespective of his murder of Eteocles, which is at the same time an act of treachery against Thebes. Irigaray says of Antigone, "Whatever her current arguments with the laws of the city may have been, another law is still drawing her along her path: identification with her mother" (Irigaray 1985a, p. 219). By returning to ancient tragedy and mythology (Baruch and Serrano 1988, p. 159), to a time in which maternal ancestry was still respected (1994, p. 70), Irigaray hopes to revive the values Antigone stood for at a time when we are taught to "consume the body of the mother (natural and spiritual) without recognition of the debt" (Jardine and Menke 1991, p. 100), in particular the relationship between women and their mothers, which she sees as "completely devalued" (1977, p. 75). Irigaray says,

> If we are not to relive Antigone's fate, the world of women must successfully create an ethical order and establish the conditions necessary for women's action. This world of female ethics would continue to have two vertical and horizontal dimensions:
> - daughter-to-mother, mother-to-daughter;
> - among women, or among "sisters."  (1993a, p. 108; see also 1985b, p. 124)

A third strategy Irigaray evinces is one that attends "to the way the unconscious works in each philosophy . . . what it does not articulate at the level of utterance: *its silences*" (1985b, p. 75). Irigaray deliberately insists upon uncovering and reworking "those *blanks* in discourse which recall the places of [woman's] exclusion" (1985a, p. 142), in retrieving woman from a tradition in which she "finds herself dispersed in the shards of a broken mirror" (1993a, p. 194). Antigone's immediate and intuitive grasp of her ethical duty to her brother is eclipsed, in Hegel, by the reflected and mediated consciousness that must be developed, where individual familial duty gives way to universal political duty. Irigaray seeks to breathe new life into Antigone's transgression of Creon's edict, in order to ensure that in the future women do not suffer the same fate as Antigone, who is walled up in an underground cave at Creon's behest.

The work of re-interpreting the traditional place of woman has "implications that, no matter how mediate they may be, are nonetheless politically determined" (1985b, p. 81). Practically, in addition to endorsing the civil rights of women, this entails making women "take responsibility for themselves socially" (Irigaray 1994, p. 81). Irigaray thinks that "it is up to [women] to become subjects" but "to do this women need rights" (1994, p. 81). Women must "demand the rights that are appropriate to them" (1994, p. 72). Irigaray regards as uncivil "men who rape, prostitute, or possess women without their responsible consent" and "men who abuse the image of women's bodies for pornography and advertising" (1994, p. 74), and suggests that "it would be a civil offence to depict women's bodies as stakes in pornography or prostitution" (1994, p. 75). In Irigaray's view, it is not only men who lack civility, women also lack civility largely because "they do not demand rights that are appropriate to them" (1994, p. 72). Among the rights that women should have she includes "a preferential right with regard to the children that they have borne" (1994, p. 76), and "the right to virginity [which] should be part of girls' civil identity as a right to respect for their physical and moral integrity" (1994, p. 74). Civil society should assist women in their "legal recourse against seduction or rape of children, against the assault and battery inflicted on them within the secrecy of the family, against the overwork that may be demanded of them" (1994, p. 76).

Women must "become fully conversant with the subjectivity–objectivity relationship – a learning experience that women are particularly lacking as a result of their cultural past of identification with the object of desire. Women can acquire this knowledge" (1994, p. 26). The issue, says Irigaray, "is not one of elaborating a new theory of which woman would be the *subject* or the *object*, but of jamming the theoretical machinery itself, of suspending its pretension to the production of a truth and of a meaning that are excessively univocal" (1985b, p. 78). Irigaray describes this process of "jamming the theoretical machinery itself," this "*crossing back through the mirror that subtends all speculation*" (1985b, p. 77) in terms that recall Merleau-Ponty's "chiasm." It is "a playful crossing," which is neither "simply situated in a process of reflection or mimesis, nor on one side of this process or the other: neither on the near side, the empirical realm that is opaque to all language, nor on the far side, the self-sufficient infinite of the God of men" (1985b, p. 77). The structure of these sentences, "neither this . . . nor that" is not incidental to that which Iriaray's language tries to capture. At crucial moments in her text she will often posit contradictory concepts that conflate traditional philosophical distinctions – for example, her use of the term "sensible transcendental," which "confounds the opposition between immanence and transcendence" (1993, p. 33). Like Merleau-Ponty, she is interested in experiences that "offer us all at once, pell-mell, both 'subject' and 'object', both existence and essence" (Irigaray 1993, p. 151 [quoting Merleau-Ponty 1968, p. 130]).

One of the most famous images in which Irigaray puts into play the chiasmic intertwining that she borrows from Merleau-Ponty is that of the lips (1993, p. 161; 1985b, pp. 205–18), which are "continually interchanging. They are neither identifiable nor separable one from the other . . . *these 'two lips' are always joined in an embrace*" (Irigaray 1977, p. 65). Jane Gallop has suggested that Irigaray is proposing, with the figure of the labial lips, an alternative to Lacan's phallus (1982). Irigaray says "I'm trying to say that the female sex would be, above all, made up of '*two lips.*' Insofar as this is a response to the masculine definition of the female sex as lack, castration, or as "no sex" it is an attempt to symbolize what cannot be symbolized within the male logic of the gaze (1985b, p. 90). As such it is one of a series of gestures that Irigaray makes to "open the possibility of a different language" (1985b, p. 80), but to do so "by going back through the dominant discourse" (1985b, p. 119). Although Irigaray recognizes the need to "speak outside" the Western canons of logic and the traditional psychoanalytic dependence upon an Oedipal structure (1977, p. 70), she still finds Freud "useful" (1977, p. 63), and the "analytical framework . . . effective" (1977, p. 70), just as she insists upon the need to "go back through the masculine imaginary . . . and at the same time, to (re)discover a possible space for the feminine imaginary" (1985b, p. 164).

## Writings

Irigaray, L.: *Speculum de l'autre femme* (Paris, Minuit, 1974); tr. Gillian C. Gill, *Speculum of the Other Woman* (Ithaca, NY: Cornell University Press, 1985a).

——: *Ce sexe qui n'en est pas un* (Paris: Minuit, 1977); tr. Catherine Porter with Carolyn Burke, *This Sex Which Is Not One* (Ithaca, NY: Cornell University Press, 1985b).

——: "Women's exile," Interview by D. Adlam and C. Venn, trans. C. Venn, *Ideology and Consciousness*, 1 (1977), pp. 62–76.

——: *Et l'une ne bouge pas sans l'autre* (Paris: Minuit, 1979).

——: *Amante marine de Friedrich Nietzsche* (Paris: Minuit, 1980); trans. Gillian C. Gill, *Marine Lover of Friedrich Nietzsche* (New York: Columbia University Press, 1991).

——: *L'Oubli de l'air* (Paris: Minuit, 1983).

——: *Ethique de la différence sexuelle* (Paris: Minuit, 1984); tr. Carolyn Burke and Gillian C. Gill *An Ethics of Sexual Difference* (Ithaca, NY: Cornell University Press, 1993a).

——: *Parler n'est jamais neutre* (Paris: Minuit, 1985).

——: *Sexes et Parentés* (Paris: Minuit, 1987); trans. Gillian C. Gill, *Sexes and Genealogies* (New York: Columbia University Press, 1993c).

——: *Je, tu, nous: pour une culture de la différence* (Paris: Grasset, 1990); tr. Alison Martin, *Je tu, nous: Toward a Culture of Difference* (New York: Routledge, 1993b).

——: *Sexes et genres à travers les langues: éléments de communication sexuée* (Paris: Grasset, 1990).

——: *J'aime à toi: esquisse d'une félicité dans l'histoire* (Paris: Grasset, 1992).

——: *Le temps de la différence: Pour une révolution pacifique*; tr. Karin Montin, *Thinking the Difference: For a Peaceful Revolution* (New York: Routledge, 1994).

## References and further reading

Baruch, E. H. and Lucienne J. Serrano (eds): *Women Analyze Women* (New York: New York University Press, 1988), pp. 149–64. (Originally published in *Women Writers Talking*, ed.

Janet Todd (New York: Holmes and Meier, 1983), pp. 231–45.)

Butler, J.: *Bodies that Matter: On the Discursive Limits of "Sex"* (New York: Routledge, 1993).

Derrida, J.: *Marges de la philosophie* (Paris: Minuit, 1972); tr. Alan Bass, *Margins of Philosophy* (Chicago, IL: University of Chicago Press, 1982).

Gallop, J.: *The Daughter's Seduction: Feminism and Psychoanalysis* (Ithaca, NY: Cornell University Press, 1982).

Heidegger, M.: "Zeit und Sein," in *Zur Sache des Denkens* (Tübingen: Max Niemeyer, 1969); tr. Joan Stambaugh, *On Time and Being* (New York: Harper & Row, 1972).

——: *Die Grundprobleme der Phänomenologie* (Frankfurt: Vittorio Klostermann, 1978); tr. A. Hofstadter, *Basic Problems of Phenomenology* (Bloomington: Indiana University Press, 1982).

Jardine, A. and Menke A. M. (eds): *Shifting Scenes: Interviews on Women, Writing, and Politics in Post-68 France* (New York: Columbia University Press, 1991).

Merleau-Ponty, M.: *The Visible and the Invisible* (Evanston, IL. Northwestern University Press, 1968).

Moi, T.: *Sexual/Textual Politics: Feminist Literary Theory* (London: Methuen, 1985).

Plaza, M.: " 'Phallomorphic power' and the psychology of 'woman,'" tr. Miriam David and Jill Hodges, *Ideology and Consciousness*, 4 (Autumn 1978), pp. 4–36.

Whitford, M.: *The Irigaray Reader* (Oxford: Basil Blackwell, 1991).

——: *Luce Irigaray: Philosophy in the Feminine* (London and New York: Routledge, 1992).

# 55

# Kristeva

KELLY OLIVER

Julia Kristeva was born in 1941 in Bulgaria. She was educated by French nuns, studied literature and worked as a journalist before going to Paris in 1966 to do graduate work with Lucien Goldmann and Roland Barthes. While in Paris she finished her doctorate in French literature, became involved in the influential journal *Tel Quel*, and began psychoanalytic training. In 1979 she finished her training as a psychoanalyst. Currently, Kristeva is a professor of linguistics as the University of Paris VII and a regular visiting professor at Columbia University. In addition to her work as a practicing psychoanalyst and her theoretical writings, Kristeva is a novelist.

Kristeva's work reflects her diverse background. Her writing is an intersection between philosophy, psychoanalysis, linguistics, and cultural and literary theory. She developed the science of what she calls "semanalysis," which is a combination of FREUD's psychoanalysis (see Article 12) and Saussure's and Peirce's semiology. With this new science Kristeva challenges traditional psychoanalytic theory, linguistic theory, and philosophy.

In most of her writing, Kristeva's goal is to bring the speaking body, complete with drives, back into philosophy and linguistics. In one of her most influential books, *Revolution in Poetic Language*, she criticizes both HUSSERLIAN phenomenology (see Article 15) and Saussurean linguistics for formulating theories of the subject and language that cannot account for the processes through which a subject speaks:

> Our philosophies of language, embodiments of the Idea, are nothing more than the thoughts of archivists, archaeologists, and necrophiliacs. Fascinated by the remains of a process which is partly discursive, they substitute this fetish for what actually produced it. . . . These static thoughts, products of a leisurely cogitation removed from historical turmoil, persist in seeking the truth of language by formalizing utterances that hang in midair, and the truth of the subject by listening to the narrative of a sleeping body – a body in repose, withdrawn from its socio-historical imbrication, removed from direct experience. (Kristeva 1974, p. 13)

There are two ways in which Kristeva brings the speaking body back into theories of language. First, she proposes that bodily drives are discharged through language. Second, she maintains that the structure or logic of signification is already operating in the material body. On Kristeva's analysis language is in the body and the body is in language.

Kristeva's most influential contribution to the philosophy of language has been her distinction between the semiotic and the symbolic elements of signification. All signification is made up of these two elements in varying proportions. The semiotic element is the organization of drives in language. It is associated with rhythms and tones that are meaningful parts of language and yet do not represent or signify something. Rhythms and tones do not represent bodily drives; rather bodily drives are discharged through rhythms and tones. The symbolic element of language, on the other hand, is the domain of position and judgment. It is associated with the grammar or structure of language that enables it to signify something. This symbolic element of language should not, however, be confused with Lacan's notion of the Symbolic (see Article 47, LACAN). Lacan's notion of the Symbolic includes the entire realm of signification, while Kristeva's symbolic is one element of that realm.

The dialectical oscillation between the semiotic and the symbolic is what makes signification possible. Without the symbolic, we have only sounds or delirious babble. But without the semiotic, signification would be empty and we would not speak. The semiotic provides the motivation for engaging in signifying processes; we have a bodily need to communicate. The symbolic provides the structure necessary to communicate. Both elements are essential to signification. And it is the tension between them that makes signification dynamic. The semiotic both motivates signification and threatens the symbolic element. The semiotic provides the negativity and the symbolic provides the stasis or stability that keeps signification both dynamic and structured. The semiotic makes change, even structural change, possible.

In addition to proposing that bodily drives make their way into language, Kristeva maintains that the logic of signification is already present in the material of the body. Once again combining psychoanalytic theory and linguistics, Kristeva relies on both Lacan's account of the infant's entrance into language and Saussure's account of the play of signifiers. Lacan points out that the entrance into language requires separation, particularly from the maternal body. Saussure maintains that signifiers signify in relation to one another through their differences. Combining these two theses, it seems that language operates according to principles of separation and difference. Kristeva argues that the principles or structures of separation and difference are operating in the body even before the infant begins to use language.

She calls the bodily structures of separation the "logic of rejection." For Kristeva the body, like signification, operates according to an oscillation between instability and stability, or negativity and stasis. For example, the process of metabolization is a process that oscillates between instability and stability: food is taken into the body and metabolized and expelled from the body. Because the structure of separation is bodily, these bodily operations prepare us for our entrance into language. From the time of birth the infant's body is engaging in processes of separation; anality is the prime example. Birth itself is also an experience of separation: one body violently separated from another.

Part of Kristeva's motivation for emphasizing these bodily separations and privations is to provide an alternative to the Lacanian model of language acquisition.

Lacan's account of signification and self-consciousness begins with the paternal metaphor's substitution of the law of the father for the desire of the mother. On the traditional psychoanalytic model of both Freud and Lacan the child enters the social or language out of fear of castration threats. The child experiences its separation from the maternal body as a tragic loss and consoles itself with words instead. Paternal threats make words the only, if inadequate, alternative to psychosis. Kristeva insists, however, that separation begins prior to the Oedipal situation and that this separation is not only painful but also pleasurable. She insists that the child enters the social and language not just due to paternal threats but also because of paternal love.

At bottom, Kristeva criticizes the traditional account because it cannot adequately explain the child's move to signification. If the only thing that motivates the move to signification is threats and the pain of separation, then why would anyone make this move? Why not remain in the safe haven of the maternal body and refuse the social and signification with its threats? Kristeva suggests that if the accounts of Freud and Lacan were correct, then more people would be psychotic. She maintains that separation must be pleasurable and this explains the move away from the maternal body and into signification. Just as the separations inherent in the material of the body are pleasurable, even if they are also sometimes painful, so too the separations that make signification possible are pleasurable. The logic of signification is already operating in the body and therefore the transition to language is not as dramatic and mysterious as traditional psychoanalytic theory makes it out to be.

Kristeva's concern to bring the body with all of its dynamic processes back into theory explains the types of discourses on which she focuses. Because traditional philosophy has revolved around fixed notions of a unitary and autonomous subject that covers over the dynamic processes that produce such a subject position, Kristeva is concerned with discourses that break down the identity of the subject. She focuses on crises in identification. For Kristeva, three models that challenge the unitary subject are poetry, psychoanalysis, and maternity.

## Poetry

Poetry challenges the unitary subject by pointing to the signifying process and the processes through which the subject is able to take a position as subject. It does so by attending to the semiotic element of language, rhythms, and tones. In poetry both the meaning and position of words and the tones and affects associated with words are important. Poetry points up the tension between the semiotic and the symbolic elements of language. Kristeva claims that poetry performs a "reversed reactivation" of the contradiction between the semiotic and symbolic. The reversed reactivation is *not* a Hegelian negation of the symbolic's negation of the semiotic which yields a new synthesis of the two. Rather, in poetry the contradiction between the semiotic and symbolic is reactivated and not sublimated. It is a reversed reactivation because the semiotic, which appears to be chronologically and logically prior to the symbolic, manifests itself through the symbolic.

Kristeva maintains that any theory of language is also a theory of the subject. If language is a dynamic process then the subject is a dynamic process. Kristeva develops the notion of a subject-in-process/on-trial [*le sujet en procès*]. The Cartesian *cogito* or Husserlian transcendental ego are only moments in this process; they are neither chronologically nor logically primary. Like signification, the subject is always in a constant process of oscillation between instability and stability or negativity and stasis.

## Psychoanalysis

Psychoanalysis challenges the notion of a unitary subject with the belief in the unconscious. For Kristeva, psychoanalysis is the only place where theories of the subject and the dynamic practice of the subject-in-process come together. The psychoanalytic session is an attempt to come to terms with the dynamic nature of the subject while opening on to its fluidity. Kristeva claims that while religious rituals and literature are only cathartic, psychoanalysis is an elaboration of the drive processes and their relation to the signifying process. This elaboration is crucial in treating the cause and not just the symptoms of neurosis. While the semiotic drive force is powerful when discharged in signifying practices, the position of judgment made possible by the symbolic element of signification is necessary not only to direct that discharge but also to redirect it.

In her recent writings, Kristeva uses psychoanalysis as a model for analyzing relations between peoples of different nations and ethnic backgrounds. Just as she brings the speaking body back into language by putting language into the body, she brings the subject into the place of the other by putting the other into the subject. Just as the pattern and logic of language is already found within the body, the pattern and logic of alterity is already found within the subject. In a Hegelian move, Kristeva makes the social relation interior to the psyche. This is why the subject is never stable but always in process/on trial. Kristeva suggests that if we can learn to live with the return of the repressed other within our own psyches, then we can learn to live with others.

## Maternity

Maternity is the most literal and dramatic model of a subject-in-process. It is the very embodiment of the subject-in-process that is necessary for the continuation of the species. Unlike poetry or psychoanalysis, maternity, in one way or another, touches all people. Until the umbilical cord is cut, who can decide if there is one subject or two? The model of an autonomous unitary subject breaks down with the maternal body. The maternal body is the limit of traditional notions of identity. Because it breaks down identity, it is what Kristeva calls, in *Powers of Horror*, "abject." The abject is not, as we might ordinarily think, what is grotesque or unclean; rather it is what calls into question borders and threatens identity. The abject is on the borderline. As such it is both fascinating and terrifying.

As Kristeva describes it, the infant must go through a stage of abjection in which it "abjects," or finds abject, its mother's body. In order to be weaned the infant must find its mother's body both fascinating and horrifying. It is this experience of horror at the lack of borders between its body and its mother's that drives the infant away from the maternal body and allows the infant to become social. With her theory of abjection Kristeva challenges Lacan's account of the acquisition of language and onset of self-consciousness through the mirror stage and castration threats.

Kristeva maintains that there are extremely important processes in operation prior to the mirror stage and the paternal castration threats. Unlike Freud and Lacan, who attribute language acquisition and socialization to the paternal function and ignore the function of the mother as anything other than the primary object, Kristeva elaborates and complicates the maternal function. She insists that there is regulation and structure in the maternal body and the child's relationship to that body. Before the paternal law is in place the infant is subject to maternal regulations, what Kristeva calls "the law before the law." While in the womb the fetus is engaged in processes of exchange with the maternal body that are regulated by that body. After birth, there are further exchanges between the maternal body and the infant. The mother monitors and regulates what goes into, and what comes out of, the infant's body. Language acquisition and socialization, in so far as they develop out of regulations and law, have their foundations in the maternal function prior to the Law of the Father of traditional psychoanalysis.

In addition to revolutionizing the position and importance of the maternal function in psychoanalytic theory, Kristeva revolutionizes the paternal function. In *Tales of Love* she suggests that the paternal function does not just include threats and law. The father is not merely the stern father of the law. Rather, she proposes a loving father, what she calls "the imaginary father." The imaginary father provides the loving support that enables the child to abject its mother and enter the social. Kristeva describes the imaginary father as a mother-father conglomerate. In her scenario the imaginary father performs the function of love. It is the child's feeling that it is loved that allows the child to separate from the safe haven of the maternal body. Threats and laws alone do not provide this necessary support. The paternal function must be more complex than Freudian or Lacanian psychoanalytic theory make it out to be.

## Feminism

Although Kristeva has an ambivalent, sometimes hostile, relation to feminism and some aspects of the feminist movement in France, her theories provide some innovative approaches for feminist theory. One of her central contributions to this is her call for a new discourse of maternity. In "Stabat Mater," an essay in *Tales of Love*, she criticizes some of the traditional discourses of maternity in Western culture, specifically the myth of the Virgin Mary, because they do not present the mother as primarily a speaking being.

Without a new discourse of maternity we cannot begin to conceive of ethics. If ethics is the philosophy of our obligations to each other, then in order to do ethics we need to analyze the structure of our relations to each other. And if, as Freudian psychoanalytic theory maintains, our relation with our mothers is the model for all subsequent relations, then we need to analyze our relation with our mothers. In Western culture, however, this relation has been figured as a relation to nature, a relation that threatens the social and any possibility of ethical relations. On this view the relation with the mother is not a social relation and therefore not a model for an ethical relation. In order to conceive of an ethical relation we need to reconceive of a relation with the mother as a social relation with a speaking social being. At this point Kristeva's theory is similar to IRIGARAY's (see Article 54). But whereas Irigaray maintains that we need a new discourse of maternity that allows us to imagine an identification with the maternal body as a social relation rather than an anti-social relation, Kristeva maintains that we need to complicate our notion of maternity in order to separate out the maternal body – which she insists must be abjected – from the mother's other functions as woman or feminine or possibly even as mother.

Kristeva suggests that women's oppression can be at least partially explained as a misplaced abjection. It is necessary to abject the maternal body *qua* the fulfiller of needs. But in Western culture woman, the feminine, and the mother have all been reduced to the reproductive function of the maternal body. The result is that when we abject the maternal body we also abject woman, the feminine, and the mother. We need a new discourse of maternity that can delineate between these various aspects and functions of women. Kristeva has set the stage by highlighting and complicating the maternal function. In her new discourse of maternity, the relation, even identification, with the mother is no longer anti-social; rather it is the primary social relation upon which all subsequent relations are modeled. It is a social relation whose obligations come from the loving embrace of the other within oneself.

To view the mother's relation to the developing infant as a function uncouples the activities performed by the care-taker from the sex of the care-taker. The mother, *qua* care-taker, is neither feminine nor masculine, neither female nor male. In "Stabat Mater" Kristeva claims that the mother is alone of her sex. Although she may believe that the maternal function should be performed by women, she does use the language of functions to separate care-taking functions from other activities performed by women. Woman, the female, the feminine, and the mother cannot be reduced to the maternal function. Women and mothers are primarily speaking social beings.

Ultimately, all of Kristeva's writing challenges traditional ethics that have presupposed an autonomous unitary subject. All of her models suggest an alternative model of ethics based on the split subject of psychoanalysis. Within her account of ethics obligations do not originate in laws of reason or universal principles that transcend the subject. Rather, ethical obligations are inherent in the process through which we become subjects, a process that is the constant negotiation with an other – language as other, the unconscious other within, or the other out of whom we were born.

# Writings

Kristeva, Julia: *Revolution in Poetic Language*, tr. from *La Révolution du langage poétique* (Paris: Seuil, 1974) by Margaret Waller (New York: Columbia University Press, 1984).

——: *Desire in Language*, tr. Thomas Gora, Alice Jardine, and Leon Roudiez, ed. Leon Roudiez (New York: Columbia University Press, 1980).

——: *Powers of Horror*, tr. Leon Roudiez (New York: Columbia University Press, 1982).

——: *Tales of Love*, tr. from *Histoires d'amour* (Paris: Éditions Denoël, 1983) by Leon Roudiez (New York: Columbia University Press, 1987).

——: *Black Sun: Depression and Melancholy*, tr. from *Soleil Noir: Dépression et Mélancolie* (Paris: Gallimard, 1987) by Leon Roudiez (New York: Columbia University Press, 1989).

——: *Strangers to Ourselves*, tr. from *Etrangers à nous-mêmes* (Paris: Fayard, 1989) by Leon Roudiez (New York: Columbia University Press, 1991).

——: *Nations without Nationalisms*, tr. Leon Roudiez (New York: Columbia University Press, 1993).

——: *New Maladies of the Soul*, tr. from *Les Nouvelles maladies de l'ame* (Paris: Fayard, 1993) by Ross Gubermann (New York: Columbia University Press, 1995).

——: *Time and Sense: Proust and the Experience of Literature*, tr. from *Le temps sensible: Proust et l'experience litteraire* (Paris: Gallimard, 1994) by Ross Gubermann (New York: Columbia University Press, 1996).

——: *Julia Kristeva Interviews*, ed. Ross Gubermann (New York: Columbia University Press, 1996).

——: *The Portable Kristeva*, ed. Kelly Oliver (New York: Columbia University Press, 1997).

# References and further reading

## Books

Gallop, Jane: *Feminism and Psychoanalysis: the Daughter's Seduction* (London: Macmillan, 1982).

Grosz, Elizabeth: *Sexual Subversions: Three French Feminists* (Sydney, London, and Boston: Allen & Unwin, 1989).

Lechte, John: *Julia Kristeva* (London and New York: Routledge, 1990).

Moi, Toril: *Sexual/Textual Politics: Feminist Literary Theory* (London and New York: Methuen, 1985).

Oliver, Kelly: *Reading Kristeva: Unraveling the Double-bind* (Bloomington IN: Indiana University Press, 1993).

## Anthologies

*The Thinking Muse. Feminism and Modern French Philosophy*, ed. Jeffner Allen and Iris Young (Bloomington: Indiana University Press, 1989).

*Abjection, Melancholia and Love: The Work of Julia Kristeva*, ed. Andrew Benjamin and John Fletcher (London and New York: Routledge, 1990).

*Body/text in Julia Kristeva: Religion, Women and Psychoanalysis*, ed. David Crownfield (Albany, NY: SUNY Press, 1992).

*Ethics, Politics and Difference in Julia Kristeva's Writings*, ed. Kelly Oliver (New York: Routledge, 1993).

## Articles

Butler, Judith: "The body politics of Julia Kristeva," *Hypatia, A Journal of Feminist Philosophy*, vol. 3, no. 3 (Winter 1989).

Jardine, Alice: "Opaque texts and transparent contexts: the political difference of Julia Kristeva," in *The Poetics of Gender*, ed. Nancy K. Miller (New York: Columbia University Press, 1986).

Jones, Ann Rosalind: "Julia Kristeva on femininity: the limits of a semiotic politics," in *Feminist Review*, 18 (Winter 1984).

Nye, Andrea: "Woman clothed with the sun: Julia Kristeva and the escape from/to language," *Signs: Journal of Women in Culture and Society*, vol. 12, no. 4, pp. 664–86 (1987).

Oliver, Kelly: "Kristeva's imaginary father and the crisis in the paternal function," in *Diacritics* (Summer 1991).

Rose, Jacqueline: "Julia Kristeva: take two," in Rose, *Sexuality in the Field of Vision* (London: NLB/Verso, 1986).

Smith, Paul: "Julia Kristeva et al., or, take three of more," in R. Feldstein and J. Roof (eds), *Feminism and Psychoanalysis* (Ithaca: Cornell University Press, 1989).

Ziarek, Ewa: "At the limits of discourse: heterogeneity, alterity, and the maternal body in Kristeva's thought," *Hypatia, A Journal of Feminist Philosophy*, vol. 7, no. 2 (Spring 1992).

# 56

# Le Doeuff

## MOIRA GATENS

Michèle Le Doeuff's research interests include British Renaissance philosophy (especially the works of Francis Bacon and Thomas More) and the writings of Shakespeare. However, she is best known in Anglo-American philosophy for her writings on the philosophical imaginary and feminism. Le Doeuff is a somewhat idiosyncratic figure in contemporary French philosophy. As Colin Gordon has remarked, her work "shows no systematic affiliation, no signs of a formative debt or repudiation" (translator's Preface, Le Doeuff 1989, p. vi). Le Doeuff does, however, mention the work of Simone DE BEAUVOIR (see Article 22), Gaston Bachelard, Michel FOUCAULT (Article 49) and Gilles DELEUZE (Article 51) as contributing to the development of her own philosophical stance. As we shall see, this issue of discipleship is pertinent to her appraisal of the historical situation of women in philosophy. She states "one is commonly asked whether one is a this man-ian or a that man-ian . . . once one becomes a whoeverian, that is the end of philosophy and of the desire for intellectual independence which should also be a characteristic of feminism" (1991, pp. 59–60).

Le Doeuff's first book, *The Philosophical Imaginary*, appears to be a collection of disparate essays on More, Bacon, Galileo, Descartes, KANT (Article 2) and others. However, her analyses of these various philosophical texts are unified by her thesis concerning the indispensability of the image to philosophical thought. She has stated that her work "is about the stock of images you can find in philosophical works, whatever they refer to: insects, clocks, women, or islands" (Mortley 1991, p. 86). Le Doeuff's notion of the imaginary should not be confused with that employed by Jacques LACAN or Luce IRIGARAY (Articles 47 and 54). Le Doeuff employs this notion to refer to a form of thinking in images, a type of pictorial writing, in which philosophy denies that it engages.

Philosophy claims, or aims for, the status of a transparent, self-aware discipline that is self-contained, complete, and free of any unthought or imaginary element. Many philosophers like to think of themselves as concerned only with the bare truth, with that which is abstract or universal – unadorned by images, metaphors, or pictures, which are seen to properly belong to literature. In this respect, philosophy may regard itself as above other forms of knowledge, literally a meta-discourse, which has the right to stand as arbiter of other disciplines. What then, Le Doeuff asks, are we to make of the fact that a casual perusal of philosophical works will reveal "clocks, horses, donkeys and even a lion, scenes of sea and storm, forests and trees"? (1989, p. 1). Even so austere a philosopher as Immanuel Kant produced a number of texts in which we encounter the image of the island (see 1989, pp. 8–18). The "scandal" of philosophy, according to Le Doeuff, is that it simply cannot exist or function without a repertoire of images. Such images are central to the philosophical enterprise and function to mask those parts of a philosopher's thought that are unable to be articulated in purely conceptual terms. The particular imaginary employed in a given philosophical system also tends to organize the fundamental values of that system. Le Doeuff maintains that not only does philosophy make use of imagery, it has its own peculiar stock of images which circulates between texts.

This specifically philosophical imaginary serves to structure the subjectivity of those who are deemed fit to become philosophers. Thus, philosophy has its own processes of socialization, through which those who are accepted into the rank of philosopher perpetuate, unawares or not, the imaginary of a social minority which is marked by a particular mode of relating to other forms of knowledge as well as by ways of relating to others who are excluded from philosophy. As we will see below, such a socializing practice presents a barrier to women who would be philosophers since they are often excluded by the masculinist nature of much philosophical imagery. This is to say that the specifically philosophical imaginary forms part of the unacknowledged induction into philosophy and so is not incidental to the types of person who become philosophers nor to the types of practice in which they engage.

A concern with the images employed in philosophy is not, then, an "anecdotal" approach to philosophy but rather one which maintains that a study of philosophical imagery has much to tell about the nature of philosophy and philosophers, as well as the values which, wittingly or not, they promote. Her analyses of specific philosophical texts lead Le Doeuff to conclude that when a philosopher resorts to thinking in images, this signals a tension, evasion, or a difficulty in the work. The deployment of an image – a clock, an island – functions to make present something which the philosophy in question needs but cannot conceptually justify. In this sense, the imaginary stands in the place of argument and so represents that which the philosophical system in question fails to, and perhaps is unable to, provide. The philosophical imaginary thus protects the system of thought which deploys it from facing up to its own necessary incompleteness. But how does philosophy justify this literary "thinking in images" since it has explicitly defined itself against such forms of thought? Le Doeuff argues that by a somewhat dishonest maneuver philosophy displaces its own deficiencies and incompleteness on to others, typically the novice or student, for whose benefit the supposedly accessible image is introduced. The image is thus presented as bridging the gap between ignorance (the student's "lack") and knowledge (the philosopher's "completion"). However, such a maneuver has its costs. Imagery is ambiguous and unstable and may work against that which it was introduced to justify. The deployment of images in a philosophical text may signal an intention or a desire to close a system of thought but may nevertheless end by working against itself by opening up the system to other interpretations. (See, for example, Le Doeuff's analysis of the imagery employed by Sartre in his

608

account of the relation between "the knower and the known" as being like "a kind of rape by sight," 1991, pp. 75–88.)

Does this mean that Le Doeuff sees philosophy as a futile and sexist practice that should be abandoned? Certainly she argues against the continuation of a particular conception of philosophy – the conception of philosophy as a closed and complete meta-discourse. However, philosophical activity is not exhausted by this description. One may conceive of philosophy as an open-ended and necessarily unfinished project which is shared between those in the present – and those in the past – who value reasoned and critical debate. Such a conception of philosophy would not need to deny that, like all forms of thought, it employs images and metaphors and necessarily contains some unthought elements. (Compare this interpretation of Le Doeuff's relation to philosophy with that offered by Morris 1981/2; and Grosz 1989.) Of course, this alternative conception of philosophy is not one to which all philosophers are likely to want to subscribe. It is one which does not exclude certain parties a priori – such as women, children, the "person on the street," or "barbarians." Le Doeuff maintains that such exclusions arise from an impossible desire for absolute knowledge which one can fool oneself into believing one possesses provided that there are others who are seen as incapable of philosophical reasoning and knowledge.

Le Doeuff argues that much philosophy, historically and in the present, constructs its own self-conception, at least partly, by treating women as incapable of philosophy. If philosophy is incapable of clearly stating what it is and what distinguishes it from other forms of rational inquiry, it can at least console itself and give itself an identity by excluding some persons from the practice of philosophy. It is not, however, women only whom it excludes but also children, "common" people, "uncivilized" people. It is for this reason that Le Doeuff rejects the suggestion of some feminists that philosophy, and reason or rationality, are irredeemably "male." By Le Doeuff's lights, this claim does not make epistemological or political sense. Just as there is no single imaginary, there is not just one form of reason. We should speak of rationalities, in the plural. It is only a hegemonic conception of philosophy which posits one reason, and this hegemonic philosophy is no less damaging to, and exclusive of, some men than it is of all women. Rather than insist on the "maleness" of philosophy, Le Doeuff prefers to speak of the masculinism of philosophy where masculinism refers not to an essence possessed by all men but to the adoption by some male philosophers of a superior attitude towards women and femininity in the first place and in the second, a disparaging attitude towards all those who are deemed incapable of reason. Far from identifying this attitude with rationality, Le Doeuff argues that it is reasonable to expose this attitude for what it is: particularist, unethical, and irrational (1991, pp. 97, 187). This conception of philosophy is not only untenable, it is also unethical since it fails to extend to others the very privileges which it assumes for itself (for example, the right to independent thought). A philosophical practice which was also an ethical practice would need to begin from at least the presumption of equality and reciprocity between persons. A form of thought that is capable of taking responsibility for its own shortcomings would not need to project its own incapacities on to others.

Unlike some "feminists of difference," Le Doeuff does not see rationality as a value which we can afford to discard. She conceives of reason as a dynamic process by which one tries to make things clearer or more accessible to scrutiny and debate. Although it is something which people have in common, it cannot be understood as a pre-given essence. Rather, reason is what should emerge from, or what is achieved by, critical engagement with others (see Le Doeuff 1990). It is with this alternative, open-ended conception of reason that we can begin to see how Le Doeuff's apparently diverse researches converge. It is in *Hipparchia's Choice, An Essay Concerning Women, Philosophy, etc.*, that one can appreciate the manner in which Le Doeuff's concerns with the imaginary and with women and feminism, are interconnected. In this book she argues that if we conceive of philosophy as a necessarily incomplete and ongoing endeavor which involves a constant reorientation of thought, then the impulse to deny the imaginary elements of such thought would not arise. This alternative conception of philosophy would not require the a priori exclusion of anyone since the motivation to maintain an identity as philosopher through the exclusion of others would be absent.

Le Doeuff's work on "woman" and "the feminine" as they figure in philosophical texts should be seen as part and parcel of her work on the philosophical imaginary. Her thesis concerning the way in which images of clocks and islands function in philosophy is valid also for the manner in which images of women are deployed in philosophy. However, there is an important difference between images of women and images of islands – what one says about imaginary islands has no effect upon existing islands, but what one says about "woman" can and does cause harm to existing women. To say, for example, that Nature is like a woman whom the philosopher – if he is to learn her secrets – must seduce, rather than violate, is to make assumptions concerning: the sex of the subject of knowledge (the philosopher), the sex of the object of knowledge (feminized nature), and normative relations between the sexes, which are damaging to women. Furthermore, such a sexualized imaginary turns women away from knowledge and philosophy since clearly it is not they who are the intended recipients of such wisdom. Here we see one of the ways in which Le Doeuff's thesis concerning the socializing function of the philosophical imaginary covertly acts to exclude women; for how could this sexualized imaginary operate to structure a philosophical subjectivity for one who is a woman? A woman who is a philosopher is more likely to feel a painful contradiction between her vocation as philosopher and her role as the "seduced" party in a masculinist imaginary. This is an important aspect of Le Doeuff's thinking on the question of women and philosophy. She maintains that what "turns women away from philosophical production is intrinsic and structural" to philosophy (1991, p. 141).

Women may be excluded from philosophy by an active prohibition, for example, by denying them access to literacy and educational institutions, but they also may be excluded by more subtle, discursive means. One may want to object and point out that even when women were actively prohibited from studying philosophy, there were exceptions: Hipparchia, Heloise, Elizabeth of Bohemia (one of Descartes's correspondents), and so on. But was the prohibition still operating even in the cases of these exceptional women? Le Doeuff responds in the affirmative since these women did not really have access to philosophy *per se*. Rather, they had access to philosophies adopted or created by particular men (Crates, Abelard, Descartes) for whom they played the part of admiring pupil. However, women do not hold a monopoly on this transferential relation between the teacher and the pupil who fantasizes that the teacher knows "everything." Men, too, can become enamored with the image of the all-knowing master. The difference between the sexes turns on at least two features of the pedagogic relation. First, men may at least aspire to the position of "he who knows all" whereas women typically have neither the gall to aspire to, nor the requisite authority to take up, the place of the master. Second, men may be enamored of a particular teacher/philosopher without thereby foreclosing their access to the work of other philosophers. These features add a further dimension to the transferential relation in the case of women which Le Doeuff names the "Heloise complex." This complex describes the dynamic whereby women tend to remain trapped in the transferential relation and so fail to develop an independent relation to philosophy.

What is perhaps most disturbing to Le Doeuff is that even when explicit prohibitions against women's access to philosophy are lifted, women still tend to accept some man's ready-made version of philosophy rather than themselves developing an independent relation to philosophy. Le Doeuff treats the relationship between Simone de Beauvoir and Jean-Paul SARTRE (see Article 21) as a paradigm case of the problematic relation between women and philosophy. De Beauvoir's famous text, *The Second Sex*, may be seen as an attempt to apply Sartre's existentialist philosophy to an analysis of the situation of women. (Of course, stated baldly, this is a rather simplistic view. For a nuanced reading of the de Beauvoir/Sartre relation, see Le Doeuff 1989, ch. 6; and 1991, notebooks 2 and 3.) The very public, and much publicized progress of the long-term relation between this couple (see Sartre's and de Beauvoir's autobiographies and their published letters) provides Le Doeuff with a wealth of material through which to analyze the transferential relation between Sartre and de Beauvoir. Le Doeuff makes much of the fact that even though de Beauvoir was one of the very few women who excelled in her philosophical studies, she nevertheless accepted Sartre's philosophy rather than seeking to develop her own. Is the contemporary situation of women in philosophy any different? Le Doeuff maintains that implicit prohibitions against women becoming philosophers still operate. However, contemporary women have the benefit of something which de Beauvoir did not – the women's movement. According to Le Doeuff, this movement has the potential to radically change not only women's social, economic, and political status, but also women's historical relation to the practice of philosophy.

Le Doeuff's approach to the tension between being a woman who is a philosopher and the image of women presented in philosophy is to put this tension or unease to work. Feminism is what allows this tension to be potentially productive or creative in the present. The existence of this social movement, which signals a collectively acknowledged disaffection among women with their social positioning, provides a means for thinking through the relation between women and philosophy. Such disaffection with one's circumstances may also be seen to result in a radical social disorientation which, though painful, obliges one to take stock of where one is, where one would like to be, and the most likely means of successfully reaching one's desired destination. This notion of orientation-disorientation ties in with Le Doeuff's understanding of a non-hegemonic practice of philosophy. The dominance of cartographical images in the latter half of *Hipparchia's Choice* is significant. To acknowledge that one feels disoriented in one's surroundings and that one is not alone in this, points to the need to collectively create new maps which will reflect the values and aims of those endeavoring to orient themselves.

Le Doeuff's project, then, is to map out an alternative non-hegemonic conception of philosophy which acknowledges the contours or the "lie of the land" that constitutes our "given" situation – our historical context – without allowing this context to entirely dominate our present and future plans to forge new paths or to set off in one direction rather than another. The point of this mapping image is that we cannot entirely alter our situation but we can acknowledge that past mappings have privileged certain aspects of our terrain and certain sorts of traveler. This amounts to the claim that women who wish to be philosophers cannot assume that existing or "ready-made" philosophies will suit their diverse purposes. Rather, they need to claim the right, and recognize the necessity, to develop an independent relation to philosophical thought.

## Writings

Le Doeuff, M.: "Operative philosophy: Simone de Beauvoir and existentialism," *I & C,* 6 (1979).

——: *Recherches sur l'imaginaire philosophique* (Paris: Payot, 1980); tr. C. Gordon, *The Philosophical Imaginary* (London: Athlone Press, 1989).

——: *L'Etude et le rouet, des femmes, de la philosophie, etc.* (Paris: Le Seuil, 1989); tr. T. Selous, *Hipparchia's Choice: An Essay Concerning Women, Philosophy, etc.* (Oxford: Blackwell, 1991).

——: "Women, reason, etc.," *differences,* vol. 2, no. 3 (1990).

## References and further reading

Grosz, E.: *Sexual Subversions: Three French Feminists* (Sydney: Allen and Unwin, 1989), ch. 6.

Morris, M.: "Operative reasoning: Michèle Le Doeuff, philosophy and feminism," *I & C,* 9 (1981/2).

Mortley, R.: *French Philosophers in Conversation* (London: Routledge, 1991), ch. 5.

# Afterword

WILLIAM R. SCHROEDER*

At least two types of readers are holding this book: specialists seeking to supplement their knowledge and initiates hoping to gain passage into this forbidding field. In the following remarks I hope to situate and integrate these essays for both types of readers. At least initially, specialists will study essays on their favorite figures to assess the quality of the author's interpretation, hoping to gain new insight and perspective; then they will explore essays on unfamiliar figures in order to broaden their understanding of the tradition. They might benefit from a map of still unresolved issues (i.e., decision-points) in order to focus their own thinking for the future. This *Companion* can serve both a Hegelian and a Nietzschean function for them. The Hegelian hope is that by reviewing and re-assessing these figures new conclusions about the tradition as a whole will emerge – steps towards a broader framework that can inform current research. The Nietzschean hope is that by reviewing one's past heroes and additional candidates for appreciation (as Nietzsche suggests in *Schopenhauer as Educator*) one can refashion one's own philosophical identity – broadening it perhaps, challenging it certainly.

Initiates will turn first to the figures who provoke their curiosity. They may benefit from an effort to integrate the contributions of these disparate thinkers, a summary that facilitates further understanding of the strengths and weaknesses of this tradition. I intend to sketch such a summary, without being reductive or simplistic. One strategy for achieving such an overview is to tell a story in which there are winners and losers – conquests and defeats – and which celebrates a present that resolves the problems of the past. I will not follow this strategy here because this picture of progressive development is not the most accurate or useful way to understand the relationships between these figures, at least not for the purposes of responding to this book. I defend a different strategy in section I below.

*I wish to thank the following people for reading an early draft of this essay and offering useful suggestions: Frithjof Bergmann, John Coker, Simon Critchley, Rod Ganiard, Kevin Hill, Richard Schacht, and the members of my spring 1997 seminar (especially Julia Simon and Craig Mataresse). I also wish to thank Simon Critchley for letting me read his Introduction to this volume before I began work on this Afterword. I am especially indebted to his remarks on the importance of the history of Continental philosophy to its practice and on its utopian vision. Beyond this, the extent of our basic agreement gave me the courage to attempt this rather sweeping synopsis.

In section II, I indicate some of the strengths of the tradition as a whole, promising features that are common to a wide range of thinkers represented here. In section III, some weaknesses in the tradition are sketched – recurrent maneuvers that seem inept or problems that have been avoided. In section IV, I try to construct a map of the important questions over which there is unresolved disagreement. I call these issues "decision-points;" the future direction of Continental philosophy will be guided by the resolution of these questions. My goal in that section is to sketch a network of decision-points, not to offer definitive resolution of the questions, although the map may facilitate such resolution. Finally, I indicate one way in which the book may enhance philosophical development; here I elaborate the Nietzschean hope described above. Sections II and III are mainly for initiates, though specialists may find my hypotheses useful. Section IV is mainly for specialists, though initiates may begin to organize their own responses to the tradition by exploring the decision-points sketched there. Section V exemplifies a project from which everyone can benefit.

I cover many issues and thinkers in this essay. In order to create a larger picture and framework, I risk neglecting subtleties and detail. Although I have tried to produce an innovative overview, other interpretations of this tradition are certainly possible.

## I The relationships among these philosophers

When Continental philosophers review the history of their discipline, they nearly always focus on past errors in order to define the path towards the Real Truth, which they are about to deliver. Hegel, Heidegger, and Habermas all followed this pattern. Sometimes they acknowledge the virtues of past positions, but often they simply dismiss them. The goal of this essay is different. Rather than assume that past positions are dead (and superseded), I propose to regard them as full of life and to search for the contributions each can make to current questions. Although these philosophers may have attacked each other, rarely has one achieved total victory. Sometimes definitive points have been scored on particular issues; most often, however, the subject is simply changed, and new projects are pursued. The older projects remain important and may even contain crucial insights for current questions, but these contributions are often missed because a narrative of historical progress is assumed.

Was Hegel refuted by Marx? No; indeed, one can argue that Hegel had a deeper comprehension of bourgeois culture and ideology than Marx, and certainly he did not ignore what Marx called "material [economic and social class] forces." Did Nietzsche disprove Kant or Hegel? His point of departure was Schopenhauer, and Schopenhauer took himself to be an inheritor of Kant, but this does not mean Nietzsche overcame Kant in answering Schopenhauer. For the most part, Nietzsche asks different questions, initiates new tasks. Brentano and the phenomenologists seem to ignore Nietzsche rather than appropriate or refute him. Twentieth-century hermeneutic thinkers developed Hegelian and Nietzschean themes, but they did not supersede either thinker. On the issues of dispute between them, the earlier figures may have the upper hand. Did the structuralists and post-structuralists refute phenomenology? They completed many criticisms of the tradition that phenomenology had already begun (e.g., challenges to both transcendental and empirical egos), but phenomenology remains a coherent and fruitful discipline despite their critique. In many of these cases new philosophical programs were adopted and new questions pursued; attention was refocused rather than predecessors refuted. Often these movements pass by each other in the night. Because it surveys the whole tradition, giving all philosophers their due, this book invites a re-examination of the relationships among the many programs of Continental philosophy.

This is perhaps the deepest impression made by the book: the sheer diversity of philosophical programs, even within the same intellectual movement. Our task – those who now wish to take stock and assess these programs – is to understand the relationships between them. This requires understanding that these programs have different goals and assumptions and work within different sets of rules, and so their results are often skewed in relation to one another. When one compares Hegel, Husserl, Heidegger, Sartre, Levinas, and Irigaray on the relationship between oneself and other people (or *any* of the figures in this tradition on *any* specific topic), they often conceive the question in entirely different ways. So their results as often complement as conflict with one another. Comprehending how the answers modify, challenge, and supplement each other is a major philosophical task in its own right. However, coherent progress on such issues cannot be made until these complex relations among the various programs are clarified. This task must be completed for each major issue because the relationships between the figures may differ significantly depending on which issue is considered.

The aim of the authors in this book was to present the achievements of their philosophers as lucidly and succinctly as possible, without grinding axes, without invidious over-simplification, and without vagueness or hyperbole. Their efforts can engender renewed appreciation of these positions. Figures long dismissed may emerge with unexpected strengths, while recent trendy figures may exhibit unacknowledged weaknesses. The book as a whole captures the vitality of the tradition, and it invites an effort to illuminate the complex relationships among the philosophers. The *Companion* makes the task of producing such comprehension easier. There is good reason to attempt this task. Too often Continental philosophy does not produce promising collaborations across movements. Instead, emerging philosophers identify themselves with one figure or movement, neglecting the contributions of the others. Achieving such overall comprehension will bring the full resources of the tradition to bear on specific questions.

Thus, for various reasons I think that a unilinear model of historical progress in Continental philosophy is misleading and fruitless. But I also believe the diverse programs in the tradition more often supplement than conflict with one another. Results on specific issues can be dovetailed without falling into dull eclecticism. Here I would suggest a Nietzschean perspectival vision of the relationship between these programs. Nietzsche believed that philosophy is inevitably interpretive, but he insisted that the different perspectives can broaden and enrich one's vision by

615

rectifying the oversimplifications produced by any one (*Genealogy of Morals*, Book III, Section 12). The perspectives function like different kinds of maps of the same territory; all can be informative in their own way; all are needed to produce a complete picture. This is how I think these figures can be best related to each other. Treat the program of each figure like a Nietzschean perspective; examine the ways in which results both supplement *and* challenge one another. Where they supplement, seek to integrate the results rather than simply conjoin them. Where they conflict, make both positions stronger through the competition. Merleau-Ponty adopted a similar vision of the relationships among styles of living or art. Their results may not always reinforce each other, but their differences may stimulate each side to push its own program further, to reach new heights or explore new territory – to become more what they are – and thus such differences can enhance the achievements of each. I find this way of relating these philosophers both a more compelling and a more useful way to respond to this book.

## II   The strengths of Continental philosophy

The strengths of the tradition can be organized into four categories: (1) major shifts introduced by Hegel (in particular, his break with Kantian tradition); (2) a focus on philosophical anthropology rather than philosophy of mind; (3) a distinctive reaction to modernist and bourgeois culture, Enlightenment ideals, and the collapse of the belief in God; and (4) a distinctive way of taking the linguistic turn. Each category includes several components, and I shall explore these categories in turn. My claim is not that these features are shared by every member of the tradition, but rather that they capture its predominant emphasis – even if there are occasional dissonant voices. Moreover, these are not simply common features, they are common strengths; they make Continental philosophy a vital field of inquiry.

To start with the first category: Hegel was to transform Continental philosophy in both substantive and methodological fashions. Some of his substantive contributions were to underline the importance of social existence in human life and thus to initiate the beginnings of social science. In addition, he established the importance of history in understanding both human and philosophical development. Essentially, he made sociality and history impossible for philosophy to ignore. His methodological contributions include a distinctive systematic approach, an integrative vision, and a willingness to challenge the value of the institutions of his day.

Until Hegel, the dominant project in modern social philosophy was social contract theory, rooted in speculations on the origins of society based on assumptions about a presocial state of nature. Against this position Hegel showed that sociality is fundamental to the human condition and that the fundamental drive in social life is not self-preservation but the struggle for recognition. Mutual recognition literally constitutes social identity and many other features of the person. For example, mutual recognition plays an important role in the constitution of reason and of one's capacity for moral action. Before Hegel the manner in which persons constitute each other's identities was ignored. In addition, universal recognition functions as a central ideal in Hegel and in the tradition thereafter

616

in Marx, Buber, Lukács, Sartre, early Foucault, and de Beauvoir. Even Nietzsche, who is often interpreted as privileging isolated, heroic individuals, acknowledged the importance of friendship, competition, and culture in the development of higher humanity. For Hegel, mutual recognition raises each person to a higher level of existence and creates a unifying spirit between what would otherwise have been isolated individuals. Although he thinks that the road to mutual recognition requires struggle and domination, he shows how domination can be overcome. Thus, he puts social existence on the agenda of Continental philosophy, and he envisions a compelling ideal that accepts the place of struggle without surrendering to it.

In addition to clarifying the importance of social life, Hegel also forged some key concepts for illuminating it. In effect, Hegel (and Marx) originated "scientific" inquiry into social phenomena; perhaps this is why their Continental heirs are not reluctant to interrogate the foundations of social science and to make real contributions to social theory. This combination of critical and creative contributions to the human sciences characterizes hermeneutics, Freud, phenomenology, philosophical anthropology, Foucault, and Deleuze. They contribute not just to history and psychoanalysis, but also to sociology, economics, and anthropology. In Continental philosophy the line between philosophy and social theory (even critical examinations of empirical research) is thin, and Continental thinkers regularly challenge the goals, methods, assumptions, research programs, and conclusions of social scientists. This provides an important critical perspective for social theory, and it also forces Continental thinkers to remain cognizant of current empirical research. They have realized that useful theoretical and empirical work are inextricably linked. This disappearance of the borders between philosophical thinking and scientific research has also become more prominent even in analytic philosophy with respect to physics and cognitive psychology.

In addition, Hegel showed that recapitulating and internalizing one's historical development is essential to achieving maturity and wisdom. One's identity is essentially related to one's own development, and the identity of one's era is essentially related to the historical process that produced it. After Hegel nearly every tradition in Continental philosophy insists on the formative role of history. Marx and Marxism simply reinterpreted Hegel's developmental picture, rooting it in economic and technological factors. Nietzsche uses genealogy (critical history) to indict those elements of the present he sought to overcome and monumental history to show that real alternatives were possible. History plays a major role in all the twentieth-century movements until its centrality is challenged in Structuralism. But even Foucault reinterprets the genealogical approach to challenge the present, and he suggests that understanding historical breaks is necessary to accurately grasp the configuration of the present. Thus, the tradition largely accepts Hegel's claim that grasping the historical process which produced one's present is essential to understanding the determining issues of one's era and oneself. History provides an essential context for making any lasting philosophical progress.

One of Hegel's most distinctive achievements is an integrated system, which answers a variety of questions with a unified vision. Many have criticized him for

617

creating a rigid, overly diagrammatic system, but I would claim that his notion of the concrete universal forced him to consider each issue on its own terms, to find a solution that would address the specificity and complexity of each problem while also fitting with the general direction of his other answers. Thus, I would suggest that Hegel is among the first to produce a philosophical system that is not mechanical or artificial, but rather is supple and capable of handling complexity. Others in the Continental tradition have been animated by this Hegelian drive towards system, and they have retained his refusal to allow the system to dominate the component theses and his efforts to create distinctive solutions in recalcitrant areas that suggest expansions of the system. Marxists, for example, develop a variety of tools for examining distinct historical eras and levels of culture. Phenomenology allows for different types of intentionality when examining the distinctive character of diverse mental activities. It thus can acknowledge the differences among perception, emotion, volition, and cognition without sacrificing a unifying thesis. Hermeneutics can be supple in the way it conceives its various objects of study – texts, persons, artworks, historical eras, social actions, and philosophy – while retaining a consistent view of the nature of interpretation itself. Even those famous in the Continental tradition for being anti-systematic (Kierkegaard, Nietzsche, Derrida, Lyotard) offer a vision that integrates many diverse sectors of reality, providing metaphors that at least partially answer this demand for system without sacrificing concreteness. The Continental tradition seeks a supple, fluid systematicity that integrates diversity without ignoring complexity. It escapes the woodenness and oversimplification that plagues much systematic thinking.

Hegel also found ways to acknowledge the relative truth of each "moment" he studied without allowing these limited truths to remain immune to the claims of other "moments." He tried to retain the positive achievements of each of the stages or concepts or capacities or types he synthesized into his larger vision. In this way, he refuses to allow limited perspectives to become absolute. Nietzsche alters Hegel's vision of how a complete overview is reached, but even Nietzsche thinks both that diverse interpretive perspectives can supplement and enhance one another and that no one perspective contains the complete truth. Only a variety of perspectives will allow one to gain the fullest vision of the phenomenon. Nietzsche sees the relation between each perspective (e.g., physiology, history, morality, psychology, art) on the model of a distinctive type of map of the same territory. Each map simplifies the total picture, but this allows it to achieve real illumination. The philosopher has to understand how all the maps of the same territory can be related, and this synoptic vision may differ in its constitution depending on the question asked. Again, each perspective is given its due, but the truth is achieved only by making a just adjudication of perspectives. This vision of how different perspectives can work together to produce a larger truth also operates in hermeneutics, phenomenology, and later versions of Marxism. No perspective can be isolated from the others; none is sufficient in itself. This vision of Reason (and its path to the fullest truth humans can reach) is challenged in Foucault and Derrida, but already Lyotard and Deleuze are operating with more synthetic strategies that attempt to grasp the complex relation of different linguistic strategies (Lyotard) or disciplines (Deleuze) to each other. The value of this approach is that it allows diverse approaches to have their say while insisting that they make a contribution to a larger vision. This vision of Reason avoids the pitfalls of radical relativism and absolutism.

Both Marx and Nietzsche challenge the value of bourgeois culture and both offer an alternative vision of what humanity can become. Yet both also demand more than utopian imagination; both try to show how their cultures could be changed and how individuals might transform themselves to achieve these ideal visions. In retrospect, one can perceive this same critical, tough-minded utopianism in Hegel, a vision of an alternative future (e.g., reciprocal recognition, a distinctive type of bureaucracy, a newly organized state) that indicates possible paths to larger changes. Existentialism and even Freud adopt this critical stance to the bourgeois order, though Freud's alternative is more restrained and limited than Sartre's. Certainly Continental feminism adopts the same critical stance, and Foucault creates immense critical distance from the present even though his utopian vision is limited. This impulse to define and revalue modern culture and bourgeois life operates throughout most postmodernists, even though their sense of alternatives is limited. Continental philosophy since Hegel has typically adopted a critical stance to the dominant order; it sought to define alternatives that are not just fanciful dreams. It has helped articulate many discontents of modern life and insisted on re-imagining human possibilities.

If this first category of strengths derives from Hegel's distinctive break with Kant, then the second category derives from the more complete view of human existence achieved by life-philosophy (Nietzsche, Dilthey, and Bergson), existential phenomenology, and philosophical anthropology (Gehlen and Plessner). Continental philosophy has sought to clarify human existence generally, rather than just the mind or intellect. This broader vision of human life includes seven key factors: the centrality of practice, the body, unconscious factors in the psyche, emotions, time-consciousness, freedom, and doubts about the self. Taken together, these factors situate human existence in nature and elaborate its unique features. They refuse to reduce persons to brains or to cognitive systems. Even when Husserl returned to Descartes in developing phenomenology, very quickly his purely cognitive vision of the mind was replaced by a more embodied, situated, practical understanding of the whole person (in Scheler, Heidegger, Sartre, and Merleau-Ponty). This more complex vision of human life not only is truer, it also comprehends more accurately the actual workings of cognition. Moreover, it faces hard questions about the interaction among these central factors.

Practical life (praxis, instrumental action) is given central emphasis in most Continental traditions (e.g., Fichte, Marxism, hermeneutics, existentialism, and feminism). In others, it is treated as having at least equal importance to theoretical reason (Hegel, Nietzsche, Foucault, and postmodernism). This focus on human action may be the common feature that unites all major types of Western philosophy in the twentieth century (American pragmatism, Wittgenstein, Austin). Continental philosophers focus on it first, however, and examine it most thoroughly. Through action, persons transcend their situations and pasts, realize goals and values, unify their desires and mesh with the instrumental environment. Practical life is also the sphere of self-realization and self-transformation. Theory and analytical reason are not dismissed or forgotten, but they are often treated as modifications or distinct types of practice, to which the general analysis of action applies.

An essential part of human action is using the body, and Continental philosophy typically analyzes the body as a system of habits, desires, or volitions. The body is important in Marx and Nietzsche, but it also plays a central role in Merleau-Ponty, Foucault, and Bordieu. As the notion of a transcendental ego (a center of selfhood existing beyond the reach of worldly forces and influences) is rejected, the body takes on many of the functions of the empirical ego. It is the source of both inertia and initiative. In the Continental tradition a passive mechanistic conception of the body is rejected in favor of a dynamic self-regulating model. The body is also shown to have its own kind of knowledge rooted in habit and practical relations with the world. It is also the site of unconscious forces, especially in Nietzsche and Freud. In Foucault this complex of bodily habits is the target of power–knowledge strategies; and Continental feminism elaborates a distinctive experience of the body among women, especially in sexual awareness and desire. In Nietzsche and Bergson the body is seen as a dynamic expression of an element that lies between matter and mind: life. By elucidating a truer vision of the body and its importance in human life, Continental philosophy transcends the Cartesian view that sees persons as pure minds and minds as cognitive instruments.

Although many movements in Continental philosophy are often dismissively summarized as "the philosophy of consciousness" by Habermas (and others), in fact it has uncovered a variety of unconscious factors operating in human action and cognition. The most famous thinkers in this category are Freud, who put the unconscious dynamics of desire on the map for Western thought, and Nietzsche, who insisted on the importance of unconscious drives in determining action and thought. Like Freud, Nietzsche felt the whole system of drives and their relationships remained largely unconscious to the agent, and both rejected Cartesian models of self-understanding through privileged access as a result. In addition, Heidegger (and much of the hermeneutic tradition) insisted on the importance of background schemes (cognitive and practical) in responding to the environment. Similarly, structuralism and later movements forcefully emphasize the constitutive role of binary oppositions, cognitive frameworks, and rules of grammar, all of which operate beneath the level of explicit consciousness. Even Sartre allows that much about human existence remains opaque because too often most people live in self-deception. If one moves beyond the level of individual action to social life and history, then most of the tradition ratifies a notion of the "cunning" of history – an implicit directedness that operates without being transparent to historical agents. Uncovering these factors allows Continental philosophers to challenge the ideal of rational autonomy and to grasp the worldly contingencies that affect thought and action.

There is also a long tradition in Continental philosophy that elucidates the nature, role, and importance of emotions in human experience. This reflection extends both to the nature of emotions generally and to the analysis of the role of particular emotions in human life. This emphasis begins with Hegel's examination of desire (and many other kinds of practical relationships with the world), through Marx's stress on the role of basic needs, to Nietzsche's examination of the centrality of resentment, pity, and the Dionysian and Apollonian drives in life itself, to Freud's examination of the dynamics of repression, to Brentano and Scheler's focus on the centrality of emotions as means to apprehend values, to Heidegger's emphasis on moods and the significance of anxiety, to Sartre's attempt to construct a general theory of emotions, to the efforts of Continental feminists and Deleuze to rethink Freud's analysis of desire and will, and, finally, to Baudrillard's reflections on the distinctive emotions defining the postmodern temperament. The whole tradition has explored the status of emotions in human life and isolated various examples for extended treatment. It has shown that human existence cannot be adequately understood without comprehending emotions.

Another feature of the broader approach to human existence characteristic of Continental philosophy is an elucidation of human temporality. Phenomenology offers a subtle analysis of time consciousness (in Bergson, Husserl, Heidegger, and Sartre), and others explore an ethically more viable relation to time's passing (in Nietzsche, Heidegger, and Levinas). Kant initiated this effort to understand the human experience of time, and the Continental tradition both challenges and advances Kant's analysis. Minkowski contends that the various psychoses are aberrations from the typical experience of time. Both Foucault and Derrida challenge their predecessors' theories of time, and this revision is central to their skepticism. Foucault challenges Hegel's dialectical analysis of history, and Derrida challenges the phenomenological comprehension of time-constituting subjectivity. The importance of these challenges further demonstrates the centrality of the issue of temporality to the tradition; it constitutes the warp and woof of human life.

In addition, the whole tradition has challenged not only Kant's transcendental ego, but also the alleged experience of the empirical ego. Hegel and Marx provide deflationary approaches to the notion of individuality, rejecting the idea that persons are atomized individuals prior to society. If individuality is to be realized, this will only occur through a reconstitution of social and economic life. Nietzsche, Freud, and Deleuze challenge the Cartesian subject that supposedly owns all of its experiences and retains a privileged access to them. Nietzsche attempts to reduce the self to a dynamic conflict of drives or wills (internal forces); Freud and Deleuze develop and amplify this approach. Although Husserl tried to return to the Cartesian ego, these efforts were quickly abandoned by both Heidegger and Sartre. Sartre describes a variety of types of selfhood, the most important of which derive from one's own projects and from the other person's perspective on one's life. But neither of these experientially viable concepts of self are static or stable throughout one's life. Hermeneutics tries to rehabilitate the experience of self through the phenomenon of self-interpretation and reflexivity, but these efforts are countered by Foucault and Derrida, both of whom see self-interpretations as a tool which the dominant order uses to control persons rather than a tactic of emancipation. Der-

621

rida challenges the efficacy and veracity of any form of self-consciousness, suggesting that reflection is an entry into a mystifying hall of mirrors that proliferates images rather than producing a coherent self. Perhaps one could summarize these critical stances by saying that Continental philosophy is suspicious of the concept of the self and tries to comprehend human life without relying on this concept.

Finally, the complexities of human freedom remain under continuing scrutiny as the tradition develops. Hegel lauds freedom as the ultimate goal of historical development, but this freedom only exists in a social context that allows the achievement of reciprocal recognition among citizens. His freedom is inherently and necessarily social and produces self-realization; it transcends the purely negative view of freedom prominent in the English tradition. Marx retains a similar concept of freedom, and makes it the main aim of revolutionary praxis. He shows that capitalism is antipathetic to the self-realized, mutually affirming form of freedom Hegel sought. Although Nietzsche was skeptical of any notion of freedom that minimized deterministic forces, he none the less attempted to define a positive notion of freedom that required self-understanding, self-challenge, and achieved self-perfection. Freedom becomes a learned talent for expressing one's best possibilities, a command of the forces (both within and without) that resist this perfectionist achievement. The concept of freedom that emerges from hermeneutics and existentialism is continuing self-transcendence, the capacity to refashion or reinterpret oneself in any situation; this capacity produces the well-known existential weight of responsibility. These traditions retain the positive ideal of reciprocal recognition derived from Hegel, and Western Marxism continues the effort to elucidate and practically overcome the forces that prevent the achievement of this freedom in the contemporary era. Even in post-structuralism some conception of freedom is retained. To be sure, Foucault details the hidden influences and unconscious domination of modern power–knowledge operations, but his last writings defined a notion of self-creation that depends on a refurbished notion of freedom. Deleuze's somewhat anarchic model of human action continues to incorporate an idea of freedom. Though different movements within the tradition may rely on different conceptions of freedom, and though many of these thinkers attack bourgeois notions of freedom, the ideal of freedom as self-realization still plays an important role throughout the tradition. It shows that such freedom continues to remain essential to a truly human life.

The dominant result of these efforts is anti-Cartesian. Persons are understood to be more than minds, and minds are understood to be more than intellects. Human existence is practical, embodied, emotional, and temporal. Many factors structuring human experience operate beneath the level of explicit consciousness, and thus persons are not transparent to themselves. Often they deceive themselves, and their most prominent delusion is this very notion of the self. Moreover, practical activity must be understood in a context of habits, institutions, and operative rules of thumb. Freedom still remains a viable ideal, but the Continental notion of freedom is thoroughly social and involves some type of self-realization.

The third category of strengths of the Continental tradition is based on a distinctive relation to the death of God and to traditional Christian-bourgeois morality.

622

Though Nietzsche made the formula "God is dead" famous, the intellectual dubiousness of the concept was already apparent to Hegel and Marx. However, these nineteenth-century figures go beyond declaring the death of God and celebrate the full implications of this event. God's death is welcomed because the world becomes something for humanity to create and by doing so it can recreate itself. Humans may now become like gods, rising to the challenge of God's death by replacing him: finding the strength and vision to create new ethical values. In addition, these philosophers elaborate the destructiveness wrought by the belief in God, e.g., Marx's opiate of the people, Feuerbach's sense of humanity's self-alienation of its own powers, and Nietzsche's belief that Christianity supported slavishness, weakness, resentment, and many other misguided forms of life. This secularization of ethics continues in Sartre and Foucault. Though Scheler remained a theist throughout most of his life, his ethical realism did not rely on theistic assumptions. Even when the experience of God is reinterpreted in Buber and Levinas, it is given a this-worldly description, and one can abandon the theistic overtones without much loss. Continental philosophy has thus not simply abandoned some metaphysical conception of God, but sketched ways of living that render faith superfluous.

Nietzsche saw the potential nihilistic implications of the death of God and as a result created a tough-minded vision that remained "true to the earth" while also avoiding nihilism and Schopenhauer's contempt for life. Since Nietzsche, many figures in the tradition have sought alternatives to nihilism while rejecting the dominant Christian–bourgeois moral consensus. In ethics this is perhaps the feature that most distinguishes Continental philosophy from other traditions. Through both deontology and consequentialism, analytic philosophy has defended the classic ideals of the Enlightenment: reason, liberty, equality, fraternity, and happiness. There is remarkable consensus about the good, and this immensely simplifies the task of developing a "justification" of morality and a theory of right action. This whole project of justification has never taken hold in Continental philosophy because the basic consensus about the good is less fixed and certain. But the experience of value and the importance of striving remain unquestioned. Nietzsche calls for the creation of new values. Scheler shows how new values can be discovered through the flourishing of basic moral tenors in personal agents. Hartmann included a number of new values in his list of virtues. Both the existentialist stress on authenticity and the post-structuralist stress on abiding with differences are efforts to produce ethical visions that offer some kind of alternative to the bourgeois–Christian consensus. I admit that Continental efforts to produce new values could be still more visionary, but at least the major figures in Continental ethics sense the flawed character of the consensus that dominates Anglo-American ethics and have begun the search for alternatives.

The fourth category of strengths derives from the manner in which recent Continental philosophy has taken the linguistic turn. From Hegel to Deleuze there has been significant reflection in the Continental tradition on the nature and status of concepts generally and philosophical concepts in particular. In general, they have shown that philosophical concepts should be related to an expanded sense of rea-

623

son, rather than to the dichotomies operating in what Kant called "the understanding." Hegel's entire logic is devoted to the distinctive character of philosophical concepts and their dynamic relationships. Other major figures in the tradition (e.g., Nietzsche on grammar, Heidegger on logic, Foucault on archeology, and Derrida on identity) probe and interrogate the foundations of logic, rather than simply assume that familiar inference patterns are legitimate. The stance of Continental philosophy is more critical and searching. Moreover, though phenomenology operates in the material mode rather than the formal mode, it nonetheless sought necessary and sufficient conditions (essences) for a wide variety of basic concepts. In its existential versions (in Heidegger, Sartre, and Merleau-Ponty) it sought a "logic" implicit in the person's practical relation to the world as well. Lyotard is producing a neo-Wittgensteinian analysis of language-programs, even if he suggests that they have less ordered relations to one another than some philosophers have hoped. Thus the first strength in the Continental treatments of language is a more concrete sense of how philosophical concepts actually function and a more critical stance towards logic.

In addition, when Continental philosophy did take the linguistic turn, it rejected the program of clarifying philosophical problems either though creating an ideal language or mining the distinctions of ordinary language, and instead focused on the linguistic features of philosophy itself. This focus raised more questions than it answered. Though language has always been an important topic of philosophical reflection in Continental philosophy, it became a dominant theme after the rise of structuralism, which uses its model of linguistic systems to study every other social and cultural system. First the limits of using a linguistic metaphor to study other systems were quickly realized. Then the critical reaction to structuralism (in Foucault and Derrida) uncovered some important truths about linguistic systems and language.

Foucault suggests that intellectual disciplines have complex but describable systems of rules governing the relationships among statements – rules that are inadequately captured by any current syntactic, semantic, or pragmatic analysis of language. Moreover, though rule-governed, these systems are far more diffuse than the model of deduction suggests. He thus shows that statements exist in skewed, angular relation to each other within discursive formations as well as between them. He also discovered that widely diverse concepts can be concealed in the use of the same word across time in the same intellectual tradition and thus that the analysis of concepts requires more than an analysis of meaning. He reveals the dynamic quality of thought, its propensity to outstrip existing distinctions and categories. He also suggests that several distinct analytical programs concerning the relation of language to the world have existed and that the shift from one to another is unmotivated. He rejects the idea that new approaches actually refute former approaches. Instead, epistemological breaks emerge, and a new program simply begins. This suggests that though argument certainly plays some role in the development of philosophy (and other intellectual disciplines), the roots of major intellectual change lie elsewhere. Similar observations can be made about the transformations among philosophical programs in the last hundred years in both analytic and Continental philosophy.

Derrida has challenged a wide variety of dominant philosophical oppositions in order to encourage more serious thinking on the issues they inform and also to introduce a sharper sense of skepticism about many past philosophical programs. In addition, Derrida has demonstrated the linguistic character of philosophy itself by examining its rhetorical operations, its narrative and metaphoric devices, and the pragmatic self-contradictions implicit in many philosophical texts. He implies that a literary analysis is necessary to truly comprehend a philosophical text. And few others in any tradition can teach the reading of texts in the way reading Derrida's own essays can. In addition, Continental feminism challenges the subtle ways in which language operates in both philosophical texts and everyday discourse to enforce patriarchal assumptions, claims, and tendencies. Rather than producing a more ordered, rational approach to philosophical questions, the linguistic turn in Continental philosophy introduced a more robust form of skepticism and challenged the strong claims of reason in much previous philosophy (both Continental and analytic). In general, recent Continental examinations of language have shown how language can stifle thought and can undermine personal and social transformation. Thus Continental philosophy introduces the same challenge and revisionary impulses into thinking about language as it has into ethics and value theory.

I have tried to indicate some common strengths among the Continental philosophers explored in this volume. These consist sometimes in a more sophisticated analysis of certain phenomena, sometimes in a fuller appreciation of certain problems, and sometimes in the formulation of ambitious projects that are at least partially realized. Most of these strengths pave the way towards a truer and more complete understanding of the phenomena they concern. My hope has been to suggest unifying themes and conclusions and perhaps the beginnings of a framework for comprehending the main achievements of the field. For many of these generalizations some counter-examples undoubtedly could be produced, but I have shown that a wide diversity of figures represented in this book can be incorporated into this modest attempt at a synoptic summary of strengths.

## III  Some weaknesses in Continental philosophy

Among the traditions in Continental philosophy can be found some recurrent weaknesses. While these may not apply to every single thinker in the tradition, they are common enough to be cause for concern. Some of these weaknesses may be the reverse sides of some of the strengths mentioned above, but they may also be avoidable. Not all the weaknesses I describe are invidious because they are not always operative. For example, in the "trapdoor" objection described below, many do not use the trapdoor to dismiss their critics. Nevertheless the weakness is there and can cause problems. The five objections I will describe are: (1) creating a trapdoor to silence objectors; (2) failing to protect the position from the trapdoor;

(3) overgeneralizing; (4) neglecting to clarify steps towards desired social change; and (5) failing to integrate the first- and third-person viewpoints. I mention these potential problems because any effort to advance Continental philosophy requires an awareness of the weaknesses that need to be overcome as well as strengths on which to build.

First, many Continental thinkers virtually immunize their positions from serious debate by including categories that undermine the legitimacy of any possible critical standpoint. The thinkers may not always use these "trapdoors" in concrete debate, but they are always present, ready to be sprung at any time. Consider some examples. Marx interprets most philosophical positions as class-biased ideologies, and thus Marxists can always suggest that critics' motives and assumptions derive from a suspect class position. Moreover, Marx sometimes argues that ideological positions derive from "false consciousness," assumptions that support the hegemonic class domination that operates beneath the level of rational assent. Thus, Marxists may claim that the standpoint from which criticisms are launched is a mystification, that critics would abandon their objections if the source of these objections were understood. Similarly, Nietzsche relates intellectual stances to the character of their proponents, suggesting that they derive from specific wills to power. Moreover, he divides visionary types (*Ubermenschen*) from less creative types (the herd), and Nietzsche can always claim that a critical stance expresses a herd viewpoint. This can function as an Olympian dismissal that makes serious response unnecessary. Freud can also claim that opponents cannot recognize the truth of his claims because they have repressed the data necessary to verify it. Heidegger can suggest that critical perspectives derive from an inauthentic approach to the world, which ultimately expresses a corrupt understanding of Being. Sartre can suggest that critics exist in a state of self-deception that prevents them from acknowledging the truth of his claims, insisting that they have not yet made the transition to purified reflection which would allow their confirmation. Derrida can suggest that critics are operating from a logocentric standpoint that blocks access to the central claims of *différance*. Foucault can suggest that his opponents assume a past, displaced discursive formation and thus have failed to accept the new episteme that supports his standpoint. Even Hegel tries to include every possible alternative position as a stage leading towards his own system. He tries to indicate their flaws before they can even enunciate their objections.

In some of these cases (Hegel and Derrida), specific criticisms of the standpoint or assumptions of the objector are or at least can be made, but in many cases these trapdoors too easily function as blanket rejections that potentially protect the position against all conceivable objections. Although proponents of these positions might see these trapdoors as strengths, I see them as weaknesses because they are too sweeping. If a critical position is rejected on the basis of some feature specific to it, then at least a substantive response has been made to the objector. But these universalistic defenses make any determinate response unnecessary. Because they can be applied to any critic, the actual force they have in any particular case is weak, perhaps even negligible. Ultimately these trapdoors derive from a sweeping diagnosis of the current condition of philosophy and culture. The problem is that such diagnoses may or may not qualify the standpoint of a potential critic. In addition, the blanket objection typically feels like an *ad hominem* response, rather than a discussion of the substance of the objection. Thus, the presence of such trapdoors weakens some positions in Continental philosophy.

A second weakness, correlative with the first, is that many of these positions do not adequately account for their own stance in relation to the trapdoor. In short, they neglect to consider their own relation to the diagnostic flaw that motivates their perspective. Does Marx account for the class-position of his own standpoint; can he show that his position is not infected with false consciousness? Does Nietzsche account for the will to power operating in his own position; can he convincingly show that his own view is not corrupted by resentment and is not a remnant of Christianity? Does Heidegger's position really transcend the conception of being as presence (Levinas argues pointedly that it does not), and can he be certain his own vision derives from an authentic stance? Has Sartre purged his own views of all self-deception and impure reflection? Do Derrida's notions of *différance*, writing, and supplement fully escape logocentricism and the metaphysics of presence? Has Foucault considered the power-knowledge effects of his own discourse? Is Hegel's own position simply one more stage in a dialectic that will continue, or can he show that his standpoint has included all possible alternative positions? In some cases, there may be legitimate and coherent answers to these questions, but if a position relies on such a trapdoor, then it must ensure that it can circumvent its own trap.

A third weakness derives from a desire for universality or all-inclusiveness that is sometimes stretched beyond the bounds of plausibility. Sometimes this drive for universality simply involves overgeneralization. For example, both Hegel and Marx operate with a sophisticated notion of dialectic that captures something important about human thought, social action, and history. But Hegel and later Engels suggest that the dialectic also operates throughout nature. Although a case can be made for this in the organic world (dialectic is an attempt to capture formally some key features of organic systems), extending the metaphor to the inorganic sphere may be questionable. Similarly, in Nietzsche, the will to power was initially developed to explain a variety of psychological and social phenomena, and in that context it is at least a serious hypothesis (or at least *part* of the full story). However, Nietzsche also sought to generalize the principle to all of nature, and in that sphere the usefulness of the notion as an explanatory principle is certainly dubious. Freud, likewise, initially used the Oedipus complex to explain a specific stage of human development; however, the attempt to extend the model to female development has drawn devastating criticisms from feminist theorists. Beyond this, Freud attempted to derive the significant symptoms of most neuroses from this stage of development, unfortunately leading to an oversimplification of his own theory. (This tendency was rightly challenged by Deleuze and Guattari in *Anti-Oedipus*.)

At other times Continental philosophers exhibit a tendency towards reductionism or oversimplification. Marx (and his followers) sought to explain the many movements and developments in history by claiming that economic factors (forces and relations of production, however broadly defined) are always the primary

627

determinants. This almost certainly does injustice to other central factors, and typically results in linguistic expansions of the notion of the "economic." Freud's initial impulse to reduce all motivation to the pleasure principle (or even to both a pleasure and destruction principle) also seems to oversimplify human action. As these sweeping explanatory principles are attacked, the meaning of the key terms gets broadened in order to cover the apparent counter-examples, and the explanatory value of the principle gets correspondingly reduced. This drive to universality operates in nearly all the movements in Continental philosophy. Hermeneutics seeks to understand all phenomena on the model of interpreting a text. Phenomenology posits intentionality as the fundamental feature of all mental states. Existentialism makes practical activity – an instrumental orientation to the world – the primordial feature of human existence, reducing all other capacities to variants of praxis. Post-structuralism insists that dispersion is the only proper metaphor for understanding relationships among statements, and thus that narrative, organicity, and dialectic never apply. All these principles have a specific range of applicability and a set of contexts in which they are informative and illuminating. But when they are extended beyond that range, then major difficulties develop.

A fourth weakness concerns Continental efforts to envision alternatives to the current political–economic–cultural order and to devise ways to realize these alternatives. Marx not only had a vivid alternative, he indicated concrete steps by which that alternative could be achieved. He is the least susceptible to this fourth weakness. Hegel's vision was equally clear, and he offered a number of specific suggestions for improving the world-order of his era, but the connection between his suggestions and the full realization of his vision is tenuous. If Nietzsche's social and cultural ideal is sketchy, then his practical proposals for its realization are barely visible. Western Marxism developed Marx's ideal and buttressed his critical analysis of the dominant order, but became gradually more pessimistic about achieving qualitative transformation, and thus reneged on the task of offering strategies to transform the present. Existentialism's social and political ideals are vague, and hence careful practical thought about how to achieve them has not been forthcoming. Similarly, though one senses a demand for some alternative in postmodernist thinkers, the exact nature of that alternative is unclear, and suggestions of how to move the whole culture in new directions are minimal. So, though I think Continental philosophy has tried to envision social and cultural alternatives to the dominant order, the means to move towards their realization remain underdeveloped. This is a significant weakness.

Some might object here that these weaknesses apply to all philosophy and thus offer no special objection to Continental philosophy. To be sure, the trapdoor strategy also operates in logical positivism (the verifiability criterion of meaning), which was skewered on its own spear, but such trapdoors are rarer in Anglo-American philosophy. In that tradition, positions are responsive to criticisms and often become stronger as a result. Also, later Wittgenstein, Austin, and cognitive philosophy are all able to account for their own standpoint and strategies. When overgeneralization or oversimplification is demonstrated, then Anglo-American philosophers typically adjust their positions, preferring informativeness to artificial universality. Finally, Anglo-American philosophers as a group tend to be uncritical of the dominant order (at least officially) and thus do not have responsibility for finding plausible paths to cultural transformation. This silence, however, is a more serious weakness than Continental philosophy's inattention to transformative strategies.

The final point is less a weakness than a problem still insufficiently addressed. The problem is the relationship between the first-person and the third-person viewpoints on human phenomena and culture. Hegel, Marx, and Nietzsche studied human existence and social life both from the standpoint of the observer (from an objective or scientific viewpoint) and also from the standpoint of the agent (from a subjective or a participant viewpoint). Hegel even sought to understand how these standpoints might be integrated (the moment of the in-and-for-itself). In the twentieth century, various movements have allowed one of these standpoints to dominate their thinking. The first-person standpoint dominates in hermeneutics, phenomenology, and existentialism while the third-person standpoint dominates in Western Marxism, in structuralism, and in post-structuralism. The ways in which these two viewpoints can be integrated have not been fully explored. Even in Marx and Nietzsche, though both viewpoints are explored, their interrelationship is unclear. Perhaps a return to Hegel is necessary in order to examine his solutions to this problem and to see if they can be elaborated, now that each standpoint has been further developed.

Thus, if the Continental philosophy of the future is to continue its strong development, it must learn to address its weaknesses. It must be less tempted to immunize itself from criticism, must learn to account for its own viewpoint, must beware of overgeneralization and oversimplification, must discover practical steps that might realize its visions for the future, and must learn to integrate the first- and third-person standpoints.

## IV   Decision-points in Continental philosophy

In this section I try to indicate some important issues that divide the major thinkers within this tradition, issues on which no synthesis or compromise is likely to be forthcoming and thus issues on which the future of the discipline may be staked. I elucidate these issues under two general rubrics: metaphysical–epistemological–methodological issues and value issues. Within the first group, I will describe five different decision-points: (1) dialectic vs dispersion; (2) ahistorical essence vs variation; (3) interpretation vs description; (4) expanded reason vs irrationalism; and (5) realities vs illusions concerning the self. Within the values group, I will describe three decision-points: (1) embracing vs rejecting the ideals of modernity; (2) the power of higher culture to promote change; and (3) foundational issues in the theory of value. Among the more disturbing facts about the tradition is that these basic disputes are rarely matters of serious debate. People adopt one side or the other without seriously considering evidence for the other side. Indeed, too often these decision-points are gulfs across which opponents shout, rather than issues subject to analysis and argument. Although I cannot attempt to provide answers to these controversies here, this section at least attempts to set out the positions of the opposing sides clearly.

Several decision-points are metaphysical disputes. Perhaps the most important of these is the contest between those who favor some version of a dialectical model of reality and thought (Hegel, Marx, Sartre, Merleau-Ponty) vs those who reject this model (e.g., Foucault, Derrida, and Deleuze). The issue contains at least three disagreements. The first question is whether history has an underlying pattern and whether this pattern ultimately yields progress. Both Hegel and Marx insist that there is a pattern and that it produces progress whereas Foucault insists that there are fundamental historical breaks that shatter any claim to pattern, and thus that progress is illusory; discourses within one era are incommensurate with those in another. These issues are actually independent, for there may be progress even if there is no inherent pattern, and there may be a pattern that reveals continuous regression. The second question is whether various movements and discourses within an era have an organic or disparate relation to one another. Hegel, Marx, Marxism, Merleau-Ponty, and Sartre hold that at least some degree of organic coherence exists within eras, while Foucault and perhaps Deleuze (with his rhizomatic metaphor) defend a model of dispersion. On this issue, historical eras might, at least in principle, differ – some may exhibit a high degree of coherence and organicity and others less so. The third question is whether there are *any* totalities or organic systems (those with internal relations among their parts), and whether thought systems are best understood with this metaphor. Obviously, organic systems themselves are prime candidates for instantiating the dialectic, but Merleau-Ponty insists that the metaphor also captures the relation between persons and their environments (natural, social, ideational). Hermeneutics also posits weak organic coherence between interpreters and their backgrounds. On this issue, if Derrida's concepts of *différance*, supplement, copula (etc.) describe a fundamental metaphysical fact, then he will probably be the strongest challenger to the dialectical model. Here, too, the real issue is probably the breadth of application of the organic-dialectical model.

A second decision-point concerns whether there are ahistorical essences either in human nature or in nature as a whole that are not affected by differences in culture, historical period, or environment. On this issue phenomenologists and structuralists as well as Nietzsche (will to power) and Freud (pleasure and destruction drives) stand on one side while all the dialecticians (Hegel, Marx, Marxists) and postmodernists (including post-structuralism) stand on the other. Most members of the hermeneutic tradition straddle this divide by claiming that interpretation is an essential, invariant feature of the mind, but that it is shaped and influenced by background, context, and historical era at every point. One could also argue than Hegel (the struggle for recognition) and Marx (productive activity) also posit a small number of invariant, essential features even though they have different forms in different eras. In the case of phenomenology, Husserl insists that intentionality is an invariant feature of mental states, and in general he is opposed to the idea that the laws of logic might vary across cultures and historical eras. Moreover, the existential phenomenologists isolate "existentials" or invariant structures by which human beings are related to the practical environment, to themselves, and to other people, regardless of culture or era. Structuralists identify invariant cognitive operations that define the mind; these underlie all cultural operations and thus cannot be altered by differences in culture or era. On the other side stand Foucault, who attacks all constants and invariants, and hermeneutic thinkers, who think every feature of the mind is conditioned by the social and intellectual background.

Answers to this question have to be examined on both a general and a specific level. Those on either side have to give some plausible basis for thinking that cultural and intellectual factors either do or do not structure the mind all the way down. On the specific level, one has to consider each proposed invariant capacity or structure to determine whether or not it has been invariant across eras and cultures. Empirical research on non-Western cultures should prove instructive on this question. Probably some invariant structures do exist, but they may be so general that nothing important will follow from this fact. Still, each specific proposal for an invariant structure has to be taken on its merits, despite the general arguments on the matter. Here, as in many other areas, the general arguments are only as strong as the particular cases that support them.

A third metaphysical–epistemological decision-point is closely related to the second. It concerns whether one's relation to reality (e.g., nature, other people, history, or one's own occurrent mental states) is invariably interpretive in the sense that it is mediated by structures (foreground or background) that alter one's access to that reality or whether one can have purely descriptive, unmediated access to that reality. On this issue, most phenomenologists and philosophers who accept a robust concept of intuition (e.g., Bergson) are on the side which believes unmediated access is possible, whereas Nietzsche, most hermeneutic thinkers, and Derrida fall on the other side. Other thinkers, such as Foucault, Marx, and Freud, think that the people they analyze can only have mediated access to reality while, at the same time, believing that they, as investigators, can have unmediated access to the conceptual system, socio-economic systems, or psychological systems conditioning their subjects. Some phenomenologists, like Husserl, think one can have unmediated access to one's own states of mind, while others, like Sartre, think such access is possible (when reflection is purified) but not typical. Moreover, those who claim one's access is always necessarily mediated differ on how damaging this fact is. Nietzsche, for example, thinks that one's relation to anything is always perspectival (and thus oversimplifying) but that one can compensate for these simplifications by examining a variety of perspectives on the same phenomenon. Although this may not provide the unvarnished truth, it does produce a more adequate and more complete assessment.

One argument, typically taken to definitively demonstrate the truth of the mediated-access position, is that all claims about reality must be formulated in language; hence language always alters one's access to that reality. This argument is not unassailable, however, since one might state or report one's unmediated access in language in a fully adequate fashion without the structure of the language corrupting one's access to reality. One might, for example, report the color of

631

an object, the psychological state that one is experiencing, or the goal one is seeking without the language in which that report is given corrupting one's access to the phenomena. On this issue, too, both general and specific arguments must be closely examined. The interpretivist position must show that any *possible* proposal for unmediated access is wrong, and often this requires considering the variety of proposals that have been made. They must also show that the mediated access is epistemologically corrupting. Also, the tensions within split positions (like Foucault's), which hold that access to discursive formations can be unmediated (at least retrospectively) but that such formations condition access to reality for agents within them, must be resolved. Those who defend unmediated access must not only provide convincing examples; they must also show why linguistic (or other) factors do not corrupt one's access to reality.

A fourth metaphysical decision-point pits those who believe that Reason must be enhanced in order to be able to comprehend complex, multidimensional, or exotic spheres against those who think Reason's limitations are so great that it cannot be enhanced. In this debate, Hegel, Nietzsche, hermeneutics, and phenomenology (the enhancers) stand opposed to post-structuralism (especially Foucault) and Lyotard (and possibly Marx) (the deflators). For example, Hegel created dialectical reason to comprehend history; Scheler explored a logic of emotions; Merleau-Ponty a logic of perception; and Nietzsche a just adjudication of perspectives. Each tried to enhance the capacities of Reason to clarify a refractory area. On the other side, Foucault contends that there are definite epistemic breaks within the history of thought and that arguments and evidence simply cannot operate across such divides because, ultimately, what constitutes evidence for one position will be irrelevant to another, and because the assumptions and rules operating in the new discursive formation are so different that they cannot be made commensurate with those in the former one. In Continental philosophy the position that the discursive reason implicit in deductive and propositional logic is sufficient to clarify all spheres of reality is viewed with skepticism. At the birth of Continental philosophy Kant insisted that Pure Reason had to be confined within specific limits, but he allowed that practical life and aesthetic judgment might require distinct types of reason in order to be adequately understood. Those who seek to enhance Reason are simply following this lead. The deflators, on the other hand, have reintroduced difficult skeptical concerns about Reason that still must be answered.

A different interpretation of the possibilities and limits of Reason concerns the role of Reason in the psyche. Here the opposition is between, on the one hand, those thinkers who take rational autonomy both as an ideal and a real possibility, and, on the other, those that think the psyche is governed by factors alien to reasons or rational rules. On the irrationalist side stand Marx, Nietzsche, Freud, Bergson, Scheler, Sartre, Foucault, and Deleuze, while on the rationalist side stand Hegel, Husserl, Habermas, and critical theory. Those who argue against the psychic hegemony of Reason do so from a variety of different standpoints. Some argue that ideologies or power–knowledge frameworks or drives infect any attempt to achieve a purely rational perspective. Others argue that feeling provides a more primordial access to reality; still others argue that Reason is the servant of the will or drives or life-force. Those who argue that Reason can at least become master of its own house suggest that its victory requires a strenuous process of transcending background influences (both cognitive and emotional), and even that battle is never completely won.

The two interpretations of this decision-point are not identical, and the main skeptical implications that follow from insisting on the limits of Reason in the first interpretation do not necessarily obtain in the second interpretation. Nietzsche provides an important example here. He thinks that drives and the will dominate the human psyche and thus rejects the very possibility of a completely objective standpoint, but this does not prevent him from asserting that various drive-based perspectives can correct and supplement one another in such a way that a more complete truth can be achieved.

A fifth decision-point is really a series of issues concerning the variety of capacities associated with human selfhood and agency, e.g., consciousness, self-consciousness, will, reflection, imagination, self-transcendence, individuality, and self-transformation. One issue is which of these capacities are essential to agency; another is whether there is or can be an autonomous self. There are probably as many distinct analyses of selfhood as there are movements in the tradition; all of them adopt diverse stances on the importance and value of the various capacities listed above. The phenomenologists, for example, place great premium on consciousness, and Sartre valorizes self-transcendence. Nietzsche, however, challenges the importance of both consciousness and self-consciousness without thereby rejecting the possibility of genuine self-transformation through reorganizing one's drives. Foucault, on the other hand, almost dismisses the will and the intellect as independent sources of initiative, but he too, in his last phase, seems to allow some capacity for self-transformation along Nietzschean lines. Thus, although nearly everyone agrees that the transcendental ego must be rejected, many disputes still exist concerning the nature and constitution of the empirical ego. The issue of autonomy is important in Continental philosophy because most of its movements assert some form of social constitution of the self. Such social constitution typically compromises autonomy (and its related notions of self-sufficiency and self-mastery).

I shall now turn my attention to the second general category of decision-points: value issues. The area subsumes debates about the value of modernity (and Enlightenment ideals), about cultural institutions, and about the foundations of value theory. These decision-points concern which direction to pursue, how to do it most effectively, and how to justify the transformation.

Perhaps the most important issue in this constellation concerns the revaluation of modernity's basic values, e.g., reason, happiness, liberty, equality, fraternity. Here, Hegel, Marx, and Habermas stand at one extreme (fundamentally enthusiastic about the possibilities of modernity) and Nietzsche and Heidegger at the other extreme (deeply skeptical about the basic directions of modernity – searching for some alternative), with a variety of thinkers enthusiastic about some of these values, but not the others (e.g., Sartre, Foucault). Those antagonistic to modernity can be forward looking (e.g., Nietzsche) or backward looking (e.g., Heidegger), and many so-called postmodernist theories do not actually revalue, but often embrace, certain features of the present (e.g., Baudrillard). Those who seek to revalue the dominant values of the modern era must produce a coherent method for doing this. Those who value modernity sometimes see its core values as subverted by the dominant political–economic order; thus, they take the social realities of modernity to be in "contradiction" with its founding ideals. They seek alternative institutions to better realize these received values. Their justificatory task is less demanding because a well-established consensus exists for these values. The critical-utopian stance described above as a strength derives from Continental efforts to make modernity fulfill its promises or to transform modernity's values into a more defensible constellation.

Equally important is the effort to understand the efficaciousness of various institutions in achieving the transition towards some future, more promising order. Some of the institutions relevant here are the state, art, popular movements, and philosophy. The disputes concern whether these institutions can produce genuine change or not and which among them are the most effective. Some are sharply critical of the state (Marx, Nietzsche) while others think a reorganization of the state can make a significant contribution to a better future (Hegel). Others regard the state as less significant and create an alternative analysis of specific institutional power practices that must be opposed and transformed by local popular movements (Foucault, Deleuze). Some believe art can make enormous contributions, not just to raising consciousness of the need for cultural transformation, but in directing and imagining this change effectively. Certainly Nietzsche and some Western Marxists (especially Bloch) believe art could play such a role. Marx himself and perhaps Freud are more skeptical of the transformative power of art. Marx and the poststructuralists strive to undermine the pretensions of philosophy to envision and justify positive change, while Hegel and Nietzsche believe philosophers have a central creative role in making the transition to a more promising future. Marx thinks only revolutionary activity which gains control of the means of production will create real change while some post-structuralists seem to think that theory can be the lever of cultural transformation. The issue here is not just the most effective strategies for change, but the most effective focus for change, the institution on which much else in modern culture depends.

Finally, the thinkers in this tradition offer various strategies to support the value assessments that underlie these cultural transformations. On this issue there is not so much focused opposition as a plurality of positions, the relationships among which are unexplored. Hegel, for example, grounds many of his value assessments in the historical process itself. Nietzsche defends his ideals naturalistically – as enhancing the processes of increased self-organization (power) already operative in the life-process. Scheler grounds his value assessments in an emotional intuition that illuminates an objective hierarchy of values and governs the organization of culture and persons. The existentialists defend a conception of heroic authenticity that articulates itself within a tradition and self-consciously defines itself amidst a clear consciousness of reality as it is. Levinas and Buber locate their ideals in a specific relation to other people that conditions the entire experience of value. None of these positions is necessarily incompatible with the others, but they are quite different. Future work in the tradition on the sources of value assessment will benefit from a close examination and critique of these attempts.

These eight issues – dialectic vs dispersion; essences vs history; interpretation vs description; expanded reason vs irrationalism; the possibilities and limits of self-hood; the revaluation of modernity's values; the role of specific institutions in achieving cultural transformation; and the sources of value assessment – provide a map of decision-points that begins to delineate the current space of Continental philosophy. These issues may provide a useful structure for reviewing and rethinking the positions summarized in this *Companion*. They may also help readers determine their own projects for contributing to the future of Continental philosophy.

The natural way to conclude this essay would be to attempt a coherent and systematic answer to these eight disputes. That is a book-length project for another occasion. Instead, I will suggest a different way to use the book: it can provide the means to refashion one's philosophical aspirations.

## V Creating the future through self-definition

The aim of this book is not just to summarize the present state of Continental philosophy but to stimulate movement towards a productive future. I call this the Nietzschean hope of the project. In *Schopenhauer as Educator* Nietzsche encourages his readers to discover their highest promise by reviewing their past identifications, passions, and teachers, recalling the force of their inspiration. He suggests that by integrating these elements readers can fashion distinctive individual identities, ideal selves that can guide their future development. This *Companion* can enable its readers to recall (or discover) their own models and define the features that give those exemplary figures their intellectual power. In order to encourage this effort, I shall attempt this myself as a kind of example. In my opinion, there are scores of promising directions in which Continental philosophy can develop as we pass through the millennium, as many promising directions as there are combinations of strengths within the tradition. The path I sketch is only one possibility. I shall outline it briefly, but fully enough to explain this possible use of the book.

The philosophers that shine most radiantly for me are Hegel, Nietzsche, Scheler, Sartre, Merleau-Ponty, and Foucault. I shall first try to state the features that make them exemplary philosophers, and then I will sketch a brief attempt at an integration. Rather than focus on their substantive positions, I will concentrate on their goals, methods, and intellectual virtues.

Hegel's *Phenomenology* is a masterpiece because it encompasses many significant intellectual and practical orientations to the world, orientations that inform philosophical positions, ways of life, phases in the development of a person and of Western culture. Hegel achieves this completeness by drawing on a rich knowledge of the sciences and history of thought. Moreover, the *Phenomenology* organizes these positions systematically, coherently relating them to one another. Hegel explores the logic of this pattern, a pattern he thinks reveals a deeper logic of thought and

635

reality. Finally, Hegel focuses on meta-philosophical, foundational questions as well as on object-level questions in philosophy; he tries to account for his point of departure, and he tries to show how his approach resolves the conundrums that plagued past positions. He often shows how apparently incompatible oppositions can be overcome to produce a standpoint that retains their best achievements.

Nietzsche's power lies in his revaluation of all values and his ability to meet the challenges of nihilism that might result from that revaluation. Although his vision for individual achievement is clear, his vision for the culture as a whole is sketchier, but at least apparent. Nietzsche also begins to create the necessary psychological tools that would make achieving higher humanity at least possible, if not likely. In order to do this, Nietzsche seeks a clear sense of human nature as it is; on this basis he shows the way to human nature as it might be. Finally, Nietzsche has enormous expectations of philosophers. Not only must they become capable of integrating a wide diversity of standpoints in order to achieve the most comprehensive vision of reality, they must achieve the creative vision and strength of character necessary to lead the culture in new directions. They are required to undergo an existential transformation necessary to produce "new values," and they are encouraged to help others achieve similar visions. If philosophy could even partly achieve this agenda, its importance for the culture would be restored.

Scheler exhibits two central virtues. First, like C. D. Broad in the Anglo-American tradition, he possesses an ability to distinguish the variety of questions at stake in a given controversy and to understand how philosophical positions offer systematic answers to a complex network of questions. He displays this quality vividly in his short essay "Other Minds" in *The Nature of Sympathy*. There he offers a penetrating survey of a field of inquiry before making his own contribution. In this way he helps readers find a basis for making their own contributions. Secondly, when he states his own position, invariably he reveals something of which one has only dimly been aware. He sees deeply into the phenomena, and is able to show others what he sees. Just as he thinks different individuals and cultures could creatively reveal new and heretofore unknown dimensions of the value hierarchy, he is able to reveal heretofore unknown features of human experience with great subtlety and astuteness. Unfortunately, there is no way to bottle and transmit this penetrating vision, but future philosophical efforts can only benefit from seeking it.

Sartre's virtues are somewhat different. He attempts an exhaustive analysis of human capacities, exploring virtually every type of mental state (except perhaps cognition), as well as action, interpersonal relations, and group life. He proposes an analysis of emotions, imagination, perception, transcendence, time-consciousness, desire, reflection, action and goal-directed behavior, intersubjectivity, self and other understanding, the body, the experience of selfhood, and the process and practice of writing. He studies these capacities from both the first-person, phenomenological viewpoint and the third-person biographical viewpoint, and thus he shows how to use his theoretical insights in analyzing the lives of particular persons. His vision is less original than synthetic; he draws key insights from Hegel, Marx, Dilthey, Husserl, and Heidegger, and weaves them together into a new tapestry that is stronger than any of its isolated components. He also exposes the strategies people use to avoid harsh truths about themselves and the world; he advances Nietzsche's critical project in this respect. Like Nietzsche, he believes that the character of persons can be measured by how much truth they can bear, and he strives to reveal the gritty truth as uncompromisingly as possible.

Merleau-Ponty shares his most prominent virtue with Scheler: an intense dialogue with scientific and empirical research on the issues that concern him. Both of these philosophers maintain a critical stance towards the sciences they knew so well, but both feel the necessity of addressing and integrating the best insights of the social and cognitive sciences. Like Hegel, Merleau-Ponty strives to overcome the divisions that divide the study of persons (e.g., between atomistic empiricism and cognitive approaches in psychology). He creates a third approach that avoids the conundrums that plague the dominant approaches. His greatest contribution is to the study of perception and the role of the body in relating individuals to their natural, practical, and social environments. Although he examines a variety of other issues, his insights in those areas all flow from his basic stance on perception. There his contributions are deep and extensive. Ideally, one should try to combine Merleau-Ponty's depth with Sartre's breadth. In addition, in his last works he struggles with the important meta-philosophical, foundational questions of phenomenology and philosophy. Like Hegel and Husserl, he probes the foundations in order to ensure that his position can account for its own practice.

Foucault's contribution is his continuation of Nietzsche's revaluation of modernity with a special focus on the human sciences and their related institutions (the asylum, the clinic, and the prison). In order to take other perspectives seriously, Nietzsche believed philosophers had to transcend their own time. Foucault engenders a sense of being alien in one's own era – creating a crucial sense of untimeliness that allows readers to transcend their present frameworks. He also critically interrogates the disciplines and practices that claim to liberate persons and casts them in a harsh, unforgiving light. He thus indicts modernity (and its underlying practices and values) as intensely as Nietzsche indicted Christianity and its successor frameworks. Foucault is much less creative than Nietzsche in envisioning alternatives, and this risks a nihilistic response (or at least diminished aspirations) that Nietzsche would have diagnosed as part of the problem. Yet among recent thinkers Foucault most forcefully challenges the claims of liberal humanism.


So how do these exemplary achievements fit together? Nietzsche, Sartre, and Foucault teach an uncompromising critical assessment of the present. This critical tendency is balanced by Hegel and Scheler who find the promising possibilities in the present – trends that can produce a better future. Nietzsche most explicitly offers a creative vision of the future; in my view, Continental philosophers must rise to his challenge to create new values, new visions. Hegel and Sartre offer a wide-ranging analysis either of human capacities or of basic ideal-typical approaches to the world (theoretical and practical). Their range and breadth of insight needs to be supplemented by the depth and penetration of Merleau-Ponty. In addition, Hegel, Scheler, and Merleau-Ponty engage in an ongoing dialogue with the best empirical research they can find. They neither worship nor dismiss the achievements of the sciences; they properly assess the limits of their achievements, but they also learn from their discoveries. Hegel and Merleau-Ponty take foundational or meta-philosophical questions to be as central as the substantive issues they seek to solve. They strive to ensure that the projects they pursue can account for themselves, without being obsessed by a constant return to beginnings that paralyzes progress. Finally, all these philosophers in their own way seek to find ways to expand Reason: Hegel's dialectic, Nietzsche's perspectivism, Scheler's logic of the heart, and Sartre and Merleau-Ponty's phenomenological reflection all seek to supplement the evidence of science (and common sense) and formal logic. Most seek to overcome enervating dichotomies. These are the goals and aspirations that I would take into the future.

These are the figures from whom I draw inspiration in this tradition, and these are the lessons or goals I take from them. No doubt each reader will compose his or her own list of model philosophers and their virtues. The benefit of this process is a fuller awareness of the direction one seeks to pursue. Without a considered sense of one's goals, one can make no progress. Reviewing the possibilities is a way of crystallizing one's identity, and at least producing a personal agenda. No doubt these personal syntheses should be tested and discussed, but creating the synthesis is a necessary first step in contributing to such a discussion. I hope this book contributes to this task of self-definition and helps steer the discipline towards some promising futures.

# Index

INDEX

*Index compiled by Meg Davies (Registered Indexer, Society of Indexers)*